Juvenile Delinquency and Rehabilitation

Juvenile Delinquency and Rehabilitation

Examining the Good Lives Model

Colinda M.B. Serie

Boom juridisch Antwerpen
Antwerpen
2023

eleven

Published, sold and distributed by Eleven
P.O. Box 85576
2508 CG The Hague
The Netherlands
Tel.: +31 70 33 070 33
Fax: +31 70 33 070 30
e-mail: sales@elevenpub.nl
www.elevenpub.com

Sold and distributed in USA and Canada
Independent Publishers Group
814 N. Franklin Street
Chicago, IL 60610, USA
Order Placement: +1 800 888 4741
Fax: +1 312 337 5985
orders@ipgbook.com
www.ipgbook.com

Boom juridisch Antwerpen
ISBN 978-94-6451-107-9
ISBN 978-94-6451-208-3 (e-book)
NUR 824
D/2023/15251/03

GPRC
Guaranteed
Peer Reviewed
Content
boekenvak.be/gprc

Eleven is an imprint of Boom uitgevers Den Haag.
ISBN 978-94-6236-425-7
ISBN 978-94-6236-428-8 (e-book)

This research project was supported by FWO (research project grant G073018N).

Man is not fully conditioned and determined but rather determines himself
whether he gives in to conditions or stands up to them.
In other words, man is ultimately self-determining.
– Viktor E. Frankl, *Man's Search for Meaning*

Table of Contents

Preface

It is with great pleasure that I present to you this book: *Juvenile Delinquency and Rehabilitation: Examining the Good Lives Model.* Although I officially began studying this research topic at the Leuven Institute of Criminology (KU Leuven) in October 2016, the journey towards it started well before this. In 2012, I was accepted for the two-year Forensic Psychology master program at Maastricht University. My passion for working with youngsters was ignited during my studies when I received the chance to intern at the Catamaran in Eindhoven, a forensic psychiatric clinic for youth. I also became interested in academic research and my aspirations to pursue a PhD-study in this field were born. Professor Corine de Ruiter, head of the masters programme, has always inspired me as a mentor and passionate scientist-practitioner in the field of Forensic Psychology. When I graduated in 2014, I was fortunate to be able to work with her as a research assistant. We applied for several funds to make my PhD dream a reality, but unfortunately they were not awarded. Thankfully, I was not deterred by these rejections. In fact, they had the opposite effect, and when a fully funded PhD vacancy in the field of youth criminology presented itself in Leuven I gladly and wholeheartedly seized the opportunity.

The guidance and work experience I was granted during my time in Maastricht by Professor Corine de Ruiter, proved to be an invaluable basis at the start of this PhD study. Furthermore, the exact topic of the PhD project initially funded by KU Leuven and later by the Research Foundation Flanders (FWO) was open to interpretation, allowing me to start off with a blank canvas. I am very grateful for the trust my supervisor Professor Stefaan Pleysier and co-supervisor Professor Johan Put instilled in me by not only hiring me, but also providing me with the space and freedom in my thinking and approach to shape my own research (skills). With both a criminologist/sociologist and legal expert as supervisors, I had full confidence that the guidance would be of an excellent standard. This indeed proved to be the case and often provided interesting complementarian views and perspectives. I am therefore very appreciative of the pleasant multi-disciplinary collaboration over all these years. In sum, – and to stay in line with my research topic – they have created a satisfying and challenging work environment for me that meets the three main human psychological needs: competence, relatedness and autonomy. As my research design began to take shape, Corine de Ruiter's forensic expertise and guidance also proved to be very helpful. As this collaboration showed to be of high value it eventually resulted in a joint degree with Maastricht University with Corine becoming a co-supervisor. This provided a larger network, more resources and an additional multi-disciplinary dimension. I want to express my gratitude to all three of my supervisors and both universities for making this valuable opportunity possible.

During this research project, the multi-disciplinary and multi-university collaboration expanded even further as I had the honour of meeting and working with several great scholars. I had the pleasure to participate in the three-day Good Lives Model training by Professor Tony Ward and Dr. Mary Barnao organized by Professor Wouter Vanderplasschen, Professor Stijn Vandevelde, and Dr. Lore van Damme, at Ghent University. While developing my research project, I also met and discussed my proposal with Dr. Shadd Maruna who provided the useful suggestion of including studying treatment engagement and motivation. Additionally, Dr. Mayumi Purvis and Dr. David Prescott were so kind to answer a number of questions regarding their perspectives on the Good Lives Model. Moreover, for the execution of my research, I collaborated with Dr. Lore van Damme, especially in the meta-analysis (Chapter 4) where we also received statistical support via email from Dr. Mark Assink. Similarly, Dr. Nick Broers was of great help with his advice on my statistical analyses. Additionally, a part of my data collection was made possible by the collaboration with the Youth Research Platform (JOP) in Flanders, Belgium. The JOP is a policy research centre funded by the Flemish government consisting of a multi-disciplinary consortium of partners from the Leuven Institute of Criminology (KU Leuven), educational studies of Ghent University and sociology of the Free University of Brussels. I am very grateful and honoured to have been a part of all these wonderful and educational collaborations.

It should furthermore be noted that this research project would not have been possible without the willingness of the participating institutions. In particular, I would like to thank the directors of the youth (detention) institutions in Flanders, Belgium: 'Fordulas' in Kortenberg, 'De Grubbe' in Everberg, and 'De Kempen' in Mol, and the Dutch Juvenile Justice Institution 'Het Keerpunt' in Cadier en Keer. However, as willing as the institutions were, the success of this study fully rests upon the willingness and openness of the participants. Their candour and commitment are the essential foundation upon which my research has been built. I am therefore more than grateful for the trust instilled in me by confiding their life stories to me. It could not have been easy opening up to a complete stranger about their personal life. Additionally, I would also like to thank all staff members (including security, receptionists, treatment coordinators, treatment providers, teachers and social workers) for their invaluable interest and assistance in the study, which made it possible to efficiently collect all the data. I also want to thank Carmen Rijk and Mirte Put for their high-quality work in assisting with the data collection and coding.

Finally, I want to mention a number of people who contributed to this work and helped me become the researcher I am today, through friendship, love and support. During all these years I had the privilege of sharing an office with Elke, a highly skilled and experienced researcher, and perhaps even more importantly a kind, patient and caring person. I am very grateful she was always there to not only share in the good times, but also to help and support me through difficult times. In addition, I have been glad to be part of our research line Youth Justice at KU Leuven and the Forensic Psychology section at Maastricht University where I was surrounded by bright and fun colleagues who ensured a pleasurable working atmosphere. Outside of work I was also fortunate to be surrounded by a network of kind and loving people. I am beyond grateful for my ever-supportive and loving parents who have always believed in me and whose hard work made it possible for me to attend university. I am also grateful for my sister who never stopped visiting and supporting me no matter where my studies and work took me. My loving family-in-law, I also want to thank you. You have welcomed me into your family with great fervour and I look forward to many more family dinners and competitive game nights. In addition, I want to mention my friends, especially those who have been there for me all of these years. In particular, I want to thank Annemarijn who has supported me since the beginning, both professionally and as a caring friend. Together we have travelled, had a lot of fun, and share great memories. The same applies to Michelle who I have known as a dear friend since we were barely able to walk. As my research has shown, humans are social beings and meaningful, loving, relationships are essential to live a happy life. That brings me to giving a special thanks to my husband Daniël, who I met at the beginning of this journey in 2012 and who has been there for me ever since. I cannot imagine a life without him by my side. Thank you for your unwavering support and unconditional love.

All in all, I am aware that I have been blessed with many wonderful opportunities and an abundance of love in my life and I hope that I can offer others the same. One way in which I hope to contribute to the happiness of others lies before you. With this book I aim to provide an understanding of how to help young offenders get their lives back on track.

Abbreviations

ADHD	Attention Deficit Hyperactivity Disorder
ANOVA	Analysis of Variance
ASO	Algemeen Secundair Onderwijs (general secondary education)
ATMQ	Adolescent Treatment Motivation Questionnaire
BSO	Beroepssecundair Onderwijs (vocational secondary education)
GLM	Good Lives Model
GLP	Good Lives Plan
GPA	Grade Point Average
GST	General Strain Theory
HAVO	Hoger Algemeen Voortgezet Onderwijs (higher general secondary education)
ICC	Intraclass Correlation Coefficient
JJI	Juvenile Justice Institution (Justitiële Jeugd Inrichting)
JOP	JeugdOnderzoeksPlatform (youth research platform)
KSO	Kunst Secundair Onderwijs (artistic secondary education)
MI	Motivational Interviewing
MORM	Multifactor Offender Readiness Model
MST	Multi-Systemic Therapy
NA	Negative Affect
PA	Positive Affect
PIC-R	Personal, Interpersonal, and Community Reinforcement perspective
PWB	Psychological Well-being
PYOP	Preventing Youth Offending Program
RNR	Risk Need Responsivity
SCT	Self-Control Theory
SDQ	Strengths and Difficulties Questionnaire
SDT	Self-Determination Theory
SE	Standard Error
SEM	Structural Equation Modelling
SES	Socio-Economic Status
SPANE	Scale of Positive and Negative Experience

SWB	Subjective Well-being
SWLS-(CV)	Satisfaction With Life Scale (Child Version)
TSO	Technisch Secundair Onderwijs (technical secondary education)
UNCRC	United Nations Convention on the Rights of the Child
VMBO	Voorbereidend Middelbaar Beroepsonderwijs (preparatory secondary vocational education)
VWO	Voorbereidend Wetenschappelijk Onderwijs (preparatory university education)
WHOQOL	World Health Organization Quality of Life assessment
YDC	Youth Detention Centre
YLS/CMI	Youth Level of Service/Case Management Inventory

1 Introduction

Responding to juvenile delinquency is a hot topic that oftentimes elicits strong opinions and emotions in society. It is also a topic that is highly ranked on the agenda of politicians and policymakers. As a result, the successful rehabilitation of young offenders and accompanying low recidivism rates are considered high-priority goals. However, practitioners in juvenile justice systems often face a dilemma, as they are confronted with the need to balance the welfare of the young offenders with the safety of society. In this book, I will examine whether and how this dilemma can be avoided and result in successful juvenile offender rehabilitation with positive effects for both the youth and society. A first step in this endeavour is to gain perspective on what exactly is the problem.

1.1 Reducing Risk or Increasing Well-being?

In general, juvenile delinquency can be subdivided in two distinct categories: an 'adolescent-limited' group and a 'life course persistent/childhood-onset' group. While in the first group antisocial behaviour starts during adolescence and remains more or less restricted to this period, the latter is characterized by persistent antisocial behaviour starting early in life (Moffitt, 1993, 2018). Research in especially the latter group has consistently revealed high prevalence rates of psychiatric disorders (and comorbidity) varying between 50% and 90%. Common diagnoses include attention deficit hyperactivity disorder (ADHD), oppositional-defiant disorder, and conduct disorder, but (comorbid) depression and anxiety disorders are also common (Boonmann et al., 2015; Colins et al., 2009, 2010; Stouthamer-Loeber & Loeber, 2002; Vermeiren et al., 2006).

Furthermore, persistent/childhood-onset offenders are more likely than adolescent-limited offenders to report victimization of childhood maltreatment (Assink et al., 2015; Hoeve, Colins, et al., 2014), which in turn is related to a higher number of psychosocial problems, such as substance abuse, family problems, peer relationship problems, school maladjustment, and mental health problems (Assink et al., 2015; Bielas et al., 2016; Chitsabesan et al., 2006; Hoeve, Colins, et al., 2014). Consequently, trauma, psychiatric disorders, and mental health problems can severely affect adolescents' well-being and quality of life, especially for those in residential settings (Bastiaansen et al., 2005; de Ruigh et al., 2019; Weber et al., 2016).

Adolescence (i.e. the life period between 12 and 18 years old) in and of itself is already known to be a turbulent period. Due to the many cognitive, social and physical changes during this period behavioural problems, emotional problems and diminished well-being can arise (Arnett, 1999; Fortune, 2018; Goldbeck et al., 2007; Miller, 2014). Compared to adolescents in the community, detained adolescent offenders in residential institutions generally experience even poorer mental and physical health, more family adversity, poorer peer relationships, poorer school attendance (Jozefiak & Sonnichsen Kayed, 2015; Leroux, 2019) and lower levels of subjective well-being (Buunk et al., 2016; Llosada-Gistau et al., 2015). During detention, mental health problems have also been related to lower levels of treatment motivation and engagement (Van Damme, Hoeve, et al., 2015), known to hamper effective offender rehabilitation (Harder et al., 2015; Olver et al., 2011; van der Laan & Eichelsheim, 2013). Subsequently, childhood trauma and (comorbid) psychiatric disorders have been related to aggression, violence and later (re-)offending in detained adolescents (Aebi et al., 2015; Hoeve et al., 2015; Hoeve et al., 2013; Vahl et al., 2016; van der Put & De Ruiter, 2016; White et al., 2016; Wibbelink et al., 2017; Wilson et al., 2009). Furthermore, when leaving closed residential settings, previously detained adolescents can encounter a range of difficulties with adapting to life outside the structured facility. These difficulties include having problems with housing, finances, school, and/or employment that can again result in diminished quality of life and well-being (Baltodano et al., 2005; Harder et al., 2011; Lanctôt et al., 2007).

Given these potentially complex and interacting problems in persistent and detained adolescent offenders, it is not surprising that successful rehabilitation of these adolescents within the juvenile justice system is considered challenging (Taylor & Leys, 2013; Underwood & Washington, 2016). For example, young mentally ill offenders in Belgium are usually refused admission to psychiatric wards because they are deemed too aggressive or too complex. As a result, they are often placed in a Youth Detention Centre where they do not always receive the specific care they need (Jongeren Welzijn, 2011). This problem exists in many countries where the juvenile justice system lacks appropriate resources to meet the specific needs of delinquent youth with mental health problems (Skowyra & Cocozza, 2007; Taylor & Leys, 2013). A fundamental issue underlying this problem may be the tension between the domain of justice and the domain of mental health care (Grisso, 2008; Henry et al., 2015). This tension unfolds in two main approaches to offender rehabilitation: (1) *a risk-focused approach* that focuses on reducing recidivism and community protection, and (2) *a psychopathology or welfare-focused approach* that is concerned with treatment and care of individuals suffering from psychological problems or symptoms (Barnao et al., 2016; Henry et al., 2015; McCormick et al., 2015). Despite these different priorities, they still share the common goal of improving outcomes for the individual as well as for society (de Ruigh et al., 2019; McCormick et al., 2015).

This tension can also be observed in the Flemish juvenile justice system that has recently moved from a welfare-focused approach (in which care and protection were the guiding principles) to a sanction-focused approach (in which the response to the offence is emphasized). This shift occurred with the passage of the new Juvenile Delinquency

Decree, which gradually took effect in September 2019 (Put & Leenknecht, 2019; Put & Pleysier, 2018). In this new approach, the law aims to provide a clear, socially norm-affirming response to offences committed by minors, not evading the responsibility of the young offender. It furthermore states that this response should be clearly separated from, but easily combined with, youth care when needed (Parliamentary Acts Flemish Parliament No. 1670/1, 2017-2018, p. 4). In responding to a juvenile offence, the court considers the severity of the crime, the personality of the juvenile, the recidivism risk, the safety of society, the living environment of the juvenile, and the safety of the juvenile (Parliamentary Acts Flemish Parliament No. 1670/1, 2017-2018, p. 12). From this goal description, it becomes clear that the situation of the offender as well as the risk and consequences for society are taken into account. Additionally, special attention is devoted to young offenders with psychiatric disorders (De Bus & Put, 2020; Put, 2020). In such cases, a combination of both care for the individual and safety of society are paramount in determining the response to juvenile delinquency (Parliamentary Acts Flemish Parliament No. 1670/1, 2017-2018, p. 13).

Moreover, from a children's rights perspective, juvenile offenders are entitled to developmentally appropriate treatment that promotes their reintegration into society. That is, the United Nations Convention on the Rights of the Child (UNCRC) requires that judicial interventions for minors "ensure that children are dealt with in a manner appropriate to their well-being and proportionate both to their circumstances and the offence" (UNCRC, 1989, Art. 40). As a result, forensic practitioners in particular may encounter problems in being a 'double agent' by trying to "strike a balance between providing care and treatment for 'patients' while simultaneously protecting society from 'offenders'" (Barnao et al., 2016, p. 1; see also Ward, 2013). Therefore, in this book I will explore whether and how risk-focused and welfare-focused approaches in offender rehabilitation can be combined to effectively improve the well-being as well as reduce the recidivism risk of detained adolescent offenders.

1.2 A Risk-focused Approach: The Risk Need Responsivity Model

Over the past decades, there has been a debate on the effectiveness of offender rehabilitation to reduce recidivism in both adult and juvenile offenders. In the 1970s, it was believed that *nothing works* in rehabilitating offenders (Martinson, 1974). Since then, several reviews and meta-analyses have contested this view by showing that offender treatment *does* work in reducing recidivism (for an overview see: Lipsey & Cullen, 2007). However, this raised a new question: exactly *what works* in the rehabilitation of offenders? In response to this question, Donald A. Andrews and James Bonta (Andrews & Bonta, 1994, 2010; Andrews, Bonta, et al., 1990; Bonta & Andrews, 2017) developed a rehabilitation model or framework that aimed to articulate how to reduce recidivism and effectively reintegrate offenders in society. They referred to this framework as the Risk Need Responsivity (RNR) model. The model contains three main principles (*risk*, *need*, and *responsivity*) that interventions or treatments should adopt to be effective in reducing recidivism. Since its development, the RNR model has received an impressive amount of support by a large number of studies and meta-analyses. These studies have demonstrated that offender rehabilitation interventions adhering to the three RNR principles are indeed more effective in reducing recidivism than those that do not, both in adults and adolescents (Andrews & Dowden, 2007; Andrews, Zinger, et al., 1990; Bonta & Andrews, 2017; Dowden & Andrews, 1999a, 1999b, 2000; Hanson et al., 2009; Koehler et al., 2013; Latessa & Lowenkamp, 2006; Smith et al., 2009).

The *risk* principle forms the basis of the RNR model and states that criminal behaviour can be predicted in terms of levels of risk. According to this principle, in order to effectively reduce recidivism, the level of treatment intensity should match the individual offender's level of risk for (re-)offending (Andrews & Bonta, 2010; Bonta & Andrews, 2017). More specifically, high-risk offenders require more intensive interventions compared to low-risk offenders. This principle is supported by many studies (in both adults and juveniles) demonstrating that reductions in recidivism are highest when low-risk offenders receive minimal amounts of treatment services or supervision, and high-risk offenders receive intensive interventions (Andrews & Bonta, 2010; Andrews & Dowden, 2006; Bonta & Andrews, 2017; Dowden & Andrews, 1999b; Koehler et al., 2013; Lipsey, 2009; Lowenkamp & Latessa, 2004; Lowenkamp et al., 2006).

The *need* principle states that effective rehabilitation efforts should target the dynamic needs and risk factors that are known to be directly related to the individual offender's criminal behaviour (i.e. *criminogenic needs*). Needs that might seem important for the benefit of the individual offender, but are actually only weakly associated with recidivism (i.e. *non-criminogenic needs*) should receive less (or even no) attention when the intervention aims at recidivism reduction. Examples of these non-criminogenic needs are low self-esteem, mental health problems, emotional distress, physical health problems, social skills deficits (Andrews & Bonta, 2010; Bonta & Andrews, 2017; Ogloff & Davis, 2004). Instead, Andrews and Bonta (2010) propose eight central criminogenic risk factors as the most important ones: criminal history, antisocial personality pattern, antisocial attitudes, antisocial associates/peers, family problems, school/work problems, lack of constructive leisure/recreation, and substance abuse (Bonta & Andrews, 2017). These risk factors have received support in a large number of studies and meta-analyses in adults (Gendreau et al., 1996; Hanson & Morton-Bourgon, 2004, 2005; Olver et al., 2014; Wooditch et al., 2014) and juveniles (Cottle et al., 2001; Glueck & Glueck, 1950; Grieger & Hosser, 2014; Olver et al., 2009). Andrews and Bonta (2010) assert that these criminogenic risk factors are dynamic (except for criminal history) and "...when changed, are associated with changes in the probability of recidivism" (p. 49). Interventions for adults and juveniles targeting these criminogenic risk factors have indeed shown to be (moderately) more effective in reducing recidivism than interventions that target primarily non-criminogenic factors, such as personal distress, physical activity, and self-esteem (Andrews & Bonta, 2010; Andrews & Dowden, 2006; Bonta & Andrews, 2017; Dowden & Andrews, 1999b; Hanson et al., 2009; Koehler et al., 2013; Singh et al., 2014; Vieira et al., 2009).

The *responsivity* principle suggests that interventions should be delivered in a manner that matches the abilities and learning styles of the offender (Andrews & Bonta, 2010; Bonta & Andrews, 2017). The responsivity concept is divided into two types: general and specific. *General responsivity* refers to the recommendation of using the most powerful strategies to influence (criminal) behaviour, currently known as *cognitive-behavioural strategies* (Andrews & Bonta, 2010; Bonta & Andrews, 2017; Dowden & Andrews, 1999b; Koehler et al., 2013; Landenberger & Lipsey, 2005; Lee & DiGiuseppe, 2018; Lösel & Schmucker, 2005). *Specific responsivity* emphasizes matching the intervention to the offender, taking into account each individual's characteristics, such as mental health issues, intelligence level, cognitive style, level of amenability and treatment engagement (Andrews & Bonta, 2010; Bonta & Andrews, 2017). Although the latter responsivity principle is the least studied of the RNR model, studies have shown that certain aspects, such as the offender's intellectual functioning, mental health issues, minimization and denial of offending, and treatment readiness and motivation can moderate treatment effectiveness (Hubbard, 2007; Looman et al., 2005; McCormick et al., 2017; Silver et al., 2020). Paying attention to treatment motivation and engagement in offender rehabilitation seems to be a particularly important factor that can positively impact the effectiveness of the intervention in both adults and adolescents (Andrews & Bonta, 2010; Bonta & Andrews, 2017; Bourgon & Bonta, 2014; Ginsburg et al., 2002; Levenson & Macgowan, 2004; Marshall & Marshall, 2012; Marshall et al., 2008; Nee et al., 2013).

In view of the above, it can be concluded that numerous studies provide support for the relevance of the RNR principles to offender rehabilitation, by demonstrating promising results in reducing recidivism of interventions that adhere to them. As a result, the focus on risk assessment and management has become standard practice in offender rehabilitation (Andrews & Bonta, 2010; Bonta & Andrews, 2017). However, the results of RNR-based interventions only show a moderate effect on recidivism reduction. Meta-analyses indicate that RNR-based interventions result in approximately 20% more recidivism reduction compared to interventions that do not adhere to the RNR principles (Andrews & Dowden, 2006; Bonta & Andrews, 2017; Dowden & Andrews, 2000; Hanson et al., 2009; Koehler et al., 2013; Latessa & Lowenkamp, 2006). The recidivism rates for both adult and juvenile offenders who completed RNR-based interventions remain substantial (on average around 30%, sometimes even higher; Hanson et al., 2009; Koehler et al., 2013; Latessa & Lowenkamp, 2006). Moreover, dropout rates in offender rehabilitation interventions are high, ranging from 20% for prison-based interventions for adult offenders to 58% for residential juvenile offender treatment programs (Olver et al., 2011). Treatment dropout has been consistently linked to negative outcomes, such as higher recidivism rates compared to treatment completers, sometimes even higher than for untreated offenders (McMurran & Theodosi, 2007; Olver et al., 2011). Consequently, these results suggest that there is still room for improvement in (juvenile) offender rehabilitation.

1.3 A Strengths-based Approach: The Good Lives Model of Offender Rehabilitation

As outlined in the previous section, offender rehabilitation interventions based on the RNR model focus mostly on targeting empirically derived risk factors that are directly linked to offending and recidivism. Partly as criticism on this focus on risk, the 'Good Lives Model of offender rehabilitation' (GLM) was developed (Ward, 2002a, 2002b).[1] The authors of the GLM criticize the RNR model's primary focus on risk reduction because, in their view, it cannot provide constructive guidance for treatment goals and ignores important aspects of human functioning (Ward, 2002a, 2002b; Ward & Maruna, 2007; Ward & Stewart, 2003a). According to the GLM's developers, an important aspect ignored by RNR-based interventions is that humans are, by nature, goal-directed beings, who experience a need to strive for approach goals instead of merely avoiding problems and minimizing deficits (Emmons, 1996; Ward, 2002a, 2002b; Ward & Brown, 2003). Furthermore, the GLM deems individuals as active, goal-seeking agents, who acquire a sense of who they are and what really matters to them from their daily activities and lifestyle (Laws & Ward, 2011; Ward & Maruna, 2007). Subsequently, negative or avoidance goals are considered as particularly difficult to implement in treatment, because they do not specify what is sought, but only what should be eliminated (Ward & Brown, 2003; Ward & Stewart, 2003c; Ward et al., 2006). Ward and Stewart (2003c) use the metaphor of offenders as pincushions to clarify their criticism towards the RNR model:

> Offenders are essentially collections of discrete risk factors (i.e., "pins") that are embedded in their lifestyles, environments, and personalities. The task of the therapist is to remove each risk factor, or pin, from an offender (i.e., target the

1 Although the GLM was initially developed for offender rehabilitation of adult sexual offenders, it is considered to be applicable to all types of offenders (Laws & Ward, 2011; Ward & Maruna, 2007). Since its development it has been advanced and applied to both men and women, violent offenders, street gangs, mentally disordered offenders, and young offenders (Barnao, Ward, & Robertson 2016; Byrne, 2020; Fortune, 2018; Langlands, Ward, & Gilchrist, 2009; Lord, 2016; Mallion, 2021; Mallion & Wood, 2020; Pflugradt & Allen, 2019; Whitehead, Ward, & Collie, 2007).

> criminogenic needs) and by doing so reduce the offender's overall level of risk. However, the danger is that when the primary focus of treatment is on individual risk factors, individuals are viewed as disembodied bearers of risk rather than as integrated agents. Just as removing all the pins from a pincushion leaves only holes, treating offenders strictly according to this [RNR] model leaves them with gaps in their lives. (p. 354)

Ward and colleagues (Ward, 2002b; Ward & Brown, 2004; Ward & Maruna, 2007; Ward & Stewart, 2003b, 2003c) further argue that risk factors merely act as red flags that signal there is a problem. Consequently, they contend that risk factors alone cannot provide guidance on what to do in interventions, other than to attempt to remove them or weaken their effects. This means that, according to the GLM, it is not enough to merely equip individuals with skills to control or manage their risk factors. Instead, interventions should provide the opportunity to build upon a more adaptive personal identity, one that gives a sense of meaning and fulfillment (Ward, 2002a, 2002b; Ward & Gannon, 2006; Ward & Maruna, 2007; Ward & Stewart, 2003c). As Ward, Mann, and Gannon (2007) propose "… offenders want better lives, not simply the promise of less harmful ones" (p. 106).

Notwithstanding their criticism, Ward and colleagues also express their appreciation for the RNR model and its extensive empirical basis (Ward, 2002b; Ward & Maruna, 2007; Ward, Melser, et al., 2007). As a result, they argue that a focus on reducing dynamic risk factors (i.e. criminogenic needs) is indeed *necessary* but *not sufficient* for effective offender treatment (Ward & Gannon, 2006; Ward & Maruna, 2007; Ward & Stewart, 2003b, 2003c). In this regard, the GLM states it should not be viewed as a replacement of the RNR model, but rather as a supplement; creating an integration in which both models can benefit from each other's strengths (Ward & Maruna, 2007; Ward, Melser, et al., 2007; Ward et al., 2012). Thus, the GLM focuses not only on criminogenic risk factors, problems, and deficits, but is also concerned with the enhancement of offenders' capabilities in order to meet their personal (non-criminogenic) human needs and goals (Ward, 2002b; Ward & Stewart, 2003a). It is believed that securing primary human needs, in a socially acceptable and personally meaningful way, will both improve well-being (i.e. result in a 'good life') and target the possible obstacles that get in the way of this goal (known as '*risk factors*'), consequently preventing recidivism (Ward, 2002b; Ward & Gannon, 2006; Ward & Stewart, 2003a; Ward et al., 2006). Focusing on capabilities and well-being makes the GLM a strengths-based approach, having its roots in positive psychology[2] (Aspinwall & Staudinger, 2003; Rapp & Goscha, 2012; Ward & Gannon, 2006; Ward & Mann, 2004; Ward & Maruna, 2007). Strengths-based approaches aim to "move away from 'disease' and

2 See also Chapter 3, Section 3.1 for a brief explanation of 'positive psychology'.

'deficits' and move toward human potential and well-being" (Rapp & Goscha, 2012, p. 14). Accordingly, Ward (2002b) states that the GLM combines the improvement of well-being with the reduction of recidivism (risk), resulting in a hybrid and holistic rehabilitation model.

The GLM is based on two, mainly theoretical, etiological assumptions. The *first etiological assumption* holds that all human beings strive to obtain, to varying extent, a universal set of human needs and goals in order to achieve a higher well-being (Ward, 2002a, 2002b; Ward & Maruna, 2007; Ward & Stewart, 2003a).[3] In the GLM these needs and goals are addressed as eleven *primary goods*: (healthy and safe) 'life'; 'knowledge'; 'excellence in work'; 'excellence in play'; 'excellence in agency'; 'inner peace'; 'relatedness' with friends, family, or a partner; (being part of a) 'community'; 'spirituality' (seeking purpose and meaning in life); 'creativity'; and 'pleasure' (see the next chapter(s) for an elaboration of these eleven primary goods; Purvis, 2010; Purvis et al., 2014; Ward, 2002a, 2002b). While primary goods are broad motivational constructs, instrumental or *secondary goods* provide the specific ways or means of securing the primary goods. There is no fixed list of possible secondary goods as it involves a wide range of specific possibilities, opportunities, and behaviours that depend on one's personal preferences, capabilities, and environment. Examples of secondary goods include: having a successful career (i.e. for the primary good of 'excellence in work'), spending time with loved ones (i.e. for the primary good of 'relatedness'), or engaging in leisure activities, such as sports and hobby's (i.e. for the primary goods of 'excellence in play' and/or 'pleasure') (Ward, 2002a, 2002b). According to the GLM, human beings strive to attain all of the primary goods, but individuals may differ in the weight they give to each, thereby reflecting their personal values and priorities in life (Ward, 2002b).

The *second etiological assumption* of the GLM is that a failure to prosocially obtain primary goods needed for well-being can result in criminal behaviour (Ward & Marshall, 2004; Ward & Maruna, 2007; Ward & Stewart, 2003a).[4] All human actions, including criminal or antisocial acts, are viewed as ultimately linked to the pursuit of human goods. Criminal behaviour, according to the GLM, can thus be seen as an alternative, antisocial attempt to obtain primary goods when an individual fails to prosocially secure the individual's primary goods. In this process, two possible routes towards offending behaviour are assumed: the direct and indirect route (Purvis, 2010; Purvis et al., 2011, 2014; Ward & Gannon, 2006; Ward & Marshall, 2004; Ward & Stewart, 2003a). The direct route is assumed to occur when primary goods are (deliberately) sought through offence-related antisocial actions (Purvis et al., 2011). The main problem presumed to underly the direct route is the use of *inappropriate (illegal) ways or means* of achieving the goods (e.g.

3 See Chapter 3 for a theoretical elaboration of the GLM's first etiological assumption.
4 See Chapter 5 for a theoretical elaboration of the GLM's second etiological assumption.

illegal sexual acts for the primary goods of 'relatedness' and/or 'pleasure'; Purvis et al., 2011; Ward & Gannon, 2006; Willis & Ward, 2013). The indirect route is assumed to occur when an individual experiences other problems in the initial prosocial pursuit of their valued goods that eventually result in an offence (Purvis et al., 2011).

The proposed potential indirect problems include a *lack of scope* (i.e. one or more primary goods are neglected), a *lack of coherence* (i.e. there is conflict between the ways certain goods are pursued), and a *lack of capacities* (i.e. a lack of skills or resources to achieve the primary goods sought in a prosocial manner; Purvis et al., 2011; Ward, 2002b; Ward & Gannon, 2006). In the latter potential problem, the prosocial attainment of primary goods can be hampered by a lack of capacities due to both *personal (internal) limitations* (e.g. a lack of knowledge or skills) and *environmental (external) disadvantages* (e.g. a lack of resources or opportunities; Purvis et al., 2011; Purvis et al., 2014; Ward & Stewart, 2003a). An example of the indirect route is when a conflict between the need for intimacy ('relatedness') and the desire for autonomy ('excellence in agency') leads to the breakup of a relationship. Subsequent feelings of loneliness and distress, combined with maladaptive coping strategies (e.g. substance use) might lead, in specific circumstances, to a loss of control and sexual offending (alternatively seeking the primary good of 'relatedness'; Purvis et al., 2011).

Grounded in these etiological assumptions, the GLM argues that effective rehabilitation interventions should thus combine the reduction of recidivism (risk) with an improvement in the offender's personal well-being (Laws & Ward, 2011; Ward, 2002b; Ward & Fortune, 2013; Ward & Gannon, 2006; Ward & Maruna, 2007; Ward & Stewart, 2003a; Ward et al., 2006).[5] It is this combination that could potentially bridge the tension between security (risk management) and treatment or care (welfare promotion) within the juvenile justice system.

1.4 AIM

Based on the above, it is hypothesized that a combination of a risk-focused approach and a welfare-focused approach, such as the GLM proposes, is a potentially promising way forward in juvenile offender rehabilitation. GLM-based rehabilitation interventions could offer this dual approach by promoting offenders' strengths, valued goods and well-being, while also reducing recidivism (risk) in an effective and sustainable manner. This integrative approach of the GLM could be especially beneficial for (detained) adolescent offenders given the complex range of problems they display as outlined in the beginning of this chapter (regarding their well-being, mental health and psychosocial problems,

5 See Chapter 9 for a theoretical elaboration of these practical assumptions.

resistance to treatment, dropout risk, and recidivism risk; Fortune, 2018; Van Damme et al., 2017; Ward et al., 2012).

Although this integrative approach suggested by the GLM seems promising in theory, the RNR model – to a certain extent justifiably – has criticized the GLM for its lack of empirical evidence: "At this point, the empirical support for GLM pales compared to that of RNR" (Andrews et al., 2011, p. 737). Ten years have passed since this comment and research into the assumptions and the effectiveness of the GLM is on the rise (see for overviews of these studies also: Fortune, 2018; Mallion et al., 2020; Netto et al., 2014; Purvis et al., 2014; Willis & Ward, 2013; Zeccola et al., 2021; Ziv, 2016, 2018). Nevertheless, compared to the vast empirical evidence base for the RNR model, the GLM lags behind in the number of studies investigating the model, especially those exploring the application of the GLM to young offenders (Fortune, 2018; Van Damme et al., 2017).

Hence, in this book I will specifically examine the applicability of the GLM's etiological assumptions and intervention recommendations in (detained) adolescent offenders.

1.5 Overview

To this end, in the next chapter (**Chapter 2**) I will first provide an overview of the differences and similarities between the RNR model and the GLM. I elaborate upon the hypothesis that the GLM's hybrid focus on both well-being promotion and recidivism (risk) reduction could potentially bridge the gap between risk- and welfare-focused approaches in juvenile justice systems.

The remainder of this book is divided in three parts. The first part entails a literature study regarding the theoretical background of the GLM's etiological assumptions about well-being and delinquency. **Chapter 3** first provides an overview of the theoretical and empirical literature of the relationship between primary goods and well-being in general (i.e. GLM's *first etiological assumption*). The theoretical background of the GLM, however, focuses heavily on adults. Therefore, **Chapter 4** provides an extensive systematic literature review and meta-analysis on the existing studies concerning the relationship between the proposed GLM primary goods and overall well-being, particularly in adolescents from the general population. Next, **Chapter 5** follows with an overview of the existing theoretical and empirical literature concerning the potential role of primary goods and well-being in the aetiology of juvenile delinquency (i.e., GLM's *second etiological assumption*).

The second part of the book comprises the empirical examination of the two etiological assumptions of the GLM in (detained) adolescents. In **Chapter 6**, the hypotheses regarding the role of primary goods and well-being in explaining juvenile delinquency are empirically tested based on survey data of a large sample of adolescents from the general population. In **Chapters 7** and **8** we aim to further uncover the mechanisms underlying the observed relations between primary goods, well-being and juvenile delinquency. In these chapters, results are presented of a study in which we quantitatively assessed (**Chapter 7**) and qualitatively interviewed (**Chapter 8**) recently arrested and detained male adolescent offenders regarding their primary goods satisfaction, overall well-being, mental health problems, criminogenic risk (factors), and committed offence(s).

In the final part, we examine the extent to which the GLM's practical assumptions are also applicable to juvenile rehabilitation interventions. **Chapter 9** starts with a literature review of the theoretical and empirical background of these practical assumptions regarding effective rehabilitation according to the GLM. Specific attention is given to the hypothesized effects of well-being and primary goods pursuit on increasing treatment motivation and reducing recidivism (risk). In **Chapter 10**, these hypotheses are then tested, based on the follow-up data of the detained adolescents from the study in Chapter 7, who were followed during their residential stay in a juvenile detention centre. More specifically, in that chapter, the longitudinal associations between primary goods satisfaction, overall well-being, mental health problems, treatment motivation, and recidivism risk are examined. In the final chapter (**Chapter 11**), I discuss the conclusions, implications, and recommendations for future research and juvenile offender rehabilitation in practice. Ultimately, with this work I aim to provide evidence-based recommendations that can help juvenile justice interventions to effectively respond to (detained) adolescent offenders' (criminogenic) needs and their potential complex problems in a constructive and positive manner.

2 The Risk Need Responsivity Model vs. The Good Lives Model

Similarities and Differences

In the Introduction, I outlined the challenging tension between risk-focused and welfare-focused approaches in juvenile justice systems. Additionally, I briefly introduced the most commonly used risk-focused approach: The Risk Need Responsivity (RNR) model and an upcoming strengths-based approach: The Good Lives Model of offender rehabilitation (GLM). In this chapter, I will first provide an overview of the differences and similarities between the views of these two rehabilitation models. Subsequently, I will argue that at least in theory a hybrid focus on both well-being promotion and recidivism (risk) reduction, as proposed by the GLM, could potentially overcome the tension between the two seemingly opposing approaches in juvenile justice.

2.1 Similarities and Differences Between the Two Rehabilitation Models

2.1.1 *Offender Rehabilitation: What Works According to Whom?*

In the past, the authors of the RNR model and GLM have been critical towards each other's work.[1] As mentioned in the Introduction, the GLM criticizes the RNR model for its primary focus on criminogenic risk factors (Ward, 2002b; Ward & Brown, 2003, 2004; Ward & Maruna, 2007; Ward, Melser, et al., 2007; Ward & Stewart, 2003a, 2003b; Ward et al., 2012). Simultaneously, the RNR model's authors mainly criticize the GLM for its focus on well-being in offender rehabilitation (Andrews & Bonta, 2010; Andrews et al., 2011; Bonta & Andrews, 2003; Wormith et al., 2012). It seems, however, that this critique in both directions is not always warranted, and the two models actually agree on important aspects of offender rehabilitation. For example, in the fifth edition of *The Psychology of Criminal Conduct*, Andrews and Bonta (2010) incorrectly criticize the GLM for promoting punishment and sanctions instead of human services. This statement is incorrect as the GLM in fact agrees with the RNR model that interventions should focus on reducing

1 See also the work of Ronen Ziv (2016, 2018) for an extensive review of the two models, their debate, and controversies.

recidivism and working towards prosocial, fulfilling lives instead of mere punishment (Laws & Ward, 2011; Ward, 2002b). Indeed, in a later and more elaborate response to the GLM, Andrews et al. (2011) retract this erroneous statement: "Both RNR and GLM offer[ed] an alternative to punishment" (p. 748). Nevertheless, Andrews and Bonta (2010) continue to be particularly critical of the GLM's focus on pursuing personal well-being and (non-criminogenic) human needs:

> It is not sufficient to highlight personal well-being or to highlight the accumulation of rewards and satisfactions. It must be made explicit that the contingencies should be supportive of noncriminal alternative routes to rewards. That is what adherence with the principles of RNR is designed to support. (Andrews & Bonta, 2010, p. 55)

The authors of the RNR even accuse GLM interventions of being potentially supportive of crime if they focus on satisfying human needs without consideration of the (possible antisocial) means to do so (Andrews et al., 2011, p. 740). Instead, they argue that to adhere to their *need* principle, effective interventions should focus primarily on criminogenic risk factors becoming strength factors (Andrews & Bonta, 2010, p. 54). The developers of the GLM countered this criticism by stating that GLM-based interventions aim to provide a more fulfilling way of living and satisfying one's primary human goods in a *prosocial instead of a criminal* manner (Ward, 2002b; Ward & Maruna, 2007; Ward & Stewart, 2003b; Ward et al., 2012). This would include reducing criminogenic risk factors, which in the GLM are deemed obstacles in the way of reaching this goal (Ward & Stewart, 2003a):

> The rehabilitation process is crucially dependent on identifying the internal and external obstacles that have been thwarting an individual's ability to meet his or her fundamental needs. These may be defensive strategies, personal and vocational skill deficits, maladaptive attitudes and beliefs, and lack of social support and integration. The basic concept that should drive rehabilitation is that of human well being and its component notion of categorical needs and basic goods.... This is in stark contrast to most current treatment programmes for offenders where the focus is on alleviating problems, or diminishing risk, rather than enhancing well being. (pp. 140-141)

As we already saw in the Introduction (Section 1.3), the GLM has acknowledged the importance of addressing criminogenic needs, but voices criticism towards the RNR model for neglecting (non-criminogenic) human needs, values, and well-being (Ward & Stewart, 2003a; Ward et al., 2012):

> The RNR promotes prosocial behavior only insofar as it functions to reduce criminal behavior, whereas the GLM promotes prosocial behavior both that has the possibility to reduce criminal behavior and that provides the individual with an opportunity to live a satisfying life, the latter with which the RNR does not concern itself. (Ward et al., 2012, p. 101)

As a defence to this criticism of the GLM, Andrews et al. (2011) assert that the RNR model does not "seek ways of making someone's life more miserable" (p. 742). Instead, they argue that they too focus on building strengths and rewarding non-criminal alternatives to the risk factors that are favouring criminal behaviour. Andrews et al. (2011) compare the GLM's *prosocial* promotion of primary human goods to the RNR-based aim of building up rewards for non-criminal activities. In their reactions to the GLM's criticism, the developers of the RNR model have also argued that the RNR model is not incompatible with the goal of helping offenders living a good life (Andrews et al., 2011; Bonta & Andrews, 2003). They stated that:

> Living the good life can be attained through the RNR by assisting offenders with employment, dealing with their substance abuse and changing attitudes and social networks that interfere with a personal and interpersonal rewarding life (Bonta & Andrews, 2003, p. 216). Furthermore, Bonta and Andrews (2003) suggest that decreasing criminogenic needs can lead to the enhancement of personal well-being and they refer to the Cambridge study of Farrington et al. (2006) to support this claim. In their report on this longitudinal study, Farrington and colleagues (2006) suggest that desistance from crime can result in the enhancement of success in other areas of life, such as housing, employment, relationships, and mental health. Although this longitudinal study seems to suggest life success in these areas follows from desistance of crime, it would take an experimental design to provide evidence for a causal relationship and rule out other possible explanations. Given the complex interaction of human behaviours, it could also be plausible that life success facilitates the desistance from crime (Ward & Fortune, 2016).

2.1.2 Goods to Pursue and/or Risks to Avoid?

As mentioned in the Introduction and the previous section, the GLM views the RNR's criminogenic needs or risk factors as the internal (i.e. *personal limitations*) or external (i.e. *environmental disadvantages*) obstacles (omissions or distortions) that interfere with an individual's capacities to prosocially achieve their primary human goods and well-being

(Purvis et al., 2011; Ward, 2002b; Ward & Stewart, 2003a, 2003b, 2003c; Ward et al., 2006). For example, according to the GLM, a lack of opportunities or skills to socialize with prosocial peers (i.e., a criminogenic RNR need) might be obstacles in obtaining meaningful relationships (i.e. GLM's primary good of 'relatedness'). In turn, this could lead to the alternative antisocial way of obtaining the good, such as committing crimes to be accepted in a criminal gang (Ward, 2002b; Ward & Stewart, 2003a; Willis et al., 2013).

In this example, effective rehabilitation according to both the RNR and the GLM should thus focus on reducing the criminogenic risk of engagement with antisocial peers, by working on strengthening social skills to engage with prosocial peers. In theory, RNR- and GLM-based interventions could both reach the same goal of reducing recidivism risk, although they depart from a different perspective. The GLM would prioritize working towards personal well-being, a fulfilling life, and satisfying the need for meaningful relationships in a non-harmful way (strengthening social skills to socialize with prosocial instead of antisocial peers; Ward & Gannon, 2006; Ward et al., 2006). The RNR model on the other hand, would focus on reducing the criminogenic risk of engaging with antisocial peers by shifting this risk into a strength (strengthening social skills to avoid engagement with antisocial peers; Andrews & Bonta, 2010; Andrews et al., 2011). Both, if successfully executed in interventions, could diminish the criminogenic risk of antisocial peers, potentially reducing the recidivism risk.

Additionally, there is also considerable similarity between the most important types of *criminogenic needs* targeted by the RNR model (i.e. the 'central eight'), and the eleven *primary goods* of the GLM (see Table 2.1; Looman & Abracen, 2013).[2] Ward and Stewart (2003b, 2003c) propose that criminogenic needs function as markers indicating there is a problem in the way individuals are seeking their primary human goods; a problem that they argue is most likely directly related to their criminal behaviour. They subsequently state that different types of risk factors are likely related to distinct clusters of primary human goods (Ward & Brown, 2004; Ward & Stewart, 2003b, 2003c). Nonetheless, all kinds of criminogenic risk factors are deemed by the GLM to potentially serve as obstacles for all types of primary goods, depending on each person and their environment. Ultimately, several life domains (relationships with family/friends/peers, school/work, leisure, and cognition/emotions) could be targeted by the RNR model with the aim of reducing criminogenic risk factors, as well as by the GLM with the aim of satisfying primary human goods in a prosocial way (Ward & Gannon, 2006; Ward & Stewart, 2003b, 2003c; Ward et al., 2006).

2 The (theoretical) relationships between primary goods and criminogenic risk factors will be discussed in more detail in Chapter 5.

Table 2.1 The GLM Primary Goods, Examples of GLM Secondary Goods, and the RNR Criminogenic Risk Factors and Needs

Good Lives Model			Risk Need Responsivity model	
Primary goods	**Prosocial secondary goods (means)**	**Antisocial secondary goods (means)**	**'Central eight' Dynamic Risk factors**	**Criminogenic needs**
In general, the GLM strives for a prosocial happy and fulfilling life in which antisocial behaviour is seen as an obstacle to this ultimate goal. **Antisocial behaviour in general should thus be countered with prosocial non-harmful alternatives.**			**Criminal history**	Build up non-criminal alternative behaviours in high-risk situations
Excellence in agency – Seeking independence and autonomy, making one's way in life	Developing and following through with life plans, being assertive	Having control over other people, abusing, or manipulating others	**Antisocial personality pattern** (impulsive, adventurous pleasure-seeking, weak self-control, restlessly aggressive)	Build problem-solving skills, self-management skills, anger management, empathy, and coping skills
Inner peace – The experience of emotional equilibrium, freedom from emotional turmoil and stress	Exercise, meditation, self-regulation skills or other activities that help manage emotions and stress	Use of alcohol or drugs, *Venting frustrations through aggression	**Antisocial attitudes** (attitudes, values, beliefs, rationalizations, and thoughts that are favourable to crime and cognitive-emotional states of anger, feeling irritated, resentful and/or defiant)	Reduce procriminal thinking, recognize risky thinking and feeling, build up alternative less risky thinking and feeling, build and practice prosocial thoughts, adopt a prosocial identity
Pleasure – The desire to experience feelings of happiness and pleasure	Socializing with friends, enjoyment of food, watching movies, sex, thrill-seeking activities	Antisocial thrill-seeking activities, drinking alcohol or taking drugs	**Substance abuse**	Reduce substance abuse, reduce the personal and interpersonal supports for substance-oriented behaviour, and enhance alternatives to drug abuse
Relatedness – Sharing close and mutual bonds with other people, including relationships with intimate partners, family and friends	Spending time with family and/or friends, having an intimate relationship with another person	Engaging in illegal intimate activities, *Spending time with antisocial friends or relatives	**Family problems** (poor quality relationships, poor parental monitoring, and disciplining)	Reduce conflict, build positive relationships, enhance monitoring and supervision, enhance warmth and caring

Good Lives Model			Risk Need Responsivity model	
Primary goods	**Prosocial secondary goods (means)**	**Antisocial secondary goods (means)**	**'Central eight' Dynamic Risk factors**	**Criminogenic needs**
Community – Being part of, or belonging to a group of people who share common interests, concerns, or values	Belonging to a service club, volunteer group, or sports team	Being a member of a criminal gang	**Antisocial associates/peers** (association with procriminal others and relative isolation from prosocial others)	Reduce association with criminal friends and associates, enhance association with prosocial friends and associates
Excellence in work – Striving for excellence and mastery in work	Being employed or volunteering in meaningful work, advancing one's career	*Advancing a criminal career	**School/Work problems** (low levels of performance, rewarding performance and satisfactions)	Enhance performance, involvement, rewards, and satisfactions in school/work, enhance work/study skills
Knowledge – Seeking knowledge about oneself, other people, the environment, or specific subjects important to the individual	Attending school or training courses, self-study (e.g., reading), mentoring or coaching, attending a treatment program	*Learning about criminal skills		
Life – Looking after physical health and/or staying alive and safe	Healthy diet, regular exercise, earning a livelihood, having a safe place to live	Stealing money to pay for rent and food		
Excellence in play – Striving for excellence and mastery in hobbies or leisure activities	Participating in sports, playing an instrument, arts and crafts	*Engaging in criminal (leisure) activities	**Lack of constructive leisure/recreation** (low levels of involvement and satisfactions)	Enhance involvement, rewards, and satisfactions in leisure/recreation, encourage participation in prosocial recreation activities
Creativity – The desire to create something, do things differently, or try new things	Painting, photography, and other types of artistic expression; participating in new or novel activities	*Trying new or creative antisocial activities		

Good Lives Model			Risk Need Responsivity model	
Primary goods	**Prosocial secondary goods (means)**	**Antisocial secondary goods (means)**	**'Central eight' Dynamic Risk factors**	**Criminogenic needs**
Spirituality – Having meaning and purpose in life; being part of a larger whole	Participating in religious activities (e.g., going to church, prayer), participating in groups that share a common purpose (e.g., environmental groups)	*Being part of a terrorist group		

Note. The descriptions of the RNR risk factors and criminogenic needs are derived from Bonta and Andrews (2017, pp. 45-46, 181 and 338), and Andrews and Bonta (2010, pp. 58 and 500). The descriptions of the primary and secondary GLM goods are derived from Willis, Prescott and Yates (2013) and Purvis, Ward and Willis (2014).

* = These antisocial secondary goods were not explicitly mentioned in Willis et al. (2013) and Purvis et al. (2014) but have been deducted from the vast amount of GLM literature cited throughout this and the following chapters.

2.1.3 *Explaining Criminal Conduct: Two Sides of the Same Coin?*

In the previous sections, we have seen that regardless of their critique of each other's work, both the GLM and the RNR models, although departing from a different perspective, are quite similar in their ultimate goals for offender rehabilitation. Andrews and Bonta (2010), however, not only developed the principles for effective offender rehabilitation (i.e. the RNR principles), but also proposed an integrated theory *explaining* criminal conduct (the Personal, Interpersonal and Community Reinforcement Perspective; PIC-R).[3] This theory holds that individual differences in the probability of criminal behaviour are due to the perceived rewards and costs of that behaviour (Andrews & Bonta, 2010; Bonta & Andrews, 2017). The chances of a criminal act occurring are believed to increase if the density[4] of the rewards is deemed higher than its costs. The theory further states that whether the rewards of the criminal behaviour outweigh the costs depends on personal, (social) environmental, and community factors (Andrews & Bonta, 2010; Bonta & Andrews, 2017). Examples of these factors that influence this cost-benefit analysis coincide with several of the RNR risk factors: impulsivity problems, antisocial attitudes, antisocial peers or family (Andrews & Bonta, 2010). They furthermore argue that "… low rates of rewards and satisfaction in conventional pursuits may motivate criminal behavior under a stress or strain interpretation …" (Andrews & Bonta, 2010, p. 148), and:

> Low scores on the measures of social power and personal competence suggest that a person is unlikely to receive many rewards for nondeviant pursuits; hence, the subtractive costs of deviance may be slight and the motivation for crime increased. (Andrews & Bonta, 2010, p. 154)

This theory seems to be in line with the GLM that views criminal behaviour as an antisocial alternative for pursuing primary human goods (similar to rewards), when the conventional, prosocial, and non-harmful way is unsatisfactory due to internal and external obstacles (i.e. risk factors; Purvis et al., 2011; Ward, 2002a, 2002b; Ward & Stewart, 2003a). For example, in this line of reasoning, the GLM and PIC-R would explain the criminal act of robbery by a person who was unable to keep a satisfactory legal job in similar ways. According to both theories, it can be hypothesized that the robber chose the quick reward of the antisocial alternative over a legal job due to a number of risk factors or obstacles,

---

3 In the latest version (sixth edition) of *The Psychology of Criminal Conduct* (Bonta & Andrews, 2017) this theory is no longer explicitly referred to as the PIC-R, but as an integrated part of the General Personality and Cognitive Social Learning theory of criminal conduct. The reasoning and arguments of the theory, however, remain the same.

4 *Density* refers to "… the number, variety, quality, and magnitude of rewards [/costs] as well as the immediacy, frequency, and regularity with which they are delivered" (Andrews & Bonta, 2010, p. 147).

such as a lack of competence, difficulties with self-control, antisocial attitudes, and/or the influence of antisocial peers (Andrews & Bonta, 2010; Bonta & Andrews, 2017; Ward & Brown, 2003; Ward & Gannon, 2006; Ward & Stewart, 2003a, 2003c). Thus, to prevent delinquency, the PIC-R (similar to the GLM) promotes the strengthening of rewards from non-criminal behaviour, while at the same time reducing the criminogenic risk factors, to make reward seeking (or in GLM terms: the pursuit of primary goods) by criminal means less appealing (Andrews & Bonta, 2010; Ward, 2002b; Ward & Stewart, 2003c; Ward et al., 2012). Although Andrews and Bonta (2010) mention a few examples of rewards (that resemble some of the primary goods of the GLM), such as money, feelings of pleasure, relief, stress-reduction, accomplishment, independence, group membership, and social approval, the PIC-R does not address explicitly what types of rewards offenders seek in their criminal acts. This is different from the GLM, which aims to discover the rewards that are important for the individual offender (i.e. the primary goods) in order to set personalized treatment goals that focus on achieving those rewards in a prosocial instead of a criminal way (Ward, 2002a, 2002b; Ward & Gannon, 2006; Ward & Maruna, 2007; Ward & Stewart, 2003a, 2003c; Ward et al., 2012).

The PIC-R also differs from the GLM by emphasizing the effect of the (potential) punishment and costs issuing from the individual, the (social) environment or the community (such as disapproval, negative self-labelling, feelings of fear, etc.) for criminal behaviour: "… but the truly dramatic effect of low levels of rewards and satisfactions from conventional activity is the near total absence of subtractive punishment for criminal behavior" (Andrews & Bonta, 2010, p. 148). Interestingly, in light of this reasoning, Andrews and Bonta (2010) even partly retract their previous statement that mental health problems are not important risk factors for delinquency and recidivism:

> … even measures of psychological discomfort (such as anxiety, low self-esteem, and alienation) may be related to criminality under very particular circumstances. Certain forms of deviance may reduce psychological distress (a subtractive reward), and with a background of low levels of self-satisfaction, the personally mediated subtractive costs of deviance will be relatively low. (Andrews & Bonta, 2010, p. 154)

This rationale is once again in line with the GLM, more specifically with the idea that in the pursuit of rewards, non-criminogenic needs can be explanatory for antisocial behaviour. In this particular example, it coincides with the GLM-based hypothesis that antisocial attempts to obtain the primary good (the 'reward' in RNR-terms) of 'inner peace' (reducing distress) can result in deviant attempts to obtain this good, for example, through substance use or venting frustration aggressively (Purvis et al., 2014; Willis et al., 2013), especially if there is not much else to lose.

In a more general sense, it is argued that both the GLM and PIC-R are (at least in part) based on the basic principles of strain theory (Andrews et al., 2011; Ward & Maruna, 2007):

> Building on a central premise of "strain theory" (see Messner and Rosenfield, 2001), the GLM proposes that crime might best be understood as the product of obstacles to the pursuit of legitimate goals. (Ward & Maruna, 2007, p. 121)

> Theoretically, GLM owes much to strain theory (Merton, 1957) and, if we go back further, to the Freudian frustration-aggression model of crime (Dollard, Doob, Miller, Mowrer, & Sears, 1939). Essentially, achieving primary goods are blocked by distortions in self-identity and criminogenic needs (Lindsay, Ward, Morgan, & Wilson, 2007; Ward & Maruna, 2007). Both the psychodynamic and strain theories have been integrated in the general personality and cognitive social learning (GPCSL) theoretical perspective that underlies RNR. (Andrews et al., 2011, p. 740)

Robert Agnew's (1992) well-known general strain theory of crime and delinquency suggests three types of strain that could lead to criminal behaviour, namely: (1) the prevention or blockage from achieving positively valued goals, (2) the (anticipated) removal or loss of positively valued stimuli that one possesses, and (3) the (anticipated) presentation to noxious or negatively valued stimuli. These types of strain resemble the (anticipated) costs and blockage of rewards that can result in criminal behaviour according to the PIC-R, as well as the possible internal and external obstacles to the pursuit of valued goals (i.e. primary goods) of the GLM.[5]

2.2 Bridging the Gap

2.2.1 *The Potential Bridge Between Risk-focused and Welfare-focused Rehabilitation Approaches*

In the face of these substantial similarities between the RNR/PIC-R and the GLM, and their shared ultimate goal, the GLM is still critical of the RNR model and the accompanying PIC-R. As became clear, the GLM's main point of criticism on the RNR model is its *primary* focus on eliminating or modifying criminogenic risk factors that are directly related to offending and are *defined by professionals* (through risk assessment). Although

5 See Chapter 5, Section 5.2.1 for an elaboration on the analogy between the GLM and strain theory.

the developers of the GLM assume that targeting criminogenic needs is necessary in offender rehabilitation, they assert that the RNR model does not address the full range of *(self-perceived)* needs of offenders and is therefore insufficient to adequately reduce recidivism (Ward & Fortune, 2013; Ward & Maruna, 2007; Ward & Stewart, 2003a, 2003b; Ward et al., 2012). Indeed, as mentioned in the Introduction (see Section 1.2), meta-analyses have shown that attending to individual criminogenic needs in rehabilitation based on the RNR model, only results in a relatively small proportion of the reduction in recidivism rates (20% more recidivism reduction compared to non-RNR interventions). Moreover, the recidivism rates for both adult and juvenile offenders who completed RNR interventions remain substantial (on average around 30%, sometimes even higher; Andrews & Bonta, 2010; Andrews & Dowden, 2006; Bonta & Andrews, 2017; Dowden & Andrews, 1999b; Hanson et al., 2009; Koehler et al., 2013; Vieira et al., 2009).

Although many empirical studies in the past have shown that dynamic criminogenic risk factors (in particular the 'central eight' of the RNR model) can statistically predict recidivism in adults (Gendreau et al., 1996) and adolescents (Olver et al., 2009), a statistical relationship with recidivism is not the same as a causal one (Fortune & Heffernan, 2019; Fortune & Heffernan, 2021; Heffernan, Wegerhoff, et al., 2019; Ward & Fortune, 2016). For a risk factor to be causal, and thus an important treatment goal for recidivism reduction, it should precede and increase the likelihood of (re)offending, and when changes occur in the risk factor, this should likewise result in a change in the likelihood of (re)offending (Mann et al., 2010).

Ongoing research into risk factors for recidivism, however, seems to suggest that most of them are rather 'symptoms' of or 'proxies' for delinquency with other underlying causal mechanisms (Heffernan & Ward, 2017; Heffernan, Wegerhoff, et al., 2019; Klepfisz et al., 2016; Ward & Fortune, 2016). That is, several meta-analyses investigating the relationship between change in criminogenic risk factors during treatment and future offending behaviour did not reveal a strong and consistent relationship (Beggs, 2010; Serin et al., 2013; van den Berg et al., 2018). For example, although they found a (small) effect of positive change in risk factors on recidivism rates, van den Berg et al. (2018) conclude that dynamic risk factors in fact:

> measure clinical features that are associated with the psychological propensities that actually cause recidivism, instead of assessing these propensities themselves … [and] If dynamic risk factors are predominantly correlates of psychological propensities, causally related to sexual (re)offending, then treatment of these dynamic risk factors would still, at best, 'treat the symptoms' and not the causes. (p. 187)

Accordingly, Wooditch, Tang, and Taxman (2014) found improvements in probationers on several criminogenic risk factors (criminal thinking, antisocial associates in friends and family, support from family, income, and substance use) over a six- and twelve-month-period follow-up. However, only reductions in associations with criminally involved family members, improved income, and decreased alcohol use were related to reductions in offending. Thus, although the presence of risk factors can increase the likelihood of (re-) offending in the form of internal (personal factors) or external (environmental factors or situations) limitations or obstacles, it does not automatically mean they directly cause the behaviour. As a result, it is assumed that risk factors alone are unable to (fully) explain (or change) criminal behaviour (Fortune & Heffernan, 2021; Heffernan & Ward, 2019; Heffernan, Ward, et al., 2019; Heffernan, Wegerhoff, et al., 2019; Ward, 2016; Ward & Fortune, 2016; Ward & Willis, 2016). As an example, we know that low impulse control increases the risk of delinquency (Andrews & Bonta, 2010; Ogilvie et al., 2011), but these impulse control problems are usually not the (only) direct cause and are deemed not to offer a complete explanation of delinquent behaviour (Ward, Melser, et al., 2007; Ward & Stewart, 2003a). It is only in combination with knowledge about the underlying mechanisms that we can explain why someone with a certain risk factor (such as impulse control problems) would or would not engage in criminal acts (known as *forensic risk/case formulation* in the structured professional judgment approach; Hart & Logan, 2011; Hart et al., 2011; Heffernan & Ward, 2015; Lewis & Doyle, 2009; Logan & Johnstone, 2010; Ward & Beech, 2015). Heffernan and Ward's (2015) conclusion on the concept of dynamic risk factors is that they

> are composite constructs, indicative of problems with agency: the absence of resources required to act successfully and prosocially toward achieving valued goods ... they are just one piece of the etiological puzzle (p. 259).

In this reasoning, according to the GLM, criminogenic risk factors can contribute to the delinquent behaviour as obstacles or limitations in the pursuit of satisfying someone's primary human goods and needs in a prosocial way, leading to committing a criminal act (Heffernan & Ward, 2015). For example, the decision to commit a robbery by someone who has impulse control problems as a risk factor can be driven by various underlying mechanisms, reasons, and motivations. The robber in this example may have had a financial need (part of the primary good of 'life' by acquiring livelihood), because they also had a drug problem due to unresolved mental health issues (primary good of 'inner peace') that contributed to their low impulse control, which on top of everything also resulted in loss of work. Another possibility is that the robber is someone with a great need for excitement and fun (primary good of 'pleasure'), partly due to an underlying diagnosis of ADHD, whose low impulse control made it more difficult to resist certain illegal activities suggested by antisocial peers. In both examples, the GLM argues that effective treatment targets for offender rehabilitation should take into account the different underlying mechanisms of the impulse control problems and the different primary human needs that were pursued by committing the crime. Subsequently, it is suggested that:

> simply relying on DRF [Dynamic Risk Factors] as treatment targets is a mistake as they do not reliably identify underlying causes at all; they are in effect summary labels for possible causes, contextual features, behavior, and mental state variables. (Heffernan, Ward, et al., 2019, p. 54)

Thus, the GLM maintains that for treatment and practitioners, it is essential to discover not only the risk factors, but also the underlying causal mechanisms, reasons, and motivations which may vary from person to person, in order to reduce recidivism effectively (Fortune & Heffernan, 2019; Heffernan, Ward, et al., 2019; Taxman & Caudy, 2015; Ward, 2016, 2019; Ward & Carter, 2019).

Theoretically, both the RNR model and GLM together could thus provide the tools to reduce recidivism on a sustainable basis. That is, the GLM could make it possible to identify the personal needs, rewards and values underlying the delinquent behaviour, while the RNR model pays attention to the risk factors that hinder the prosocial attainment of those needs (Ward, 2019; Ward & Maruna, 2007; Ward & Stewart, 2003c). Therefore, the GLM suggests that offender rehabilitation should be an integration of both focusing on primary human goods and values while simultaneously identifying and targeting the various obstacles (i.e. risk factors) that prevent offenders from living a prosocial, balanced and fulfilling life (Ward & Gannon, 2006; Ward & Maruna, 2007; Ward & Stewart, 2003c; Ward et al., 2012). Consequently, the GLM is said to shift from a narrower risk-reduction focus (such as the RNR model), towards a broader *dual* focus on both enhancing offender well-being (through primary human need attainment), in addition to reducing recidivism risk (Ward & Brown, 2004; Ward & Fortune, 2013; Ward & Maruna, 2007; Ward & Stewart, 2003c; Ward et al., 2012). It is because of this dual focus of the GLM on well-being promotion and recidivism risk reduction that this model could serve as a possible 'bridge' to overcome the problematic tension between the risk-focused approach and the welfare-focused approach when treating juvenile offenders.

2.2.2 The Potential Additional Value of the GLM: Treatment Motivation and Engagement

Besides its potential to form a bridge between the risk-focused and welfare-focused approaches in offender rehabilitation, the GLM could potentially be of incremental value to the RNR model in terms of responsivity. Offenders in general – and juvenile offenders in particular – may be quite reluctant to participate in involuntary treatment and services imposed upon them by the (juvenile) justice system (Case & Haines, 2015; Fortune, 2018; Ginsburg et al., 2002; Howells & Day, 2003, 2007; McMurran & Ward, 2004, 2010; Olver et al., 2011), making rehabilitation efforts a real challenge (McMurran, 2002).

Therefore, the RNR model stresses the importance of increasing treatment motivation, especially in high-risk offenders who have a tendency to drop out of treatment (Andrews & Bonta, 2010; Andrews et al., 2011; Bonta & Andrews, 2017; McMurran & Theodosi, 2007; Olver et al., 2011). In order to adhere to the *risk* principle of the model, interventions should ensure that high-risk offenders remain in treatment to receive the appropriate amount of services (Andrews & Bonta, 2010; Bonta & Andrews, 2017). Simultaneously, according to the *responsivity* principle of the RNR model, offender rehabilitation programmes should be matched to offender characteristics, such as motivation and cognitive style to be effective (Andrews & Bonta, 2010; Bonta & Andrews, 2017). In this sense, the RNR model contradicts itself when it contends that (consistent with their *need* principle) rehabilitation interventions should mainly focus on criminogenic needs while non-criminogenic needs (for example personal distress and interpersonal distrust) are deemed less important. That is, these non-criminogenic needs, according to their *responsivity* principle, could be particularly important to increase treatment motivation and engagement (especially for high-risk offenders who tend to drop out more easily), improving the effectiveness of the intervention.

Thus, in line with both their *risk* and *responsivity* principle, non-criminogenic needs could be just as important as criminogenic needs when they have motivational purposes and indirectly reduce criminogenic risk (Andrews & Bonta, 2010; Bonta & Andrews, 2017). It is in this *responsivity* principle where the RNR model and GLM meet, since they both highlight the importance of treatment readiness and motivation (Ogloff & Davis, 2004; Stephenson et al., 2013; Ward et al., 2004; Ward & Maruna, 2007; Ward & Stewart, 2003a). As Ward and Stewart (2003a) argue in their response to the RNR:

> Before persons are capable of acquiring coping skills, prosocial attitudes etc. they need to be motivated to participate in the whole process of therapy (responsivity principle!). And this means that therapists should intentionally aim to increase offenders' sense of safety, esteem, and well being. (p. 131)

Ward and colleagues further assert that in order to adhere to RNR's *responsivity* principle and to target criminogenic needs effectively, it is often necessary to target non-criminogenic needs as well (McMurran & Ward, 2004; Ward & Maruna, 2007; Whitehead et al., 2007; Wilson & Yates, 2009). This is because non-criminogenic (according to the RNR) needs, such as personal distress, financial crises, or interpersonal distrust, could negatively impact treatment readiness, treatment engagement, and the development of the therapeutic alliance, which make it difficult for the therapist to deliver standard RNR model interventions (Guebert & Olver, 2014; Nee et al., 2013; Stephenson et al., 2013; Ward et al., 2004; Ward & Maruna, 2007).

Although the RNR model underlines the importance of treatment motivation and responsivity (Bourgon & Bonta, 2014), it lacks a comprehensive framework or guidelines on how to implement it in practice. Apart from briefly mentioning motivational interviewing as a possible responsivity technique to increase treatment motivation (Andrews & Bonta, 2010; Andrews et al., 2011; Bonta & Andrews, 2017; McMurran, 2009), the RNR model does not elaborate on how to effectively engage offenders in treatment (Ward et al., 2012). Andrews and Bonta (2010) agree with this point as they state: "You may have noted that we have not developed the principle of specific responsivity to any serious degree. We have not done so because it remains unexplored" (p. 507).

When taking a closer look at motivational interviewing techniques proposed by Andrews and Bonta as a potential responsivity tool, we see they rely on values and ideas similar to those of the GLM.[6] Motivational interviewing (MI) is defined as: *a client-centered, directive method for enhancing intrinsic motivation to change by exploring and resolving ambivalence* (Miller & Rollnick, 2002, p. 25). With respect to the application of MI in criminal justice populations, Ginsburg and colleagues (2002) maintain that the same principles apply: eliciting client concerns, reflecting on ambivalence and discrepancies between actual behaviour and personal values, and allowing the clients to develop a plan for change that best suits them. This is where the GLM could be of additional value, as it is said to trigger internal motivation and increase treatment engagement by not only focusing on risk reduction, but also on addressing offenders' strengths and self-determined personal goals to enhance their well-being (McMurran & Ward, 2004, 2010; Ward et al., 2004; Ward & Fortune, 2013; Ward & Maruna, 2007; Ward, Melser, et al., 2007; Ward & Stewart, 2003c; Ward et al., 2006; Ward et al., 2012).

In fact, Andrews and Bonta (2010) seem to acknowledge the potential value of the GLM by stating:

> Collaborative treatment planning may establish the motivational value of targeting selected non-criminogenic needs for particular offenders. The earliest statements of RNR were not sufficiently clear on these points. (p. 508), and: We do like the idea that PIC-R and RNR be integrated with a powerful model of human motivation. (p. 512)

6 These similarities will be further discussed in Chapter 9, Section 9.3.3.

In this consideration that non-criminogenic needs may be important as well, especially for responsivity and motivational purposes, Andrews et al. (2011) agree that targeting emotional well-being could be associated with less recidivism, as long as the rehabilitation services are consistent with the RNR principles. This viewpoint contends with several recent studies that indeed find significant relationships between the so-called non-criminogenic factors, such as psychological problems and well-being, on the one hand and recidivism (risk) on the other (Basanta et al., 2018; Bouman et al., 2009; Hanniball et al., 2018; Wibbelink et al., 2017).[7]

2.3 Moving Forward: To an Integrative Approach in (Juvenile) Offender Rehabilitation

From this chapter we can conclude that, theoretically, the GLM aims to incorporate and proposes an expansion of the RNR principles by promoting a life worth living through the pursuit of primary human goods or goals that individuals value, using prosocial means (see also: Andrews et al., 2011; Ward & Maruna, 2007; Ward et al., 2012; Willis & Ward, 2013; Ziv, 2016, 2018).

First, the *need principle* is believed to be incorporated within the GLM framework because promoting human goods and well-being – in a non-harmful way – includes the reduction of internal or external criminogenic needs or risk factors (Ward & Fortune, 2013). Second, the application of the *risk principle* in the GLM stems from the idea that high-risk individuals (compared to low-risk individuals) tend to have more problems with regard to their internal and external capacities (i.e. have more criminogenic risk factors) to meet their valued human needs. Thus, according to both the RNR and the GLM, these higher-risk individuals require more intensive interventions (Lowenkamp & Latessa, 2004; Lowenkamp et al., 2006; Willis & Ward, 2013). Finally, the GLM aims to apply and complement the *responsivity principle* through its focus on enhancing treatment engagement by complementing risk reduction, with the enhancement of offenders' strengths and self-determined (non-criminogenic) personal goals to improve their well-being (Willis et al., 2013).

This way, as a strengths-based approach, the GLM aims to combine the risk-focused approach with a welfare-focused approach, a potential promising way forward for juvenile offender rehabilitation. Nevertheless, the number of studies investigating the theory of the GLM are scarce, especially those exploring the application to young offenders (Fortune, 2018; Mallion et al., 2020; Van Damme et al., 2017). Therefore, in the next chapters, a

---

7 These studies will be discussed in more detail in the following chapters.

detailed overview of the GLM, its underlying theories and etiological assumptions will be given, along with the accompanying research evidence to date.

3 Theoretical and Empirical Background of GLM's First Etiological Assumption

Associations Between Primary Goods and Well-being

In the previous chapters, I argued that theoretically the 'Good Lives Model of offender rehabilitation' (GLM) could combine the enhancement of well-being with the reduction of recidivism (risk), potentially resulting in an integrative (juvenile) offender rehabilitation model. Since the GLM's two main etiological assumptions about well-being and delinquency form the basis of their practical recommendations for effective (juvenile) offender rehabilitation, we will now explore them in more detail. We begin, in this chapter, with an elaboration of the underlying theories and empirical background of GLM's *first main assumption*. To reiterate, this first assumption holds that all human beings strive to obtain, to varying extent, a universal set of eleven human needs and goals in order to achieve a higher well-being, or in other words 'to have a good life' (Ward, 2002b; Ward & Maruna, 2007; Ward & Stewart, 2003a). In the GLM, all human behaviour is thus seen as a way to acquire these needs and goals, called *primary goods*, to reach a state of well-being.

3.1 What is a Good Life?

As the GLM emphasizes the enhancement of individual well-being, an important first step is to consider the conceptual meaning of human well-being and what is actually meant by the term *good life*. The GLM's focus on well-being makes it a strengths-based approach that stems from positive psychology (Ward & Maruna, 2007). Since the 1990s, psychological research started to shift from a deficit and psychopathology focus to more positive topics, such as well-being, happiness, flourishing, optimism, hope, strengths, capabilities, and so on. Subsequently, in 2000, Martin Seligman and Mihaly Csikszentmihalyi (2000) published the seminal paper on the introduction of a new field in psychology: positive psychology. A shift to studying positive human traits as proposed in positive psychology by Seligman and Csikszentmihalyi (2000) was believed to advance science by uncovering: "how to build the qualities that help individuals and communities, not just to endure and survive, but also to flourish" (p. 13). Later positive psychology was defined as:

> The scientific study of positive experiences and positive individual traits, and the institutions that facilitate their development. A field concerned with well-

> being and optimal functioning, positive psychology aims to broaden the focus of clinical psychology beyond suffering and its direct alleviation. (Duckworth et al., 2005, p. 629)

Nowadays, within the positive psychology and 'happiness literature', a confusing amount of well-being concepts exists (see for a discussion of different conceptualizations e.g. Ben-Arieh et al., 2014; Diener, 2006; Ryan & Deci, 2001; Wallander & Koot, 2016). Seligman (2004, 2011) proposed an influential theory of well-being in which he made a distinction between three different categories of human well-being or 'good lives': the pleasant life (*affective subjective well-being*), the engaged life (*cognitive subjective well-being*), and the meaningful life (*eudaimonic well-being*), which will be discussed in more detail in the next sections.

3.1.1 Well-being Approaches

Broadly speaking, the current modern conceptualizations of well-being can be divided according to the ancient Greek philosophical concepts of *Hedonism* on the one hand and *Eudaimonia* on the other (Holte et al., 2014; Kashdan et al., 2008; King et al., 2004; Ryan & Deci, 2001; Waterman, 2008). Hedonism is derived from the Greek word 'hēdonē (ἡδονή)', which translates to 'pleasure' and holds the idea that well-being consists of seeking pleasure and avoiding pain. *Eudaimonia* (εὐδαιμονία) consists of the words 'eu (εὐ)', translated as 'good', and 'daimōn (δαίμων)' translated as 'spirit' or 'demon', that combined can be roughly translated into 'human flourishing' (Aristotle, 1985; Holte et al., 2014). The Greek philosopher Aristotle (1985) suggested, in his *Nichomachean Ethics*, that all human action is directed towards certain goals or end states. In his view, discovering these end states equals finding the human goods (virtues, such as friendship, honour, justice, and intellect) and subsequently the highest good: *Eudaimonia* (i.e. human flourishing). Furthermore, Aristotle considered *Eudaimonia*, resulting from the pursuit of virtues, to be superior to *Hedonism*, which consisted of searching happiness and pleasure, only for its own sake (Aristotle, 1985; Holte et al., 2014; Jørgensen & Nafstad, 2004). In modern *hedonic* well-being approaches, however, a good life constitutes not only of balancing pleasant and negative feelings (*affective subjective well-being*) but is combined with a positive cognitive evaluation of life, that is, life satisfaction (*cognitive subjective well-being*) (Eid & Larsen, 2008; Holte et al., 2014; Seligman, 2004). The most renowned modern hedonic well-being theory is the one of Ed Diener, who defines subjective well-being (SWB) as:

> All of the various types of evaluations, both positive and negative, that people make of their lives. It includes reflective cognitive evaluations, such as life satisfaction and work satisfaction, interest and engagement, and affective reactions to life events, such as joy and sadness. Thus, subjective wellbeing is an umbrella term for the different valuations people make regarding their lives, the events happening to them, their bodies and minds, and the circumstances in which they live. (Diener, 2006, p. 153)

On the other hand, modern *eudaimonic* well-being approaches contend that well-being consists of more than subjective feelings and judgments of (life) satisfaction (Holte et al., 2014; King et al., 2004; Seligman, 2004). In fact, eudaimonic theories maintain that not all attained subjective human desires result in well-being, even though they might produce positive feelings (Ryan & Deci, 2001; Seligman, 2004; Waterman, 2008). An example of an eudaimonic theory is Ryff's theory of psychological well-being (Ryff, 1989; Ryff & Singer, 1998), which conceptualizes well-being as positive human functioning in the sense of self-actualization. Based on several theories of successful ageing, Ryff (1989) defines this psychological well-being (PWB) as being comprised of six dimensions: self-acceptance, positive interpersonal relations, autonomy, environmental mastery, meaning in life and personal growth.

Building on Ryff's dimensions of PWB, Keyes (2002) developed a taxonomy of 'human flourishing' in which 'the good life' consists of both the happy life (*hedonic well-being, SWB*) and the meaningful or fulfilling life (*eudaimonic well-being, PWB*) that have been found to be distinct, but strongly related to each other (Chen et al., 2013; Keyes et al., 2002; Waterman, 2008; Waterman et al., 2008). Keyes and colleagues explain the overlap between hedonic and eudaimonic well-being by arguing that, humans positively evaluate and have positive feelings (hedonic well-being) towards a life in which they are functioning well (eudaimonic well-being) and feel negative emotions and judgments about a life in which they are functioning poorly (Keyes & Annas, 2009; Keyes et al., 2002).

This integrative approach is similarly adopted by Deci and Ryan (2000), who proposed the Self-determination Theory (SDT) in which the fulfilment of three basic psychological needs – 'relatedness', 'competence', and 'autonomy' – are deemed essential for intrinsic human motivation and well-being (Deci & Ryan, 2000; Ryan & Deci, 2000b, 2017b). The SDT shares the eudaimonic hypothesis with Ryff (1989) and Keyes (2002) that being related, competent and autonomous are important factors for well-being. Furthermore, the SDT agrees with Keyes and colleagues (2002) that hedonic subjective well-being and eudaimonic well-being are distinct concepts of well-being, but are also strongly related. The SDT differs, however, from Ryff (1989) and Keyes (2002) who use the concepts of 'relatedness', 'competence', and 'autonomy' (amongst others) to *define* eudaimonic well-being, while according to the SDT, fulfilment of these three psychological needs will *foster* both subjective (hedonic) well-being and eudaimonic well-being (Ryan & Deci, 2001; Ryan et al., 2013). The SDT even takes the eudaimonic approach a step further by asserting that psychological (eudaimonic) need fulfilment and a resulting state of well-being is a natural aim of human life and the driving force of human motivation and actions (Deci & Ryan, 2000).

3.1.2 *The Good Life According to the GLM*

Within these different well-being approaches, GLM's assumptions about well-being seem to be most compatible with the integrative approach of the SDT (see Figure 3.1). That is, Ward (2002a) describes 'the good life' as a happy *and* a fulfilling life that can be achieved by satisfying primary human needs, called *primary goods*[1]:

> A good life becomes possible when an individual possesses the necessary conditions for achieving primary goods, has access to primary goods, and lives a life characterized by the instantiation of these goods. (Ward, 2002a, p. 515)

Ward (2002a) goes on to explain that these primary goods are necessary for optimal human functioning and will result in higher levels of well-being. They are:

> actions or states of affairs that are viewed as intrinsically beneficial to human beings and are therefore sought for their own sake rather than as means to some more fundamental ends. (Ward, 2002a, p. 515)

1 The term 'primary goods' has also been used before by political philosopher John Rawls (1978) in his theory of justice. Although the GLM does not directly refer to Rawls' work, it is possible Rawls' primary goods are somehow related to the GLM's primary goods. Rawls' primary goods, however, were proposed in a societal/political context to provide justice which is distributed fairly and are considered "things that every rational man is presumed to want" (p. 62). He subdivided them in basic and social primary goods, in which basic goods are the basic mental and bodily human abilities, such as health, strength, intelligence, memory, creativity etc., and the social goods include income, wealth, and certain liberties such as the freedom of speech and movement. Thus, despite being named 'primary goods', they are actually resources and means that help to promote someone's end goals, which make them – in GLM terms – secondary goods (see Section 3.4.1). Nevertheless, Nussbaum (2001) and Sen (2001) in proposing the capabilities approach, and Doyal and Gough (1991) in their theory of human need, refer to Rawls' work.

Figure 3.1 Overview of Different Well-being Concepts and Their Relationships

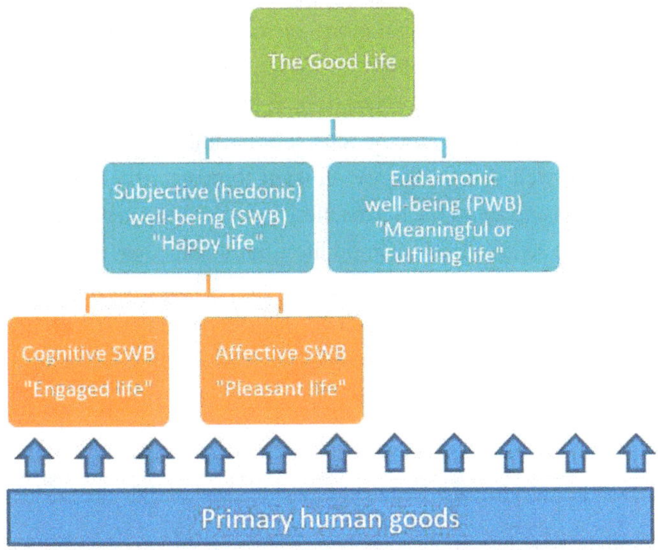

Relying on several philosophical works from Rasmussen (1999) and Kekes (1989, 1995), Ward (2002a, 2002b) further states that all human behaviour is driven by strivings and goals resulting from the primary goods; goods that are also intrinsically valuable and lie at the heart of human nature.

> That is, Rasmussen (1999) theorized that human well-being or flourishing stems from the fulfilment or realization of human nature. According to him (based on the Aristotelian notion of Eudaimonia), human flourishing is the ultimate end goal of human behaviour and consists of certain activities that result in the actualization of potentialities that are distinctly human, yet are also worthwhile in themselves. Rasmussen proposes examples of these potentialities of humans, or human goods (but does not elaborate on them), such as knowledge, health, friendship, creative achievement, beauty, and pleasure. In his view, when we seek knowledge, engage in loving relationships, strive for health, etc., humans are able to flourish as they express their human nature (Rasmussen, 1999).

Furthermore, Ward's Good Lives Model is strongly inspired by philosopher John Kekes (1989, 1995), who published several books on ethics and what he considers to be a good life. Kekes' work builds on the writings of Aristotle, David Hume and John Stuart Mill.[2] He asserts that universal human characteristics consist of the facts of the body (physiological characteristics, such as our bodily functions, senses, etc.), the self (psychological characteristics, such as capacities, talents, attitudes, etc.), and the social life (social organization characteristics, such as cooperation, rules, customs, etc.). These universal human characteristics are believed to be the foundation of human motivation and are the necessary conditions for well-being: "For we all want to protect the conditions in which we can obtain the benefits and avoid the harms these human characteristics define" (Kekes, 1989, p. 28). According to Kekes (1995), a good life consists of values which are connected to those benefits and harms that can make life better if we respectively obtain and avoid them. Furthermore, Kekes (1995) states that human nature dictates that some values will normally benefit all human beings and some values will normally harm everyone, for which he used the terms *primary goods*[3] and *primary evils* (p. 19).

3.1.3 *Goal-directed Human Nature*

To further back their claim about the goal-directedness of human nature, Ward and colleagues (Ward, 2002a; Ward & Maruna, 2007; Ward & Stewart, 2003a, 2003c) refer to psychological literature on motivation and self-regulation that maintains humans are naturally inclined to seek a range of universal goals, needs or goods (Austin & Vancouver, 1996; Baumeister & Heatherton, 1996; Deci & Ryan, 2000; Doyal & Gough, 1991; Emmons, 1996, 1999; Schmuck & Sheldon, 2001).

A vast amount of research exists that examined the role of goal pursuit in human life, mostly in adult samples. These studies (both cross-sectional and longitudinal) consistently find that being committed to and attaining personally valued goals results in higher levels of well-being (Cantor & Sanderson, 1999; Diener et al., 1999; Emmons, 1996, 1999; Kelly et al., 2015; Klug & Maier, 2015; Lent, 2004; Sheldon et al., 1996). Personal goals[4] in these studies are defined as future-oriented representations of what individuals are striving for in their life and what they try to attain or avoid in various life domains (Brunstein et al., 1999; Cantor & Sanderson, 1999; Emmons, 1996, 1999; McGregor & Little, 1998; Schmuck

---

2 Although their writings are undoubtedly important and interesting philosophical works, it goes beyond the scope of this chapter to elaborate on them here.

3 Kekes (1995) briefly mentions some of these primary goods as examples throughout his texts (some very similar to those of the GLM), such as the primary values of intimacy, pleasure, social order, independence, creativity, honour, privacy, comfort, and success. However, he does not explain or define them in depth.

4 Sometimes also referred to as *current concerns* (Cox & Klinger, 2004), *personal strivings* (Emmons, 1996), *ultimate concerns* (Emmons, 1999), *life tasks* (Cantor & Sanderson, 1999), *personal projects* (McGregor & Little, 1998), and '*possible selves*' (Markus & Nurius, 1986).

& Sheldon, 2001). Examples include making a career, starting a family, getting or staying fit and healthy etc.

However, not all personal goals are believed to lead to higher levels of well-being. That is, studies find that in order to lead to a state of well-being and fulfilment, goal pursuit should be focused on goals that are intrinsically motivating (Cantor & Sanderson, 1999; Emmons, 1996; Schmuck & Sheldon, 2001). Accordingly, the pursuit and attainment of extrinsic, materialistic goals (i.e., wealth, fame, or status that are related to external approval) have been found to be associated with lower levels of well-being and negative affect. In contrast, the pursuit and fulfilment of intrinsic goals have been shown to be related to higher levels of well-being and positive affect (Dittmar et al., 2014; Emmons, 1996, 1999; Kasser, 2002; Ryan & Deci, 2000b; Schmuck et al., 2000; Sheldon & Houser-Marko, 2001; Van Den Broeck et al., 2019).

Intrinsic goal pursuit that can lead to a happy and fulfilling life includes goals that are personally relevant, valued and self-determined instead of controlled or imposed by external sources (Oishi et al., 1999; Ryan & Deci, 2000b; Sheldon & Elliot, 1998, 1999; Sheldon, Elliot, et al., 2004; Sheldon & Kasser, 1998; Sheldon, Ryan, et al., 2004). They are intrinsically motivating as they reflect universal innate human needs, such as relatedness and community contribution/belonging (Deci & Ryan, 2000; Emmons & Diener, 1986; Ryan & Deci, 2000a, 2017b; Schmuck et al., 2000; Schmuck & Sheldon, 2001). As Emmons (1996) concluded from his work:

> Goal attainment per se will not lead to subjectively satisfying long-term states, unless these goals are intrinsically meaningful and integrated within an overall structure of the individual in his or her social context. (p. 333)

3.2 The Development of the GLM Primary Goods

The initially proposed primary human goods in the GLM, as necessary for a 'good life' and human well-being, consisted of: 'life' (i.e. healthy living and functioning), 'knowledge' (i.e. the desire to understand aspects of themselves, their environments, and other people), 'excellence in play and work' (i.e. the need for mastery experiences), 'excellence in agency' (i.e., the need for autonomy and self-directedness), 'inner peace' (i.e. freedom from emotional turmoil and stress), 'friendship (i.e. relatedness, including intimate, romantic and family relationships) and community' (i.e. the need to belong), 'spirituality' (in the broad sense of finding meaning and purpose in life), 'creativity' (i.e. the need for novelty, innovation and individuality), and 'happiness' (i.e., pleasure, the need to feel good in the here and now; Ward, 2002b).

The question that arises, however, is how the GLM arrived at this initial set of primary goods deemed necessary for human well-being. In one of his first articles on the GLM, Ward (2002b) refers to Murphy (2001) as his inspiration for unravelling these fundamental primary human goods. Mark C. Murphy is a professor of philosophy and a natural law theorist who outlined 'a theory of practical rationality'. Murphy's (2001) theory of practical rationality aims to identify and characterize reasons for human action and asserts that the basic reasons are intrinsic goods grounded in the nature of human beings. Murphy (2001), like many other philosophers discussed in this chapter, refers to Aristotle (1985) as a source of inspiration. Murphy (2001) argues that there are two methods for the detection of these basic reasons for human action or in other words the intrinsic human goods: 'derivationism' and 'inclinationism'.

In the derivationist approach, the intrinsic human goods are believed not to be self-evident, but ought to be derived by means of logical analysis and speculative reason (i.e. logical deductive thoughts), enabling us to gradually uncover certain facts about human beings and their fundamental functioning and nature (Murphy, 2001; Ward, 2002b). On the other hand, the inclinationist approach holds that every human being has some implicit knowledge of what the basic goods are, and this implicit knowledge results in a tendency to pursue and desire certain things. In this way, intrinsic goods can become self-evident by "examining the particular things that one is inclined to pursue and asking what goods ultimately make those things worth seeking" (Murphy, 2001, p. 42). Murphy suggests that both approaches should be used, as neither method alone is sufficient to fully understand the nature of primary human goods needed for optimal human functioning, or as he terms it *human flourishing* (Murphy, 2001).

This dual philosophical approach led Murphy to suggest a set of nine basic human goods, including: life (healthy functioning), knowledge, aesthetic experience (experiencing the beauty of paintings, music, nature, etc.), excellence in play and work (feeling challenged and being productive), excellence in agency (being able to act and choose reasonably), inner peace (being in a state of equilibrium), friendship and community, religion (being in harmony with the spiritual world) and finally happiness (being able to structure the goods in one's life; Murphy, 2001). Comparing these nine goods with the initially proposed primary goods by Ward (2002b), we can see striking similarities (see Appendix A[5]). Asserting the idea that human well-being consists of (at least) a number of universal, objectively determined aspects, makes Ward, drawing heavily on Murphy's work, an objectivist (Taylor, 2013). However, up until this point it remains unclear why exactly these initial nine (and later eleven) GLM primary human goods were chosen over others as necessary to live a 'good life' (e.g., Ward, 2002a, 2002b; Ward & Brown, 2004; Ward & Marshall, 2004; Ward & Maruna, 2007; Ward & Stewart, 2003a, 2003c).

5 See https://www.elevenpub.com/en/content/appendices-9789462364257.

In constructing the GLM primary goods, Ward and colleagues did not solely rely on Murphy's philosophy, but drew from a variety of theories, in particular from psychological (Aspinwall & Staudinger, 2003; Cummins, 1996; Deci & Ryan, 2000; Emmons, 1996, 1999)[6] and philosophical work (Arnhart, 1998; Becker, 1992; Griffin, 1996; Nussbaum, 2001; Rescher, 1990). Therefore, in the next section, I will elaborate on these theories that have been put forward by Ward and colleagues as the GLM's inspiration (Ward, 2002a, 2002b; Ward & Brown, 2004; Ward & Gannon, 2006; Ward & Marshall, 2007; Ward & Maruna, 2007; Ward & Stewart, 2003c).

3.3 THEORIES UNDERLYING THE GLM PRIMARY GOODS

To gain a better understanding of what the primary goods entail and where they come from, the different theories underlying the primary goods will be outlined in this section. As a summary, Appendix A (see fn 5) represents an overview of the different theories and their proposed 'goods' we discuss here.

3.3.1 *Self-Determination Theory (SDT)*

As briefly discussed in Section 3.1, GLM's conceptualization of well-being resembles the integrative (eudaimonic) approach of Deci and Ryan's (2000) Self-Determination Theory (SDT). Similarly, the GLM has adopted the three basic psychological human needs as proposed by the SDT into its list of primary goods (Ward, 2002a, 2002b). According to SDT, the three psychological needs for 'relatedness', 'competence', and 'autonomy' are: "innate psychological nutriments that are essential for ongoing psychological growth, integrity, and well-being" (Deci & Ryan, 2000, p. 229). These basic human needs are deemed to motivate behaviour towards their fulfilment and will – when fulfilled – promote well-being. *Relatedness* constitutes seeking attachments and experiencing feelings of security, belongingness and intimacy with others. *Competence* is a sense of mastery in which people feel effective in their ongoing interactions with the social environment and experience opportunities to exercise and express their capacities. *Autonomy* refers to

6 Although not explicitly mentioned in any of the GLM writings (as far as I have found), Maslow's well-known theory on motivation and human behaviour bears similarities to some of the GLM ideas. Maslow (1962) explains human behaviour as the pursuit of a number of innate human needs, which can be reached in a hierarchical manner: first, physiological needs (e.g. food, water), followed by safety needs (e.g. protection from pain, fear, disorder, anxiety), belongingness and love (e.g. affection, security, social acceptance), and esteem needs (e.g. gaining approval, recognition). Once these lower-level needs are (partly) satisfied, humans could be able to reach a level of self-actualization, being able to actualize their authentic human potentialities and capacities. Comparing these to some of the GLM's primary human goods, we can see resemblances with Maslow's hierarchy of needs.

volition and the desire to self-organize experience and behaviour in accordance with one's integrated sense (Deci & Ryan, 2000).

Both the GLM and SDT view human beings as "inherently active, self-directed organisms who are naturally predisposed to seek autonomy, relatedness, and competence" (Ward, 2002a, p. 517). In both theories, the human needs are treated as essential and universal, conditions for a happy and fulfilling life. Failure to meet the three basic needs is believed to inevitably cause psychological distress and result in maladaptive functioning (Deci & Ryan, 2000; Ward, 2002a; Ward & Maruna, 2007; Ward & Stewart, 2003a, 2003c). Correspondingly, a vast range of studies across different countries and cultures has indeed found support for the universality of the three basic psychological human needs proposed by SDT (Deci & Ryan, 2000). These studies consistently find that greater satisfaction of these three needs is related to higher levels of well-being (e.g. Church et al. 2013; Emmons, 1999; Gunnell et al.,2014; Milyavskaya & Koestner, 2011; Milyavskaya et al., 2013; Reis et al., 2000; Sheldon & Elliot, 1999; Sheldon et al., 2001; Sheldon et al., 1996; Tang et al., 2020; Tay & Diener, 2011; Vansteenkiste et al., 2010).

3.3.2 *Psychological Theories*

The remaining primary goods are derived from a range of other psychological theories, among them the work of Emmons (Emmons, 1996, 1999) on goal achievement, personal strivings and their relationship to well-being. The goals associated with subjective well-being in Emmons' work include: the goals of achievement (success, accomplishment, competing with a standard of excellence), affiliation (approval and acceptance, and preventing loneliness), intimacy (establishing deep, mutually gratifying relationships), power (influence and effect on others), personal growth and health (improving or maintaining mental and physical health), self-presentation (making a favourable impression on others), independence (autonomy and self-assertion), emotionality (emotional regulation), generativity (giving of oneself to others and having an influence on future generations), and spirituality (searching for the sacred; Emmons, 1996; Emmons, 1999). Most of these have some similarity with the GLM's primary goods (Ward, 2002b).

Furthermore, the GLM (Ward & Gannon, 2006) refers to the extensive work on positive psychology of Aspinwall and Staudinger (2003), which outlines several human strengths. Although their work does not provide a fixed list of human strengths, the chapters provide an overview of several aspects of human beings that have been proven to provide personal growth and well-being, such as physical health, relationships, intelligence, self-regulation, agency, positive affect, coping, and creativity. Additionally, an example of a psychological study that did provide a fixed list which Ward (2002b) refers to, is the work of Cummins (1996) who studied quality of life. Based on empirical research, he identified a number of life domains important for life satisfaction: finances, health, work and productivity, personal relationships, safety, community belonging and religion/spirituality.

3.3.3 *Philosophical Theories*

As has become clear in this chapter, the GLM draws heavily on philosophical works addressing the issues of well-being and 'the good life'. One philosophical discipline that inspired Ward (2002b) to construct his primary goods is philosophical anthropology, which is defined as "a fundamentally normative discipline whose mission is to study what is involved in 'the good life'" (Rescher, 1990, p. 1). As a normative philosopher, Rescher (1990) asserts that 'the good life' consists not only of the pursuit of happiness (i.e. feelings of satisfaction and pleasure), but should include important goals beyond personal happiness resulting in being a fuller and better person. He describes the following goals as important:

> Gaining respect from one's associates and the love of some among them; pride of achievement in some area of activity, vocational or avocational; appreciation of the accomplishments of the [human] race in art and science; and the enjoyment of hobbies or sports. (pp. 31-32)

According to Rescher (1990), these goals are necessary for self-development and fulfilment of a person. Furthermore, he mentions seven fundamental conditions that are essential for being a person: intelligence and self-understanding (being able to process information, acquire, maintain and modify consciously held beliefs about the world and one's place within it); affectivity (being able to emotionally react to developments); agency (being capable of goal-oriented action as a free agent); rationality (actions must proceed from reasons that are grounded in ones aims and values); mutual recognizance (having fellow-feeling, functioning in a context of community) and self-esteem (having self-respect and valuing oneself). Finally, he concluded that:

> The crux of the imperative to personhood is thus the fundamental duty to make good use of the opportunities that come our way to realize ourselves as fully as possible – the fundamental duty of self-realization. (Rescher, 1990, p. 20)

Furthermore, adopting a typical philosophical eudaimonic approach to well-being, the capabilities theories of Sen (2001) and Nussbaum (2001) assert that although life satisfaction might be an important aspect, well-being also consists of positive human *functioning* which can only be attained by certain capabilities (Nussbaum, 2001; Sen, 2001). Every human being is believed to be entitled to have basic capabilities to function properly, much like human rights (Nussbaum, 2001; Sen, 2001). According to Sen (2001) these capabilities include being able to live a healthy life, to obtain the education and skills needed to effectively achieve one's goals, and having the freedoms to engage in the activities an individual values. Whereas Sen (2001) declines to provide a list of specific capabilities, Nussbaum (2001) explicitly defines ten essential and universal capabilities that seemingly inspired Ward (2002b), consisting of being able to: live a life of normal length (life); have good health including reproductive health, being adequately nourished and having adequate shelter (bodily health); to move freely and being secure (bodily integrity); use the senses, think and reason (to be informed and cultivated by education, to be self-expressive and search for one's meaning in life); love and care for others, not having one's emotional development blighted (emotions); form a life plan (practical reason); live with concern for others (affiliation); and for other species; to play, laugh and enjoy; and control one's environment.

Becker (1992) is another philosopher from whom the developers of the GLM (Purvis et al., 2014; Ward & Marshall, 2007) drew their inspiration in the construction of the list of primary goods. Becker (1992), somewhat similar to Ward (see below), adopts a more pluralistic view on what can be considered a good life. He argues it is not possible to construct one final ultimate good in life (e.g. happiness). Rather, he proposes a list of things that can all be regarded as ultimate goods, not reducible to any of the others on the list; they are intrinsic, necessary or widely instrumental, and definitive, at least in part, of a good life. Becker identified seventeen goods: material conditions to sustain life and consciousness; a certain state of consciousness; a form of knowledge or comprehension of the nature, value and meaning of things; the possession of a sound self-concept and the ability to decide, choose and act; the harmonization of reason, desire and will; the excellence or realization of human characteristics; meaningful opportunity (liberty and autonomy to make choices and carry out valuable projects); meaningful activity (actual pursuit of valuable projects); meaningful necessity (being compellingly called to a valuable role outside one's own life); self-esteem and self-respect; benevolence (concern or affection for others); mutual love (reciprocal affection, benevolence and empathy); sexuality (erotic love, sexual behaviour and reproduction); achievement (productive activity); rectitude (morally right conduct); integrity (an intact and coherent identity); a life as an aesthetic object (a life that is beautiful or sublime).

Similarly inspiring the GLM's views (Ward, 2002b), Arnhart (1998) argues that certain human goods – or as he calls them: 'desires' – are innate and universal:

> There are at least twenty human desires that are universal because they are part of the biological nature of human beings as manifested in all societies throughout human history. (p. 17)

Based on philosophical and evolutionary theory, Arnhart (1998) proposes twenty different kinds of human desires: a complete life (living a full lifespan), providing parental care, sexual identity, sexual mating, familial bonding, friendship, social ranking, justice as reciprocity, political rule, war, health, beauty, wealth, speech, practical habituation, practical reasoning, practical arts, aesthetic pleasure, religious understanding and intellectual understanding.

Finally, in Section 3.2 we have already discussed the striking similarities between the GLM's primary goods and the nine basic human needs of the objectivist Murphy (2001). At the same time, Ward (2002b) seems to draw his objectivist ideas not only from Murphy (2001), but also from Griffin (1996), who asserts that not all our personal desires are able to result in a good life, only prudential values will. Griffin (1996) considers prudential values for a good life to be things valuable for any human. He lists five prudential values: accomplishment (giving life weight or point), the components of human existence (choosing one's own course through life, agency, and autonomy), understanding (knowing about oneself and one's place in the world), enjoyment (pleasures, perception of beauty and enjoyment in life), and deep personal relations (reciprocal relations of friendship and love).

Despite this mainly objectivistic view of a definitive set of values, Griffin (1996) incorporates a pluralistic notion in his theory of a good life as well. He emphasizes the possibility of individual differences in the extent and the manner of how people can achieve the important goods or values: "There being just one profile of prudential values for humans is compatible with there being very many forms that a good human life could take" (p. 31). Like Griffin (1996), Ward is more lenient and pluralistic in his views than Murphy. That is, Ward (2002a, 2002b) also accepts the possibility of personal and social influence in determining which human goods are more or less important for an individual's well-being, and the manner in which they can be achieved (Griffin, 1996; Murphy, 2001; Ward, 2002a, 2002b). It is this combination of an objectively determined set of primary goods and the pluralistic ways in which they can lead to a good life that lies at the core of the GLM and will be discussed in the next section.

3.4 Good Lives: Social, Cultural and Personal Differences

In the previous sections, I outlined the various theories that led to the GLM's proposal of eleven primary goods essential for human well-being. As we have seen, these goods are generally believed to be universal, objective, broad motivational constructs. Nevertheless, we also concluded that the GLM does not only adopt a strict objectivist view of 'the good life', but accepts a more lenient pluralistic view:

> The term 'good lives' is preferred to the singular 'good life' as I accept the view that there is no one ideal or preferred lifestyle for any given individual. (Ward, 2002a, p. 516)

Again, based on the theoretical work of several philosophers (Den Uyl, 1991; Kekes, 1989; Rasmussen, 1999) and cognitive anthropology (d'Andrade, 1995), Ward (2002a; 2002b) argues that although a number of natural, basic or primary human goods exist, the nature of the primary goods sought by individuals, their weight, and the way they are met, are believed to be influenced by personal and cultural circumstances, beliefs, values and norms (Ward & Maruna, 2007).

This latter notion seems to be strongly inspired by Kekes' (1989) eudaimonistic views:

> Our nature and society provide many of our wants and the conventions that guide their satisfaction. Yet, how we regard our wants, which ones we aim to satisfy and how we rank their respective importance is within our personal control. And so are our conceptions of good lives. (p. 111)

Likewise, while Deci and Ryan (2000) assert that their psychological needs from the SDT are universal they also argue that: "…these three needs can be satisfied while engaging in a wide variety of behaviors that may differ among individuals and be differentially manifest in different cultures" (p. 231). In a similar vein, Den Uyl (1991) interprets the universal goods (virtues) proposed by Aristotle as necessary for human flourishing as

> generic characteristics of our nature as a package of capacities whose realization is required for self-perfection, but whose form is individualized by each person's attributes, circumstances and interests. (p. 167)

In line with this reasoning, and again based on Aristotle's notion of Eudaimonia, Rasmussen (1999) argues that no two cases of human flourishing are the same, nor are they interchangeable. The way in which an individual can reach the person's full potential differs, depending on the individual's particular talents, potentialities and circumstances. Similarly, d'Andrade (1995) states that there are certain universal motivational goals, such as being healthy, safe and maintaining relationships. Yet, how these goals are fulfilled differs according to the specifics of life in particular societies and cultures. Consequently, human well-being, in Ward's (2002a) view, is individualized and only exists in relation to a person's particular set of values, circumstances, abilities and opportunities:

> A conception of good lives is closely associated with explicit assumptions about what constitutes a fulfilling or worthwhile life and therefore has a strong normative basis (i.e., embodies fundamental values). This life is chosen by the individual, fashioned to some conceptualization of good lives, and yields a sense of personal identity and meaning. There may be room for the notion of natural basic goods, ... but this needs to be tempered by the recognition that any conception of a worthwhile life is at least partly a social construction.... Different people will require slightly different weightings of the basic goods or valued activities, although all will have the same set of basic goods. (Ward, 2002a, pp. 516-517)

For example, research between individualistic and collectivistic cultures has found differences in which needs are considered more important for well-being. These studies demonstrated that in collectivist cultures, the expectations of friends and family played a larger role in goal setting rather than self-determination. Likewise, compared to people living in wealthy nations, people in poor nations tend to prioritize basic physical and safety needs more than others (Oishi & Diener, 2009; Oishi et al., 2009). Thus, cultural and social environments (e.g. values and norms) combined with personal characteristics (e.g. preferences, capabilities, and opportunities) are believed to influence (i.e. construct) the different weightings people place on the primary goods and how they aim to pursue them in specific strategies and behaviours.

3.4.1 Secondary Goods

The different ways in which the GLM's primary goods can be attained are called *secondary goods*: instrumental needs that point out the specific goals (desired states, activities or experiences), actual strategies and behaviours. Because of their wide variability there is no fixed list of the possible secondary goods. For example, an individual might attain the primary good of 'excellence in work' by working as a car mechanic, while another might train to be a doctor (Ward, 2002a, 2002b; Ward & Stewart, 2003a). Secondary goods can be sources for more than one primary good at one time. For instance, being employed can provide for the primary good of 'life' by means of a stable income, while also contributing to the primary goods of 'relatedness' (through friendships with coworkers), being part of a 'community' (i.e. being part of the company), being challenged to 'excel in work' activities, feelings of autonomy (i.e. 'excellence in agency') and perhaps also experiencing fun and 'pleasure'.

All the different ways in which people strive for and realize the goods that are important to them are deemed to shape their way of life or lifestyle and reflect their personal identity (Emmons, 1986; Ward & Marshall, 2004; Ward & Maruna, 2007). This distinction between primary and secondary goods seems to be inspired by Kekes (1995) who argued that

> universally human benefits and harms are 'primary goods' and 'primary evils.' Correspondingly, 'secondary goods' and 'secondary evils' are benefits and harms that derive their status from historically, socially and culturally variable aspects of a good life. (p. 19)

Thus, he concluded:

> It must be recognized, therefore, that in addition to universal primary values derivable from human nature, there are also secondary values whose identity varies with social and personal circumstances. Good lives depend on both primary and secondary values. (Kekes, 1995, p. 22)

3.5 Empirical Evidence Supporting the GLM's Primary Goods

Up to this point we have mainly discussed the theoretical and philosophical background of the GLM's assumption about well-being and primary goods. Additionally, Ward and Maruna (2007) have provided a number of references as empirical evidence for the relevance of the primary goods:

> there is accumulating evidence for all the ones outlined earlier: life or healthy physical functioning (e.g. Martin, 2005; Kyvsgaard, 1991); play (e.g. Wrzesniewski, Roszin and Bennett, 2003); work (e.g. Theodossiou, 1998); autonomy or agency (e.g. Dobransky, 1999; Emmons, 1999); inner peace or emotional equilibrium (e.g. Kelly, 2003; Maruna, 2001); relatedness and community (e.g. Berscheid, 2003); spirituality or meaning (e.g. Emmons, 2003); pleasure (e.g. Martin, 2005); creativity (e.g. Cassandro and Simonton, 2003); and knowledge (e.g. Emmons, 1999; Lippke, 2003). (p. 145)

Later, Purvis (2010) set out to empirically test the assumptions of the GLM applied to adult sex offenders. She described the primary goods in detail in her doctoral dissertation and assessed the role they played in the offender's lives, based on 26 in-depth qualitative interviews. From her research she concluded that instead of the nine initial primary goods (Ward, 2002b), there were actually eleven; she separated 'work' from 'play', and 'relatedness' from 'community'. Based on this line of work (Purvis, 2010; Purvis et al., 2014; Willis et al., 2013), in the text that follows, the definitions of the current set of eleven primary goods are outlined. In addition, I will integrate and briefly discuss the references that were put forward by Purvis (2010), and Ward and Maruna (2007) as empirical evidence supporting the relationship between the GLM's primary goods and well-being.

3.5.1 *Life*

The primary good of 'life' refers to people's need for healthy and quality living, the need to feel safe and secure. It incorporates all the physical needs and factors that are important for healthy living and physical functioning: food, water, shelter and a physically healthy body. Ideal fulfilment of this good would mean that the person presents as a physically healthy person whose physical functioning and living circumstances are of a high standard. Examples of prosocial secondary goods that could provide for this need include gaining secure and stable accommodation, engaging in physical exercise or sports, being diet conscious, preparing healthy meals, legally managing one's own finances to ensure basic needs are met, and managing specific health problems (Purvis, 2010; Purvis et al., 2014; Willis et al., 2013).

Physical health has proven to be a characteristic of happy people as set out in Martin's (2005) overview of the 'happiness literature':

> Various studies have found that happiness relates more strongly to people's mental health than it does to their objective physical health – that is their health as assessed independently by a doctor. However, reasonably strong associations are found between happiness and people's perception of their own health: their so-called subjective health. (p. 105).

Furthermore, both Purvis (2010) and Ward and Maruna (2007) refer to the large file-study of Kyvsgaard (1991) to emphasize the relevance of the good of healthy living. Kyvsgaard (1991) analysed statistical file data from 12,254 law violators in Denmark and reported that poor living conditions (i.e. being unemployed, low income, living on welfare, not owning a house) were related to offending, where more severe conditions coincided with more serious offending.

3.5.2 *Knowledge*

The primary good of 'knowledge' refers to one's interest in, access to and possession of information. It is not related to how intelligent someone is, but rather to how well informed an individual feels about things that are important to that person. The good of knowledge is based on the notion that people are fundamentally curious beings with the desire to understand aspects of themselves, their environments and other people. Examples of prosocial secondary goods are asking questions, studying, participating in training, vocational pursuits, self-study activities, belonging to a discussion group or taking lessons to acquire a new skill (Purvis, 2010; Purvis et al., 2014; Willis et al., 2013).

Martin (2005) concluded that research revealed a consistent, but modest, association between educational level and happiness. That is, people who received more years of education tended to be somewhat happier than those who had been educated at a lower level. From a different perspective, Emmons (1999) argues that research has shown that intelligence – in the sense of problem-solving and adaptive processing of information – is positively related to successful goal attainment, which is in turn linked to higher levels of well-being. Additionally, Purvis (2010), and Ward and Maruna (2007) cite the work of Lippke (2003) who proposes that a lack of knowledge or a lack of interest in learning about new things can lead to social deprivation, reduced opportunities and diminished capacities, which in turn can lead to maladaptive functioning and crime:

> They lack opportunities for gainful employment, sufficient education or training to take advantage of such opportunities, and are surrounded by pressures and temptations toward illegal conduct, conduct that in one way or another may help them get what they so desperately need. (p. 466)

3.5.3 *Excellence in Work*

The primary good of 'excellence in work' refers to the need to engage in work, which provides the person with a sense of pride, achievement, satisfaction and skill development. Meaningful employment will have both an intrinsic value (accomplishment for the sake of it, i.e. for personal fulfilment) and an instrumental value (accomplishment for a specific purpose, i.e. a promotion, greater responsibility or salary increase) and should be in accordance with an individual's personal set of skills, interests, preferences and desires. Examples of prosocial secondary goods are having a legal meaningful paid job, volunteer work, undergoing apprenticeships, and taking professional development courses (Purvis, 2010; Purvis et al., 2014 Willis et al., 2013).

In their study, Wrzesniewski et al. (2003) found that people who experienced their work as a calling instead of 'just a job' reported a more rewarding relationship to their work, associated with gaining more enjoyment and satisfaction from it. Similarly, Martin (2005) concluded that having a satisfying job is strongly related to more happiness. Furthermore, he argues that work can also meet other needs, in the sense that it not only provides money but also provides meaning and structure to a person's life, mental and emotional stimulation, personal relationships, opportunities to use and develop skills, social status, self-esteem and a sense of identity. In the other direction, Purvis (2010), and Ward and Maruna (2007) also refer to the research of Theodossiou (1998) who found that being unemployed is associated with higher levels of anxiety, depression, loss of confidence, a reduction in self-esteem and lower levels of general happiness.

3.5.4 *Excellence in Play*

The primary good of 'excellence in play' refers to the need to engage in leisure or fun activities that provide the person with a sense of pride, achievement, satisfaction or skill development. It involves engaging in activities for the purpose of both enjoyment and achieving mastery in a certain area. Examples of prosocial secondary goods are participating in team or individual sports, having hobbies (such as playing an instrument or arts and crafts), and participating in organized discussion groups, such as movie or book clubs (Purvis, 2010; Purvis et al., 2014; Willis et al., 2013).

Purvis (2010) and Wrzesniewski et al. (2003) stated that there is a notable absence of research investigating the significance of play (i.e. leisure activities, hobbies) to human happiness. Nevertheless, Wrzesniewski et al. (2003) concluded from their survey study that passions or hobbies, such as music, art or sports were described by the respondents as positive, enriching activities in their lives that offered amusement and fun. Likewise, Csikszentmihalyi (2000) asserts that play in the form of enjoyable activities is able to provide people with 'flow', which is a mental state in which a person performing an activity is fully immersed in a feeling of energized focus, full involvement and enjoyment in the process of the activity that encourages optimal functioning. Moreover, Martin (2005) mentions playfulness as one of the characteristics of happy people, while concluding: "Sports and games are common forms of adult play, and common sources of happiness" (p. 66).

3.5.5 *Excellence in Agency*

The primary good of 'excellence in agency' refers to the human need to formulate each person's own goals and to seek ways to realize them in actions and activities of the person's own choice. It encompasses the need for autonomy, self-directedness, personal power, control and mastery, which becomes especially salient during the period of adolescence

(Arnett, 1999). It includes the desire to stand on one's own two feet, to be able to pursue the things one values most and to shape one's life in a way that is consistent with one's deepest values and concerns. Examples of prosocial secondary goods are being assertive, self-reflective and legally achieving a form of (financial) independence (Purvis, 2010; Purvis et al., 2014; Willis et al., 2013).

The empirical evidence base for this good can be found in the work of Dobransky (1999),[7] who identified the freedom to engage in self-directed decision making as a key factor in achieving a consistently fulfilling life. Likewise, Martin (2005) concluded from his review: "Happy people tend to feel more empowered and more in control of their lives than unhappy people" (p. 55). In a more general sense, Emmons (1999) concluded from his empirical work on the relationship between personal strivings (goals) and well-being (as we saw earlier in this chapter) that pursuing and achieving goals is important in itself, but it is even more important that these goals form a self-asserted, integrated whole in line with a person's identity and life plan.

3.5.6 *Inner Peace*

The primary good of 'inner peace' refers to the need for freedom from emotional turmoil and stress. It includes emotional self-regulation and achieving a state of emotional balance. It also refers to the need for emotional competence. Emotional competence is the application of self-regulation processes in the emotional domain. It consists of a number of skills, such as awareness and understanding of one's own emotional state, the ability to express how one feels, the capacity to identify other people's emotions, the capacity to respond empathetically to other people, and the ability to manage aversive emotions through a range of adaptive strategies. Examples of prosocial secondary goods include learning emotional control and other self-regulation skills, meditation, counselling, or physical exercise (Purvis, 2010; Purvis et al., 2014; Willis et al., 2013).

As evidence for the good of 'inner peace', Purvis (2010), and Ward and Maruna (2007) refer to the studies of Kelly (2003), who found that worrying was significantly related to higher levels of stress, depression, anxiety, lower levels of happiness and less life satisfaction. Martin (2005) similarly concluded that research confirms that anxious individuals who frequently worry tend to be less happy, while happy people are less inclined to feel anxious. He furthermore states that resilience, the ability to cope with a certain number of setbacks and stress in one's life, plays an important part in maintaining well-being. Purvis (2010), and Ward and Maruna (2007) additionally refer to the work of Maruna (2001) on the

7 Unfortunately, I was not able to retrieve the original unpublished manuscript of this reference and had to rely on the conclusion drawn by Purvis (2010).

desistance process of ex-offenders. He found that offenders who had managed to desist from crime were less likely to suffer from depression and other types of psychological distress (Maruna, 2001).

3.5.7 Relatedness

The primary good of 'relatedness' refers to the innate need of human beings to establish affectionate, mutual bonds with an intimate partner, family members, and close friends. Examples of prosocial secondary goods include: personal disclosure, communication, support, consensual sexual activity and physical contact, spending time together, sharing interests, etc. It entails forming relationships with a partner, maintaining friendships, spending time with family and having/parenting children (Purvis, 2010; Purvis et al., 2014; Willis et al., 2013).

As empirical evidence for this fundamental human need, Purvis (2010), and Ward and Maruna (2007) refer to Berscheid's (2003) chapter in Aspinwall and Staudinger's book on human strengths (2003), wherein she concluded that humans are innately inclined to form strong, enduring attachments with other human beings. Relationships with others provide us with meaning and purpose, positive feelings of love, happiness and satisfaction, which can support us to overcome physical and mental challenges (Berscheid, 2003). Martin (2005) similarly identified connectedness with other people as the most important characteristic of happy people.

3.5.8 Community

The primary good of 'community' refers to the human need to belong to social groups, to feel connected to groups that reflect their interests, concerns and values. It entails the feeling of being part of, being able to rely on and contributing to a wider social or cultural network. Examples of prosocial secondary goods include belonging to special interest or social groups (e.g. a political party, a sports club, a crafts group, book club, nature/wildlife group, social activism group or religious affiliations), engaging in volunteer work, or being part of a school group (Purvis, 2010; Purvis et al., 2014; Willis et al., 2013).

The empirical background of this good can – similar to the good of 'relatedness' – be found in the work of Berscheid (2003) and Martin (2005) on the fundamental importance of social interactions and feelings of belonging.

3.5.9 Spirituality

The primary good of 'spirituality' refers to the need to discover a sense of meaning and purpose in life. This could involve seeking religious inspiration and affiliation, a spiritual connection with a transcendent being or reality, or simply the experience of being part of a larger whole. Examples of prosocial secondary goods to attain this need include belonging to a church, environmental association, volunteer group, or living one's life according to a particular set of ethical values (Purvis, 2010; Purvis et al., 2014; Willis et al., 2013).

According to Emmons (2003) "Meaning-making is an activity that is distinctly human, a function of how the human brain is organized" (p. 105). In his studies, spiritual strivings were found to be positively related to subjective well-being, were rated as more important and requiring more effort than non-spiritual strivings. Similarly, Martin (2005) stated that people who regard their lives as meaningful tend to be happier and more satisfied. He furthermore concluded that religion and spirituality can boost happiness by giving individuals a strong sense of purpose and meaning in their lives.

3.5.10 Creativity

The primary good of 'creativity' refers to a need for novelty, innovation and individuality in one's life. 'Creativity' does not just refer to the ability to produce artistic work, it may also be present in the way a person solves problems, or the way the person appreciates beauty or nature. It is essentially the expression of oneself through creative forms of activity. Examples of prosocial secondary goods are painting, gardening, solving problems, attending art exhibitions, playing a musical instrument. Creativity may also be expressed in the way people dress or present themselves (e.g. with tattoos, jewellery, etc.) (Purvis, 2010; Purvis et al., 2014; Willis et al., 2013).

Purvis (2010), and Ward and Maruna (2007) refer for this good to Cassandro and Simonton (2003) who concluded from their review that research has linked creative behaviour (expressing novel, creative ideas and products) to optimal human functioning, both physical and mental health and well-being.

3.5.11 Pleasure

The primary good of 'pleasure' refers to the need to feel good in the here and now, and includes a range of feelings and sensations, such as joy, merriment, delight, elation and hedonic pleasure. Ward (2002b) initially referred to this good as 'happiness' but in later work changed it to 'pleasure', to not confuse the good with the overarching goal of happiness in terms of overall well-being (Purvis, 2010; Purvis et al., 2014; Ward & Maruna, 2007). Examples of prosocial secondary goods include the enjoyment of food, massage, legal thrill-seeking activities and engaging in consensual sexual activity (Purvis, 2010; Purvis et al., 2014; Willis et al., 2013).

Purvis (2010), and Ward and Maruna (2007) refer to Martin (2005) to explain the distinction between the overarching goal of overall well-being and the good of happiness/ pleasure. Martin (2005) argues that pleasure is the presence of pleasant and positive moods or emotions (i.e. a state of happiness), while the overarching goal of overall well-being, which is often referred to as *being happy* requires more than just feeling good at a certain point in time. For example, someone can be unhappy in life overall, but feel pleasure or states of happiness at some points in time, because of, for example, contextual factors, such as eating chocolate, enjoying a massage, shopping, etc. He goes on to state that although pleasure can be related to higher levels of well-being, it is not enough on its own:

> Sprinkling our lives with small pleasures clearly can give a lift, and research has confirmed that people who deliberately build more pleasurable activities into their daily lives do indeed feel better as a result. There is nothing inherently wrong with pleasure. The problem is that the quick fix of pleasure alone is not a reliable route to lasting happiness. (Martin, 2005, p. 123)

3.6 Possible Problems

As we have seen in the theories outlined earlier, it is assumed that the successful attainment of *all the primary goods* (by means of *secondary goods*) will lead to a happy and fulfilling life. Conversely, when the primary goods are not obtained, they are assumed to cause psychological distress, leading to mental health problems and social maladjustment. Four types of problems in the attainment of the primary goods have been identified, which will be elaborated in the following text: problems with *capacity, scope, means*, and *coherence* (Purvis, 2010; Purvis et al., 2011; Ward, 2002a, 2002b; Ward & Marshall, 2004; Ward & Maruna, 2007).

3.6.1 Lack of Capacities and Scope

First, a problem with *capacities* can occur when internal or external obstacles stand in the way of attaining a good in a successful manner. Internal obstacles are believed to arise when a person lacks skills or abilities to secure certain goods. According to the GLM, these obstacles can occur on several levels: cognitive (e.g. when an individual lacks knowledge or mental ability), psychological (e.g. when an individual lacks belief in himself or has motivational problems), and behavioural (e.g. when an individual has limited abilities and/or lacks certain skills). External obstacles consist of environmental disadvantages (e.g. lack of resources or opportunities), such as limited availability of social support, employment opportunities and access to education (Purvis, 2010; Purvis et al., 2011; Ward, 2002a). The second problem that can get in the way of seeking a fulfilling and happy life is a *lack of scope* in the primary goods. A lack of scope is said to occur when someone fails to strive for or secure (to some degree) each of the eleven primary goods. Problems in scope can be caused by a disinterest in one or more goods, but are also believed to be caused by problems in *capacity* (Purvis, 2010; Purvis et al., 2011; Ward, 2002a, 2002b).

Empirical studies support the importance of *both internal and external capacity* and conclude that well-being promoting goals should be realistically specific and attainable given someone's personal skills, capacities, resources, environment and support (Cantor & Sanderson, 1999; Diener et al., 1999; Emmons, 1999; Massey et al., 2008, 2009; Nurmi & Salmela-Aro, 2002; van Vianen, 2018). For example, Diener and Fujita (1995) found that individuals with the highest level of well-being had the highest level of congruence between the goals they reported as most relevant in their lives and the number of available resources that are necessary for attaining those goals (e.g. possessions, such as money, social roles, opportunities as well as internal characteristics or skills). This is in line with Brunstein et al. (1999) who concluded from their studies on the relationship between goal pursuit and well-being that:

> high investments in the pursuit of personal goals do not necessarily produce happiness and elation. Rather, to achieve well-being and avoid distress, individuals also require access to social and environmental resources that they can use to materialize their commitments. (p. 170)

Brunstein (1993) and his colleagues (Brunstein et al., 1998) found that well-being increased over time for those who reported favourable conditions (e.g., many opportunities to work on goals, control over goal-relevant outcomes, and support of personal goals by others) for the goals they were strongly committed to. On the other hand, poor conditions (indicated by a lack of opportunity, control and support) to accomplish the goals they were committed to, were predictive of a decline in well-being.

3.6.2 *Inappropriate Means and Lack of Coherence*

A third problem that can occur is related to the *means*, or secondary goods, that were used to obtain the primary goods. Some secondary goods might not be appropriate to successfully (and prosocially) obtain the desired primary good. Moreover, it is argued that the ways in which goods are fulfilled should not only be personally satisfying to result in a good life, but should also conform to moral standards (Kekes, 1989; Ward, 2002a, 2002b). The use of inappropriate means could result from a *lack of capacities* in earlier (failed) attempts to attain the primary goods. An example of an inappropriate pursuit can be found in (excessive) alcohol and drug use to create inner peace and feelings of pleasure when other (appropriate) attempts have failed. The use of alcohol and drugs might suppress negative feelings for a while, but will not be sufficient to result in long-term inner peace. When the use of alcohol and drugs results in substance abuse or addiction, it may even negatively affect the attainment of other primary goods by causing relationship, work or health problems (Purvis, 2010; Purvis et al., 2011; Ward, 2002a, 2002b).

The latter issue, in which the attempt to attain one good conflicts with the attainment of others, can result in the fourth problem of a *lack of coherence*. According to the GLM, it is important that in each person's life, the eleven goods are coherently related to each other. A lack of coherence is said to occur when a conflict arises in the attainment of the different primary goods. According to the GLM, two types of coherence are necessary: horizontal and vertical.[8] *Horizontal coherence* refers to the harmonious attainment of several goods alongside one another, without conflict. The attainment of one good should not be in conflict with the attainment of another as was just depicted in the example of alcohol and drug use to attain 'inner peace', causing relationship, work and health problems. *Vertical coherence* refers to a structured (hierarchical) ranking of the goods. Although the GLM specifies all eleven goods are important for well-being, the importance assigned to each of them is believed to differ per person, depending on preferences, skills, social norms and cultural values of the person. As a result, the GLM asserts that the most important goods should be given the most priority, commitment and resources and should be reflected in important specific life goals. Thus, for example, a vertical conflict could occur when someone values 'relatedness' and family relationships more than 'excellence in work' yet spends most of his or her time at the office. Both horizontal and

8 The distinction between vertical and horizontal coherence is most likely inspired by Emmons (1999), and Sheldon and Kasser (1995) who first described the importance of the two types. According to Emmons (1999): "Optimal health and well-being occur when different elements of personality are integrated into a more-or-less coherent whole" (p. 116). Such a coherent whole can be reached vertically and horizontally according to Sheldon and Kasser (1995). They propose that vertical coherence occurs when lower-level (more concrete/practical) goals are consistent with or regulated by higher-level (more abstract) goals. Horizontal coherence occurs when different, same-level goals are not conflicting and help or strengthen each other (Sheldon & Kasser, 1995).

vertical conflicts may arise on a daily basis, and/or could also comprise a more general problem in a person's life (Purvis, 2010; Purvis et al., 2011; Ward, 2002a, 2002b).

Several of the theories underlying the GLM stress the importance of having a balanced and structured life plan; one in which all necessary goods for human well-being are attained in a coherent manner without conflict (Arnhart, 1998; Den Uyl, 1991; Emmons, 1996, 1999; Kekes, 1989, 1995; Murphy, 2001; Rasmussen, 1999). Emmons (1996) summarizes how primary good attainment is believed to be linked to well-being, as adopted by the GLM:

> Why are goals important for well-being? Simply, it is because that is how people are designed. Goal-directedness is a human enterprise. Yet something more than the possession of and progression toward important life goals is needed in order for individuals to experience well-being. What seems to be missing is an overall organizing principle that brings together and integrates separate goal strivings into a coherent structure. Conflict and differentiation are such prepotent predictors of well-being precisely because they reflect incoherence and lack of harmony in the system. It is clear that people should strive for outcomes that are consistent with the types of persons they envision becoming. (pp. 331-332)

Empirical research indeed indicates that well-being not only depends on the progress and fulfilment of goals, but also on the harmonious integration of all goals together in a structured and coherent life plan (Boudreaux & Ozer, 2013; Diener et al., 1999; Emmons, 1996, 1999; Gray et al., 2017; Kelly et al., 2015; McGregor & Little, 1998; McGregor et al., 2006; Schmuck & Sheldon, 2001; Sheldon & Kasser, 1995). With regard to horizontal conflict, two meta-analyses, by Kelly et al. (2015) based on 83 studies and Gray et al. (2017) based on 54 studies, concluded that (horizontal) conflict between goals was related to more psychological and physical symptoms, as well as poor subjective well-being. Additionally, studies show that individuals experiencing less (horizontal) conflict between their goals tended to report that their goals were also more aligned with their overall life plan and their personalities (vertical coherence), in turn resulting in higher levels of well-being (Emmons, 1996, 1999; Kelly et al., 2015; McGregor & Little, 1998; McGregor et al., 2006; Sheldon & Kasser, 1995). Regarding vertical conflict, studies find that an imbalanced allocation of resources and commitment to valued goals can result in the neglect of certain important goods, which have been demonstrated to create stress and even more conflict ultimately resulting in a variety of negative consequences for health and well-being (Brunstein et al., 1998; Deci & Ryan, 2000; Sheldon & Niemiec, 2006; Vansteenkiste et al., 2010).

3.7 Conclusion

In the current chapter, I have outlined the theoretical and empirical background of the first GLM assumption on primary goods and well-being put forward by Ward (2002a, 2002b) and his colleagues (e.g. Purvis, 2010; Purvis et al., 2014; Ward & Brown, 2004; Ward & Marshall, 2004; Ward & Maruna, 2007; Ward & Stewart, 2003a, 2003c). However, a major problem lies in the fact that this assumption is almost entirely based on theoretical work and only on a relatively small number of empirical studies. Additionally, these studies have not explicitly tested the GLM's assumptions, but rather indirectly provide some degree of support. What is more, these theories and studies focus largely on adults. Although the GLM is believed to be applicable to all human beings, including adolescents, this assumption lacks an empirical foundation (Fortune, 2018; Van Damme et al., 2017). Therefore, in the next chapter, we will assess the existing empirical support for the first GLM assumption regarding the relationship between primary goods and well-being, specifically for adolescents.

4 Different Phase, Different Needs?

Associations Between Primary Goods and Overall Subjective Well-Being in Adolescents: A Systematic Multi-Level Meta-analysis

As seen in the previous chapter, it has consistently been found that – in adults – well-being can be achieved by the fulfilment of needs and attainment of personal goals that are: intrinsically valuable and motivating, autonomously chosen, realistically achievable, and form a structured coherent life plan. Similarly, the Good Lives Model's (GLM) theoretical and empirical background of the specific primary goods are based on studies and theories that focused on adults. Although the GLM is believed to be applicable to all human beings, including adolescents, this assumption lacks an empirical foundation (Fortune, 2018). It could potentially be problematic to apply the GLM assumptions and principles, developed for adults, to young people without substantiation. Because of their developmental phase, adolescents may have different needs or they may prioritize them differently (Fortune, 2018; Richards, 2011). That is, research suggests that well-being might be related to different types of personal goals and needs across the lifespan, as a result of changing expectations, values, resources and opportunities (Cantor & Sanderson, 1999; Massey et al., 2008). An adequate adaptation to these changes throughout one's life is believed to be important to maintain well-being (Cantor & Sanderson, 1999).

Especially the period of adolescence (between the ages of 12 and 18 years) has long been known as a turbulent phase of life, with a greater risk of mental and behavioural problems due to the many mental, physical and social changes (Arnett, 1999; Žukauskienė, 2014). During this period of development and change, adolescents are exploring their own identity and are starting to build their own life and future (Erikson, 1968; Proctor et al., 2009; Ryan & Deci, 2017a; Zirkel, 1992; Zirkel & Cantor, 1990; Žukauskienė, 2014). Accordingly, studies have found that adolescents pursue goals that are unique to this particular developmental phase (Marttinen & Salmela-Aro, 2012; Massey et al., 2008, 2009; Messersmith & Schulenberg, 2010; Nurmi, 1991; Ogilvie et al., 2001; Salmela-Aro, 2010). The type of goals that people strive for can vary greatly between individuals, influenced by personal, cultural and social contexts. In general, however, adolescent goals seem to follow a 'cultural prototype' in which they are expected to achieve educational goals first, followed by occupational and relationship/family goals. Additionally, social needs become more important when adolescents gain independence from their parents and spend a greater amount of time in the company of peers (Massey et al., 2008;

Messersmith & Schulenberg, 2010; Nurmi, 1991). Hence, it is quite conceivable that adolescents prioritize other GLM primary goods for their well-being than adults.

Although a vast number of studies exist on what contributes to adolescents' overall well-being (see e.g. for reviews: A. Ben-Arieh et al., 2014; Gilman & Huebner, 2003; Holte et al., 2014; Proctor et al., 2009), to the best of our knowledge, a single comprehensive (systematic) review of the specific *GLM primary goods* and their relation to well-being in adolescents is lacking. That is why, in this chapter, the existing literature on adolescents' well-being will be systematically reviewed. More specifically, we conducted a multi-level meta-analysis to assess the extent to which the eleven GLM primary goods are related to overall well-being in this specific age group.

4.1 Method

4.1.1 *Included and Excluded Well-being Measures*

As discussed in detail in previous chapters, the concept of well-being can vary greatly according to the underlying views, theories and research areas. Depending on these different views, theories, and research areas the concept of 'well-being' is also measured differently. In the current systematic review we only included studies that operationalized 'well-being' with global or overall, context-free measures such as the components of Diener's (2006) conceptualization of subjective well-being (SWB; overall life satisfaction, positive and negative affect) and overall happiness (e.g. items such as: 'To what degree do you feel happy in general?'; 'To what degree do you feel satisfied overall with your life?'; 'To what extent have you felt happy/sad in the past four weeks?'). Importantly, we included only studies with well-being measures that were based on subjective or self-perceived experiences, feelings or evaluations by the participants in the form of self-report. As SWB is by definition subjective, self-reports are preferred as they emphasize the personal experience rather than relying on external judgments of someone else's happiness or well-being (Diener et al., 2000).

Ultimately, measures that assessed well-being as the sum or mean of specific (life) domains were excluded. Examples of excluded well-being measures are the Oxford Happiness Scale, Multidimensional Students Life Satisfaction Scale, Personal Well-being scale, Kidscreen-10, Ryff's Psychological Well-being scale, Rosenberg's self-esteem scale, and the WHO-5 of the World Health Organization.[1] Examples of the overall, context-free subjective well-being questionnaires that were included as outcome variables are the

---

1 Nevertheless, some of the subscales or items of these measures were included as primary goods proxy-measures (see Appendix B, https://www.elevenpub.com/en/content/appendices-9789462364257).

Satisfaction With Life Scale (Diener et al., 1985), Students Life Satisfaction Scale (Huebner, 1995), Subjective Happiness Scale (Lyubomirsky & Lepper, 1999), Positive and Negative Affect Schedule (Watson et al., 1988); Scale of Positive and Negative Experience (Diener et al., 2010), Affect Balance Scale (Bradburn, 1969), and single item scales on life satisfaction and happiness with life and in general, such as Cantril's Ladder (Cantril, 1965).

4.1.2 *Included and Excluded Primary Goods Proxy-measures*

The eleven primary goods of the GLM consist of theoretical, broad motivational constructs, which cannot easily be assessed with a single item or scale. Therefore, we had to rely on proxy-measures that tap into the more concrete ways or means used to satisfy the primary goods (i.e. the secondary goods) as outlined in the work of Ward, Purvis, Willis, and colleagues (Purvis, 2010; Purvis et al., 2014; Ward, 2002a, 2002b; Ward & Maruna, 2007; Willis et al., 2013). Examples of secondary goods are: having a successful career (i.e. for 'excellence in work'), spending time with family and friends (i.e. for 'relatedness'), or going to church (i.e. for 'spirituality') (Ward, 2002a, 2002b; Ward & Maruna, 2007; Willis et al., 2013). It was not always easy to decide which type of measure was best able to tap into the primary goods and which was not. When in doubt, the author and the second reviewer discussed the measures to reach consensus on whether or not it reflected a certain primary good. In this process, decisions were always based on the detailed descriptions of the primary and secondary goods of Ward, Purvis, Willis, and colleagues (see Chapter 3; Purvis, 2010; Purvis et al., 2014; Ward, 2002a, 2002b; Willis et al., 2013). If a measure assessed a certain secondary good for which it was not clear or ambiguous to which primary good it was related (for example, secondary goods that could clearly satisfy more than one primary good), it was excluded. In this way, we aimed to include only assessment measures that tapped into a specific primary good (see Appendix B[2] for an overview of included and excluded primary goods proxy-measures).

4.1.3 *Search Strategy and Selection*

A systematic literature search was conducted using the PsycINFO, Pubmed, Web of Science, ERIC, and SocIndex databases first in April 2017 and subsequently updated in May 2021 (see Figure 4.1). We searched for combinations of search terms related to well-being and adolescence in publication titles, with no restriction of time period or publication type. The specific search terms and combinations that were entered were: well-being,

2 See https://www.elevenpub.com/en/content/appendices-9789462364257.

wellbeing, 'satisfaction with life', 'life satisfaction', happiness, and happy, combined with youth*, young*, juvenile*, adolescen*, and child*. This search strategy resulted in 16,746 publications, which were imported into Endnote, a software tool for managing references. Duplicates were (hand-) searched and removed, leaving 9,274 publications.

In the first phase, these 9,274 publication titles were reviewed one by one to identify publications that were irrelevant for the current study. Publications were excluded in this phase if it became clear from the title that the publication met one or more of the exclusion criteria (see Table 4.1 for a list of all exclusion and inclusion criteria). Examples of clearly irrelevant publications were articles reporting on studies with animals, very young children and babies, book reviews, intervention or methodological studies. If there were no indicators of exclusion criteria and the publication seemed to meet the inclusion criteria, or if the title did not hold sufficient information to make a clear decision, the publication was included and reviewed in more detail in the second phase: the abstract review. This first phase led to the exclusion of 6,498 publications.

The remaining abstracts (n = 2,776) were examined on whether they met exclusion and/or inclusion criteria. Most important in this phase was to check whether the publication studied possible determinants of adolescents' well-being. When there was a strong sense of doubt whether the article should be included in the next, full-text screening phase, the Introduction and/or Method section was already screened briefly. After the abstract screening phase, 2,196 publications were excluded, of which 198 titles/abstracts were checked by a second reviewer on whether they indeed met the exclusion criteria, to assess reviewer reliability. Only one of the publications assessed by the second reviewer was mistakenly excluded by the first author and was thus included in the set of publications to be reviewed in full.

The remaining 580 full-texts were imported in Endnote and examined in detail. First, we recorded which sample was used: whether or not the sample was from the general population, its gender distribution, age range, mean age and country of origin. Only those with samples from the general population with their (mean) age between 12 and 18 years were included. Second, it was recorded what type of well-being assessment was used as an outcome measure. Only studies that assessed self-reported well-being or a closely related concept (e.g. life satisfaction, happiness, positive or negative affect) in a global manner were included. This resulted in 345 included publications that were categorized according to the primary good(s) they measured in relation to well-being. While categorizing, 158 publications were excluded as they did not adequately measure any of the primary goods according to our included proxy-measures (see Appendix B[3]), leaving 187 publications for the final data-extraction phase.

3 See https://www.elevenpub.com/en/content/appendices-9789462364257.

We checked the reference lists of these 187 publications for other relevant publications that we might have missed. In addition, reference lists of literature reviews, books, book chapters, book reviews and conference papers excluded in earlier phases, but seemed relevant, were searched. This cross-referencing strategy yielded eight publications that we added to the final set, resulting in a total number of 195 publications. Again, the reference lists of these eight publications were checked, but no new publications were retrieved for inclusion.

Table 4.1 Inclusion and Exclusion Criteria

Inclusion criteria	Exclusion criteria
– included studies on human adolescents between 12 and 18 years old	– included only non-human (animal) samples – included mainly adults (mean age 18+) – included mainly young children (mean age <12)
– reported on the general population	– focused on a subgroup compared to general population – compared subgroups with each other – included only specific patient or subgroup samples (no general population)
– assessed overall well-being, such as happiness and/or life satisfaction, using standardized questionnaires (self-report) as an outcome measure	– clearly did not assess any concept related to well-being – assessed and analysed well-being as a predictor – assessed well-being using an external rater (not self-report)
– assessed one of the GLM primary goods or concepts related to them in relation to well-being – reported sample size and correlation coefficient(s)	– did not report on a study at all (e.g. reported only on policy, opinion, or editorial issues) – reported on purely methodological issues – reported on intervention effects or pilot studies – did not report sample size or correlation coefficients
– peer-reviewed	– not peer-reviewed/grey literature – quality score of 4 or less[4]
– written in English	– not written in English
– abstract and full text available	– no abstract and full text available

4 A quality score for each publication was assessed using a slightly adapted form of the Joanna Briggs Institute Critical Appraisal Tool (see https://joannabriggs.org/sites/default/files/2020-08/Checklist_for_Analytical_Cross_Sectional_Studies.pdf). We omitted question 4 and changed question 3 to: 'Was the independent variable measured in a valid and reliable way?'.

The data from each of these 195 articles was extracted in a structured format, including title, author(s), publication year, country/countries in which the study was conducted, sample size(s), age range and mean, gender distribution, ethnicity distribution, study design (cross-sectional or longitudinal), analysis method, type and details of the well-being measure(s), type and details of the primary good(s) proxy measure(s), and the reported correlation coefficient(s) between the two measures.

While extracting the data, the quality of each publication was assessed using a slightly adapted form of the Joanna Briggs Institute Critical Appraisal Tool (see this chapter, fn 4). The publications were assessed on whether they clearly defined inclusion criteria for the sample; whether subjects and setting were described in detail; whether the independent (primary good measure(s)) and dependent (well-being measure(s)) variables were assessed in a valid and reliable way, whether there were confounding factors identified and dealt with; and finally, whether appropriate statistical analyses were used. Each of these items was scored with 2 points if it could be answered with *yes*, 1 if *unclear* and 0 if *no*. This yielded a quality score ranging from 0 to 14.

During this quality check, the principal researcher and the second reviewer discussed to reach consensus in ambiguous cases. Publications without the adequate statistical data (correlation coefficients and sample size) or a quality score of 4 or less were excluded (n = 47), leaving 148 publications to be included (see Appendix C[5] for an overview and details of these 148 included publications). Nine of these publications reported on a sample and data that was already included in another included publication. Therefore, we excluded the duplicate data by selecting the most recent publication that reported the data. One of these publications was excluded because it reported on the follow-up data of the same sample of another publication. This resulted in 139 publications covering 532 effect sizes for data-analysis entered in SPSS (version 27).

5 See https://www.elevenpub.com/en/content/appendices-9789462364257.

Figure 4.1 Flow-chart of Included and Excluded Publications

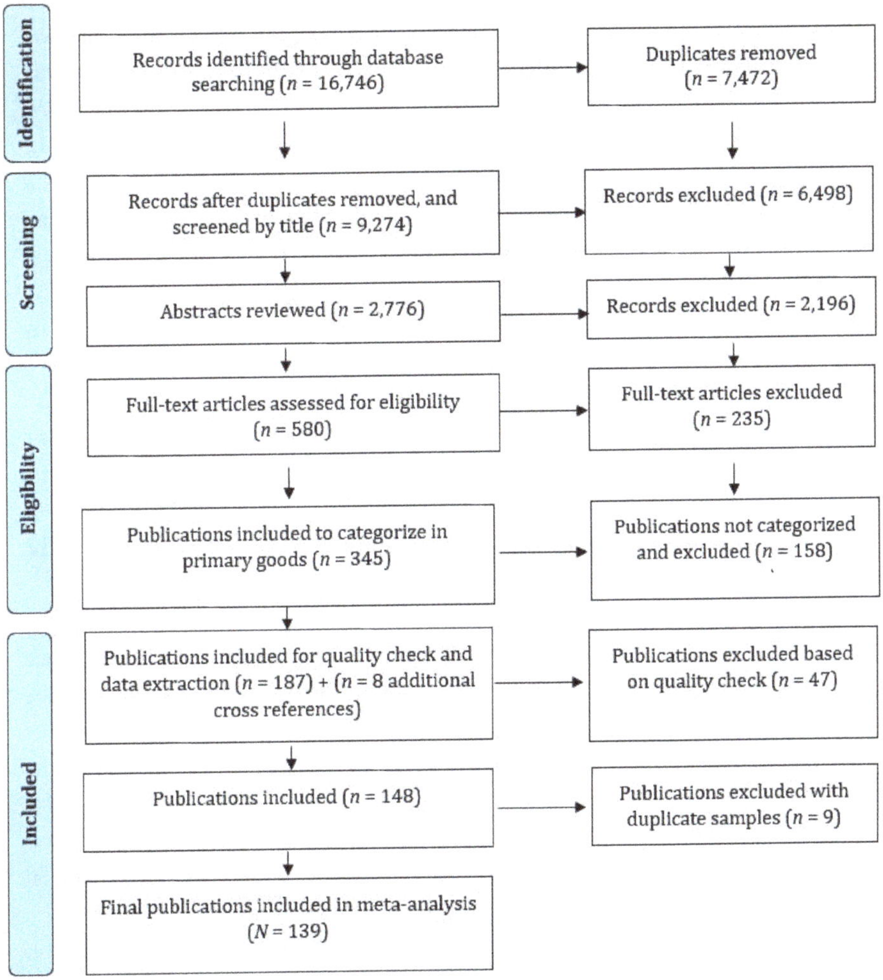

4.1.4 *Data-analysis*

A large number of studies in the dataset used multiple measures for one primary good and/or well-being, resulting in multiple effect sizes per study. This led to the violation of the assumption of independent effect sizes that underlie classical meta-analytic strategies (Lipsey & Wilson, 2001). Therefore, we opted to analyse the overall effect size (Pearson's correlation coefficient r) for the association between each primary good and overall well-being, using a multilevel random effects model. The meta-analyses were conducted in R (a statistical software environment; version 3.6.3) with the metafor package of Viechtbauer (2010), using the syntax from Assink and Wibbelink (2016). A multilevel approach takes into account both the within and the between study variance. In this way, multiple effect sizes can be extracted from each included study, so that all information in the studies can be preserved and maximum statistical power is achieved (Assink & Wibbelink, 2016). We used a three-level random effects model to account for three levels of variance: the sampling variance of each effect size (level 1), the variance between effect sizes of different outcomes extracted from the same study (level 2), and the variance between the different studies (level 3). All model parameters were estimated using the Restricted Maximum Likelihood estimation method. The log-likelihood-ratio-tests were performed one-tailed; all other tests were performed two-tailed and p-values < .05 were considered statistically significant.

We first analysed the overall estimate of the effect size for each of the eleven primary goods in relation to overall well-being by conducting eleven separate meta-analyses. The t-distribution was used for testing individual regression coefficients of the meta-analytic models and for calculating the corresponding confidence intervals of the overall estimates of the effect size. Next, to determine whether the variance between effect sizes from the same study (level 2) and the variance between studies (level 3) was significant, two separate one-tailed log-likelihood-ratio tests were performed for each primary good, in which the fit of the full model was compared to the fit of a model excluding one of the variance parameters. Subsequently, in case of significant variation between effect sizes from the same study and/or between studies, the analysis was extended by including moderator variables to determine whether this variation could be explained by the type of the measures that were used. When possible, we ran moderator analyses to assess for differences in the type of primary good proxy measure (for example, the primary good 'life' was assessed with questionnaires on the sub-goods 'physical health', 'financial situation' and 'living situation'). An omnibus test was performed to determine whether a (potential) effect of one or more moderator variables included in the model was significant.

To prepare the dataset for these analyses the correlation coefficients (r) were transformed to Fisher's Z scores as reported by Cooper (2017) using the formula:

$$Zr = (1/2)[loge(1+r) - loge(1-r)]$$

The accompanying variance was calculated as: 1/[N-3]. In general, the reported total sample size (N) was used to calculate this variance, unless it was explicitly specified in the Method/Results section that the number of participants who completed the relevant questionnaires, or the number of participants on which the correlation coefficient was based, differed from the total sample size. When, throughout the text, different numbers of participants were used to calculate the correlation coefficient, and the exact sample size was unclear, the smallest number was chosen to be conservative. When the number of participants for whom the correlations in a correlation matrix were calculated was ranging between two different numbers, the smallest number was chosen. If a study was longitudinal in nature, only the data of the first assessment were used. When a publication reported on two or more different independent samples (female/male samples, or samples from different countries) but used the same measures and study procedure in both samples, we first calculated a single weighted mean correlation coefficient for the study before transforming it to Fisher's Z scores.

After the analyses in R, the Fisher's *Z* scores were transformed back to correlation coefficients for interpretation and reporting purposes. Forest plots were made for all meta-analyses showing the correlation coefficients and confidence intervals of all included studies (see Appendix D[6]). *Positive* correlation coefficients indicate that a greater primary good attainment or satisfaction is related to a *higher* level of reported well-being, life satisfaction, positive affect, *or lower* negative affect. *Negative* correlation coefficients indicate that a greater primary good attainment or satisfaction is related to a *lower* level of reported well-being, life satisfaction, positive affect *or higher* negative affect. In order to achieve this parallel way of reporting, the direction of the correlation coefficient was reversed when a higher score on the primary good questionnaire corresponded to lower or worse well-being. We adopted the empirical guidelines for interpreting the magnitude of correlation coefficients, suggested by Hemphill (2003) based on a reflection of a multitude of psychological studies and meta-analyses: $r < .20$ reflects a small effect, $r = .20$ to .30 a moderate effect and $r > .30$ a large effect.

4.2 RESULTS

In this section, the results of the eleven meta-analyses are reported separately per primary good, each including the overall correlation coefficient and whether or not there was significant between and/or within study variance. If applicable, the results of the moderator analyses of the different subtypes of goods are reported as well (see **Table** for an overview of these results). All overall correlation coefficient estimates were positive, which means that for all statistically significant primary goods a greater attainment or satisfaction is related to a higher level of subjective well-being.

6 See https://www.elevenpub.com/en/content/appendices-9789462364257.

Table 4.2 Overall Estimates per Primary Good and Moderator Analyses over Sub-goods

(Sub) Goods$^{(N)}$	Overall estimates $^{(K)}$	(Sub) Goods$^{(N)}$	Overall estimates $^{(K)}$
Life$^{(50)}$	.31 [.27 - .35]$^{***(88)}$	**Relatedness$^{(67)}$**	.37 [.34 - .40]$^{***\ (180)}$
Physical health	.31 [.26 - .36]$^{ab\ (43)}$	Family	.44 [.40 - .47]$^{a\ (65)}$
Living situation	.37 [.31 - .43]$^{b\ (20)}$	Peers	.32 [.28 - .36]$^{b\ (53)}$
Financial situation	.26 [.20 - .32]$^{a\ (25)}$	General/Others	.35 [.31 - .39]$^{b\ (62)}$
Knowledge$^{(5)}$	.25 [.14 - .36]$^{***\ (10)}$	**Community$^{(8)}$**	.29 [.22 - .35]$^{***\ (27)}$
Excellence in work$^{(24)}$	.28 [.24 - .31]$^{***\ (38)}$	**Spirituality$^{(28)}$**	.28 [.23 - .33]$^{***\ (84)}$
Life achievement	.36 [.30 - .42]$^{a\ (8)}$	Religion/spirituality	.24 [.18 - .31]$^{a\ (48)}$
School achievement	.29 [.24 - .33]$^{b\ (21)}$	Meaning/purpose	.31 [.16 - .45]$^{a\ (36)}$
GPA	.21 [.14 - .27]$^{c\ (9)}$		
Excellence in play$^{(3)}$	.32 [.16 - .46]$^{**\ (4)}$	**Creativity$^{(4)}$**	.18 [.06 - .30]$^{**\ (7)}$
Excellence in agency$^{(10)}$	.35 [.27 - .43]$^{***\ (16)}$	**Pleasure$^{(5)}$**	.13 [-.09 - .33]$^{ns\ (7)}$
Goal pursuit	.44 [.35 - .51]$^{a\ (5)}$		
Control	.28 [.20 - .36]$^{b\ (11)}$		
Inner peace$^{(32)}$	.51 [.48 - .54]$^{***\ (71)}$		
Mental health	.54 [.49 - .58]$^{a\ (33)}$		
Anxiety	.40 [.33 - .47]$^{b\ (13)}$		
Depression	.52 [.48 - .57]$^{a\ (25)}$		

Note. K = number of effect sizes, N = number of studies. GPA = Grade Point Average. Different superscript letters (a, b, c,) indicate statistically significant differences when they differ from each other within one moderator analysis. $^{**}p < .01$; $^{***}p < .001$.

4.2.1 *Primary Goods in Relation to Adolescents' Well-being*

Life

The overall effect size estimate of the primary good 'life' is analysed on the basis of 50 studies and 88 effect sizes that assessed the relationship with overall well-being in adolescents in 19 countries. The overall correlation coefficient of .31, 95% CI [.27, .35] represents a large effect. Significant heterogeneity was found for both within study variance ($p < .001$) and between study variance ($p < .001$). We identified three types of measures that assessed sub-goods of 'life': physical health, financial situation and living situation. The moderator analysis showed that living situation (as a sub-good of 'life') was more strongly correlated with overall well-being ($r = .37$) than measures reporting on the financial situation ($r = .26$), $F(2,85) = 4.06$, $p = .021$.

Excellence in Work

The overall effect size estimate of the primary good 'excellence in work' is analysed on the basis of 24 studies and 38 effect sizes that assessed the relationship with overall well-being in adolescents in 12 countries. The overall correlation coefficient of .28, 95% CI [.24, .31] represents a moderate effect. Significant heterogeneity was found for both the within study variance ($p < .001$) and the between study variance ($p = .021$). We identified three types of measures that assessed sub-goods of 'excellence in work' for adolescents: subjective feelings of achievement and mastery in life in general, subjective feelings of achievement at school and their Grade Point Average (GPA) as an objective academic achievement score. The moderator analysis revealed these three types of measures differed significantly from each other in their relation to well-being, $F(2,35) = 6.35$, $p = .004$. Subjective achievement in life in general showed the strongest correlation with overall well-being ($r = .36$), followed by self-reported achievement at school ($r = .29$), and GPA scores ($r = .21$).

Inner Peace

The overall effect size estimate of the primary good 'inner peace' is analysed on the basis of 32 studies and 71 effect sizes that assessed the relationship with overall well-being in adolescents in 21 countries. The overall correlation coefficient of .51, 95% CI [.47, .54] represents a large effect. Significant heterogeneity was found for both the within study variance ($p < .001$) and the between study variance ($p = .015$). We identified three types of measures that assessed 'inner peace' for adolescents: questionnaires that assessed general mental health, anxiety and depression. These three types of measures differed significantly from each other in their relation to well-being, $F(2,68) = 8.34$, $p < .001$. Anxiety measures showed a significantly smaller correlation with overall well-being ($r = .40$) than mental health in general ($r = .54$), and depression ($r = .52$).

Relatedness

The overall effect size estimate of the primary good 'relatedness' is analysed on the basis of 67 studies and 180 effect sizes that assessed the relationship with overall well-being in adolescents in 23 countries. The overall correlation coefficient of .37, 95% CI [.34, .40] is considered a large effect. Significant heterogeneity was found for both the within study variance ($p < .001$) and the between study variance ($p < .001$). We identified three types of measures that assessed 'relatedness' for adolescents: questionnaires that assessed relatedness with people in general (including feelings of loneliness), relatedness with family, and relatedness with peers. The moderator analysis showed that the three types of measures differed significantly from each other in the strength of their relation to well-being, $F(2,177) = 18.43$, $p < .001$. The correlation between family relatedness and overall well-being was significantly stronger ($r = .44$) than relatedness in general ($r = .35$), and relatedness with peers ($r = .32$).

Community

The overall effect size estimate of the primary good 'community' is analysed on the basis of eight studies and 27 effect sizes that assessed the relationship with overall well-being in adolescents in six countries. The overall correlation coefficient of .29, 95% CI [.22, .35] reflects a moderate effect size. Significant heterogeneity was found for both within study variance ($p < .001$) and between study variance ($p = .029$). All questionnaires categorized as assessing 'community' were related to group belonging and social acceptance, no sub-goods were identified.

Spirituality

The overall effect size estimate of the primary good 'spirituality' is analysed on the basis of 28 studies and 84 effect sizes that assessed the relationship with overall well-being in adolescents in 20 countries. The overall correlation coefficient of .28, 95% CI [.23, .33] is considered a moderate effect. Significant heterogeneity was found for both the within study variance ($p < .001$) and the between study variance ($p < .001$). We identified two measures that assessed 'spirituality' for adolescents: questionnaires that assessed religiosity and being/feeling spiritual on the one hand, and having a sense of or searching for meaning and purpose in life on the other. The moderator analysis showed that these two types of measures did not statistically differ from each other in relation to well-being, $F(1,82)=2.79$, $p = .099$.

4.2.2 *Primary Goods Under-represented in the Research Literature*

Several primary goods were under-represented in the empirical literature: 'goal pursuit' (a sub-good of 'excellence in agency'), 'knowledge', 'excellence in play', 'pleasure', and 'creativity'. Results based on these rather small numbers of studies and effect sizes (five or less) should be interpreted with caution and require more research to be able to draw more robust conclusions (Jackson & Turner, 2017). Nevertheless, we will present the results of these goods here to provide a complete picture of all eleven goods. Appendix D[7] provides forest plots of all meta-analyses in which all effect sizes and their confidence intervals are reported in detail.

Excellence in Agency

The overall effect size estimate of the primary good 'excellence in agency' is analysed on the basis of ten studies and sixteen effect sizes that assessed the relationship with overall well-being in adolescents in nine countries. The overall correlation coefficient of .35, 95% CI [.27, .43] represents a large effect. Significant heterogeneity was found for the between study variance ($p = .004$) but not the within study variance ($p = .381$). We identified two types of measures that assessed 'excellence in agency' for adolescents: questionnaires that assessed perceived control over life on the one hand, and goal pursuit on the other. The moderator analysis showed that the two types of measures differed significantly from each other in their relation to well-being, $F(1,14)=9.12$, $p = .009$. Goal pursuit was more strongly related to overall well-being ($r = .44$) than perceived control ($r = .28$). However, it must be noted that only five effect sizes were found for goal pursuit, in comparison to eleven for perceived control.

Knowledge

The overall effect size estimate of the primary good 'knowledge' is analysed on the basis of five studies and ten effect sizes that assessed the relationship with overall well-being in adolescents in five countries. The overall correlation coefficient of .25, 95% CI [.14, .36] reflects a moderate effect size. Significant heterogeneity was found for within study variance ($p < .001$) but not for between study variance ($p = .50$). All questionnaires categorized as assessing 'knowledge' were related to learning and curiosity, no sub-goods were identified.

Excellence in Play

The overall effect size estimate of the primary good 'excellence in play' is analysed on the basis of three studies and four effect sizes that assessed the relationship with overall well-being in adolescents in five countries. The overall correlation coefficient of .32, 95% CI [.16, .46] represents a large effect. Significant heterogeneity was found for within study variance ($p < .001$) but not for the between study variance ($p = .375$). All questionnaires categorized as assessing 'excellence in play' measured satisfaction with leisure and free time, no sub-goods were identified.

7 See https://www.elevenpub.com/en/content/appendices-9789462364257.

Creativity

The overall effect size estimate of the primary good 'creativity' is analysed on the basis of four studies and seven effect sizes that assessed the relationship with overall well-being in adolescents in three countries. The overall correlation coefficient of .18, 95% CI [.06, .30] is considered a small effect. Significant heterogeneity was found for the within study variance ($p < .001$) but not for the between study variance ($p = .50$). All questionnaires categorized as assessing 'creativity' measured the tendency of seeking novel and challenging experiences, no sub-goods were identified.

Pleasure

The overall effect size estimate of the primary good 'pleasure' is analysed on the basis of four studies and five effect sizes that assessed the relationship with overall well-being in adolescents in seven countries. The overall correlation coefficient of .13, 95% CI [-.09, .33] was found not to be statistically different from zero ($p = .189$), meaning we found no overall effect between the primary good of 'pleasure' and overall well-being. There was, however, significant heterogeneity for the within study variance ($p < .001$) but not for between study variance ($p = .229$). The questionnaires categorized as assessing 'pleasure' measured different assessments of enjoyment and sensation seeking, but no clear sub-goods were identified.

4.3 Discussion

Based on this multilevel meta-analysis, it can be concluded that for almost all the eleven GLM primary goods a greater attainment or satisfaction is related, in varying degrees, to higher levels of overall subjective well-being in adolescents between the ages of 12 and 18. Most of the primary goods were well represented in various studies, including a diverse number of relevant predictor variables and outcome measures for well-being. Moreover, most primary goods were studied in numerous countries representing a variety of cultures, indicating a certain degree of generalizability of the findings. The results are discussed in more detail in the following text.

4.3.1 *Psychological Needs: Relatedness, Competence and Autonomy*

The strongest relationships with adolescent subjective well-being were found for the GLM primary goods derived from the three psychological needs of Deci and Ryan's Self-determination Theory (SDT; 2000): 'relatedness' ('relatedness' and 'community' in GLM terms), 'competence' ('excellence in work' and 'excellence in play' in GLM terms), and 'autonomy' ('excellence in agency' in GLM terms). SDT posits that the satisfaction of these three needs is essential for positive development and well-being in all human beings (Deci & Ryan, 2000; Ryan & Deci, 2017b). The results confirm that this also applies to adolescents.

The primary good of 'relatedness' seemed to be one of the most important factors for adolescents' well-being. For adolescents, peer, and 'community' relationships (i.e. the need to belong) were both strongly positively related to their subjective well-being. Supportive peer relationships are consistently found to be related to positive psychological and social development (Proctor & Linley, 2014). That is, peer relationships can be important sources of affection, intimacy, alliance, feelings of inclusion, enhancement of self-worth, and have been linked to both current and future well-being of adolescents (Brown & Braun, 2013; Proctor & Linley, 2014; Van Ryzin et al., 2009; Žukauskienė, 2014). Furthermore, being part of a social group has been found to be a source of pride and a sense of identity (Sheldon & Bettencourt, 2002).

While it is widely assumed that for adolescents their friends are gradually more important than their family (Massey et al., 2008; Messersmith & Schulenberg, 2010; Nurmi, 1991), we found that family relationships correlated more strongly with their subjective well-being compared to peer relationships. Studies on family relationships in general, and parental attachment in particular, consistently show that secure attachment relationships and good communication within the family fosters the experience of support and trust in which youth can (learn to) express their feelings (Ainsworth, 1989; Bowlby, 1969; Cava et al., 2014; Proctor et al., 2009). Furthermore, a stable and secure attachment between children and their parents is known to positively contribute to the development of social relationships, emotion regulation, and the way the children cope with development issues (Ainsworth, 1989; Rask et al., 2003; Žukauskienė, 2014).

Interestingly, for the GLM primary good of 'excellence in work', a sense of mastery and achievement in life was more important for adolescents' well-being than academic achievement alone. Perhaps not all adolescents value academic achievement and some might be more focused on vocational achievement or other competencies (Proctor & Linley, 2014; Proctor et al., 2009). Accordingly, 'excellence in play' showed an overall large positive effect size in relation to well-being, while 'excellence in work' (subjective and objective academic achievement) was moderately related to higher levels of overall well-being in adolescents. These results indicate that although, in general, school is an important part of adolescents' life and they are often encouraged to succeed academically, for them it is not the only and most important source of feelings of mastery and competence related to their well-being. Adolescents might experience school or work as something that is obligatory, while leisure activities are pursued voluntarily, and mastery in these are an important source of well-being. Although 'excellence in play' was under-represented in our meta-analysis, this finding is in line with studies evidencing the importance of leisure activities on subjective well-being, in both adults and adolescents (Csikszentmihalyi, 2000; Kuykendall et al., 2018; Kuykendall et al., 2015).

As for autonomy or 'excellence in agency', we found that goal pursuit was more important for adolescent subjective well-being than perceived control. This might be related to the fact that adolescents are gradually developing independence and do not have full autonomy over their lives as long as they live with their parents or caregivers. This fits with the developmental stage that adolescents go through while forming their own identities and starting to build their own lives and futures (Proctor et al., 2009; Zirkel, 1992; Zirkel & Cantor, 1990; Žukauskienė, 2014). Consequently, they might attach more value to the possibility of pursuing their own goals rather than having full control over their own lives (which they obviously do not yet have). Accordingly, SDT argues that a certain level of perceived control may be necessary, but insufficient condition for experiencing a high level of autonomous motivation (motivation which is self-determined and intrinsic), instead of other-determined and extrinsic, and subsequent well-being as a consequence (Ryan & Deci, 2000b).

In addition, studies suggest that a combination of both perceived control *and* being able to pursue intrinsically valuable goals might be necessary for autonomous motivation and well-being (Hortop et al., 2013; Van Petegem et al., 2012). For example, in adolescents, whether they were able/allowed to make their own independent decisions in life (having control) did not contribute to their personal and social well-being, unless the motives behind these decisions were intrinsic and autonomous (Van Petegem et al., 2012). Similarly, Hortop and colleagues (2013) followed young adult students over a 6-month period and assessed their life goals, motivation, perceived control, and emotional well-being. They found that students who felt autonomously motivated to pursue their goals (instead of feeling pressured by others to pursue them) and who also perceived high levels of control over their own lives showed the largest improvements in well-being. However, students with generally low levels of autonomous motivation – independent of their perceived control – showed the smallest improvements in well-being. These results underline the importance of perceived autonomy and self-directedness regardless of (perceived) control.

4.3.2 *Emotional Needs*

Our analyses further confirmed that emotion processing and coping skills are important for overall well-being in adolescents: of the eleven primary goods, 'inner peace' showed the strongest relationship with adolescent subjective well-being, that is, better mental health, less depression, and less anxiety were related to higher levels of overall well-being. The strong relationship between emotional well-being and overall well-being in adolescents is reflected not only in the large number of studies in our analyses, but has also been demonstrated in other reviews that have concluded that the two types of well-being reinforce each other both positively and negatively (Lent, 2004; Proctor et al., 2009).

In our analysis, the large effect size for the primary good of 'inner peace' could be explained by the fact that the developmental phase of adolescence is marked by greater mood disruptions and extreme emotions (Arnett, 1999). Furthermore, this could also be (partly) explained by the fact that various studies have shown that someone's mood at the time of completing the questionnaires can affect the answers on emotional and overall well-being, thus artificially increasing the correlation found between emotional well-being and overall well-being (Diener et al., 1991; Eid & Diener, 2004; Gamble & Gärling, 2012). Although it seems that 'inner peace' is one of the most important factors related to adolescents' well-being, we must be cautious to interpret the magnitude of this effect, because there is a risk of spurious correlation.

4.3.3 Basic Needs

Another important primary good appears to be the good of 'life', comprising of adolescents' living situation, financial situation and physical health. The overall positive effect size for physical health and living situation in relation to subjective well-being was large. This is in line with the GLM's theory that the primary good of 'life' mainly concerns the need for healthy living, the need to feel safe and secure (Purvis, 2010; Purvis et al., 2014; Ward, 2002a, 2002b; Willis et al., 2013). In Maslow's (1962) 'hierarchy of needs', physiological (food, water, warmth, rest) and safety needs form the basic needs that are deemed necessary to secure the higher-level needs of, for example, relatedness, belonging, feelings of achievement and self-actualization, which resemble the psychological needs of the SDT. However, a moderate positive effect was found for a better and more satisfying financial situation on adolescents' well-being. Although the GLM mentions that 'life' consists of living circumstances that are of a high standard, and possible secondary goods include earning an adequate livelihood to achieve this (Purvis, 2010; Purvis et al., 2014; Ward, 2002a, 2002b; Willis et al., 2013), it appears that the financial situation as such is of lesser importance for adolescents' well-being compared to perceived physical health and living situation.

An explanation of this finding can be found in the fact that adolescents, compared to adults, are usually not (fully) responsible for their own financial situation. It is furthermore in line with a large body of research that shows there seems to be a threshold for basic needs: only in low income/developing countries, economic status is related to subjective well-being, but not in high income/developed countries (Cummins, 2000; Easterlin, 1995; Howell & Howell, 2008). Moreover, studies typically show that the pursuit of extrinsic or material goals, such as money and wealth, are less important for well-being in general and might even be detrimental for both adults and adolescents (Dittmar et al., 2014; Easterbrook et al., 2014; Kasser, 2002; Massey et al., 2008). Those studies suggest that striving for a sense of self-worth via external rewards reflects a lack of personal/inner self-worth (Massey et al., 2008). Moreover, materialistic attitudes and lifestyles are believed to conflict with the pursuit of goals and needs deemed necessary for personal growth and finding meaning in life, such as relatedness or spirituality (Kasser, 2016).

4.3.4 *Spiritual Needs*

Unlike extrinsic goals, achieving intrinsic goals, which are deemed to be satisfying in and of themselves, such as community contribution or personal growth, are consistently found to be related to higher levels of well-being in both adults and adolescents (Davids et al., 2017; Ryan & Deci, 2000b; Schmuck et al., 2000; Sheldon, Ryan, et al., 2004; Van Den Broeck et al., 2019; Veronneau et al., 2005). In this sense, finding a purpose or meaning in life (i.e. the primary good of 'spirituality') – whether or not in the form of religiosity – can be considered an intrinsic goal (Emmons, 2005; Emmons et al., 1998; van Dierendonck, 2012; van Dierendonck & Mohan, 2006), which was found to be moderately related to higher levels of overall well-being in adolescents. It is believed that adolescence is a developmental phase of search for identity and discovery of a purpose in life (Bronk et al., 2009; Damon et al., 2003; Erikson, 1968; Ryan & Deci, 2017a).

This purpose or meaning in life can be achieved through several means, one of them being religion (van Dierendonck, 2012; van Dierendonck & Mohan, 2006). However, as our results show, religion is definitely not the only way. Spirituality, or philosophy of life, in the broad sense can be important for adolescents as well (Dankulincova Veselska et al., 2018). An example of spirituality in the broad sense that was found to be positively related to adolescents' well-being is connectedness with nature (Holder et al., 2016; Howell et al., 2013). This finding is in line with the GLM's description of the need for spirituality that can involve seeking religious inspiration and affiliation, a spiritual connection with a transcendent being or reality, or simply the experience of being part of a greater whole (Purvis, 2010; Purvis et al., 2014; Ward, 2002a, 2002b; Willis et al., 2013). Accordingly, Howell et al. (2013) found that for undergraduate students, a sense of meaning in life mediated the positive relationship between religiosity and well-being as well as the positive relationship between connectedness with nature and well-being. From this, we can conclude that finding meaning in life is an important factor in relation to adolescents' well-being, regardless of the source.

4.3.5 *Curiosity and Expressive Needs*

The primary goods of 'knowledge' and 'creativity' are both related to the need for novelty, curiosity and expression. 'Knowledge' was found to be positively moderately related to adolescents' well-being. The GLM describes the need for 'knowledge' as resulting from the fact that human beings are fundamentally curious and possess the desire to understand aspects of themselves, their environments and other people (Purvis, 2010; Purvis et al., 2014; Ward, 2002a, 2002b; Willis et al., 2013). Especially for adolescents this seems a logical need in the development of their identities and world views. In our meta-analysis, the goods of 'knowledge' or 'curiosity' were under-represented, yet studies in adults have shown that being curious and interested promotes exploration and learning which contributes to personal growth and well-being (Gallagher & Lopez, 2007). Exploration, in turn, can lead to being challenged, gaining new knowledge, meeting new people and developing new skills and competencies (Kashdan & Silvia, 2009).

Similarly, we found that 'creativity' was positively related to adolescents' well-being, albeit with a small effect size. In the few included studies, 'creativity' was conceptualized as relating to experiencing/seeking novel activities. The GLM, however, describes 'creativity' not only as the need for novelty, but also in the broader sense of individual, creative expression of oneself through alternative forms of activity, such as art or creative problem-solving (Purvis, 2010; Purvis et al., 2014; Ward, 2002a, 2002b; Willis et al., 2013). Although we found no studies examining the latter to be more specific conceptualization of creativity, studies with young children find that self-expression through music, arts and crafts – other than through words – allowed them to express complex feelings and identities (Lo & Matsunobu, 2014; Silvey, 2014). It is therefore also recommended to study these broader conceptualizations of 'creativity' in relation to adolescents' well-being in future research.

4.3.6 *Pleasure and Happiness: A Paradox?*

Finally, we found no statistically significant relationship between the primary good of 'pleasure' and adolescent subjective well-being. Aristotle already suggested that seeking pleasure just for the fun of it (i.e. hedonism) was not the (preferred) way towards happiness or well-being (i.e. eudaimonia). He argued quite harshly: "The many, the most vulgar, seemingly conceive the good and happiness as pleasure, and hence they also like the life of gratification. Here they appear completely slavish, since the life they decide on is a life for grazing animals…." (Aristotle, 1985, p. 7). As seen in Chapter 3, many modern-day scholars still hold the idea that pleasure and positive emotions are insufficient to live a good life, especially those considered to be eudaimonic theorists. The latter argue that well-being comes from finding meaning and purpose in life (Huta & Ryan, 2010; Ryff & Singer, 2008; Waterman, 2008).

Studies that examined the contributions to well-being of both these orientations to happiness: hedonic (i.e., pleasure) and eudaimonic (i.e., meaning and purpose in life), usually find that although pleasure (positive emotions and enjoyment) is positively related to subjective well-being, purpose and meaning are more important (Diener et al., 2012; Peterson et al., 2005; Vella-Brodrick et al., 2009). On the other hand, research indicates that pleasurable emotions, such as joy and contentment, can have a positive effect on several life domains and well-being. One example is the Broaden-and-Build Theory of Fredrickson (2004) which states that positive emotions are able to broaden an individual's perspective by causing them to set more personal growth and approach goals. Several studies have indeed found that the experience of positive affect enables success across multiple life domains including work performance, social relationships, physical well-being, coping, problem-solving, and creativity (Lyubomirsky et al., 2005).

The absence of a relation in our analysis could therefore also be explained by the limited power resulting from the very few studies that were included for the analysis of this primary good, which also revealed large heterogeneity in individual effect sizes (see the forest plots in Appendix D[8]). The proxy-measures for this primary good in our meta-analysis varied greatly in content; some measured the tendency to seek sensation, while others asked about the satisfaction with enjoyment in general. The way people seek pleasure and joy may differ from individual to individual, hence explaining the varying effect sizes and the null finding.

For that matter, in all our analyses, we were limited by the proxy-measures for the primary goods as found in the existing empirical literature. Yet there are many ways in which people can obtain these goods, as Laws and Ward (2011) conclude:

> At the level of the abstract primary good, there is a degree of universality apparent in people's motives and their associated actions. However, at the level of everyday actions, there is frequently a bewildering variety of ways of seeking and realizing these abstract values. (p. 215)

4.4 Limitations and Remaining Questions

Although the data enabled us to uncover some interesting findings on the relationship between primary goods and overall well-being in adolescents, our meta-analysis has some limitations that should be taken into consideration. First, as mentioned in the Method

8 See https://www.elevenpub.com/en/content/appendices-9789462364257.

section, we aimed to include only reliable and valid measures for assessing the primary goods and well-being. With regard to the well-being questionnaires, we were strict in only including overall, context-free self-report scales/items reflecting the components of overall subjective well-being (life satisfaction/happiness, positive and negative affect). These questionnaires, however, have been criticized in the past. One of the major critical arguments is that these self-report measures are vulnerable to several biases (Kahneman, 1999). A commonly suggested bias is the tendency of people to judge their life satisfaction or well-being based on momentary experiences, memory and context, thereby not reflecting a general or even accurate assessment (Garcia et al., 2020; Kahneman, 1999). Based on a number of studies examining contextual influences on life satisfaction judgments, Schwarz and Strack (1999) conclude that overall life satisfaction assessments are extremely sensitive to mood, memory or temporarily accessible information (triggered by preceding questions or events). More recent studies, however, have refuted this claim, as Schimmack and Oishi's (2005) meta-analyses and replication studies revealed high retest reliability of life satisfaction judgments and weak effects of the item order on domain and overall well-being judgments (Diener et al., 2013).

Another possible bias arises from 'shared method variance', where strong correlations between life satisfaction in general (overall life satisfaction) and satisfaction with important life domains (domain satisfaction) may become inflated by similarities in assessment method. Indeed, studies find that similar methods and responses can account for some of the shared variance between domain and life satisfaction; still most of the variance is explained by the actual satisfaction with important life domains (Diener et al., 2013; Larsen et al., 1985; Schimmack, 2008; Schimmack & Oishi, 2005).

Regarding the proxy-measures, we aimed to conceptualize the primary goods rather 'pure' and excluded studies that measured primary goods with variables that were non-exclusive and could relate to several other primary goods as well. An example is the exclusion of measures about sports participation, because engaging in sports as a hobby can serve a variety of primary goods, such as 'life' (physical health), 'relatedness' (engaging in group sport activities), 'excellence in play', etc. This resulted, for some of our analyses, in the inclusion of only a limited number of proxy-measures for a particular good. Consequently, considerable differences exist in the number of studies and effect sizes found per primary good, which makes it difficult to compare the overall effect sizes. Moreover, as previously mentioned in the Results section, the data on 'goal pursuit' (a sub-good of 'excellence in agency'), 'knowledge', 'excellence in play', 'creativity', and 'pleasure' had very few studies and effect sizes (five or less), resulting in limited statistical power. These meta-analytic findings thus need to be interpreted with caution as more research is needed to draw more robust conclusions (Jackson & Turner, 2017). To be uniform, only those studies were included that reported correlation coefficients and excluded those who only reported beta-coefficients. Future meta-analyses however could include beta-coefficients to compensate for some of the missing data (see for this suggestion: Peterson & Brown, 2005) as well as assess and take into account the possible effects of publication bias (Sutton A. J. et al., 2000).

Although some studies suggest there may be gender differences in the relationships between different life domains and overall well-being (Jovanović et al., 2016; Kroll, 2011), we did not control for gender in our analyses. Nonetheless, some of the included studies did find support for gender differences, where overall well-being in girls was more strongly related to social indicators (such as family, friends and community satisfaction), while for boys, school and achievement satisfaction seemed to be stronger predictors of well-being (Chui & Wong, 2016; Vera, Moallem, et al., 2012). In contrast, no gender differences were found with regard to the relationship between physical health and well-being (Mahon et al., 2005). Future meta-analyses could include gender as an additional moderator variable. Finally, it must also be noted that this meta-analysis relied on cross-sectional studies and correlation coefficients, which precludes conclusions on causality and the direction of the effects.

As a final remark, the GLM (Purvis, 2010; Purvis et al., 2011; Ward, 2002a, 2002b) and its underlying theories (Arnhart, 1998; Emmons, 1996; Murphy, 2001; Rasmussen, 1999) stress the importance of having a balanced and structured life plan; one in which all necessary goods for human well-being are attained in a coherent manner without conflict (see also Chapter 3). However, few studies have examined the interaction between different types of needs/goods and the role of balance in subjective well-being. In adults, studies have shown that a balanced allocation of commitment and resources to valued goals and needs is important for well-being (Brunstein et al., 1998; Deci & Ryan, 2000; Gray et al., 2017; Kelly et al., 2015; Sheldon & Niemiec, 2006; Vansteenkiste et al., 2010). More specifically, Sheldon and Niemiec (2006) found that adults who simultaneously felt autonomous, competent and related to others reported the highest level of subjective well-being, compared to those who satisfied only one or two of these goods.

Theoretically, it is suggested that the involvement in multiple life domains is necessary to satisfy the full spectrum of human needs (Sirgy & Lee, 2018; Sirgy & Wu, 2009). Furthermore, it is believed that subjective well-being can only be attained when both higher-order (emotional, psychological or personal growth) and basic (physical and survival) needs are met (Maslow, 1962; Sirgy & Wu, 2009). Empirically, this hypothesis was tested by Petrie (2013) in young adults (18-21 years) who found that being able to integrate a broad range of life activities in the domains of physical health, friendship, recreation, creativity, self-esteem, work and community resulted in an increase in well-being. Likewise, Sheldon, Cummins et al. (2010) found that for adults, it is not the amount of time spent on each life domain, but the (perceived) balance between them that is important for need satisfaction and well-being.

Even fewer studies exist on the role of balanced need satisfaction for well-being in adolescents. One study by Milyavskaya et al. (2009), however, found the same results as for adults: the findings showed that adolescents who experience a balance of need satisfaction (i.e., balancing 'relatedness', 'competence', and 'autonomy') across important life contexts, including at school, at home, with friends and in part-time jobs, reported higher well-being. Nevertheless, none of these studies in adults or adolescents assessed the interaction and balance between all GLM primary goods. Thus, further studies are necessary to examine the interaction between the eleven primary goods and possible interactions in relation to well-being (see Chapters 6 and 7). To achieve this, it is also important to include qualitative studies in addition to quantitative ones. What is understood as 'well-being' by individuals can vary considerably and is dependent on personal, developmental, cultural and social factors (see e.g.: Bourke & Geldens, 2007a; Bourke & Geldens, 2007b; Carlquist et al., 2017; Chaplin, 2009; Delle Fave et al., 2011; Fattore et al., 2007; Navarro et al., 2017; Oishi et al., 2009; Sutton C., 2021; Vujcic et al., 2019). Qualitative research into how young people define well-being and the importance they attach to the eleven primary goods suggested by the GLM could thus contribute to more profound insights (see Chapter 8).

4.5 CONCLUSION

For now, we can conclude that most of the 11 GLM primary goods are related, in varying degrees, to overall subjective well-being in adolescents. Some goods, however, may be more salient in their particular developmental phase, such as 'relatedness' (with family) and 'inner peace'. Others might manifest itself differently in adolescents compared to adults, such as achieving competence (i.e. 'excellence in work' and 'excellence in play'), their financial situation (i.e. 'life'), and autonomy (i.e., 'excellence in agency'). Knowing which primary goods are related to well-being (i.e. the *first GLM assumption*), however, will not be sufficient to guide successful offender rehabilitation. Therefore, in the next chapters, we will also examine the *second GLM assumption* that a failure to obtain primary goods and well-being in a prosocial manner can result in criminal behaviour.

5 Theoretical and Empirical Background of GLM's Second Etiological Assumption

Associations Between Primary Goods, Well-Being, and Juvenile Delinquency

In the previous chapters, I focused on the *first assumption* of the 'Good Lives Model of offender rehabilitation' (GLM). We unravelled the existing theories and research on the associations between the eleven primary goods and adolescents' well-being. We now shift to the theoretical and empirical background of the *second assumption* that presupposes that criminal behaviour is triggered when the fulfilment of these primary goods is thwarted or disrupted (Ward & Stewart, 2003a). To reiterate, primary goods and the pursuit of well-being are viewed as the major drivers behind all human behaviour. When these primary goods are not satisfied, they not only compromise one's well-being, but they are also believed to lead to social maladjustment and delinquent behaviour (Ward, 2002a, 2002b; Ward & Marshall, 2004; Ward & Maruna, 2007; Ward & Stewart, 2003a, 2003b). According to the GLM, criminal behaviour is an alternative, antisocial attempt to obtain primary goods and well-being when individuals fail to prosocially secure their primary goods.

5.1 Pathways to Delinquency According to the GLM

In Chapter 3 (Section 3.6), we have already identified four types of problems or difficulties in the attainment of the primary goods: problems with *capacity, scope, means* and *coherence* (Purvis, 2010; Purvis et al., 2011, 2014; Ward & Stewart, 2003a). In brief, this means individuals can: (1) *lack the capacities* and opportunities to satisfy their primary goods prosocially, (2) *lack scope* in the range of goods they pursue and achieve, (3) use *inappropriate (antisocial) means* to obtain primary goods, and/or (4) *lack coherence* in pursuing various primary goods. A *lack of capacities* or *inappropriate means* to successfully pursue one's primary goods can subsequently also result in a *lack of scope* resulting in one or more goods being neglected and/or unsatisfied, leaving the individual with an unfulfilling and incomplete life. Likewise, *conflict* or *incoherence* between goods could result in poor fulfilment of one or more primary goods. For example, when the good of 'excellence in work' takes precedence over the need for 'relatedness' by working late and not having any time left to spend with family (Purvis, 2010; Purvis et al., 2011; Ward, 2002a, 2002b; Ward & Maruna, 2007).

Purvis et al. (2011) empirically assessed the different ways in which these problems with primary good pursuit could lead to offending behaviour. They interviewed 26 adult male sex offenders about the details of and rationale behind their offences. They discovered two routes that can lead to the onset of offending: *direct* and *indirect* (Purvis, 2010; Purvis et al., 2011). Problems with the pursuit of primary goods can lead to offending behaviour in a direct way through the (deliberate) use of *inappropriate (antisocial) means* (e.g. illegal sexual acts to obtain the good of 'relatedness' or 'pleasure'; Purvis, 2010; Purvis et al., 2011; Ward, 2002a, 2002b). The indirect route was found to occur when the problems with primary good fulfilment generate an accumulation of negative effects on the individual's life, such as problems at work or within the family, resulting in feelings of loneliness, incompetence and/or distress. In turn, these negative feelings, combined with maladaptive coping strategies (i.e. inadequate coping, such as substance use) might lead – in specific circumstances – to a loss of control and offending behaviour to pursue one's primary goods after all. The proposed potential indirect problems include *inadequate scope, incoherence* or *conflict* and a *lack of capacities* (Purvis et al., 2011; Ward, 2002b; Ward & Gannon, 2006). In the latter potential problem, the prosocial attainment of primary goods can be hampered by a lack of capacities due to both *personal (internal) limitations* (e.g. a lack of knowledge or skills) and *environmental (external) disadvantages* (e.g. lack of resources or opportunities; Purvis et al., 2011; Purvis et al., 2014; Ward & Stewart, 2003a). Criminogenic risk factors, such as the 'central eight' of the Risk Need Responsivity (RNR) model, are seen as omissions or distortions in these internal (i.e. skills, values, beliefs) and external (i.e. resources, support, opportunities) conditions required for prosocially satisfying one's primary goods and ultimately living a fulfilling and good life (Laws & Ward, 2011; Ward & Maruna, 2007; Ward & Stewart, 2003a).

5.2 Need and Goal Frustration

The notion that a lack of need satisfaction can have adverse effects on well-being and result in antisocial or criminal behaviour is not entirely new. In Chapter 2 (Section 2.1.3) we already briefly mentioned that GLM's second etiological assumption has its roots in the central premise of 'strain theory', that is, the GLM proposes that crime can be understood as the result of obstacles (causing strain) in the pursuit of prosocially obtaining certain goals (i.e. the primary goods; Ward & Maruna, 2007). However, it was suggested long before that failing to satisfy human needs and goals can result in frustration and compensating strategies, such as antisocial or criminal behaviour. In the text that follows, I will briefly discuss these existing theories and their relationship to the GLM.

5.2.1 *Strain Theory*

Earlier examples of theories on need and goal frustration are found in criminology, such as Robert Merton's theory of limited opportunity and anomie. Merton (1938) explained criminal behaviour as an innovative route to the same rewards and successes of legal employment, when legitimate routes were unavailable in certain social structures. According to Merton (1938), frustration and strain arise especially when cultural demands promote the prospect of accumulating wealth and status, while lower-class individuals are largely denied legitimate opportunities to do so. This incompatible combination is thought to result in frustration and sets the stage for alternative, antisocial pursuits of the valued rewards among the lower classes. Cohen (1955), and Cloward and Ohlin (1960) extended Merton's ideas by addressing the status of frustration of lower-class youth in delinquent gangs. They emphasized adolescents' lack of interest in legitimately pursuing middle-class success and the subsequent adoption of delinquent subculture norms.

Robert Agnew (1985) further adapted these ideas by offering a psychological explanation for crime and de-emphasizing the role of social class. He stated that individuals in general, and adolescents in particular, pursue a variety of (immediate) goals, not only long-term, social class-related goals, such as future monetary success and status. Consequently, Agnew explained criminal behaviour in his 'general strain theory of crime and delinquency' (GST) as a consequence of general frustration and difficulties at home, school and work. This theory suggests that certain types of strain can induce negative affect, such as anger and frustration. In turn, anger and frustration create pressure for corrective action, with delinquency being one of the possible coping strategies (Agnew, 1985, 1992, 2006; Agnew & White, 1992). Thus, GST's ideas are quite similar to the GLM's explanation of criminal behaviour (Ward & Maruna, 2007). Analogous to the GLM, GST views delinquency as an alternative, antisocial way to reduce strain by achieving or protecting valued goals (direct route) and/or managing the resulting negative affect through, for example, (aggressive, antisocial) venting or illicit drug use (indirect route; Agnew, 1985, 1992, 2013; Ward & Maruna, 2007).

Agnew (1985, 1992, 2006) proposes three major types of strain. The first type of strain is believed to arise when someone is blocked and prevented from achieving positively valued goals, such as academic success, having fun and being popular. The second type can occur when positively valued stimuli that a person possesses are actually removed or threatened to be removed. Examples include: loss of a parent or moving out of one's neighbourhood. The third type of strain comes from actual or anticipated exposure to negative or noxious stimuli. This final type of strain is said to occur when adolescents are placed in aversive situations from which they cannot legally escape, such as being bullied at school, abused at home or other adverse situations imposed on them. These situations are believed to block legal pain-avoidance behaviour that subsequently results in frustration (Agnew, 1985, 1992, 2006). Especially the first two types of strain are consistent with the GLM's assumption that delinquent behaviour can result from hampered primary goods (i.e. valued goals) pursuit.

Furthermore, GST argues that certain strains are more likely to contribute to criminal behaviour than others (Agnew, 2006). A first characteristic that is assumed to render strain more likely to lead to crime is its magnitude, such as strains that are objectively or subjectively more severe, frequent or central to someone's core values. Additionally, strains that are assumed to more likely result in crime are those that are experienced as unjust or undeserved, are associated with low social control and create incentive or pressure to engage in antisocial coping. The latter includes strains that are believed to foster the social learning of crime, increasing the likelihood that individuals will view crime as desirable or justifiable. Consequently, although Agnew (2006) states that GST examines a broad range of possible strains (hence the word 'general' in the name), he proposes a number of strains as the most likely to be related to criminal behaviour: parental rejection, child abuse or neglect, abusive peer relations, negative school experiences, low-paying jobs, chronic unemployment, homelessness, parental supervision that is erratic, excessive and/or harsh and failure to achieve high levels of autonomy (pp. 194-195). Recalling the criminogenic risk factors proposed by the RNR model (see Chapter 2), we can see similarities between some of the 'central eight' (e.g. family problems, school/work problems and peer problems) and what GST defines as important strains. Furthermore, these strains are similarly linked to a number of GLM primary goods, such as 'relatedness', 'excellence in work' (school), 'life' (having a livelihood and safe place to live), and 'excellence in agency' (autonomy).

Whether strain results in antisocial or criminal behaviour instead of an adaptive coping strategy is, according to Agnew (1992, 2006, 2013), contingent on a number of factors. First, criminal coping is deemed more likely when people lack the ability, resources and/or (social) support to employ adaptive, legal coping strategies. In GLM terms this relates to the problem of *lack of capacities*. Second, if the goals and values affected by strain are of high importance and if there are few alternative goals or values, it is expected to be more difficult to compensate for the strain in other life domains. In GLM terms, when some values are not met at all and/or neglected, this relates to the problem of *lack of scope*. Third, whether or not someone engages in delinquency as a result of strain is also thought to be dependent on the access to or the possession of illegitimate means and antisocial associates. In GLM terms, this relates to the problem of *inadequate (illegal) means* and some of the RNR model's criminogenic needs (e.g. antisocial associates and attitudes). Furthermore, the GLM's and RNR's criminogenic risk factors relate to the GST in its idea that some individuals are believed to be more disposed than others to respond to strains with criminal behaviour due to individual traits, such as impulsivity and negative emotionality or antisocial beliefs. Additionally, according to the GST (Agnew, 1992, 2006, 2013), individuals are deemed more likely to use antisocial coping when costs of crime are low. This can happen, for example, when someone does not have much to lose (such as a legal job or prosocial relationships) or lives in an environment with less social control. Finally, *lack of coherence*, the fourth problem in GLM primary good achievement, is not explicitly mentioned by Agnew in his explanation of delinquent behaviour. Nevertheless, in GLM terms, strain (blockage or removal of valued goals) could be the result of a conflict between different types of goals (Agnew, 2013; Ward & Maruna, 2007). Thus, the factors that according to GST render someone more inclined to behave illegally are quite similar to the four problems in GLM primary good achievement and the (GLM's and RNR's) internal and external criminogenic risk factors as obstacles to legal, prosocial coping mechanisms.

Nevertheless, Agnew's conceptualization of strain has been criticized in the past for being too broadly defined and missing a structural framework. That is, Agnew's types of strain can be operationalized in many different ways (e.g. as subjective feelings about certain events or as objectively experienced stressful events) and can result from all sorts of goals and (negative/unjust) situations or (life) events. While many studies have found a link between strain and delinquent behaviour, they generally do not identify which type of strain is important in explaining the relationship (Agnew, 2013; Op de Beeck, 2012). As Agnew (2006) stated it: "Researchers and policymakers are left wondering which of the hundreds of specific strains they should consider in their work" (p. 53). Contrarily, the GLM postulates a coherent overall framework with a specific number of universal needs (i.e. the eleven primary goods) that – when thwarted (because of criminogenic risk factors) – could result in negative affect and (subsequent) delinquent behaviour. Thus, although GST lies at the root of the GLM and they share the same core ideas, theoretically the GLM seems to offer more specific hypotheses.

5.2.2 Self-Determination Theory

As outlined in previous chapters, the GLM is also inspired by Deci and Ryan's (2000) Self-Determination Theory (SDT) in its conceptualization of well-being and the conceptualization of some of their primary goods, based on the human needs of 'relatedness', 'competence', and 'autonomy' (Ryan & Deci, 2017b). In this section, I will discuss how SDT seemingly also inspired the GLM's ideas on how maladaptive behaviours can arise, that is, SDT argues that when an individual's primary human needs, which are deemed necessary for well-being, are thwarted, they turn to need substitutes or compensatory behaviour to provide some substitute satisfaction (Deci & Ryan, 2000; Ryan & Deci, 2017b). For instance, someone who has not been successful in satisfying the need for meaningful relationships ('relatedness'), a sense of pride in one's skills ('competence'), or a sense of agency ('autonomy'), might compensate by attempting to gain approval, a sense of worth, or status, by pursuing extrinsic goals, such as acquiring fame, money and material possessions (Deci & Ryan, 2000). In more extreme cases, Deci and Ryan (2000) suggest that when need satisfaction is hindered by environments that are rejecting (i.e. thwarting 'relatedness'), overchallenging (i.e. thwarting 'competence'), or excessively controlling (i.e. thwarting 'autonomy'), alternative responses can consist of psychological withdrawal or antisocial activity. Vansteenkiste and Ryan (2013) further argue that *low need satisfaction*, such as low levels of experienced relatedness to others is not the same as *need frustration*, such as explicit rejection by others. Low need satisfaction could result in negative effects over the course of time, while active need frustration is believed to have an immediate negative effect.

Empirical studies have indeed found that 'need thwarting environments' in adolescents' lives, such as controlling parenting, physical punishment and a lack of support and love, result in frustration of the basic psychological needs of 'competence', 'relatedness', and 'autonomy' (Vansteenkiste & Ryan, 2013). For example, Thogersen-Ntoumani et al. (2010) found that adolescent girls raised in families that lack support and nurturance are more likely to value and pursue extrinsic (e.g. looking attractive) over intrinsic goals (e.g., being physically healthy). Although extrinsic goals can seem appealing at first, these goals are considered to only provide a fleeting type of satisfaction. In the long run, they may interfere with genuine (intrinsic) need satisfaction and well-being.

People who tend to overfocus on getting rich, attractive and famous have less time and energy left to serve other basic psychological needs. A focus on extrinsic goals can even have adverse effects on psychological need satisfaction (Dittmar et al., 2014; Kasser, 2002, 2004). For example, excessive striving for financial success and gaining fame may diminish deep social contacts. Another example can be found in people who use substances or shopping to cope with their unpleasant feelings. Extrinsic activities such as these might temporarily distract people from their negative emotional states, but they will not solve the underlying problems. They can even lead to more problems, such as addiction, debt, conflicts and diminished well-being (Dittmar et al., 2014; Kasser, 2002, 2004; Schmuck & Sheldon, 2001; Sebire et al., 2009; Thogersen-Ntoumani et al., 2010; Vansteenkiste & Ryan, 2013). Need frustration without adaptive coping can subsequently result in negative outcomes, such as psychopathology and aggression in adolescent boys and girls (Bartholomew et al., 2011; Chen et al., 2015; Rodríguez-Meirinhos et al., 2020; Vansteenkiste & Ryan, 2013). Rodríguez-Meirinhos et al. (2020), for example, found that adolescents' need satisfaction for 'relatedness', 'competence' and 'autonomy' correlated with well-being, while the frustration of these needs was related to both internalizing and externalizing behaviour problems.

The adverse outcomes of need frustration can be explained by compensatory behaviours that can arise as a response to need thwarting (Vansteenkiste & Ryan, 2013). A first type of response to need frustration is the development of rigid behaviour patterns. In response to the frustration of needs, people are believed to set perfectionistic standards in an attempt to prove one's worth. Self-critical perfectionism can give rise to intense feelings of guilt and inferiority when these high standards are out of reach (Shafran & Mansell, 2001; Vansteenkiste & Ryan, 2013). In turn, it can increase need frustration and result in internalizing problems, such as anxiety and depression (Shafran & Mansell, 2001; Vansteenkiste & Ryan, 2013). On the other hand, need frustration could also elicit oppositional defiance by which the person actively resists the socially acceptable activity. Consequently, they seek other (illegal or antisocial) ways to satisfy their needs instead (Vansteenkiste & Ryan, 2013). For instance, Van Petegem et al. (2019) found that adolescents who experienced more autonomy frustration, due to over-controlling parenting, demonstrated more oppositional-defiant behaviour. Similar results were found in a clinical sample of male adolescents who were referred to a residential mental health care centre as a result of their antisocial behaviour (Van Petegem et al., 2015).

A related type of compensatory behaviour is a release or even an active revolt against the execution of self-control (Vansteenkiste & Ryan, 2013). Examples of this behaviour can be seen when need frustration in the form of experienced pressure and control (i.e. a lack of 'autonomy') are related to higher levels of alcohol abuse (Knee & Neighbors, 2002), smoking (Williams et al., 2009), and aggression (Joussemet et al., 2008). Both the loss of self-control and active oppositional defiance in response to need frustration can go hand in hand, to result in antisocial and criminal behaviour.

5.3 Combining Primary Goods and Risk Factors to Explain Juvenile Delinquency

Against the backdrop of the theories discussed earlier, we will now focus on the GLM primary goods and how problems in the achievement of each of them are believed to result in delinquent behaviour.

In criminological theories on the explanation of delinquency, a distinction is often made between background and foreground factors. *Background factors* are contextual and relate to known criminogenic risk factors, while *foreground factors* comprise the motivations, perceptions and justifications of the offenders themselves at the time of the criminal behaviour (Jacobs & Wright, 1999; Wright & Topalli, 2013).

Certain *background factors* are considered *criminogenic risk factors* because of their statistical co-occurrence with crime. However, they do not provide information on the underlying *reasons why* (i.e. *the foreground factors*) someone with those background (or risk) factors would engage in criminal behaviour. Moreover, many of these background (or risk) factors can also be present in people who do not commit offences, that is, they fail to explain why two individuals with an identical risk factor profile do not offend to a similar extent or why individuals with certain risk factors go long periods without offending. Rather, these risk factors are viewed as red flags that could predispose someone to criminal behaviour, but do not fully explain the delinquent behaviour (see also the discussion on the relevance of risk factors according to the GLM in Chapter 2, Section 2.2.1; Heffernan & Ward, 2020; Jacobs & Wright, 1999; Ward, 2016; Ward & Beech, 2015).

Similarly, authors (Cohen & Felson, 1979; Farrington, 1986; Verdonck, 2017; Warr & Stafford, 1991) have argued that *foreground factors*, such as universal desires, motivations, and needs are also not sufficient to fully explain delinquent behaviour; that is, they fail to explain why those motivations would result in criminal behaviour instead of prosocial ways to secure those needs. For example, Sutherland and Cressey (1960) stated that while thieves might be motivated to secure money, so are honest labourers. Others have stressed that even though someone has a strong motivation to commit crimes, there has to be the opportunity to do so as well (see e.g. the Routine Activities Theory, Cohen & Felson, 1979; and Situational Action Theory, Wikström, 2014).

Hence, in order to adequately explain delinquency, the GLM argues that it is important to uncover the underlying needs and motivations (related to the eleven primary goods, i.e. the *foreground factors*), as well as the criminogenic obstacles that block the prosocial ways and/or encourage the antisocial ways to satisfy those needs (i.e. the *background factors*) (Ward & Maruna, 2007; Ward & Stewart, 2003a, 2003c; Yates & Ward, 2008). Combining *foreground* and *background factors* in explaining delinquency is however also not something new. In the 1980s, Farrington (1986) already suggested a theory in which juvenile (property) delinquency is explained as an end product of a four-stage process. In the first stage, a motivation or desire arises, such as the desire for material goods, peer status or excitement (i.e., *foreground factors*). During the second stage, a method is chosen to satisfy the desire. Whether someone chooses a legal or an illegal method depends on certain *background factors*, what we nowadays call risk factors:

> It is suggested that some people (e.g., children from poorer families) are less able to satisfy their desires for material goods, excitement and social status by legal or socially approved methods, and so they tend to choose illegal or socially disapproved methods. (Farrington, 1986, p. 381)

Once an illegal method is selected, the motivation to commit a crime becomes magnified in the third stage when beliefs and attitudes that delinquency is legitimate (i.e. well-known criminogenic risk factors) are becoming internalized. In the final stage, the *foreground factors* become relevant again when a decision process takes place in a particular situation. Whether or not people act on their desires and motivations in an illegal manner is assumed to depend on the opportunities, costs, benefits and probabilities of the situation at hand (e.g. the available goods to be stolen, peer approval, chances of getting caught, etc.;

Farrington, 1986). As human behaviour constitutes a complex combination of different processes on different levels, it is important to consider both *foreground* (i.e. primary goods) and *background factors* (i.e. criminogenic risk factors) if we want to adequately explain it.

5.4 THE ANTISOCIAL AND CRIMINAL PURSUIT OF PRIMARY GOODS

Recall at this point that the GLM's primary goods are considered broad motivational concepts, which can be pursued with both legal/prosocial means (i.e. appropriate secondary goods) and illegal/antisocial means (i.e. inappropriate secondary goods). When it comes to offender rehabilitation, we are of course particularly interested in the aetiology of the latter. Therefore, in the remainder of this chapter, I will focus on how and why adolescents may attempt[1] to fulfil each of the GLM primary goods through antisocial or delinquent behaviour. To this end, I will discuss existing theories and research evidence on the hypothesized relationship between (the antisocial pursuit of) the primary goods and juvenile delinquency. Furthermore, for each primary good – where applicable – I will discuss the RNR's criminogenic risk factor(s) that are most probably associated with it.

As we will see in the following text, most criminogenic risk factors of the RNR model's 'central eight' (i.e. antisocial personality pattern, antisocial attitudes, antisocial associates/peers, family problems, school/work problems, lack of constructive leisure/recreation, and substance abuse) appear to be directly related to at least one conceptually similar GLM primary good (see also Table 2.1 in Chapter 2). However, in practice it is likely that a combination of risk factors can serve as obstacles in the prosocial pursuit of multiple primary goods in a complex interaction. Similarly, criminal behaviour can serve as an attempt to attain several primary goods. When applying the GLM in practice, it is thus important to assess which primary goods and risk factors interact in what way to explain a specific individual's criminal behaviour (known as *forensic case formulation* in the structured professional judgment approach; Hart & Logan, 2011; Hart et al., 2011; Heffernan & Ward, 2015; Lewis & Doyle, 2009; Logan & Johnstone, 2010; Ward & Beech, 2015). What will become clear is that the eleven primary goods of the GLM could offer a comprehensive framework in which different theories and perspectives can be integrated to explain adolescent/juvenile delinquency.

---

1 Note that these attempts are usually not considered successful as antisocial behaviour more likely only works as a quick fix that is not satisfying in the long run and can cause a range of (other) problems (Ward, 2002a, 2002b; Ward & Maruna, 2007).

5.4.1 *Life*

The primary good of 'life' refers to people's need for healthy and quality living, the need to feel safe and secure. It incorporates all the basic physical needs and factors that are important for healthy living and physical functioning: food, water, shelter and a physically healthy body (Purvis, 2010; Purvis et al., 2014; Willis et al., 2013).

Studies on the direct relationship between physical health and juvenile delinquency are scarce. Nevertheless, some studies have found a positive relationship between adolescent delinquency and health problems, such as lack of exercise, poor diet, lack of sleep and somatic (chronic) illness (Meldrum et al., 2015; Peach & Gaultney, 2013; Penner, 1982; Schoenthaler & Bier, 1985; Semenza, 2018; Stogner & Gibson, 2010, 2011; Woods et al., 2013). Semenza (2018) explains these findings by suggesting that:

> Adolescents may find that the negative effects of a poor health lifestyle may result in not feeling healthy, socially engaged, physically fit, or attractive according to conventionally agreed-upon standards. All these outcomes may lead to a decrease in self-attitude and greater motivation to engage in delinquency. (pp. 1409-1410)

Other authors refer to general strain theory in their explanation of how frequent minor somatic complaints (as noxious stimuli) can create strain by blocking the universal goal of good health subsequently making it more difficult for an individual to reach other important goals (Stogner & Gibson, 2010, 2011). Again, others have concluded that low self-control, as a result of sleep deprivation or malnutrition, as a mediator accounted for the relationship with juvenile delinquency (Meldrum et al., 2015; Peach & Gaultney, 2013; Schoenthaler & Bier, 1985). Hence, although a positive relationship between physical health problems and juvenile delinquency has been found, knowledge on the underlying mechanism(s) remains limited.

Important for the primary good of 'life' in general, and physical health in particular, is the financial capacity to provide for one's basic physical needs. In general, minors have few legal opportunities to obtain a (well-paying) job, leaving them financially dependent on their parents and/or caregivers. For some, this might put them in a situation in which they lack sufficient resources to meet their needs. Additionally, problems at school and/or work, central criminogenic risk factors in the RNR model (Andrews & Bonta, 2010; Bonta & Andrews, 2017), could also interfere with the capacity to financially provide for one's needs (see 'excellence in work' below). Financial strain and a resulting lack of satisfaction of basic physical needs are often mentioned by young offenders themselves as their primary motivations for offending (Agnew, 1990; Farrington, 1993; Gudjonsson & Sigurdsson, 2007; Lopez, 2008; Putniņš, 2010; Shong et al., 2019). In a large qualitative study (the National Survey of Youth), 1,395 adolescent offenders were interviewed about their motives for a range of offences (Agnew, 1990). Based on these accounts, Agnew (1990) concluded that in property crimes the most common motive, besides seeking pleasure and fun (see Section 5.4.11), is utilitarian in the sense of obtaining material gains to provide for the basic needs of food and shelter. Similarly, material gain is a frequently mentioned motive for juvenile property offenders (Troonbeeckx et al., 2015; Verdonck, 2017), juvenile drug offenders (Nguyen & Bouchard, 2013).

These findings are corroborated by quantitative studies that found financial strain to be related to adolescents' problem behaviour, including substance abuse, running away, truancy, stealing and burglary (Baron, 2004, 2007; Hoeve, Stams, et al., 2014; Shek, 2003; van Beek et al., 2021). Yet, not all studies find a significant relationship between perceived financial situation and adolescent delinquency (Hamilton et al., 2009). Importantly, these quantitative results were found in cross-sectional studies from which the direction of the relationship could not be determined. In response to this shortcoming, Hoeve et al. (2016) conducted a three-wave, longitudinal study and concluded that the relationship between financial problems (such as debts) and delinquency in adolescents and young adults is reciprocal. Youth with financial problems were more likely to engage in delinquent behaviour, and delinquent youth were more likely to develop financial problems.

Apart from financial resources to provide for livelihood and healthy living, the primary good of 'life' also concerns the need for (physical) safety. Related to this, violence and carrying (or using) weapons are sometimes referred to as self-defence and a way to feel safe. This motive is especially relevant for youth who are involved in a criminal network and have rivals or enemies (Mallion & Wood, 2020; Verdonck, 2017). In support of this, Reid et al. (2017) found that male adolescents who were exposed to violence were more likely to report weapon carrying. In a more general context, Van Geel et al. (2014) concluded in their meta-analysis that youth involved in bullying (as victims, bullies and victim-bullies) reported more weapon carrying than other peers. Especially victims of bullying whose sense of safety had been violated or threatened successively were at increased risk of weapon carrying (Lu et al., 2020; Pham et al., 2017).

5.4.2 *Knowledge*

The primary good of 'knowledge' refers to one's interest in, access to, and possession of information. It is not related to how intelligent someone is, but rather to how well informed an individual feels about things that are important to him/her (Purvis, 2010; Purvis et al., 2014; Willis et al., 2013).

As far as I have found, no prior studies examined the relationship between the primary good of 'knowledge' and juvenile delinquency. In adults, Purvis (2010) did not find a direct relationship between 'knowledge' and sexual offending, but concluded that a lack of knowledge could form an obstacle to the achievement of other primary goods. For example, a failure in the acquisition of knowledge could negatively affect one's education and career prospects (i.e. 'excellence in work'). Similarly, Taylor (2017) concluded that some of the male adult residential burglars that she interviewed about the relationship between primary goods and delinquent behaviour, regarded themselves as 'experts' in their field. They perceived their knowledge and skill to break into a house successfully, quietly and without being caught, as an 'art' and 'expertise' (Taylor, 2017). In the latter context, having knowledge of things that one is interested in seems to be more closely related to feeling competent and skilled, which overlaps with the next two primary goods: 'excellence in work' and 'excellence in play' (see Sections 5.4.3 and 5.4.4). As Purvis (2010) concluded from her research with adult sex offenders: "[knowledge] could be implicit in the goals of employment, achievement and leisure" (p. 219).

5.4.3 *Excellence in Work*

The primary good of 'excellence in work' refers to the need to engage in work, which provides the person with a sense of pride, achievement, satisfaction and skill development (Purvis, 2010; Purvis et al., 2014; Willis et al., 2013). For adolescents, this good is usually equated with educational performance instead of employment. Still, adolescents from the age of 15 (in Europe) are legally allowed to hold a (part-time) job, so for them excellence in school and work can both be considered relevant.

Problems with school and academic achievement are important criminogenic risk factors (Andrews & Bonta, 2010; Bonta & Andrews, 2017; Christle et al., 2005; Cottle et al., 2001; Grieger & Hosser, 2014; Hoffmann, 2020; Katsiyannis et al., 2008; Maguin & Loeber, 1996; Pyle et al., 2016) that can mainly (but not exclusively) serve as obstacles in the prosocial achievement of 'excellence in work' (or 'competence' in SDT terms; Deci & Ryan, 2000). There are several explanations that could account for the relationship between poor academic achievement and delinquency.

The first explanation can be found in the (partly) mediating effect of executive dysfunction, such as attention problems and low self-control (Hoffmann, 2020; Maguin & Loeber, 1996). Another explanation for the relationship between poor academic performance and delinquency could be related to punitive reactions by schoolteachers to problem behaviour at school (i.e. the school-to-prison pipeline; Wald & Losen, 2003). Exclusionary disciplinary practices, such as (temporary) suspension can result in early school dropout and delays in academic progress. This, in turn, delays or diminishes the opportunity to graduate or obtain certificates that are necessary for legal employment (Christle et al., 2005; Moore & McArthur, 2014). Without a certificate or degree to acquire a well-paying position, criminality is often viewed as more profitable than a low-paying legal job (Cullen et al., 1997; Jacobs & Wright, 1999; Troonbeeckx et al., 2015; Wright & Topalli, 2013).

Additionally, some forms of delinquency require a specific set of 'criminal skills' that are not challenged in most legal activities. An example of this can be found in car theft, where male adolescents take pride in being able to disable a security measure on a vehicle and to start the engine without the key (Drozda, 2006). Moreover, some young offenders view their criminal activities as a full-time job in which they are able to challenge and even improve their skills, gain promotion, status and respect (Brezina & Topalli, 2012; Nguyen & Bouchard, 2013; Verdonck, 2017; Wood, 2014; Wood & Alleyne, 2010). For example, Nguyen and Bouchard (2013) found that high-earning adolescent offenders who were specialized in drug cultivation developed the necessary criminal skills over time and expanded their illegal network.

5.4.4 *Excellence in Play*

The primary good of 'excellence in play' refers to the need to engage in leisure or fun activities that provides the person with a sense of pride, achievement, satisfaction or skill development (e.g. participating in individual or group sports; Purvis, 2010; Purvis et al., 2014; Willis et al., 2013). Besides school or work, a sense of achievement, pride and skill development (or 'competence' in SDT terms) can be obtained from leisure activities (see also Chapter 4, Section 4.3.1; Deci & Ryan, 2000; Purvis, 2010).

A *lack* of prosocial constructive leisure activities is a central criminogenic risk factor (Agnew & Petersen, 1989; Andrews & Bonta, 2010; Bonta & Andrews, 2017; Cottle et al., 2001; Grieger & Hosser, 2014). One explanation for the association between this risk factor and delinquency is that a lack of structured leisure can result in boredom, which in turn could lead to antisocial behaviour as a means to kill time (Drozda, 2006; Newberry & Duncan, 2001; Wainwright & Nee, 2014). Other explanations are related to a combination of spending unstructured time with antisocial peers and a lack of supervision from authority figures and/or caregivers (Hoeben & Weerman, 2016). Youth who report committing crimes as their leisure activity mention a number of barriers to other socially acceptable activities. Examples of these barriers include: legal activities not being sufficiently challenging, a lack of financial resources, a lack of legal activity opportunities nearby, and a lack of skills to engage in the available activities (Farnworth, 2000; Robertson, 1994, 2001).

The latter can be partly explained by Csikszentmihalyi's (2014) famous theory on 'flow', which argues that activities are deemed enjoyable and intrinsically rewarding when: "a person perceives that his capacity to act (or skills) matches the opportunities for action perceived in the environment (or challenges)" (p. 276). In this sense, Csikszentmihalyi (2014) argues that criminal acts, and especially violence, can provide enjoyment, leisure and a state of 'flow' when alternatives are lacking:

> While specialized training is required for a symbolic confrontation such as chess or for noncompetitive challenges, no special skill is needed to perceive the challenge of a confrontation and to act in a setting that requires violence. (p. 278)

Relatedly, a popular leisure activity for adolescent boys is combat sports and martial arts, such as wrestling and kickboxing (van der Kooi, 2020; van Gemert, 2019; Verdonck, 2017). Although martial arts can serve as a constructive way to safely improve and express one's physical skills, promoting adolescents' well-being (Gubbels et al., 2016; Harwood et al., 2017; Tadesse, 2017; van der Kooi, 2020), some adolescents improperly use these skills 'on the street' to prove their strength and status with violence and fights (van Gemert, 2019; Verdonck, 2017).

5.4.5 *Excellence in Agency*

The primary good of 'excellence in agency' refers to the human need to formulate one's own goals and seek ways to realize them in actions and activities of their own choice, similar to the SDT's concept of 'autonomy' (Deci & Ryan, 2000). It encompasses the need for autonomy, self-directedness, personal power, control and mastery (Purvis, 2010; Purvis et al., 2014; Willis et al., 2013), which becomes especially salient during the period of adolescence (Arnett, 1999).

This is an important developmental milestone as adolescents continue to acquire more independence gradually on their way to adulthood (Arnett, 1999). In this context, Moffitt (1993) explains the large prevalence of adolescent-onset delinquency by the so-called 'maturity-gap'. This theory posits that adolescents engage in (minor) delinquent behaviour when they experience a 'gap' between their biological (physical) maturity and a lack of autonomy they are granted through society-determined roles and regulations for their age group (social maturity). This idea also reflects in the SDT's concept of 'autonomy' frustration, which is deemed as an important factor underlying oppositional-defiant behaviour in adolescents (Brenning et al., 2019; Van Petegem et al., 2015; Van Petegem et al., 2019).

Empirical studies have indeed found that in adolescent boys and girls, a larger discrepancy between physical maturity and granted autonomy (by societal and parental rules) is related to conflict with parents and a higher prevalence of (rebellious) minor (but not serious) delinquency and drug use (Barnes & Beaver, 2010; Dijkstra et al., 2015; Piquero & Brezina, 2001). Referring to general strain theory, Dijkstra et al. (2015) argue: "The strain resulting from the absence of legitimate means to express their maturity motivates adolescents to express it in alternative, illegitimate ways, such as delinquency" (p. 749). In line with these findings, a strong desire for finding one's own way in life and the tendency to seek autonomy has been related to problem behaviour and delinquency in adolescents (Loney & Harkins, 2018; Noom et al., 1999; Troonbeeckx et al., 2012; Troonbeeckx et al., 2015). As we saw for the good of 'excellence in work' (Section 5.4.3), some juveniles deliberately choose to pursue a criminal career. An often-mentioned motive for this choice is their need to be free and not (financially) dependent on parents, an academic career or an employer (Jacobs & Wright, 1999; Troonbeeckx et al., 2015; Verdonck, 2017; Wright & Topalli, 2013).

Additionally, a lack of agency defined by low self-efficacy (Bandura, 1977, 1982) has also been related to adolescents' engagement in criminal behaviour (Bandura et al., 2003; Carroll et al., 2013; Chung & Elias, 1996; Del Bove et al., 2008; Troonbeeckx et al., 2012). Self-efficacy is the belief that one can produce desired effects by one's own actions (Bandura, 1977). The amount of perceived self-efficacy is assumed to influence the amount of (coping) effort, commitment and how long someone will persist in a certain behaviour or action in the face of obstacles and aversive experiences (Bandura, 1977, 1982; Baumeister & Vohs, 2004). A lack of self-efficacy could thus render people more susceptible to cease prosocial attempts towards their goals, when faced with obstacles and turn to (seemingly easier) antisocial alternatives. This could occur, for example, when someone experiences problems at school, feels unable to improve their performance and drops out to start a criminal career (Troonbeeckx et al., 2012; Troonbeeckx et al., 2015). Accordingly, Oyserman and Saltz (1993) found that impulsivity was related to a lack of attempts to achieve one's goals in delinquent boys. A lack of striving towards future goals was in turn related to truancy and hooliganism. In contrast, more positive future expectations in adolescents have been related to less problem behaviour over time (Dubow et al., 2001). Taken together, Carroll et al. (2013) conclude that delinquent adolescents, compared to nondelinquents, have significantly fewer goals in life, lower (academic and self-regulatory) self-efficacy, and lower commitment to their goals.

Moreover, an important criminogenic risk factor related to the primary good of 'excellence in agency' is an antisocial personality pattern characterized by aggressiveness, impulsiveness and a lack of self-control (Andrews & Bonta, 2010; Bonta & Andrews, 2017; DeLisi & Vaughn, 2008; Grieger & Hosser, 2014). For someone who lacks a sense of control, interpersonal crimes such as assault or sexual offences can serve as an alternative way to experience power and control over others instead (Barnett & Wood, 2008; Loney & Harkins, 2018; Mann & Hollin, 2007; Maruna, 2001; Ward et al., 1993; Yates, Simons, et al., 2009).

5.4.6 *Inner Peace*

The primary good of 'inner peace' refers to the need for freedom from emotional turmoil and stress. It includes emotional self-regulation and achieving a state of emotional balance (Purvis, 2010; Purvis et al., 2014; Willis et al., 2013). Since adolescents are known to have a higher risk of experiencing emotional problems (Arnett, 1999) and mental health problems are especially prevalent in detained adolescents (Colins et al., 2010; Colins et al., 2009; Vermeiren et al., 2006), the primary good of 'inner peace' could be particularly relevant for them.

Although mental health problems (especially internalizing disorders) are not explicitly listed among the 'central eight' risk factors, they have been found to be strongly related to a higher risk of juvenile delinquency (Aebi et al., 2015; Hoeve et al., 2015; Hoeve et al., 2013; Pyle et al., 2016; Vahl et al., 2016; van der Put & De Ruiter, 2016; Wibbelink et al., 2017; Wilson et al., 2009). This relationship can be especially salient for adolescents who experienced childhood trauma, rendering some adolescents more susceptible to stressors (Wells et al., 2017) and more likely to engage in antisocial behaviour (Case & Haines, 2007; Miller, 2014; Ruchkin et al., 2002; Wells et al., 2017). Subsequently, mental health problems (both internalizing and externalizing) are hypothesized to serve as important obstacles to the achievement of all primary goods, suggesting the pursuit of 'inner peace' can be a driving force for all types of offending behaviour (Barnao et al., 2016).

Some authors have suggested that substance use (disorder) is an important mediating (criminogenic) factor explaining the relationship between mental health issues and adolescent antisocial behaviour (Guebert & Olver, 2014), that is, emotional dysregulation in adolescence has been related to a higher risk of substance abuse (Wills et al., 2016). According to juveniles themselves, drug use is an easy way to cope with negative emotions and mental health problems (Agnew, 1990; Caffray & Schneider, 2000; Loney & Harkins, 2018; Skrzypiec, 2017; Teevan & Dryburgh, 2000). In a large sample of adjudicated youth, Craig et al. (2018) examined the effects of having (a history of) serious mental health problems and drug use on their reported reasons for offending. Youth with a history of drug use were found to be more likely to offend for reasons of feelings of excitement and material gain. This could partly be explained by committing (property) crimes to be able to finance their substance abuse (Craig et al., 2018; Nguyen & Bouchard, 2013; Troonbeeckx et al., 2015).

Furthermore, a history of serious mental health problems significantly increased the odds of having anger and revenge as motivators for offending, while offending for material gain, excitement or to gain peer status were less likely (Craig et al., 2018). Accordingly, offending behaviour could also be triggered by the pursuit of 'inner peace' through venting feelings of stress, frustration, anger and aggression on property (i.e., vandalism) and people (i.e., assault; Agnew, 1990; Berkowitz, 1989; Dollard et al., 1939; Farrington, 1993;

Skrzypiec, 2017; Verdonck, 2017). A specific example of this is found in sexual offences, which are explained by offenders themselves as a way for stress relief and alleviating negative emotional states to achieve 'inner peace' (Barnett & Wood, 2008; Chu et al., 2015; Mann & Hollin, 2007; Ward et al., 1993; Wylie & Griffin, 2013; Yates, Simons, et al., 2009). In combination, taking drugs or alcohol could additionally trigger an easier resort to violence and criminality through arousal and disinhibition (Barnett & Wood, 2008; Gottfredson & Hirschi, 1990; Verdonck, 2017). This resonates with both substance abuse and emotional states, such as anger, aggressiveness, feeling irritated and resentful, as part of the central criminogenic risk factors (Andrews & Bonta, 2010; Bonta & Andrews, 2017).

5.4.7 Relatedness

The primary good of 'relatedness' refers to the innate need of human beings to establish affectionate, mutual bonds with an intimate partner, family members and close friends (Purvis, 2010; Purvis et al., 2014; Willis et al., 2013), similar to SDT's concept of 'relatedness' (Deci & Ryan, 2000).

Adolescence is generally known as a period in which parents and family become less important to make room for peer relationships (Warr, 2002), but this is largely a misconception that needs to be refined. Although adolescents might spend more time with peers, and peer relationships become more important over the years, the relationships they have with family in general – and parents in particular – continue to have a major influence on their lives[2] (Aumeboonsuke, 2017; Bowlby, 1969; Wang et al., 2007; Warr, 2002). Earlier, in the 1940s, Glueck and Glueck (1950) studied risk factors for delinquent boys and concluded that family relationships and parenting were the most important. A vast amount of research has accumulated since then, confirming that especially single parent families, parental conflict, and parenting practices characterized by a lack of supervision, support and affection, are important risk factors for youth delinquency (Demuth & Brown, 2004; Derzon, 2010; Hoeve et al., 2011; Hoeve et al., 2009; Loeber & Stouthamer-Loeber, 1986; Pinquart, 2017; Sampson & Laub, 1995; Vanassche et al., 2014; Wright & Cullen, 2001; Yalçın, 2012).

Based on these (meta-analytic) findings, Bonta and Andrews (2017) include family problems, and especially relational issues with parents, as part of the 'central eight' criminogenic risk factors. Having a secure attachment relationship with parents or caregivers serves as a reliable basis to develop positively into adulthood. The attachment

2 See also Chapter 4, Section 4.3.1 in which we found that family relatedness showed one of the strongest relationships with adolescents' well-being (stronger than friendships).

relationship with parents influences how children develop social ties with others, build resilience, self-reliance and emotional regulation skills. A lack of secure attachment to parents or caregivers can play an important role in a youth's positive development when they find their way into society and establish their own peer relationships (Bowlby, 1969; Gottfredson & Hirschi, 1990; Patterson & Dishion, 1985; Sroufe, 2005).

This reasoning is in line with Hirschi's (2017) Social Control Theory, in which he states that delinquency can result from weak social bonds with conventional others, mainly parents, friends and at school. These bonds are believed to comprise four elements: attachment, commitment, involvement and belief. *Attachment* refers to the affection and respect someone holds towards others such as parents, peers and teachers. Individuals are less likely to deviate from conventional norms when they are sensitive to the opinion and approval of others to whom they are attached. *Commitment* refers to the rational component of a bond in which an individual does not want to risk losing the time and energy invested in conventional behaviour, such as an education or a career. *Involvement* refers to the idea that time and energy are limited, and the more people are involved in conventional activities the less time they will have to engage in deviant behaviour. The last element consists of belief, which refers to the extent to which individuals believe they should obey the rules of society. The less people believe they should obey the rules, the more likely they will violate them. Although Hirschi (2017) acknowledges all four elements are important in social bonds, he focuses mainly on attachment in his explanation of delinquency. Especially attachment to parents plays an important role in his Social Control Theory, that is, weak affectional relationships with parents are believed to weaken other relationships with conventionally adult authorities as well, such as at school or institutions in general (Hirschi, 2017; Sampson & Laub, 1995).

The latter is corroborated by more recent studies where they similarly conclude that especially adolescents who experience little or no supervision, support and affection from their families aim to seek recognition and social support from delinquent peers (Baron, 2015; Brezina & Azimi, 2018; Colvin et al., 2002; Patterson & Dishion, 1985; Rebellon, 2002; Verdonck, 2017; Warr, 2002; Wood & Alleyne, 2010). In turn, association with delinquent peers (including friends, partners and siblings) is considered one of the most important central criminogenic risk factors (Andrews & Bonta, 2010; Baron, 2015; Bonta & Andrews, 2017; Cottle et al., 2001; Dishion & Tipsord, 2011; Glueck & Glueck, 1950; Grieger & Hosser, 2014; Patterson & Dishion, 1985).

The relationship between delinquency and association with delinquent peers can be explained by several mechanisms. Social learning theories offer a general explanation for this relationship. For instance, Bandura's (1971, 1978) Social Learning Theory proposes that all sorts of human behaviour (including criminality) can be acquired by observing, modelling, and imitating others. This reasoning builds upon Sutherland's theory of differential association, which holds that criminality can be best explained by learning criminal behaviour by association with delinquent others (Sutherland & Cressey, 1960). Burgess and Akers (1966) further developed Sutherland's ideas by elaborating on the (social) learning processes underlying human behaviour, focusing on positive and negative reinforcements (operant conditioning) as the main influence on criminality. More specifically, association with delinquent peers is considered to provide strong positive reinforcement for criminal behaviour and attitudes, and modest or low levels of reinforcement for prosocial behaviour and attitudes, known as *deviancy training* (Dishion et al., 1996; Dishion & Tipsord, 2011; Patterson & Dishion, 1985; Shortt et al., 2003).

Warr (1993, 2002) took Sutherland's differential association theory even a step further to assess which aspects of association with delinquent peers are particularly important for adolescents. He found that the time spent with delinquent peers, the importance of these relationships and loyalty towards each other are strongly related to influencing one's behaviour. Other studies similarly found that a sense of loyalty between peers is an important aspect that can contribute to juvenile delinquency (Baron, 2015; Baron & Hartnagel, 1998; Brezina & Azimi, 2018; Colvin et al., 2002; Dishion & Tipsord, 2011; Troonbeeckx et al., 2015). For example, group fights were oftentimes rationalized as helping out a friend (Baron & Hartnagel, 1998; Farrington, 1993; Teevan & Dryburgh, 2000; Verdonck, 2017). Another well-known way in which the need for relatedness can result in offending is peer pressure, that is, juveniles can engage in delinquent behaviour to build a reputation and gain recognition, status, and respect from their peers (Agnew, 1990; Buelga et al., 2008; Warr, 2002). In particular, less severe offences, such as shoplifting, drug use and vandalism are oftentimes attributed to showing off, being dared, gaining peer status, and/or getting friends' approval (Dijkstra et al., 2010; Teevan & Dryburgh, 2000; Warr, 2002).

Finally, a specific need for relatedness in the form of intimacy is a frequently mentioned driving force for adult sex offenders (Barnett & Wood, 2008; Mann & Hollin, 2007; Purvis, 2010; Ward et al., 1993; Yates, Simons, et al., 2009) as well as juvenile male sex offenders (Chu et al., 2015; Wylie & Griffin, 2013).

5.4.8 Community

Related to the earlier mentioned primary good of 'relatedness' is the need to belong and be part of a group. People are known to be social creatures who do not merely need to feel connected to others but also have the need to feel socially included. The primary good of 'community' thus refers to the human need to belong to social groups, to feel connected to groups that reflect their interests, concerns and values. It entails the feeling of being part of, being able to rely on, and contribute to a wider social or cultural network (Purvis, 2010; Purvis et al., 2014; Willis et al., 2013). Thus, peer pressure to engage in antisocial behaviour is not only linked to 'relatedness', but also to the primary good of 'community', that is, using illicit drugs in a group (Teevan & Dryburgh, 2000), joining group fights (Verdonck, 2017) and being involved in criminal gangs (Dishion & Tipsord, 2011; Mallion & Wood, 2020; Sharkey et al., 2011; Wood, 2014; Wood & Alleyne, 2010) can all be prompted by the wish to belong.

Furthermore, the neighbourhood in which the adolescents grow up plays a major role in this primary good. High-crime or disadvantaged neighbourhoods are a known risk factor for (adolescent) delinquent behaviour (Jacobs et al., 2020; Sampson et al., 2002; Wikström & Loeber, 2000). This influence is particularly strong when juveniles grow up surrounded by a network of people (i.e. a community) who they value, feel connected to and who engage in criminal behaviour (Troonbeeckx et al., 2015). These findings provide support for the Social Disorganization Theory of Shaw and MacKay (1969), which holds that a community's social organization could be disrupted by low economic status, ethnic heterogeneity and residential mobility, which in turn results in high (juvenile) delinquency rates. In this theory, high rates of (juvenile) delinquency in disadvantaged communities are explained as:

> the existence of a system of values supporting criminal behavior … since it is only where such a system exists that the person through criminal activity may acquire the material goods so essential to status in our society and at the same time increase, rather than lose, his prestige in the smaller [delinquency supporting] group system of which he has become an integral part. (Shaw & MacKay, 1969, p. 189)

Building on this theory, other authors have focused not only on economic deprivation in communities, but also on the role of social capital. They argue that living in a disadvantaged neighbourhood leads to higher rates of delinquency due to less cohesion, trust and social control from the conventional community (Bursik Jr & Grasmick, 1993; Oberwittler, 2004; Putnam, 2001; Sampson & Groves, 1989; Sampson et al., 2002; Sampson et al., 1997; Sutherland & Cressey, 1960).

5.4.9 Spirituality

The primary good of 'spirituality' refers to the need to discover a sense of meaning and purpose in life. This could involve seeking religious inspiration and affiliation, a spiritual connection with a transcendent being or reality, or simply the experience of being part of a larger whole (Purvis, 2010; Purvis et al., 2014; Willis et al., 2013).

The good of 'spirituality' is another example of a good that is not often directly related to engagement in delinquent behaviour. In fact, pursuing religiosity or spirituality is often considered a protective factor for deterring delinquency (Baier & Wright, 2001; Eryılmaz, 2018; Hirschi & Stark, 1969; Johnson et al., 2000; Laird et al., 2011; Miller & Vuolo, 2018; Sumter et al., 2018).[3] Still, one way in which a search for meaning and purpose in life could lead to antisocial behaviour is being a member of, or identifying with antisocial/violent activist or terrorist groups. Terrorism or acts of violence out of religious, social or political convictions are believed to arise out of a collective strain experienced by all group members (Agnew, 2010; Blazak, 2001). Such an affiliation can subsequently give rise to adhering to antisocial group norms, values and having a common higher purpose in life (Agnew, 2010; Mallion & Wood, 2020). Examples of these so-called 'hate groups' are right-wing or white-supremacy terrorist groups (e.g. 'Skinheads', 'Neo-Nazis'); Christian terrorist groups (e.g. 'Ku Klux Klan', 'Army of God'); Islamic terrorist or militant groups (e.g. 'Taliban', 'Islamic State', 'Al-Qaida'); and political militant organizations (e.g. 'Irish Republican Army', 'Tamil Tigers'; Blazak, 2001; Desmarais et al., 2017).

Based on in-depth interviews with 65 skinhead recruiters, Blazak (2001) concluded that, in order to recruit youth for their violent (political/societal) cause, they aim to make them believe they are warriors defending the white race, providing them with a sense of purpose in their lives. With regard to terrorism out of religious convictions, a recent systematic review on risk factors for terrorist group membership and terrorist attacks, identified that being religious in itself was not related to terrorism, but rather the underlying ideological (i.e. higher purpose) motivations were (Desmarais et al., 2017). Similarly, a meta-analytic study on risk factors for radicalization concluded that while religious practice (such as prayer or attendance at places of worship) does not play a significant role, underlying religious fundamentalist identity and attitudes are important risk factors (Wolfowicz et al., 2020).

5.4.10 *Creativity*

The primary good of 'creativity' refers to a need for novelty, innovation and individuality in one's life. 'Creativity' does not just refer to the ability to produce artistic work, it may also be present in the way a person solves problems or the way they appreciate beauty or nature. It is essentially the expression of oneself through creative forms of activity (Purvis, 2010; Purvis et al., 2014; Willis et al., 2013). In the latter sense, gang membership or affiliation with delinquent peers or groups can be seen as a way to express oneself as living

3 However, there does not yet seem to be any consensus on the possible underlying mechanisms of this relationship (e.g. social control, moral values and/or self-control, etc.; Sumter et al., 2018).

a 'gangster' or deviant lifestyle in search of identity and self-expression. Examples of this expression include tattoos, a certain way of dressing, hairstyles, and graffiti tags (Blazak, 2001; Jacobs & Wright, 1999; Mallion & Wood, 2020; Wooden & Blazak, 1995).

Furthermore, curiosity (i.e. a need for novelty, innovation and individuality) can also be viewed as part of 'creativity', which has often been found as a motive for adolescents to engage in antisocial behaviour (Agnew, 1990). Juveniles, especially adolescents, are curious and explore what the world has to offer, and they test the limits (Arnett, 1999). It is therefore not unusual that this sometimes results in the exploration of deviant behaviour, particularly minor offences, and drug use (Arnett, 1992, 1999; Mayone & Arneklev, 2015; Teevan & Dryburgh, 2000).

5.4.11 Pleasure

The primary good of 'pleasure' refers to the need to feel good in the here and now, and includes a range of feelings and sensations, such as joy, merriment, delight, elation and hedonic pleasure (Purvis, 2010; Purvis et al., 2014; Willis et al., 2013).

Adolescents are known for their tendency to seek out thrills, sensation and excitement for their enjoyment (Arnett, 1992, 1999; Fortune, 2018; Miller, 2014). Violence and aggression in general, particularly for adolescent boys, have been found to serve as a way to seek these thrills and (adrenaline) kicks. Especially when more conventional ways are less available or less attractive (Arnett, 1992, 1996; Verdonck, 2017; Wilson & Scarpa, 2011). Accordingly, a number of studies have confirmed that, for crime in general, an important motive for young offenders consists of thrillseeking and pleasureseeking. Usually, to pass the time and prevent boredom (Drozda, 2006; Farrington, 1993; Gordon & Caltabiano, 1996; Hansen & Breivik, 2001; Newberry & Duncan, 2001; Putniņš, 2010; Robertson, 1994; Troonbeeckx et al., 2015). In particular, drug offences and less severe crimes (such a shoplifting, vandalism and fights) are oftentimes driven by the need for excitement and pleasure (Agnew, 1990; Arnett, 1992, 1996; Caffray & Schneider, 2000; Farrington, 1993; Gudjonsson & Sigurdsson, 2007; Loney & Harkins, 2018; Lopez, 2008; Teevan & Dryburgh, 2000; Thakker & Ward, 2010; Verdonck, 2017).

Furthermore, as we saw for the primary good of 'life', the need for monetary and material gain is a major motivation for criminal behaviour. Although gainful offending can serve to support oneself and provide for basic needs, it is also a fast way to be able to finance products just for pleasure, such as luxurious clothing, electronic devices, vehicles, alcohol or drugs and to go out partying (Farrington, 1986, 1993; Jacobs & Wright, 1999; Lopez, 2008; Taylor, 2017; Troonbeeckx et al., 2015; Verdonck, 2017; Wright & Topalli, 2013). Another specific type of pleasure that has been mentioned as a motive for sexual offences specifically is sexual gratification for adult sex offenders (Mann & Hollin, 2007;

Ward et al., 1993; Yates, Simons, et al., 2009), as well as for juvenile male sex offenders (Chu et al., 2015). Adventurous pleasure-seeking is furthermore related to the central criminogenic risk factor of antisocial personality pattern, characterized by impulsivity and lack of self-control (Andrews & Bonta, 2010; Bonta & Andrews, 2017; DeLisi & Vaughn, 2008; Grieger & Hosser, 2014; Ogilvie et al., 2011; Pratt & Cullen, 2000).

An important theory supporting impulsive pleasure and thrill-seeking as major driving forces of (youth) delinquency is the self-control theory (SCT) of Gottfredson and Hirschi (1990). This theory views humans as hedonists who aim to maximize pleasures and minimize pain. SCT assumes everyone behaves to pursue the same universal hedonistic desired ends, such as free money, quick revenge and uncomplicated sex. Similar to the GLM, SCT thus argues that "Criminal events can be explained using principles that explain all other human conduct" (Gottfredson & Hirschi, 1990, p. 14). Consequently, crime is assumed for humans to be an easy, efficient means to pleasure. Nevertheless, SCT also states that because we all have the same desired ends, those desires cannot account for why some engage in offending behaviour and others do not. Considering this assumption, the sole variable responsible for offending, according to SCT, is a lack of self-control, defined as the "... tendency of individuals to pursue short-term gratification without consideration of the long-term consequences of their acts" (Gottfredson & Hirschi, 1990, p. 177). A lack of self-control subsequently results in deficient impulse control, boredom susceptibility, having difficulty controlling one's temper and taking (high) risks, all aspects that are related to sensation seeking (Zuckerman, 1971, 1994).

The SCT, however, largely ignores and rejects the possibility that individual differences in universal motivations, such as thrill- and pleasure-seeking, may influence attraction to crime as a means for these ends. Subsequently, Burt and Simons (2013) partly refuted the SCT assumptions as they found that youth who differed in the need for thrill-seeking differed also in their levels of self-control. More specifically, adequate self-control was most strongly related to less offending among those low in thrill-seeking needs. Whereas for juveniles who scored high on the need for thrill-seeking, self-control did not significantly reduce offending. Hence, the authors conclude that motivation for crime, here in the form of the need for excitement and pleasure, is an important factor in the explanation of criminal behaviour, over and above self-control and impulsivity.

The latter resonates with the idea that criminogenic risk factors, such as impulsivity, can play an important role in offending behaviour but are not its (only) cause and explanation. These findings are furthermore in line with the GLM's idea that although we all strive to obtain a set of universal goods (including pleasure), individuals differ in how they prioritize and try to realize them in specific and concrete ways, reflecting their personal resources, capabilities and values in life (Ward, 2002a; Ward & Maruna, 2007). A lack of self-control or impulsivity can however serve as an important criminogenic risk factor that renders someone more inclined to pursue antisocial ways of sensation and pleasure-seeking (Burt & Simons, 2013; Verdonck, 2017). Especially the combination of a strong need for sensation and thrills with a lack of self-control, analogous to 'a strong engine with weak brakes', could result in deviant risky behaviour (Feij, 2006). A strong tendency for sensation seeking and impulsivity could eventually express itself in criminality in combination with other known criminogenic risk factors such as delinquent peers, alcohol and drug use, lack of parental care and supervision, poor academic/work/financial prospects etc., which can push or pull someone towards criminal behaviour (Farrington et al., 2017; Hansen & Breivik, 2001; Robertson, 1994).

5.5 Adolescent Well-being and Delinquency

In the previous chapters, we have already concluded that adolescents may be confronted with a range of strains and stressors, characteristic of their developmental period which can result in problems with primary good attainment and lower levels of well-being (Gilman & Huebner, 2003; Op de Beeck, 2012). As we have seen, the GLM assumes that offenders who experience lower levels of well-being due to their unfulfilled primary goods, aim to compensate this by means of criminal behaviour.

Existing empirical research partly corroborates this assumption, as numerous studies find that in adolescents lower levels of well-being (conceptualized as life satisfaction) are indeed related to higher levels of drug use, problem behaviour, and delinquency, both in cross-sectional (Buelga et al., 2008; Gonzalez et al., 2021; MacDonald et al., 2005; McKnight et al., 2002; Olson et al., 2020; Suldo & Huebner, 2004; Sun & Shek, 2010, 2012; Valois et al., 2001, 2002, 2006; Zullig et al., 2001) and longitudinal studies (Hanniball et al., 2018; Haranin et al., 2007; Jung & Choi, 2017; Lyons et al., 2014; Shek & Lin, 2016; Sun & Shek, 2013; Zhu & Shek, 2020b). All of these longitudinal studies suggest that well-being has an influence on problem behaviour, yet there are exceptions: Lyons et al. (2013) and Zhu and Shek (2020a, 2021) also found evidence for a causal effect in the opposite direction.

Other studies show that the ability to adequately cope with strain, stress and obstacles in one's life is important in the relation between well-being and delinquency. Olson et al. (2020) studied the relationship between strain (negative emotional reactions to events or obstacles), life satisfaction and delinquency in young adult students. They found that strain was positively related to offending behaviour, but this relationship disappeared when life satisfaction was taken into account. Higher levels of life satisfaction were then associated with less delinquency. This is not surprising, as high levels of life satisfaction and well-being are known to be able to serve as a buffer for experienced strain and stress (Park, 2004). In the other direction, Rask et al. (2002) conclude that low levels of life satisfaction in adolescents can lead to inadequate coping, alcohol misuse, a sense of meaninglessness and self-destruction. Additionally, Hanniball et al. (2018) found that substance abuse mediated the link between life satisfaction and offending behaviour in adolescents, that is, low levels of life satisfaction were related to more substance abuse, which in turn was related to an elevated risk of offending. These combined results lead us to the hypothesis that strain and obstacles in obtaining primary goods in a prosocial way, together with inadequate coping (such as substance abuse) and (other) criminogenic risk factors, can result in both lower levels of well-being and more delinquent behaviour in adolescents.

5.6 Conclusion

Based on this chapter, we can conclude that on a theoretical level, the GLM's etiological assumptions can be applied to adolescent offenders. However, there still exists a number of unresolved issues, mainly regarding the lack of empirical studies that include all primary goods in relation to the well-being and juvenile delinquency of adolescents. Furthermore, criticism exists on the GLM's theoretical explanation of delinquency, particularly concerning the extent to which the primary goods are truly universal. As Ogloff and Davis (2004) have argued: "More work is needed to understand the extent to which offenders' human needs are similar to – or satisfied in similar or dissimilar ways from – non-offenders" (p. 238). However, according to the GLM, antisocial behaviour is assumed to be motivated by the same universal needs as any other form of human behaviour. Changing norms and values over time and in different cultures determine what kind of behaviour is or is not permissible in a certain society (Ward & Carter, 2019). Some forms of 'antisocial' behaviour were once viewed and even encouraged as conventional behaviour (e.g. the use of cocaine). Conversely, some behaviours are now (in most countries) considered legal, while they were punishable in the past and still are in certain parts of the world (e.g. homosexuality). Consequently, Ward and Carter (2019) state:

> A bold claim is that criminal behaviour is remarkably like normal behaviour and may well have adaptive outcomes for the person concerned, despite it being necessarily undesirable from a social/legal perspective. The trick is not to look at it through a lens of deviancy but rather work from the assumption that the person is motivated by normal needs and desires. (p. 2)

Still, I agree with Ogloff and Davis (2004) that more research is needed in the ways that (adolescent) offenders aim to pursue well-being, satisfy their primary goods and what role criminogenic risk factors play in this process. In the next chapters, I will therefore empirically assess the GLM's etiological assumptions regarding primary goods, well-being, and the explanation of delinquency in both a general adolescent sample (Chapter 6) and a sample of detained adolescent boys (Chapters 7 and 8).

6 Examining Direct and Indirect Pathways to Juvenile Delinquency in the General Population

Testing the Associations Between Primary Goods, Well-Being, and Delinquency in Adolescents from the General Population

Up until now, I have discussed the existing theoretical and empirical evidence underlying the GLM's assumptions about the role of primary goods in well-being and delinquency. From this discussion we concluded that the GLM can, at least theoretically, serve as a comprehensive framework for explaining delinquency in adolescents.

To reiterate, the GLM assumes that humans strive to attain 11 primary goods to experience well-being (i.e. *the first GLM assumption*). The pursuit of these primary goods and well-being are viewed as the major drivers behind all human action, including criminal and antisocial behaviour. People who turn to offending behaviour are assumed to experience lower levels of well-being, because the fulfilment of their primary goods is hampered. As a result, they are believed to aim directly or indirectly to achieve their primary goods by means of antisocial or criminal behaviour (i.e. *the second GLM assumption*), that is, problems with the prosocial pursuit of primary goods and well-being (e.g., due to criminogenic risk factors) can lead to the (deliberate) use of antisocial means (i.e. the direct route). Indirectly, problems with primary good fulfilment can also generate an accumulation of negative effects on the individual's life, such as problems with work or within the family. Those problems can result in feelings of loneliness, incompetence, and/or distress, compromising one's well-being. In turn, these negative feelings, combined with maladaptive coping strategies and other criminogenic risk factors (e.g. substance use or aggression regulation problems) might lead to a loss of control and offending behaviour to pursue one's primary goods and well-being (i.e. the indirect route; Purvis, 2010; Purvis et al., 2011; Ward, 2002a, 2002b; Ward & Marshall, 2004; Ward & Maruna, 2007).

Although the existing research literature generally supports this theory for adults, for adolescents slightly different assumptions might be appropriate, especially regarding the relative importance and manifestation of some of the primary goods. The meta-analyses reported in Chapter 4 revealed that for almost all 11 primary goods a greater attainment or satisfaction is related, in varying degrees, to higher levels of overall well-being in adolescents. The primary goods of 'inner peace' (mental health), 'relatedness' (with family and friends), 'community' (group belonging and social acceptance), 'excellence in agency' (in the sense of self-directed goal pursuit), and 'excellence in work' (manifested as feelings of competence and achievement) had the strongest associations with adolescents' well-being. Regarding the primary good of 'life', physical health and living situation had a stronger effect on adolescents' well-being than their financial situation. This latter finding and the different manifestation of 'excellence in agency' in adolescents, might be explained by the fact that adolescents, compared to adults, are usually not yet (fully) responsible for their own financial situation and life in general. Furthermore, attaining the primary good of 'spirituality' showed a positive relationship with adolescents' well-being through searching and finding a sense of purpose or meaning in life, not only through religion per se. A limited number of studies examined the relationship between adolescents' well-being and the primary goods of 'excellence in play', 'creativity', 'knowledge', and 'pleasure'; more research is needed before any firm conclusions can be drawn about these goods.

Additionally, from the literature review in Chapter 5 we can infer that adolescents' delinquent behaviour can potentially be explained by all GLM primary goods. For explaining adolescents' delinquent behaviour, problems with the attainment of 'relatedness' (with family and peers), 'community', 'pleasure', 'knowledge', 'excellence in work', 'excellence in play', 'inner peace', and 'excellence in agency' seem particularly relevant. Although they could potentially play an important role in adolescent delinquency, the primary goods of 'spirituality' and 'creativity' have received relatively less attention in the research literature. Interestingly, while financial situation, an aspect of the primary good of 'life', was less strongly related to well-being (compared to other goods), it seems to play a salient role in the explanation of juvenile delinquency. Still, the primary goods that are most relevant for explaining juvenile delinquency appear to be the same goods that were found to be important for adolescents' well-being. Furthermore, research (as discussed in Chapter 5) has shown that overall lower levels of well-being are related to higher levels of substance use, problem behaviour and delinquency in adolescents.

In sum, adolescents can experience a range of possible problems with primary good satisfaction that can lead to lower levels of well-being as well as antisocial behaviour and delinquency. To the best of my knowledge, however, no prior study has examined the combined effects of all primary goods and well-being on juvenile delinquency. Therefore, in this chapter, we first examine the hypothesis that overall subjective well-being is related to delinquent behaviour in adolescents (*the second assumption*). Using path analyses, we further investigate the hypothesis that (dis)satisfaction with the 11 primary goods can predict adolescents' well-being (*the first assumption*) and (in)directly predict delinquency (*the second assumption*).

6 *Examining Pathways to Juvenile Delinquency in the General Population*

6.1 Method

6.1.1 *Sampling Procedure*

The GLM's etiological assumptions were tested using part of the survey data from the 'JOP School Monitor 2' of the Youth Research Platform (Jeugd Onderzoeks Platform [JOP]; Bradt et al., 2019; JeugdOnderzoeksPlatform, 2018). This is a recurring large-scale survey study among school-age youth in Flanders, Belgium. The study was conducted at 80 secondary schools[1] in the period between February and May 2018. Of these schools, one class per academic year per type of education (general, including art school 'ASO/KSO', technical 'TSO', and vocational 'BSO')[2] was randomly selected to participate in the survey. In this way, 9,987 students were selected.

The selected students were informed about the study and asked for their active consent. The privacy of the participants and the anonymity of their answers was guaranteed during the entire procedure. Both the students and their parents (the latter had been informed about the study via a letter sent by the school) were given the option to refuse or stop participation at any time.[3] Through this procedure, 147 students (and/or their parents; 1.47% of the selected sample) refused to participate. Another 1,293 students from the selection (12.95%) could not participate because they were absent at the time the study took place or due to technical problems with the electronic tablets on which the survey was administered. In the end, 8,547 students[4] between the ages of 11 and 23 participated in the study. During the initial data cleaning process, participants with impossible answer combinations (e.g. participants who indicated to be active members of all 13 possible associations when asked a question about their leisure time activities) and participants who had not filled in more than 80% of the questions were removed (n = 108) from the dataset. This resulted in an initial sample of 8,439 participants. Two different questionnaires were used, one (less elaborate) for the younger students between 12 to 13 years, and another (more elaborate) one for the older students from the age of 14 and up. Only the latter questionnaire included all the necessary data for the current study. Furthermore, as

1 The majority of the schools were situated in the cities of Brussels, Antwerp and Ghent, while a smaller sample (around 25%) were situated in non-urban areas. For the entire selection procedure, see Bradt et al. (2019).

2 In the Belgian education system 'aso' is the Dutch abbreviation of *algemeen secundair onderwijs* (general secondary education), 'kso' is *kunst secundair onderwijs* (artistic secondary education), 'bso' is *beroepssecundair onderwijs* (vocational secondary education), and 'tso' is *technisch secundair onderwijs* (technical secondary education).

3 This study received ethical approval from the Social Ethical Committee (SMEC) of the KU Leuven (G-2017 03 813).

4 Which is about 1% (0.78%) of the total number (1,101,936) of youth between the ages of 11 and 23 residing in Flanders and Brussels on 1 January 2018 retrieved from Statbel.

the focus in this research is on adolescents, in our analyses we only used the data from the participants aged 14 to 18 at the time of participation (n = 6,131).

To adequately conduct the path analyses, 1,863 participants who had missing values on at least one of the variables included in the path model(s) were removed from the dataset, resulting in a dataset of 4,268 complete cases. Further, preparatory analyses of this sample revealed eight participants with a highly improbable response pattern that significantly distorted the results (i.e. extreme outliers), whose data were subsequently removed from the dataset[5] (Field, 2009; Mortelmans & Dehertogh, 2007). This resulted in a final sample of 4,260 participants.

6.1.2 *Measures*

Subjective Well-Being

Well-being was operationalized as subjectively experienced overall well-being, consisting of a standardized composite score of general life satisfaction (Satisfaction with Life Scale–Child Version; Diener et al., 1985; Gadermann et al., 2010) and emotional well-being, both positive and negative (Scale of Positive and Negative Experience; Diener et al., 2010). In this way, well-being is measured at both the cognitive (general life satisfaction) and affective (emotional well-being, positive and negative) level. This tripartite structure of subjective well-being (life satisfaction, positive affect and negative affect) is based on a large number of studies that describe this operationalization as reliable and valid (Metler & Busseri, 2017; Wallander & Koot, 2016).[6]

Satisfaction with Life Scale-Child Version (SWLS-CV). To assess general life satisfaction the five items of the Satisfaction with Life Scale-Child Version were used (SWLS-CV; Diener et al., 1985; Gadermann et al., 2010). We opted for the child version so that the questions were understandable for a broad age group. For the JOP School Monitor 2, the original English scale was officially translated into Dutch (Serie et al., 2017a). The items (e.g. 'I am happy with my life') are answered on a 5-point Likert scale (from 1 = *strongly*

5 This removal was based on an exploratory regression analysis predicting one of the outcome measures (total score of the Satisfaction With Life Scale – Child version, SWLS-(CV), 5 to 25) with the 16 primary goods proxy-items, age and gender as predictors. This analysis revealed various statistics to identify extreme outliers: Studentized residuals larger than (–)3, leverage larger than three times the average leverage (0.013), and DFits larger than $2*\sqrt{(18/4268)}$ (Field, 2009; Mortelmans & Dehertogh, 2007). If one of these statistics indicated a possible problem with a case, it was examined in more detail (n = 88). A participant's data was only removed if a highly improbable response pattern was found characterized by the following indications: (1) they scored high on SWLS-CV (≥ 19) but did not report *(very) satisfied* in at least one domain; (2) they scored low on SWLS-CV (≤ 11) but did not report *(very) dissatisfied* in at least one domain; or (3) they scored average on SWLS-CV (12 – 18) but scored on all domains either *very dissatisfied* or *very satisfied.* Eight participants met one of these three indicators and in combination with their outlier statistics, it was decided to remove them from the dataset.

6 See also the elaboration on the operationalization of well-being in Chapter 4, Section 4.2.1.

disagree to 5 = *strongly agree*). Adding the items results in a sum score between 5 and 25, which has been found to be reliable and valid in measuring the cognitive evaluation of general life satisfaction from a context-free perspective (Gadermann et al., 2010; Ortuno-Sierra et al., 2019). The reliability analysis in the current sample showed high internal consistency for this scale (Cronbach's α = .83).

Scale of Positive and Negative Experience (SPANE). Emotional well-being was measured with the Scale of Positive and Negative Experience (SPANE; Diener et al., 2010). For the JOP School Monitor 2, the original English scale was officially translated into Dutch (Serie et al., 2017b). The scale consists of six positive and six negative emotions, for which participants indicate how often these emotions were experienced in the past four weeks (from 1 = *very rarely or never* to 5 = *very often or always*). The scores can be added up to form the following subscales: positive affect (PA; with a possible sum score ranging from 6 to 30), negative affect (NA; with a possible sum score ranging from 6 to 30) and an affect balance scale for which the NA is subtracted from the PA score. The SPANE has been found to be reliable and valid for measuring emotional well-being in adults and adolescents (Jovanović, 2015; Telef, 2013). In accordance with these earlier studies, the reliability analyses in the current sample showed high internal consistency for both the positive emotion (Cronbach's α = .83) and the negative emotion subscale (Cronbach's α = .83).

The exploratory factor analysis (principal component analysis) of the items of the three scales together (SWLS-CV, PA and NA) in the current sample revealed a clear three-component factor structure of subjective well-being, which taken together produced high internal consistency (Cronbach's α = .90). Subsequently, to arrive at a composite score of subjective overall well-being,[7] the sum scores of the SWLS-CV, the positive affect scale

7 Although employing Structural Equation Modelling (SEM; for example in SPSS AMOS) to estimate subjective well-being (SWB) as a latent composite variable, resulting from its three primary indicators (SWLS-CV, PA, and NA), is suggested to be a more adequate and sophisticated way to operationalize well-being compared to composite scores (Metler & Busseri, 2017), this was not possible in the current analyses, that is, the dependent continuous delinquency outcome (frequency sum score) was heavily skewed and the assumption of normally distributed errors (residuals) for SEM (using linear regression analysis) was violated (Field, 2009; Mortelmans & Dehertogh, 2007). It was also not possible to use SPSS AMOS including a dependent dichotomous delinquency measure, as SPSS AMOS is not well-suited to perform logistic regression analysis. To accommodate this problem, I used the computational tool PROCESS v3.5 in SPSS v27, which performs mediation, moderation and conditional process analyses; somewhat similar to SEM but it uses bootstrapping to simulate the sampling distribution. Therefore, the normality assumption is no longer necessary in large sample sizes (Hayes, 2017; Hayes et al., 2017). However, in PROCESS it is not possible to estimate a latent factor and it was necessary to compute an observed composite score for well-being/SWB (Hayes, 2017). Therefore, I computed different possible composite scores of SWB (Busseri & Sadava, 2011) and checked whether the different operationalizations would produce different results compared to each other and a latent factor in SEM. I computed a 0 to 100 SWB index by summing the raw sum scores SWLS-CV + PA – NA and converting them to the 0-100 index (using the formula in fn 8); an SWB factor score based on the principal component factor analysis (PCA) of the sum scores of SWLS-CV, PA, and NA; a weighted SWB sum-score by summing the weighted (according to their PCA component coefficients) sum scores of the SWLS-CV, PA and NA; and a standardized 0 to 100 SWB index by converting each of the sum

(PA), and the negative affect scale (NA) of the SPANE were first standardized by converting each of them separately to a scale from 0 to 100.[8] The standardized SWLS-CV sum score was then added to the standardized PA sum score, minus the standardized NA sum score (as proposed by e.g.: Busseri & Sadava, 2011; Metler & Busseri, 2017). This calculation provided a standardized sum score with a possible range between -100 and 200. To facilitate its interpretation, this composite score was again converted to an index ranging from 0 to 100 (from here on referred to as 'the well-being index'), where 0 indicates the lowest overall subjective well-being and 100 indicates the highest.

GLM Primary Goods Satisfaction

The attainment of the GLM primary goods was measured with domain-specific life satisfaction as proxy-measures. Given the conceptual complexity of the primary goods, some of the goods were measured with more than one item (see Table 6.1 for an overview). This resulted in 15 items (in Dutch) for which the participants were asked how satisfied they were on a 5-point Likert scale (from 1 = *very dissatisfied* to 5 = *very satisfied*) for the following domains: financial situation, living situation, safety, physical health, education, leisure activities, information access, social contacts with friends (i.e. friendships), love life, family relationships, other social contacts in the neighbourhood/clubs/associations, mental health, autonomy (agency), pleasure/enjoyment and creativity. The wording of these items is based on existing, validated quality of life instruments (Gilman & Huebner, 2000),[9] such as the Personal Well-being Index (Tomyn et al., 2013), the Perceived Life Satisfaction Scale (Adelman et al., 1989), the (Brief) Multidimensional Student's Life Satisfaction Scale (Gilman et al., 2000; Huebner et al., 2006), and the World Health Organization's Quality of Life Scale (WHOQOL, 1995). Finally, the domain of religion/spirituality was also assessed, but because it was deemed conceptually difficult to answer the question whether one is satisfied with one's spirituality, participants were asked: 'How important is religion/spirituality for you?' This question could be answered from 0 = *not important at all* to 10 = *very important*. To be consistent with the other items, this item was recoded to a 5-point Likert scale (JeugdOnderzoeksPlatform, 2018). Finally, for the

---

scores of SWLS-CV, PA and NA from 0 to 100, before summing them (SWLS-CV + PA – NA) and again converting that sum score to an index from 0 to 100 (as described in Section 6.1.2). These composite scores of SWB did not differ from each other (Pearson's $r > .999$). Moreover, the linear regression analyses with the 16 primary goods proxy-items, age and gender as predictors did not produce different conclusions when using each of the different SWB operationalizations as a dependent variable, also not compared to the SEM analysis in SPSS AMOS using the estimation of SWB as a latent factor. Consequently, I used the standardized SWB index (from 0 to 100) as a stand-in for a higher order latent SWB factor, because this type of composite score is also recognized as a common and easy to interpret operationalization of well-being (Busseri & Sadava, 2011; Metler & Busseri, 2017).

8 (Raw score - Minimum score) * (100/ Maximum-Minimum score).

9 Also inspired by the systematic literature review in Chapter 4.

purpose of this study, all 16 primary goods proxy-items were recoded in such a way that a higher score indicates lower levels of satisfaction (i.e. more dissatisfaction), and for religion/spirituality: less importance.

Table 6.1 Description of the 11 GLM Primary Goods and the Accompanying Proxy-Items

Primary Goods	Description	Proxy-Items: How Satisfied Are You with …
Life	*The need for healthy and quality living, the need to feel safe and secure. It incorporates all the basic physical needs and factors that are important for healthy living and physical functioning: food, water, shelter, a physically healthy body and so on.*	… how much money you have? … where you live? … how safe you feel? … your physical health?
Knowledge	*One's interest in, access to, and possession of information. It is not related to how intelligent someone is, but rather to how well informed an individual feels about things that are important to them.*	… your access to information about things that interest you (e.g. on the internet, in magazines or courses)?
Excellence in work	*The need to engage in work, which provides the person with a sense of pride, achievement, satisfaction, and skill development.*	… your education?
Excellence in play	*The need to engage in leisure or fun activities that provide the person with a sense of pride, achievement, satisfaction, and skill development.*	… your leisure activities (hobby's, sports, music …)?
Excellence in agency	*The need to formulate their own goals and seek ways to realize them in actions and activities of their own choice. It encompasses the need for autonomy, self-directedness, personal power, control, and mastery.*	… how much you can decide about your own life?
Inner peace	*The need for freedom from emotional turmoil and stress. It includes emotional self-regulation and achieving a state of emotional balance.*	… your mental health?
Relatedness	*The need of human beings to establish affectionate, mutual bonds with an intimate partner, family members, and close friends.*	… your love life? … your social contacts with friends? … your relationships with your family?

Primary Goods	Description	Proxy-Items: How Satisfied Are You with …
Community	*The need to belong to social groups, to feel connected to groups that reflect their interests, concerns, and values. It entails the feeling of being part of, being able to rely on, and contributing to a wider social or cultural network.*	… your social contacts with other people (in your neighbourhood, clubs/associations)?
Spirituality	*The need to discover a sense of meaning and purpose in life. This could involve seeking religious inspiration and affiliation, a spiritual connection with a transcendent being or reality, or simply the experience of being part of a larger whole.*	How important is religion/spirituality for you?
Creativity	*The need for novelty, innovation and individuality in one's life. It does not just refer to the ability to produce artistic work, it may also be present in the way a person solves problems, or the way they appreciate beauty or nature. It is essentially the expression of oneself through creative forms of activity.*	… how creative you can be (with trying new things, art, music, solving problems)?
Pleasure	*The need to feel good in the here and now. It includes a range of feelings and sensations, such as joy, merriment, delight, elation, and hedonic pleasure.*	… how much you can enjoy yourself (with e.g. good food, a trip, a movie)?

Notes. The descriptions of the primary goods are based on the work of Purvis (2010); Purvis et al. (2014); and Willis et al. (2013). The items in this table are translated from the original items in Dutch to English for the purpose of this chapter.

Self-Reported Delinquency

To assess delinquency, a five-item scale was used to ask the participants (in Dutch) how often (0 = *never*, 1 = *once*, 2 = *twice*, 3 = *three times*, or 4 = *more than three times*) they had committed five types of offences in the preceding 12 months. The types of offences included in the survey were: vandalism ('deliberately damaging or breaking something in the street, at school or in another public place'), shoplifting ('stealing something from a shop or department store'), theft ('stealing something from another person, e.g. money, bicycle, cell phone, or something else'), harassment ('harassing or threatening someone'), and physical assault ('beating up somebody so badly that he/she sustained injuries'). These questions were based on the 2005 monitor of the Dutch Scientific Research and Documentation Center (Wetenschappelijk Onderzoek-en Documentatiecentrum) of the Ministry of Justice and Security concerning self-reported juvenile delinquency (van der

Laan et al., 2006). Combining the five frequency scores resulted in a total delinquency frequency score ranging from 0 to 20.[10]

6.1.3 Statistical Analyses

First, to describe the sample we used descriptive statistics of the participants' gender, age, school background, ethnic background, family situation, well-being scores, primary goods proxy-items and self-reported offences. Next, the association between overall subjective well-being and juvenile delinquency was assessed. Independent-samples *t*-tests were used to compare the mean well-being index scores between self-reported 'offenders' and 'non-offenders'. This was done for all five offences combined (where adolescents were considered 'offender' if they reported to have committed at least one of the five offences once in the preceding 12 months), as well as for the five offences separately. We also examined the relationship between the well-being index and the number of self-reported offences (based on the total frequency score of the five offence items). This was done using a Pearson correlation analysis and a one-way Analysis of Variance (ANOVA) assessing the differences in well-being between four groups: adolescents who reported committing none of the five offences, one offence, two offences, and three or more offences. All analyses were conducted in SPSS (version 27).

Subsequently, to assess the hypothesized (direct and indirect) pathways between the primary goods (the 16 proxy-items), adolescents' overall subjective well-being (the well-being index), and delinquency frequency (total score of all five offences taken together), we used the computational tool PROCESS version 3.5 in SPSS (version 27).[11] PROCESS performs mediation, moderation and conditional process analyses similar to structural

10 It is sometimes recommended to prefer 'variety' scores of delinquency over 'frequency' scores (Sweeten, 2012). Nevertheless, similar results were obtained using a 'variety' score of delinquency (measured as the number of different offences committed 1 to 5) in the analyses compared to the 'frequency' score (the sum of the self-reported frequency of the five offences combined). Moreover, the 'frequency' scores were preferred in this study because we were interested in the extent of delinquent behaviour in general, not just the number of types committed.

11 In the exploratory linear regression analyses predicting well-being and delinquency the necessary statistical assumptions were assessed. Multicollinearity was not an issue as all VIF values were below 2.14 (see Appendix E, https://www.elevenpub.com/en/content/appendices-9789462364257). The error terms were independent. Checks for the linearity and homoscedasticity assumptions revealed there might have been a slight violation of both, but non-linear transformations of the (in)dependent variables did not improve the fit or made it worse (Mortelmans & Dehertogh, 2007). Moreover, when using inferential methods in the regression analysis in PROCESS that do not assume homoscedasticity, no differences in the results occurred. This suggests that even though there was evidence of a possible assumption violation (i.e., heteroscedasticity), it did not significantly affect the results. Finally, as already explained in fn 7, for total delinquency (but not well-being) as a dependent variable the residuals of the linear regression analyses were not normally distributed. However, as PROCESS uses bootstrapping to simulate the sampling (and error) distribution the normality assumption is no longer necessary (Hayes, 2017; Hayes et al., 2017).

equation modelling (SEM), but uses bootstrapping to simulate the sampling distribution (see this chapter fn 7 and 11 for a more detailed explanation of this choice; Hayes, 2017; Hayes et al., 2017). The number of bootstrap samples for percentile bootstrap confidence intervals (95%) was set at 5,000. Age and gender were included as control variables because evidence suggests that these variables may be related to both well-being (Proctor et al., 2009) and delinquency (Cottle et al., 2001).

For interpreting the magnitude of correlation coefficients, the guidelines by Hemphill (2003) were used: $r < .20$ reflects a small effect, $r = .20$ to .30 a moderate effect, and $r > .30$ a large effect. When interpreting Cohen's d effect sizes the following guidelines were used: $d = 0.20$ reflects a small effect, $d = 0.50$ a medium effect, and $d = 0.80$ a large effect (Cohen, 1988). In all analyses, p-values less than .05 were considered statistically significant.[12]

6.2 Results

6.2.1 *Sample Characteristics*

The 4,260 included adolescents (aged 14 to 18) had a mean age of 16.05 ($SD = 1.25$). About half (44.9%, $n = 1{,}912$) were boys and 55.1% ($n = 2{,}348$) were girls. In terms of education, 48.8% ($n = 2{,}079$) attended general (including art school) secondary education ('aso'/'kso'), about a third (32.7%, $n = 1{,}393$); attended technical secondary education ('tso'), and the minority (18.3%, $n = 778$) vocational secondary education ('bso'). Most of the participants in the sample went to school in one of the larger cities in Flanders (Antwerp, Brussels, or Ghent; 68.9%, $n = 2{,}935$), while about 40% (41.2%, $n = 1{,}753$) also lived there. The majority of participants were born in Belgium (87.7%, $n = 3{,}734$). Of the 12.2% ($n = 519$) of participants born abroad, the most common countries of origin were the Netherlands (2.7%, $n = 114$), Poland (0.8%, $n = 33$), Spain (0.7%, $n = 28$), Bulgaria (0.5%, $n = 20$), and Russia (0.5%, $n = 20$). Almost half (45.2%, $n = 1{,}927$) of the participants' father and/or mother were born abroad. The most common countries of origin of the parent(s) were Morocco (10.9% fathers, 8.5% mothers), Turkey (4.2% fathers, 3.7% mothers), the Netherlands (2.4% fathers, 2.4% mothers) and Congo (1.6% fathers, 1.8% mothers). The majority of the participants' parents lived together (66.6%, $n = 2{,}839$). About a quarter of the participants' parents were divorced (27.4%, $n = 1{,}167$) and in 4.4% ($n = 188$) one or both parents were unknown or deceased.

12 Or 95% confidence intervals that did not include 0.

6.2.2 *Descriptive Statistics*

Subjective Well-Being

On the overall subjective well-being index (ranging from 0 to 100), participants scored on average 61.83 (*SD* = 14.76). In terms of general life satisfaction (measured with the sum score of the SWLS-CV ranging from 5 to 25), the participants scored on average 16.85 (*SD* = 3.82), which converted to the 0 to 100 index corresponds to a mean score of 59.23 (*SD* = 19.08). Regarding emotional well-being (measured with the sum scores of the subscales of the SPANE, ranging from 6 to 30), the participants scored on average 21.45 (*SD* = 3.86) on the positive affect scale (PA), and 15.15 (*SD* = 4.28) on the negative affect scale (NA), which corresponds on the 0 to 100 index to a mean score of 64.40 (*SD* = 16.08) for PA and 38.14 (*SD* = 17.84) for NA.

GLM Primary Goods Satisfaction

Most participants reported to be *(very) satisfied* with the primary goods proxy-items, ranging from 44.4% with their love life to 87.3% with their access to information. Nevertheless, for all items there is a small but noteworthy minority who report to be *(very) dissatisfied*, ranging from 2.3% with their access to information to 27.4% with their love life. See Table 6.2 for an overview of the frequency scores, means and standard deviations of all satisfaction items. In contrast to the satisfaction items, for 'religion/spirituality' participants were asked how important they considered it to be. About a quarter reported religion/spirituality to be *very important* (23.5%, *n* = 1,002), 12.0% consider it to be *important* (*n* = 512), 20.8% (*n* = 885) report it to be *neither important nor unimportant*, 12.6% (*n* = 538) consider it *unimportant*, and a third considers it to be *not important at all* (31.3%, *n* = 1,323).

Table 6.2 Primary Goods Proxy-Items Satisfaction Frequencies *N* (%) and Descriptive Statistics

How satisfied are you with …	Very satisfied	Satisfied	Neither satisfied nor dis-satisfied	Dis-satisfied	Very Dis-satisfied	*M* (*SD*)
… how much money you have?	840 (19.7%)	2,101 (49.3%)	841 (19.7%)	368 (8.6%)	110 (2.6%)	**2.25** (0.95)
… where you live?	1,359 (31.9%)	2,026 (47.6%)	579 (13.6%)	229 (5.4%)	67 (1.6%)	**1.97** (0.90)
… how safe you feel?	1,383 (32.5%)	2,209 (51.9%)	523 (12.3%)	111 (2.6%)	34 (0.8%)	**1.87** (0.78)
… your physical health?	940 (22.1%)	1,826 (42.9%)	970 (22.8%)	387 (9.1%)	137 (3.2%)	**2.29** (1.01)
… your access to information about things that interest you (e.g., on the internet, in magazines or courses…)?	1,446 (33.9%)	2,276 (53.4%)	440 (10.3%)	65 (1.5%)	33 (0.8%)	**1.82** (0.74)
… your education?	760 (17.8%)	2,152 (50.5%)	964 (22.6%)	289 (6.8%)	95 (2.2%)	**2.25** (0.90)
… your leisure activities (hobby's, sports, music…)?	1,334 (31.3%)	1,924 (45.2%)	717 (16.8%)	210 (4.9%)	75 (1.8%)	**2.01** (0.92)
… how much you can decide about your own life?	849 (19.9%)	2,201 (51.7%)	832 (19.5%)	288 (6.8%)	90 (2.1%)	**2.19** (0.90)
… your mental health?	1,011 (23.7%)	1,964 (46.1%)	779 (18.3%)	348 (8.2%)	158 (3.7%)	**2.22** (1.01)
… your relationships with your family?	1,584 (37.2%)	1,618 (38.0%)	720 (16.9%)	236 (5.5%)	102 (2.4%)	**1.98** (0.99)
… your social contacts with friends?	1,364 (32.0%)	2,159 (50.7%)	560 (13.1%)	133 (3.1%)	44 (1.0%)	**1.90** (0.81)
… your love life?	848 (19.9%)	1,045 (24.5%)	1,200 (28.2%)	690 (16.2%)	477 (11.2%)	**2.74** (1.26)

How satisfied are you with …	Very satisfied	Satisfied	Neither satisfied nor dis-satisfied	Dis-satisfied	Very Dis-satisfied	*M* (*SD*)
… your social contacts with other people (in your neighbourhood, clubs/ associations)?	685 (16.1%)	1,866 (43.8%)	1,218 (28.6%)	380 (8.9%)	111 (2.6%)	**2.38** (0.95)
… how creative you can be (with trying new things, art, music, solving problems)?	929 (21.8%)	1,980 (46.5%)	1,007 (23.6%)	248 (5.8%)	96 (2.3%)	**2.20** (0.92)
… how much you can enjoy yourself (with e.g., good food, a trip, a movie)?	1,403 (32.9%)	2,146 (50.4%)	528 (12.4%)	130 (3.1%)	53 (1.2%)	**1.89** (0.82)

Notes. $N = 4{,}260$. A higher score on the primary goods proxy-items (ranging from 1 to 5) corresponds to lower levels of satisfaction (i.e., more dissatisfaction).

Delinquency Frequencies

In terms of delinquency frequencies, 61.2% (n = 2,609) reported not having committed any of the five offences in the preceding 12 months. The remaining 38.8% (n = 1,651) reported having committed at least one of the five offences once in the preceding 12 months. One-third of this group of offenders (33.5%; n = 553) reported having committed only one offence in the preceding 12 months and 19.0% (n = 314) reported two offences. Slightly less than half of the offenders (47.5%; n = 784) reported having committed three or more offences. Approximately half (49.5%; n = 818) of the 1,651 offenders reported having committed only one of the five types of offences, while the other half (50.5%; n = 833) reported a combination of different types. See Table 6.3 for an overview of the frequencies per offence.

Table 6.3 Self-Reported Frequencies of the Five Types of Offences in the Preceding 12 Months

Offence type	Never n (%)	Once n (%)	Twice n (%)	Three or more n (%)
Vandalism	3,227 (75.8%)	538 (12.5%)	218 (5.1%)	283 (6.7%)
Shoplifting	3,362 (78.9%)	432 (10.1%)	180 (4.2%)	286 (6.7%)
Theft	3,716 (87.2%)	297 (7.0%)	89 (2.1%)	158 (3.7%)
Harassment	3,985 (93.5%)	147 (3.5%)	52 (1.2%)	76 (1.8%)
Physical assault	3,934 (92.3%)	179 (4.2%)	58 (1.4%)	89 (2.1%)

Note. N = 4,260.

6.2.3 *Relationship Between Well-Being and Delinquency*

To assess the relationship between overall subjective well-being and delinquency, we first conducted an independent-samples t-test to analyse the difference in overall subjective well-being (the 0-100 well-being index) between those who reported having committed at least one of the five offences once in the preceding 12 months ('offenders') and those who reported not having committed any of the offences ('non-offenders'). The results show that the self-reported offenders scored significantly lower on overall subjective well-being (n = 1,651; M = 59.54, SD = 14.84) than those who reported no offences (n = 2,609, M = 63.28, SD = 14.53), t(3,453.38) = 8.06, $p < .001$ (Cohen's d = 0.26), corresponding to a small effect size. See Table 6.4 for an overview of the differences in well-being index scores between self-reported 'offenders' and 'non-offenders' for each of the different offence types separately. All effect sizes for each of the different offence types were considered small.

Table 6.4 Differences in Overall Subjective Well-Being (the 0-100 Well-Being Index) Between Self-Reported 'Offenders' and 'Non-offenders'

	Offenders		Non-offenders		*T*-test	
Offence type	*M (SD)*	*n*	*M (SD)*	*n*	Cohen's *d*	*p*
Vandalism***	**59.53** (14.52)	1,033	**62.56** (14.76)	3,227	0.21	<.001
Shoplifting***	**58.66** (15.11)	898	**62.67** (14.55)	3,362	0.27	<.001
Theft***	**58.41** (14.64)	544	**62.33** (14.71)	3,716	0.27	<.001
Harassment**	**59.17** (13.59)	275	**62.01** (14.82)	3,985	0.19	.002
Physical assault***	**58.63** (15.78)	326	**62.09** (14.64)	3,934	0.24	<.001

Notes. $N = 4{,}260$. 'Offenders' reported to have committed the offence at least once in the preceding 12 months, whereas the 'non-offenders' reported to not committing the offence in the preceding 12 months. *** = $p < .001$, ** = $p < .01$, based on independent-samples *t*-tests. A higher score on the well-being index (ranging from 0 to 100) corresponds to higher levels of subjective overall well-being.

Next, we assessed the relationship between overall subjective well-being (the 0-100 well-being index) and the number of self-reported offences committed in the preceding 12 months (for all five offence types combined) with a one-way ANOVA and Tukey-Kramer Post-Hoc tests. Results showed a statistically significant relationship between well-being and the number of offences committed, $F(3, 4256) = 27.17$, $p < .001$ (see Table 6.5). Specifically, the post-hoc results showed that adolescents who reported not having committed any of the offences scored significantly higher on overall well-being ($n = 2{,}609$, $M = 63.28$, $SD = 14.53$) compared to all other groups: those who committed one offence, $p = .009$; who committed two, $p = .007$, and who committed three or more offences, $p < .001$. Additionally, adolescents who reported having committed three or more offences in the preceding 12 months ($n = 784$) scored also significantly lower on well-being ($M = 58.06$, $SD = 15.16$) than adolescents who reported one offence ($n = 588$, $M = 61.37$, $SD = 14.25$), $p < .001$. Furthermore, a statistically significant negative correlation was found between the well-being index and the total number of self-reported offences (Pearson's $r = -.13$, $p < .001$), which is considered a small effect.

Table 6.5 Differences in Overall Subjective Well-Being (the 0-100 Well-Being Index) According to the Number of Self-Reported Committed Offences

Number of offences	*M (SD)*	*n*
No offences	**63.28** (14.53)[a]	2,609
One offence	**61.12** (14.42)[b]	553
Two offences	**60.46** (14.45)[b,c]	314
Three or more offences	**58.06** (15.16)[c]	784

Notes. $N = 4{,}260$. Different superscripts (a, b, c) correspond to statistically significant differences based on Tukey-Kramer post-hoc tests ($p < .05$). A higher score on the well-being index (ranging from 0 to 100) corresponds to higher levels of subjective overall well-being.

6.2.4 *Direct and Indirect Pathways Between Primary goods, Well-Being, and Delinquency*

To examine the hypothesized routes between the primary goods (the 16 proxy-items), the well-being index, and self-reported offending frequency, a path analysis was conducted in PROCESS (see this chapter, fn 7 and 11 for a more detailed explanation of this choice; Hayes, 2017; Hayes et al., 2017). Figure 6.1 shows the summarized results of this path analysis, which are explained in detail below.

Figure 6.1 Path Analysis Model of Associations Between Primary Goods Proxy-Items, Well-Being, and Total Delinquency, Controlling for Age and Gender

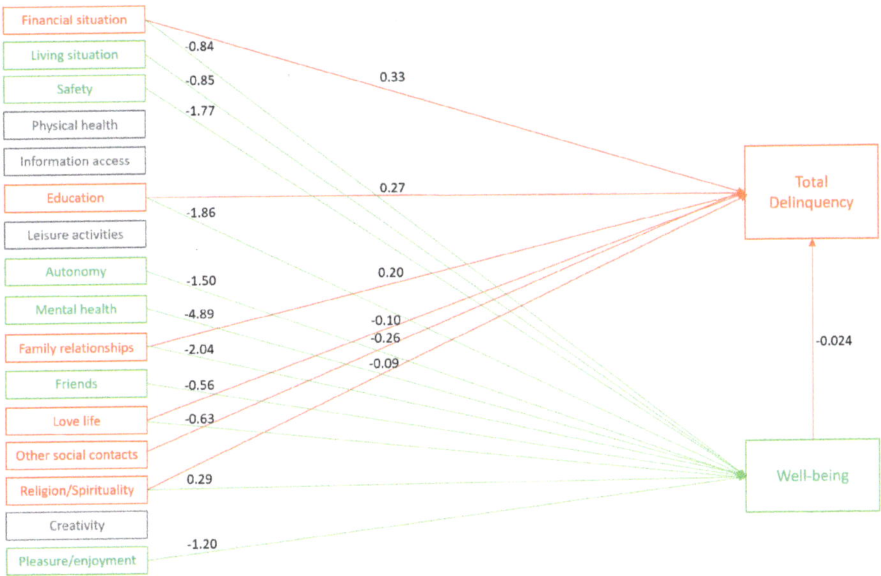

Notes. N = 4,260. The path analysis model shows the statistically significant ($p < .05$) associations, controlling for age and gender. Coefficients presented are unstandardized bootstrap estimates (B). A higher total delinquency frequency score (0 to 20) corresponds to more reported committed offences. A higher score on the well-being index (0 to 100) corresponds to higher levels of subjective overall well-being. A higher score on the primary goods proxy-items (1 to 5) corresponds to lower levels of satisfaction (i.e. more dissatisfaction), with one exception: a higher score on religion/spirituality (1 to 5) corresponds to lower levels of attributed importance. Predictors in green are only directly related to well-being and indirectly (but not directly) to delinquency. Predictors in red are (also) directly related to delinquency. Predictors in grey were found to be non-significant.

Direct Effects of the Primary Goods on Well-Being

First, the path analysis showed the direct effects of the primary goods on well-being. The ordinary least squares path analysis on overall subjective well-being showed that 53.2% of the variance in the well-being index could be explained by the primary goods proxy-items, controlling for gender and age, $F(18, 4241) = 267.71$, $p < .001$. The unstandardized bootstrap estimates (B) of the direct effects on well-being can be found in Table 6.6.

Gender was found to be a significant predictor of well-being, with boys reporting higher well-being than girls (B = -2.18, 95% CI [-2.85, -1.56]). In addition, age was also a significant predictor; reported well-being decreased with age (B = -0.33, 95% CI [-0.58, -0.08]). Of the primary goods proxy-items, more dissatisfaction with one's mental health appeared to be the strongest predictor of lower levels of subjective well-being (B = -4.89, 95% CI [-5.33, -4.43]), followed by more dissatisfaction with family relationships

(B = -2.04, 95% CI [-2.45, -1.63]), and more dissatisfaction with education (B = -1.86, 95% CI [-2.25, -1.46]).

Other significant predictors of lower levels of well-being were more dissatisfaction with: one's feelings of safety (B = -1.77, 95% CI [-2.30, -1.24]), sense of autonomy (B = -1.50, 95% CI [-1.98, -1.04]), pleasure/enjoyment (B = -1.20, 95% CI [-1.75, -0.67]), living situation (B = -0.85, 95% CI [-1.28, -0.42]), financial situation (B = -0.84, 95% CI [-1.24, -0.44]), love life (B = -0.63, 95% CI [-0.91, -0.36]), and social contacts with friends (B = -0.56, 95% CI [-1.10, -0.04]). For all these primary goods proxy-items more dissatisfaction predicted lower levels of overall subjective well-being. Finally, we found that less importance attributed to religion and/or spirituality predicted higher levels of well-being (B = 0.29, 95% CI [0.08, 0.50]).

Table 6.6 Unstandardized Bootstrap Estimates (B) of the Direct Effects and Bootstrap Inferences (SE and CI) of the Primary Goods Proxy-Items on Overall Subjective Well-Being Based on the PROCESS Path Analysis, Controlling for Age and Gender

	B (SE)	95% CI B
Control variables		
Age	-0.33 (.13)*	[-0.58, -0.08]
Gender (0 = boy, 1 = girl)	-2.18 (.33)*	[-2.85, -1.56]
Primary goods proxy-items		
Financial situation	-0.84 (.21)*	[-1.24, -0.44]
Living situation	-0.85 (.22)*	[-1.28, -0.42]
Safety	-1.77 (.27)*	[-2.30, -1.24]
Physical health	-0.26 (.21)^{ns}	[-0.68, 0.16]
Information access	0.11 (.30)^{ns}	[-0.48, 0.71]
Education	-1.86 (.21)*	[-2.25, -1.46]
Leisure activities	-0.33 (.22)^{ns}	[-0.76, 0.10]
Autonomy	-1.50 (.24)*	[-1.98, -1.04]
Mental health	-4.89 (.23)*	[-5.33, -4.43]
Family relationships	-2.04 (.21)*	[-2.45, -1.63]
Friendships	-0.56 (.27)*	[-1.10, -0.04]
Love life	-0.63 (.14)*	[-0.91, -0.36]
Other social contacts	-0.12 (.21)^{ns}	[-0.53, 0.30]
Religion/spirituality	0.29 (.11)*	[0.08, 0.50]

	B (SE)	95% CI B
Creativity	-0.30 (.21)^{ns}	[-0.71, 0.12]
Pleasure/enjoyment	-1.20 (.28)*	[-1.75, -0.67]

Notes. N = 4,260. R^2 = .532; model $F(18, 4241) = 267.71$, $p < .001$; * = significant p < .05; ns = not significant. The unstandardized estimates (B), standard error (SE), and the 95% confidence intervals (CI) were obtained using percentile bootstrapping based on 5,000 bootstrap samples. A higher score on the well-being index (0 to 100) corresponds to higher levels of subjective overall well-being. A higher score on the primary goods proxy-items (1 to 5) corresponds to lower levels of satisfaction (i.e. more dissatisfaction), with one exception: a higher score on religion/spirituality (1 to 5) corresponds to lower levels of attributed importance.

Direct Effects of the Primary Goods on Total Delinquency

Next, the path analysis showed the direct and indirect effects of the primary goods on total delinquency with well-being as a possible mediator. The ordinary least squares path analysis on total delinquency showed that 9.8% of the variance in the total frequency of committed offences (all five types combined) could be explained by the primary goods proxy-items, with well-being as mediator, controlling for gender and age, $F(19, 4240)$ = 24.26, $p < .001$. The unstandardized bootstrap estimates (B) of the direct effects on total delinquency can be found in Table 6.7.

Gender was found to be a significant predictor of total delinquency, with girls reporting a lower frequency of committing offences than boys (B = -1.26, 95% CI [-1.46, -1.06]). A higher level of well-being significantly predicted less total delinquency, albeit with a small effect (B = -0.024, 95% CI [-0.03, -0.02]). Of the primary goods proxy-items, more dissatisfaction with one's financial situation was the most important significant predictor of more delinquency (B = 0.33, 95% CI [0.20, 0.46]). The second most important predictor of more reported offences was more dissatisfaction with one's education (B = 0.27, 95% CI [0.14, 0.40]), followed by more dissatisfaction with family relationships (B = 0.20, 95% CI [0.10, 0.31]). In the opposite direction, more dissatisfaction with other social contacts (B = -0.26, 95% CI [-0.37, -0.14]) and more dissatisfaction with one's love life (B = -0.10, 95% CI [-0.18, -0.03]), significantly predicted less reported offences. Finally, we also found that less importance attributed to religion and/or spirituality significantly predicted less delinquency (B = -0.09, 95% CI [-0.15, -0.03]).

Table 6.7 Unstandardized Bootstrap Estimates (B) of the Direct Effects and Bootstrap Inferences (SE and CI) of the Primary Goods Proxy-Items on Total Delinquency Frequency Based on the PROCESS Path Analysis, With Well-Being as Mediator, Controlling for Age and Gender

	B (SE)	95% CI B
Control variables		
Age	-0.009 (.03)^{ns}	[-0.08, 0.06]
Gender (0 = boy, 1 = girl)	-1.26 (.10)*	[-1.46, -1.06]
Mediator		
Well-being	-0.024 (.01)*	[-0.03, -0.02]
Primary goods proxy-items		
Financial situation	0.33 (.07)*	[0.20, 0.46]
Living situation	0.07 (.06)^{ns}	[-0.05, 0.19]
Safety	0.02 (.08)^{ns}	[-0.15, 0.18]
Physical health	0.03 (.05)^{ns}	[-0.08, 0.13]
Information access	0.08 (.08)^{ns}	[-0.07, 0.24]
Education	0.27 (.07)*	[0.14, 0.40]
Leisure activities	-0.08 (.06)^{ns}	[-0.20, 0.03]
Autonomy	-0.03 (.06)^{ns}	[-0.15, 0.09]
Mental health	-0.03 (.07)^{ns}	[-0.16, 0.10]
Family relationships	0.20 (.05)*	[0.10, 0.31]
Friendships	-0.12 (.08)^{ns}	[-0.27, 0.03]
Love life	-0.10 (.04)*	[-0.18, -0.03]
Other social contacts	-0.26 (.06)*	[-0.37, -0.14]
Religion/spirituality	-0.09 (.03)*	[-0.15, -0.03]
Creativity	0.04 (.06)^{ns}	[-0.08, 0.15]
Pleasure/enjoyment	-0.06 (.07)^{ns}	[-0.19, 0.08]

Notes. N = 4,260. R^2 = .098; model $F(19, 4240) = 24.26$, $p < .001$; * = significant $p < .05$; ns = not significant. The unstandardized estimates (B), standard error (SE), and the 95% confidence intervals (CI) were obtained using percentile bootstrapping based on 5,000 bootstrap samples. A higher total delinquency frequency score (0 to 20) corresponds to more reported committed offences. A higher score on the well-being index (0 to 100) corresponds to higher levels of subjective overall well-being. A higher score on the primary goods proxy-items (1 to 5) corresponds to lower levels of satisfaction (i.e. more dissatisfaction), with one exception: a higher score on religion/spirituality (1 to 5) corresponds to lower levels of attributed importance.

Indirect Effects of the Primary Goods on Total Delinquency Through Well-Being
Table 6.8 shows the unstandardized bootstrap estimates (B) of the indirect effects of age, gender and the primary goods proxy-items on total delinquency (all five types combined) through their effects on well-being. Except for more dissatisfaction with other social contacts (B = 0.003, 95% CI [−0.007, 0.01]), all items that significantly directly predicted total delinquency (as found in Table 6.7), also significantly predicted more delinquency indirectly through lower levels of well-being: gender (B = 0.05, 95% CI [0.03, 0.08]), less importance of religion/spirituality (B = -0.007, 95% CI [-0.01, -0.002]), more dissatisfaction with one's: financial situation (B = 0.02, 95% CI [0.009, 0.03]), education (B = 0.04, 95% CI [0.03, 0.07]), family relationships (B = 0.05, 95% CI [0.03, 0.07]), and love life (B = 0.02, 95% CI [0.007, 0.03]).

The predictors that were not directly related to delinquency frequency, but indirectly predicted more offences through lower levels of well-being were: age (B = 0.008, 95% CI [0.002, 0.02]), more dissatisfaction with one's: living situation (B = 0.02, 95% CI [0.008, 0.03]), feelings of safety (B = 0.04, 95% CI [0.02, 0.06]), sense of autonomy (B = 0.04, 95% CI [0.02, 0.06]), mental health (B = 0.12, 95% CI [0.07, 0.16]), social contacts with friends (B = 0.01, 95% CI [0.001, 0.03]), and pleasure/enjoyment (B = 0.03, 95% CI [0.01, 0.05]). The predictors that were not directly related to delinquency and also not significantly indirectly through well-being were: dissatisfaction with one's physical health (B = 0.006, 95% CI [-0.004, 0.02]), information access (B = -0.003, 95% CI [-0.02, 0.01]), leisure activities (B = 0.008, 95% CI [-0.002, 0.02]) and creativity (B = 0.01, 95% CI [-0.003, 0.02])..

Table 6.8 Unstandardized Bootstrap Estimates (B) of Indirect Effects and Bootstrap Inferences (SE and CI) of the Primary Goods Proxy-Items on Total Delinquency Frequency Score Through Well-Being Based on the PROCESS Path Analysis, Controlling for Age and Gender

	B (SE)	95% CI B
Control variables		
Age	0.008 (.004)*	[0.002, 0.02]
Gender (0 = boy, 1 = girl)	0.05 (.013)*	[0.03, 0.08]
Primary goods proxy-items		
Financial situation	0.02 (.006)*	[0.009, 0.03]
Living situation	0.02 (.007)*	[0.008, 0.03]
Safety	0.04 (.010)*	[0.02, 0.06]
Physical health	0.006 (.005)^{ns}	[-0.004, 0.02]
Information access	-0.003 (.007)^{ns}	[-0.02, 0.01]

	B (SE)	95% CI B
Education	0.04 (.010)*	[0.03, 0.07]
Leisure activities	0.008 (.005)ns	[-0.002, 0.02]
Autonomy	0.04 (.010)*	[0.02, 0.06]
Mental health	0.12 (.023)*	[0.07, 0.16]
Family relationships	0.05 (.011)*	[0.03, 0.07]
Friendships	0.01 (.007)*	[0.001, 0.03]
Love life	0.02 (.005)*	[0.007, 0.03]
Other social contacts	0.003 (.005)ns	[-0.007, 0.01]
Religion/spirituality	-0.007 (.003)*	[-0.01, -0.002]
Creativity	0.007 (.005)ns	[-0.003, 0.02]
Pleasure/enjoyment	0.03 (.009)*	[0.01, 0.05]

Notes. N = 4,260. * = significant $p < .05$; ns = not significant. The unstandardized estimates (B), standard error (SE), and the 95% confidence intervals (CI) were obtained using percentile bootstrapping based on 5,000 bootstrap samples. A higher total delinquency frequency score (0 to 20) corresponds to more reported committed offences. A higher score on the well-being index (0 to 100) corresponds to higher levels of subjective overall well-being. A higher score on the primary goods proxy-items (1 to 5) corresponds to lower levels of satisfaction (i.e. more dissatisfaction), with one exception: a higher score on religion/spirituality (1 to 5) corresponds to lower levels of attributed importance.

6.3 Discussion

In this study, the etiological assumptions of the GLM were tested in a large sample of adolescents from the general population in Flanders, Belgium. More specifically, it was examined to what extent satisfaction with the 11 primary goods was related to adolescents' well-being (*GLM's first assumption*) and indirectly (through well-being) or directly related to delinquent behaviour (*GLM's second assumption*). To answer these questions, we collected self-report data from students in 80 secondary schools (as part of the 'JOP School Monitor 2'; Bradt et al., 2019; JeugdOnderzoeksPlatform, 2018) on overall subjective well-being (a combination of general life satisfaction and emotional well-being), life domain-specific satisfaction based on the primary goods, and delinquent behaviour. In the following sections, I elaborate on the findings from this study. Specific attention is paid to the most important primary goods that were found to be related to both adolescents' well-being and delinquency.

6.3.1 *The Relationship Between Well-being and Adolescent Delinquency*

Based on the self-report data of 4,260 adolescents we can conclude that there is a relatively small but statistically significant association between overall subjective well-being and self-reported delinquent behaviour. When taking a closer look into this relationship, we find that adolescents who reported committing at least one offence in the preceding year reported significantly lower overall well-being than adolescents who reported not having committed any offences. This was true for all five types of offences taken together (vandalism, shoplifting, theft, harassment and physical assault), as well as for each type of offence separately. The more offences someone committed in the preceding year, the lower their reported overall well-being. These results are consistent with the second assumption of the GLM, which states that offenders experience lower levels of well-being. They are also in line with previous cross-sectional studies examining the relationship between adolescent life satisfaction and delinquency (Buelga et al., 2008; Gonzalez et al., 2021; MacDonald et al., 2005; McKnight et al., 2002; Olson et al., 2020; Suldo & Huebner, 2004; Sun & Shek, 2010, 2012; Valois et al., 2001, 2002, 2006; Zullig et al., 2001).

Because of the cross-sectional nature of our study, we cannot draw conclusions on the direction or causality of this relationship. Based on the GLM and on previous findings, it could be inferred that the associations are in the hypothesized direction: from well-being to delinquency. However, the relationship could also be in the opposite direction, and/or well-being and offending behaviour may be influencing each other reciprocally. An additional problem with the self-report data lies in the fact that subjective well-being (and primary goods satisfaction) was assessed at the time of participation in the survey, while delinquency was self-reported about the preceding 12 months. In a strict sense, this means the self-reported delinquency preceded the primary goods satisfaction and well-being in terms of time. In line with this, longitudinal studies examining the relationship between adolescents' well-being and delinquency have found evidence for a relationship in both directions (Hanniball et al., 2018; Haranin et al., 2007; Jung & Choi, 2017; Lyons et al., 2013, 2014; Shek & Lin, 2016; Sun & Shek, 2013; Zhu & Shek, 2020a, 2020b, 2021).

6.3.2 *The Role of Primary Goods in Adolescents' Well-Being and Delinquency*

From the path analysis it can be inferred that primary goods (dis)satisfaction is related to adolescents' well-being and delinquency. For almost all primary goods, *more dissatisfaction* predicted *lower levels of well-being*. Some primary goods were both indirectly (through well-being) and directly related to delinquency: 'life' (financial situation), 'excellence in work' (education), 'relatedness' (with family and love life), and 'spirituality' (religion). For most of these primary goods, *more dissatisfaction* predicted *more delinquency*. As the exceptions from this list, *more dissatisfaction* with one's love life (as part of 'relatedness') and *less importance* of religion/'spirituality' predicted *less delinquent behaviour.* Furthermore, the primary good of 'community' was exclusively directly (and not indirectly) related to delinquency, where *more dissatisfaction* with 'community' (i.e. other social contacts) predicted *less delinquency.* Other goods were only indirectly (through well-being) related to delinquency: 'life' (living situation and safety), 'excellence in agency', 'inner peace', 'relatedness' (with friends), and 'pleasure'. In these cases, *more dissatisfaction* predicted *more delinquency* through *lower levels of well-being.* However, other primary goods were not related to either of the two outcome measures: 'life' (physical health), 'knowledge', 'excellence in play' and 'creativity'.

Based on these findings taken together, some tentative conclusions can be drawn about which primary goods could be especially relevant for both adolescents' well-being and juvenile offending. Particularly in line with the conclusions from Chapters 4 and 5, the data showed that the primary goods that are based on the three psychological needs of the Self-determination Theory ('relatedness', 'competence' and 'autonomy'; Deci & Ryan, 2000; Ryan & Deci, 2000b, 2017b) play an important role in both adolescents' well-being and delinquency, which will be detailed in the next sections.

6.3.3 *Relatedness: Family, Peers and Community*

Satisfaction with family relationships (as part of the GLM primary good and SDT need of 'relatedness') appeared as the second most important predictor of overall subjective well-being among adolescents, after mental health (i.e. 'inner peace'), that is, both more dissatisfaction with family relationships and more dissatisfaction with mental health was related to lower levels of well-being. This is consistent with many previous studies showing that family relationships have a large impact on adolescents' well-being (see also Chapter 4). Through supportive relationships with their parents, adolescents can (learn to) express their feelings in a safe environment (Bowlby, 1969; Cava et al., 2014; Proctor et al., 2009). Moreover, a secure attachment relationship with parents/caregivers serves as a basis to develop into a mentally healthy and well-adjusted adult. The attachment with parents influences how children develop social interactions with others, build resilience, self-reliance and emotion regulation skills (Bowlby, 1969; Gottfredson & Hirschi, 1990; Patterson & Dishion, 1985; Sroufe, 2005).

Additionally, from our analyses it appears that more dissatisfaction with family relationships was related to higher levels of delinquent behaviour. This resonates with one of the eight central criminogenic risk factors proposed by Andrews and Bonta (2010), namely family problems. As already discussed in Chapter 5, a vast amount of research confirms that especially single parent families, parental conflict and parenting practices characterized by a lack of supervision, support and affection, are important risk factors for (youth) delinquency (Bonta & Andrews, 2017; Demuth & Brown, 2004; Derzon, 2010; Glueck & Glueck, 1950; Gottfredson & Hirschi, 1990; Hoeve et al., 2009, 2011; Loeber & Stouthamer-Loeber, 1986; Onder & Yilmaz, 2012; Patterson & Dishion, 1985; Pinquart, 2017; Sampson & Laub, 1995; Vanassche et al., 2014; Wright & Cullen, 2001).

It has been assumed that during adolescence peers gain more importance over family, especially regarding their influence on delinquent behaviour (Burgess & Akers, 1966; Dishion et al., 1996; Massey et al., 2008; Messersmith & Schulenberg, 2010; Sutherland & Cressey, 1960). In our analyses, however, we only found an indirect effect of friendships, where more dissatisfaction about contacts with friends was related to more delinquency through lower levels of well-being, but no direct relationship. A direct relationship was found for satisfaction with one's love life (also part of 'relatedness') and social contacts with other people in their neighbourhood, clubs and associations (i.e. the primary good of 'community'), where greater satisfaction increased self-reported delinquency. Still, these effects were smaller - and in the opposite direction - compared to the ones found for family satisfaction. This finding suggests that although peers are relevant for adolescents' well-being and they can play a role in delinquent behaviour, they seem less important compared to the influence of family. These findings could also indicate that when adolescents are not satisfied with their family relationships, they may turn to their peers (including romantic partners) and other contacts in their community instead (Barnert et al., 2015). If these contacts engage in antisocial behaviour, they could encourage delinquency, which is again in line with one of the eight criminogenic risk factors: antisocial peers (Andrews & Bonta, 2010; Bonta & Andrews, 2017; Hirschi, 2017; Jacobs et al., 2020; Patterson & Dishion, 1985; Shortt et al., 2003; Troonbeeckx et al., 2015; Van Damme, Colins, Pauwels, et al., 2015; Van Damme et al., 2016; Wikström & Loeber, 2000).

Although we can only speculate about the explanation of these findings, it suggests that despite the satisfaction that juveniles derive from their social contacts, this does not always contribute to their prosocial development and can even predict more delinquent behaviour (Van Damme, Colins, Pauwels, et al., 2015; Van Damme et al., 2016). This also emphasizes the importance of considering whether the means used to fulfil the primary goods (i.e. the 'secondary goods') are appropriate and prosocial. For effective rehabilitation, this means it would not be enough to work on the satisfaction of primary goods and increase well-being without paying attention to exactly how they are pursued. The latter is in line with the GLM's recommendation of combining primary good achievement with criminogenic risk reduction in offender rehabilitation interventions (Ward & Fortune, 2013; Ward & Maruna, 2007).

6.3.4 *Competence: Excellence in Work and Life*

The second most important GLM primary good for both well-being and delinquent behaviour of adolescents appears to be 'excellence in work' ('competence' in SDT). Satisfaction with education was used as a proxy measure in this study to measure the need to work towards a career in which one can develop skills that provide a sense of pride, accomplishment and/or satisfaction (i.e., excellence or competence). We found that more dissatisfaction with education was related to lower levels of well-being and more delinquency. This is consistent with previous research showing that working towards a meaningful and successful life, in terms of education and a career, is an important factor in well-being (Ng et al., 2015; Proctor et al., 2009; Salmela-Aro & Tynkkynen, 2010).

When one's education fails to provide a sense of accomplishment and/or satisfaction, antisocial behaviour could serve as a substitute for one's needs and/or an outlet of frustration. Accordingly, problems with school and academic achievement are known to be important criminogenic risk factors (see also Chapter 5; Andrews & Bonta, 2010; Bonta & Andrews, 2017; Christle et al., 2005; Cottle et al., 2001; Grieger & Hosser, 2014; Hoffmann, 2020; Katsiyannis et al., 2008; Maguin & Loeber, 1996). Furthermore, without a certificate or diploma to acquire a well-paying position, criminality is often viewed as more profitable than a low-paying lawful job (Cullen et al., 1997; Jacobs & Wright, 1999; Troonbeeckx et al., 2015; Wright & Topalli, 2013).

Similarly, more dissatisfaction with one's financial situation (part of the primary good of 'life') appears to be an important predictor of more delinquency. As minors have few opportunities to obtain a well-paying lawful job, they are often financially dependent on their parents and/or caregivers. For some, this might put them in a situation in which they lack sufficient resources to meet their (basic) needs and want to fulfil these in other ways. Indeed, as discussed in Chapter 5, financial problems are related to juvenile delinquency (Hoeve et al., 2016; van Beek et al., 2021) and numerous studies have shown that financial gain is an important motivation for young offenders (Agnew, 1990; Farrington, 1993; Gudjonsson & Sigurdsson, 2007; Lopez, 2008; Nguyen & Bouchard, 2013; Putniņš, 2010; Shong et al., 2019; Troonbeeckx et al., 2015; Verdonck, 2017).

6.3.5 *Autonomy: Excellence in Agency*

As mentioned before, adolescence is a transition phase in which juveniles gain more independence but are also still (partly) bound by rules, regulations and parental influence which determine what they can or cannot do (Arnett, 1999; Soenens et al., 2017). This does not mean they do not have the freedom to make their own choices within the limitations of being a minor. Furthermore, despite their lack of (full) independence, adolescents can experience a sense of 'autonomy' (in SDT terms) and 'agency' (in GLM terms) through self-endorsement of their behaviour. Self-endorsed behaviours concern actions that are accepted as personally valuable and meaningful (Soenens et al., 2017; Van Petegem et al., 2012). For example, some can choose to follow their parent's decision and still feel autonomous, because they fully endorse their opinion and understand the importance of the decision. However, when parental and/or legal rules and regulations restrict juveniles in such a way that they feel coerced without a sense of self-endorsement, this can result in autonomy frustration (Soenens et al., 2017; Van Petegem et al., 2012).

Several studies showed that autonomy frustration can result in oppositional behaviour in adolescents (see Chapter 5; Brenning et al., 2019; Van Petegem et al., 2015, 2019), but in our study we did not find a direct relationship between delinquency and autonomy satisfaction (measured as satisfaction with how much the juveniles can decide about their own life). Nonetheless, more autonomy dissatisfaction significantly predicted lower levels of overall well-being in adolescents. Subsequently, we also found an indirect relationship of autonomy dissatisfaction on delinquency, via well-being, that is, in our sample, more dissatisfaction with their level of autonomy was related to lower levels of well-being, which in turn was related to more delinquency. The latter is in line with research demonstrating the benefits of self-endorsed functioning for subjective well-being (Ryan & Deci, 2000b; see also Chapter 4). These findings suggest that although a sense of autonomy or agency in adolescence might not be a direct contributor to delinquency, it can play an indirect role in offending behaviour with subjective well-being serving as a mediator.

6.3.6 *Inner Peace*

Another example of an indirect predictor of delinquency is the primary good of 'inner peace'. 'Inner peace' was measured as the satisfaction with one's mental health and was the strongest predictor of adolescent subjective well-being, that is, more dissatisfaction with one's mental health significantly was related to lower levels of well-being. This finding is in line with the results of the meta-analysis reported in Chapter 4. As in the meta-analysis, we should be cautious to interpret the magnitude of this effect, because there is a risk of spurious correlations. Various studies have demonstrated that someone's mood at the time of completing the questionnaires can affect the answers about mental health, emotional and overall well-being, thus artificially increasing the correlation (Diener et al., 1991; Eid & Diener, 2004; Gamble & Gärling, 2012). Nonetheless, a range of studies confirms the importance of mental health for adolescents' well-being. Furthermore, mental health could be especially salient throughout the period of adolescence because of the major changes and developments in emotion regulation that can impact their well-being (Arnett, 1999; Houben et al., 2015; Proctor et al., 2009; see also Chapter 4).

Although we did not find a direct relationship between mental health satisfaction and delinquency, we found an indirect relationship through adolescent subjective well-being. More dissatisfaction with one's mental health was related to lower levels of well-being, which in turn was related to more delinquency. This finding of an indirect relationship is in line with the GLM's assumption that mental health problems can present as obstacles in the pursuit of primary goods achievement and well-being (Barnao et al., 2016). Maladaptive coping and emotion regulation, such as substance abuse, can subsequently result in a loss of control and (in combination with other criminogenic risk factors) in offending behaviour (Barnao et al., 2016; Purvis et al., 2011). The latter is also in accordance with studies demonstrating the mediating role of substance abuse in the relationship between mental health problems and offending behaviour in juveniles (see also Chapter 5, Section 5.4.6; Craig et al., 2018; Guebert & Olver, 2014). At the same time, this finding resonates with the fact that substance abuse is one of the eight central criminogenic risk factors (Andrews & Bonta, 2010).

Furthermore, the fact that we did not find a direct relationship between mental health satisfaction and delinquency is consistent with the exclusion of mental health problems as a criminogenic risk factor (Andrews & Bonta, 2010; Bonta & Andrews, 2017). Yet, it contradicts several (meta-analytic) studies that found a relationship between mental health problems and adolescent (re-)offending (Colins et al., 2009, 2010; Hoeve et al., 2015; Wibbelink et al., 2017). This may be attributable to the fact that these studies (mostly) relied on bivariate studies, whereas we controlled for several factors (including all primary goods, overall well-being, gender, and age). Another explanation could be found in the fact that these studies primarily included detained adolescents with diagnosed (psychiatric) disorders, which reflects more extreme manifestations of delinquency and mental health problems compared to our sample from the general population. Despite these contradictory findings we can conclude that the primary good of 'inner peace' can play an important role in adolescents' well-being and delinquency.

6.3.7 *Spirituality*

Notably, we measured the primary good of 'spirituality' differently compared to the other primary goods, that is, we used an item that assessed the perceived importance of the good rather than satisfaction with it. Higher levels of importance were related to lower levels of well-being and (subsequently) more reported delinquency. This finding contradicts many studies that reported religiosity as a protective factor in deterring delinquency (Baier & Wright, 2001; Eryılmaz, 2018; Hirschi & Stark, 1969; Johnson et al., 2000; Miller & Vuolo, 2018; Sumter et al., 2018) and well-being (Diener et al., 2011; Lim & Putnam, 2010; Regnerus, 2003; Tay et al., 2014). This unexpected finding may be explained by the different approach in measurement (importance vs. satisfaction), that is, previous work showed that difficult circumstances (such as poverty, low education level and safety issues) can lead to higher levels of religiosity (i.e. attaching more importance to religion) and lower levels of subjective well-being (Diener et al., 2011; Tay et al., 2014). Thus, for some youth, (focusing on) religion could provide solace in difficult circumstances, which is simultaneously linked to both lower well-being and a higher likelihood of delinquent behaviour.

However, attaching a high level of importance to religion does not always equate to a high degree of religiosity, religious practice and/or adherence to religious beliefs (Desmond et al., 2010). Furthermore, as also discussed in Chapter 4, GLM's definition of 'spirituality' expands beyond religiosity. It refers to the need to discover a sense of meaning and purpose in life (Purvis, 2010; Purvis et al., 2014; Willis et al., 2013), which can be achieved through several means, including religion (van Dierendonck, 2012; van Dierendonck & Mohan, 2006). Based on our meta-analysis in Chapter 4, we concluded that finding meaning in life is an important factor for adolescents' well-being, regardless of the source of this meaning (Dankulincova Veselska et al., 2018; Holder et al., 2016; Howell et al., 2013). Thus, in future research (see the following chapters), the primary good of 'spirituality' should also be assessed in a broader sense, including satisfaction with finding one's meaning in life as well as satisfaction with one's religion/religious practice.

6.3.8 *Less Important Goods*

In our analyses, several primary goods proxy-items were not directly related to adolescents' well-being nor to delinquency: 'knowledge', 'creativity', 'excellence in play', and physical health as part of 'life'. The fact that these primary goods were not directly related, however, does not mean they do not or cannot contribute via other primary goods. Although we found no indications of multi-collinearity, our path model included the possibility of covariance between all predictors, and most goods were found to be significantly related to each other (see Appendix E[13] for the correlation matrix and VIF values). For example, regarding the primary good 'excellence in play', fun leisure activities such as playing a team sport with friends could also provide for 'relatedness' and 'pleasure' (Zullig & White, 2011); goods that are directly related to adolescents' well-being and (in)directly to delinquent behaviour. Similarly, the primary good of 'knowledge' (access to information about things that are of interest to a person) relates to education satisfaction and could in that way serve as 'excellence in work'.

13 See https://www.elevenpub.com/en/content/appendices-9789462364257.

Obviously, an alternative interpretation of these null findings is that some primary goods are just not (as) important to adolescents. For example, adolescents' physical health (as part of healthy 'life') might be less important to them as they do not often experience (serious) illness due to their young age. Nonetheless, we should keep in mind that our self-report assessment may have also played a role; the primary goods encompass theoretically complex and broad concepts that are difficult to capture in a single item.

It is also important to mention that these results are based on the entire group of adolescents, but there may be differences at the individual level in the degree of relevance that adolescents assign to the various goods (Oishi et al., 1999). The developers of the GLM also recognize this as they argue that the relative importance of certain goods and the many possible ways how people aim to achieve them (by means of secondary goods) may vary according to one's personal situation, norms, values and priorities (Ward & Fortune, 2013; Ward & Maruna, 2007). In line with this, a number of studies found a moderating effect of importance ratings attached to life-domain satisfaction effects on overall subjective well-being (Hsieh, 2016; Sirgy & Lee, 2018; Sirgy et al., 2019).

6.4 Conclusion

In conclusion, the etiological assumptions of the GLM regarding well-being and the explanation of delinquent behaviour are largely applicable to adolescents from the general population. Almost all primary goods were indirectly (through well-being) and/or directly related to adolescent delinquency. Especially primary goods that are based on the psychological needs of the Self-determination Theory ('relatedness', 'competence' and 'autonomy'; Deci & Ryan, 2000; Ryan & Deci, 2000b, 2017b) play an important role in both adolescents' well-being and delinquency. Furthermore, a notable conclusion from our study is that while greater satisfaction with primary goods was usually related to less self-reported delinquency, the opposite was true for 'relatedness' (with partner) and 'community' (other social contacts). It is therefore deemed essential for rehabilitation interventions to not only focus on how satisfied juveniles are with their primary goods achievement, but also examine the ways in which they (try to) fulfil them.

6.5 Limitations and Remaining Questions

Despite the clear conclusions derived from the current study, some important concerns and questions remain. Although we have attempted to avoid some of the methodological limitations of previous studies by using a large sample, including all 11 primary goods, using a context-free well-being measure and including several types of delinquent behaviour, this study also has its limitations. First, we used self-report measures, which may be subject to several biases. A commonly suggested bias is the tendency of people to answer self-report measures of well-being based on momentary experiences, memory and context, thus not reflecting a general or even accurate assessment (Kahneman, 1999; Schwarz & Strack, 1991). Additionally, the relationship between well-being and delinquent behaviour could potentially be explained (in part) by social desirability (Gilman & Barry, 2003; Singh, 1979), that is, youth who want to answer the questions in a socially desirable way could report both high levels of well-being and none or little delinquent behaviour. As already discussed in Chapter 4 regarding the well-being measures (Section 4.4), more recent studies have largely refuted these claims (Diener et al., 2013; Larsen et al., 1985; Schimmack & Oishi, 2005). With regard to the measures of delinquency, some suggest self-report (in youth) might be biased (Junger-Tas & Marshall, 1999; Van Widenfelt et al., 2003), while others have shown that they can be deemed reliable and valid for research purposes (Bernasco, 2013; Junger-Tas & Marshall, 1999; Muris et al., 2003; Singh, 1979).

Second, as mentioned before, the GLM's primary goods and well-being are complex and broad theoretical constructs, which are not easily captured with a few items.[14] Although for our data a linear relationship between primary goods, well-being and delinquency was most appropriate, there were statistical indications that a non-linear relationship might have also been a possibility (see this chapter, fn 11). This is in accordance with other studies that demonstrated a non-linear and more complex relationship between life domain–specific satisfaction and overall well-being (González et al., 2010; Rojas, 2006). Furthermore, we did not include a measure of the relative importance that juveniles attach to the primary goods and how they (aim to) achieve them (i.e. the secondary goods). Which primary goods are more important than others and how a person aims to fulfil their primary goods can differ according to a person's particular set of (cultural, social and personal) values, circumstances, abilities and opportunities (d'Andrade, 1995; Den Uyl, 1991; Griffin, 1996; Kekes, 1989; Rasmussen, 1999; Ward, 2002a, 2002b; Ward & Maruna, 2007). Moreover, as discussed in previous chapters, the GLM (Purvis, 2010; Purvis et al., 2011; Ward, 2002a, 2002b), its underlying theories (Arnhart, 1998; Emmons, 1996; Murphy, 2001; Rasmussen, 1999) and empirical research (Milyavskaya et al., 2009; Petrie, 2013; Sheldon & Niemiec, 2006; Sirgy & Lee, 2018; Sirgy & Wu, 2009; Van den Broeck et al., 2019) stress the importance of having a balanced and structured life plan; one in which all goods necessary for well-being are attained in a coherent manner without conflict. More detailed and qualitative research on how young offenders view well-being, what is important to them regarding the primary goods, how they (aim to) achieve them,

14 In 2020, when our data-collection was already completed, Harper et al. (2020) published the Good Lives Questionnaire, which contains 35 items aimed to measure the 11 GLM primary goods. However, based on their factor analysis they found only 5 factors rather than 11. This suggests, once again, that the primary goods are not easily measured and a number of the primary goods are likely to be correlated.

what obstacles can get in the way and how this relates to their delinquent behaviour, could shed light on those more complex mechanisms (see Chapters 7 and 8).

Finally, although the effects in our results proved to be statistically significant, most were (very) small, this was especially true for the indirect effect sizes. This is probably because of the large statistical power provided by our large sample size. Very small effect sizes indicate that these relationships are rather weak, raising the question of whether they are meaningful in real life. Therefore, we should be cautious about generalizing the results and translating them into practice. Additionally, our results are based on a sample of adolescents from the general population, which may differ from detained adolescent offenders. Moreover, as already mentioned regarding the association between well-being and delinquency, the relationships between primary goods and delinquency are similarly correlational in nature and may be bi-directional. Therefore, we cannot infer causality from our statistical models (Hayes, 2017). To use the etiological assumptions of the GLM as a basis for the rehabilitation of juvenile offenders, more research is necessary with (detained) adolescent offenders (see the next chapters).

7 Examining Direct and Indirect Pathways to Juvenile Delinquency in Detained Adolescents

Testing the Associations Between Primary Goods, Well-Being, Mental Health Problems, Criminogenic Risk and Delinquency in Detained Adolescent Boys

In the previous chapter, I empirically tested the etiological assumptions of the Good Lives Model (GLM) for explaining well-being and delinquency in a sample of adolescents from the general population. Based on this analysis, we found a small but statistically significant relationship between adolescents' subjective well-being and self-reported delinquency. Furthermore, the statistical models showed indirect (through overall well-being) as well as direct effects of primary goods satisfaction on adolescent delinquency. Satisfaction with several GLM primary goods showed a significant and direct association with both the adolescents' well-being and delinquency ('life' in the form of financial situation, 'excellence in work' in the form of education, 'relatedness' with family and a partner and 'spirituality'), while some primary goods were only directly related to well-being ('life' in the form of living situation and safety, 'excellence in agency', 'inner peace', 'relatedness' with friends and 'pleasure') or to delinquency ('community'). All primary goods that were directly related to the adolescents' well-being were also indirectly related to delinquency through well-being. Other primary goods (i.e. 'knowledge', 'creativity', 'excellence in play' and 'life' in the form of physical health) appeared less important and showed no statistically significant relationships with either outcome measure.

However, to adequately explain the complexity of delinquent behaviour it is not enough to merely determine the existence of an association between delinquency, well-being and primary goods satisfaction. To explain juvenile delinquent behaviour more in depth, it is also necessary to examine the mechanisms that account for these relationships. Four types of problems that can hamper primary good attainment have been proposed and identified (in adult offenders). That is, individuals can: (1) *lack the capacities* and opportunities to satisfy their primary goods in a prosocial way, (2) *lack scope* in the range of goods they pursue and achieve, (3) use *inappropriate (antisocial) means* to obtain primary goods, and/or (4) *lack coherence* in pursuing different goods (Purvis, 2010; Purvis et al., 2011; Ward, 2002a, 2002b; Ward & Marshall, 2004; Ward & Maruna, 2007). Furthermore, the GLM states that the prosocial attainment of primary goods can be hampered due to both personal (*internal*) limitations (e.g. a lack of knowledge or skills) and environmental (*external*) disadvantages (e.g. lack of resources or opportunities). In particular, the criminogenic risk factors from the Risk Need Responsivity (RNR) model (Bonta & Andrews, 2017) are suggested as important (internal and external) obstacles to obtaining primary goods via prosocial means (Purvis, 2010; Purvis et al., 2011, 2014; Ward & Stewart, 2003a).

Based on the literature study in Chapter 5, we concluded that several criminogenic risk factors (a number of which are specific to the developmental period of adolescence), such as: emotional problems, family problems, impulsivity and antisocial peer influences are indeed hypothesized to hinder adolescents in the prosocial ways, and/or encourage the antisocial ways, to satisfy their primary goods and pursue well-being. Furthermore, although it is usually not considered a criminogenic risk factor, mental health problems are hypothesized to present salient obstacles for detained adolescents (Barnao et al., 2016; Colins et al., 2010; Cottle et al., 2001; Vermeiren et al., 2006; Wibbelink et al., 2017; see the Introduction in Chapter 1 and the elaboration of the primary good of 'inner peace' in Chapter 5, Section 5.4.6). The potential role of the RNR model's criminogenic risk factors and other possible obstacles (i.e. mental health problems) for the pursuit of primary goods satisfaction and well-being, however, have not yet been (quantitatively) examined together in relation to adolescent delinquency.

Therefore, in this chapter, we will not only examine the relationships between primary goods satisfaction, well-being and offending behaviour in adolescents, but we will also examine the hypothesized underlying obstacles in the prosocial pursuit of their goods and well-being. For this purpose, a sample of 170 male detained adolescents filled out a survey within two weeks after their arrest about their subjective well-being and primary goods satisfaction in the 4-week period before their arrest. Based on the findings in the previous chapter, some changes and additions were made in the primary goods proxy-items, to assess them in more detail (see Table 7.1). Additionally, self-reported offending behaviour in the preceding year and experience of (internalizing and externalizing) mental health problems were measured. The survey questions were combined with a recidivism risk assessment interview (using the Youth Level of Service/Case Management Inventory), to identify potential criminogenic risk factors. These data together serve to test the hypothesis that obstacles in (prosocially) obtaining primary goods (i.e., due to criminogenic risk factors and mental health problems), result in lower levels of well-being and explain offending behaviour in adolescents.

7.1 Method

7.1.1 Setting and Sampling Procedure

This study was conducted in two secure juvenile detention institutions for male[1] adolescents: one in Belgium (Flanders) and one in the Netherlands. The study received (ethical) approval by the director of the Flemish Youth Detention Centres, the Dutch Custodial Institutions Agency (Dienst Justitiële Inrichtingen), and the Social and Societal Ethics Committee of the Catholic University of Leuven (G-2017 10 945). The recruitment period ran between July 2018 and December 2019.

Most of the participants (90.6%) were recruited in the Youth Detention Centre (YDC)[2] in Everberg, Belgium (Flanders), where they were awaiting their trial and sentence after arrest. During the data collection period the new Flemish Juvenile Delinquency Decree had not yet (fully) taken effect. This meant that, within five days the judge decided whether the juvenile's pre-trial detention was extended by one month. After one month, the judge could again prolong the pre-trial detention for a last time with one extra month. During their stay, a team of criminologists, psychologists, teachers and social workers assessed and observed the juveniles to provide the court with a substantiated written advice on the recidivism risk and need for detention. Both the infrastructure (i.e. aggravated locked doors, high fences and barred windows) and the daily regime (i.e., strict rules, scheduled activities, limited and scheduled contact with close relatives) of the YDC are meant to secure and protect the juveniles and society. Adolescents (aged 14 to 17 years old) admitted to the YDC who had committed a criminal offence, whose pre-trial detention had been prolonged for at least one month, who were capable of understanding, speaking and reading Dutch, and who were prosecuted by a court in the east of the country[3] were eligible

1 The initial aim of the study was to include both adolescent boys and girls. The two participating institutions, however, only admitted boys. Initially, one other secure residential institution (a forensic psychiatric institution) in Belgium (Flanders) participated in the study. This institution admitted both boys and girls, but only two met the inclusion criteria during the recruitment period. Of these two, only one was a girl. The other eligible participant in this forensic psychiatric institution was a boy, but because of the large differences in setting, regime and treatment methods compared to the detention institutions, he was excluded from the study as well.

2 Gemeenschapsinstelling (GI) De Grubbe, Everberg (BE).

3 This inclusion criterion was meant to ensure that participants included in the follow-up study (see Chapter 10), who were sentenced by the judge to be transferred to detention, would be admitted to an institution within travel distance of the researcher. Being prosecuted by a court in the eastern part of the country usually meant that a juvenile, who was sentenced to a longer detention period of more than two months and five days, was transferred to another secure residential institution, also in the eastern part of the country (i.e., Gemeenschapsinstelling (GI) De Kempen, Mol, BE). Compared to GI De Grubbe in Everberg that is focused on orientation and assessment, GI De Kempen in Mol is focused more on rehabilitation and re-integration (see Chapter 10).

for inclusion. Eligible participants were addressed individually and personally by the researcher, receiving oral and written information about the aims, content, and duration of the study (including the follow-up study, see Chapter 10, and for a random sub-sample of the qualitative interview, see Chapter 8).

To increase the number of participants we chose to include a youth detention institution in the south of the Netherlands as well. In this Dutch Juvenile Justice Institution (JJI),[4] some juveniles were awaiting their trial, while others were serving their sentence. The infrastructure and daily regime were quite similar to that of the Flemish YDC. Similar inclusion criteria as in the Flemish YDC were used: adolescents (aged 14 to 17 years old) admitted to the JJI who had committed a criminal offence and were sentenced to (pre-trial) detention, who were capable of understanding, speaking, and reading Dutch, were eligible for inclusion. Different from the Flemish YDC, for the Dutch sample we did not take into account which court had sentenced them. Additionally, unlike the procedure in the Flemish YDC, the researcher was not permitted access to eligible participants before they agreed to participate. Therefore, a staff member of the institution first had to provide the verbal and written information about the aims, content and duration of the study. Juveniles who agreed to participate were then addressed by the researcher personally.

Written and verbal active informed consent was asked from the juveniles before participation. The parent(s)/caregiver(s) of the participants also received a letter including information about the aims and practical aspects of the study. In the Flemish YDC, when their child was younger than 16 years old, the parent(s)/caregiver(s) were given the opportunity to refuse participation (i.e. passive informed consent). In the Dutch JJI, all parent(s)/caregiver(s) (independent of the boys' age)[5] were given the opportunity to refuse participation (i.e. passive informed consent). Participants were guaranteed that their information would be treated anonymously, confidentially (e.g. not shared with the police, the court, the residential institution or others), in accordance with European and national privacy laws.[6] Furthermore, they were assured that participation was voluntary, they could stop their participation at any time and refusal or acceptance to participate in the study would not affect their judicial status or stay in the institution.

During the recruitment period, 457 juveniles were admitted to the Flemish YDC, of which 182 met inclusion criteria and were asked to participate. Twenty-six (14.3%) refused participation themselves and in one case (0.5%) the parents refused participation of their

4 Justitiële Jeugd Inrichting (JJI) Het Keerpunt, Cadier en Keer (NL).

5 This differed from the procedure in the Flemish YDC because of restrictions placed by the Dutch Custodial Institutions Agency.

6 Except for information suggesting an immediate threat of severe danger for someone else or the juveniles themselves, which would be shared with the appropriate authorities. This only included information about acts in the future and did not include information about (criminal or deviant) acts in the past.

son, leading to 155 consenting participants (85.2%). In the Dutch JJI, to my knowledge,[7] 120 juveniles were admitted, of which only 28 met inclusion criteria and were asked to participate.[8] Twelve (42.9%) refused participation, resulting in 16 consenting participants (57.1%). Taking participants from these two institutions together led to a total sample of 171 participants. During the data cleaning process, it became apparent that one participant did not complete any of the questionnaires (he only participated in the risk assessment) and was therefore removed from the dataset, resulting in a final sample of 170 participants.[9]

7.1.2 Study Procedure

About two weeks (on average 16 days) after their arrest, participants were asked to fill out a survey on an electronic tablet. This two-week period gave them time to get used to the new situation, but was considered short enough to still remember four weeks before their arrest. The first part of the survey consisted of questions concerning demographic information (i.e. age, ethnic background, school background, family and living situation). Secondly, the participants were asked about their overall subjective well-being (internalizing and externalizing), mental health problems and primary goods satisfaction, for the four weeks prior to their arrest. Specifically, participants were asked to retrospectively (while thinking about the four weeks before their arrest, when they were still in the community) fill out the Satisfaction With Life Scale (SWLS-CV; five items on a 5-point Likert scale), the Scale of Positive and Negative Experiences (SPANE; 12 items on a 5-point Likert scale), the Strengths and Difficulties Questionnaire (SDQ; 25 items on a 3-point Likert scale), and items concerning their level of satisfaction with the proxy primary goods (20 items on a 5-point Likert scale). Additionally, participants were asked to retrospectively answer six self-report items about their offending behaviour in the preceding year (12 months). After they finished the survey, the participants were interviewed about the preceding year (12 months) up until the time of their arrest, using the Youth Level of Service/Case Management Inventory (YLS/CMI) to assess their criminogenic risk factors and recidivism risk level. These assessment sessions varied in duration from approximately 45 to 90 minutes.

---

7 In contrast to the procedure in the Flemish YDC, I had no insight into who was admitted to the Dutch JJI but was dependent on the information passed on by staff members.

8 This is partly because a substantial number of juveniles admitted to the Dutch JJI were 18 years or older (because of the Dutch adolescent delinquency law) or were not able to speak and understand Dutch (usually unaccompanied refugee minors). Additionally, near the end of the study's recruitment period, it was decided by the Dutch government that the institution was being shut down due to a national reorganization.

9 Nevertheless, the numbers of included participants in the analyses in this chapter varies because of missing values on the different items.

7.1.3 *Measures*

Subjective Well-Being

Similar to the previous chapter (see Section 6.1.2), well-being was operationalized as subjectively experienced overall well-being, consisting of a standardized composite score of general life satisfaction (Satisfaction With Life Scale-Child Version; Diener et al., 1985; Gadermann et al., 2010) and emotional well-being, both positive and negative (Scale of Positive and Negative Experience; Diener et al., 2010). In this way, well-being is measured at both the cognitive (general life satisfaction) and affective (emotional well-being, positive and negative) level. This tripartite structure of subjective well-being (life satisfaction, positive affect and negative affect) is based on a large number of studies that describe this operationalization as reliable and valid (Metler & Busseri, 2017; Wallander & Koot, 2016).[10]

Satisfaction with Life Scale-Child Version (SWLS-CV). To assess general life satisfaction, the five items of the Dutch version of the Satisfaction with Life Scale-Child Version were used (SWLS-CV; Diener et al., 1985; Gadermann et al., 2010; Serie et al., 2017a). The items (e.g., 'I am happy with my life') are answered on a 5-point Likert scale (from 1 = *strongly disagree* to 5 = *strongly agree*). Adding the items results in a sum score between 5 and 25, which has been found to be reliable and valid in measuring the cognitive evaluation of general life satisfaction from a context-free perspective (Gadermann et al., 2010; Ortuno-Sierra et al., 2019). The reliability analysis in the current sample showed high internal consistency for this scale (Cronbach's $\alpha = .86$).

Scale of Positive and Negative Experience (SPANE). Emotional well-being was measured with the Dutch version of the Scale of Positive and Negative Experience (SPANE; Diener et al., 2010; Serie et al., 2017b). The scale consists of six positive and six negative emotions, for which participants indicate how often these emotions were experienced during the past four weeks (from 1 = *very rarely or never* to 5 = *very often or always*). The scores can be added up to the following subscales: positive affect (PA; with a possible sum score ranging from 6 to 30) and negative affect (NA; with a possible sum score ranging from 6 to 30). The SPANE has been found to be reliable and valid for measuring emotional well-being in adults and adolescents (Jovanović, 2015; Telef, 2013). In accordance with these earlier studies, the reliability analyses in the current sample showed high internal consistency for both the positive emotion (Cronbach's $\alpha = .82$) and the negative emotion subscale (Cronbach's $\alpha = .81$).

10 See also the elaboration on the operationalization of well-being in Chapter 4, Section 4.1.1.

The principal component analysis[11] of the items of the three scales together (SWLS-CV, PA, and NA) in the current sample confirmed that a three-component factor structure of subjective well-being was possible, but favoured taking them together as a single factor which produced high internal consistency (Cronbach's α = .81). Subsequently, the standardized composite sum score was used as 'the well-being index' (see Chapter 6, Section 6.1.2 for a more elaborate description of this sum score), where 0 indicates the lowest overall subjective well-being and 100 indicates the highest.

GLM Primary Goods Satisfaction

The attainment of the GLM primary goods was measured with domain-specific life satisfaction as proxy-measures. The same proxy-items were used as in the previous chapter (see Section 6.1.2) with a few exceptions (see Table 7.1 for an overview). The primary good of 'spirituality' was now measured by asking about the level of satisfaction with religion/spirituality as well as having meaning in life.[12] Furthermore, three items were added to measure 'relatedness'; they asked about the satisfaction of the participants with their number of friends,[13] the relationship with their mother and the relationship with their father.[14] This resulted in 20 items for which the participants were asked how satisfied they were on a 5-point Likert scale (from 1 = *very dissatisfied* to 5 = *very satisfied*) for the following domains: financial situation, living situation, safety, physical health, access to information, education, leisure activities, autonomy (agency), mental health, family relationships, (number of) friends, love life, other social contacts in the neighbourhood/clubs/associations, religion/spirituality, meaning in life, creativity and pleasure/enjoyment. For the purpose of this study, all 20 primary goods proxy-items were recoded in such a way that a higher score indicates lower levels of satisfaction (i.e. more dissatisfaction).

---

11 The exploratory factor analysis (principal component analysis) did not reveal the clear three-component factor structure as found in Chapter 6 without fixing the number of factors to three, probably due to the small(er) sample size.

12 To increase consistency of the items, the proxy-item for the primary good of 'spirituality' was now assessed in the same format as all others (asking about satisfaction instead of importance). Furthermore, from the previous chapters it became clear that the primary good of 'spirituality' does not only refer to religion, but also to a sense of meaning and purpose in life. Therefore, compared to the study in Chapter 6, two items were now added: one concerning satisfaction with religion/spirituality and one concerning satisfaction with the meaning of one's life.

13 In Chapter 6 it became clear that, contrary to expectations based on literature claiming that peer relationships are important for adolescents, 'satisfaction with friendships' was not (strongly) related to either well-being or delinquency. To further examine this finding, we included an extra item asking about the satisfaction with the number of friends (quantity) in addition to the satisfaction with the relationships with friends (quality).

14 This was because we aimed to examine the differential effect of the relationship with parents compared to the relationship with family in general.

Table 7.1 Proxy-Measures of the 11 GLM Primary Goods

Primary goods	Proxy-items: How satisfied are you with …
Life	… how much money you have? … where you live? … how safe you feel? … your physical health?
Knowledge	… your access to information about things that interest you (e.g., on the internet, in magazines or courses)?
Excellence in work	… your education?
Excellence in play	… your leisure activities (hobby's, sports, music …)?
Excellence in agency	… how much you can decide about your own life?
Inner peace	… your mental health?
Relatedness	… your relationships with your family? … your relationship with your mother? * … your relationship with your father? * … your social contacts with friends? … your number of friends? * … your love life?
Community	… your social contacts with other people (in your neighbourhood, clubs/ associations)?
Spirituality	… your religion/spirituality? * … how much meaning your life has? *
Creativity	… how creative you can be (with trying new things, art, music, solving problems)?
Pleasure	… how much you can enjoy yourself (with e.g. good food, a trip, a movie)?

Notes. *These items were added compared to the study in Chapter 6. The items in this table are translated from Dutch to English.

Mental Health Problems: Strengths and Difficulties Questionnaire (SDQ)

To assess mental health problems, the Dutch version of the Strengths and Difficulties Questionnaire – Self-Report (SDQ; Treffers & Van Widenfelt, 2000) was administered. The SDQ is a 25-item questionnaire developed by Goodman (1997) for assessing psychosocial adjustment of children and adolescents. The items ask about both strengths and difficulties in five domains (sum scores): emotional problems, behavioural/conduct problems, hyperactivity, peer problems, and prosocial behaviour. For each item, three response categories are possible: 0 = *not true*, 1 = *somewhat true*, and 2 = *certainly true*. Five of the 25 items are positively worded 'strengths' that are reversed coded when contributing to the emotional problems, peer problems, conduct problems or hyperactivity subscales. The five items of the prosocial behaviour subscale are not used in this study.

Adding the sum scores of the emotional problems (five items), conduct problems (five items), peer problems (five items), and hyperactivity (five items) subscales results in a 'total difficulties' score (20 items; with a sum score ranging from 0 to 40). The 'total difficulties' score can be divided into 'normal' (≤ 15), 'borderline' (16-19), and 'abnormal' or 'problematic' (≥ 20). Furthermore, it is possible to construct two overarching subscales to discriminate between internalizing problems (by summing the emotional and peer problems subscales) and externalizing problems (by summing the conduct problems and hyperactivity subscales). Each of these subscales has a possible sum score ranging from 0 to 20 (Goodman et al., 2010). The internal consistency, test-retest reliability, and validity of the various SDQ scales were found to be acceptable to good (Goodman, 2001; Muris et al., 2003; Van Widenfelt et al., 2003). The reliability analyses in the current sample showed high internal consistency for the 'total difficulties score' (Cronbach's α = .75) and the externalizing problems subscale (Cronbach's α = .76), but a low internal consistency was found for the internalizing problems subscale (Cronbach's α = .50).

Self-Reported Delinquency

To assess delinquency, participants were asked how often (0 = *never*, 1 = *once*, 2 = *twice*, 3 = *three times*, or 4 = *more than three times*) they had committed six different types of offences in the preceding 12 months. The types of offences were: vandalism ('deliberately damaging or breaking something in the street, at school, or in another public place'), shoplifting ('stealing something from a shop or department store'), theft ('stealing something from another person, e.g. money, bicycle, cell phone or something else'), harassment ('harassing or threatening someone'), physical assault ('beating up somebody so badly that he/she sustained injuries'), and drug dealing ('selling drugs'). The same scale was used in the previous chapter (see Section 6.1.2), except now drug dealing is included as an extra item, because a large proportion of the detained adolescents were arrested for drug dealing. Combining the six frequency scores resulted in a total delinquency frequency score ranging from 0 to 24.[15]

15 It is sometimes recommended to use 'variety' scores of delinquent behaviours over 'frequency' scores (Sweeten, 2012). We examined whether this made a difference, but similar results were obtained using a delinquency 'variety' score (measured as the number of different offences committed: a score between 1 and 6) compared to the 'frequency' score (the sum of the self-reported frequency of the six offences combined). Moreover, 'frequency' scores were preferred in this study because we were interested in the extent of delinquent behaviour, not just the number of offence types committed.

Recidivism Risk Assessment: Youth Level of Service/Case Management Inventory (YLS/CMI)

To assess recidivism risk and criminogenic risk factors, a structured risk assessment was conducted using the Dutch version of the Youth Level of Service/Case Management Inventory (YLS/CMI; de Ruiter & Hildebrand, 2009; Hoge & Andrews, 2006). The YLS/CMI is designed to assess the level of recidivism risk and criminogenic needs in youth aged 12 to 18. It is based on the Level of Service Inventory-Revised (LSI-R), developed for recidivism risk assessment of adult offenders by Andrews and Bonta (1995). The YLS/CMI consists of 42 items (scored as 1 = *present* or 0 = *absent*) divided into eight subscales (sum scores) representing the 'central eight' criminogenic risk factors of the RNR model of Andrews and Bonta (1995, 2010): prior and current offences/dispositions (five items), family circumstances/parenting (six items), education/employment (seven items), peer relations (four items), substance abuse (five items), leisure/recreation (three items), personality/behaviour (seven items), and attitudes/orientation (five items). A higher score corresponds to more risk factors present and a higher risk of recidivism. The total risk score can range from 0 to 42, which can be divided into 'low' (0 to 8), 'moderate' (9 to 22), 'high' (23 to 34) and 'very high' (35 to 42) risk. The instrument has proven good to excellent inter-rater reliability (de Ruiter & Hildebrand, 2009; Hoge & Andrews, 2006; Koh et al., 2020; Rocque & Plummer-Beale, 2014) and acceptable concurrent and predictive validity (de Ruiter & Hildebrand, 2009; Hilterman et al., 2014; Hoge & Andrews, 2006; Koh et al., 2020; Olver et al., 2009, 2012, 2009; Schwalbe, 2007).

The guidelines for the administration of the YLS/CMI recommend that the scoring is based on information from an interview with the juvenile, a review of clinical and judicial records, and retrieval of information from other collateral sources, such as the school, family members and parents (de Ruiter & Hildebrand, 2009; Hoge & Andrews, 2006). However, in our study it was not possible/permitted to access the participants' records or collateral informants. Therefore, the scoring was based solely on the YLS/CMI interview conducted with the participants. Rating YLS measures based on a single information source (e.g. only the interview) is, however, a common and accepted practice for research purposes (Labrecque et al., 2018; Rocque & Plummer-Beale, 2014).

The inter-rater reliability of the YLS/CMI scoring based only on the interview was examined. The intraclass correlation coefficient (ICC) was calculated for 25 cases that were independently scored by the principal researcher and a second rater. We calculated the ICCs and their 95% confidence intervals in SPSS (version 27), based on a single-rater, absolute agreement, two-way mixed-effects model (Koo & Li, 2016; McGraw & Wong, 1996; Shrout & Fleiss, 1979). The ICCs were calculated for all risk domains and for the total score. For the single measure ICCs, the following critical values were selected: $ICC \geq .90$ = *excellent*, $.75 \leq ICC < .90$ = *good*, $.50 \leq ICC < .75$ = *moderate*, $ICC < .50$ = *poor*

(Koo & Li, 2016). The ICCs for the risk domains and total score ranged from .82 to .99, and can thus be classified as 'good' to 'excellent' (see Table 7.2).

Table 7.2 Intraclass Correlation Coefficients (ICCs) for YLS/CMI Risk Domains and Total Score

YLS/CMI risk domains	ICC	95% CI	*F*
1. Prior and current offences/ Dispositions	.98	[.96, .99]	109.32***
2. Family Circumstances/Parenting	.91	[.80, .96]	21.72***
3. Education/Employment	.93	[.84, .97]	30.68***
4. Peer relations	.86	[.72, .93]	13.50***
5. Substance abuse	.99	[.97, .99]	142.39***
6. Leisure/Recreation	.82	[.63, .92]	9.56***
7. Personality/Behavior	.86	[.71, .94]	13.78***
8. Attitudes/Orientation	.86	[.71, .94]	12.79***
Total score	.98	[.95, .99]	89.50***

Notes. *** = $p < .001$; $df1 = 24$, $df2 = 24$. The ICCs and their 95% confidence intervals are based on a single-rater, absolute agreement, two-way mixed-effects model. YLS/CMI = Youth Level of Service/Case Management Inventory.

7.1.4 Statistical Analyses

First, to describe the sample we used descriptive statistics of the participants' age, school background, ethnic background, family situation, well-being scores, primary goods proxy-items, self-reported offences, mental health problem scores and criminogenic risk. Next, the association between overall subjective well-being and juvenile delinquency was examined. We examined the relationship between the well-being index and the number of self-reported offences (based on the total frequency score of the six offence items). This was done using a correlational analysis and a one-way Analysis of Variance (ANOVA) examining the differences in well-being between four groups: adolescents who reported having committed none of the six offences,[16] one offence, two offences, and three or more offences. All analyses were conducted using SPSS (version 27).

Subsequently, to examine the hypothesized (direct and indirect) paths between the primary goods (the 20 proxy-items), the well-being index and delinquency frequency

16 Some stated they were innocent of committing any of the surveyed offences in the preceding year ($n = 4$), while most ($n = 9$) reported other offences not included in this study, such as truancy, drug use, online offences and sexual assault.

(total score of all six offences), we used the computational tool PROCESS version 3.5 in SPSS (version 27).[17] PROCESS performs mediation, moderation and conditional process analyses similar to structural equation modelling (SEM), but uses bootstrapping to simulate the sampling distribution (Hayes, 2017; Hayes et al., 2017). The number of bootstrap samples for percentile bootstrap confidence intervals (95%) was set at 5,000.

In the next step, we examined the role of possible obstacles by conducting the same path analyses again, but including internalizing and externalizing mental health problems (total subscales of the SDQ) and criminogenic risk (total score of the YLS/CMI) as covariates. Furthermore, in all path analyses, age was included as a control variable because evidence suggests that it may be related to both well-being (Proctor et al., 2009; see also Chapter 6) and delinquency (Cottle et al., 2001).

For interpreting the magnitude of correlation coefficients, the guidelines by Hemphill (2003) were used: $r \leq .20$ reflects a small effect, $r = .20$ to $.30$ a moderate effect, and $r \geq .30$ a large effect. In all analyses, p-values less than .05 were considered statistically significant.[18]

7.1.5 Power Analysis

Prior to the start of the study, we conducted a power analysis using G*Power 3.1 (Faul et al., 2009) to determine the appropriate number of participants based on a linear regression model predicting delinquency with 25 predictors (the well-being index, 20 primary goods proxy-items, internalizing and externalizing problems, criminogenic risk, and age). For this analysis, G*Power suggested a total sample of 172 participants, in order to detect a moderate effect size ($f^2 = 0.15$) in explained variance by the model (R^2; with 80% power ($\alpha = .05$, *two-tailed*). To detect moderate effect sizes ($f^2 = 0.15$) in the single regression coefficients with these 25 predictors and 80% power ($\alpha = .05$, *two-tailed*), a total sample of 56 participants was suggested to be adequate. Thus, we aimed to include at least 172 participants. As previously described, we ultimately included 170 participants, but we did

17 In the exploratory linear regression analyses predicting well-being and delinquency, the necessary statistical assumptions were examined. Multicollinearity was not an issue as all VIF values were below 3.33 (see Appendix F, https://www.elevenpub.com/en/content/appendices-9789462364257). The error terms were independent. Although there were no signs indicating heteroscedasticity, checks for the linearity assumption revealed there might have been a slight violation of that assumption in predicting well-being (but not delinquency). Nevertheless, non-linear transformations of the (in)dependent variable(s) did not improve the fit or make it worse (Mortelmans & Dehertogh, 2007). The results, furthermore, showed that although the error terms/residuals in predicting the dependent variables well-being and delinquency were generally normally distributed, the residuals in predicting delinquency seemed slightly skewed. This is, however, accommodated by using bootstrap estimates in PROCESS, which takes into account the actual sample (and error) distribution (Hayes, 2017; Hayes et al., 2017). Furthermore, this method was also used in Chapter 6, which ensures consistency and enables comparability across chapters.

18 95% confidence intervals that did not include 0.

not reach this number in all our analyses because of missing values (the number of participants ranged from 132 to 170).

7.2 RESULTS

7.2.1 Sample Characteristics

The 170 adolescent boys (aged 14 to 17) had a mean age of 16.14 years (*SD* = 0.88). In terms of education and employment, the majority (77.1%, *n* = 131) attended school before they were arrested, 13.5% (*n* = 23) were temporarily suspended from school, 7.6% (*n* = 13) did not attend school and were unemployed, and 1.8% (*n* = 3) were employed full time. From those who attended school or were temporarily suspended (*n* = 154), 40.3% (*n* = 62) attended vocational secondary education ('bso'/'vmbo'), 22.1% (*n* = 34) attended part-time secondary education (combined with part-time employment and/or traineeship), 13.0% (*n* = 20) attended special secondary education, 10.4% (*n* = 16) attended technical secondary education ('tso'/'havo'), 7.6% (*n* = 12) attended general (including art school) secondary education ('aso'/'kso'/'vwo'), 3.2% (*n* = 5) attended primary school and 3.2% (*n* = 5) attended higher (vocational) education.[19] The majority of participants were born in Belgium (67.1%, *n* = 114) and 15.9% (*n* = 27) were born in the Netherlands. The other participants (17.01%, *n* = 29) were born in other countries: Angola, Bulgaria, Congo, Ethiopia, Gambia, Ghana, Italy, Macedonia, Morocco, Mauritania, Dutch Antilles, Nigeria, Romania, Russia, Senegal, Serbia, Somalia, Spain, Surinam and South Africa. The most common countries of origin of the parent(s) were Belgium (34.6% fathers, 37.6% mothers), Morocco (18.2% fathers, 12.9% mothers), the Netherlands (5.9% fathers, 9.4% mothers), Turkey (5.9% fathers, 2.9% mothers), and Surinam (3.5% fathers, 3.5% mothers). About half of the participants' biological parents were divorced (47.1%, *n* = 80), 40% (*n* = 68) lived together, and in 12.9% cases (*n* = 22) one or both parents were unknown or deceased. Before their arrest, about a third (34.7%, *n* = 59) lived together with both parents, 37.6% (*n* = 64) lived (most of the time) with their mother, 5.3% (*n* = 9) lived (most of the time) with their father, 13.5% (*n* = 23) lived in a residential institution, and 8.8% (*n* = 15) lived somewhere else (e.g. with foster parents, other family members, friends or alone).

19 In the Belgian education system 'aso' is the Dutch abbreviation of *algemeen secundair onderwijs* (general secondary education), 'kso' is *kunst secundair onderwijs* (artistic secondary education), 'bso' is *beroepssecundair onderwijs* (vocational secondary education), and 'tso' is *technisch secundair onderwijs* (technical secondary education). Compared to the education system in the Netherlands, 'aso/kso' is roughly comparable to *Voorbereidend Wetenschappelijk Onderwijs* (VWO; preparatory university education) and *Hoger Algemeen Voortgezet Onderwijs* (HAVO; higher general secondary education), while 'tso' and 'bso' are roughly comparable to *Voorbereidend Middelbaar Beroepsonderwijs* (VMBO; preparatory secondary vocational education).

7.2.2 *Descriptive Statistics*

Subjective Well-Being

On the overall subjective well-being index (ranging from 0 to 100), participants (n = 164) scored on average 59.69 (SD = 15.94). On general life satisfaction (measured with the sum score of the SWLS-CV, ranging from 5 to 25), the participants (n = 167) scored on average 15.08 (SD = 4.48), which converted to the 0 to 100 index corresponds to a mean score of 50.40 (SD = 22.38). Regarding emotional well-being (measured with the sum scores of the SPANE subscales, ranging from 6 to 30), participants scored on average 21.43 (SD = 3.90) on the positive affect scale (PA, n = 166), and 14.51 (SD = 4.06) on the negative affect scale (NA, n = 167), which corresponds to a mean score of 64.28 (SD = 16.25) for PA and 35.45 (SD = 16.93) for NA on the 0 to 100 index.

GLM Primary Goods Satisfaction

Most participants reported to be *(very) satisfied* with the primary goods proxy-items, ranging from 47% with their education to 90% with their number of friends. Still, for all items there is a small but relevant minority who report to be *(very) dissatisfied*, ranging from 3.5% with their number of friends to 28.8% with the relationship with their father. See Table 7.3 for an overview of the frequencies of all item responses.

Table 7.3 Primary Goods Proxy-Items Satisfaction Frequencies *N* (%) and Descriptive Statistics

How satisfied are you with …	Very satisfied	Satisfied	Neither satisfied nor dissatisfied	Dis-satisfied	Very Dis-satisfied	*M (SD)*
… how much money you have? (n = 169)	40 (23.5%)	62 (36.5%)	35 (20.6%)	23 (13.5%)	9 (5.3%)	**2.40** (1.15)
… where you live? (n = 170)	73 (42.9%)	60 (35.3%)	22 (12.9%)	10 (5.9%)	5 (2.9%)	**1.91** (1.03)
… how safe you feel? (n = 170)	62 (36.5%)	73 (42.9)	25 (14.7%)	8 (4.7%)	2 (1.2%)	**1.91** (0.90)
… your physical health? (n = 170)	66 (38.8%)	66 (38.8%)	28 (16.4%)	8 (4.7%)	2 (1.2%)	**1.91** (0.92)
… your access to information about things that interest you (e.g. on the internet, in magazines or courses …)? (n = 168)	65 (38.2%)	59 (34.7%)	38 (22.4%)	4 (2.4%)	2 (1.2%)	**1.92** (0.90)
… your education? (n = 170)	31 (18.2%)	49 (28.8%)	44 (25.9%)	30 (17.6%)	16 (9.4%)	2.7 (1.22)
… your leisure activities (hobby's, sports, music …)? (n = 170)	46 (27.1%)	70 (41.2%)	29 (17.1%)	15 (8.8%)	10 (5.9%)	**2.25** (1.13)
… how much you can decide about your own life? (n = 167)	50 (29.4%)	62 (36.5%)	39 (22.9%)	9 (5.3%)	7 (4.1%)	**2.17** (1.05)
… your mental health? (n = 170)	60 (35.3%)	62 (36.5%)	28 (16.5%)	12 (7.1%)	8 (4.7%)	**2.09** (1.11)
… your relationships with your family? (n = 170)	72 (42.4%)	31 (18.2%)	31 (18.2%)	24 (14.1%)	12 (7.1%)	**2.25** (1.32)
… your relationship with your mother? (n = 169)	92 (54.1%)	26 (15.3%)	23 (13.5%)	10 (5.9%)	18 (10.6%)	**2.03** (1.37)
… your relationship with your father? (n = 164)	56 (32.9%)	25 (14.7%)	34 (20.0%)	17 (10.0%)	32 (18.8%)	**2.66** (1.52)

How satisfied are you with …	Very satisfied	Satisfied	Neither satisfied nor dissatisfied	Dis-satisfied	Very Dis-satisfied	*M (SD)*
… your social contacts with friends? (n = 168)	70 (41.2%)	66 (38.8%)	25 (14.7%)	5 (2.9%)	2 (1.2%)	**1.83** (0.88)
… your number of friends? (n = 169)	80 (47.1%)	73 (42.9%)	10 (5.9%)	5 (2.9%)	1 (0.6%)	**1.66** (0.77)
… your love life? (n = 170)	64 (37.6%)	47 (27.6%)	40 (23.5%)	10 (5.9%)	9 (5.3%)	**2.14** (1.15)
… your social contacts with other people (in your neighbourhood, clubs/ associations)? (n = 170)	47 (27.6%)	83 (48.8%)	31 (18.2%)	8 (4.7%)	1 (0.6%)	**2.02** (0.84)
… your religion/spirituality? (n = 164)	60 (35.3%)	65 (38.2%)	29 (17.1%)	8 (4.7%)	2 (1.2%)	**1.95** (0.92)
… how much meaning your life has? (n = 170)	46 (27.1%)	65 (38.2%)	42 (24.7%)	14 (8.2%)	3 (1.8%)	**2.19** (0.99)
… how creative you can be (with trying new things, art, music, solving problems)? (n = 170)	59 (34.7%)	73 (42.9%)	27 (15.9%)	7 (4.1%)	4 (2.4%)	**1.96** (0.94)
… how much you can enjoy yourself (with e.g. good food, a trip, a movie)? (n = 170)	84 (49.4%)	56 (32.9%)	18 (10.6%)	8 (4.7%)	4 (2.4%)	**1.78** (0.98)

Notes. A higher score on the primary goods proxy-items (ranging from 1 to 5) corresponds to lower levels of satisfaction (i.e. more dissatisfaction).

Delinquency Frequencies

In terms of delinquency frequencies, 7.6% (n = 13) of the 170 detained adolescents reported not having committed any of the six offences in the preceding 12 months (see fn 16 in this chapter). Seven participants (4.1%) did not answer one or more of the six offence frequency items. The majority (88.3%, n = 150) reported having committed at least one of the six offences once in the preceding 12 months. Of these, 15.3% (n = 23) reported committing only one offence in the preceding 12 months and 4.7% (n = 7) reported two offences. The majority (80%, n = 120) reported having committed three or more offences. Regarding the types of offences, 22% (n = 33) reported having committed only one type of offence in the preceding 12 months, while the majority (78%, n = 117) reported a combination of different types. See Table 7.4 for an overview of the frequencies per offence.

Table 7.4 Self-Reported Frequencies of the Six Types of Offences in the Preceding 12 Months

Offence type	None n (%)	Once n (%)	Twice n (%)	Three or more n (%)	Missing values n (%)
Vandalism	95 (55.9%)	16 (9.4%)	15 (8.8%)	42 (24.7%)	2 (1.2%)
Shoplifting	68 (40.0%)	23 (13.5%)	18 (10.6%)	59 (34.7%)	2 (1.2%)
Theft	67 (39.4%)	17 (10.0%)	15 (8.8%)	69 (40.6%)	2 (1.2%)
Harassment	97 (57.1%)	23 (13.5%)	10 (5.9%)	36 (21.2%)	4 (2.4%)
Physical assault	71 (41.8%)	27 (15.9%)	26 (15.3%)	42 (24.7%)	4 (2.4%)
Drug dealing	77 (45.3%)	7 (4.1%)	0 (0.0%)	81 (47.6%)	5 (2.9%)

Note. N = 170.

Mental Health Problems

The participants (n = 163) scored on average 13.04 (SD = 5.56) on the 'total difficulties' scale of the SDQ (ranging from 0 to 40). Based on their total difficulties score, the majority (68.7%, n = 112) scored in the 'normal' range, 17.2% (n = 28) scored 'borderline' and 14.1% (n = 23) scored 'abnormal/problematic'. Concerning the subscales (ranging from 0 to 20) the participants (n = 166) scored on average 5.54 (SD = 2.70) on internalizing problems and 7.49 (SD = 3.96, n = 164) on externalizing problems.

Criminogenic Risk

Regarding their total recidivism risk level of the YLS/CMI (ranging from 0 to 42), the participants (n = 166) scored on average 19.78 (SD = 7.88). Based on their total risk level, about half (52.4%, n = 89) of the total sample were classified as 'moderate' risk. About a third (34.7%; n = 59) were classified as 'high', 9.4% (n = 16) as 'low', and 1.2% (n = 2) as 'very high' according to the cut-offs.

7.2.3 *Relationship Between Well-Being and Delinquency*

To assess the relationship between overall subjective well-being and the number of self-reported offences committed in the preceding 12 months (for all six offence types combined), we conducted a one-way ANOVA and Tukey-Kramer post-hoc tests. Results showed a statistically significant relationship between well-being and the number of offences committed, $F(3, 153) = 2.73$, $p = .046$ (see Table 7.5). Nevertheless, the post-hoc tests revealed no significant differences ($p > .05$) between the four groups. This could have been due to a lack of statistical power because of the rather small group sizes in the 'no' (n = 13), 'one' (n = 23) or 'two' (n = 7) offence groups, compared to the 'three or more offences' group (n = 114). However, a statistically significant negative correlation was found between the well-being index and the total number of self-reported offences (Pearson's $r = -.29$, $p < .001$), which is considered a moderate effect.

Table 7.5 Differences in Overall Subjective Well-Being (the 0-100 Well-Being Index) According to the Number of Self-Reported Committed Offences

Number of offences	*M (SD)*	*n*
None of the six offences	**66.77** (17.44)	13
One offence	**63.99** (15.12)	23
Two offences	**69.33** (16.89)	7
Three or more offences	**57.99** (15.58)	114

Notes. $N = 157$. Tukey-Kramer post-hoc tests revealed no significant differences ($p > 0.05$). A higher score on the well-being index (ranging from 0 to 100) corresponds to higher levels of subjective overall well-being.

7.2.4 *Direct and Indirect Pathways Between Primary Goods, Well-Being and Delinquency*

To examine the hypothesized routes between the primary goods (the 20 proxy-items), the well-being index and self-reported delinquency frequency, a path analysis was conducted in PROCESS (Hayes, 2017; Hayes et al., 2017). Figure 7.1 shows the summarized results of this path analysis, which are explained in detail in the following pages.

Figure 7.1 Path Analysis Model of Associations Between Primary Goods Proxy-Items, Well-Being and Total Delinquency, Controlling for Age

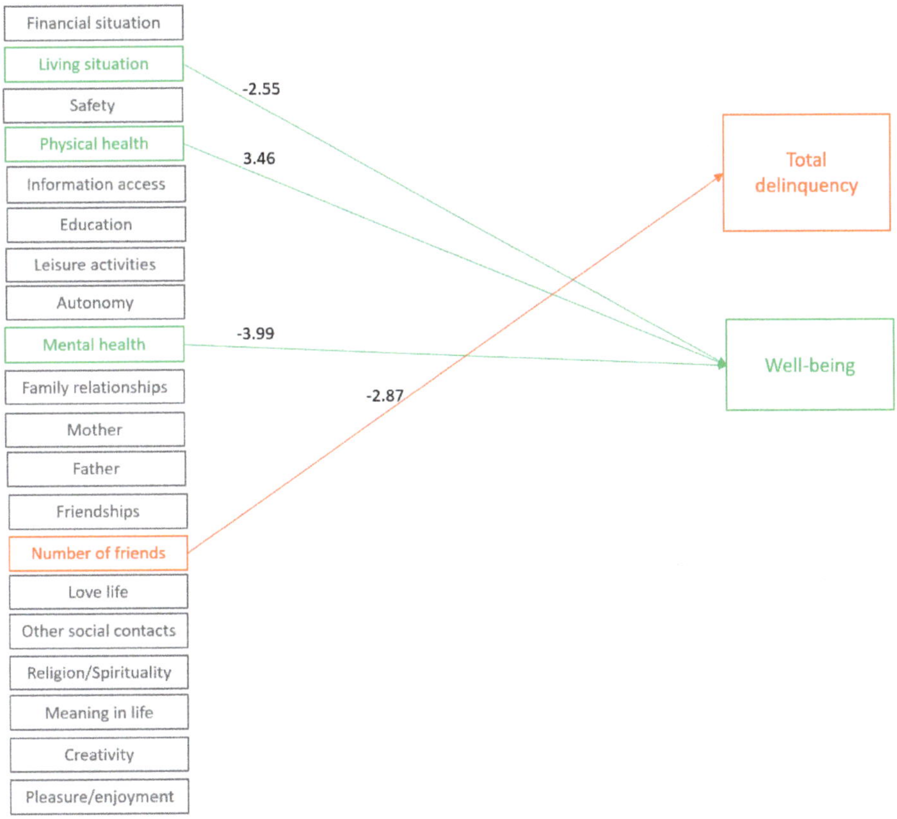

Notes. $N = 138$. The path analysis model shows statistically significant ($p < .05$) associations, controlling for age. Coefficients presented are unstandardized bootstrap estimates (B). A higher total delinquency frequency score (0 to 24) corresponds to more reported committed offences. A higher score on the well-being index (0 to 100) corresponds to higher levels of subjective overall well-being. A higher score on the primary goods proxy-items (1 to 5) corresponds to lower levels of satisfaction (i.e. more dissatisfaction). Predictors in green are only directly related to well-being. Predictors in red are only directly related to delinquency. Predictors in grey were found to be insignificant.

Direct Effects of the Primary Goods on Well-Being

First, the path analysis showed the direct effects of the primary goods on well-being. The ordinary least squares path analysis on overall subjective well-being showed that 61.4% of the variance in the well-being index could be explained by the primary goods proxy-items, controlling for age, $F(21, 116) = 8.79, p < .001$. The unstandardized bootstrap estimates (B) of the direct effects on well-being can be found in Table 7.6.

Of the primary goods proxy-items, more dissatisfaction with one's mental health appeared to be the strongest predictor of lower levels of well-being (B = -3.99, 95% CI [-6.51, -1.28]). Additionally, more dissatisfaction with one's living situation significantly predicted lower levels of well-being (B = -2.55, 95% CI [-5.10, -0.02]) and in the opposite direction: more dissatisfaction with one's physical health predicted higher levels of well-being (B = 3.46, 95% CI [0.46, 6.62]). The other primary goods proxy-items and age as a control variable did not turn out to be significant predictors (see Table 7.6).

Table 7.6 Unstandardized Bootstrap Estimates (B) of the Direct Effects and Bootstrap Inferences (SE and CI) of the Primary Goods Proxy-Items on Overall Subjective Well-Being Based on the PROCESS Path Analysis, Controlling for Age

	B (SE)	95% CI B
Control variable		
Age	1.04 (1.04)^{ns}	[-0.98, 3.09]
Primary goods proxy-items		
Financial situation	-1.18 (1.10)^{ns}	[-3.28, 0.99]
Living situation	-2.55 (1.30)*	[-5.10, -0.02]
Safety	-1.75 (1.32)^{ns}	[-4.39, 0.84]
Physical health	3.46 (1.58)*	[0.46, 6.62]
Information access	-0.61 (1.47)^{ns}	[-3.26, 2.55]
Education	-1.16 (1.11)^{ns}	[-3.35, 1.04]
Leisure activities	-1.63 (1.03)^{ns}	[-3.54, 0.52]
Autonomy	-1.60 (1.15)^{ns}	[-3.82, 0.68]
Mental health	-3.99 (1.32)*	[-6.51, -1.28]
Family relationships	-0.97 (1.57)^{ns}	[-4.08, 2.09]
Mother	-0.06 (1.18)^{ns}	[-2.33, 2.23]
Father	-0.70 (1.04)^{ns}	[-2.74, 1.35]
Friendships	-0.14 (1.66)^{ns}	[-3.88, 2.86]
Number of friends	0.87 (1.61)^{ns}	[-2.24, 4.03]
Love life	-0.18 (0.92)^{ns}	[-1.72, 1.98]
Other social contacts	-0.03 (1.52)^{ns}	[-3.07, 2.94]
Religion/spirituality	0.91 (1.35)^{ns}	[-1.85, 3.48]
Meaning in life	-2.75 (1.73)^{ns}	[-6.11, 0.76]
Creativity	-0.44 (1.49)^{ns}	[-3.14, 2.80]

	B (SE)	95% CI B
Pleasure/enjoyment	-1.78 (1.68)^{ns}	[-4.85, 1.85]

Notes. $N = 138$. $R^2 = .614$; model $F(21, 116) = 8.79$, $p < .001$; * = significant $p < .05$; ns = not significant. The unstandardized estimates (B), standard error (SE), and the 95% confidence intervals (CI) were obtained using percentile bootstrapping based on 5,000 bootstrap samples. A higher score on the well-being index (0 to 100) corresponds to higher levels of subjective overall well-being. A higher score on the primary goods proxy-items (1 to 5) corresponds to lower levels of satisfaction (i.e. more dissatisfaction).

Direct and Indirect Effects of the Primary Goods on Total Delinquency

Next, the path analysis showed the direct and indirect effects of the primary goods on total delinquency with well-being as possible mediator. The ordinary least squares path analysis on total delinquency showed that 30.2% of the variance in the total frequency of committed offences (all six types combined) could be explained by the primary goods proxy-items, with well-being as mediator, controlling for age, $F(22, 115) = 2.26$, $p = .003$. The unstandardized bootstrap estimates (B) of the direct effects on total delinquency can be found in Table 7.7.

Of the primary goods proxy-items, only more dissatisfaction with one's number of friends significantly predicted less total delinquency (B = -2.87, 95% CI [-5.16, -0.79]). The other primary goods proxy-items, with age as a control variable, and overall subjective well-being as mediator did not turn out to be significant predictors (see Table 7.7).

As the path analysis revealed no significant direct effect between well-being and total delinquency (B = -0.01, 95% CI [-0.15, 0.12]), no significant indirect effects were found.

Table 7.7 Unstandardized Bootstrap Estimates (B) of the Direct Effects and Bootstrap Inferences (SE and CI) of the Primary Goods Proxy-Items on Total Delinquency Frequency Based on the PROCESS Path Analysis, with Well-Being as Mediator, Controlling for Age

	B (SE)	95% CI B
Control variable		
Age	-0.53 (0.86)^{ns}	[-2.25, 1.14]
Mediator		
Well-being	-0.01 (0.07)^{ns}	[-0.15, 0.12]
Primary goods proxy-items		
Financial situation	-1.54 (0.84)^{ns}	[-3.20, 0.11]
Living situation	-0.11 (0.98)^{ns}	[-2.08, 1.78]

	B (SE)	95% CI B
Safety	1.45 (0.95)^{ns}	[-0.37, 3.38]
Physical health	-0.43 (1.09)^{ns}	[-2.46, 1.75]
Information access	-0.21 (0.99)^{ns}	[-2.20, 1.67]
Education	0.50 (0.66)^{ns}	[-0.83, 1.79]
Leisure activities	0.43 (0.77)^{ns}	[-1.08, 2.00]
Autonomy	0.60 (0.79)^{ns}	[-0.97, 2.12]
Mental health	-0.26 (0.98)^{ns}	[-2.12, 1.70]
Family relationships	1.60 (0.83)^{ns}	[-0.14, 3.16]
Mother	0.18 (0.67)^{ns}	[-1.10, 1.56]
Father	0.17 (0.61)^{ns}	[-1.04, 1.35]
Friendships	1.04 (1.43)^{ns}	[-1.28, 4.27]
Number of friends	-2.87 (1.11)*	[-5.16, -0.79]
Love life	0.26 (0.63)^{ns}	[-0.93, 1.54]
Other social contacts	0.60 (1.18)^{ns}	[-1.79, 2.86]
Religion/spirituality	-1.22 (0.84)^{ns}	[-2.93, 0.40]
Meaning in life	0.70 (1.07)^{ns}	[-1.35, 2.77]
Creativity	0.54 (0.95)^{ns}	[-1.36, 2.40]
Pleasure/enjoyment	0.95 (1.02)^{ns}	[-1.00, 3.08]

Notes. $N = 138$. $R^2 = .302$; model $F(22, 115) = 2.26$, $p = .003$; * = significant $p < .05$; ns = not significant. The unstandardized estimates (B), standard error (SE), and the 95% confidence intervals (CI) were obtained using percentile bootstrapping based on 5,000 bootstrap samples. A higher total delinquency frequency score (0 to 24) corresponds to more reported committed offences. A higher score on the well-being index (0 to 100) corresponds to higher levels of subjective overall well-being. A higher score on the primary goods proxy-items (1 to 5) corresponds to lower levels of satisfaction (i.e. more dissatisfaction).

7.2.5 *Examining the Role of Obstacles in Explaining Well-Being and Delinquency*

To examine the role of obstacles in the relationships between the primary goods (the 20 proxy-items), the well-being index, and self-reported offending frequency, the same path analysis as in Section 7.2.4 was conducted in PROCESS (Hayes, 2017; Hayes et al., 2017), now including internalizing and externalizing mental health problems (total subscales of the SDQ) and criminogenic risk (total score of the YLS/CMI) as additional covariates. Figure 7.2 shows the summarized results of this path analysis, which are explained in detail below.

Figure 7.2 Path Analysis Model of Primary Goods Proxy-Items, Criminogenic Risk, Internalizing and Externalizing Mental Health Problems, Well-Being, and Total Delinquency, Controlling for Age

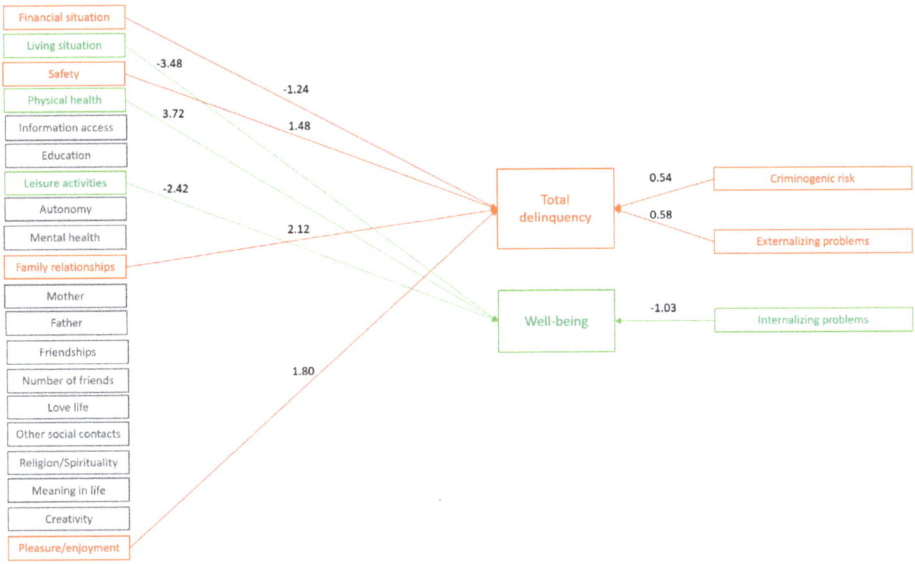

Notes. $N = 132$. The path analysis model shows the statistically significant ($p < .05$) associations, controlling for age. Coefficients presented are unstandardized bootstrap estimates (B). A higher total delinquency frequency score (0 to 24) corresponds to more reported committed offences. A higher score on the well-being index (0 to 100) corresponds to higher levels of subjective overall well-being. A higher score on internalizing and externalizing problems (0 to 20) corresponds to more symptoms. A higher score on criminogenic risk (0 to 42) corresponds to more criminogenic risk factors present and a higher risk of recidivism. A higher score on the primary goods proxy-items (1 to 5) corresponds to lower levels of satisfaction (i.e. more dissatisfaction). Predictors in green are only directly related to well-being. Predictors in red are only directly related to delinquency. Predictors in grey were found to be insignificant.

Direct Effects of the Primary Goods and Possible Obstacles on Well-Being

First, the path analysis showed the direct effects of the primary goods on well-being, now including internalizing and externalizing mental health problems and criminogenic risk factors as covariates. The ordinary least squares path analysis on overall subjective well-being showed that 65.2% of the variance in the well-being index could be explained by the primary goods proxy-items, internalizing and externalizing problems, and criminogenic risk, controlling for age, $F(24, 107) = 8.35$, $p < .001$. The unstandardized bootstrap estimates (B) of the direct effects on well-being can be found in Table 7.8.

Of the possible obstacles, more internalizing problems significantly predicted lower levels overall subjective well-being (B = -1.03, 95% CI [-1.93, -0.13]). Different from the direct effects of the primary goods proxy-items on well-being without mental health problems and criminogenic risk as control variables (see Table 7.6), dissatisfaction with one's mental health was no longer a significant predictor of well-being (B = -2.59, 95% CI [-5.55, 0.55]) and more dissatisfaction with one's leisure activities now also significantly predicted lower levels of well-being (B = -2.42, 95% CI [-4.45, -0.23]). Similar to the direct effects without the possible obstacles as covariates, more dissatisfaction with one's living situation remained a significant predictor of lower levels of well-being (B = -3.48, 95% CI [-6.13, -0.98]) and in the opposite direction, more dissatisfaction with one's physical health remained as a significant predictor of higher levels of well-being (B = 3.72, 95% CI [0.49, 7.07]). The other primary goods proxy-items and control variables did not turn out to be significant predictors (see Table 7.8).

Table 7.8 Unstandardized Bootstrap Estimates of the Direct Effects (B) and Bootstrap Inferences (SE and CI) of the Primary Goods Proxy-Items, Internalizing and Externalizing Problems, and Criminogenic Risk on Overall Subjective Well-Being Based on the PROCESS Path Analysis, Controlling for Age

	B (SE)	95% CI B
Control variable		
Age	0.37 (1.12)^{ns}	[-1.90, 2.56]
Covariates		
Internalizing problems	-1.03 (0.46)*	[-1.93, -0.13]
Externalizing problems	-0.44 (0.33)^{ns}	[-1.09, 0.25]
Criminogenic risk	-0.11 (0.16)^{ns}	[-0.41, 0.21]
Primary goods proxy-items		
Financial situation	-1.48 (1.19)^{ns}	[-3.71, 0.89]
Living situation	-3.48 (1.28)*	[-6.13, -0.98]
Safety	-0.45 (1.44)^{ns}	[-3.24, 2.41]
Physical health	3.72 (1.66)*	[0.49, 7.07]
Information access	0.29 (1.50)^{ns}	[-2.55, 3.48]
Education	-0.52 (1.12)^{ns}	[-2.72, 1.68]
Leisure activities	-2.42 (1.08)*	[-4.45, -0.23]
Autonomy	-1.45 (1.18)^{ns}	[-3.74, 0.92]
Mental health	-2.59 (1.55)^{ns}	[-5.55, 0.55]
Family relationships	-1.05 (1.45)^{ns}	[-4.02, 1.69]
Mother	0.53 (1.14)^{ns}	[-1.78, 2.88]
Father	-0.84 (1.04)^{ns}	[-2.88, 1.27]

	B (SE)	95% CI B
Friendships	0.90 (1.77)^{ns}	[-3.01, 4.18]
Number of friends	-0.52 (1.95)^{ns}	[-4.40, 3.42]
Love life	0.07 (0.90)^{ns}	[-1.76, 1.80]
Other social contacts	-0.41 (1.55)^{ns}	[-3.52, 2.61]
Religion/spirituality	0.77 (1.34)^{ns}	[-2.01, 3.32]
Meaning in life	-2.68 (1.75)^{ns}	[-6.05, 0.75]
Creativity	-0.02 (1.42)^{ns}	[-2.55, 3.08]
Pleasure/enjoyment	-1.21 (1.67)^{ns}	[-4.48, 2.19]

Note. $N = 132$. $R^2 = .652$; model $F(24, 107) = 8.35$, $p < .001$; * = significant $p < .05$; ns = not significant. The unstandardized estimates (B), standard error (SE), and the 95% confidence intervals (CI) were obtained using percentile bootstrapping based on 5,000 bootstrap samples. A higher score on the well-being index (0 to 100) corresponds to higher levels of subjective overall well-being. A higher score on internalizing and externalizing problems (0 to 20) corresponds to more symptoms. A higher score on criminogenic risk (0 to 42) corresponds to more criminogenic risk factors present and a higher risk of recidivism. A higher score on the primary goods proxy-items (1 to 5) corresponds to lower levels of satisfaction (i.e. more dissatisfaction).

Direct and Indirect Effects of the Primary Goods and Possible Obstacles on Total Delinquency

Next, the path analysis showed the direct and indirect effects of the primary goods on total delinquency with well-being as possible mediator, now including internalizing and externalizing mental health problems and criminogenic risk factors as covariates. The ordinary least squares path analysis on total delinquency showed that 64.5% of the variance in the total frequency of committed offences (all six types combined) could be explained by the primary goods proxy-items, internalizing and externalizing problems, and criminogenic risk, with well-being as mediator, controlling for age, $F(25, 106) = 7.71$, $p < .001$. The unstandardized bootstrap estimates (B) of the direct effects on total delinquency can be found in Table 7.9.

Of the possible obstacles, more externalizing problems (B = 0.58, 95% CI [0.22, 0.94]) and higher criminogenic risk (B = 0.54, 95% CI [0.40, 0.69]) significantly predicted more total delinquency. Different from the direct effects of the primary goods proxy-items on delinquency without mental health problems and criminogenic risk as control variables (see Table 7.7), dissatisfaction with one's number of friends was no longer a significant predictor (B = -1.36, 95% CI [-3.45, 0.63]). Additionally, more dissatisfaction with one's safety (B = 1.48, 95% CI [0.06, 2.91]), family relationships (B = 2.12, 95% CI [0.80, 3.47]) and pleasure/enjoyment (B = 1.80, 95% CI [0.16, 3.46]), now significantly predicted more total delinquency. Furthermore, in the other direction, more dissatisfaction with one's financial situation (B = -1.24, 95% CI [-2.49, -0.03]) predicted less delinquency. The other primary goods proxy-items, control variables and overall subjective well-being as mediator did not turn out to be significant predictors (see Table 7.9).

As, the path analysis revealed no significant direct effect between well-being and total delinquency (B = 0.06, 95% CI [-0.05, 0.16]), no significant indirect effects were found.

Table 7.9 Unstandardized Bootstrap Estimates of the Direct Effects (B) and Bootstrap Inferences (SE and CI) of the Primary Goods Proxy-Items, Internalizing and Externalizing Problems and Criminogenic Risk on Total Delinquency Frequency Score Based on the PROCESS Path Analysis, With Well-Being as Mediator, Controlling for Age

	B (SE)	95% CI B
Control variable		
Age	-0.42 (0.65)^{ns}	[-1.74, 0.82]
Covariates		
Internalizing problems	-0.42 (0.21)^{ns}	[-0.81, 0.004]
Externalizing problems	0.58 (0.18)*	[0.22, 0.94]
Criminogenic risk	0.54 (0.08)*	[0.40, 0.69]
Mediator		
Well-being	0.06 (0.06)^{ns}	[-0.05, 0.16]
Primary goods proxy-items		
Financial situation	-1.24 (0.64)*	[-2.49, -0.03]
Living situation	-0.23 (0.75)^{ns}	[-1.66, 1.28]
Safety	1.48 (0.71)*	[0.06, 2.91]
Physical health	-1.76 (0.94)^{ns}	[-3.60, 0.04]
Information access	0.39 (0.75)^{ns}	[-1.17, 1.83]
Education	-0.10 (0.54)^{ns}	[-1.18, 0.95]
Leisure activities	0.68 (0.70)^{ns}	[-0.61, 2.14]
Autonomy	0.30 (0.62)^{ns}	[-0.90, 1.50]
Mental health	1.17 (0.73)^{ns}	[-0.26, 2.60]
Family relationships	2.12 (0.68)*	[0.80, 3.47]
Mother	-0.41 (0.51)^{ns}	[-1.40, 0.63]
Father	-0.85 (0.47)^{ns}	[-1.77, 0.06]
Friendships	1.00 (1.09)^{ns}	[-0.90, 3.39]
Number of friends	-1.36 (1.05)^{ns}	[-3.45, 0.63]

	B (SE)	95% CI B
Love life	0.03 (0.51)^{ns}	[-0.99, 1.04]
Other social contacts	0.51 (0.93)^{ns}	[-1.40, 2.19]
Religion/spirituality	-0.95 (0.66)^{ns}	[-2.24, 0.38]
Meaning in life	-0.45 (0.90)^{ns}	[-2.23, 1.32]
Creativity	-0.54 (0.77)^{ns}	[-2.27, 0.85]
Pleasure/enjoyment	1.80 (0.84)*	[0.16, 3.46]

Notes. $N = 132$. $R^2 = .645$; model $F(25, 106) = 7.71$, $p < .001$; * = significant $p < .05$; ns = not significant. The unstandardized estimates (B), standard error (SE), and the 95% confidence intervals (CI) were obtained using percentile bootstrapping based on 5,000 bootstrap samples. A higher total delinquency frequency score (0 to 24) corresponds to more reported committed offences. A higher score on internalizing and externalizing problems (0 to 20) corresponds to more symptoms. A higher score on criminogenic risk (0 to 42) corresponds to more criminogenic risk factors present and a higher risk of recidivism. A higher score on the well-being index (0 to 100) corresponds to higher levels of subjective overall well-being. A higher score on the primary goods proxy-items (1 to 5) corresponds to lower levels of satisfaction (i.e. more dissatisfaction).

7.3 DISCUSSION

In this chapter we aimed to assess the etiological assumptions of the Good Lives Model (GLM) in explaining well-being and delinquency in a sample of 170 detained adolescent males. We first examined the associations between primary goods satisfaction, well-being and self-reported delinquency. Based on the findings of the previous chapter, a number of changes and additions were made in the present study, to investigate the primary goods in more detail. Furthermore, we took the analyses a step further by investigating which pathways might explain the observed relationships. Specifically, we examined the role of criminogenic risk factors, as they are suggested by the GLM to be important obstacles in the prosocial attainment of primary goods (Purvis, 2010; Purvis et al., 2011, 2014; Ward & Stewart, 2003a). Additionally, we examined the role of internalizing and externalizing problems, because mental health problems have also been hypothesized to serve as significant obstacles for adolescents' attainment of primary goods and well-being (Barnao et al., 2016; Colins et al., 2010; Vermeiren et al., 2006; Wibbelink et al., 2017). In the following sections, I elaborate on the findings from this study.

7.3.1 *The Relationship Between Well-Being and Adolescent Delinquency*

Based on the self-report data of 170 detained adolescent males, our results showed a moderate negative relationship between overall subjective well-being and self-reported delinquency frequency, where lower levels of well-being were associated with more delinquent behaviour. These results are again in line with previous research and largely confirm the second assumption of the GLM, which states that offenders experience lower levels of well-being (Buelga et al., 2008; Gonzalez et al., 2021; MacDonald et al., 2005; McKnight et al., 2002; Olson et al., 2020; Suldo & Huebner, 2004; Sun & Shek, 2010, 2012; Valois et al., 2001, 2002, 2006; Zullig et al., 2001). It must be noted that the same caution in interpreting the direction of these findings remains as in the previous chapter, because of the cross-sectional nature of our study. Hence, we cannot infer whether a lower level of well-being results in offending behaviour and/or vice versa.

7.3.2 *The Role of Primary Goods in Detained Adolescents' Well-Being and Delinquency*

Contrary to the GLM model and the findings in the general population sample reported in Chapter 6, in the current study we only found direct effects of the primary goods on well-being and delinquency. The path analyses revealed no indirect effects of primary goods on delinquency through well-being. The fact that the indirect route to delinquency via well-being was not present in the detained adolescent could lie in the combination of small effects, a relatively small sample size and a subsequent lack of statistical power, that is, the indirect effects in the general population sample were (very) small and most likely reached statistical significance because of the large sample size ($N = 4{,}260$). Our detention sample was considerably smaller ($N = 170$, and even smaller for the path analyses due to missing values, resulting in less statistical power to detect (very) small effects (see also the limitations in Section 7.5).

In the following text, we will focus and elaborate on those primary goods that were found to directly relate to detained adolescents' well-being and/or delinquency. Based on the path analyses we found that only the primary goods of 'life' was directly related to both detained adolescents' well-being and delinquency. The primary goods of 'relatedness' and 'pleasure' were only directly related to detained adolescents' delinquent behaviour, but not well-being. The primary good of 'inner peace' appeared to be only related to detained adolescents' well-being in the form of dissatisfaction with mental health and internalizing problems, while externalizing problems were only related to delinquent behaviour. These findings will be discussed in more detail in the next sections.

7.3.3 *Life: Basic Physical Needs*

Based on the results of this study, we can conclude that for detained adolescents the primary good of 'life' is an important factor for their well-being, especially regarding their living situation and physical health. When taking into account the possible obstacles of mental health problems and criminogenic risk factors, both living situation and physical health remained significant predictors of well-being. First, more dissatisfaction with one's living situation was related to lower levels of overall well-being. This finding is in line with the results of the meta-analysis (Chapter 4) and our own study (Chapter 6) in adolescents from the general population. Contrarily, however, in our sample of detained adolescents we found that the less satisfaction they reported with their physical health, the higher their overall well-being levels.

This finding could be explained by the fact the detained adolescents in our current sample were asked about their well-being and satisfaction levels thinking about the time before their arrest. In that period, some of them were living with friends or on the streets and were running away from home or the police. Many of them did not attend school, partied a lot and lacked structure in their lives. This may suggest that although the adolescents' physical health suffered from their lifestyles, other aspects of that same lifestyle could increase their overall well-being. Moreover, in such an unhealthy environment and lifestyle, one's basic physical needs might become more prominent and emphasized over other needs. This is in line with Maslow's (1962) 'hierarchy of needs', which states that physiological (food, water, warmth, rest) and safety needs form the basic necessities before the higher-level needs (i.e. such as the psychological needs of the Self-determination Theory; Ryan & Deci, 2017b) come in to play.

Regarding the relationship between the primary good of 'life' and adolescent delinquency, our study shows that especially satisfaction with one's financial situation is an important factor. As discussed in previous chapters, financial problems have been related to juvenile delinquency (Hoeve et al., 2016; van Beek et al., 2021) and numerous studies have shown that financial gain is an important motivation for young offenders (Agnew, 1990; Farrington, 1993; Gudjonsson & Sigurdsson, 2007; Lopez, 2008; Nguyen & Bouchard, 2013; Putniņš, 2010; Shong et al., 2019; Troonbeeckx et al., 2015; Verdonck, 2017). For detained adolescents, while taking into account criminogenic risk and mental health problems, more satisfaction with their financial situation became a significant predictor of their delinquent behaviour. In our study with adolescents from the general population (see Chapter 6), however, we found the opposite, more dissatisfaction with one's financial situation was a significant predictor of adolescent delinquency. Because of the cross-sectional nature of both our studies, we cannot infer conclusions about the direction of the relationships, that is, offending behaviour could be motivated by a lack of money, but just as well alleviate prior financial worries. Either way, we can conclude from these studies that financial situation plays an important role in adolescent delinquency. Longitudinal and qualitative research could provide more of an understanding of this phenomenon.

Furthermore, when taking into account criminogenic risk and mental health problems, more dissatisfaction with one's safety additionally appeared as a significant predictor of more offending. This finding could again, as all associations, be interpreted in both directions. Engagement in delinquency may expose someone to a risky lifestyle and various dangers that can compromise their safety (Cops & Pleysier, 2014; Mallion & Wood, 2020). For example, Cops and Pleysier (2014) found in a large group of adolescents that a riskier lifestyle was related to a higher prevalence of offending, which in turn also led to higher levels of victimization. In the other direction, not feeling safe can also incite violent behaviour as a defence mechanism and protection (Mallion & Wood, 2020; Reese et al., 2001; Verdonck, 2017; Verdonck et al., 2011).

7.3.4 Relatedness: Family and (Fun with) Friends

Previous chapters have outlined the importance of relationships with family and friends, for both adolescents' well-being and juvenile delinquency. It was therefore surprising to find that none of the relatedness items showed a significant effect on the detained adolescents' well-being. This may be related to the possible explanation that this group of adolescents are typically more focused on their basic physical needs, placing other needs in the background. On the other hand, both family and friends did seem to play important roles in their delinquent behaviour, that is, greater satisfaction with one's number of friends was related to more delinquent behaviour. In the other direction, when taking into account criminogenic risk and mental health problems, greater dissatisfaction with family relationships was related to more offending.

These findings are similar to the results from the general population of adolescents (see Chapter 6), where an increase in satisfaction with peers predicted more delinquency, and more delinquency was simultaneously also predicted by a decrease in satisfaction with family relationships. We explained this by the possibility of a tension and conflict between satisfaction with (antisocial) peer relationships on the one hand and dissatisfaction with family bonds on the other (Barnert et al., 2015). This is in line with theories and studies stating that during adolescence peers can gain more influence over family, especially regarding the influence in delinquent behaviour (Burgess & Akers, 1966; Dishion et al., 1996; Massey et al., 2008; Messersmith & Schulenberg, 2010; Sutherland & Cressey, 1960; Warr, 2002). Despite (or even because of) their satisfaction with (their number of) social contacts with peers, it can increase the likelihood of (together) engaging in delinquency (Van Damme, Colins, Pauwels, et al., 2015; Van Damme et al., 2016). Moreover, in general, a greater number of friends may increase the possibility of having antisocial friends among them.

Accordingly, when adding criminogenic risk factors and mental health problems as covariates, satisfaction with one's number of friends no longer significantly predicted adolescents' delinquent behaviour. This finding supports our earlier explanation and many studies (Andrews & Bonta, 2010; Baron, 2015; Bonta & Andrews, 2017; Cottle et al., 2001; Dishion & Tipsord, 2011; Glueck & Glueck, 1950; Grieger & Hosser, 2014; Patterson & Dishion, 1985) that it is probably not merely the satisfaction with one's number of friends that increases the likelihood of delinquent behaviour, but specifically the engagement with antisocial friends (as part of the criminogenic risk factors). In doing so, they might aim to seek the primary good of 'pleasure' (which also became a significant predictor of delinquency), fun and excitement they are not experiencing in legal activities. Furthermore, these findings correspond to numerous studies demonstrating that sensation seeking to pass the time and prevent boredom is a common motive for engaging in illegal activities, such as fights, vandalism, drug use and shoplifting (see also Chapter 5; Arnett, 1992, 1996; Drozda, 2006; Farrington, 1993; Gordon & Caltabiano, 1996; Hansen & Breivik, 2001; Newberry & Duncan, 2001; Putniņš, 2010; Robertson, 1994; Troonbeeckx et al., 2015; Verdonck, 2017; Wilson & Scarpa, 2011). Thus, our results once again confirm the importance of assessing the specific ways in which juveniles aim to achieve their primary goods.

7.3.5 *Inner Peace: Mental Health*

In line with previous chapters, for detained adolescents, mental health appeared as the strongest predictor of overall subjective well-being. To reiterate these previous chapters, we emphasized being careful in interpreting the magnitude of this effect, because of the risk of a spurious correlation and assessment biases (Diener et al., 1991; Eid & Diener, 2004; Gamble & Gärling, 2012). However, in this study, we also included an additional measure of mental health problems, to assess mental health (both internalizing and externalizing symptoms) in more detail. When adding these variables to the path analyses, we saw that satisfaction with mental health was no longer related to well-being, but internalizing problems were, that is, more internalizing problems was related to less overall well-being. This solidifies the basis on which we can conclude that mental health indeed plays an important role in adolescents' well-being (Arnett, 1999; Houben et al., 2015; Proctor et al., 2009; see also Chapters 4 and 6). Additionally, when adding internalizing problems as a covariate, more dissatisfaction with leisure activities appeared as an additional predictor of lower levels of well-being. This could suggest that mental health problems may act as an obstacle for adolescents to successfully participate in leisure activities, a life domain deemed important for adolescents (Csikszentmihalyi, 2000; Kuykendall et al., 2015, 2018). Still, we should be careful when interpreting the effects of internalizing mental health problems as the subscale that was used in this sample showed a rather low internal consistency. More research is recommended to delve deeper into these findings with different measurements, such as more elaborate psychopathology questionnaires and diagnostic information.

7.3.6 *Obstacles: Criminogenic Risk Factors and Mental Health Problems*

Regarding the possible obstacles, we found that internalizing problems were only directly related to the detained adolescents' lower levels of well-being, while externalizing problems and criminogenic risk factors were specifically related to more delinquent behaviour. These findings thus partly confirm our hypothesis that obstacles (i.e. in the form of criminogenic risk factors and mental health problems) can result in lower levels of well-being and explain offending behaviour in adolescents. As for mental health problems, our results add to the often-conflicting findings on the relationship between psychopathology and (juvenile) delinquency (Wibbelink et al., 2017). In their meta-analysis, Wibbelink et al. (2017) concluded that, in general, internalizing disorders (i.e. depression and anxiety disorders) are not significantly related to criminal recidivism, while externalizing disorders are.

Furthermore, regarding the criminogenic risk factors, our findings confirm the long-standing empirical legacy of the RNR that criminogenic risk factors play an important role in explaining juvenile delinquency, that is, they could form the obstacles that facilitate or foster criminal behaviour. Hence, criminogenic risk factors could play a more important role than merely signalling a problem area, as previously stated by the GLM (Ward, 2002b; Ward & Brown, 2004; Ward & Maruna, 2007; Ward & Stewart, 2003b, 2003c). Instead, rehabilitation interventions could address the criminogenic risk factors as obstacles in the way to achieve primary goods and well-being in a prosocial manner.

As discussed earlier, taking into account these obstacles, some GLM primary goods appeared to be significant additional predictors of adolescent delinquency, that is, we saw that while satisfaction with one's number of friends was no longer a significant predictor, more dissatisfaction with one's safety (i.e. 'life'), family relationships (i.e. 'relatedness') and 'pleasure' became significant predictors of more adolescent delinquency. Additionally, but in the other direction, more dissatisfaction with one's financial situation (i.e. 'life') was related to less delinquency. These findings indicate that independent of criminogenic risk factors and mental health problems, primary goods (dis)satisfaction can play an explanatory role in understanding juvenile delinquency.

7.3.7 *Less Important Goods(?)*

As in the previous chapter, a number of primary goods were unrelated to adolescents' well-being and delinquency. In detained adolescent boys these were 'knowledge', 'excellence in work', 'excellence in agency', 'community', 'spirituality' and 'creativity'. This could indicate these goods are indeed less important for the detained boys and/or contribute in some other indirect way to either their well-being or delinquent behaviour. Although we, again, found no indications of multi-collinearity, the models included the possibility of covariance between all predictors, and most were found to be significantly related to each other (see Appendix F[20] for the correlation matrix and VIF values). Another explanation can be found in a lack of statistical power. Especially smaller effects could go undetected because of our relatively small sample (see the limitations in Section 7.5).

7.4 Conclusion

In conclusion, the results of this study suggest that the etiological assumptions of the GLM in explaining well-being and delinquency can partially be applied to detained adolescents, that is, in this study we found no support for the hypothesized indirect routes of primary goods satisfaction, through well-being, on delinquency. Nonetheless, support was found for a bivariate relationship between adolescents' well-being and delinquency, and direct associations with a limited number of the primary goods. Primary goods satisfaction demonstrated additional explanatory value beyond criminogenic risk factors of the RNR in predicting juvenile delinquency. In practice, however, it is important to assess exactly how the juveniles aim to achieve primary goods satisfaction, as for some primary goods more satisfaction was related to more delinquency. In those cases, focusing on merely increasing satisfaction in rehabilitation interventions, without considering how (antisocial vs. prosocial) that satisfaction is achieved, will not be sufficient to reduce recidivism. Additionally, along with mental health problems, criminogenic risk factors can be seen as potential obstacles in prosocially fulfilling one's primary goods, representing important treatment targets for rehabilitation.

7.5 Limitations and Remaining Questions

In general, the same limitations that applied to the previous study in the general population, also apply to this study (see Chapter 6, Section 6.5). In both studies, based on statistical associations, we cannot infer conclusions about the direction and causality of the observed relationships (Hayes, 2017). Additionally, in the current study we might have lacked statistical power to find small(er) effects as a result of our smaller samples size. Nevertheless, despite the fact that we found fewer statistically significant predictors compared to the

20 See https://www.elevenpub.com/en/content/appendices-9789462364257.

previous chapter, the variances explained by our path analyses (R^2) in the current study were still medium to large. It should be noted, however, that PROCESS does not provide an adjusted R^2 and therefore does not take into account the number of predictors added to the model. Nevertheless, these findings can still indicate that the (unstandardized) effects of the statistically significant predictors in our current study are probably relevant and meaningful in explaining well-being and juvenile delinquency in detained adolescents.

Another potential limitation in the current study lies in the gender of our sample of detained adolescents. Although the initial intention was to include both girls and boys (as in Chapter 6), this proved not to be feasible (see this chapter, fn 1). Other studies have pointed towards the importance of (the lack of research into) gender differences in detained adolescents. Detained female adolescents could have specific needs, different from their male counterparts, such as higher prevalence of psychopathology and traumatic experiences (Van Damme et al., 2014, 2016, 2017, 2019). Future studies are advised to include both boys and girls.

Furthermore, although in the current study we aimed to add and change some of the primary goods proxy-items to be able to assess the observed relationships in more detail, the quantitative analyses remain limited in explanatory depth, that is, the results cannot shed light on how adolescents define their own well-being, what influences their well-being according to them, the importance they attach to the eleven primary goods, and what role the primary goods satisfaction and well-being might have played in their (own) explanation of their delinquent behaviour. Moreover, in the current study we only indirectly assessed the proposed problems that can hamper primary good attainment by taking into account the hypothesized obstacles in the form of criminogenic risk factors and mental health problems. The other four possible problems according to the GLM (*lack of capacities* and opportunities, *lack of scope*, use of *inappropriate means*, and *lack of coherence*) are more difficult to measure quantitatively. Therefore, in the next chapter we will pay attention to whether and how these problems (can) play a role in the explanation of the detained adolescents' delinquent behaviour based on a qualitative method.

8 Examining the Self-Perceived Pathways to Juvenile Delinquency in Detained Adolescents

Self-Perceived Views on Primary Goods, Well-Being and Delinquency in Detained Adolescent Boys

In the previous two chapters, we examined the etiological assumptions of the Good Lives Model (GLM) in (detained) adolescents using quantitative methods. Taken together, these two studies revealed some interesting relationships between primary goods satisfaction, well-being and adolescent delinquency.

We concluded that both psychopathology and criminogenic risk factors may be obstacles in the pursuit of well-being and can promote delinquent behaviour. Still, taking into account these obstacles, some primary goods (i.e., 'relatedness', 'life' and 'inner peace') remained or became significant predictors of adolescent well-being and/or delinquency. These findings indicate that beyond criminogenic risk factors, the primary goods can play an explanatory role in adolescent well-being and delinquent behaviour. From this finding we also concluded that criminogenic risk factors may play a bigger role than merely signalling a problem area, as previously stated by the GLM (Ward, 2002b; Ward & Brown, 2004; Ward & Maruna, 2007; Ward & Stewart, 2003b, 2003c). In fact, they could guide rehabilitation interventions in how to address the primary goods achievement in a prosocial manner.

Still, not all primary goods proved to be related to either well-being and/or delinquency in adolescents. We also did not find (strong) support for the hypothesized indirect route that problems (*lack of capacities* and opportunities, *lack of scope*, *use of inappropriate means* and *lack of coherence*) with primary goods achievement result in an accumulation of negative effects on the individual's life and overall well-being, and in this way lead to offending behaviour (Purvis, 2010; Purvis et al., 2011). These statements, however, warrant some caution as the cross-sectional nature of the studies and the almost exclusive reliance on self-report data limit drawing of conclusions regarding causality. In general, quantitative research provides a broad overall picture of associations within a group that cannot be extended to the individual case. Moreover, as repeated throughout the chapters, well-being and the primary goods constitute complex and rather broad theoretical constructs that are difficult to fully capture in a few quantitative survey items.

Consequently, qualitative research could expand our knowledge about the self-perceived insights, motivations and the narrative explanations of the detained youth themselves (see e.g., Horstkötter et al., 2012). In our quantitative studies we structured and predefined our variables to test our hypotheses, whereas a qualitative study allows for the youths' own interpretation and input. Subsequently, where quantitative data can provide a more generalizable picture of associations between variables and uncovers group variance, qualitative data delves into personal experiences, understandings, details and specific situations of individuals (Mortelmans, 2020; Silverman, 2013).

Hence, qualitative data can provide knowledge on how detained adolescents define well-being, what according to them influences their well-being, the importance they attach to the primary goods and how they view the role of primary goods satisfaction and well-being in their delinquent behaviour (see e.g., also the qualitative studies on the GLM's assumptions in adults; Purvis et al., 2011; Taylor, 2017). Therefore, in the current study, we examine the GLM's assumptions about well-being and delinquency, by analysing qualitative interviews that were conducted with a sub-sample (n = 31) of the detained adolescents that also participated in the study described in the previous chapter.

8.1 Method

8.1.1 Study Procedure

For this study, the sampling procedure described in Chapter 7 (see Section 7.1.1) is applicable. The sample (N = 170) in that study was additionally asked to potentially participate in an additional interview for the current study. Of that sample, 82 refused to participate in the additional interview and 88 detained adolescents agreed to participate. Of these 88 consenting participants, 31 were randomly selected to participate in this part of the study. After they filled out the survey and completed the risk assessment interview (at T1, see Section 7.1.2 for the full procedure), participants were interviewed using a semi-structured interview (see Appendix G[1]) based on the GLM interview guide developed by Yates, Kingston, et al. (2009). Questions were asked about how the detained adolescents viewed their primary goods attainment and its relationship to their well-being and past offending behaviour. Additionally, we questioned them about possible experiences of problems or obstacles in the pursuit of primary goods and well-being. These interviews ranged in duration from 13 to 59 minutes. The interviews were transcribed verbatim by another researcher who pledged confidentially in accordance with ethical and privacy guidelines. Although the interviews were held and transcribed in Dutch, the quotes used

1 See https://www.elevenpub.com/en/content/appendices-9789462364257.

in the Results section were translated into English for the purpose of this study (the original Dutch quotes are added in the accompanying footnotes).

8.1.2 *Qualitative Analyses*

The data of the verbatim interview transcripts were analysed using thematic analysis (Braun & Clarke, 2006; Mortelmans, 2020). Thematic analysis is a qualitative approach for analysing and reporting patterns or themes within data. This type of analysis can take the form of an inductive as well as a deductive approach. An inductive approach means that the themes are derived from the data themselves in a bottom-up fashion. This type of analysis is exploratory in nature and ensures that the results closely reflect the statements, experiences and perceptions of the participants themselves. In contrast, a 'theoretical thematic analysis' is considered a deductive and theory-driven approach. In this approach the emerging themes are deduced based on previous research. This type of analysis is suitable to test specific research questions (Braun & Clarke, 2006; Mortelmans, 2020). Although we aimed to explore the youth's own ideas and experiences openly, with as little suggestion as possible from the researcher, the current study is also focused on examining the GLM theory. As a result, the data are not analysed in a theoretical and epistemological vacuum. Consequently, we used both an inductive and a deductive analytic approach, which will both be explained in more detail in this section.

In a first step, qualitative research software (NVivo 1.4.1, QSR International, 2021) was used to organize the verbatim interview transcripts. The transcripts of the qualitative interviews were then analysed line-by-line using the iterative bottom-up (i.e., inductive) approach as described by informed grounded theory and thematic analyses (Creswell & Poth, 2016; Glaser & Strauss, 1967; Mortelmans, 2020; Thornberg, 2012). First, I identified concepts in codes in an open coding phase. Examples of codes that emerged in this phase included the specific things, situations, experiences and people that were mentioned as important to the youths' well-being on the one hand, and the specific self-perceived obstacles and problems they experienced in their lives on the other. After a first round of coding, all interviews were analysed again to check whether they consisted of additional data for the codes that had emerged in the first round. This inductive approach allowed for the identification of recurring categories and concepts voiced by the youth and ensured that their own words and expressions were preserved in the results (Braun & Clarke, 2006; Mortelmans, 2020).

In a next step, we analysed the emerged codes in a deductive manner as described in 'theoretical thematic analysis' (Braun & Clarke, 2006; Mortelmans, 2020), that is, the categories that had emerged in the previous inductive approach were examined, compared, and – when possible – categorized in terms of the theoretical higher-order themes of the

GLM: the importance and pursuit of the eleven primary goods for well-being and the four problems with primary goods attainment in general and in relation to the youths' delinquent behaviour. This resulted in a thematic framework in which the theoretical assumptions of the GLM could be tested against the views of the detained adolescents. More specifically, this technique allowed for the translation of the GLM assumptions into the words and perspectives of the detained adolescents themselves.

8.2 Results

8.2.1 *Sample Description*

The 31 adolescent boys (aged 14 to 17) had a mean age of 16.16 (SD = 0.86). In terms of education and employment, the majority of the participants (64.5%, n = 20) attended school before they were arrested; 12.9% (n = 4) were temporarily suspended from school; 19.4% (n = 6) did not attend school and were unemployed; and one (3.2%) was employed full-time. Of the youth who attended school or were only temporarily suspended (n = 24), 33.3% (n = 8) attended vocational secondary education ('bso'/'vmbo'), 20.8% (n = 5) attended part-time secondary education (combined with part-time employment and/or traineeship), 20.8% (n = 5) attended technical secondary education ('tso'/'havo'), 8.4% (n = 2) attended general (including art school) secondary education ('aso'/'kso'/'vwo'), one (4.2%) attended primary school and one (4.2%) attended higher (vocational) education. The majority of participants were born in Belgium (64.5%, n = 20) and 12.9% (n = 4) were born in the Netherlands. The other participants (22.6%, n = 7) were born in a number of different countries: Bulgaria, Ghana, Dutch Antilles, Russia, Spain and South Africa. About half of the participants' biological parents were divorced (41.9%, n = 13), 45.2% (n = 14) lived together, and in 12.9% (n = 4) of the cases one or both parents were unknown or deceased. Before their arrest, about a third of the participants (38.7%; n = 12) lived with both their parents, 35.5% (n = 11) lived (most of the time) with their mother, 5.3% (n = 9) lived (most of the time) with their father, 19.4% (n = 6) lived somewhere else (e.g., with foster parents, other family members, friends or alone), and two (6.5%) lived in a residential institution.

This sub-sample of 31 detained adolescents did not significantly differ from those adolescents who only participated in the study of Chapter 7 in terms of demographic variables and self-report measures of primary goods satisfaction, well-being and delinquency.

8.2.2 The Importance of Primary Goods According to Detained Adolescents

First, the participants were asked what their lives would look like if they could have it exactly how they wanted it to be. Additionally, they were asked why the things they mentioned were important to them and how they aim(ed) to achieve them.

Loved Ones

When asked about what their dream lives would look like, all adolescents mentioned they wanted to be at home, with family (parents, brothers and sisters), friends, a partner and/or a family of their own.

> Uh. At home. Uhm. Just with my mom, my sisters … Just happy. Nothing more. (Participant 11, age 15)[2]

> When I am older, I would uh … I would like to have, maybe a child that would be running around the house. And … just, a small, but loving family. And that my parents would come over or we'd go over to my parents' house. And that we'd just have breakfast together or lunch or dinner. And just … have a nice atmosphere between us. (Participant 151, age 16)[3]

> The happy things I already had in my life. I didn't need much more. I had my girlfriend, I had my mates … and that uh, that was enough for me. (Participant 19, age 17)[4]

Family relationships (from the primary good of 'relatedness'), often the relationship with their parent(s), were consistently identified as (the most) important in their lives. Friends or partners were also mentioned as important by most participants, but usually as less important and less often than family and parents.

> Interviewer: Were there certain things more important than others?

2 "Euh. Thuis. Euhm. Gewoon met mijn moeder, mijn zussen … Gewoon vrolijk. Meer niet."
3 "Als ik ouder zou zijn, dan euh … zou ik een, misschien een klein kindje willen hebben dat dan rondloopt door het huis. En … gewoon, een klein, maar liefdevol gezinnetje. En dat mijn ouders dan langskomen of wij gaan langs bij mijn ouders. En dat we dan gewoon samen ontbijten of middag eten of avondeten. En gewoon … een leuke sfeer hebben onder elkaar."
4 "De gelukkige dingen had ik in mijn leven. Ik had niet veel meer nodig. Ik had mijn vriendin, ik had mijn maten … en dat euh, dat was genoeg voor mij."

> Participant: Yes. Parents are more important than friends. (Participant 2, age 17)[5]

> They are the two people who brought me here on earth. They took care of me. My mother carried me for nine months. (Participant 127, age 17)[6]

> Being with family is the most important thing to me, always. And that will never change. (Participant 25, age 17)[7]

> Without your family, you're nothing anyway. Family members are the ones who stand by you in case of need. (Participant 58, age 14)[8]

The realization of the importance of relationships appeared to be triggered by the fact that their detention was depriving them of regular contact with their families and loved ones.

> I would just [want to] wake up at home ..., with my parents, for example, yeah. Then, just spend all day with them.... Because, you know, now see ... I am here without them, and ... I actually miss them. (Participant 117, age 15)[9]

> Interviewer: What was most important for you?
> Participant: Family. My parents really. Yeah ... just having moments with them. I was detained for a long time ... So, I thought just being with them is very important. (Participant 35, age 16)[10]

Parents

However, the majority of participants also had experience with conflict(s) at home, consisting of chronic problems in their relationships with parents and/or problems that were caused by their delinquent behaviour. Despite these conflicts at home, most youth still valued the bond they have with their parent(s). For example, when asked why his parents were so important to him, one participant answered:

---

5 "Ja. Ouders zijn belangrijker dan vrienden."

6 "Hun zijn de twee mensen die mij hier op aarde hebben gebracht hé. Die hebben voor mij gezorgd. Mijn moeder heeft mij negen maanden in haar, alee, negen maanden gedragen."

7 "Sowieso met familie zijn is het belangrijkst voor mij altijd. En dat zal nooit veranderen"

8 "Zonder je familie ben je toch niks. Familie is diegene die bij jou staat in de geval van nood."

9 "Ik zou gewoon thuis [willen] wakker worden ..., met mijn ouders, bijvoorbeeld, ja. Dan, gewoon heel de dag met hun ... Omdat ja, nu zie ... zit ik hier zonder hun en ... ik mis hun eigenlijk wel, ja."

10 "Familie. Mijn ouders echt. Ja ... gewoon momenten met hun hebben. Ik heb lang vastgezeten toen hè ... Dus ik dacht gewoon met hun zijn, is heel belangrijk."

> Because uh, I had noticed that when grandpa died. Then I saw dad was crying, but before that, dad was always fighting with my grandpa. They never said anything to each other. When grandpa died, daddy had to cry and then I thought 'he often fights with him, but he still loves him'. The same with my mother … It is your mother, it will always stay that way. (Participant 10, age 16)[11]

Another participant explained that despite and/or maybe because of the problems he experienced with his father he wanted to make him proud:

> I, uh, I have a bad relationship with my father. And then … When you're standing … on the sports field … with him and you suddenly see him smiling … that does something. And, uh … making sure his team wins … because of you, that does something to you. That he is happy. (Participant 35, age 16)[12]

Friends

Aside from family, most boys reported they enjoyed hanging out with friends.

> … just being with friends, that is what I liked to do, I didn't do much more. (Participant 1, age 17)[13]

> When I am with my mates that makes me happy. When I'm at home, with my mother or my family, that's what makes me happy. (Participant 5, age 15)[14]

> I liked being with friends, nothing more. (Participant 6, age 17)[15]

Especially for youth who had experienced problems at home or who had a poor relationship with their parent(s), friends seemed to play an important role:

11 "Omdat euh, ik had dat gemerkt toen opa dood was. Dan had ik gezien dat papa moest wenen en daarvoor had papa altijd ruzie met mijn opa. Die praatte nooit tegen elkaar. Toen opa dood was moest papa wenen en toen dacht ik wel van 'hij heeft daar vaak ruzie mee, maar hij houdt er wel van'. En bij mijn mama ook … bij mama is het gewoon van ja, dat is uw moeder he, dat blijft."

12 "Ik euh, ik heb een slechte band met mijn vader. En dan … Als ge dan euh, op het sportveld staat … met hem staat en ge ziet ineens hem lachen en … dat doet iets hé. En euh … ervoor zorgen dat zijn team wint … door u, ja, dat doet u iets hé. Dat die blij is."

13 " … gewoon bij vrienden, dat is wat ik graag deed, ik deed niet veel anders."

14 "Als ik met kameraden ben daar word ik gelukkig van. Als ik bij mijn thuis ben, bij mijn moeder of mijn familie, daar ben ik blij om."

15 "Ik was graag met mijn vrienden. Meer niet."

> We talked about all kinds of things. Everyone was open. Well, the three of us, when the three of us were together we could talk about anything. We trusted each other. We knew the most about each other. They knew more about me than my parents. I knew more about them than their parents. Like this. When he had a fight with his father and his mother, we would meet up, he would tell us what had happened. (Participant 10, age 16)[16]

Usually 'true' friends were distinguished as important compared to other more superficial friends. Feelings of mutual trust and understanding appeared to play an important role in these true friendships.

> [those true friends] they the ones with … are who I actually grew up with. They stay with me, even if things are bad, even if I'm here [in detention]. Because some friends I will not see again, that's why. Now I see who my real friends are. Because those guys from my neighbourhood they also came to my house 'how is [name] doing?'. So, I know, those are my real friends. (Participant 58, age 14)[17]

> Because, for example, my friends, who I only hang out with, that small circle, they also understand me. I understand them. We come from the same situations, uh, have gone through the same things or are going through the same things right now. (Participant 64, age 16)[18]

Reasons Why Loved Ones are Important

When asked why being around people close to them mattered to them, most youth referred to the importance of being loved and supporting each other.

---

16 "We praten over van alles. Iedereen is open. Alee wij met zen drieën, als we met zen drieën waren konden we over alles praten. We vertrouwden elkaar. Wij wisten het meeste van elkaar. Hun wisten meer over mij dan mijn ouders. Ik wist meer over hun dan hun ouders. Zo. Als die ruzie had met zijn vader en zijn moeder dan he, we spraken af, dan vertelde die wat er was gebeurd."

17 "[mijn echte vrienden] hun zijn degene met … met wie ik eigenlijk ben opgegroeid. Zij blijven bij mij, ook al gaat het slecht, ook al zit ik hier [in detentie]. Want sommige vrienden die zie ik niet terug, daarom. Nu zie ik wie mijn echt vrienden zijn. Want die jongens van mijn buurt die zijn ook naar mijn huis gekomen 'hoe gaat het met [naam]?'. Dus ik kan weten, dat zijn mijn echte vrienden."

18 "Want bijvoorbeeld mijn vrienden, waar ik ook alleen maar mee omga, die kleine cirkel, die begrijpen mij ook. Ik begrijp hun. Wij komen uit zelfde situaties, euh, hebben hetzelfde meegemaakt of maken nu hetzelfde mee."

> Because I love her. She's my only support right now. She also supports me through these times. She won't drop me. She will always be there for me. That's really something that I appreciate. (Participant 19, age 17)[19]

> I can always go there if there is something or with my problems, I can always talk to them about it. Just like a confidant or something like that, but then it's my own family. (Participant 71, age 17)[20]

Others mentioned the importance of feeling comfortable and being themselves around loved ones.

> When I'm with my girlfriend, I can really ..., then, then, it does not matter whether I am sober, high, or drunk ..., time always flies by. So ... Spending time with her is ... a one hundred topic, when I am out of here. So [I want] to be with her as much as possible in my free time.... She understands me completely. (Participant 16, age 16)[21]

> My mother accepts me the way I am. That's the most important thing ... She always loves me. No matter what I did. (Participant 28, age 17)[22]

Again, others talked about the importance of making their loved ones happy, for example, by doing something to make them proud or giving them presents.

> When my mom is happy, I get happy too. And if my girlfriend is happy and such then.... Yeah, I just like to see them smile. (Participant 39, age 16)[23]

> That my parents ... are just proud of me. (Participant 28, age 17)[24]

19 "Omdat ik die graag zie. Zij is mijn enigste steunbeleid momenteel. Zij steunt mij ook door deze tijden. Zij laat mij niet vallen. Zij zal er altijd zijn voor mij. Dat is echt wel iets dat ik apprecieer."

20 "Ik kan daar altijd terecht als er iets is of met mijn problemen kan ik er met hun over praten. Net zoals de vertrouwenspersoon zoiets, maar dan is het wel mijn eigen familie."

21 "Als ik bij mijn lief ben kan ik mij echt, dan dan, maakt niet als ik nuchter ben, high, zat ... de tijd vliegt voorbij. Dus ... Tijd spenderen met haar is ... a one hundred topic wanneer ik buiten ben. Dus [ik wil] zoveel mogelijk bij haar zijn in mijn vrije tijd ... Zij begrijpt mij totaal."

22 "Mijn moeder mij accepteert hoe ik ben. Dat is het belangrijkste ... Zij had mij altijd graag. Maakt niet uit wat ik deed."

23 "Als mijn moeder blij is ofzo, dan word ik ook zo blij. En als mijn vriendin ook zo blij is enzo dan ... Ja, ik zie hun gewoon graag lachen."

24 "Dat mijn ouders ... dat zij gewoon trots zijn op mij."

> Because my parents did so much for me, and they also always gave me everything I wanted. They would put me in the best school, they would do anything for me. Especially my mom. She would really do everything for me. So, I have to pay her back somehow. (Participant 67, age 16)[25]

A few boys also mentioned the joy pets brought to their lives.

> [I would want] maybe some pets, some joy in the house
> (Participant 17, age 17)[26]

Livelihood

Most participants said they aimed to have a nice house to live in (with their loved ones) and have enough money at their disposal to make ends meet (i.e., the primary good of 'life').

> [I want to be] in my own little house of course. Then uh … just make it my own. Because I would like to either build a house or buy something and renovate it. So that I can … make it my own. Make it cozy, the way I want it. (Participant 60, age 16)[27]

> Uh, yeah just being able to have a good life. Later. Being able to take care of my family. (Participant 2, age 17)[28]

Most boys who emphasized the importance of money (over other goods) did so because they and/or their parent(s) had little money to spend.

> Just that like, for example, you want to go buy something, but you don't have enough money. Or you see your mother … in the store … she sees a dress that she wants to buy, but she doesn't have enough [money], because she still has to

25 "Omdat mijn ouders zo veel voor mij hebben gedaan en zij hebben mij ook altijd alles gegeven wat ik wou. Zij hebben mij … als ik … ze zouden mij in de beste school steken, ze zouden alles voor mij doen. Zeker mijn mama. Zij zou echt alles voor mij doen. Dus, ik moet haar dat terugbetalen op één of andere manier."

26 "[Ik wil] misschien wat huisdieren, wat vreugde in huis."

27 "[Ik wil] in mijn eigen huisje [zijn] natuurlijk. Dan euh … gewoon eigen, eigen ding maken. Want ik wil graag ofwel een huis bouwen ofwel iets kopen en renoveren. Dat ik zo … ja een beetje mijn eigen ding ervan kan maken. Beetje gezellig kan maken, hoe ik dat wil."

28 "Euh, ja gewoon een goei leven kunnen hebben. Later. Voor mijn gezin kunnen zorgen."

> buy bread for the children. And that affected me when that happened. (Participant 127, age 17)[29]

> You start the month, you're with your parents, your parents barely earn anything, not even enough to feed everyone enough. Uh ... Then you're going to want to do something about that, you are going to want to make some money, extra money right? (Participant 138, age 17)[30]

Living a 'Normal' Life

Up until now, we have seen that the achievement of the primary goods of 'relatedness' (spending time with family and friends) and 'life' (having a livelihood and a place to live) are important life goals. Some of the boys referred to this dream life as 'wanting to live a normal life', being 'like everybody else' and being a part of society (i.e., the primary good of 'community').

> I would just like to have a job, a house, a pension also later. And yeah, make enough money. Also a car, family, children and yeah ... like everyone else, just be a normal family. And not having difficulties or things like that with money and so on, just decent, that you can participate in society. (Participant 5, age 15)[31]

> Yes, a roof over your head. Of course, a house, a garden, settling down. Just a normal life, not like we have now, an apartment in a neighbourhood behind the station. (Participant 138, age 17)[32]

---

29 "Gewoon dat als bijvoorbeeld, ge wilt iets gaan kopen, maar ge hebt niet genoeg geld ofzo om dat te kopen. Of ge ziet uw moeder ... die ziet in de winkel ... die ziet zo een kleedje ofzo en die wilt die kopen, maar die heeft niet genoeg [geld], want die moet nog brood kopen ofzo voor de kinderen. En dat raakte mij wel als dat gebeurde."

30 "Je begint met de maand, je bent bij je ouders, je ouders verdienen amper iets, niet eens genoeg om iedereen eten te geven, deftig genoeg eten. Euh ... Dan ga jij daar willen iets op doen, ga jij geld, extra geld willen gaan verdienen toch?"

31 "Ik zou gewoon willen dat ik werk heb, een huis, een pensioen ook later. En ja, geld verdienen, genoeg. Ook een auto, gezin, kinderen en ja ... zoals iedereen ja, gewoon zo een normaal gezin zijn. En niet moeilijkheden of zo een dingen hebben met geld enzo, gewoon fatsoenlijk dat ge in de maatschappij kunt meeleven."

32 "Ja, een dak om onder te kunnen leven. Tuurlijk een huis, een tuin, alles rustig toch. Gewoon een normaal leven, niet zoals we nu hebben appartement in een wijk achter het station."

> I'm planning on just quitting everything [crimes] anyway and just going to work. No more hanging out with bad friends and stuff, just yeah, normal. Like other boys my age. (Participant 11, age 15)[33]

Money, Cars, Freedom and Fun

About half of the participants, however, took this a step further and wanted to pursue not just a 'normal' life, but wished for a wealthy lifestyle, characterized by possession of extreme amounts of money, luxury, parties and enjoyment (i.e., the primary good of 'pleasure') and the freedom to buy, go and do according to their own life goals (related to the primary good of 'excellence in agency').

> Waking up in my villa in Miami. Near the water. With a garden where I can chill by the water. With boat, a yacht…. Yes, I want to be rich…, take drugs occasionally with friends. Just such a chill life. I would want to be Dan Bilzerian [famous rich Armenian-American poker player and actor]. (Participant 3, age 16)[34]

> I'm quite materialistic. I, as a person, because, you see, I want … to have the freedom to step into a store and buy what I want and step outside. I want to be able to get fines and not care. Give me a 10.000 euro fine and I want to say: 'okay here it is, done'. That's how I want to live. That freedom. (Participant 67, age 16)[35]

Being detained triggered the need to be free in most of the participants.

> See with money, you have the freedom to go everywhere. You can do almost anything. When you have been detained … then you realize what freedom is. (Participant 16, age 16)[36]

33 "Ik ben sowieso van plan om gewoon te stoppen met alles [delicten] en gewoon te gaan werken. Niet meer met slechte vrienden optrekken enzo, gewoon ja, normaal. Zoals anderen jongens van mijn leeftijd."

34 "Ik word in mijn villa in Miami wakker. Zo aan, zo aan water daarzo. Zo een tuin en dan chillen aan het water. Met boot daar, een jacht … ik wil zo rijk zijn … drugs pakken af en toe met vrienden. Gewoon zo een chill leven. Dan Bilzerian zou ik willen zijn."

35 "Ik ben vrij materialistisch. Ik, als persoon, want, zie je, ik wil … ik wil zo graag de vrijheid hebben om in een winkel te stappen en te kopen wat ik wil en buiten te stappen. Ik wil boetes kunnen krijgen en mij niks ervan aantrekken. Geef mij een boete van 10.000 euro en gewoon 'oké hier, klaar'. Zo wil ik leven. Die vrijheid."

36 "Zo met geld, je hebt vrijheid overal hé … Je kan bijna alles doen. Als je hebt vastgezeten … je beseft dan wel wat vrijheid is."

> I just want more freedom … I did have some freedom, but I still had to stick to the agreements with my probation officer and … those community service hours and stuff, you know? That wasn't really freedom. (Participant 39, age 16)[37]

Related to this need to be free, the participants voiced a need to be free from problems (with justice authorities), worries (about money) and stress. A significant number of participants repeatedly referred to their wish for 'peace and quiet' (i.e., the primary good of 'inner peace'). They appeared to be troubled by many problems and worries they wanted to disappear.

> that you are away from the neighbourhood for a while. That you have no more worries. You don't have to think for a while about getting arrested at any moment. That you're away from everything for a while. (Participant 28, age 17)[38]

> I'm telling you, the day that I am happy is when I can quietly smoke a joint. That's because I think too much, but at that moment I don't think about anything anymore and I am just 'bam' laying there. Everything is behind me. No more stressing and no more being insecure. Rest. Aah … That's what I'd really like to do on the Matterhorn in Switzerland: smoking a joint. All the way up there. (Participant 35, age 16)[39]

While many of the youth considered wealth and fun (i.e., the primary good of 'pleasure') to be extremely important for their well-being, there were some who recognized or had experienced (usually those who are a bit older) that those goals were not always the most important in life.

> In first place comes love. That's above money and everything else. That's something you can't buy. And the moment you really get it and you feel that

37 "Ik wil gewoon meer vrijheid … Ik had wel vrijheid enzo, maar ik moest mij nog steeds wel aan de afspraak met mijn mpt-begeleider en … die taakstraffen enzo, snap je? Dat was niet echt vrijheid."

38 " … dat ge efkes weg bent van de buurt. Dat ge efkes geen zorgen meer hebt. Dat ge efkes niet meer moet denken, ja, ik kan elk moment opgepakt worden of iets. Dat ge efkes weg bent van alles."

39 "Ik zegt het, de dag dat ik gelukkig ben is dat ik rustig een joint kan smoren. Dat is, want dan … ik denk, denk zoveel, maar de moment dat ik niks meer denk en gewoon 'baam' lig. Alles is achter de rug. Niet meer stressen en niet meer onzeker zijn. Rust. Aah. Dat zou ik echt graag willen doen op de Matterhorn in Zwitserland een joint smoren. Daar helemaal vanboven."

> love, that's it ... Then you don't need the best car or the best house, you know ... Because when you have love, you have happiness. (Participant 17, age 17)[40]

> As you see, I have committed a number of crimes.... I've already seen a lot of money. In those times I uh bought a lot of things for my brothers, or uh, getting spoiled. It's not that I was always happy, no.... And in terms of finance, being, uh, financially wealthy, rich ... being rich, for example. I think that's also important. But it just makes me feel happy, not fulfilled, just happy. (Participant 85, age 17)[41]

One of the participants went on to explain the difference between the fleeting feeling of being happy and the fulfilling type of happiness:

> Happiness is, uh, is that you just don't have any worries anymore. You are just, uh, how do you say that, that's a difficult one. Just that you don't disappoint anyone in life and, uh, no one has to ... my parents don't have to worry about me anymore, or about me, or my brothers and sisters, or anything like that. They don't have to miss me. That's actually, uh, happiness for me. While being happy is just ... more the material thing, really. When ... when you have the latest car or a beautiful house or the latest cell phone and such. Then I would just be happy. If I ... if I, for example, got a cellphone from my parents, the new iPhone 6 plus, for example, I was always happy with it. But it did not bring me happiness. (Participant 85, age 17)[42]

Achieving

When asked how they would pursue their dream lives, about half of the youth referred to the importance of graduating from school and being employed to make a livelihood. In

---

40 "Sowieso op één staat liefde. Dat staat boven geld en alles. Dat is iets dat ge niet kunt betalen hé. En het moment dat ge het echt krijgt en ge voelt die liefde dat is zo ... Dan hebt ge niet de beste auto of het best huis nodig, weet ge ... Want ge hebt u liefde en dan zijt ge blij."

41 "Zoals u ziet, heb ik wel wat feiten gepleegd ... Ik heb al heel veel geld gezien. In die tijden dat ik euh, dingen kon halen voor mijn broertjes of euh, mij eigenlijk kon verwennen. Het is niet dat ik altijd gelukkig was, nee ... En sowieso op vlak van financieel zijn, financieel echt wel euh geld hebben, rijk ... rijk zijn bijvoorbeeld. Vind ik wel ook belangrijk. Maar dat maakt mij gewoon blij, niet gelukkig, blij gewoon."

42 "Gelukkig is euh, is dat ge gewoon geen zorgen meer hebt. Ge bent gewoon euh, hoe moet ge dat zeggen, dat is wel een moeilijke. Pff, ja echt gewoon dat ge niemand teleurstelt in het leven en euh, niemand hoeft ... mijn ouders hoeven zich geen zorgen meer te maken over mij, over mij, broertjes en zussen ook niet enzo. Dat die mij niet hoeven te missen eigenlijk. Dat is eigenlijk euh, gelukkig zijn voor mij. Blij zijn is eigenlijk gewoon ... meer het materiële eigenlijk, zo. Van dat ... dat ge misschien de nieuwste auto hebt of mooi huis of de nieuwste gsm enzo. Dan zou ik gewoon blij zijn. Als ik ... als ik bijvoorbeeld een gsm kreeg van mijn ouders, de nieuwe Iphone 6 plus bijvoorbeeld, was ik altijd wel blij mee, maar gelukkig niet."

their view, school and work were primarily means to an end (earning money related to the primary good of 'life').

> Interviewer: And so what is the purpose of getting a diploma in your view?
> Participant: Work, but if I would have everything I wanted, I wouldn't need to work, and I wouldn't need a diploma. I would not get a diploma for fun. I need to have a reason. (Participant 1, age 17)[43]

> For me going to school part-time is easier because that allows me to work … Going to school full-time is not for me, that's why I started playing truant. I need to work more … Oftentimes I went to work, but then I didn't go to school. So those other two days I got paid illegally. So … if went to school I didn't get paid. (Participant 5, age 15)[44]

At the same time most participants emphasized the importance of accomplishing something they were good at or enjoyed (the primary good of 'excellence in work').

> My goal is to have a technical diploma in carpentry. So I can become self-employed. Woodwork has always inspired me and that's something that I'm good at and I'm not going to drop it. It is something that appeals to me, that's what I like to do. (Participant 19, age 17)[45]

> [I want to do …] something that I like. I like entrepreneurship, for example. I also really like soccer or rapping, for example. But, for example, being a lawyer or a teacher, who is also very successful … I would not be happy. I might make a lot of money and so on, but I wouldn't be happy with what I do. I also want to enjoy what I do. (Participant 85, age 17)[46]

---

43 "Werk, maar als ik toch alles heb, heb ik geen werk nodig en ook geen diploma. Een diploma da ga ik nie halen voor de lol hé. Ik moet een reden hebben."

44 "Ik vind voor mij deeltijds gemakkelijker want daardoor kan ik rapper gaan werken. Als ik, voltijds is niks voor mij. Daardoor ben ik zo begonnen met spijbelen enzo, Ik moet meer werken … Vaak omdat ik ging werken ging ik dan niet naar school. Dus die andere twee dagen kreeg ik zwart [betaald]. Dus … als ik niet naar school ging kreeg ik mijn loon niet."

45 "Het is mijn bedoeling om een technisch diploma schrijnwerkerij vast te hebben. Dat ik zelfstandige kan worden. Hout heeft mij altijd al geïnspireerd en dat is iets wat dat ik goed kan en ik ga dat niet laten vallen. Dat spreekt mij aan, dat vind ik leuk om te doen."

46 "[Ik wil] iets sowieso … dat ik leuk vind. Ik vind ondernemen bijvoorbeeld leuk. Ik vind voetbal of rappen vind ik bijvoorbeeld ook heel leuk. Maar bijvoorbeeld, een advocaat zijn of een leerkracht zijn, die ook heel succesvol … ik zou niet gelukkig zijn dan. Dus ik wel misschien heel veel geld verdienen enzo, maar ik zou niet blij zijn met wat ik doe. Ik wil ook plezier hebben in wat ik doe."

Although most boys referred to school and regular employment as the means to achieve competence and a livelihood, a significant number of them saw this as a back-up plan and aimed to make a career out of their hobby (i.e. the primary good of 'excellence in play'), such as becoming a famous soccer player, boxer or rapper.

> I dream of the fact … of becoming an artist … in terms of music or an actor … I will show them [the fans] that there is always still hope. (Participant 4, age 15)[47]

> I rap too, but in English. So … I want to become famous with that. (Participant 16, age 16)[48]

> Thai boxing, I went from fifteenth place in my weight class to third place in just two years. So, I thought that was going to be something big. I had put all my hopes on Thai boxing. I was too focused on Thai boxing. So that's why I had, uh, dropped school and had bad grades. (Participant 127, age 17)[49]

> Plan A is actually more uh, the rapping, the soccer actually, I do see that as plan A. Plan B is always school so if … if something fails in my life, then … plan B is school. (Participant 85, age 17)[50]

Status, Reputation and Pride

Status symbols, such as big houses, expensive cars or expensive clothes were viewed as the ultimate proof of having achieved something.

> Participant: I would definitely want a DSquared pants of 200 euros with a shirt of 700 euros …[51]
> Interviewer: What makes you want that? Why is that important?
> Participant: Getting attention. The attention you get from everyone. If you have Balenciaga's and you have DSquared pants and you have a shirt from

47 "Ik droom toch wel van het feit … van een artiest worden … Op vlak van muziek of een acteur … Dat ik ze [de fans] toch wel laat zien dat er altijd nog hoop is."

48 "Ik rap ook, maar in het Engels. Dus … daardoor bekend mee willen worden."

49 "Thai box, ik ging van vijftiende plaats van heel mijn gewichtsklasse ging ik in twee jaar naar drie. Dus ik dacht dat gaat wel iets worden. En dan heb ik al mijn hoop op thai box gestoken, maar ik had school. Alee, ik was te veel gefocust op thai box. Dus daarom had ik, euh, mijn school gelaten en had ik slechte punten."

50 "Plan A is eigenlijk meer euh, het rappen, het voetbal eigenlijk, dat zie ik wel als plan A. Plan B is altijd school dus als … als iets mislukt in mijn leven, dan is … plan B, school."

51 "Ik wil sowieso een DSquared broek van 200 euro met een hemd van 700 euro …"

> Armani and … sunglasses from Cartier. People start looking at you like … someone who has money. (Participant 16, age 16)[52]

> Money is important. If you don't have money you are just nothing. In my view, without money you are nothing. (Participant 71, age 17)[53]

> Just ask any man. Nobody wants to drive around in an ugly car. A house and car, they are status symbols for any person. If you drive a nice car, you're rich. If you drive an, yes, Opel Corsa you're poor. Things like that. (Participant 58, age 14)[54]

Status symbols simultaneously seemed to serve the purpose of pursuing the feeling of belonging to a group they looked up to (i.e., the primary good of 'community'), mainly by portraying themselves as belonging to the 'big guys'.

> Belonging to the big guys. Everyone wants to belong to the big guys. Reputation. Just … proving yourself. (Participant 16, age 16)[55]

> At first, I always had to get money from my parents and sometimes they didn't give me anything. That was frustrating for me and uh … yes see my friends, they went to do something nice and I couldn't go. Yes, they were also much older than me. And yes … that frustrated me too. [But now] when I walk into the neighborhood, older people also look at me. I get respect from them too. (Participant 28, age 17)[56]

Some youth used social media to achieve this goal, and felt they had accomplished something once they had many online followers, received 'likes' and were 'famous'.

---

52 "Aandacht krijgen. De aandacht dat je van iedereen krijgt dan. Als je Balenciaga's hebt en je hebt een DSquared broek en je hebt een hemd van Armani en … zonnebril van Cartier. Mensen gaan wel kijken van … die, die heeft geld."

53 "Geld is belangrijk. Als je geen geld hebt ben je gewoon niks. In mijn ogen, ben je gewoon niks."

54 "Vraag maar aan elke man. Niemand wil in een lelijke auto rondrijden. Een huis en auto is gewoon een statussymbool voor elke persoon. Als je in een mooie auto rijdt ben je rijk. Als je in een, ja, Opel Corsa rijdt ben je arm. Zulke dingen."

55 "Bij de grotere … Iedereen wilt bij de grotere horen. Reputatie. Gewoon … jezelf bewijzen"

56 "Eerst moest ik altijd geld halen bij mijn ouders en soms gaven ze mij ook niks. En toen was dat ook frustrerend en euh … ja kijk mijn vrienden toen gingen ze wel iets leuks doen en ik niet. Ja, zij waren ook veel ouder dan mij. En ja … dat frustreerde mij ook. Als ik [nu] gewoon in de buurt stap kijken ook oudere mensen naar mij. Ik krijg ook respect van hun."

> What is also important for me is still the social media and, uh, yes, the circle of friends, the social media … For example, the followers you have and the likes you get and so on. I still think that's important too. That I still have to keep up that standard … [When I get out] I will have to work twice as hard because now I'm kind of gone. Everyone forgets about you at some point and then you have to work twice as hard to have everything back that you had achieved. (Participant 4, age 15)[57]

Although achieving competence was seen primarily as a means towards financial gain, status or reputation in relation to others, some boys also considered it a goal in itself.

> Becoming really good at one thing. Just, it doesn't matter what … but just being good at something. Whether it's painting or rugby, I would prefer rugby, but just … yeah. Becoming known by doing something I'm really super good at. (Participant 16, age 16)[58]

Nonetheless, most participants agreed that the main goal was to achieve something in life to be proud of.

> That I realize I accomplished something and … That I made it. (Participant 39, age 16)[59]

> At the end of the day, I'm a youngster who started from scratch, right. If I could achieve that [being famous], then, uh, I could show everyone that it is possible and that your dreams can come true. (Participant 4, age 15)[60]

Meaning in Life

A smaller subset of boys also referred to their need to achieve something in life as accomplishing something bigger than themselves: to do something meaningful, such as

57 "Wat ook belangrijk natuurlijk was voor mij is nog steeds de social media en euh, ja, de vriendencirkel, de social media … Bijvoorbeeld volgers die je hebt en de likes die je krijgt enzo. Dat vind ik ook nog belangrijk. Dat ik dat nog steeds op standaard moet houden … [Als ik buiten ben], dat wordt twee keer harder werken omdat ik dan, nu toch wel een beetje verdwenen ben. Dan vergeet iedereen je op een gegeven moment en dan moet je twee keer harder werken om alles terug te hebben dat je had bereikt."

58 "Goed worden echt in één ding. Gewoon, maakt niet uit wat … maar gewoon in iets. Of het nu schilder is of rugby, liever rugby he, maar gewoon … ja. Bekend worden in iets waar ik echt super goed in ben."

59 "Dat ik ook gewoon besef zo van ja, ik heb ook iets bereikt en … ik heb het eigenlijk gemaakt."

60 "Uiteindelijk ben ik toch wel een jongere die van nul is begonnen he. Als ik dat [beroemd zijn] zou kunnen bereiken dan, euh, kan je toch laten zien dat het mogelijk is en dat je dromen waar kunnen worden."

giving back to the community (i.e., the broader conceptualization of the primary good of 'spirituality').

> Because well, being rich and all, I don't really think that's something, but if you give something back to the people then I think it is much better. (Participant 35, age 16)[61]

> Maybe I will go into politics. Being progressive ... making progress. That's ... making things better. Giving money to people who don't have jobs ... making sure they get jobs. Giving homeless people shelter. Things like that. (Participant 58, age 14)[62]

One of these participants also explained that he wanted to invest in sustainable energy to support a brighter future for his offspring.

> I think that's important because uh ... I'm here now [on earth] and uh.. I hope that my children will be here as well. That they also get that opportunity. You know what I mean? I think that's a little more important than myself. (Participant 35, age 16)[63]

Only one participant referred to the importance of being religious (the narrower conceptualization of the primary good of 'spirituality').

> [Religion] ...that's just very important. Without it, I would still be ... I would have committed other crimes, for example. Then maybe I would have done something worse or ... It just sets me straight more than anything else. (Participant 10, age 16)[64]

61 "Want ja, dat rijk zijn, ik vind dat eigenlijk niks hé, maar als gij iets teruggeeft aan de mensen dan denk ik dat gij daar veel meer mee bent."

62 "Misschien ga ik ook politiek in. Dat is gewoon, progressief ... progressie maken. Dat is ... dingen beter maken. Mensen die geen werk hebben geld ... zorgen dat ze werk krijgen. Mensen die zwervers zijn onderdak bezorgen. Ja. Zulke dingen."

63 "Ik vind dat belangrijk voor euh ... Ik ben hier nu [op aarde] en euh, ik hoop ook dat mijn kinderen er dan zijn. Dat die ook die kans krijgen. Snapt ge? Dat vind ik een beetje belangrijker als mezelf."

64 "[Religie] ...dat is gewoon heel belangrijk. Zonder dat was ik zeg maar nog, dan was ik hier met andere feiten gekomen bijvoorbeeld. Dan zou ik misschien iets erger hebben gedaan of ... Het brengt me gewoon meer op het rechte pad dan iets anders."

Staying True to Oneself

While talking about their well-being, life goals and needs, about half of the participants also stressed the importance of being themselves, having their own identity and staying true to themselves (i.e., the primary good of 'excellence in agency').

> I would just stay myself. I wouldn't want to be like anybody else. Because now, I have a girlfriend and she has fallen for the person that I am. Not the person I would want to be. (Participant 19, age 17)[65]

Less Frequently Mentioned Primary Goods

Other primary goods were less often identified as important to the detained youth. One example was pursuing physical health, as part of the primary good of 'life'. Only those boys who were at some point confronted with illness of themselves or people around them, indicated physical health as important.

> I just want to feel healthy.... and that my leg heals well, that is still one of my goals. (Participant 25, age 17)[66]

> A lot of money and health, those are the two things important to me ... My father is ill. So, health is ... You only notice that someone is healthy when they become ill. (Participant 58, age 14)[67]

The primary good of 'knowledge' was also rarely mentioned. When it was mentioned as important, it mainly related to the primary good of 'excellence in work', as a means to become more skilled or knowledgeable about something.

> I am interested in business management. I don't know why, but I would like to know everything about marketing. Here they also give me books about it, so I can read about that. (Participant 3, age 16)[68]

> Especially, looking up things was the most fun. Because, see, you don't know the feeling ... you're sitting in your room and you have a question. And you

65 "Ik zou gewoon mezelf blijven. Ik zou op niemand willen lijken. Omdat nu, ik heb een vriendin en zij is gevallen op de persoon dat ik ben. Niet op de persoon dat ik wil zijn."

66 "Ik wil mij gewoon gezond voelen ... en dat mijn been goed geneest, dat is sowieso nog steeds mijn doel."

67 "Veel geld en gezondheid. Dat zijn de twee dingen die ik het belangrijkste vind ... Mijn vader is ziek. Gezondheid is ... je ziet pas dat iemand gezond is als hij ziek wordt."

68 "Ik heb wel veel interesse voor bedrijfsbeheer. Ik weet niet waarom, maar ik zou graag alles weten van marketing. Ze hebben hier ook zo boeken dat zij aan mij hebben gegeven zodat ik daar over kan lezen."

> search all day and at the end of the day you have the answer to your question. That's the best feeling you can have. (Participant 67, age 16)[69]

Similarly, the primary good of 'creativity' was only mentioned in relation to the primary good of 'excellence in play', as a skill, useful for gaining competence in leisure activities. One participant explained that his creativity shows when he is engaging in hobbies and leisure activities.

> In writing rap lyrics, for example, or in the past when … in elementary school we had to work with clay and so on. People often said that I was very creative, that I could make beautiful statues and so on. And drawing, so … I thought I was creative. And in making up stories and jokes for example, I can also be very creative in that. (Participant 85, age 17)[70]

8.2.3 *Secondary Goods in the Pursuit of Primary Goods*

An important finding is that, in line with GLM's theory, most secondary goods play a role as the concrete means to achieve multiple primary goods at the same time. The secondary goods most often talked about included going to school/work, participating in sports and hanging out with friends.

School and Work

Going to school served several primary goods including:

- 'Knowledge', to gain information on the things the boys were interested in.
  I want to go to university. So, I'm going to study something that teaches me about the stock market and stuff…. (Participant 67, age 16)[71]
- 'Life', to achieve the necessary degree(s) to become gainfully employed and make a living.

---

69 "Vooral opzoeken, dat was het leukste. Want, zie, ge weet niet het gevoel … ge zit in uw kamer en ge hebt een vraag. En ge zoekt de hele dag en op het einde van de dag hebt ge het antwoord op uw vraag gekregen. Dat is het beste gevoel dat ge kunt hebben."

70 "Met rapteksten schrijven, bijvoorbeeld, of vroeger toen … in de basisschool moesten we zo werken met klei enzo. Werd er heel vaak gezegd dat ik heel creatief ben, dat ik van die mooie beeldjes kon maken enzo. En tekenen enzo, dus … Dat vond ik, was ik wel creatief. En zo echt verhaaltjes verzinnen en grapjes maken bijvoorbeeld, ik kan daar ook heel creatief in zijn."

71 "Ik wil universiteit studeren, ook met aandelen. Dus ik ga iets studeren dat mij leert over aandelen enzo …"

When I'm out of here I'm going to start school and apply for a student job right away. So … Then I'll have a steady income anyway. And after that I can get a real job and I won't be short of money. (Participant 7, age 17)[72]
Interviewer: And so what is the purpose of getting a diploma in your view?
Participant: Work, but if I would have everything I wanted, I wouldn't need to work, and I wouldn't need a diploma. I would not get a diploma for fun. I need to have a reason. (Participant 1, age 17)[73]

- 'Excellence in work', to become skilled at something they enjoyed or were good at.
  Because I … I actually want to become a prison guard. And then you have to, yeah … finish school before you can start that. (Participant 27, age 15)[74]
- 'Relatedness', to meet with friends and peers at school.
  My parents have now enrolled me in school … where, uh, a few friends of mine are also going, and then we'll be together in class. That's really the only reason for me to go back to school. (Participant 120, age 16)[75]

Sports

Likewise, participating in sports fulfilled several primary goods. Most often mentioned was the role it played in achieving the primary good of 'pleasure' and it was perceived as something fun.

> I've been doing that [taekwondo] for three years now. I just really enjoy doing it (Participant 11, age 15)[76]

When asked why they perceived it as a fun activity, some participants talked about the joy of accomplishment, such as winning games or just being good at it (i.e., the primary good of 'excellence in play').

> I think … The winning, the … the fun after winning especially. The feeling when you've tackled somebody [in a rugby game]. The good feeling you get

72 "Als ik hierbuiten ben ga ik sowieso direct beginnen met school en studentenjob. Dus … Dan heb ik sowieso een vast inkomen zeg maar. En, en daarna ga ik werken. Dus dan heb ik geen gebrek aan geld."

73 "Werk, maar als ik toch alles heb, heb ik geen werk nodig en ook geen diploma. Een diploma da ga ik nie halen voor de lol hé. Ik moet een reden hebben."

74 "Omdat ik … ik wil eigenlijk cipier worden. En dan moet ge, ja … school afmaken voor dat te kunnen beginnen."

75 "Mijn ouders hebben me nu ingeschreven op school … waar dat euh … een paar vrienden van mij ook zitten en dan kom ik ook bij hun in de klas. Dat is echt het enige voor mij om terug naar school te gaan."

76 "Ik doe dat [taekwondo] al drie jaar nu. Ik vind dat gewoon echt leuk."

when you've tackled someone or the good feeling you get when you've turned … and scored a goal. (Participant 16, age 16)[77]

To accomplish something with it, playing in tournaments. (Participant 27, age 15)[78]

Other boys talked about the joy of being with friends and peers (i.e., the primary good of 'relatedness') and being part of a specific group of people sharing the same values and interests (i.e., the primary good of 'community').

It's just … the friends I have there and my coach … Just that all the people there have respect for each other and don't argue with each other. We are like one family, one big family. (Participant 11, age 15)[79]

A small number also referred to sports as beneficial for their physical health (i.e., the primary good of 'life') and mental health (i.e., the primary good of 'inner peace').

[I would] …play soccer maybe weekly, uh, or even every day … stay healthy. But being happy is actually also a form of health for me. If I feel stressful, uh, and depressed and such, I feel sick. (Participant 85, age 17)[80]

Participant: That's a form of martial arts. That's an outlet for me too. And it is nice to know all the combinations. To work on your physical strength, that is nice.[81]

Interviewer: You mention an outlet. An outlet for what exactly?
Participant: When you had a bad day and you go kick boxing, you can punch everything out of your system so to speak. (Participant 27, age 15)[82]

77 "Ik denk … Het winnen, het … alee het plezier na het winnen vooral. Het gevoel, als je iemand hebt getackeld [in een rugbywedstrijd]. Het goed gevoel dat je krijgt als je iemand hebt getackeld of het goed gevoel dat je krijgt als je hebt gedraaid … en een goal gescoord."

78 " …voor daar iets mee te bereiken, toernooien spelen."

79 "Gewoon, met de … de vrienden die ik daar heb en mijn coach … Gewoon dat alle mensen gewoon respect hebben en echt geen ruzie met elkaar maken. Wij zijn zoals één familie, grote familie."

80 "[Ik zou] … wel wekelijks euh, gaan voetballen en misschien elke dag … gezond blijven. Gelukkig zijn is voor mij eigenlijk ook een vorm van gezondheid, eigenlijk hé. Als je … als ik mij stressvol voel en euh, depressief enzo, voel ik mij wel ziek."

81 "Dat is zo een vechtsport. Dat is een uitlaatklep ook. En dat is ook zo fijn zo die combinaties kennen. Ook aan conditie werken, dat is fijn."

82 "Dat is als ge zo een beetje een mindere dag hebt gehad dan gaat ge kick boxen en dan slaat ge alles eruit zeg maar."

Hanging Out with Friends

Hanging out with friends primarily served the primary goods of 'relatedness' and 'pleasure'.

> [I like] being outside actually. I don't really like being inside. [When I'm outside] then I'm not alone … Then I'm around other people that I can really talk to and stuff. (Participant 11, age 15)[83]

> Just chilling, relaxing, with friends. Just having fun together. (Participant 127, age 17)[84]

> We were usually with a group, smoking weed or something. Just perfect. (Participant 14, age 16)[85]

For a significant number of boys being outside with friends also served other primary goods, namely the primary good of 'excellence in agency', where they stressed the importance of being able to go outside.

> [I enjoyed] being social, having social contacts. And also the freedom I had. (Participant 2, age 17)[86]

> Just being free … Walking about, yes. (Participant 8, age 17)[87]

Finally, there was the primary good of 'community', especially for those youth who would hang out in their neighbourhood.

> My neighbourhood was my life. And I grew up with those men. They are not … They are not ordinary people, they are … just, they are friends, they are brothers. (Participant 138, age 17)[88]

83 "[Ik vind] het buiten zijn eigenlijk [leuk]. Ik ben niet zo graag binnen eigenlijk. [Wanneer ik buiten ben] dan ben ik niet alleen zo … Dan heb ik andere mensen waarmee ik echt kan praten enzo."

84 "Gewoon chillen. Gewoon, ontspannen, gewoon rustig met vrienden. Gewoon gezelligheid."

85 "We zaten zo meestal met een groepje, dan zo gingen wij zo, zo jointjes smoren ofzo. Was het wel af."

86 "[Ik vond] gewoon da contact, sociaal zijn enzo [leuk]. En gewoon de vrijheid die ik had."

87 "Gewoon vrij zijn … Gewoon rondstappen, ja."

88 "Mijn wijk was ook mijn leven hé. En ik ben opgegroeid met die mannen hé. Het is niet … het niet alsof dat, dat zijn niet gewone personen hé, dat zijn … gewoon, dat zijn vrienden, dat zijn broeders."

8.2.4 *Delinquency and the Role of (Problems in) Primary Goods Achievement Explained by Adolescents*

All interviewed boys reported having experienced at least one or more problems in achieving their goals (i.e., in the pursuit of their primary goods) before their arrest. These problems were classifiable into the four categories of potential problems in primary good achievement as proposed by the Good Lives Model: internal and external obstacles (including inadequate or lack of capacities), lack of scope, inappropriate (illegal) means and lack of coherence (i.e., conflicts between goals).

We found that (combinations of) internal and external obstacles could lead to a lack of opportunity and/or ability to satisfy one's primary goods (i.e., the problem of inadequate capacities). These obstacles could contribute to the other problems by resulting in certain goods not being met or pursued at all (i.e., the problem of lack of scope); conflicts between goals when trying to satisfy one's primary goods anyway (i.e., the problem of lack of coherence); and ultimately to the problem of using inappropriate (illegal) ways to satisfy one's primary goods and well-being.

When asked if they experienced any difficulties in their lives, the most commonly identified internal obstacles consisted of aggression and impulsivity problems.

> The crimes I've committed are not nice. So why would I want to do that? Uh, I didn't achieve anything with it, why should I do it? And before that, I had these little fights at school, were they fun? No. Then why did I do it? Nobody knows. Those kids provoked me and made me angry. (Participant 10, age 16)[89]

> When I have that angry feeling … Usually it's like a bucket of water overflowing … If I get angry and the guy stays in my view … then it gets worse and worse. (Participant 16, age 16)[90]

> If I had thought a little bit longer, I probably could've avoided that, but … I didn't think long enough and … I just thought for a minute and then I thought 'okay, that's easy money, I'm just going to do it'. You know? (Participant 39, age 16)[91]

---

89 "De feiten die ik heb gedaan is niet leuk. Dus waarom zou ik die feit willen doen. Euh, wat ik bereikt daarmee heb is niks dus, waarom zou ik het moeten doen. En daarvoor ook, van zo die kleine ruzies op school, waren die leuk? Nee. Waarom heb ik die dan gedaan? Dat weet niemand. Die kinderen die mij hebben uitgedaagd waardoor ik boos werd."

90 "Als ik dat boze gevoel heb … Het is meestal bij mij zo, zoals de emmer loopt over … Als ik word boos en die gast blijft in mijn zicht … wordt dat hoger en hoger."

91 "Als ik wat langer had nagedacht dan had ik dat waarschijnlijk kunnen vermijden, maar … ik dacht niet lang genoeg na en … ik dacht gewoon effe na en dan dacht ik van 'oké, dat is snel geld, ik ga dat gewoon effe

Some of these youths were also easily influenced by their peers.

> I shouldn't get carried away too quickly, I get carried away too easily. I let myself be influenced too quickly. (Participant 14, age 16)[92]

In contrast to experiencing externalizing problems, such as aggression and impulsive behaviour, a significant number of participants also reported internalizing emotional problems, such as worries, stress and insecurities.

> I was depressed a lot, and uh … I wanted … to find my peace somewhere. [I thought] if I make a lot of money … I can get the life that I want. With that, I always forgot about all the stress and all the, uh, all the depression I had. (Participant 85, age 17)[93]

> I am very insecure, but you don't see this [on the outside]. (Participant 35, age 16)[94]

About a third of the participants reported dealing with substance use problems. Almost all of these youth reported emotional problems as well.

> Drugs, that brings out the aggression in me a little. (Participant 11, age 15)[95]
> Some days it [drugs] brought paranoia in my head. (Participant 35, age 16)[96]

Some of the boys explained their drug and/or alcohol use explicitly as means to alleviate their symptoms.

> [I smoked weed] for my sleep problems, for my concentration and staying calm, so I wouldn't explode … fall into a fit of rage or something. (Participant 138, age 17)[97]

---

doen'. Snap je?"

92 "Ik moet mij niet snel laten meeslepen, ik laat mij te snel meeslepen. Ik laat me te snel beïnvloeden."

93 "Ik was wel vaak depressief, en euh … Ik wou sowieso wel … ergens mijn rust vinden. [Ik dacht] als ik nu heel veel geld maak, kan ik het leventje krijgen die ik wou hebben. Daarmee vergat ik altijd alle stress en alle, euh, alle depressie die ik had hé."

94 "Ik ben heel onzeker, maar ge ziet dat niet [aan de buitenkant]."

95 "Drugs, dat brengt de agressie een beetje naar boven."

96 "Ik had wel sommige dagen dat dat [drugs] wat … paranoia in mijn kop bracht."

97 "[Ik rookte wiet] voor mijn slaapproblemen, voor mijn concentratie en mijn rustig blijven dat ik niet ontplof … in een woede-uitbarsting val ofzo."

> Some moments I really need a joint. If I don't have one at that moment … I lose my mind … Then you get angry for no reason. I hated that. (Participant 35, age 16)[98]

> If I hadn't smoked [weed] I'd really be … yeah, I'd get stressed out by, yeah just, everything. (Participant 5, age 15)[99]

These internal obstacles usually interfered with their family relations and/or school.

> [I can] be obnoxious. I would get in trouble again and I had to go to the head mistress or to the principal. Then I got suspended. (Participant 59, age 15)[100]

> [I fight] with my parents … On a daily basis. (Participant 120, age 16)[101]

> I had conflicts with my mom … we were just like water and fire. (Participant 17, age 17)[102]

External Obstacles

The external obstacle that was most often mentioned consisted of having antisocial friends and being involved in a criminal environment or network.

> I know that if I go to my old friends, that I'm going to end up the same as what I came here for. And then this month, these two months that I'm here will have been totally useless. And I don't want that. (Participant 19, age 17)[103]

> I don't think of them as bad friends, but I know they've done things. You know what I mean? … If I didn't know some of them, I probably wouldn't be here. But that's with everybody, that's … You can't lie about that, it's the same for

98 "Sommige momenten heb ik wel echt een joint nodig zen. Als ik dan geen joint heb … word ik gek. Dan wordt ge kwaad voor geen reden. Dat haatte ik dan gewoon."

99 "Als ik niet had gerookt [wiet] dan was ik echt … Ja, dan kreeg ik stress van, ja gewoon, door alles."

100 "[Ik kan] gewoon ambetant doen. Kreeg ik weer problemen en moest ik zo naar de directrice gaan of naar de directeur. Dan kreeg ik schorsing."

101 "[Ik maak ruzie] met mijn ouders … Dagelijks wel."

102 "Ik had conflicten met mijn moeder … het was gewoon precies water en vuur."

103 "Ik weet dat ik als ik naar mijn oude vrienden ga gaan, dat ik het terug ga eindigen gelijk als voor wat ik naar hier ben gekomen. En dan heeft die maand, twee maand dat ik hier zit eigenlijk gewoon totaal geen nut gehad. En dat wil ik ook niet."

> everyone. A lot is just a matter of the people you hang out with, the environment you end up in. (Participant 2, age 17)[104]

> Interviewer: Would you want to get out [of that environment]?
> Participant: Yes. But can I? No. Just walk into [city] if you know half the drug lords. Even though I don't contact them. They will know I'm there … I really need to move. (Participant 35, age 16)[105]

For some boys, the family environment also served as an external obstacle.

> The police asked if, uh, if my mother came to get me. My mother replied that she couldn't. Because she was working or she was just busy at home, with something more important. So then … it's like you just got left behind anyway. (Participant 4, age 15)[106]

> My mom actually always argued with my family. (Participant 64, age 16)[107]

> I do not like it at home. (Participant 3, age 16)[108]

Additionally, a significant number of participants reported financial problems, either having little to spend and/or having debts.

> Surviving. I didn't grow up with wealth. I didn't grow up with a silver spoon in my mouth. I grew up in difficult circumstances. I couldn't ask my parents for some money to get a bag of chips or something or buy new clothes. It wasn't like that. (Participant 138, age 17)[109]

---

104 "Ik zie dat niet als slechte vrienden, maar ik weet wel dat die dingen hebben gedaan. Snapt ge? … Als ik sommige van hen niet zou kennen, dan zou ik hier waarschijnlijk niet zitten. Maar da's bij iedereen, dat … daar kunt ge niet over liegen, da's bij iedereen zo. Veel draait om, met wie da je omgaat, in welke milieus ge terecht komt."

105 "Ja. Kunt ge dat? Nee. Loop maar in [stad] als ge de helft van de drugsbaronnen kent. Ook al maak ik geen contact met hun. Die weten dat ik hier zit … Ik moet echt verhuizen."

106 "De politie vroeg of ik euh, of mijn moeder mij kwam halen. Mijn moeder antwoordde dat ze niet kon. Omdat ze aan het werken was of omdat ze gewoon druk was thuis, met iets belangrijkers. Dus dan … is het alsof je toch gewoon achtergelaten bent."

107 "Mijn ma heeft eigenlijk altijd ruzie gemaakt met mijn familie."

108 "Ik vind het thuis niet leuk."

109 "Overleven. Ik ben niet opgegroeid met rijkdom. Ik ben niet opgegroeid met een zilveren lepel in de mond. Ik ben opgegroeid in moeilijke omstandigheden. Niet van zo bijvoorbeeld ik vraag een beetje geld aan mijn ouders en ik ga een zakje chips halen ofzo of nieuwe kleren kopen. Dat was niet zo."

> [I don't want] any more problems with that [committing crimes, using drugs]. And no more debts anywhere. (Participant 5, age 15)[110]

About a third of the participants had dropped out of school, either temporarily or permanently. Most of them did not have a legal job either.

> School also caused me to end up in [institution]. Well, I did ... but uh, that was actually the final straw. That I didn't go to school. (Participant 28, age 17)[111]

> Before I was here, I had work and so some money. But then I stopped [working] and those things [crimes] happened. (Participant 5, age 15)[112]

> Really just hanging out with my friends or being with my girlfriend. That's really uh ... that's almost daily what I did. And otherwise I just sat at home. (Participant 19, age 17)[113]

Finally, the detained youth viewed their involvement with the juvenile justice system and/ or being detained as an important obstacle in achieving their goals.

> The judge ... is the one who closes doors. He doesn't let you work on your future. He locks you up. (Participant 14, age 16)[114]

> I don't think I have achieved any dreams yet. If I dreamed of being in jail, then I have achieved that. Other than that, I haven't achieved anything ... I wanted to finish school..., but yeah ... those bastards from justice took away my appointments [with school] (Participant 35, age 16)[115]

110 "[Ik wil] ook geen problemen daarmee [feiten plegen, drugs gebruiken]. En nergens schulden hebben."

111 "School zorgde ook ervoor dat ik in [instellingnaam] ben beland. Alee, ikzelf ... maar euh, dat was eigenlijk de druppel. Dat ik niet naar school ben gegaan."

112 "Voordat ik hier zat, werk had ik al dus geld had ik ook al. Maar dan was ik gestopt [met werk] en gebeurde die dingen [feiten]."

113 "Echt gewoon rondhangen met mijn vrienden of bij mijn vriendin zijn. Dat is echt euh ... dat is bijna dagelijks dat ik dat deed. En anders zat ik gewoon thuis."

114 "De jeugdrechter ... die sluit deuren. Die laat u niet werken aan u toekomst. Die sluit u op."

115 "Ik denk dat ik nog geen dromen heb bereikt. Als ik droomde van de bak dan heb ik dat bereikt. Verder heb ik niks bereikt. Ik wou mijn school doen via midden jury, maar ja ... die rotzakken van justitie hebben mijn afspraken [met school] afgepakt."

Lack of Scope

About a third of the participants talked about having a lack of motivation or scope in their lives. This manifested itself in setting few goals for themselves, in having few aspirations for the future and especially in showing little commitment to the responsibilities expected of them.

> Before I was here, not really. I played truant a lot, I, I didn't think much about school. Uh, but I don't, I don't really have any goals in my life. (Participant 2, age 17)[116]

> I never looked at what I was going to do the next day ... When I got up, I would look at myself like what are we going to do today. I didn't have a bigger outlook before I came here. (Participant 19, age 17)[117]

Four participants identified this lack of scope as (one of) the reasons for their delinquent behaviour, usually referred to as 'just being bored'.

> It [drug use] turned into a habit. It was just, pff, more out of boredom too. (Participant 67, age 16)[118]

> It [crimes] was just for fun. I didn't have ... we really didn't have anything to do ... I didn't go to school anymore ... It was just to pass the time. (Participant 19, age 17)[119]

Explaining Delinquency: Inappropriate (Illegal) Means

Although all participants experienced the problems mentioned up until now, at least to some extent, as difficulties in their lives in general, they did not always consider them to be linked specifically to their delinquent behaviour. Nevertheless, in explaining their deviant behaviour, either using drugs and/or committing crimes, several illegal means to achieve their goals were mentioned.

---

116 "Voor dat ik hier zat, niet echt. Ja, ik weet dat niet, ik spijbelde veel, ik, ik dacht niet veel aan school. Euh, maar ik heb niet, ik heb niet echt doelen in mijn leven."

117 "Ik keek nooit wat dat ik de volgende dag ging doen ... Als ik opstond, dan keek ik mezelf zo van wat gaan we vandaag doen. Een groter vooruitzicht heb ik niet gehad voordat ik naar hier kwam."

118 "Gewoonte, was het [drugs gebruiken] geworden. Het was gewoon zo, pff, meer uit verveling ook."

119 "Dat [criminaliteit] was gewoon voor het plezier. Ik had niet ... wij hadden echt niks te doen ... Ik ging niet meer school ... Dat was gewoon voor dag-invulling te doen."

Substance Use

Substance use was explained as a way to feel good, forget about worries and stress (i.e., the primary good of 'inner peace'), to have fun (i.e., the primary good of 'pleasure') and to impress or try to belong to their peer group (i.e., the primary goods of 'relatedness' and 'community').

> I don't really know why I use it. Just, when you're so bored or, when you're sad, then you are smiling again, then you're happy again. (Participant 59, age 15)[120]
> Because it made me happy, gave me a good feeling, relaxing, uh, it also made me sleep well. (Participant 7, age 17)[121]

> Because you want to belong, and not be alone .... I had no friends, that was a new school. And then yeah, that's how it happened. (Participant 17, age 17)[122]

Two participants explained that they started using drugs because they were curious about it (i.e., the primary good of 'creativity', trying something new).

> Someone offered it to me and I wanted to try it anyway. (Participant 1, age 17)[123]
> I wanted to know how it felt. The feeling, in my head. (Participant 67, age 16)[124]

Property Crimes and Drug Dealing

Property crimes, such as stealing and drug dealing appeared most often motivated by the need for money. Some participants saw it as legitimate means to make ends meet (i.e., the primary good of 'life'), while others pursued a life of wealth, luxury and fun (i.e., the primary good of 'pleasure').

> Yeah, I don't have that much money at home. I didn't get that much pocket money either and then uh ... you really do earn quite a lot with it [drug dealing]. (Participant 19, age 17)[125]

120 "Ik weet eigenlijk niet waarom dat ik gebruik. Gewoon, als ge u zo verveelt ofzo, als ge droevig zijt, dan lacht ge gewoon terug, dan wordt ge terug blij."

121 "Omdat mij dat blij maakte, goed gevoel, ontspannend, euh, ik kon er ook goed van slapen."

122 "Omdat ge er bij wilt horen, niet alleen wilt zijn ... Ik had geen vrienden, dat was een nieuwe school. En dan ja, zo is dat gebeurd hé."

123 "Iemand biedt dat aan en ik wou dat sowieso al proberen."

124 "Ik wou weten hoe het voelde. Het gevoel, in mijn hoofd."

125 "Ja, ik heb niet zoveel geld thuis. Ik kreeg ook niet zo veel zakgeld en dan euh ... verdient ge daar [drugsdealen] wel echt tamelijk veel mee."

> As society puts it, [I will] recidivate. I'll fall into old habits because that is what I'm used to. Because if I'm not going to have money in my pockets and I'm not going to get anything from my parents, and I want to go to a party, or I want a nice tracksuit … What am I going to do then? Otherwise, I can't survive one or two weeks. (Participant 35, age 16)[126]

A few participants reported being motivated to make money illegally to finance their own drug habit. Thus, depending on what primary good(s) they aimed to achieve with their substance use (for example, 'inner peace' and 'pleasure'), those goods indirectly played a role in committing property offences as well.

> All of it [crimes]. Really everything, was because I was addicted. (Participant 16, age 16)[127]

Trying to belong to a peer group or in the neighbourhood (i.e., the primary goods of 'relatedness' and 'community') also played an important role in their delinquent behaviour, according to some youth.

> You see the big guys in your neighbourhood … who had nice clothes but lived in the suburbs. I asked, 'how come you have all that'? And then they helped me. (Participant 138, age 17)[128]

> Just impress them … being the talk of the day … I didn't handle it well, when I think about it now. We don't all have to commit crimes to have a group of friends. (Participant 4, age 15)[129]

Several participants pointed out that they aimed to build a career and/or achieve something to be proud of with their illegal activities (i.e., the primary good of 'excellence in work').

126 "Zoals de maatschappij het zegt hé, [ik zal] recidiven. Ik ga terug in herhaling vallen, want wat ben ik gewend. Want als ik geen geld in mijn zakken ga hebben en ik krijg niks van mijn ouders, en ik wil naar een feestje of ik wil een mooi trainingspak … Wat ga ik dan doen? Anders kan ik geen week of twee weken overleven hé."

127 "Allemaal. Echt, alles [feiten]. Was om het verslaafd zijn dus."

128 "Je ziet de grote van de wijk … Die zo mooie kleding hadden enzo, maar toch in de achterstandswijk waren, vroeg ik van 'hoezo heb je dat allemaal?'. En dan hebben zij geholpen."

129 "Gewoon de indruk maken … en dat ik toch wel het onderwerp ben … het was toch verkeerd aangepakt, nu ik erover nadenk. Want we moeten niet allemaal feiten plegen om een goede vriendengroep te hebben."

> Financially uh, everything is still working just as, uh, it worked. I have people outside who still work for me so to speak. And, I don't have to do anything so to speak. I'm just doing my time here. (Participant 25, age 17)[130]

> So, the higher [in rank] you can go … There is also a level where you don't get caught … And then you don't make a lot of money, but you can provide good quality [drugs] to people. That's what I would do … I'm just a businessman. (Participant 35, age 16)[131]

Violent Crimes

Violent crimes, on the other hand, were often motivated by peer pressure (i.e., the primary goods of 'relatedness' and 'community') and sometimes sparked by emotional issues (i.e., the primary good of 'inner peace'), including aggression and impulsivity.

> [It was] pure peer pressure … because if someone suddenly would have left … I would like that people know me as uhm, not the one who is afraid or, uh, the loser or something. No. (Participant 85, age 17)[132]

> Belonging to the big guys. Everyone wants to belong to the big guys. Reputation. Just … proving yourself. (Participant 16, age 16)[133]

> Sometimes I do think: 'I don't care what he thinks' … But it's when I meet that guy that I … I want to, yeah … how do you say that. Something snaps inside me. (Participant 16, age 16)[134]

Others attributed their violent behaviour to the idea that they helped their friends (i.e., the primary good of 'relatedness').

---

130 "Financieel euh, alles loopt zoals euh, ja als het liep. Ik heb gewoon zeg maar mensen buiten die gewoon nog steeds voor mij werken. En ik hoef niks te doen zeg maar. Zit mijn tijd effe uit."

131 "Dus hoe hoger [in de rangorde] dat ge kunt komen … Er is ook een niveau waar ge niet gepakt wordt … En dan verdient ge ook niet veel geld, maar ge kunt goede kwaliteit [drugs] leveren aan mensen. Dat zou ik wel doen. Ik ben gewoon businessman."

132 "[Dat was] echt pure groepsdruk … Als er opeens iemand weg gaat … Ik zou wel graag willen dat euhm, dat mensen mij niet kennen als dat dat de bangerik is of euh, de loser ofzo, nee."

133 "Bij de grotere … Iedereen wilt bij de grotere horen. Reputatie. Gewoon … jezelf bewijzen"

134 "Ik denk dat soms wel hè, 'dat maakt me niet uit wat die denkt.' … Maar het is als ik die gast tegenkom dat ik … ik wil ja … Hoe zeg je dat. Dat er iets in mij schiet."

> Because I didn't know what was coming down on him and I didn't want to say to him 'just go alone'. I wanted to be there to show him … that I was there for him. (Participant 10, age 16)[135]

Sometimes violent crimes were also referred to as something fun to do (i.e., the primary good of 'pleasure'). One boy in particular mentioned television and films as an inspiration.

> It's actually fun to watch, I like watching a bank get robbed and stuff. (Participant 4, age 15)[136]

Lastly, one boy also said he got into fights to protect himself (i.e., the primary good of 'life'; safety).

> To prove yourself … that you shouldn't pick a fight with me. That people should be afraid of me. That they should not directly hit me because they know that I'm going to do something back to them anyway. (Participant 16, age 16)[137]

Lack of Coherence

Finally, the fourth problem in the achievement of primary goods that arises from the interviews was lack of coherence, or conflicting goals. This lack of coherence was identified by six participants, and it primarily concerned the negative effects of committing crimes and using drugs on other life domains. None of the participants mentioned a lack of coherence as a problem that could cause or underlie their delinquent behaviour; rather, it turned out to be a consequence of it.

> With my family [relationships], I was not satisfied with that. But that … that was all on me. It was just because I did drugs that things got bad. And since I stopped doing drugs things have been going really well again. (Participant 67, age 16)[138]

> I lived with a level of stress. Most criminals die from heart disease and stuff you know. Because of stress … You don't feel good about yourself when you

135 "Omdat ik niet wist wat er op hem afging en ik wou niet tegen hem zeggen van 'ga maar alleen'. Ik wou er wel bij zijn om te laten zien van … dat ik er voor hem was."

136 "Het is eigenlijk leuk om naar te kijken, ik vind het wel leuk om te kijken hoe een bank beroofd wordt enzo."

137 "Jezelf bewijzen … dat je geen ruzie moet zoeken. Dat mensen bang van u moeten zijn. Dat die niet direct mij moeten slagen want dat die weten dat ik sowieso iets ga terug doen."

138 "Mijn familie [relaties], was ik niet tevreden mee. Maar dat … dat lag allemaal aan mij. Dat was gewoon omdat ik drugs deed dat het slecht ging. En vanaf dat ik gestopt ben met drugs ging het weer kei goed."

> know you're lying to your parents. You don't feel good about yourself if you think that there's an undercover policeman in every car and you get paranoid. (Participant 35, age 16)[139]

> You can't do anything other than that during the day. You can't do anything else than selling drugs in your life. You don't sleep well. You're out all day. You see your parents less … that's not really a life. (Participant 28, age 17)[140]

8.3 Discussion

In this study, we aimed to examine the relationships between primary goods, well-being and delinquency, as perceived by detained adolescents themselves. For this purpose, we explored the GLM's assumptions about well-being and delinquency by analysing 31 qualitative interviews with detained adolescent boys. In a first step, the interviews were coded using an inductive thematic analysis to capture the youths' own views and experiences on well-being and their delinquent behaviour. In a second step, the codes were examined, compared and categorized in terms of the theoretical higher-order themes of the GLM: the importance and pursuit of the eleven primary goods for well-being and the four problems with primary goods attainment in general and in relation to the youths' delinquent behaviour. This resulted in a thematic framework in which the theoretical assumptions of the GLM could be tested against the views of the detained adolescents. More specifically, this technique allowed for the translation of the GLM assumptions into the words and perspectives of the detained adolescents themselves. In what follows, these results are discussed in more detail.

8.3.1 *The Role of Primary Goods in Adolescent Well-Being*

When asked what was most important for the detained boys, loved ones were usually mentioned first, notably family and friends. Family was often referred to as more important than friends, except when the youth experienced problems at home and turned to their friends instead. This could be explained by research demonstrating that those youth who experience little or no supervision, support and affection from their family aim to seek

139 "Ik leefde wel met een stressgehalte. De meeste criminelen gaan dood van hartziekten enzo hé. Door stress … Ge voelt u niet goed in uw vel hé, als gij weet dat gij liegt tegen uw ouders. Ge voelt u niet goed in uw vel hé, als gij denkt dat in elke auto een undercover politieagent zit en dat ge paranoia wordt."

140 "Ge kunt niks anders doen dan dat in jouw dag. Ge kunt ge niks anders doen dan drugs verkopen in uw leven eigenlijk. Ge slaapt slecht. Ge bent de hele dag buiten. Ge ziet uw ouders minder … dat is eigenlijk geen leven."

recognition and social support from their (delinquent) peers (Baron, 2015; Brezina & Azimi, 2018; Colvin et al., 2002; Patterson & Dishion, 1985; Rebellon, 2002; Verdonck, 2017; Warr, 2002; Wood & Alleyne, 2010). This result, furthermore, supports the conclusion from previous studies that a tension and conflict can occur between the involvement with (antisocial) peer relationships on the one hand and family bonds on the other (Barnert et al., 2015). Although we did not find a direct statistical effect of 'relatedness' on well-being in the previous chapter, the results of the present qualitative study are in line with Chapters 4 and 6, and with studies in the general population indicating the significance of 'relatedness', especially with family, for (adolescent) well-being (Berscheid, 2003; Delle Fave et al., 2011; Navarro et al., 2017; Proctor & Linley, 2014; Proctor et al., 2009; Reis et al., 2000; Ryan & Deci, 2000b; Vujcic et al., 2019).

To reiterate, both the GLM and Self-determination Theory (SDT) state that humans are naturally inclined to seek (at least) three psychological needs (or primary goods): 'relatedness', 'competence' and 'autonomy' (Deci & Ryan, 2000; Ryan & Deci, 2017b; Ward, 2002a). The basic human psychological need for 'relatedness' refers to seeking attachments and experiencing feelings of security, belongingness and intimacy with others (Deci & Ryan, 2000; Ward, 2002a). Accordingly, the detained adolescent boys emphasized relationships with family and ('true') friends as sources of love, comfort and support. The primary good of 'relatedness', furthermore, appears to overlap somewhat with the primary good of 'community', in the sense that adolescent relationships often also serve their need to belong. A significant number of detained youth dreamt of having a family of their own (i.e., the primary good of 'relatedness'), a house and attaining a legal job (i.e., the primary good of 'life'). They referred to this goal as living a life that, in their view, was 'normal', to be like everybody else and to be part of society (i.e., the primary good of 'community'). Previous research has demonstrated that these life goals are the major goals and developmental tasks in (Western) adolescents (Massey et al., 2008; Messersmith & Schulenberg, 2010; Nurmi, 1991). What is important to note here, however, is that research has found differences between individualistic and collectivistic cultures in what needs are considered more important for well-being. For example, it has been observed that in collectivist cultures, expectations of friends and family play a larger role in goal setting than self-determination (see also Chapter 3, Section 3.4; Oishi & Diener, 2009; Oishi et al., 2009).

Consistent with our previous studies in Chapters 4, 6 and 7, this 'normal' dream life emphasizes the importance of basic physical needs for well-being, in particular gaining a proper living in the form of having enough money and a safe place to live (i.e., the primary good of 'life'). As already suggested in the previous chapter, in line with Maslow's (1962) hierarchy of needs, the current findings show that youth, especially those who come from disadvantaged backgrounds, emphasize their basic physical needs over other, higher needs. This is in line with studies demonstrating that basic physical and safety needs are deemed more important in poorer nations compared to wealthy ones (Oishi et al., 2009).

A part of the detained youth took their dreams a step further and wanted a life of status among their peers (i.e., the primary good 'community'), luxury, parties, fun (i.e., the primary good of 'pleasure'), being financially independent and having the freedom to go their own way in life (related to the primary good of 'excellence in agency'). Despite their wish for this luxurious life, most still emphasized that money could not buy them everything, such as love and fulfilling happiness. This is consistent with numerous studies demonstrating that the pursuit and attainment of extrinsic, materialistic goals (i.e., wealth, fame or image that are related to external approval) is in fact related to lower levels of well-being (Dittmar et al., 2014; Emmons, 1996, 1999; Kasser, 2002; Ryan & Deci, 2000b; Schmuck et al., 2000; Sheldon & Houser-Marko, 2001; Van Den Broeck et al., 2019). Striving for a sense of self-worth via external rewards is believed to reflect a lack of personal/inner self-worth (Massey et al., 2008). Moreover, materialistic attitudes and lifestyles can conflict with the pursuit of goals and needs deemed necessary for personal growth and finding meaning in life, such as relatedness and spirituality (Kasser, 2016).

When asked how they want to achieve their dream lives, all boys expressed their desire to do so by excelling in something they could be proud of. Some mentioned school and lawful work (i.e., 'excellence in work'), while others wanted to become successful in their hobbies, such as rap music or sports (i.e., 'excellence in play'). As in our previous studies (in Chapters 4, 6 and 7), the goods of 'knowledge' and 'creativity' appeared less important to these youth, that is, they were rarely mentioned on their own and for some they seemed to serve as a means to strive for 'excellence in work' and 'excellence in play'.

Apart from how they aim to do it, what they all had in common is that they wanted to succeed in life. They wanted to strive for their own goals (i.e., the primary good of 'excellence in agency') and have a purpose in their lives (i.e., the primary good of 'spirituality'). In all this, several boys stressed the importance of being their own person, having their own identity and staying true to themselves (i.e., 'excellence in agency'). In that sense, the primary goods of 'excellence in work', 'knowledge', 'excellence in play', 'creativity', 'excellence in agency' and 'spirituality', all seem to fall under an overarching goal of 'achieving one's aspirations in life'. This finding is in line with SDT's two other important psychological needs for well-being: 'competence' and 'autonomy'. 'Competence' consists of a sense of mastery and experiencing opportunities to exercise and express one's capacities. 'Autonomy' refers to feeling self-directed and being the perceived origin or source of one's own behaviour (Deci & Ryan, 2000; Ryan & Deci, 2017b). Attaining one's own goals in life can promote both (Massey et al., 2009; Messersmith & Schulenberg, 2010; Ryan & Deci, 2017a).

Finally, despite these dreams for a bright future, the majority of our detained youth expressed feeling troubled and emphasized their need to be free of problems, worries and stress (i.e., the primary good of 'inner peace'). This corresponds with previous studies that consistently revealed mental health as the most important factor in adolescent well-being (see Chapters 4, 6, and 7).

8.3.2 *Problems in Primary Goods Achievement: Criminogenic Risk Factors as Obstacles*

The latter finding leads us to the problems that were voiced by the detained youth in achieving their goals. In our results, *internal and external obstacles* for primary goods achievement were mainly *inadequate capacities* to achieve these goods in a prosocial manner. Interestingly, these self-identified obstacles are fully consistent with the eight criminogenic risk factors of the Risk Need Responsivity (RNR) model: criminal history, antisocial personality pattern, antisocial attitudes, antisocial associates/peers, family problems, school and/or work problems, lack of constructive leisure activities and substance abuse (Andrews & Bonta, 2010; Bonta & Andrews, 2017; Ward & Brown, 2004; Ward & Stewart, 2003b, 2003c).

The most commonly identified internal obstacles were *aggression and impulsivity problems*. These obstacles can be categorized under the 'antisocial personality pattern', one of the central eight RNR risk factors, which includes impulsivity, adventurous pleasure-seeking, weak self-control and aggression (Andrews & Bonta, 2010; Bonta & Andrews, 2017; see also Chapter 5, Section 5.4.11). Some youth tried to remedy these emotional problems through substance use, which in itself was referred to as an internal obstacle and likewise constitutes one of the central eight criminogenic risk factors (i.e., 'substance abuse'; Andrews & Bonta, 2010; Bonta & Andrews, 2017; see also Chapter 5, Section 5.4.6).

The most frequently mentioned external obstacle was having antisocial friends and being involved in a criminal environment or network. For some youth, problems at home with their family and parents served as an external obstacle. Both obstacles are represented in the central eight risk factors as 'antisocial associates/peers' and 'family problems', respectively (Andrews & Bonta, 2010; Bonta & Andrews, 2017). Furthermore, an interaction between problems at home and subsequently resorting to delinquent peers could amplify their potential criminogenic risk (Barnert et al., 2015). The fact that friends and family are so important to adolescent well-being (see also Chapters, 4, 6, 7 and Section 8.3.1) may also explain its strong criminogenic impact when youth experience family problems and start to interact mainly with antisocial peers (see also Chapter 5, Sections 5.4.7 and 5.4.8).

Another set of problems often mentioned as external obstacles consisted of having financial problems (including poverty and debts), dropping out of school and not having a legal job. These youth did not have any structured activities during the day and often experienced boredom. This finding shows the relevance of the criminogenic risk factors of 'school/work problems' and a 'lack of constructive leisure activities' (Andrews & Bonta, 2010; Bonta & Andrews, 2017; see Chapter 5, Sections 5.4.1, 5.4.3, and 5.4.4).

Finally, several boys mentioned being involved in the juvenile justice system and/or being detained as an important (external) obstacle in achieving their life goals. For some, their criminal history, subsequent involvement with the justice system and a lack of trust in the authorities were major sources of frustration. These obstacles correspond with having a 'criminal history' and 'antisocial attitudes' (more specifically as being resentful and defying authorities) as criminogenic risk factors (Andrews & Bonta, 2010; Bonta & Andrews, 2017).

8.3.3 *Problems in Primary Goods Achievement: Lack of Scope and Coherence*

These (combinations of) internal and external obstacles can contribute to other problems in primary goods achievement. One of the problems that could occur is not achieving or pursuing certain goods at all (i.e., *lack of scope*). Problems in scope are assumed to be caused by problems in capacity as described above, but they may also occur because of a disinterest in one or more goods (Purvis, 2010; Purvis et al., 2011; Ward, 2002a, 2002b). In line with this, some detained boys talked about an overall lack of motivation in their lives. This manifested itself in (and/or resulted from) the boys setting few goals for themselves, having few expectations for the future and most importantly, showing little commitment to the responsibilities expected of them. Similar to previous studies, a lack of motivation and scope was even mentioned as a cause for their delinquent behaviour (out of boredom; Drozda, 2006; Newberry & Duncan, 2001; Taylor, 2017; Wainwright & Nee, 2014). To the best of our knowledge only one study explicitly examined goal-setting behaviour in delinquent adolescents and found similar results: compared to a nondelinquent control group, delinquent adolescents reported less (challenging) goals and were less committed to their goals (Carroll et al., 2013).

The other problem we identified consisted of a *lack of coherence* in trying to achieve one's primary goods. According to the GLM, a lack of coherence can occur when a conflict arises in the attainment of the different primary goods. It also states that a coherent life should involve giving the most important goods the highest priority, commitment and resources (Purvis, 2010; Purvis et al., 2011; Ward, 2002a, 2002b). Contrary to the GLM's hypothesis, in our study this lack of coherence did not appear to be a problem that caused the adolescents' delinquent behaviour, but rather turned out to be a consequence of it. That is, the detained adolescents' antisocial behaviour conflicted with the achievement of other primary goods they deemed important, such as family relationships. This finding provides further evidence that tension can occur between family relationships and being involved with delinquent peers (Barnert et al., 2015). Conflicts between life goals have been found to result in lower levels of well-being for the individual (Emmons, 1996, 1999; Gray et al., 2017; Kelly et al., 2015; McGregor & Little, 1998; McGregor et al., 2006; Sheldon & Kasser, 1995), which could also explain the previously observed negative relationships between adolescent delinquency and well-being (Buelga et al., 2008; Gonzalez et al., 2021; MacDonald et al., 2005; McKnight et al., 2002; Olson et al., 2020; Suldo & Huebner, 2004; Sun & Shek, 2010, 2012; Valois et al., 2001, 2002, 2006; Zullig et al., 2001).

8.3.4 Problems in Primary Goods Achievement: Inappropriate Means

The final problem that was identified was the use of alternative, *inappropriate (illegal) means* to satisfy one's primary goods and well-being. It is the most direct way in which primary goods achievement can lead to delinquent behaviour. Supporting this GLM assumption, the detained adolescents reported various primary goods underlying the different types of delinquent behaviour, especially combined with the presence of criminogenic risk factors (see also Chapter 5, and Section 8.3.2). This corresponds with the hypothesis of the GLM that certain types of risk factors relate to distinct clusters of primary human goods (Andrews & Bonta, 2010; Bonta & Andrews, 2017; Ward & Brown, 2004; Ward & Stewart, 2003b, 2003c; see also Table 2.1 in Chapter 2). In what follows, we will elaborate which GLM primary goods relate to which types of RNR risk factors. We will furthermore discuss how they may interact and thus result in different types of delinquency.

Most of the detained boys reported using several substances, mostly alcohol and soft drugs. These boys reported they used substances to feel good, forget about worries and stress (i.e., the primary good of 'inner peace'). Additionally, they used them as a means to have fun with friends (i.e., the primary goods of 'pleasure' and 'relatedness'). Some used substances offered by friends to impress them and to belong (i.e., the goods of 'relatedness' and 'community'). Finally, curiosity and the need to try something new (i.e., the primary good of 'creativity') were mentioned by some. From this, we can conclude that the criminogenic risk factor of substance (ab)use can be related to several primary goods, but it is most often mentioned in relation to finding 'inner peace' and 'pleasure'. This finding corresponds with previous studies stating that substance use serves as a way for youth to feel better (Agnew, 1990; Caffray & Schneider, 2000; Loney & Harkins, 2018; Skrzypiec, 2017; Teevan & Dryburgh, 2000; Thakker & Ward, 2010).

The most common type of delinquencies committed by the detained youth were property crimes and drug dealing. In line with our previous quantitative studies (see Chapters 6 and 7), the most frequently mentioned motivation for these types of offences was fast and 'easy' material and financial gain. Similar to the existing literature, this was either to make ends meet (i.e., the primary good of 'life') and/or to seek luxury (i.e., the primary good of 'pleasure'; see also Chapter 5; Agnew, 1990; Farrington, 1993; Gudjonsson & Sigurdsson, 2007; Hoeve et al., 2016; Hoeve, Stams, et al., 2014; Jacobs & Wright, 1999; Lopez, 2008; Putniņš, 2010; Shong et al., 2019; Troonbeeckx et al., 2015; van Beek et al., 2021; Verdonck, 2017). For some youth, their own drug use became a source of motivation to commit crimes in order to finance their habit (Craig et al., 2018; Nguyen & Bouchard, 2013; Troonbeeckx et al., 2015).

Similar to substance use, antisocial peers and environments played a large role in steering youth towards property crimes and drug dealing, posing important criminogenic risk factors (Andrews & Bonta, 2010; Baron, 2015; Bonta & Andrews, 2017; Cottle et al., 2001; Dishion & Tipsord, 2011; Glueck & Glueck, 1950; Grieger & Hosser, 2014; Jacobs et al., 2020; Patterson & Dishion, 1985; Sampson et al., 2002; Wikström & Loeber, 2000). They were seduced by the quick financial gains they saw others make (i.e., for the goods of 'life' and 'pleasure') and/or wanted to impress them to belong to a deviant peer group (i.e., the goods of 'relatedness' and 'community'). Several boys also stated they aimed to build a career and/or achieve something to be proud of with their illegal activities (i.e., the good of 'excellence in work'). This could be an especially important motivator for youth who experience problems with school, have less prospect of a degree and a well-paying legal job and additionally have not much to lose (Andrews & Bonta, 2010; Bonta & Andrews, 2017; Christle et al., 2005; Cottle et al., 2001; Grieger & Hosser, 2014; Hoffmann, 2020; Katsiyannis et al., 2008; Maguin & Loeber, 1996). Moreover, as evidenced in previous studies, for some offenders a ('successful') criminal career can indeed form a source of pride, status and respect that they do not receive or experience in 'normal' society (Nguyen & Bouchard, 2013; Taylor, 2017; Verdonck, 2017; Wood, 2014; Wood & Alleyne, 2010).

Violent offending appeared to be motivated by slightly different primary goods. Contrary to property offending, emotional issues (related to the primary good of 'inner peace') were often pointed out as underlying reasons for violent behaviour. This could either be attributed to disinhibition and an inability to resist impulses or the violence forms a direct way to explicitly vent one's feelings of anger and frustration (Agnew, 1990; Berkowitz, 1989; Dollard et al., 1939; Farrington, 1993; Gottfredson & Hirschi, 1990; Skrzypiec, 2017; Verdonck, 2017). Although (internalizing) mental health symptoms are not considered criminogenic risk factors, externalizing problems are (i.e., impulsivity and aggression, see also Chapter 7; Andrews & Bonta, 2010; Bonta & Andrews, 2017). Sometimes impulsivity and aggression were also triggered in combination with substance abuse. Accordingly, substance abuse has been shown to play a mediating role in the relationship between mental health problems and adolescent delinquency (Gottfredson & Hirschi, 1990; Guebert & Olver, 2014; Verdonck, 2017).

Less frequently mentioned, but specific for violent behaviour – and corresponding to our results in the previous chapter – was the need for safety and defending oneself (i.e., related to the primary good of 'life'). Youth who are involved in a criminal network and are exposed to violence have been shown to behave violently as a way of defending themselves (Mallion & Wood, 2020; Reid et al., 2017; Verdonck, 2017). Similar to property delinquency, and again in line with the previous studies in Chapters 6 and 7, the influence of peers played an important role in explaining violent offending (Andrews & Bonta, 2010; Bonta & Andrews, 2017). The detained youth explained their violence as a means of trying to belong and impress others and/or helping friends in fights (i.e., the goods of 'community' and 'relatedness'). While the former relates to peer pressure (Buelga et al., 2008; Dijkstra et al., 2010; Teevan & Dryburgh, 2000; Warr, 2002), the latter has been attributed to a sense of loyalty among peers that tends to become especially salient in group fights (Baron & Hartnagel, 1998; Farrington, 1993; Teevan & Dryburgh, 2000; Verdonck, 2017). Finally, violence was also referred to as something fun and to pass the time (i.e., the primary good of 'pleasure'). Other studies have demonstrated that adolescent antisocial behaviour in general, and violence in particular, can serve as a means to kill time (Drozda, 2006; Newberry & Duncan, 2001; Taylor, 2017; Wainwright & Nee, 2014) and to seek kicks and thrills (Arnett, 1992, 1996; Verdonck, 2017; Wilson & Scarpa, 2011).

Overall, the findings from this qualitative analysis are highly consistent with (our) previous studies that explain adolescent delinquency through motivations related to primary goods and criminogenic risk factors (see also Chapters 5, 6 and 7). They highlight the fact that different types of crimes can have different motivations and risk factors underlying them, contingent upon a person's cultural, social and personal values; abilities; and circumstances. This supports the suggestion by Ward and Carter (2019) that effective offender rehabilitation should refrain from assigning offenders to interventions based on a specific type of crime. Specific crime-based interventions run the risk of falsely assuming that people who commit a particular type of crime all manifest the same behaviour, underlying difficulties and motivations.

8.4 Conclusion

Based on the qualitative analysis in this chapter, we expanded our knowledge about the role that primary goods can play in explaining adolescent well-being and delinquency by including the self-perceived insights, motivations and explanations of the detained youth themselves. Regarding the goals in life that the detained youth considered important to their well-being, all primary goods were mentioned, some more frequently and explicitly than others. The secondary goods that were essential for the achievement of a variety of primary goods included the following: going to school/work, participating in sports and hanging out with peers. Furthermore, the obstacles that were identified by the detained boys could be classified into the four categories of potential problems in primary good achievement as proposed by the GLM: internal and external obstacles (including *inadequate or lack of capacities*), *lack of scope*, *inappropriate (illegal) means* and *lack of coherence* (Purvis, 2010; Purvis et al., 2011; Ward, 2002a, 2002b; Ward & Marshall, 2004; Ward & Maruna, 2007). All these issues were mentioned to varying degrees in association with the youths' delinquent behaviour. Contrary to one of the GLM's assumptions, however, a *lack of coherence* appeared to be a consequence of the detained adolescents' delinquent behaviour, rather than a cause (Purvis, 2010; Purvis et al., 2011, 2014; Ward & Stewart, 2003a).

8.5 LIMITATIONS AND REMAINING QUESTIONS

In the current study we aimed to unravel the motivations and explanations of the youths' behaviour from their own perspective, as emphasized by the GLM. Nevertheless, when relying on self-report and qualitative methods, particularly in offenders, some problems may arise that threaten the reliability and validity of the information.

First, offenders could be answering in a socially desirable manner, unwilling to talk (truthfully) about their illegal behaviour. This can be especially the case for offenders who are awaiting their trial. On the other hand, some youth might exaggerate and brag about their offence(s) (Bernasco, 2013). Therefore, to elicit truthful statements as much as possible, the interviewer emphasized anonymity of the interviews and survey data throughout the studies. Moreover, investing in rapport-building from the start of the study was a key component in obtaining sincere disclosures. As a result, most participants seemed genuinely pleased to be heard and to tell their stories. The current interviews about the youths' well-being, primary goods, aspirations and their own perspectives, appeared to generate more openness and willingness to disclose, compared to the risk assessment interview that was conducted first. Nonetheless, not all types of delinquency (e.g., sex offences) were discussed in the interviews. This could either be because the participants did not commit these crimes, or they chose not to disclose this information during the interviews.

Other factors could have also influenced the current results. First, although we selected the boys at random if they wanted to participate in the qualitative interview, self-selection may have occurred. That is, the youth who were willing to participate, could have also been the ones who could more easily express themselves and were therefore willing to do so. However, the analyses comparing the current sub-sample to those who did not participate in the interview (see Section 8.2.1) revealed no substantive differences. Additionally, the interviews asked the detained youth about the period before their arrest.

Thus, their stories may have been influenced by their memories and/or by conversations they previously had with the judge, other (juvenile justice) professionals, parents, other family members and peers. Finally, the interviews were coded by a single researcher which prevents assessing the (inter-rater) reliability of the analysis.

Besides these limitations, the current qualitative analysis shows what we can learn from viewing (juvenile) delinquency from the individual offender's perspective. For each person, different risk factors may interact, and different motives may underlie different types of delinquency. In this process, the GLM and RNR approach can be useful in explaining and targeting delinquent behaviour. That is, the GLM makes it possible to identify the personal needs, rewards and values underlying the delinquent behaviour, while the RNR model uncovers the criminogenic risk factors that hinder the prosocial and promote the antisocial attainment of those needs (Ward, 2019; Ward & Maruna, 2007; Ward & Stewart, 2003c).

However, at this point, we have only examined the GLM's etiological assumptions about adolescent well-being and juvenile delinquency. We did not yet examine the GLM's practical assumptions and recommendations for effective offender rehabilitation, and their applicability to juveniles. Thus, before we examine these practical assumptions empirically in detained adolescent offenders (see the study reported in Chapter 10), we will discuss the existing theoretical models and empirical research underlying the GLM's assumptions about successful rehabilitation in the next chapter.

9 Theoretical and Empirical Background of the Pathways to Sustainable Desistance

Associations Between Primary Goods, Well-Being, Treatment Motivation and Recidivism

In the previous chapters, I focused on the etiological assumptions underlying the 'Good Lives Model of offender rehabilitation' (GLM). I elaborated on the GLM's theoretical basis and conducted empirical tests of its assumptions about the link between well-being, primary goods and delinquent behaviour in (detained) adolescents. This was an important first step because the GLM's recommendations for effective rehabilitation interventions are based on these etiological assumptions. We now turn to the elaboration of the GLM's practical assumptions and recommendations that follow from its etiological assumptions.

To reiterate, the GLM states that to effectively reduce criminal recidivism, rehabilitation interventions should not only target the well-known criminogenic risk factors from the Risk Need Responsivity (RNR) model, but also focus on strengthening the offender's abilities to meet personally relevant human needs (i.e., the primary goods), which will also improve their well-being and quality of life. Working towards a better life could subsequently reduce recidivism risk more sustainably by promising a happier and prosocial life, rather than merely a less risky one. Understanding the offenders' behaviour as a function of achieving one or more primary goods can guide interventions to help them secure those goods that are important to them, in a socially acceptable manner. Moreover, working towards personally relevant goals and well-being, instead of merely working to reduce risk factors determined by professionals, is believed to increase treatment motivation and further reduce recidivism risk (Laws & Ward, 2011; McMurran & Ward, 2004; Ward, 2002b; Ward & Fortune, 2013; Ward & Gannon, 2006; Ward & Maruna, 2007; Ward & Stewart, 2003a; Ward et al., 2006). In comparison to risk-focused perspectives, Polaschek (2012) argues that:

> One of the most useful aspects of critiques from strength emphasizing perspectives is in reminding us of the importance of giving offenders reasons to want to engage in desistance and change (e.g., Porporino, 2010; Ward & Maruna, 2007), not just the capacities to do so. (p. 8)

Therefore, in this chapter, I will elaborate on the theoretical and empirical background of these practical GLM assumptions, especially in relation to treatment motivation of (adolescent) offenders. This chapter starts with an overview of the academic literature on desistance and the importance of treatment motivation and engagement for successful rehabilitation, in both adults and youth. Several theories and frameworks will be discussed that are deemed important for enhancing treatment motivation in light of the GLM: the Multifactor Offender Readiness Model (MORM; Day et al., 2010; Ward et al., 2004), the Stages of Change Model (Prochaska et al., 1992), Motivational interviewing (MI; Miller & Rollnick, 2002) and the Self-determination Theory (SDT; Deci & Ryan, 2000). Furthermore, we discuss the existing empirical evidence on the effect of GLM-based treatment goals and interventions on well-being, motivation and recidivism. In this way, this chapter provides a sound theoretical foundation for the empirical test of the GLM's practical assumptions in the next chapter (Chapter 10).

9.1 Achieving Sustainable Desistance

According to the GLM, treatment goals of successful (juvenile) offender rehabilitation should consist of personal, realistic and approach goals. Avoiding criminogenic risk factors alone is hypothesized to be insufficient for achieving sustainable desistance from crime (McMurran & Ward, 2004; Porporino, 2010; Serin & Lloyd, 2017; Ward & Fortune, 2013; Ward & Marshall, 2007; Ward & Maruna, 2007; Ward, Melser, et al., 2007). This line of thought concurs with criticism from the desistance literature on risk factor research and approaches (McNeill, 2012; Porporino, 2010). That is, advocates of desistance theories argue that risk factors for offending and recidivism are not always the same as (or even related to) the relevant factors for desistance. In this view, explanations of why people offend are deemed less important for offender rehabilitation than explanations of why people desist from crime (McNeill, 2012; Porporino, 2010).

Although the developers of GLM also criticize avoiding risk factors as the single treatment focus, they nuance the viewpoint of the desistance literature by arguing that the underlying needs and motivations for criminal behaviour *can* provide good starting points to help offenders desist from crime by satisfying these needs in a prosocial way (Serin & Lloyd, 2009; Ward & Laws, 2010). Notably, pursuing personally relevant needs merely for individual well-being will also not be sufficient for successful rehabilitation. Critics argue that strengths-based interventions focusing on well-being alone could potentially create "dangerous but happy individual[s]" (Andrews et al., 2011, p. 740; Ward & Maruna, 2007, p. 125). The GLM, thus, emphasizes the importance of supporting offenders to *prosocially* pursue their needs and well-being. In accordance with risk-focused approaches, such as the RNR, the GLM views criminogenic risk factors as obstacles that should be dealt with (Ward & Fortune, 2013; Ward & Maruna, 2007).

Similarly, in line with the desistance literature, offender rehabilitation according to the GLM should support *prosocial identity* development (Ward & Marshall, 2007; Ward & Maruna, 2007). We have seen in previous chapters that the GLM holds that we form our identity and the lives we want to live by attaching different levels of importance to the primary goods and by the ways we seek to satisfy them (Ward & Marshall, 2007; Ward & Maruna, 2007). Generally, the problem in offending behaviour is considered not to reside in the fundamental underlying needs, values and motivations (i.e., the primary goods) of the offenders, but in the actual antisocial behaviours themselves (i.e., inappropriate secondary goods). Offender rehabilitation according to the GLM will therefore not aim to try to change these underlying human values and motivations, but address the inappropriate ways in which offenders aim to pursue them (Ward, 2002a, 2002b, 2010; Ward & Fortune, 2013; Ward & Maruna, 2007). The latter is a process that shows similarities with several desistance theories, that will be elaborated on in the following sections (Laws & Ward, 2011; Ward & Laws, 2010).

9.1.1 Desistance Theories

Desistance can be defined as the process of moving from active offending to gradual reduction and eventually the complete cessation of delinquent behaviour (Laws & Ward, 2011; Maruna, 2001). A classic theory of desistance is the one of Laub and Sampson (1993, 2001, 2003) who concluded from their work[1] that desistance is a rather passive process that (unconsciously) happens to persons, especially for young offenders as part of their natural 'maturation'. In this view, certain life events inherent to the transition to adulthood, called 'turning points', are related to desistance, such as marriage, obtaining a legal stable job and going into military service. These ideas are consistent with Moffitt's previously mentioned taxonomy in which most young offenders are 'adolescence-limited' and cease their antisocial behaviour once they are older and more mature (Moffitt, 1993, 2018). Accordingly, studies have shown that maturation plays an important role in desistance during the transition from adolescence to adulthood, mainly due to reduced impulsivity, becoming more responsible, and being more considerate of others and long-term consequences (Hill et al., 2016; McCuish et al., 2020; Rocque et al., 2019).

Other desistance theories, however, have criticized this relatively passive view of the desistance process and emphasize the agentic and deliberate role people play in their life

1 A reevaluation of the longitudinal data of adolescent offenders published by the 'Gluecks' (Glueck & Glueck, 1950; see Chapter 5).

plans, choices and changes (Giordano et al., 2002; Healy, 2013; Leibrich, 1994; Paternoster & Bushway, 2009). They argue that although 'turning points', also referred to as 'hooks of change', can serve as catalysts or transition events (Giordano et al., 2002), it is the actor's own intentional role in transforming towards a more prosocial identity that matters for sustained desistance (Giordano, 2020; Giordano et al., 2002, 2003; LeBel et al., 2008; McMahon & Jump, 2018; Mulvey et al., 2004; Paternoster & Bushway, 2009; Weijers, 2020).

Theories of desistance that attribute an important role to human agency, however, differ in the motivations that underlie the transformation towards a prosocial identity. For example, according to Maruna (2001), offenders can leave their antisocial lifestyle behind when they are able to develop a new prosocial identity according to a so-called 'redemption script', in which they define themselves as essentially good persons trying to 'make good'. Others have argued that these moral motivations do not guide the desistance process, but rather more rational choices when offenders decide that the rewards and benefits of delinquency no longer outweigh the costs and disadvantages (Healy, 2013; Mulvey et al., 2004; Paternoster & Bushway, 2009; Thomas & Vogel, 2019). Paternoster and Bushway (2009) refer to this process as a 'crystallization of discontent', in which offenders experience a dissatisfaction and/or thwarting of their needs because of their antisocial lifestyle that calls for a deliberate changing of behaviour and identity (Petrich, 2020).

The latter is in line with the theory of 'possible selves' (Markus & Nurius, 1986), which suggests that having a positive expectation of one's 'possible future self' can serve as a standard against which one's current and past (antisocial) self can be compared (Oyserman & Markus, 1990). A divergence between these identities is believed to motivate people to engage in behaviours that align their current self with their aspired, possible self (Iselin et al., 2012). For example, Iselin et al. (2012) have shown that adolescent offenders' perceptions of the importance of having a legal job are indeed related to more hours worked in a community job, and a decrease in illegal activity. Mahler et al. (2018) replicated these findings in another sample of adolescent offenders. They concluded that youth who expected to graduate from college (i.e., academic self-efficacy) obtained higher grades and those who expected to stay out of trouble (i.e., desistance self-efficacy; Brezina, 2020) reported less offending behaviour. In turn, their behaviour (obtaining good grades and desisting from crime) raised their positive expectations of themselves. This also indicates that the development of a sense of self always occurs within a social context or environment; contingent on the possibilities, restraints, expectancies and values in that context (Markus & Nurius, 1986; Massey et al., 2008; Nurmi, 1991; Oyserman & Saltz, 1993).

9.1.2 *Prosocial Identity Development*

From the above theories, we can conclude that to successfully assist this process towards a prosocial self and desistance, it is important to support (young) offenders in developing appealing alternatives (e.g., proper education, legal work, housing, social support, etc.) to their criminal lifestyle (Clinkinbeard & Murray, 2012; McNeill et al., 2012; Van Hecke, Meulewaeter, Vanderplasschen, et al., 2021; Walters, 2002). This is especially important for adolescents who are still in the early stages of learning and developing their skills, resources and identity (McCuish et al., 2020; Mulvey et al., 2004). Studies into the desistance process of adolescent offenders confirm that to attain sustained desistance, it is not only important that offender rehabilitation interventions motivate youth to develop a prosocial identity, but also provide them with the appropriate (social) support to do so, enhancing their (confidence in their) ability to desist (Abrams & Aguilar, 2005; Amemiya et al., 2017; Brezina, 2020; Mahler et al., 2017; McMahon & Jump, 2018; Na & Jang, 2019; Panuccio et al., 2012; Tracey & Hanham, 2015; Van Hecke, Meulewaeter, Vanderplasschen, et al., 2021; Villeneuve et al., 2019; Wainwright & Nee, 2014).

Taken together, these desistance ideas are in line with the GLM's view on how a focus on important primary goods and well-being can guide the way to desistance, through enhancing psychological need satisfaction in a prosocial manner (Ward & Laws, 2010; Ward & Maruna, 2007). Exactly how offender rehabilitation interventions can support this process is deemed contingent on the offender's specific needs and capacities (i.e., psychological capital) combined with their social and physical circumstances (i.e., social capital; Ward & Stewart, 2003c). The GLM's aim is to make sure that the capacity and resource building process also reduces the existing obstacles (i.e., the criminogenic risk factors) towards a prosocial identity (Ward & Laws, 2010; Ward & Maruna, 2007; Ward et al., 2006). Furthermore, both the GLM and desistance theories target the offender's goals, needs and the consequences of delinquency in their lives as important opportunities to enhance treatment motivation (McMurran & Ward, 2004; Ward & Laws, 2010). In what follows, we will elaborate on why and how treatment motivation can be enhanced to improve (juvenile) offender rehabilitation.

9.2 The Importance of Treatment Motivation and Engagement for Successful Rehabilitation

In general, a lack of treatment motivation, disengagement (e.g., poor attendance and/or low cooperation) and (subsequent) treatment dropout are very common in (young) offender rehabilitation interventions (Ginsburg et al., 2002; Howells & Day, 2003, 2007; McMurran & Ward, 2004, 2010; Olver et al., 2011). In particular, detained adolescent offenders might have motivational issues concerning the mandatory interventions that are imposed upon them by authorities (Carl et al., 2020; Fortune, 2018; Harder et al., 2015). As we have seen in previous chapters, adolescents can experience difficulties relevant to their developmental period, such as psychological and emotional problems (Arnett, 1999; Fortune, 2018; Goldbeck et al., 2007; Miller, 2014). On top of that, childhood trauma and psychopathological disorders are highly prevalent in detained adolescent offenders (Boonmann et al., 2015; Colins et al., 2009, 2010; Hoeve, Colins, et al., 2014; Vermeiren et al., 2006). Both psychopathology and trauma are related, depending on the type and severity, to treatment motivation and engagement (DiGiuseppe et al., 1996; DiPierro-Sutton et al., 2021; Leenarts et al., 2013; Roedelof et al., 2013; van Binsbergen et al., 2001; Van Damme, Hoeve, et al., 2015).

Youth who suffer from emotional trauma and internalizing symptoms (e.g., anxiety and depression) are generally more aware of their problems and experience more emotional discomfort, which can enhance their willingness to engage in treatment (DiGiuseppe et al., 1996; DiPierro-Sutton et al., 2021; Leenarts et al., 2013; Van Damme, Hoeve, et al., 2015). Comparatively, externalizing disorders (e.g., conduct disorder) and symptoms of severe mental illness (e.g., psychotic disorder) are known to hinder treatment engagement, due to a lack of problem insight, social adjustment problems, interpersonal distrust and authority issues (Brooks & Khan, 2015; DiGiuseppe et al., 1996; Roedelof et al., 2013; van Binsbergen et al., 2001). Additionally, youth detention interventions tend to be highly structured and can sometimes be (experienced as) repressive. Such an environment can restrict the youth's (sense of) autonomy, reduce treatment motivation and create resistance (De Valk et al., 2019; Schubert et al., 2012; van der Helm et al., 2014, 2018).

Working with offenders who do not want and even refuse to engage in changing their behaviour makes successful rehabilitation difficult (Carl et al., 2020; McMurran, 2002; Parhar et al., 2008). Whereas higher levels of treatment motivation in offender rehabilitation are related to better treatment outcomes in both adults (Higley et al., 2019; Mann et al., 2002) and adolescents (van der Stouwe et al., 2018), low treatment motivation and engagement are related to adverse outcomes, such as treatment dropout and higher levels of recidivism (Carl et al., 2020; Drieschner & Verschuur, 2010; Harder et al., 2012; Yang et al., 2013). Numerous studies show that treatment dropouts have higher recidivism rates compared to treatment completers, and sometimes even higher than untreated control participants, in both adults as well as adolescents (Edwards et al., 2005; McMurran & Theodosi, 2007; Olver et al., 2011). In the other direction, high-risk (young) offenders also tend to have a higher chance of dropping out of treatment. Generally, those offenders who tend to drop out have more criminogenic risk factors initially than those who complete treatment (Carl et al., 2020; Olver et al., 2011; Wormith & Olver, 2002).

Thus, to effectively adhere to the risk, need and responsivity principles of the RNR model, it is deemed imperative that interventions pay attention to motivational issues in order to ensure that high-risk offenders remain (actively engaged) in treatment to receive the appropriate level of services (Andrews & Bonta, 2010; Bonta & Andrews, 2017). Paying special attention to the responsivity factors, such as treatment motivation and engagement in offender rehabilitation is therefore an important factor in effective interventions (Andrews & Bonta, 2010; Bonta & Andrews, 2017; Bourgon & Bonta, 2014; Ginsburg et al., 2002; Higley et al., 2019; Marshall & Marshall, 2012; Nee et al., 2013). For example, Higley et al. (2019) found that higher levels of treatment motivation in adult offender rehabilitation programmes were associated with improved treatment outcomes (e.g., less recidivism), over and above the effects of the level of recidivism risk.

Although the RNR model underlines the importance of treatment motivation as a responsivity factor (Bourgon & Bonta, 2014), it does not elaborate on how to effectively engage offenders in treatment (Ward et al., 2012). As already discussed in Chapter 2, this is where the GLM can be of additional value. In addition to the risk-focus of the RNR, the GLM also focuses on offenders' strengths and self-determined personal goals (i.e., one's primary goods) to enhance their well-being and motivation to change and successfully desist. As Laws and Ward (2011) explain:

> It is easier to motivate individuals to change their offense-related characteristics by focusing on the perceived benefits (primary goods) they accrue from their offending and by exploring more appropriate means (secondary goods) to achieve what is of value to them. By proceeding in this manner, individuals do not need to abandon those things that are important to them – only to learn to acquire them differently. (p. 198)

9.3 Enhancing Treatment Motivation and Engagement

9.3.1 *Multifactor Offender Readiness Model*

To further elaborate on the underlying processes in which the GLM could enhance treatment motivation, Ward et al. (2004) proposed the Multifactor Offender Readiness Model (MORM). This model states that to increase the chance that an intervention will engage an offender's readiness for treatment and change, it should consider several external (contextual) and internal (in-person) factors.

Regarding the external readiness conditions, the MORM states that firstly the appropriate interventions and skilled staff should be available to the offender, to be effective (i.e., fitting programme characteristics, opportunity and resource factors).

Furthermore, the offender's personal circumstances surrounding the intervention constitute an important factor for treatment readiness. An example of such a circumstance consists of whether the intervention is mandated (legally referred) or voluntary (self-referred). Voluntary interventions are found to be more effective than mandated ones (Parhar et al., 2008). The level of perceived coercion in mandated interventions can, however, vary to the extent that the intervention is perceived to be helpful in meeting the individual's personal goals (Day et al., 2010; Knight et al., 2000; Parhar et al., 2008; Ward et al., 2004). The location (e.g., community or institution-based) can also be relevant in this process, as it can influence the extent to which the offender is able to apply the learned skills and changes in day-to-day life. Finally, the availability of social support in the offender's surroundings is believed to be of great importance for treatment readiness, engagement and successful completion (Day et al., 2010; Ward et al., 2004).

Concerning the internal readiness conditions, the affective properties that are hypothesized to enhance treatment readiness include moderate to high levels of experienced distress (e.g., depression and anxiety) and aversive emotional reactions to their offence or status as 'offender' (e.g., guilt, shame or remorse). Behavioural factors include problem insight, help-seeking behaviour and having the capacities, such as social and communication skills, to participate and actively engage in the therapeutic process. However, before these behavioural factors come into play, it is argued that there should also be a certain level of treatment motivation consisting of the intention (i.e., the will) to seek a number of goals, of which one should be the desire to behave in a prosocial way (Ward et al., 2004). Several cognitive aspects are hypothesized to be important for treatment readiness, such as the belief that one is capable of exercising choice and control over one's life (i.e., internal locus of control, agency, and autonomy), the belief that one is capable of changing their behaviour (i.e., self-efficacy), the belief that the intervention's benefits outweigh the barriers and having positive and realistic expectations about the intervention (Day et al., 2010; Ward et al., 2004).

Finally, identity factors related to having a prosocial identity (e.g., identifying with being a hard and honest worker, a reliable partner and/or parent, a loving and peaceful person etc.) are hypothesized as important aspects of treatment readiness. The MORM, in line with the GLM, argues that human behaviour is ultimately directed at the achievement of primary goods through pursuing personal valuable goals. The individual way in which we realize these goods and goals, the weightage and priority we give to each of them is contingent on several factors, such as culture, gender, circumstances, opportunities, values and abilities. In this view, these different realizations and our behaviour are believed to constitute our identity and spell out the kind of life we seek (see also Chapter 3; Emmons, 1996, 1999; Ward, 2002a; Ward et al., 2004). For treatment readiness, it is therefore deemed important that the individual's personal identity allows the possibility of an offence-free lifestyle, is not based on being an offender and includes the potential of change (Day et al., 2010; Ward et al., 2004).

Studies empirically examining the MORM find that the internal readiness factors, in particular, are related to treatment engagement and successful treatment outcomes in adult offenders (Bosma et al., 2017; Sheldon, Howells et al., 2010; Sturgess et al., 2016). Sturgess et al. (2016) assessed the MORM by conducting a meta-analysis of the reasons why detained adult offenders fail to attend or successfully complete treatment interventions. Factors that often recurred in studies as important for treatment engagement were cognitive factors (e.g., beliefs of self-efficacy, problem recognition, treatment expectations); affective factors (e.g., distress and feelings of guilt); behavioural factors (e.g., treatment compliance, memory and concentration); and volitional and identity factors, where realizing and acknowledging the need for change was related to the establishment of prosocial goals (Sturgess et al., 2016). The studies conclude that an incongruence between treatment goals and the offenders' personal goals is associated with poor treatment engagement and noncompletion. Moreover, having little choice, feeling powerless, lacking in autonomy and feeling coerced to participate in treatment are factors related to poor engagement. Additionally, the researchers found support for external factors that enhanced treatment readiness, such as a calm, therapeutic and safe environment; perceived support from staff; and a variety of available treatments (Sturgess et al., 2016). Taken together, treatment readiness (as defined by the MORM factors) is found to be related to enhanced treatment engagement (e.g., active participation and therapeutic alliance) and successful treatment completion in adult offenders (Bosma et al., 2017; Casey et al., 2007; Sturgess et al., 2016). To the best of my knowledge, however, no studies examined the MORM in young offenders.

9.3.2 *Stages of Change Model*

Treatment readiness is not a new concept and has been frequently studied in the context of Prochaska and DiClemente's (1986) 'transtheoretical model of behavioural change', better known as the 'stages of change model' (Prochaska et al., 1992). Although this model was initially developed, studied and applied to improve addiction treatment, it is increasingly being applied to other domains as well, including offender rehabilitation (Casey et al., 2005; Day et al., 2006; McMurran, 2002; Prochaska & Levesque, 2002). According to this model, modification of (addictive) behaviour is a dynamic process that cycles through five stages: precontemplation, contemplation, preparation, action and maintenance.

In the precontemplation stage, individuals are unaware of their problems and have no intention of changing their behaviour. In the contemplation stage, individuals are aware that problems exist, and they are considering addressing them, but have not taken any action. When individuals develop the intention to take action in the near future, they have progressed to the preparation stage. Actively modifying one's behaviour (action stage) and continuing to work on preventing relapse and making continued progress (maintenance stage) are the final stages of the cycle (Prochaska & Levesque, 2002; Prochaska et al., 1992). People mostly do not go through the stages in a linear fashion, but spiral back and forth between them because relapses are common. Going through these stages is furthermore contingent upon the process of change. That is, whether or not a person goes on to a next (or previous) stage depends on their estimation of the benefits and costs of the behavioural change; their self-efficacy (i.e., the belief that they are able to succeed); and what an individual actually does to modify their behaviour (Casey et al., 2005; Prochaska et al., 1992).

Despite its widespread clinical application, criticism has also been voiced about the model, particularly regarding the proposed distinctiveness of the stages. According to this criticism, human behaviour is too complex to be categorized in discrete stages, and most likely occurs along a dimensional continuum (Burrowes & Needs, 2009; Casey et al., 2005; Hemphill & Howell, 2000; Yong et al., 2015). Furthermore, the stages of change model in itself does not provide specific guidelines on how to influence treatment readiness, but merely states that there should be a match between the offender's stage of readiness to change and the intervention provided (Casey et al., 2005; Prochaska et al., 1992). Also, most studies of treatment readiness in offenders focus exclusively on adults. Although some studies have identified (part of) the stages of change in adolescent offenders, research in this specific population is scarce (Cohen et al., 2005; Hemphill & Howell, 2000; van Binsbergen et al., 2001; Weijers, 2020). A better understanding of how to successfully influence (adolescent) offenders' readiness to change could potentially enhance treatment engagement and improve the effectiveness of offender rehabilitation interventions (Burrowes & Needs, 2009; Tierney & McCabe, 2002; Ward et al., 2004).

9.3.3 *Motivational Interviewing*

One intervention that is commonly used to address and improve treatment readiness is motivational interviewing (MI), developed by Miller and Rollnick (2002). MI is defined as "a client-centered, directive method for enhancing intrinsic motivation to change by exploring and resolving ambivalence" (Miller & Rollnick, 2002, p. 25). MI does not consist of a fixed protocol, but provides a number of motivational and collaborative techniques that can precede the treatment, such as developing discrepancy between values, goals and current behaviour of the client; avoiding conflicts; showing empathy; expressing understanding for resistance; and supporting self-efficacy. By using these techniques, the interviewer seeks to collaboratively elicit 'change talk' in the client, which consists of verbal expression of desires, abilities, reasons and the need for change (Mann et al., 2002; McMurran, 2002; Miller & Rollnick, 2002). MI is used in a wide variety of clinical domains including addiction treatment and offender rehabilitation, and is hypothesized to assist individuals in progressing through the stages of change (Day et al., 2010; DiClemente & Velasquez, 2002; Mann et al., 2002; Prochaska & Levesque, 2002).

In the precontemplation stage, a motivational interview can raise awareness of a problem and create dissonance between the offender's goals and their current behaviour. During the contemplation stage, the interview can elicit reasons to change and strengthen the confidence in the possibility of change. At the preparation stage, MI can evoke the intention to actively work towards change, while at the action and maintenance stage it can elicit optimism about the achieved changes and success (Birgden, 2004). Several meta-analyses and reviews have shown that the use of MI, compared to treatment without MI, results in better treatment adherence and improvements in health and addictive behaviour in both adults and adolescents (DiClemente et al., 2017).

Although less common, studies assessing the effects of MI in adult and adolescent offender rehabilitation also find improvements in treatment engagement, antisocial attitudes and problem behaviour (i.e., less drug- and alcohol use, less aggression) compared to interventions without MI (Harper & Hardy, 2000; McMurran, 2009). Studies examining the effects of MI on recidivism rates specifically, however, are rare and report mixed evidence for reduced offending behaviour (Alexander et al., 2013; McMurran, 2009). Nonetheless, as will become clear in the next sections, MI is believed to be especially valuable for improving offender rehabilitation interventions (Andrews & Bonta, 2010; Bonta & Andrews, 2017; Ginsburg et al., 2002; Harder et al., 2017; Miller & Rollnick, 2002) and shares several aspects with the GLM (McMurran & Ward, 2004; Stephenson et al., 2013).

9.4 Effective Treatment Goals for (Juvenile) Offender Rehabilitation

9.4.1 *Well-Being and Quality of Life*

The common theme in the GLM and its assumptions is improving offenders' well-being and quality of life. Adolescent offenders in general and detained adolescents in particular experience diminished levels of well-being (Buunk et al., 2016; Llosada-Gistau et al., 2015; see also the previous chapters). Still, little is known about the effects of well-being or quality of life on desistance in detained (adult or adolescent) offenders (Fortune, 2018; Mallion et al., 2020; van Nieuwenhuizen et al., 2002; Zeccola et al., 2021). One of the few studies examining this longitudinal relationship is conducted by Bouman et al. (2009) in a sample of 135 adult forensic psychiatric outpatients. They assessed the relationship between subjective well-being (overall life satisfaction and satisfaction with different life domains), short-term recidivism (self-reported offending three months later) and long-term violent recidivism (official reconvictions two years later). Short-term re-offending was negatively related to satisfaction with (mental) health and satisfaction with achieving their own life goals, even after controlling for recidivism risk level. Long-term violent recidivism was (modestly) negatively related to general subjective well-being and satisfaction with (mental) health. Although the latter relationships became non-significant when controlling for recidivism risk, satisfaction with (mental) health and general life satisfaction did buffer a high-risk level for violent reconvictions.

Regarding adolescent detained boys, Barendregt et al. (2018) assessed their quality of life at admission (as a proxy measure of well-being, measured as satisfaction with social participation, health, family relationships, living situation, safety, finances, self-esteem and spirituality) in relation to delinquent behaviour 12 months after discharge, but found no significant relationships. In contrast, Van Damme et al. (2016) found that a lower quality of life at admission in detained adolescent girls (measured as satisfaction on the life domains of physical health, psychological health and environment) was related to more recidivism six months after discharge, indirectly through mental health problems. Four years after their discharge, Van Damme et al. (2022) reassessed 49 of these, now adult, women, and found that personal resilience at follow-up (i.e., attitudes about their own competence and acceptance of themselves and their life) was related to both higher levels of quality of life and less offending behaviour after their discharge.

However, none of the aforementioned studies considered within-person changes in the quality of life during treatment that could influence subsequent treatment motivation, treatment outcomes and recidivism. Partly addressing this limitation, Van Damme et al. (2020), Van Hecke et al. (2019) and Van Hecke, Meulewaeter, Vanderplasschen, et al. (2021) held in-depth interviews with previously detained adolescent boys and girls to investigate what helped them in the process of leaving their former (antisocial) lifestyle behind them. On the basis of these interviews, they concluded, in line with the GLM, that the important turning points promoting motivation and desistance were related to achieving the skills (i.e., 'competence') together with the appropriate social support (i.e., 'relatedness') to build their own lives (i.e., 'autonomy').

9.4.2 *Psychological Needs: Self-Determination Theory*

The latter finding is also in line with Deci and Ryan's (2000) Self-Determination Theory (SDT; McMurran & Ward, 2004; van der Kaap-Deeder et al., 2017; Vansteenkiste & Sheldon, 2006). We already saw that SDT underlies the etiological assumptions of the GLM about well-being and primary goods. We discussed that the GLM relies on the importance of SDT's three basic psychological needs ('relatedness', 'competence' and 'autonomy') for attaining well-being (see Chapter 3) as well as explaining psychosocial outcomes including externalizing disorders and delinquency (see Chapter 5). In this section we will see that SDT also plays an important role in the conceptualization of motivation, in both MI and the GLM (McMurran, 2009; McMurran & Ward, 2004; Vansteenkiste & Ryan, 2013; Vansteenkiste & Sheldon, 2006).

SDT approaches motivation as a continuum, ranging from a complete lack of motivation or 'amotivation', through 'extrinsic motivation' that is externally regulated from outside pressure or control, to 'intrinsic motivation', which originates from within the self, is fully intrinsically regulated, autonomous and self-determined (Deci & Ryan, 2000; Ryan & Deci, 2000a, 2017b). These different types of motivation resonate with Prochaska and DiClemente's (1986) stages of change model used in MI (see Sections 9.3.2 and 9.3.3), which argues that people generally progress from a 'precontemplation stage' ('amotivation') through a 'contemplation' and 'action stage' ('extrinsic motivation') to long-term 'maintenance' of the changes ('intrinsic motivation'; McMurran & Ward, 2004; Prochaska et al., 1992). Accordingly, behaviour that is extrinsically motivated will most likely only last as long as the extrinsic controls are in place. On the other hand, intrinsic motivation is related to maintenance of sustainable change (Deci & Ryan, 2000, 2008; Ryan & Deci, 2017b). In this reasoning, an offender who is only extrinsically motivated to desist from crime because of the risk of incarceration and parole requirements that only lasts a limited amount of time, will have a higher chance to recidivate than an offender who is intrinsically motivated to leave their criminal lifestyle behind.

Based on this conceptualization of motivation by SDT, both MI and the GLM focus on enhancing *intrinsic motivation* for behavioural change. To accomplish this goal, as in MI, the GLM aims to promote prosocial treatment goals that are personally relevant to the offender and their well-being. Likewise, in line with the SDT, the GLM emphasizes the importance of pursuing and achieving goals that are intrinsically meaningful (i.e., related to the basic psychological needs and the GLM's primary goods) instead of those that are extrinsically controlled or imposed (Tyler et al., 2020; Ward et al., 2006). In Chapter 3, we already saw that intrinsic goal pursuit is important for human well-being in general (Sheldon, Ryan, et al., 2004). In this chapter, we see that it is not only relevant for well-being, but also improves intrinsic motivation (Cox & Klinger, 2004; Deci & Ryan, 2000,

2008; Emmons, 1996; McMurran & Ward, 2004; Ryan & Deci, 2017b; Vansteenkiste et al., 2010).

Numerous studies in adults and adolescents have found that intrinsic goal pursuit is related to satisfaction of the three basic psychological needs of the SDT ('relatedness', 'competence' and 'autonomy'). In turn, the satisfaction of these three needs is linked to higher levels of intrinsic motivation, treatment engagement and positive behavioural change in different life domains, such as school, work, family, relationships, sports, physical health and mental health (Hope et al., 2019; Jochems et al., 2017; Milyavskaya & Koestner, 2011; Ng et al., 2012; Rodríguez-Meirinhos et al., 2020; Ryan & Deci, 2017b). The same conclusions can be drawn from studies in adult offenders where psychological need satisfaction is related to higher levels of quality of life, intrinsic motivation and persistence to desist from crime (Petrich, 2020; van der Kaap-Deeder et al., 2017). In the next sections, I will elaborate on each of the three SDT psychological needs in relation to (offender) treatment motivation and outcomes.

9.4.3 *Relatedness: Therapeutic Alliance*

Both MI and the GLM are hypothesized to improve treatment readiness and success in (adolescent) offenders through fostering a therapeutic alliance. A strong therapeutic alliance may additionally contribute to the psychological need for 'relatedness' and the need for social support (McMurran & Ward, 2004; Ward et al., 2004). Nevertheless, establishing a therapeutic alliance in offender rehabilitation can be challenging due to the dual-role problem faced by professionals working in (juvenile) justice systems. As explained in the Introduction (Chapter 1), professionals who work in the field of (juvenile) justice often find themselves in the dilemma between helping 'patients' and protecting society from 'offenders' (Barnao et al., 2016; Ward, 2013). Furthermore, (adolescent) offenders might react distrustful, defensive and oppositional to authorities and the mandated interventions imposed upon them (see Section 9.2), especially when they suffer from psychopathology, trauma and stigma (Wittouck & Vander Beken, 2019).

Negotiation of goals, and subsequent agreement, between a therapist and a client, such as promoted by both MI and the GLM, are hypothesized to be essential for the development of trust and a therapeutic alliance in (juvenile) offender rehabilitation (DiGiuseppe et al., 1996; Marshall & Serran, 2004). Such a collaborative approach is believed to address non-criminogenic needs (e.g., low self-esteem, personal distress, interpersonal distrust and well-being), that might not be directly related to recidivism risk according to the RNR model, but are found to facilitate responsivity, treatment motivation and the therapeutic alliance (Basanta et al., 2018; Marshall, Fernandez, et al., 2003; Ward & Mann, 2004; Ward & Maruna, 2007). Consequently, a positive therapeutic alliance has been linked to higher levels of treatment motivation, positive behaviour change and less re-offending (risk), in both adult and adolescent offenders (Florsheim et al., 2000; Hachtel et al., 2019; Harder et al., 2012; Hart & Collins, 2014; Holmqvist et al., 2007; Hughes, 2012; Marshall, Serran, et al., 2003; Polaschek & Ross, 2010; Roest et al., 2016; Van Hecke, Meulewaeter, Vanderplasschen, et al., 2021; Ward & Laws, 2010).

9.4.4 *Competence: Self-Efficacy and Internal Locus of Control*

Another important mechanism to improve treatment readiness and successful rehabilitation is supporting self-efficacy, according to both MI and the GLM (McMurran & Ward, 2004; Ward et al., 2004). Self-efficacy is people's belief in their ability and 'competence' to make progress in behavioural change. Self-efficacy beliefs are an important foundation for motivation, goal commitment, performance accomplishment and well-being (Bandura, 1977, 1982, 2006). Self-efficacy is even considered a fundamental prerequisite for behavioural change as Bandura (2006) stated: "Unless people believe they can produce desired effects by their actions, they have little incentive to act, or to persevere in the face of difficulties" (p. 170).

Accordingly, several studies found that delinquent youth with more prosocial self-efficacy beliefs (e.g., positive expectations for work, family, law-abidance and the belief that they could resist antisocial behaviour) reported more prosocial aspirations for a better and more positive future regarding employment, education, family and other prosocial goals (Cuevas et al., 2017; Iselin et al., 2012; Petrich et al., 2020). Both prosocial self-efficacy and aspirations were related to shorter lengths of stay in residential placements and less recidivism one year later (Cuevas et al., 2017). Self-efficacy also relates to the experience of an internal locus of control, which is the belief that consequences are contingent upon one's own actions rather than external forces, such as chance, faith or other people (Rotter, 1966; Tyler et al., 2020). Having an internal locus of control in offender rehabilitation interventions has been related to higher levels of treatment success in both adults (Fisher et al., 1998) and adolescents (Page & Scalora, 2004).

To increase self-efficacy beliefs and internal locus of control, the GLM argues that treatment goals should not only be intrinsically valuable, but also realistically specific and attainable given someone's skills, capacities, resources, environment and support (McMurran & Ward, 2004). Studies indeed find that working towards these types of goals is related to higher levels of motivation and well-being (See Chapter 3; Brunstein, 1993; Cantor & Sanderson, 1999; Cox & Klinger, 2004; Diener et al., 1999; Emmons, 1999; Nurmi & Salmela-Aro, 2002; Rudd et al., 2014; Ryan & Deci, 2017b; van Vianen, 2018). Furthermore, the GLM argues that successful treatment goals should also consist of approach – instead of avoidance-related goals. While avoidance goals consist of negative consequences to be resisted and prevented, approach goals are considered positive incentives to be sought and moved towards (Elliot, 1999; Emmons, 1999).

Offender rehabilitation interventions that operate according to the RNR principles are said to focus on *avoiding* criminogenic risk factors (Andrews & Bonta, 2010). However, it has been proven that it is less intrinsically motivating to avoid certain consequences rather than to actively approach specific goals (Cox & Klinger, 2004; Elliot & Church, 1997; Elliot & Harackiewicz, 1996; Emmons, 1999; Laws & Ward, 2011; Mann et al., 2004; Ward et al., 2006). This is especially so because compared to focusing on reaching one specific goal, avoidance goals require considerable (cognitive) resources to monitor all the different types of potential threats to failure (Ward et al., 2006). Moreover, only avoiding risk factors in offender rehabilitation is believed to leave 'holes' in people's lives if the avoided behaviours and values are not replaced by constructive alternatives (McMurran & Ward, 2004; Ward & Stewart, 2003c). Studies indeed find that mainly striving for avoidance goals (instead of approach goals) is related to lower levels of well-being (Elliot et al., 1997). In this sense, the GLM emphasizes supporting offenders to identify approach goals that are personally meaningful, resulting in a fulfilling life (Laws & Ward, 2011; Tyler et al., 2020; Ward & Mann, 2004).

9.4.5 *Autonomy: Pursuing Personally Relevant Goals*

Risk-focused interventions tend to diminish a sense of autonomy as they aim to avoid criminogenic risk factors that are usually determined by others, such as professionals conducting risk assessments (Mann et al., 2002; Ward et al., 2006). Additionally, being detained likely elicits feelings of external control and coercion, also negatively impacting a person's sense of 'autonomy' (De Valk et al., 2019; Tyler et al., 2020; Van der Helm et al., 2018; Zamble & Porporino, 1988). Seeking to counteract this, both MI and the GLM encourage offenders to pursue their personal, prosocial goals and argue for intrinsically motivated change, rather than having it imposed upon them. By working together towards the offender's personal goals and enhancing their self-efficacy, a sense of autonomy can be regained, even while being incarcerated (Mann et al., 2002; McMurran & Ward, 2004; Tyler et al., 2020; van der Kaap-Deeder et al., 2017; Ward et al., 2006).

This approach allows offenders to experience ownership over their personal goals (i.e., having agency and autonomy), but also ensures they are in line with the treatment goals, potentially reducing the likelihood of treatment disengagement and dropout (Sturgess et al., 2016; Tyler et al., 2020). Moreover, providing choice and opportunities for self-direction and a greater sense of autonomy enhances a person's well-being and intrinsic motivation (Brown & Ryan, 2004; Deci & Ryan, 2008; Ryan & Deci, 2017b; van der Kaap-Deeder et al., 2017). Specifically in sex offender treatment, Levenson et al. (2009, 2010) conclude that the majority of adult sex offenders in their studies valued their rehabilitation therapy most for learning to meet their own needs in more adaptive ways and creating a more satisfying life. Furthermore, these studies revealed a significant correlation between treatment satisfaction and treatment engagement (i.e., attending, actively contributing and working; Levenson et al., 2009, 2010). In turn, treatment engagement was positively related to treatment progress as defined by therapist ratings on changes in insight, deviant thoughts, awareness of situational risks, motivation, victim empathy and offence disclosure (Levenson & Macgowan, 2004).

9.4.6 *Primary Goods Attainment in Adult Offenders*

The GLM, however, does not only target the three psychological needs of the SDT (i.e., 'relatedness', 'competence' and 'autonomy') to enhance quality of life and treatment readiness, but considers a broader range of personally relevant human needs: the 11 primary goods (Laws & Ward, 2011; Ward, 2002a; Ward & Brown, 2004; Ward & Maruna, 2007; Ward & Stewart, 2003a, 2003c). Interestingly, the authors of the GLM were not the only ones who proposed a focus on quality of life in offender rehabilitation as a way to improve treatment motivation. Around the same time the GLM was developed, Williams and Strean (2002, 2003) suggested that a focus on quality of life could trigger offenders' internal motivation and readiness to change their behaviour. Similar to the GLM's primary goods, Williams (2003) concludes from a qualitative study interviewing 23 detained adult sex offenders that they aspired to reach a quality of life that consists of freedom, control over their own life, good health, good family relationships, positive emotions, leisure, education, job and career success.

Research that assessed the GLM's primary goods attainment in adult offender rehabilitation revealed that desisting adult (sex) offenders strive for all primary goods to some extent (Harris et al., 2019, based on 42 interviews; Lindsay et al., 2007, based on two case studies; Whitehead et al., 2007, based on one case study; Willis & Ward, 2011, based on 16 interviews). Yet, upon re-entry to society significant obstacles were experienced in the pursuit of many primary goods, especially due to restrictions of probation, difficulty in finding a job and accommodation and damaged relationships with family and friends (Harris et al., 2019; Willis & Ward, 2011). Moreover, criminogenic risk factors (e.g., impulsivity or lack of concern for others) were negatively related to primary goods attainment (Willis & Ward, 2011). Willis and Grace (2008) assessed the difference in the GLM's primary goods attainment (assessed as the presence of secondary goods) between 39 recidivists (i.e., sexual and other offenders) and 42 desisters who completed a prison-based reintegration planning programme for sex offenders seven years earlier. Compared to the recidivists, the desisters scored better on reintegration planning in total, in terms of housing, employment and the GLM's secondary goods attainment. No differences were found concerning violent recidivism (Willis & Grace, 2008).

Assessing the difference between a risk-focus and a primary goods-focus in offender rehabilitation,[2] Barnett et al. (2014) analysed the differences in treatment change between two groups of adult sex offenders. One group was treated with a traditional relapse prevention programme (n = 321) targeting risk factors only, while the other programme (n = 202) was based on the GLM. The latter focused not only on risk factors, but also on building motivation for a better life, including identification of the primary goods that group members wished to acquire. Although they found few differences between the two programmes, those who completed the GLM-based programme showed more improvements regarding their child abuse attitudes. Furthermore, a larger proportion of those who completed the GLM-based programme attained a 'treated profile', which meant their psychometric assessment scores (on personal distress, coping skills, self-esteem, empathy, loneliness, assertiveness, locus of control and child abuse attitudes) were indistinguishable from those of a group of non-offenders. This finding, however, did not take into account that those who completed the risk-focused programme showed more dysfunctional scores pre-treatment (Barnett et al., 2014).

Similarly, Harkins et al. (2012) assessed two rehabilitation programmes for sex offenders: one relapse prevention intervention focused on risk reduction (n = 701) and one GLM-based intervention (n = 76). Despite the large difference in sample size between the two groups, the authors concluded they found no differences in the attrition rates or the rates of treatment change between the two programmes, indicating they were equally effective. Nonetheless, participants of the GLM-based intervention (based on 15 interviews) were reported to be more optimistic and opportunity-focused compared to the participants of the risk-focused relapse prevention intervention (based on five interviews; Harkins et al., 2012).

Specifically for detained, mentally disordered sex offenders, Gannon et al. (2011) evaluated a GLM group intervention based on five case studies. In general, the five offenders easily grasped the GLM components, such as the meaning of primary and secondary goods, yet some struggled with understanding the links between the GLM and their own risk factors due to their lower IQs and mental disorders. Nevertheless, asking about the offenders' important life goals played a key role in promoting their treatment engagement.

2 Simons et al. (2006) also compared sex offenders treated with a GLM approach (n = 96) to sex offenders in a traditional risk approach (n = 100) and concluded that offenders in the GLM approach were more likely to complete treatment and remain in treatment longer. They were also rated by therapists as more motivated to participate in treatment compared to offenders who received traditional relapse prevention treatment (Willis & Ward, 2013). This study, however, was only presented at a conference but never published, which is why I was not able to find detailed information about the study or the evaluated programmes.

The latter is in line with a more elaborate evaluation of two GLM-based community outreach forensic psychological services by Ward and Attwell (2014), based on semi-structured interviews with 10 violent and/or sex offenders who completed the programme. They concluded that most participants reported improvements in motivation to change, together with improved therapeutic alliance, problem-solving and goal setting, mood and confidence and perspective-taking abilities.

More recently, Ryan et al. (2019) demonstrated similar results in eight adult male sex offenders who were still participating in a community GLM-based treatment and five men who had completed the treatment. The participants mentioned the therapeutic alliance, improved treatment engagement as they realized addressing their difficulties resulted in a happier offence-free life, addressing non-criminogenic needs and understanding the root causes of their offending behaviour as the essential elements in their process of change during treatment. Despite these promising preliminary results, they are predominantly based on qualitative studies in (very) small samples of male adult (sex) offenders.

9.4.7 *Primary Goods Attainment in Young Offenders*

Only a handful of studies examined GLM-inspired interventions for young offenders. Yet, they found comparable results as observed in adult interventions. An example is the evaluation of the British 'Preventing Youth Offending Programme' (PYOP); a positive, goal-focused approach that is said to fit well with the GLM's assumptions. The programme includes one-on-one mentoring for reintegration and encompasses a strengths-based approach by aiming to improve the lives of young offenders (Nee et al., 2013; Wainwright & Nee, 2014). Compared to the control group who did not receive treatment (n = 24), targeting criminogenic risk factors together with non-criminogenic personal needs significantly reduced recidivism levels by about half in the PYOP group (n = 67; Nee et al., 2013). Wainwright and Nee (2014) concluded from seven qualitative interviews with PYOP participants that gaining a sense of responsibility, acquiring the necessary skills and supportive relationships enhanced their motivation. It furthermore enabled them to form a positive identity.

Another example from the United Kingdom is a GLM-based intervention for adolescent sex offenders developed at G-Map: an intervention explicitly adapted for young sex offenders (Fisher et al., 2010; Fortune et al., 2014; Print, 2013; Wylie & Griffin, 2013). This intervention aims to collaboratively explore which primary goods are important to the individual offender, what role they played in the offence and how they can be fulfilled in a prosocial manner. To fit with the developmental stage of adolescence, the terminology of the GLM's primary goods were adapted and reduced from eleven to eight: 'having fun', 'performing', 'having an identity and autonomy', 'having people in my life', 'having a purpose and making a difference', 'being emotionally healthy', 'being sexually healthy' and 'being physically healthy'. Based on this, in the United States, Prescott and Dent also recently developed a GLM rehabilitation intervention specifically for juvenile offenders (Prescott, 2018; Prescott & Dent, 2018). Professionals who use this method (Fisher et al., 2010; Print, 2013; Wylie & Griffin, 2013) and a few young participants ($n = 4$; Print, 2013) reported more treatment motivation and optimism, yet solid evidence for its effectiveness is lacking. To draw well-founded conclusions for offender rehabilitation in general and for adolescents in particular, controlled experimental trials by independent researchers are needed.

9.5 Conclusion

Successful GLM-based offender rehabilitation interventions (for both adults and adolescents) not only increase offenders' autonomy and motivation by identifying their personally relevant primary goods but should also adequately strengthen their abilities to prosocially obtain those goods and deal with the obstacles that may exist or arise (Laws & Ward, 2011; Tyler et al., 2020; Ward & Mann, 2004). This approach is then hypothesized to ensure that the different problems in the pursuit of primary goods and well-being (see also Chapter 3, Section 3.6; Chapter 5, Section 5.1; Chapters 7 and 8) are adequately addressed (McMurran & Ward, 2004). At the same time, sound empirical studies into the combined relationships between the GLM's primary goods attainment, well-being, treatment motivation and their effect upon recidivism (risk) and/or desistance in detained (adolescent) offenders are still very scarce. Therefore, in the next chapter, we will empirically examine these relationships in a sample of detained adolescent offenders.

10 Examining the Pathways to Desistance in Detained Adolescents

Testing the Associations between Primary Goods, Well-Being, Mental Health Problems, Treatment Motivation and Recidivism Risk during Detention

In the previous chapter, I argued that empirical research into the assumptions about effective offender rehabilitation according to the Good Lives Model (GLM) is scarce, especially for detained adolescents. In theory, a focus on primary goods attainment and well-being could potentially increase detained adolescents' treatment motivation. Combined with addressing the criminogenic risk factors, which may obstruct the prosocial attainment of a person's personally relevant human needs, rehabilitation based on the GLM is hypothesized to achieve more sustainable desistance (Laws & Ward, 2011; McMurran & Ward, 2004; Ward, 2002b; Ward & Fortune, 2013; Ward & Gannon, 2006; Ward & Maruna, 2007; Ward & Stewart, 2003a; Ward et al., 2006).

A common problem in (young) offender rehabilitation is that of negative outcomes, such as treatment dropout and high recidivism rates, partly as a result of a lack of treatment motivation (Carl et al., 2020; Drieschner & Verschuur, 2010; Ginsburg et al., 2002; Howells & Day, 2003, 2007; McMurran & Ward, 2004, 2010; Olver et al., 2011). Detained adolescent offenders, in particular, may experience low levels of motivation concerning the mandatory interventions imposed upon them by authorities (Carl et al., 2020; Fortune, 2018; Harder et al., 2015). Both internalizing and externalizing mental health problems are prevalent in detained adolescents and have been shown to affect their treatment motivation and engagement. Whereas internalizing problems are related to more treatment engagement because of more awareness and emotional discomfort, externalizing problems are found to hamper treatment engagement due to a lack of problem insight, social adjustment problems, interpersonal distrust and authority issues (DiGiuseppe et al., 1996; DiPierro-Sutton et al., 2021; Leenarts et al., 2013; Roedelof et al., 2013; van Binsbergen et al., 2001; Van Damme, Hoeve, et al., 2015). Consequently, for detained adolescent offenders, their treatment motivation is expected to improve by working towards personally relevant primary goods and well-being (Fortune, 2018; Fortune et al., 2014; McMurran & Ward, 2004, 2010; Ward & Fortune, 2013; Ward & Laws, 2010; see also Chapter 9 for an elaboration of the possible mechanisms behind this hypothesis).

Although according to the GLM an increase in well-being is theoretically assumed to improve offender rehabilitation and reduce recidivism rates through increasing treatment motivation, empirically, little is known about the effects of well-being or quality of life on recidivism or desistance over time in detained (adult or adolescent) offenders (Fortune, 2018; Mallion et al., 2020; van Nieuwenhuizen et al., 2002; Zeccola et al., 2021). Among the few studies examining the longitudinal effects of quality of life and well-being on (juvenile) offender rehabilitation, thus far none have investigated the effects of within-person change over time (Barendregt et al., 2018; Bouman et al., 2009; Van Damme et al., 2016). Moreover, studies examining the combined relationships between (changes in) GLM's primary goods attainment, well-being, treatment motivation and its effect upon recidivism (risk) and/or desistance in detained (adolescent) offenders are lacking. Therefore, in this chapter, we will examine these relationships in a sample of detained adolescent offenders.

For this purpose, at the beginning and at follow-up during their detention, we evaluated a sample of adolescent offenders who participated in the first study (see Chapter 7) and were sentenced to detention for a prolonged period in a Juvenile Justice Institution (in the Netherlands) or Youth Detention Centre (in Belgium). The follow-up assessment (T2) was performed about three months after the first baseline assessment (i.e., T1, the first assessment about two weeks after their arrest asking about the four weeks before their arrest). At both assessment points, a recidivism risk assessment interview was conducted to identify potential changes in criminogenic risk factors and recidivism risk level (using the Youth Level of Service/Case Management Inventory). Additionally, the same set of questionnaires from the first study was administered at both assessment points.

Using these questionnaires, we evaluated possible changes over time in self-reported mental health problems, primary goods satisfaction, subjective well-being and treatment motivation. These data enable us to test the GLM's hypotheses that positive changes in the pursuit of primary goods and well-being can improve treatment motivation and (subsequently) reduce recidivism risk in detained adolescent offenders (Laws & Ward, 2011; McMurran & Ward, 2004; Ward, 2002b; Ward & Fortune, 2013; Ward & Gannon, 2006; Ward & Maruna, 2007; Ward & Stewart, 2003a; Ward et al., 2006). Additionally, we can assess the role of mental health problems in this process, which is hypothesized to affect adolescents' well-being and treatment motivation (see also Chapters 4, 7 and 9; de Ruigh et al., 2019; DiGiuseppe et al., 1996; DiPierro-Sutton et al., 2021; Leenarts et al., 2013; Roedelof et al., 2013; van Binsbergen et al., 2001; Van Damme, Hoeve, et al., 2015).

10.1 METHOD

10.1.1 Setting and Sampling Procedure

This follow-up study expands on the study on detained adolescents reported in Chapter 7. The current study received (ethical) approval as part of our larger study, by the director of the Flemish Youth Detention Centres, the Dutch Custodial Institutions Agency (Dienst Justitiële Inrichtingen) and the Social and Societal Ethics Committee of the Catholic University of Leuven (G-2017 10 945).

This follow-up study was conducted in secure youth detention institutions: two in Belgium (Flanders) and one in the Netherlands. In Belgium (Flanders), adolescents whose detention in the Youth Detention Centre (YDC) De Grubbe in Everberg[1] is prolonged after a maximum of five days and two months (or earlier) can be transferred to one of four different residential YDCs in the Flemish part of Belgium; two in the east and two in the west of the country. For practical reasons, only those adolescents who were transferred to the YDCs in the eastern part of the country[2] were eligible for inclusion in the follow-up study. In the Netherlands, youth who are sentenced to detention after the pre-trial phase mostly stay in the same Juvenile Justice Institution (JJI) where they had been awaiting trial. Some, however, are transferred to a JJI elsewhere in the country. For practical reasons, only those adolescents who stayed in the initial Dutch JJI to serve their sentence (in the south of the country)[3] were included in the follow-up study.

Both the Flemish YDCs and the Dutch JJI were characterized by restrictive infrastructures (i.e., aggravated locked doors, high fences and barred windows) and daily regimes (i.e., strict rules, scheduled activities, limited and scheduled contact with close relatives). For those sentenced to (prolonged) detention, the JJI and residential YDCs focus on rehabilitation and reintegration instead of observation and orientation. By providing the juveniles with a structured and a stable environment where they can receive treatment if needed (such as aggression or emotion regulation interventions and cognitive-behavioural therapy), the institutions prepare the juveniles to ensure a positive reintegration into society. Within this reintegration process, juveniles are gradually granted more liberties and periods of leave to practice what they have learned within the institution.

Of the 170 detained adolescents who were included in the first study (see Chapter 7), only 63 (37.1%) were eligible to participate in the current follow-up study. The other 107 (62.9%) were unable to participate because they were either released (n = 62), transferred

1 Gemeenschapsinstelling (GI) De Grubbe, Everberg (BE).
2 Gemeenschapsinstelling (GI) De Kempen, Mol (BE).
3 Justitiële Jeugd Inrichting (JJI) Het Keerpunt, Cadier en Keer (NL).

to a different (not included) institution ($n = 31$) or had left the facility for reasons unknown to the researcher ($n = 14$). Of the remaining 63 adolescents who were sentenced to (prolonged) detention and eligible to participate in the follow-up study, one refused further participation. This resulted in a sample of 62 boys who had given their active written informed consent for the follow-up assessments during the first assessment (see Chapter 7, Section 7.1.1 for details of the informed consent procedure). To reconfirm, verbal informed consent was obtained prior to the start of each of the follow-up assessments. The participants were reminded that their information would be treated anonymously, confidentially (e.g., not shared with the police, court, the institution or any others) and in accordance with European and national privacy laws.[4] They were reassured that participation was voluntary, they could stop their participation at any time and refusal or acceptance to participate in the study would not affect their judicial status or stay in the institution.

At T2, the majority of the 62 included participants (93.5%, $n = 58$) had been transferred from the Flemish YDC in Everberg to one of the two residential YDCs in the eastern part of the country, while only four (6.5%) were serving their sentence in the same Dutch JJI where they had been awaiting trial (see Table 10.1 for an overview of the number of participants at each assessment point). The 62 adolescent offenders who were included in the follow-up study spent an average of seven months (219 days) in detention from the moment of their arrest to the day of their release. The first follow-up assessment (T2) was conducted on average three and a half months (105 days) after their arrest, which was about three months (on average 89 days) after the first baseline assessment (T1). At the time of the T2 assessment, those who were transferred had been in the residential YDC for about one to two months. At that point in time, about half of the adolescents had not been granted any liberties or periods of leave yet, while the other half had been granted one or two short day visits at home.

Although not included in the current chapter (see Section 10.1.4), we also assessed participants at T3 (about three months after T2). However, only 27 of the 62 included participants (43.5%) remained to participate in the second follow-up assessment. This was because 35 of the 62 (56.45%) included participants at T2 were unable to complete the second follow-up assessment (T3). The majority of these dropouts ($n = 24$) had left the detention centre soon (on average 52 days) after T2. The reasons for their early departure included: discharge/release ($n = 13$), transfer to another residential/open juvenile institution ($n = 10$) and reasons unknown to the researcher ($n = 1$). Another 11 adolescents were unable to participate at T3 due to the COVID-19 pandemic regulations.

4 This is except for information suggesting an immediate threat of severe danger to someone else or the youth themselves, which would be shared with the appropriate authorities. This only included information about acts in the future and did not include information about (criminal or deviant) acts in the past.

This resulted in 27 participants (26 who remained in the Flemish YDC, and one adolescent who remained in the Dutch JJI) who completed the baseline assessment (T1), the first (T2) and the second follow-up assessment (T3). The T3 assessment was performed about six and a half months (on average 200 days) after their arrest, about six months (on average 186 days) after T1, about three months (99 days) after T2 and about a month (on average 38 days) before the adolescents' release from the JJI or YDC. At the time of the T3 assessment, those in the residential YDCs had been there for about four to five months. At that point, all had been granted some liberties and longer periods of leave on the weekends. By then, most of them also knew when their release was planned.

Table 10.1 Overview of the Participants at Each Assessment Point

	T1 included in the first study in Chapter 7	T1 included in current follow-up study	T2 included in current follow-up study	T3
Flemish YDCs	154	58	58	26
Dutch JJI	16	4	4	1
Total	170	62	62	27

10.1.2 Study Procedure

At each assessment point, the participants were asked to fill out a survey on an electronic tablet. Additionally, they were interviewed using the Youth Service Level/Case Management Inventory (YLS/CMI) to assess their level of recidivism risk.

At T1 (as in Chapter 7), the included participants had been in the institution for an average of 16 days. This period gave them some time to get used to the new situation, but it was considered short enough to still remember the period (four weeks) before their arrest (i.e., a baseline assessment). At T1, first, participants were asked to answer questions concerning their demographic information (i.e., age, ethnic background, school background, family and living situation). Second, participants were asked to retrospectively (while thinking about the four weeks before their arrest, when they were still in the community), fill out the Satisfaction With Life Scale (SWLS-CV; five items on a 5-point Likert scale), Scale of Positive and Negative Experiences (SPANE; 12 items on a 5-point Likert scale), the Strengths and Difficulties Questionnaire (SDQ; 25 items on a 3-point Likert scale) and the items concerning their level of satisfaction with the proxy primary goods (20 items in total on a 5-point Likert scale). Additionally, they were asked to fill out the Adolescent Treatment Motivation Questionnaire (ATMQ; 11 items on a 5-point Likert scale) thinking about their current situation (recently arrested and detained). After they finished the self-report survey, participants were interviewed about the preceding year until the time of their arrest, using the Youth Service Level/Case Management Inventory (YLS/CMI) to assess their recidivism risk. These assessment sessions varied in duration between 45 and 90 minutes.

At T2 and T3, participants filled out the same questionnaires (except for the demographic data) now with their current situation in mind. After they finished the survey, participants were again interviewed about their current situation and the preceding period (the period between T1 and T2, or between T2 and T3, respectively), using the Youth Service Level/Case Management Inventory (YLS/CMI) to assess their recidivism risk. These assessment sessions varied in duration between 30 and 60 minutes.

10.1.3 Measures

Subjective Well-Being

At each assessment point, well-being was operationalized as subjectively experienced overall well-being, consisting of a standardized composite score of general life satisfaction (Satisfaction With Life Scale-Child Version; Diener et al., 1985; Gadermann et al., 2010) and emotional well-being, both positive and negative (Scale of Positive and Negative Experience; Diener et al., 2010). In this way, well-being is measured at both the cognitive (general life satisfaction) and affective (emotional well-being, positive and negative) level. See Chapter 6, Section 6.1.2 and Chapter 7, Section 7.1.3, for a more detailed description of these measures.

Satisfaction with Life Scale-Child Version (SWLS-CV). Adding the five items of the Dutch version of Satisfaction With Life Scale-Child Version (SWLS-CV; Diener et al., 1985; Gadermann et al., 2010; Serie et al., 2017a) results in a sum score between 5 and 25, which is found to be valid and reliable in measuring the cognitive evaluation of general life satisfaction from a context-free perspective (Gadermann et al., 2010). The reliability analyses at each assessment point showed high internal consistency for this scale (Cronbach's α = .86 at T1; Cronbach's α = .82 at T2; Cronbach's α = .85 at T3).

Scale of Positive and Negative Experience (SPANE). Emotional well-being was measured with the Dutch version of the Scale of Positive and Negative Experience (SPANE; Diener et al., 2010; Serie et al., 2017b). The scale consists of six positive and six negative emotions, which can be added up to create the following subscales: positive affect (PA; with a sum score ranging from 6 to 30), negative affect (NA; with a sum score ranging from 6 to 30). The SPANE has been found to be valid and reliable for measuring emotional well-being in adults and adolescents (Jovanović, 2015; Telef, 2013). In accordance with these earlier studies, the reliability analyses at each assessment point showed a high internal consistency for both the positive emotion (Cronbach's α = .82 at T1; Cronbach's α = .74 at T2; Cronbach's

α = .89 at T3) and the negative emotion sub scale (Cronbach's α = .81 at T1; Cronbach's α = .81 at T2; Cronbach's α = .85 at T3).

At each assessment point, the exploratory[5] factor analyses (principal component analysis) of the items of the three scales together (SWLS-CV, PA and NA) confirmed that a three-component factor structure of subjective well-being was possible, but favoured taking them together as a single factor which produced good to excellent internal consistency (Cronbach's α = .81 at T1; Cronbach's α = .69 at T2; Cronbach's α = .82 at T3). Subsequently, the standardized composite sum score was used as 'the well-being index' (see Chapter 6, Section 6.1.2 for a more elaborate description of this sum score), where 0 indicates the lowest overall subjective well-being and 100 indicates the highest.

GLM Primary Goods Satisfaction

The attainment of the GLM primary goods was measured with domain-specific life satisfaction as a proxy measure. The same 20 proxy-items were used as in the first assessment (see Chapter 7, Table 7.1 for an overview) at follow-up. These 20 items assessed how satisfied the participants were on a 5-point Likert scale from 1 = *very dissatisfied* to 5 = *very satisfied* for the following domains: financial situation, living situation, safety, physical health, information access, education, leisure activities, autonomy (agency), mental health, family relationships, (number of) friends, love life, other social contacts in the neighbourhood/clubs/associations, religion/spirituality, meaning in life, creativity and pleasure/enjoyment. All 20 primary goods proxy-items were recoded in such a way that a higher score indicates lower levels of satisfaction (i.e., more dissatisfaction). Subsequently, all 20 items were added to form a total primary goods dissatisfaction score, with a possible range from 20 (most satisfied) to 100 (least satisfied).

Mental Health Problems: Strengths and Difficulties Questionnaire (SDQ)

At each assessment point, mental health problems were assessed using the Dutch version of the Strengths and Difficulties Questionnaire – Self-Report (SDQ; Treffers & Van Widenfelt, 2000). The SDQ is a 25-item questionnaire developed by Goodman (1997) for assessing psychosocial adjustment of children and adolescents (see Chapter 7, Section 7.1.3 for a detailed description of this measure). Adding the sum scores of the emotional problems (five items), conduct problems (five items), peer problems (five items) and hyperactivity (five items) subscales results in a 'total difficulties' score (20 items; with a sum score ranging from 0 to 40). The 'total difficulties' score can be divided in 'normal' ($\leq$ 15), 'borderline' (16 to 19) and 'abnormal' or 'problematic' ($\geq$ 20). It is possible to

5 The exploratory factor analysis (principal component analysis) did not reveal the clear three-component factor structure as found in Chapter 6 without fixing the number of factors to three, probably due to the small(er) sample size.

construct two overarching subscales to discriminate between internalizing problems (by summing the emotional and peer problems subscales) and externalizing problems (by summing the conduct problems and hyperactivity subscales). Each of these subscales has a sum score ranging from 0 to 20 (Goodman et al., 2010).

The internal consistency, test-retest reliability and validity of the various SDQ scales were found to be acceptable to good in Dutch samples (Goodman, 2001; Muris et al., 2003; Van Widenfelt et al., 2003). The reliability analyses at each assessment point showed high internal consistency for the 'total difficulties score' (Cronbach's α = .75 at T1; Cronbach's α = .76 at T2; Cronbach's α = .76 at T3) and the externalizing subscale (Cronbach's α = .76 at T1; Cronbach's α = .76 at T2; Cronbach's α = .70 at T3), but low internal consistency was found for the internalizing subscale (Cronbach's α = .50 at T1; Cronbach's α = .55 at T2; Cronbach's α = .63 at T3).

Treatment Motivation: Adolescent Treatment Motivation Questionnaire (ATMQ)

At each assessment point, treatment motivation was measured using the 11 items of the Dutch Adolescent Treatment Motivation Questionnaire (ATMQ; Van der Helm et al., 2012). The ATMQ is based on the 'stages of change model' of Prochaska and DiClemente (1986) and developed to measure the 'active change' stage (see Chapter 9, Section 9.3.2 for an explanation of this model). Participants are asked how much they agree with the items on a 3-point Likert scale: 0 = *Not true*, 1 = *Somewhat true* and 2 = *True*. An example of an item from the active stage of motivational change is 'I want to work on my problems.' A mean total score (ranging from 0 to 2) is calculated by averaging the answers on all 11 items. A higher mean total score indicates a higher level of treatment motivation. The scale has proven good construct and concurrent validity and high internal consistency (Van der Helm et al., 2012). In our sample, the reliability analyses at each assessment point also demonstrated high internal consistency of the scale (Cronbach's α = .79 at T1; Cronbach's α = .87 at T2; Cronbach's α = .88 at T3).

Recidivism Risk Assessment: Youth Level of Service/Case Management Inventory (YLS/CMI)

To assess recidivism risk, a structured risk assessment was conducted at each assessment point about the preceding period, using the Dutch version of the Youth Level of Service/Case Management Inventory (YLS/CMI; de Ruiter & Hildebrand, 2009; Hoge & Andrews, 2006). The YLS/CMI is designed to assess the level of recidivism risk and criminogenic needs in youth aged 12 to 18 (see Chapter 7, Section 7.1.3 for a detailed description). The YLS/CMI consists of 42 items (scored as 1 = *present* or 0 = *absent*) that are divided into eight subscales (sum scores) representing the 'central eight' criminogenic risk factors of Andrews and Bonta (1995, 2010). The total risk score can range from 0 to 42, which can be divided into 'low' (0 to 8), 'moderate' (9 to 22), 'high' (23 to 34) and 'very high' (35 to 42) risk.

The instrument has proven good to excellent inter-rater reliability (de Ruiter & Hildebrand, 2009; Hoge & Andrews, 2006; Koh et al., 2020; Rocque & Plummer-Beale, 2014) and acceptable concurrent and predictive validity (de Ruiter & Hildebrand, 2009; Hilterman et al., 2014; Hoge & Andrews, 2006; Koh et al., 2020; Olver et al., 2009, 2012; Schwalbe, 2007). At T1 (for the study in Chapter 7), we examined the inter-rater reliability of the YLS/CMI (intraclass correlation coefficients; ICCs), based on a single-rater, absolute agreement, two-way mixed-effects model (see Chapter 7, Section 7.1.3 for a more detailed explanation of this procedure; Koo & Li, 2016; McGraw & Wong, 1996; Shrout & Fleiss, 1979). The ICC of the total YLS/CMI score was .98 and classified as 'excellent' (see Chapter 7, Table 7.2).

10.1.4 Statistical Analyses

Initially, we intended to test our hypotheses across the three time points (T1, T2 and T3) using path analyses in the computational tool PROCESS in SPSS.[6] However, these planned path analyses were not possible because of the small sample size at T3 (n = 27; see Section 10.1.1 for the reasons for attrition), which resulted in low statistical power.[7] Additionally, path analyses in PROCESS are not suitable for multiple imputation techniques. Hence, we had to limit our analyses to the data of the detained adolescents (n = 62)[8] at T1 (four weeks before arrest) and T2 (three and a half months later).[9]

---

6 PROCESS performs mediation, moderation and conditional process analyses similar to structural equation modelling (SEM), but uses bootstrapping to simulate the sampling distribution (Hayes, 2017; Hayes et al., 2017). Although the assumptions for linear regression in all path analyses in this chapter were not violated (normality, linearity, no heteroscedasticity, independent error terms, no significant outliers, no multicollinearity, all VIFs below 2.6; see also the correlation matrix in Appendix H, https://www.elevenpub.com/en/content/appendices-9789462364257, this method was also used in Chapters 6 and 7, which ensures consistency and comparability across the studies. Furthermore, bootstrap estimation takes into account the actual sample (and error) distribution.

7 Additional missing values resulted in 24 participants for the cross-sectional path analyses at T3. Post-hoc power analyses in G*Power 3.1 (Faul et al., 2009) revealed a power of 20% to detect a moderate effect size (f^2 = 0.15) in explained variance by the model (R^2) and a power of 57% to detect a moderate effect size (f^2 = 0.15, α = .05, *two-tailed*) for the single regression coefficients with the sample of 24 in a linear regression predicting recidivism risk at T3 with five predictors. For the longitudinal path analyses predicting recidivism risk change between T2 and T3 with five predictors, the power dropped to 16% and 50% respectively as those analyses were limited to 20 participants due to more missing values. Subsequently, the explained variance of the path analysis models at T3 and between T2 and T3 predicting recidivism risk (reduction) turned out not to be significant.

8 Nevertheless, the numbers of included participants in the analyses in this chapter varies because of missing values on the different items.

9 Additionally, this decision was justified because attrition analyses between those who remained at T3 (n = 27) and those who dropped out after T2 (n = 35) revealed no statistically significant differences on any

First, we described the demographic characteristics (age, school background, ethnic background and family situation) of these 62 participants. Subsequently, we provide means and standard deviations on participants' well-being scores, primary goods proxy-items, mental health problems, treatment motivation and recidivism risk (factors). Paired-samples *t*-tests were conducted in SPSS (version 28) to examine within-person changes on these variables between T1 and T2.

Cross-Sectional Analyses

Next, we examined the cross-sectional associations between primary goods dissatisfaction, mental health problems, subjective well-being, treatment motivation and recidivism risk at T2. We hypothesized that at T2 (during detention), detained adolescents' primary goods dissatisfaction would predict their level of well-being, treatment motivation and recidivism risk. Additionally, adolescents' level of well-being was hypothesized to predict their level of treatment motivation. Subsequently, both their level of well-being and treatment motivation were hypothesized to predict the adolescents' recidivism risk, both serving as mediators. Furthermore, we examined whether and how internalizing and externalizing mental health problems (at T2) influenced these pathways as predictors.

Longitudinal Analyses

In a next step, we examined the longitudinal pathways between primary goods dissatisfaction, mental health problems, subjective well-being, treatment motivation and recidivism risk between T1 and T2. We hypothesized that a positive change (between T1 and T2) in the detained adolescents' primary goods satisfaction predicted a positive change (between T1 and T2) in their levels of overall well-being, more treatment motivation (at T2) and a reduction in recidivism risk (between T1 and T2). Additionally, a positive change in adolescents' level of well-being (between T1 and T2) was predicted to increase their treatment motivation (at T2). Subsequently, a positive change in well-being (between T1 and T2) and higher levels of treatment motivation (at T2) were hypothesized to predict a reduction in the adolescents' recidivism risk level (between T1 and T2), both serving as mediators. Furthermore, we examined whether and how internalizing and externalizing mental health problems (at T2) influenced these pathways as predictors. We included treatment motivation, internalizing and externalizing mental health problems at T2 (instead of the change between T1 and T2) as they[10] did not significantly change over time (see the results of the paired-samples *t*-tests in Section 10.2.2). Furthermore, they represent the levels of motivation and mental health problems during detention, the time during which they are expected to influence the recidivism risk.

---

of the variables (at T2 and between T1 and T2) included in our analyses.

10 Except for externalizing mental health problems, which declined over time, see Table 10.4.

To examine these longitudinal pathways, change scores were computed between T1 and T2 for the total primary goods dissatisfaction score, well-being index and recidivism risk. A higher score on the total primary goods dissatisfaction change score corresponds with an increase in satisfaction levels. A higher score on the well-being index change score corresponds to an increase in subjective overall well-being. A higher score on the recidivism risk change score corresponds to an increase in recidivism risk. The total primary goods dissatisfaction change score (between T1 and T2) was examined as a predictor combined with internalizing and externalizing mental health problems (at T2) as covariates. Recidivism risk change (between T1 and T2) served as the dependent variable, with the well-being change score (between T1 and T2) and (subsequent) treatment motivation (at T2) as mediators.[11] This method was chosen as it has been suggested that within-individual change scores need to be examined to be able to draw conclusions about causal effects (Farrington, 2008; Serin et al., 2013).

The hypothesized pathways were examined conducting path analyses in the computational tool PROCESS version 4.0 in SPSS (version 28). The number of bootstrap samples for percentile bootstrap confidence intervals (95%) was set at 5,000. For all analyses, p-values less than .05 were considered statistically significant.[12] When interpreting Cohen's d effect sizes, the following guidelines were used: d = 0.20 reflects a small effect, d = 0.50 a medium effect and d = 0.80 a large effect (Cohen, 1988).

10.2 RESULTS

10.2.1 Sample Characteristics

At T1, the 62 adolescent boys included from the initial sample of 170 detained adolescents in Chapter 7 had comparable demographic sample characteristics to that of the initial sample (see Section 7.2.1). The 62 adolescent boys in this study had a mean age of 16.15 (SD = 0.90). In terms of education and employment, the majority (n = 45, 72.6%) attended school before they were arrested, 16.1% (n = 10) were temporarily suspended from school, 8.1% (n = 5) did not attend school and were unemployed and 3.2% (n = 2) were employed full-time. Of those who attended school or were only temporarily suspended (n = 55), 36.4% (n = 20) attended vocational secondary education ('bso'/'vmbo'), 30.9% (n = 17) attended part-time secondary education (combined with part-time employment and/or

11 Compared to Chapters 6 and 7, in all path analyses age was no longer included as a control variable since the previous analyses showed that age had no significant effect in our sample. Consequently, we kept the model as simple as possible without age as an additional variable.

12 95% confidence intervals that did not include 0.

traineeship), 14.5% (n = 8) attended special secondary education, 5.5% (n = 3) attended technical secondary education ('tso'/'havo'), 9.1% (n = 5) attended general (including art school) secondary education ('aso'/'kso'/'vwo'), 1.8% (n = 1) attended primary school and 1.8% (n=1) attended higher (vocational) education (see fn 19 in Chapter 7 for an explanation of the school type abbreviations). The majority of the participants were born in Belgium (n = 44, 71%) and 11.3% (n = 7) were born in the Netherlands. The other participants (n = 11, 17.7%) were born in a number of different countries: Italy, Macedonia, Morocco, Mauritania, Dutch Antilles, Nigeria, Romania, Servia, Spain and Suriname. The most common countries of origin of the parent(s) were Belgium (30.6% fathers; 40.3% mothers), Morocco (19.4% fathers; 12.9% mothers), the Netherlands (9.7% fathers; 9.7% mothers), Turkey (3.2% fathers; 4.8% mothers) and Suriname (3.2% fathers; 4.8% mothers). About half of the participants' biological parents were divorced (n = 36, 58.1%), 29% (n = 18) lived together and in 12.9% (n = 8) of cases one or both parents were unknown or deceased. Before the arrest, 25.8% (n = 16) lived together with both their parents, 43.5% (n = 27) lived (most of the time) with their mother, 6.5% (n = 4) lived (most of the time) with their father, 16.1% (n = 10) lived in a residential institution and 8.1% (n = 5) lived somewhere else (i.e., with foster parents, other family members, friends or alone).

10.2.2 *Descriptive Statistics*

Subjective Well-Being

Based on the overall subjective well-being index (ranging from 0 to 100), participants (n = 57) reported on average significantly lower levels of well-being at T2 (M = 50.63, SD = 14.38) compared to T1 (M = 57.71, SD = 18.00), $t(56) = 2.69$, p = .009 (Cohen's d = 0.38), corresponding to a small effect size. See Table 10.2 for an overview of all the well-being scores over time.

Table 10.2 Well-Being Scores at T1 and T2

	T1		T2		*T*-test	
Well-being measures	*M (SD)*	*N*	*M (SD)*	*N*	**Cohen's *d***	*p*
SWLS-CV ns	**14.19** (5.11)	59	**13.41** (3.84)	59	0.16	.232
SPANE PA***	**21.33** (4.13)	58	**18.34** (3.92)	58	0.51	<.001

	T1		T2		*T*-test	
Well-being measures	*M (SD)*	*N*	*M (SD)*	*N*	Cohen's *d*	*p*
SPANE NA ns	**14.77** (4.50)	60	**15.98** (4.46)	60	-0.24	.070
Well-Being Index**	**57.71** (18.00)	57	**50.63** (14.38)	57	0.38	.009

Notes. *** = $p < .001$, ** = $p < .01$, ns = not significant, based on paired-samples *t*-tests. SWLS-CV = Satisfaction With Life Scale – Child Version, a higher score on this measure (ranging from 5 to 25) corresponds to more life satisfaction; SPANE PA = Positive Affect scale of the Scale of Positive and Negative Experience, a higher score on this measure (ranging from 6 to 30) corresponds to more positive affect; SPANE NA = Negative Affect scale of the Scale of Positive and Negative Experience, a higher score on this measure (ranging from 6 to 30) corresponds to more negative affect. A higher score on the well-being index (0 to 100) corresponds to higher levels of subjective overall well-being.

GLM Primary Goods Satisfaction

Based on the total primary goods dissatisfaction score (ranging from 20 to 100), participants (n = 50) were significantly more dissatisfied at T2 (M = 45.30, SD = 12.38) compared to T1 (M = 41.44, SD = 12.32), $t(49) = -2.23$, $p = .031$ (Cohen's d = 0.32), corresponding to a small effect size. See Table 10.3 for an overview of all primary goods dissatisfaction scores at T1 and T2. As becomes clear from this table, for some primary goods the participants' satisfaction decreased, while for others it increased.

Table 10.3 Primary Goods Proxy-Items Dissatisfaction Scores at T1 and T2

	T1		T2		*T*-test	
Proxy primary goods	*M (SD)*	*N*	*M (SD)*	*N*	Cohen's *d*	*p*
Financial situation ns	**2.47** (1.08)	62	**2.44** (1.07)	62	0.02	.848
Living situation ns	**1.90** (1.12)	61	**2.08** (0.95)	61	-0.15	.247
Safety ns	**1.92** (1.01)	61	**1.80** (0.70)	61	0.10	.452
Physical health*	**2.11** (0.99)	62	**1.84** (0.89)	62	0.33	.012
Information access***	**1.68** (0.79)	60	**2.70** (1.09)	60	-0.73	<.001
Education ns	**2.75** (1.29)	61	**2.79** (1.08)	61	-0.02	.861

	T1		T2		T-test	
Proxy primary goods	*M (SD)*	*N*	*M (SD)*	*N*	**Cohen's *d***	*p*
Leisure activities ns	**2.26** (1.02)	61	**2.46** (1.25)	61	-0.14	.273
Autonomy*	**2.32** (1.27)	60	**2.82** (1.37)	60	-0.33	.014
Mental health ns	**2.32** (1.28)	62	**2.19** (1.07)	62	0.13	.297
Family relationships*	**2.45** (1.39)	62	**2.13** (1.18)	62	0.32	.014
Mother***	**2.21** (1.50)	58	**1.78** (1.19)	58	0.49	<.001
Father***	**2.82** (1.53)	60	**2.27** (1.49)	60	0.43	.001
Friendships***	**1.69** (0.84)	62	**2.50** (1.11)	62	-0.61	<.001
Number of friends ns	**1.60** (0.86)	62	**1.77** (0.82)	62	-0.25	.055
Love life ns	**2.13** (1.09)	62	**2.42** (1.24)	62	-0.21	.101
Other social contacts***	**1.80** (0.77)	61	**2.31** (0.98)	61	-0.43	.001
Religion/spirituality ns	**2.03** (1.03)	59	**1.92** (0.84)	59	0.10	.436
Meaning in life ns	**2.35** (1.09)	62	**2.35** (0.98)	62	0.00	1.00
Creativity**	**1.94** (0.96)	62	**2.55** (1.12)	62	-0.41	.002
Pleasure/enjoyment***	**1.77** (0.92)	61	**2.64** (1.18)	61	-0.63	<.001
Total dissatisfaction score	**41.44** (12.32)	50	**45.30** (12.38)	50	0.32	.031

Notes. *** = $p < .001$, ** = $p < .01$, * = $p < .05$, ns = not significant, based on paired-samples *t*-tests. A higher score on the primary goods proxy-items (ranging from 1 to 5) corresponds to lower levels of satisfaction (i.e., more dissatisfaction). A higher score on the total dissatisfaction score (ranging from 20 to 100) corresponds to lower levels of satisfaction (i.e., more dissatisfaction).

Mental Health Problems

Based on the 'total difficulties' scale of the SDQ (ranging from 0 to 40), participants ($n = 59$) reported on average less difficulties at T2 ($M = 12.88$, $SD = 5.83$) compared to T1 (M = 14.17, $SD = 6.46$), $t(58) = 2.18$, $p = .033$ (Cohen's $d = 0.28$), corresponding to a small effect size. See Table 10.4 for an overview of the SDQ scale scores at T1 and T2. As becomes clear from this table, while internalizing problems did not significantly change from T1 to T2, externalizing problems decreased significantly.

Table 10.4 Mental Health Problems (Measured with SDQ scales) at T1 and T2

	T1		T2		*T*-test	
SDQ Subscales	*M (SD)*	*N*	*M (SD)*	*N*	Cohen's *d*	*p*
Internalizing problems [ns]	**5.75** (3.26)	59	**5.90** (2.99)	59	-0.05	.689
Externalizing problems***	**8.36** (4.19)	61	**6.90** (3.88)	61	0.56	<.001
Total difficulties*	**14.17** (6.46)	59	**12.88** (5.83)	59	0.28	.033

Notes. *** = $p < .001$, * = $p < .05$, ns = not significant, based on paired-samples *t*-tests. SDQ = Strengths and Difficulties Questionnaire – Self-Report. A higher score on the SDQ subscales (0 to 20) and on the 'total difficulties' score (0 to 40) corresponds to more problems.

Based on their 'total difficulties' score at T1, the majority (62.3%, n = 38) scored in the 'normal' range, 37.7% (n = 23) scored 'borderline' and none (0.0%) scored 'abnormal/ problematic'. At T2, 71.7% (n = 43) scored 'normal', 28.3% (n = 17) scored 'borderline' and none (0.0%) scored 'abnormal/problematic' (see Table 10.5).

Table 10.5 Mental Health Norm Categories According to the SDQ 'Total Difficulties' Score at T1 and T2

	T1		T2	
SDQ total score categories	*N*	%	*N*	%
Normal	38	62.3	43	71.7
Borderline	23	37.7	17	28.3
Abnormal/ Problematic	0	0.0	0	0.0
Total	61	100	60	100

Note. SDQ = Strengths and Difficulties Questionnaire – Self-Report.

Treatment Motivation

Regarding the mean treatment motivation score (ranging from 0 to 2), participants (n = 61) did not score significantly different at T2 (M = 0.87, SD = 0.53) compared to T1 (M = 0.81, SD = 0.46), $t(60)$ = -1.06, p = .293 (Cohen's d = -0.14).

Recidivism Risk

Based on the total recidivism risk level on the YLS/CMI (ranging from 0 to 40), participants' (n = 60) recidivism risk was significantly lower at T2 (M = 19.08, SD = 7.10) compared to T1 (M = 22.98, SD = 6.44), $t(59)$ = 8.47, p < .001 (Cohen's d = 1.09), corresponding to a large effect size. See Table 10.6 for an overview of scores of all eight risk domains at T1 and T2.

Table 10.6 Recidivism Risk Scores on the YLS/CMI at T1 and T2

	T1		T2		*T*-test	
YLS/CMI risk domains	***M (SD)***	***N***	***M (SD)***	***N***	**Cohen's *d***	***p***
1. Prior and current offenses/ Dispositions*	**1.70** (1.62)	60	**1.77** (1.63)	60	-0.27	.045
2. Family Circumstances/ Parenting***	**3.28** (1.26)	60	**2.63** (1.37)	60	0.61	<.001
3. Education/Employment***	**4.03** (1.55)	60	**2.32** (1.57)	60	1.18	<.001
4. Peer relations***	**2.87** (0.98)	60	**2.62** (1.14)	60	0.53	<.001
5. Substance abuse***	**2.17** (1.61)	60	**1.90** (1.46)	60	0.60	<.001
6. Leisure/Recreation ns	**2.08** (0.91)	60	**1.98** (0.95)	60	0.20	.135
7. Personality/Behavior**	**4.28** (1.72)	60	**3.93** (1.89)	60	0.44	.001
8. Attitudes/Orientation***	**2.57** (1.42)	60	**1.93** (1.31)	60	0.63	<.001
Total risk score* **	**22.98** (6.44)	60	**19.08** (7.10)	60	1.09	<.001

Notes. *** = p < .001, ** = p < .01, * = p < .05, ns = not significant, based on paired-samples t-tests. YLS/CMI = Youth Level of Service/Case Management Inventory. A higher score corresponds to more risk factors present and a higher risk of recidivism. The number of items (scored as 1 = *present* or 0 = *not present*) varies by risk domain: prior and current offences/dispositions (5 items), family circumstances/parenting (6 items), education/employment (7 items), peer relations (4 items), substance abuse (5 items), leisure/recreation (3 items), personality/behavior (7 items), and attitudes/orientation (5 items).

Based on their total risk level, at T1, half of the participants (n = 31, 50.8%) were classified as 'moderate' risk. The other half (n = 29, 47.5%) were classified as 'high' risk, one as (1.6%) as 'very high' risk and no one was classified as 'low' risk (0.0%). At T2, 61.7% (n = 37) were classified as 'moderate' risk, 31.7% (n = 19) as 'high', 6.7% (n = 4) as 'low' and no one (0.0%) as 'very high' risk (see Table 10.7).

Table 10.7 Risk Categories According to the YLS/CMI Total Risk Level at T1 and T2

	T1		T2	
YLS/CMI total risk categories	*N*	%	*N*	%
Low risk	0	0.0	4	6.7
Moderate risk	31	50.8	37	61.7
High risk	29	47.5	19	31.7
Very high risk	1	1.6	0	0.0
Total	61	100	60	100

Note. YLS/CMI = Youth Level of Service/Case Management Inventory.

10.2.3 Cross-Sectional Associations at T2 during Detention

To examine the cross-sectional effects of primary goods dissatisfaction and subjective well-being on treatment motivation and recidivism risk at T2, with mental health problems as covariates, a path analysis was conducted in PROCESS (Hayes, 2017; Hayes et al., 2017). Figure 10.1 shows the summarized results of this path analysis, which are explained in detail below.

Figure 10.1 Path Analysis Model of Associations Between Primary Goods, Mental Health Problems, Well-Being, Treatment Motivation and Recidivism Risk at T2

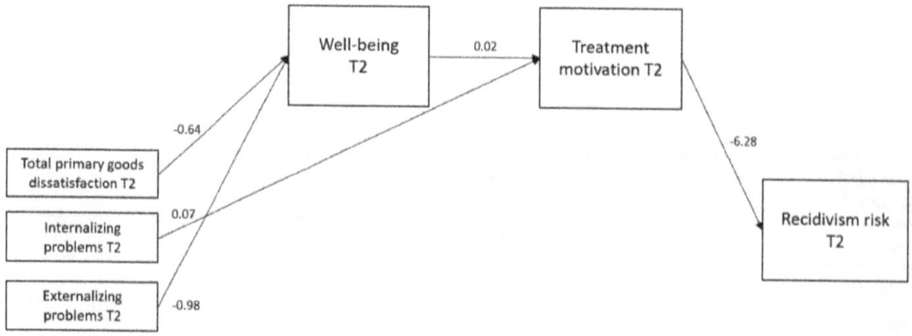

Notes. $N = 50$. The path analysis model shows the statistically significant ($p < 0.05$) associations. Coefficients presented are unstandardized bootstrap estimates (B). A higher score on the total primary goods dissatisfaction score (20 to 100) corresponds to lower levels of satisfaction. A higher score on the internalizing and externalizing subscales (0 to 20) corresponds to more problems. A higher score on the well-being index (0 to 100) corresponds to higher levels of subjective overall well-being. A higher score on the mean treatment motivation score (0 to 2) corresponds to higher levels of motivation. A higher score on the total recidivism risk score (0 to 42) corresponds to higher levels of recidivism risk.

Direct Effects of Primary Goods and Mental Health Problems on Well-Being

First, the path analysis showed the direct effects of primary goods dissatisfaction and mental health problems on well-being at T2. The ordinary least squares path analysis showed 56.2% of the variance in the well-being index could be explained by total primary goods dissatisfaction and mental health problems, $F(3, 46) = 19.63$, $p < .001$. The unstandardized bootstrap estimates (B) of the direct effects on well-being at T2 are presented in Table 10.8. A higher score on total primary goods dissatisfaction (B = -0.64, 95% CI [-0.94, -0.37]) and more externalizing problems (B = -0.98, 95% CI [-1.83, -0.19]) significantly predicted lower levels of overall subjective well-being.

Direct Effects of Primary Goods, Mental Health Problems and Well-Being on Treatment Motivation

Second, the path analysis showed the direct effects of primary goods dissatisfaction, mental health problems and well-being on treatment motivation at T2. The ordinary least squares path analysis revealed that 19.4% of the variance in treatment motivation could be explained by primary goods dissatisfaction, well-being and mental health problems, $F(4, 45) = 2.71$, $p = .042$. The unstandardized bootstrap estimates (B) of the direct effects on treatment motivation at T2 can be found in Table 10.8. More internalizing problems (B = 0.07, 95% CI [0.01, 0.13]) and higher levels of well-being (B = 0.02, 95% CI [0.004, 0.03]) significantly predicted more treatment motivation.

Direct and Indirect Effects of Primary Goods, Mental Health Problems, Well-Being and Treatment Motivation on Recidivism Risk

Finally, the path analysis showed the direct and indirect effects of primary goods dissatisfaction and mental health problems, (via) well-being and (via) treatment motivation on recidivism risk at T2. The ordinary least squares path analysis showed that 36.6% of the variance in total recidivism risk could be explained by primary goods dissatisfaction, well-being, treatment motivation and mental health problems, $F(5, 44) = 5.07$, $p < .001$. The unstandardized bootstrap estimates (B) of the direct effects on recidivism risk at T2 can be found in Table 10.8.

Higher levels of treatment motivation predicted lower levels of recidivism risk (B = -6.28, 95% CI [-9.53, -3.05]). Furthermore, a significant indirect effect was found where more total primary goods dissatisfaction predicted a higher recidivism risk through lower levels of well-being and subsequent lower treatment motivation (B = 0.07, 95% CI [0.01, 0.15]). Another significant indirect effect was found where more internalizing problems predicted lower recidivism risk through more treatment motivation (B = -0.43, 95% CI [-0.93, -0.07]). Finally, more externalizing problems predicted higher levels of recidivism risk through lower levels of overall well-being and subsequent less treatment motivation (B = 0.11, 95% CI [0.004, 0.30]).

Table 10.8 Unstandardized Bootstrap Estimates (B) of the Direct Effects and Bootstrap Inferences (SE and CI) at T2 of the Total Primary Goods Dissatisfaction on Well-Being, Mean Treatment Motivation Score and Recidivism Risk, with Mental Health Problems (Internalizing and Externalizing) as Covariates, Based on the PROCESS Path Analysis at T2

	Well-being T2		Treatment motivation T2		Recidivism risk T2	
Predictor	B (SE)	95% CI	B (SE)	95% CI	B (SE)	95% CI
Total Primary goods dissatisfaction T2	-0.64 (.15)*	[-0.94, -0.37]	0.002 (.01)^{ns}	[-0.01, 0.01]	0.01 (.11)^{ns}	[-0.19, 0.24]
Covariates						
Internalizing problems T2	-1.28 (.65)^{ns}	[-2.48, 0.17]	0.07 (.03)*	[0.01, 0.13]	0.20 (.43)^{ns}	[-0.58, 1.13]

	Well-being T2		Treatment motivation T2		Recidivism risk T2	
Predictor	**B (SE)**	**95% CI**	**B (SE)**	**95% CI**	**B (SE)**	**95% CI**
Externalizing problems T2	-0.98 (.41)*	[-1.83, -0.19]	0.003 (.02)^{ns}	[-0.04, 0.04]	0.60 (.35)^{ns}	[-0.06, 1.30]
Mediators						
Well-being T2			0.02 (.01)*	[0.004, 0.03]	-0.02 (.09)^{ns}	[-0.19, 0.16]
Treatment motivation T2					-6.28 (1.64)*	[-9.53, -3.05]

Notes. Well-being T2: $R^2 = .562$; model $F(3, 46) = 19.63, p < .001$; Treatment motivation T2: $R^2 = .194$; model $F(4, 45) = 2.71, p = .042$; Recidivism risk T2: $R^2 = .366$; model $F(5, 44) = 5.07, p < .001$; * = significant $p < .05$; ns = not significant. The unstandardized estimates (B), standard error (SE) and the 95% confidence intervals (CI) were obtained using percentile bootstrapping based on 5,000 bootstrap samples. A higher score on the total primary goods dissatisfaction score (20 to 100) corresponds to lower levels of satisfaction. A higher score on the internalizing and externalizing subscales (0 to 20) corresponds to more problems. A higher score on the well-being index (0 to 100) corresponds to higher levels of subjective overall well-being. A higher score on the mean treatment motivation score (0 to 2) corresponds to higher levels of motivation.

A higher score on the total recidivism risk score (0 to 42) corresponds to higher levels of recidivism risk.

10.2.4 Longitudinal Relationships between T1 and T2

To examine the hypothesized routes between T1 and T2 of changes in primary goods dissatisfaction and changes in well-being on treatment motivation and recidivism risk reduction, with mental health problems as covariates, a path analysis was conducted in PROCESS (Hayes, 2017; Hayes et al., 2017). Figure 10.2 shows the summarized results of this path analysis, which are explained in detail below.

Figure 10.2 Path Analysis Model of Associations between Primary Goods Changes, Mental Health Problems, Well-Being Changes, Treatment Motivation, and Recidivism Risk Changes

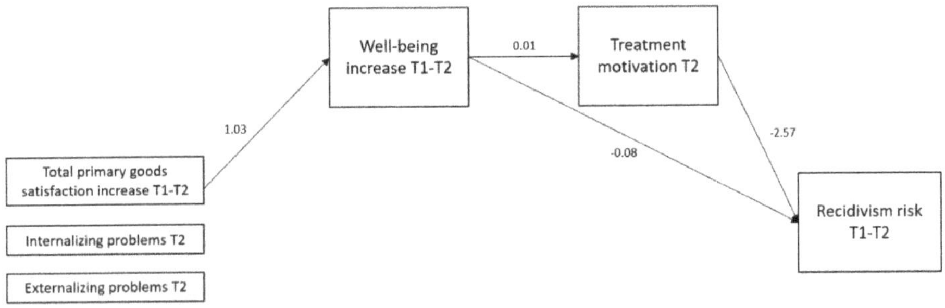

Notes. $N = 44$. The path analysis model shows the statistically significant ($p < 0.05$) associations. Coefficients presented are unstandardized bootstrap estimates (B). A higher score on the primary goods dissatisfaction change score (−80 to 80) corresponds to an increase in satisfaction levels. A higher score on the internalizing and externalizing problems subscales (0 to 20) corresponds to more mental health problems. A higher score on the well-being index change score (−100 to 100) corresponds to an increase in subjective overall well-being. A higher score on the mean treatment motivation score (0 to 2) corresponds to higher levels of motivation. A higher score on the recidivism risk change score (−42 to 42) corresponds to an increase in recidivism risk.

Direct Effects of Mental Health Problems and Changes in Primary Goods on Change in Well-Being

First, the path analysis showed the direct effects of changes between T1 and T2 in primary goods dissatisfaction between T1 and T2 and mental health problems at T2 on well-being change between T1 and T2. The ordinary least squares path analysis showed that 30.7% of the variance in the change between T1 and T2 on the well-being index could be explained by change between T1 and T2 in primary goods dissatisfaction and mental health problems at T2, $F(3, 40) = 5.92$, $p = .002$. The unstandardized bootstrap estimates (B) of the direct effects on well-being change (between T1 and T2), can be found in Table 10.9.

An increase in primary goods satisfaction between T1 and T2 significantly predicted an increase in overall subjective well-being between T1 and T2 (B = 1.03, 95% CI [-1.46, -0.55]). Internalizing problems at T2 (B = 0.06, 95% CI [-2.09, 2.41]) and externalizing problems at T2 (B = -0.97, 95% CI [-2.60, 0.47]) turned out not to be significant direct predictors of well-being change.

Direct Effects of Changes in Primary Goods and Well-Being on Treatment Motivation

Second, the path analysis showed the direct effects of changes between T1 and T2 in primary goods dissatisfaction, mental health problems at T2 and changes between T1 and T2 in well-being on treatment motivation at T2. The ordinary least squares path analysis showed that 26.8% of the variance in treatment motivation at T2 could be explained by changes between T1 and T2 in primary goods dissatisfaction, mental health problems at T2 and changes between T1 and T2 in well-being, $F(4, 39) = 3.57$, $p = .014$. The unstandardized bootstrap estimates (B) of the direct effects on treatment motivation (T2) can be found in Table 10.9.

An increase in well-being between T1 and T2 predicted higher levels of treatment motivation at T2 (B = 0.01, 95% CI [0.003, 0.02]). Primary goods satisfaction change (B = 0.005, 95% CI [-0.01, 0.02]), Internalizing problems (B = 0.03, 95% CI [-0.04, 0.09]) and externalizing problems (B = -0.01, 95% CI [-0.05, 0.03]) turned out not to be significant direct predictors of treatment motivation.

Direct and Indirect Effects of Changes in Primary Goods, Changes in Well-Being, and Treatment Motivation on Recidivism Risk Change

Finally, the path analysis showed the direct and indirect effects of changes in primary goods dissatisfaction between T1 and T2 on changes between T1 and T2 in well-being, (via) treatment motivation at T2 on recidivism risk change between T1 and T2. The ordinary least squares path analysis showed that 39.4% of the variance in total recidivism risk change between T1 and T2 could be explained by changes between T1 and T2 in primary goods dissatisfaction, mental health problems at T2, changes between T1 and T2 in well-being and treatment motivation at T2, $F(5, 38) = 4.93$, $p = .001$. The unstandardized bootstrap estimates (B) of the direct effects on recidivism risk change (between T1 and T2) can be found in Table 10.9.

An increase in well-being between T1 and T2 (B = -0.08, 95% CI [-0.14, -0.02]) and more treatment motivation at T2 (B = -2.57, 95% CI [-4.83, -0.25]) significantly directly predicted a decrease in total recidivism risk between T1 and T2. A change in primary goods satisfaction (B = 0.03, 95% CI [-0.08, 0.14]), Internalizing problems (B = 0.19, 95% CI [-0.21, 0.55]) and externalizing problems (B = -0.07, 95% CI [-0.31, 0.20]) turned out not to be significant direct predictors of recidivism risk change. Nevertheless, a significant indirect effect was found: an increase in total primary goods satisfaction between T1 and T2 predicted a decrease in recidivism risk between T1 and T2 through an increase in well-being between T1 and T2 (B = -0.08, 95% CI [-0.16, -0.02]).

Table 10.9 Unstandardized Bootstrap Estimates (B) of the Direct Effects and Bootstrap Inferences (SE and CI) of the Changes between T1 and T2 on Primary Goods Dissatisfaction and Well-Being, Treatment Motivation at T2, and Recidivism Risk Change between T1 and T2, with Mental Health Problems (Internalizing and Externalizing) at T2 as Covariates, Based on the PROCESS Path Analysis.

	Well-being increase T1-T2		Treatment motivation T2		Recidivism risk T1-T2	
Predictor	B (SE)	95% CI	B (SE)	95% CI	B (SE)	95% CI
Total primary goods satisfaction increase T1-T2	1.03 (.23)*	[0.57, 1.48]	0.005 $(.01)^{ns}$	[-0.01, 0.02]	0.03 $(.05)^{ns}$	[-0.08, 0.14]
Covariates						
Internalizing problems T2	0.06 $(1.15)^{ns}$	[-2.09, 2.41]	0.03 $(.03)^{ns}$	[-0.04, 0.09]	0.19 $(.19)^{ns}$	[-0.21, 0.55]
Externalizing problems T2	-0.96 $(.80)^{ns}$	[-2.60, 0.47]	-0.01 $(.02)^{ns}$	[-0.05, 0.04]	-0.07 $(.13)^{ns}$	[-0.31, 0.20]
Mediators						
Well-being increase T1-T2			0.01 (.004)*	[0.003, 0.02]	-0.08 (.03)*	[-0.14, -0.02]
Treatment motivation T2					-2.57 (1.18)*	[-4.83, -0.25]

Notes. Well-being change T1-T2: $R^2 = .307$; model $F(3, 40) = 5.92$, $p = .002$; Treatment motivation T2: $R^2 = .268$; model $F(4, 39) = 3.57$, $p = .014$; Recidivism risk change T1-T2: $R^2 = .393$; model $F(5, 38) = 4.93$, $p = .001$; * = significant $p < .05$; ns = not significant. The unstandardized estimates (B), standard error (SE) and the 95% confidence intervals (CI) were obtained using percentile bootstrapping based on 5,000 bootstrap samples.

A higher score on the primary goods dissatisfaction change score (-80 to 80) corresponds to an increase in satisfaction levels. A higher score on the internalizing and externalizing problems subscales (0 to 20) corresponds to more mental health problems. A higher score on the well-being index change score (-100 to 100) corresponds to an increase in subjective overall well-being. A higher score on the mean treatment motivation score (0 to 2) corresponds to higher levels of motivation. A higher score on the recidivism risk change score (-42 to 42) corresponds to an increase in recidivism risk.

10.3 DISCUSSION

In this chapter, we examined the GLM's practical assumptions about effective offender rehabilitation in a follow-up study of 62 detained adolescent boys. We tested the hypotheses based on the GLM's notion that positive changes in the pursuit of primary goods and well-being improve treatment motivation and (subsequently) reduce recidivism risk in detained adolescent offenders. Furthermore, we examined whether and how mental health problems can affect this process. Our hypotheses were largely supported by our findings at T2 (cross-sectional analyses) and also largely confirmed by our longitudinal findings on the changes between the period before the adolescents' arrest (T1) and three and a half months later (T2).

In line with our hypotheses, we found that higher levels of primary goods satisfaction at T2 was related to higher levels of well-being, which in turn predicted more treatment motivation. Subsequently, more treatment motivation predicted lower levels of recidivism risk. Nevertheless, contrary to our hypotheses, no direct effects were found for primary goods satisfaction and well-being on recidivism risk. Furthermore, we found that externalizing mental health problems during detention were related to lower levels of well-being, which resulted in less treatment motivation and subsequent higher recidivism risk. On the other hand, more internalizing of mental health problems during detention predicted more treatment motivation and consequentially less recidivism risk.

Our longitudinal analyses showed that recidivism risk reduction between the period before the adolescents' arrest (T1) and after three and a half months detention (T2) was directly predicted by an increase in well-being over that period and higher treatment motivation. An increase in primary goods satisfaction between T1 and T2 only indirectly (contrary to our hypothesis, not directly) predicted a decrease in recidivism risk between T1 and T2 through an increase in well-being in that same period. Additionally, and in line with our hypotheses, an increase in well-being between T1 and T2 predicted higher levels of treatment motivation at T2. No effects of mental health problems were found in these analyses. In the following sections, we discuss these findings and their possible explanations.

10.3.1 The Role of Primary Goods, Well-Being and Treatment Motivation in Recidivism Risk Reduction

In both the cross-sectional and longitudinal path models of recidivism risk (reduction), treatment motivation turned out to be an essential link. This finding confirms the hypothesized importance of treatment motivation in recidivism risk reduction during rehabilitation of young offenders (Andrews & Bonta, 2010; Bonta & Andrews, 2017; Bourgon & Bonta, 2014; Ginsburg et al., 2002; Higley et al., 2019; Marshall & Marshall, 2012; Nee et al., 2013). Being detained and coerced into treatment by the authorities can reduce treatment motivation and engagement in young offenders (De Valk et al., 2019; Schubert et al., 2012; van der Helm et al., 2014, 2018). In turn, low levels of treatment motivation have been shown to negatively affect offender treatment outcomes, dropout rates and recidivism risk (Carl et al., 2020; Drieschner & Verschuur, 2010; van der Stouwe et al., 2018; Yang et al., 2013).

Hence, it is relevant to examine what predicts detained adolescents' treatment motivation. From our findings it became clear that adolescents' treatment motivation during detention (at T2) was predicted by their overall subjective well-being at that time. Additionally, increases in well-being between the period before their arrest (T1) and three and a half months later (T2) predicted more treatment motivation and more recidivism risk reduction. In turn, in both path analyses, increases in well-being were predicted by increases in primary goods satisfaction. Contrary to the GLM's theory, we found no direct effects of primary goods satisfaction on recidivism risk (reduction), only indirectly through well-being and/or treatment motivation. Still, these findings together support the GLM's hypothesis that promoting personal well-being (by working towards primary goods satisfaction) can both increase treatment motivation and (subsequently) reduce recidivism risk (see also Chapter 9, Section 9.3; Laws & Ward, 2011; McMurran & Ward, 2004; Ward, 2002b; Ward & Fortune, 2013; Ward & Gannon, 2006; Ward & Maruna, 2007; Ward & Stewart, 2003a; Ward et al., 2006). Consequently, a focus on well-being next to recidivism risk could improve juvenile offender rehabilitation for both the adolescents as well as society (de Ruigh et al., 2019; Nee et al., 2013; Van Damme et al., 2016).

10.3.2 *The Role of Mental Health Problems during Detention*

Our findings furthermore support the hypothesis (and previous studies) that psychopathology in young offenders affects their treatment motivation during detention (DiPierro-Sutton et al., 2021; Leenarts et al., 2013; van Binsbergen et al., 2001; Van Damme, Hoeve, et al., 2015). That is, during detention at T2, externalizing mental health problems were related to lower levels of well-being, which resulted in less treatment motivation and subsequent higher recidivism risk. On the other hand, more internalizing of mental health problems predicted less recidivism risk through more treatment motivation. These findings are in line with studies demonstrating that youth who suffer from internalizing symptoms (e.g., anxiety and depression) experience more emotional discomfort, which can enhance their willingness to engage in treatment (DiGiuseppe et al., 1996; DiPierro-Sutton et al., 2021; Leenarts et al., 2013; Van Damme, Hoeve, et al., 2015). In contrast, externalizing problems (e.g., attention deficits, impulsivity and aggression) can hamper treatment engagement due to a lack of problem insight, social adjustment problems, interpersonal distrust and authority issues (Brooks & Khan, 2015; DiGiuseppe et al., 1996; Roedelof et al., 2013; van Binsbergen et al., 2001).

However, contrary to existing research findings (de Ruigh et al., 2019; Van Damme, Colins, De Maeyer, et al., 2015) and our previous study reported in Chapter 7 that showed a significant negative relationship between internalizing problems and well-being, we did not find an effect of internalizing problems on well-being during detention nor on well-being changes over time. This may have been due to the fact that internalizing problems remained stable over time and thus had no effect on (changes in) well-being. At the same time, we saw that treatment motivation also remained stable. Although we found that during detention (at T2) more internalizing problems were related to more treatment motivation, alleviating these internalizing mental health symptoms over time could perhaps improve treatment motivation even more. That is, when youth experience the beneficial effect on their symptoms, their motivation might increase over time as well. Taken together, these results point to the fact that although (internalizing) psychopathology is not considered a criminogenic risk factor by the RNR model (Andrews & Bonta, 2010; Bonta & Andrews, 2017; Ogloff & Davis, 2004), it could play an important role in improving rehabilitation of detained adolescents through increased treatment motivation (Guebert & Olver, 2014). Still, we should be careful when interpreting the 21 effects of internalizing mental health problems, as the subscale that was used in this sample showed a rather low internal consistency. More research is recommended to delve deeper into these findings with different measurements, such as more elaborate psychopathology questionnaires and diagnostic information.

10.4 Conclusion

To the best of our knowledge, this study is the first that quantitatively examined the longitudinal effects of changes in primary goods satisfaction and well-being on treatment motivation and recidivism risk reduction in detained adolescents. Our findings generally support the GLM's hypotheses that, in detained adolescent offenders, an increase in primary goods satisfaction increases their well-being over time, which in turn is related to more treatment motivation and (subsequent) recidivism risk reduction. These results support the idea that strengths-based rehabilitation interventions such as those based on the GLM could bridge the gap between the risk-focused approach and the welfare-focused approach in juvenile justice (see Chapters 1 and 2). That is, it presents initial evidence that promoting well-being can simultaneously and subsequently lower the recidivism risk of young offenders. Moreover, it suggests that working on 'non-criminogenic' factors, such as primary goods satisfaction and internalizing (as well as externalizing) mental health problems may improve juvenile offender rehabilitation.

10.5 Limitations and Remaining Questions

Despite these interesting findings, we must be careful when translating them to practice, as our study has a number of important limitations. One of the main limitations was the lack of a direct measure of recidivism or desistance. For practical reasons (mostly time related) we were not able to collect data on actual or self-reported recidivism rates. Instead, we used recidivism risk (reduction) on the YLS/CMI as a proxy-outcome variable, which has been proven to be predictive of re-offending and re-arrest (de Ruiter & Hildebrand, 2009; Hilterman et al., 2014; Mulvey et al., 2016; Viljoen et al., 2017). Still, in future studies it would be necessary to use official recidivism rates (and desistance), as well as self-reported recidivism (for longer periods of time), as outcome variables.

In that way, the interaction between primary goods satisfaction and criminogenic risk factors and their influence on recidivism can be further investigated. As we saw in Chapters 5 and 7, criminogenic risk factors can influence the predictive effects of primary goods satisfaction in explaining juvenile delinquency. For example, in Chapter 7, we found that more satisfaction with peers was only related to more delinquent behaviour when criminogenic risk factors were not added as covariates. That is, when taking into account criminogenic risk factors, including engagement with antisocial peers, the effect of satisfaction with peer relationships (part of the primary good of 'relatedness') disappeared. These findings show that criminogenic risk factors are not completely independent of primary goods satisfaction and can affect their influence on delinquency or recidivism. It could furthermore indicate that primary goods satisfaction per se might not explain delinquency and recidivism, but only the interaction between primary goods satisfaction and criminogenic risk factors together does. In our current analyses, primary goods satisfaction was not directly related to recidivism risk reduction, but (changes in) primary goods satisfaction may interact with (changes) in criminogenic risk factors and vice versa (Ward & Fortune, 2013; Ward & Laws, 2010; Ward & Maruna, 2007; Ward et al., 2006; Willis & Ward, 2011; see also Chapters 5 and 7), which in turn could (directly) influence recidivism rates.

Additionally, in the current study we were only able to include total primary goods satisfaction and total recidivism risk (to maximize the statistical power of the analyses), but the individual primary goods and recidivism risk factors could each produce their own (possibly interactive) effects. For example, Van Damme, Hoeve, et al. (2015) found that satisfaction with physical health, psychological health and living environment in adolescent detained girls was positively related to treatment engagement, while it was negatively related to satisfaction with social relationships. Therefore, future research requires a larger sample to be able to examine the effects of the separate criminogenic risk domains and primary goods. Partly because of our smaller sample, we chose to use PROCESS and bootstrap inferences. This however did not allow us to obtain standardized effects (only unstandardized), which will be possible with larger samples and other types of analysis (such as SEM).

Furthermore, it would be interesting to delve deeper into the mechanisms underlying the associations we found in the current study. For example, we do not know what led to increased (or decreased) primary goods satisfaction and well-being levels over time. Future studies could consider other (confounding) variables, which were not included in our study, that may impact these increases and/or decreases. Examples of these variables are therapeutic alliance, goal-pursuit and institutional factors, such as structure, restrictions and repression (see Chapter 9 for a discussion of these factors).

Moreover, individual differences, for example related to gender and culture, also deserve due consideration. Although we did not include gender, cultural and ethnic aspects, existing studies suggest that they can exert a profound effect on offender rehabilitation (Abate & Venta, 2018; Piquero et al., 2016; Van Damme et al., 2014, 2017). For instance, studies find that ethnic minority youth experience lower prosocial self-efficacy and more barriers in rehabilitation in terms of education and career opportunities (Abate & Venta, 2018). Additionally, detained girls display higher rates of trauma exposure, more mental health problems and lower levels of self-esteem compared to detained boys (Van Damme et al., 2014).

We also did not assess the role of the GLM's different proposed problems in the pursuit of primary goods and well-being over time (i.e., problems with *capacity*, *scope*, *means* and *coherence*). Like the qualitative study in Chapter 8, qualitative research could give insights into how the detained adolescents experience changes in primary goods and well-being during detention. In addition, it could provide us with more in-depth knowledge on what (de-)motivates them to engage in treatment and work towards desistance and a prosocial identity. This knowledge could, in turn, provide more detailed recommendations on how to adequately support the strengthening of (young) offenders' abilities to prosocially meet the needs that are important to them (i.e., the primary goods) and deal with the obstacles and conflicts that may exist and/or arise (Laws & Ward, 2011; Tyler et al., 2020).

Additionally, as in all studies in this research, we relied on self-report of the participants. While this offers interesting insights, it may also be worthwhile to include collateral information (e.g., from court files, parents, teachers, etc.), as that is usually the recommended approach in forensic practice (Cording et al., 2016; Heffernan, Wegerhoff, et al., 2019). Collateral information from multiple informants can provide insights that youth may not always realize or report themselves. As mentioned before, specifically for the internalizing mental health subscale we found a rather low internal consistency. Including more elaborate diagnostic information (from different sources) could shed more light on the effects we found.

Finally, although the current longitudinal analyses provide some indications of causality and direction, we cannot rule out relationships in the other direction. To further investigate the causal relationships hypothesized by the GLM, experimental studies should be the next step in future research. For example, an experimental study could investigate whether adolescents who receive interventions based on the GLM obtain different outcomes (e.g., in terms of motivation, well-being and desistance) compared to adolescents who receive treatment as usual (i.e., primarily risk-focused based on the RNR principles). In future studies it would be interesting to increase the follow-up periods and collect enough data to adequately analyse more than two points in time. In our study we were only able to assess two points in time with an average duration of three and a half months between the assessment points. On average, the juveniles in our sample stayed in the institution for seven months. Although within three and a half months the structured stable environment and treatment opportunities focusing on emotional and behavioural regulation were able to ensure some changes between T1 and T2 (as seen in our analyses), larger effects could be found when the complete detention period can be considered.

Taking these limitations into account, we conclude that juvenile offender rehabilitation could benefit from working on primary goods satisfaction, mental health problems and well-being, which was found to improve treatment motivation and (subsequent) recidivism risk reduction in detained adolescents. In the next and final chapter of this book, we turn to the recommendations for future research and the practical implications of the GLM in juvenile justice interventions.

11 General Discussion: The GLM Applied to Adolescent Offenders

Conclusions, Recommendations and Practical Implications

We began this book introducing the tension that can arise in juvenile justice systems when balancing the welfare of young offenders with the safety of society (Chapter 1). In the chapter that followed (Chapter 2), we argued that the 'Good Lives Model of offender rehabilitation' (GLM) could potentially bridge this tension. The GLM assumes that effective rehabilitation interventions should combine the reduction of recidivism (risk) in accordance with the Risk Need Responsivity (RNR) model, with the improvement of offenders' personal well-being. Although promising in theory, little empirical research exists examining the GLM's underlying etiological assumptions, especially in adolescents. Hence, as a first step, we examined the GLM's etiological assumptions about well-being and delinquency in (detained) adolescents.

11.1 The GLM' First Etiological Assumption: Primary Goods and Adolescents' Well-Being

Based on a mixed method approach we aimed to assess the GLM's *first etiological assumption* regarding the importance of achieving the proposed 11 primary goods necessary for overall well-being. The 11 primary goods proposed by the GLM consist of the following motivational needs and goals (see Chapter 3 for a more elaborate description of these primary goods): 'life' (being healthy and safe); 'knowledge' (having access to information one is interested in); 'excellence in work' (mastery in work); 'excellence in play' (mastery in hobbies or leisure activities); 'excellence in agency' (seeking independence and autonomy); 'inner peace' (emotional equilibrium); 'relatedness' (close relationships with friends, family or a partner); 'community' (group belonging); 'spirituality' (seeking purpose and meaning in life); 'creativity' (creating or trying new things) and 'pleasure' (feelings of enjoyment and fun).

Altogether, our findings (see Chapters 4, 6, 7 and 8) demonstrated support for all 11 primary goods in relation to adolescents' well-being. A greater attainment or satisfaction of these goods is related to higher levels of overall subjective well-being in adolescents. However, some primary goods seem to be more important for adolescents' well-being than others. Furthermore, the 11 primary goods seem to cluster together in such a way that we propose a specific structure in how they can relate to adolescents' well-being (see Figure 11.1). In what follows, we will explain this proposed structure in more detail.

Figure 11.1 The Structure of the GLM's Primary Goods in Relation to Adolescents' Well-Being

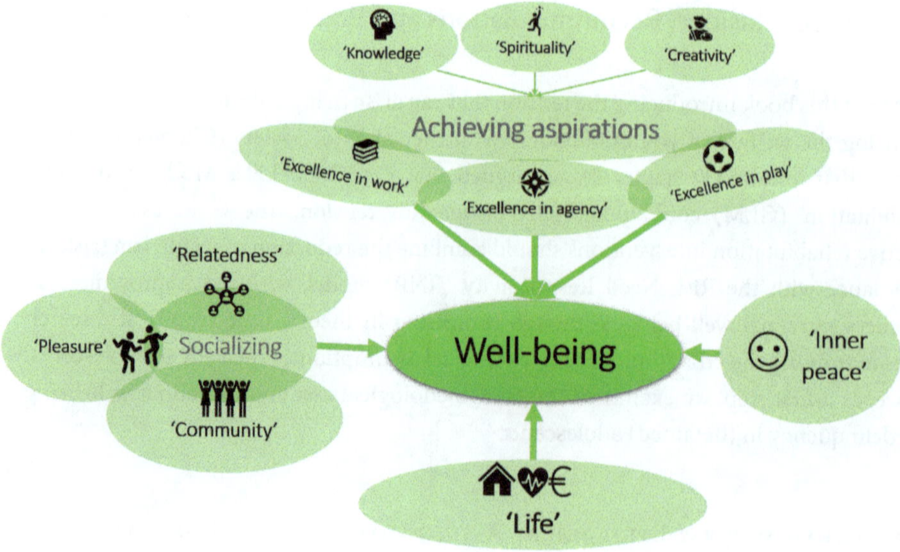

More specifically, our studies into (detained) adolescents' well-being demonstrated the particular importance of the primary goods based on the psychological needs of Self-determination Theory (SDT): 'relatedness' and 'community' (i.e., 'relatedness' in SDT), 'excellence in work' and 'excellence in play' (i.e., 'competence' in SDT) and 'excellence in agency' (i.e., 'autonomy' in SDT; Deci & Ryan, 2000; Ryan & Deci, 2000b, 2017b).

The primary goods of 'relatedness' and 'community' proved to be essential factors for (detained) adolescents' well-being, that is, relatedness with friends and particularly with family, can provide a supportive environment for adolescents on their way to adulthood (Massey et al., 2008). Previous research has demonstrated that stable and secure attachment between children and their parents makes a positive contribution to the development of social relationships, emotion regulation and the way children cope with developmental challenges (Rask et al., 2003; Žukauskienė, 2014). Additionally, supportive (prosocial) peer relationships have also been proven to promote higher levels of well-being and foster psychological, social and identity development. Peer relationships and being part of a social (peer) group can serve as important sources for *socializing* among adolescents: experiencing affection, intimacy, alliance, feelings of inclusion and fun (i.e., 'relatedness', 'community' and 'pleasure'; Brown & Braun, 2013; Hartup & Stevens, 1997; Peets & Hodges, 2018; Proctor & Linley, 2014; Sheldon & Bettencourt, 2002; Van Ryzin et al., 2009; Žukauskienė, 2014).

Furthermore, in our proposed structure, we suggest that a combination of the three primary goods of excellence – 'agency', 'work' and/or 'play' – can cluster together as a higher-order need of *achieving one's aspirations* that we found to be important for adolescents' well-being. The goods of 'spirituality', 'knowledge' and 'creativity' then appear to serve as subsidiary 'means' to this higher goal, more like intermediate goods instead of primary goods. An important developmental task for adolescents consists of finding a purpose in life by aiming to accomplish something (Damon et al., 2003; Massey et al., 2008; Messersmith & Schulenberg, 2010). This accomplishment can be achieved by pursuing one's own goals ('agency') through personally meaningful 'work' and 'play', to which 'knowledge' and 'creativity' can contribute as helpful means to excel in these goals. Additionally, pursuing one's aspirations could also be achieved by means of religion or 'spirituality' (i.e., seeking/finding a higher cause). Finding one's purpose and meaning through setting personal life goals and aspirations is considered an essential part of identity development, especially during adolescence (Bronk, 2011; Damon et al., 2003; Emmons, 1999; Erikson, 1968). Subsequently, several studies demonstrated that in adolescents, a lack of purpose and aspirations for the future can result in negative outcomes, including depression and low levels of well-being (see also Chapter 4; Bronk et al., 2009; Bronk & Finch, 2010; Damon et al., 2003; Russo-Netzer & Shoshani, 2020).

Consistent across our studies and evidenced in many other studies (see Chapters 4, 6 and 7) is also the major importance of the primary good of 'inner peace' or mental health for adolescents' well-being. Due to the many cognitive, social and physical changes they experience, the specific developmental phase of adolescence is marked by greater mood disruptions and extreme emotions (Arnett, 1999; Fortune, 2018; Goldbeck et al., 2007; Houben et al., 2015; Miller, 2014). To effectively cope with these emotions and disruptions, emotional self-regulation, and one's ability to achieve a state of emotional balance (i.e., 'inner peace') are paramount (Proctor et al., 2009; Salavera & Usan, 2020; Salavera et al., 2020).

Lastly, as a foundation of achieving well-being, lies the necessity of fulfilling the basic physical human needs for healthy and safe living (i.e., the primary good of 'life'). While this was not as evident for adolescents whose physical needs are usually well met, we found it was an important basic requirement to build upon. This finding became especially clear when the detained adolescents (see Chapters 7 and 8), often from disadvantaged backgrounds, prioritized their basic physical needs over other primary goods. This finding is furthermore in line with the idea that the basic physical needs are a prerequisite to attain one's higher-order psychological needs and well-being (Maslow, 1962; Oishi et al., 2009; Taormina & Gao, 2013). In practice, however, it should always be kept in mind that the weights of the primary goods sought, and the way in which they are met, may vary from one individual to another, as a result of personal, cultural and social circumstances, beliefs, values and norms (Ward & Maruna, 2007; see also Chapters 3 and 8).

11.2 The GLM's Second Etiological Assumption: Explaining Adolescent Delinquency

Next, we set out to examine the GLM's *second etiological assumption* that a failure to prosocially obtain primary goods needed for well-being can result in criminal behaviour. Our studies (in Chapters 6 and 7) consistently demonstrated a negative relationship between overall subjective well-being and juvenile delinquency. Nonetheless, we found little support for the indirect route suggested by the GLM, where problems in primary goods achievement result in an accumulation of negative effects on the individual's life and overall well-being, spiralling towards delinquency (Purvis, 2010; Purvis et al., 2011). This means that either this indirect route is not as common or prominent in juvenile delinquency and/or more difficult to unravel with the current datasets, that is, assessing these complex indirect interactions (over longer periods of time) would require a large longitudinal dataset over long time intervals. Hence, more research is needed to draw firm conclusions about the indirect effects.

Interestingly, we found some differences in the effects of primary goods satisfaction on delinquency in the detained adolescents (see Chapter 7) compared to the ones observed in the general population sample (see Chapter 6). In adolescents from the general population, more dissatisfaction with their family relationships ('relatedness'), education ('excellence in work') and financial situation ('life'), and more satisfaction with one's love life ('relatedness') and 'community' predicted more delinquent behaviour. In detained adolescents, more dissatisfaction with one's safety ('life'), family relationships ('relatedness') and 'pleasure', and more satisfaction with one's financial situation ('life') and peers ('relatedness') predicted more delinquent behaviour.

The observed differences between the adolescents from the general population and the detained adolescent boys may be explained by the large statistical power in the former compared to relatively low statistical power in the latter. However, another possible explanation for these differences is that the offences reported by detained boys could be more serious than those reported by the general population and/or motivated by different needs. Perhaps that is also the reason why the youth in that sample were detained and the ones from the general population were not.[1] In addition, the two samples may differ on

1 Of note, detained juveniles constitute only a minority in the population of juvenile offenders. In Flanders, Belgium, each year (on average in 2018, 2019 and 2020) about 2% of all youth who were prosecuted for

other factors that can have an impact on our results, such as demographic variables (gender, SES, family background, level of education, etc.).

Despite the observed differences, some similarities appeared as well. Both studies confirm the importance of the primary goods for healthy and safe living (i.e., 'life'), 'relatedness' with friends and family and 'inner peace' in explaining adolescent delinquency. Overall (considering Chapters 6, 7 and 8 combined), the primary goods that seemed to be most often pursued directly through juvenile offending were ones that were also important for adolescents' well-being: 'life', 'excellence in work', 'relatedness' with family and peers, 'community', 'pleasure' and 'inner peace'. In what follows, these primary goods and their relation to adolescent delinquency will be elaborated on in more detail.

A consistent finding was the importance of the satisfaction with one's financial situation (part of the primary good of 'life') in explaining juvenile delinquency. As minors have few opportunities to obtain a well-paying lawful job, they are often financially dependent on their parents and/or caregivers. For some, this might put them in a situation in which they lack sufficient resources to meet their (basic) needs and want to fulfil these in other ways (Agnew, 1990; Farrington, 1993; Gudjonsson & Sigurdsson, 2007; Lopez, 2008; Nguyen & Bouchard, 2013; Putniņš, 2010; Shong et al., 2019; Troonbeeckx et al., 2015; Verdonck, 2017).

Moreover, when one's education fails to provide a sense of accomplishment and/or satisfaction (due to problems with school and academic achievement, and known criminogenic risk factors), antisocial behaviour could additionally serve as a substitute for one's needs and/or an outlet of frustration (Andrews & Bonta, 2010; Bonta & Andrews, 2017; Christle et al., 2005; Cottle et al., 2001; Grieger & Hosser, 2014; Hoffmann, 2020; Katsiyannis et al., 2008; Maguin & Loeber, 1996). Furthermore, without a certificate or diploma to acquire a well-paying position, criminality is often viewed as more profitable than a low-paying lawful job (Cullen et al., 1997; Jacobs & Wright, 1999; Troonbeeckx et al., 2015; Wright & Topalli, 2013).

Regarding 'relatedness', we conclude that when adolescents are not satisfied with their family relationships, they may turn to their peers (including romantic partners) and other contacts in their community to satisfy their needs (Barnert et al., 2015). If these contacts engage in antisocial behaviour, it could encourage delinquency (which is in line with one of the eight criminogenic risk factors: antisocial peers; Andrews & Bonta, 2010; Bonta & Andrews, 2017; Hirschi, 2017; Jacobs et al., 2020; Patterson & Dishion, 1985; Shortt et al.,

---

offences were sentenced to detention (www.jaarverslagjeugdhulp.be/thematische-cijfers/jeugddelinquentie-gemeenschapsinstellingen). In the Netherlands, each year (on average in 2018, 2019 and 2020) about 8% of all youth who were prosecuted for offences were sentenced to detention (https://opendata.cbs.nl/statline/#/CBS/nl/dataset/83944NED/table?ts=1629880231731).

2003; Troonbeeckx et al., 2015; Van Damme, Colins, Pauwels, et al., 2015; Van Damme et al., 2016; Wikström & Loeber, 2000).

Finally, antisocial behaviours, including substance abuse, can be explained by the adolescents' need to seek the primary good of 'pleasure' in the form of feeling good, having fun, and seeking thrills and excitement. These findings correspond to numerous studies demonstrating that sensation-seeking to pass the time and prevent boredom is a common motive for engaging in illegal activities, such as fights, vandalism, drug use and shoplifting (see also Chapter 5; Arnett, 1992, 1996; Drozda, 2006; Farrington, 1993; Gordon & Caltabiano, 1996; Hansen & Breivik, 2001; Newberry & Duncan, 2001; Putniņš, 2010; Robertson, 1994; Troonbeeckx et al., 2015; Verdonck, 2017; Wilson & Scarpa, 2011). At the same time, this relates also to the primary good of 'inner peace', as we found that youth can resort to antisocial behaviour to feel good and forget about their worries and stress. This finding is consistent to the fact that although mental health problems (especially internalizing disorders) are not explicitly listed as criminogenic risk factors, they have been found to be strongly related to a higher risk of juvenile delinquency (Aebi et al., 2015; Hoeve et al., 2013, 2015; Pyle et al., 2016; Vahl et al., 2016; van der Put & De Ruiter, 2016; Wibbelink et al., 2017; Wilson et al., 2009).

In general, more dissatisfaction with these primary goods was consistently related to more delinquency. The opposite was, however, true for 'life' (specifically financial situation), 'relatedness' with peers and 'community': for these goods, more satisfaction was related to more delinquency. Thus, despite the satisfaction the adolescents derive from these primary goods, it does not always contribute to their prosocial development. This finding subsequently highlights the importance of also assessing exactly how the primary goods are pursued or achieved. Accordingly, as outlined above, the primary goods that were associated with adolescent delinquency were usually also obstructed by obstacles, particularly in the form of the RNR's central eight criminogenic risk factors (e.g., problems at school/work, family relationship problems, engaging with antisocial peers, impulsivity and substance use). Additionally, we found that internalizing mental health problems were negatively related to well-being, while externalizing problems were positively related to delinquency. Hence, both mental health problems and criminogenic risk factors can form obstacles that can block the prosocial pursuit of, and/or promote alternative, illegal ways of achieving, one's primary goods and well-being (see also Chapter 5; Andrews & Bonta, 2010; Bonta & Andrews, 2017; Laws & Ward, 2011; Ward & Maruna, 2007; Ward & Stewart, 2003a).

In sum, with our mixed methods approach (see Chapters 6, 7 and 8) we found support for the direct link between the experienced problems with primary goods achievement and adolescent delinquency as proposed by the GLM: *lack of capacities* and opportunities (i.e., due to criminogenic risk factors and mental health problems), *lack of scope* and the use of *inappropriate means*. Contrary to the GLM's assumption, however, a *lack of coherence* seemed to be the consequence of the detained adolescents' delinquent behaviour rather than a cause. Thus, based on our findings we can conclude that the second GLM etiological assumption about explaining delinquency is largely applicable to (detained) adolescents (see Figure 11.2). The findings, however, suggest that (dis)satisfaction with some primary goods (i.e., 'life', 'excellence in work', 'pleasure', 'inner peace', 'relatedness' and 'community') may be more important for explaining adolescent delinquency than others. Moreover, we also found some (slight) differences in terms of which primary goods seemed more important than others according to different types of offending behaviour (e.g., violent offending, property offending and drug related offending, see Chapter 8). These findings confirm that, in practice, it is important to identify the specific primary goods for each individual and for each type of delinquency.

Figure 11.2 Etiological Pathways of the GLM: Relationships between Primary Goods, Mental Health Problems, Criminogenic Risk Factors, Well-Being and Adolescent Delinquency

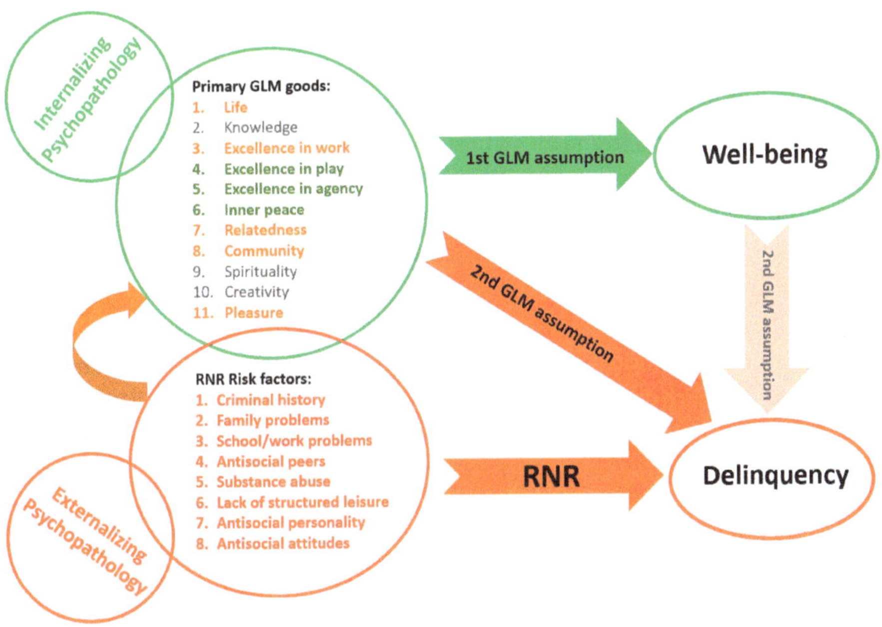

Notes. Primary goods and internalizing problems in green were found only to be related to adolescents' well-being. Primary goods in orange were related to both adolescents' well-being and juvenile delinquency. Primary goods in grey were not directly related to either. RNR risk factors (total score) and externalizing problems in red were positively related to juvenile delinquency.

11.3 The GLM's Practical Assumptions: Effects on Treatment Motivation and Recidivism (Risk)

Subsequently, we turned to the examination of the *GLM's practical assumptions* that follow from its etiological assumptions. We assessed the GLM's assumptions that to effectively reduce criminal recidivism, rehabilitation interventions should not only target the RNR's well-known criminogenic risk factors, but also focus on prosocially satisfying the offenders' primary goods, which improves their well-being and quality of life. Moreover, working on primary goods and well-being instead of only avoiding risk factors determined by professionals, is assumed to increase treatment motivation, and consequently reduce recidivism risk even more (see Chapter 9). These assumptions were tested based on the follow-up data of the detained adolescents from the study in Chapter 7, who were followed during their residential stay in a juvenile detention centre (see Chapter 10). More specifically, we tested the hypotheses that positive changes in the pursuit of primary goods and well-being during detention can improve treatment motivation and (subsequently) reduce recidivism risk in detained adolescent offenders. Additionally, we assessed what role mental health problems play in this process.

Our findings generally support the GLM's hypotheses that, in detained adolescent offenders, positive changes in primary goods satisfaction improve their well-being over time, which in turn increases treatment motivation and (subsequently) reduces recidivism risk. Furthermore, during detention, externalizing problems were related to lower levels of well-being, which resulted in lower treatment motivation and subsequent higher recidivism risk. On the other hand, more internalizing problems were related to lower recidivism risk through more treatment motivation (see Figure 11.3).

In sum, these results support the hypothesis that GLM-based rehabilitation interventions can indeed bridge the gap between the risk-focused approach and the welfare-focused approach in juvenile justice, that is, they present initial evidence that promoting well-being can lower the recidivism risk of young offenders. These findings furthermore suggest that working on 'non-criminogenic' factors, such as primary goods satisfaction and mental health problems may improve juvenile offender rehabilitation (de Ruigh et al., 2019; Nee et al., 2013; Van Damme et al., 2016; Van Hecke, Meulewaeter, Rowaert, et al., 2021).

Figure 11.3 Rehabilitation Pathways of the GLM: Relationships between Primary Goods, Mental Health Problems, Well-Being, Treatment Motivation and Recidivism Risk during Detention

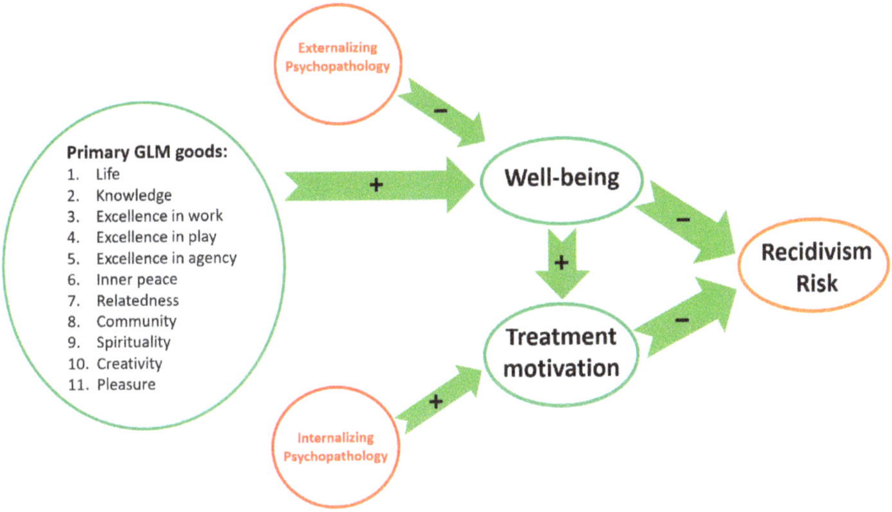

11.4 Study Limitations and Research Recommendations

Despite our interesting findings, some caution is needed when implementing them in practice. Over the course of the chapters, I have outlined several limitations of our studies. The most important limitation was our reliance on self-report data. The relationships we found reflect the adolescents' own perceptions. Although it is considered a limitation since self-report can be vulnerable to several biases (such as social desirability, memory and mood) and may affect validity, it can also be considered as a strength, considering that the concepts of the GLM are largely subjective and social constructs. For example, as we have seen, what is understood as well-being by individuals can vary considerably and is dependent on personal, developmental, cultural and social factors. The same applies to primary goods attainment, treatment motivation and self-reported mental health problems. Therefore, we believe it is important to include (and even focus) on the subjective perceptions of the (detained) adolescents themselves.

Nevertheless, future studies could include different questionnaires and measures as some scales in our studies revealed some limitations. For instance, the subscale of the SDQ measuring internalizing mental health problems showed a rather low internal consistency. Therefore, it is recommended to also include other and more elaborate psychopathology questionnaires and diagnostic information. Furthermore, as mentioned in each study, the

GLM's primary goods and well-being are complex and broad theoretical constructs, which are not easily captured with a few quantitative items. Future studies are recommended to build upon the results of this research to further develop more elaborate and sophisticated measures to adequately capture the complex phenomenon of primary good attainment.

Additionally, although we aimed to include a sufficient number of participants in all of our studies, for some analyses the number of included participants turned out to be relatively low, reducing statistical power and generalizability of our results. Moreover, our choice of statistical analyses in Chapters 6, 7 and 10 prevented us from obtaining standardized effects. Although this makes it more difficult to compare our study to previous and other studies, it makes it easier to interpret the unstandardized 'raw' effects of the scores on the scales. Future studies would benefit from larger samples and other statistical analyses (e.g., SEM) to gain more information on the effect sizes and their relevance in the real world. These studies are encouraged to consider the 'smallest effect size of interest' (Anvari & Lakens, 2021), which was not taken into account in our analyses. We relied on the general benchmarks of effect size magnitude as we had no other information to rely on, being one of the firsts conducting this type of specific research into the GLM and its assumptions. Finally, our statistical models are correlational in nature and the direction of the observed effects can go either way, making it difficult to infer causality.

Thus, (our) quantitative analyses cannot fully capture the complex and individual patterns, mechanisms and interactions between the importance of primary goods, the multiple ways in how people aim to achieve them and the internal and external obstacles in relation to both well-being and delinquency. Our qualitative study accommodates this to some extent and provides some more insight, but that method also has its own limitations. More specifically, qualitative interviews also rely on the individuals' own perception, memory, ability to self-reflect and express themselves, which can all be vulnerable to biases and (external or internal) influences. Additionally, the sample size of the qualitative interviews was even smaller than that of the quantitative analyses, which may again compromise generalizability of the results.

Regarding the generalizability, it should also be noted that we found some differences in the results with respect to the important primary goods for well-being and delinquency between the adolescents residing in the community (Chapter 6) and the detained adolescents (Chapters 7, 8 and 10). These differences could have occurred because of the difference in sample size and statistical power. Another explanation can also be found in the actual differences between these two groups. The offences reported by detained adolescents could be more serious than those reported by the adolescents from the general population and could be motivated by different needs. Additionally, the sample from the general population included both boys and girls, while the detained adolescents consisted of only boys. Gender differences may exist with regard to the role of well-being, primary goods and risk factors in juvenile delinquency and rehabilitation (see e.g., Van Damme et al., 2017). Furthermore, a large proportion of juvenile offenders are not detained in residential facilities (see this chapter, fn 1). We should thus keep in mind that the results from our studies may not be generalizable to all adolescent offenders.

Finally, we did not have access to official recidivism rates (over longer periods of time). Thus, when we draw conclusions about rehabilitation and recidivism, we rely on short-term recidivism *risk*, a proxy measure for recidivism. Research has shown that risk assessment scores (such as that of the YLS/CMI™) can be predictive of re-offending and re-arrest (de Ruiter & Hildebrand, 2009; Hilterman et al., 2014; Mulvey et al., 2016). Some scholars, however, criticize the use of recidivism risk factors as an outcome measure, because they are deemed to be measuring correlates of the underlying propensities which are related to criminal behaviour instead of causing it (see also Chapter 2, Section 2.2.1; Heffernan & Ward, 2017; Heffernan, Wegerhoff, et al., 2019; Klepfisz et al., 2016; Ward & Fortune, 2016). An additional limitation of the use of the YLS/CMI in our studies is that the scoring was based solely on the in-depth YLS/CMI interview conducted with the participants themselves. While this is a common and accepted practice for research purposes (Labrecque et al., 2018; Rocque & Plummer-Beale, 2014), it could have resulted in different risk scores compared to when additional collateral information had been used. The latter is considered the recommended best-practice for conducting a well-founded risk assessment in practice (de Ruiter & Hildebrand, 2009; Hoge & Andrews, 2011).

Keeping these limitations in mind, future research could add data from more diverse samples and use collateral sources to assess the concepts from multiple perspectives. Examples of these collateral sources are recidivism rates derived from criminal justice databases; court records; psychological assessment data; information from teachers, parents and other family members. In this way, a more complete and holistic understanding of the complex relationships between primary goods, well-being, mental health problems, delinquency, treatment motivation and recidivism (risk) could be developed. Additionally, examining other confounding variables, not included in our studies, could uncover more complex (underlying) mechanisms. Examples of variables yet to be examined within the GLM framework applied to adolescents are gender, ethnicity, cultural aspects, intervention duration, socio-economic background, neighbourhood aspects, family and living situation.

It is essential to continue to study and develop the GLM and its underlying assumptions in order to provide well-founded practical implications. This is particularly relevant in the light of the newly enacted Juvenile Delinquency Decree in Flanders, Belgium, which emphasizes the importance of employing evidence-based interventions (Pleysier, 2019; Put & Leenknecht, 2019). Similarly, in the Netherlands, the juvenile justice system also pays attention to evidence-based practice, such as reflected in the existence of Dutch Youth Institute (Nederlands Jeugd Instituut; NJI), which is committed to the description and accreditation of effective youth care methodologies. Another example of this attention for evidence-based practice is found in the existence of the Scientific Research and Documentation Centre (Wetenschappelijk Onderzoek-en Documentatiecentrum) of the Dutch Ministry of Justice and Security that contributes to their policy. At the same time, a growing number of juvenile (justice) interventions have started to implement the GLM framework in their approach.[2]

Accordingly, as repeated throughout the chapters, the next step in future research should include experimental studies, using control groups, to further investigate the causal relationships and effects hypothesized by the GLM. This will contribute to a sound, scientific and evidence-based foundation of the GLM to be applied in practice with young offenders.

11.5 Practical Recommendations

Even considering the limitations of our studies, some valuable recommendations can still be made based on this research, which will be outlined below. As the GLM consists of a broad theoretical framework, it does not propose specific treatment methods or fixed guidelines (Prescott & Willis, 2021). Nevertheless, since the GLM's introduction, several authors have suggested its practical implications for both adults (Purvis et al., 2011; Ward, Mann, et al., 2007; Willis et al., 2012; Yates, Kingston, et al., 2009; Yates & Prescott, 2011; Yates et al., 2010) and juveniles (Fortune et al., 2014; Prescott, 2018; Prescott & Dent, 2018; Print, 2013). Based on these authors and our own work, in what follows, we aim to translate our findings into more specific and practical recommendations for enhancing juvenile offender rehabilitation.

11.5.1 Complying with the Risk Need Responsivity Principles

A first step towards integrating the GLM into the rehabilitation of (young) offenders lies in the initial assessment phase. In addition to a traditional recidivism risk assessment, it is recommended to include an assessment of the primary goods that are important to the individual offender as well as how they expect and aim to achieve them (Ward, Mann, et al., 2007; Ward & Stewart, 2003c; Willis et al., 2012, 2013).

2 See for example, the e-learning module (in Dutch) provided by the Flemish government: www.jeugdhulp.be/leermodule/integratief-begeleidingsmodel-rnrglm/scormcontent/index.html#/ and the description of the recent changes (since 2020) in the approach of the Flemish juvenile justice institutions which combine a focus of recidivism risk with the improvement of the youth's needs satisfaction and well-being: www.jeugdrecht.be/node/42.

Such an integration ensures that while applying the GLM, the principles of the RNR model are adhered to as well. First, a recidivism risk assessment can serve the *risk principle* of the RNR by distinguishing low-risk from high-risk youth, to determine the appropriate intensity of the intervention (i.e., the higher the risk, the higher the intensity; Andrews & Bonta, 2010; Bonta & Andrews, 2017; Lipsey, 2009; Lowenkamp & Latessa, 2004; Lowenkamp et al., 2006; Willis & Ward, 2013). Second, integrating a risk assessment[3] with a primary goods assessment (see Section 11.5.3) will clarify which criminogenic risk factors hamper the prosocial attainment of the young offender's stated primary goods and how they facilitate criminal behaviour as an antisocial alternative. This knowledge can guide the intervention towards working on the offenders' personal (approach) goals in a prosocial manner, instead of merely avoiding the known risks. Consequently, setting intervention goals in a collaborative manner, while focusing on offender well-being, can increase the juveniles' treatment motivation and thus complies with the *responsivity principle*. Enhanced treatment motivation and shared intervention goals can, in turn, facilitate decreasing criminogenic risk factors (according to the *need principle*), by explaining them to the juveniles as obstacles to achieving their goals and well-being (Ward & Fortune, 2013; Ward, Mann, et al., 2007; Ward & Stewart, 2003b; Willis et al., 2013).

11.5.2 Forensic Case Formulation

The assessment of the important primary goods, how the juveniles aim to achieve them and uncovering the (criminogenic) obstacles is an important first step. A recently developed way to combine all this information on the individual offender is forensic case formulation (Hart & Logan, 2011; Hart et al., 2011; Heffernan & Ward, 2015, 2020; Lewis & Doyle, 2009; Logan & Johnstone, 2010; Ward & Beech, 2015). Case formulation in mental health practice is known as:

> the preparation of an evidence-based explanation of a person's difficulties – their form, their origins, and their development and maintenance over time (Johnstone & Dallos, 2006; Tarrier, 2006). Drawing on either one or many theories and practices, the process of formulation is intended to generate an idiographic treatment plan that will provide a response to the difficulties presented that is both effective and proportionate – more so than a generic treatment plan, such as one based on diagnosis or practice guidelines. (Hart et al., 2011, p. 118)

3 Such as the Youth Level of Service/Case Management Inventory (de Ruiter & Hildebrand, 2009; Hoge & Andrews, 2006) or the Structured Assessment of Violence Risk in Youth (Hilterman et al., 2014).

Thus, *forensic* case formulation is essentially an individualized etiological explanation of the onset, interrelations and maintenance of antisocial and criminal behaviour (Heffernan & Ward, 2020; Lewis & Doyle, 2009). In constructing a forensic case formulation, a structured professional risk judgment (in accordance with the RNR model) can be combined with the assessment of the primary goods' importance and ways to realize them. Important in this process is to obtain information from the offender themselves combined with observations, existing (justice and/or client) files and other collateral sources (such as information from family members, work or school). By combining these assessments, the individual's criminal behaviour can be explained on multiple levels, including the neurobiological, psychological, social and cultural mechanisms. This approach then shifts the focus away from simply identifying risk factors to explaining how these risk factors interact with primary goods achievement and can cause criminal behaviour. Subsequently, such a forensic case formulation can serve as the foundation for effective individualized treatment, probation supervision and rehabilitation plans (see Section 11.5.4; Gatner et al., 2021; Heffernan & Ward, 2020; Lewis & Doyle, 2009).

11.5.3 Primary Goods Assessment

Several authors have outlined guidelines on how to assess offenders' important primary goods (i.e., what is most important to them in life), the ways in which they aim to satisfy them (i.e., both prosocial and antisocial secondary goods) and any problems experienced in attaining each good.

Willis et al. (2012) propose that "Heavily weighted goods are identified through asking increasingly detailed questions about a client's past and current core commitments in life and valued day-to-day activities and experiences" (p. 129), and:

> the process of identifying heavily weighted goods should be one of extraction, whereby the clinician identifies the goods evident in client's responses through reflective listening, paraphrasing, and summarizing – rather than presenting clients with a list of primary goods and asking them to identify the relative importance they place/placed on each. This is because the concept of primary goods is relatively abstract and clients will be more likely to focus on secondary goods – the means used to attain primary goods – from which the primary goods must be extracted and inferred. (p. 129)

As a result, an assessment with young offenders to uncover their important primary goods should ideally consist of detailed semi-structured interview questions. One way to start this conversation is asking about the juvenile's dream life (also known as the miracle question used in solution-focused therapy; Clark, 1998, 1999). Asking about what the juveniles' lives would look like if a miracle occurred and they could have anything they wished for, can elicit their most salient and important values and goods. Although this might spark unrealistic expectations and dreams at first, it provides the opportunity to identify the underlying primary goods and explore more realistic alternative options to satisfy them. Additionally, the GLM-based semi-structured interview questions should ideally consist of asking about the evaluation of the primary goods' level of importance over time and whether they would like to have more of each good in their lives (Ward, Mann, et al., 2007; Willis et al., 2012). It must be noted, however, that this type of assessment method requires a certain level of cognitive and verbal ability (see also Section 11.5.5 for alternative assessment methods specifically for youth). Preferably, the assessment is also embedded within a longer period of therapeutic alliance to uncover the juvenile's interests, drives, skills, talents, etc.

Furthermore, identifying secondary goods (i.e., the specific ways the juvenile aims or has aimed to achieve their primary goods) provides information on the strengths and opportunities (i.e., appropriate ways that successfully and prosocially satisfy their primary goods), as well as the inappropriate or antisocial ways and the (criminogenic) internal and external obstacles (Willis et al., 2012, 2013). To uncover these secondary goods, it is recommended to ask about strategies that have been effective (i.e., strengths, protective factors)[4] and ineffective (i.e., obstacles, risk factors) in achieving the juvenile's primary goods, what has prevented them from achieving them and what they would like to achieve over time. More indirect questions could consist of asking about family members, people they know and/or fictional characters (from TV, movies, novels, etc.) whom they would most (not) like to be and why. These types of questions are deemed to tap into fantasies and possible lives (Ward, Mann, et al., 2007). As mentioned before, although in some juveniles this might elicit unrealistic or exaggerated ideas, expectations and wishes at first, it can still form the basis to further explore the underlying drives and primary goods.

Ultimately, such detailed primary goods interview questions can also highlight the four possible problems with primary goods achievement proposed by the GLM: problems with capacity, scope, means and coherence (Yates, Kingston, et al., 2009; Yates & Prescott, 2011; Yates et al., 2010). Additionally, discussing the juvenile's offending behaviour in an open and genuinely curious manner (see for example: Clark, 1999) can provide more information on how primary and secondary goods could have played a role in the crimes committed:

4 These strengths and opportunities are sometimes also referred to as 'protective factors' (Ward, 2017), consisting of positive attributes that reduce the likelihood of violence or offending behaviour (Viljoen et al., 2018) or factors that can buffer the elevated risk for offending behaviour of at-risk individuals (Farrington et al., 2016).

> It is a process of understanding what they were trying to achieve via offending and the purpose that offending served for them in relation to attaining primary goods. (Willis et al., 2012, p. 130)

Importantly, as became clear from our findings, many juveniles expressed satisfaction with the antisocial or criminal ways in which they aimed to achieve their important primary goods. For example, even though it increases their likelihood of offending behaviour, adolescent offenders may express satisfaction with their achievement of the important primary goods such as 'relatedness' and belonging to social groups ('community') by engaging with antisocial peers. Another example is the primary good of 'life', where earning a livelihood with criminal behaviour was associated with higher satisfaction with one's financial situation. Thus, being satisfied with important primary goods is not sufficient for reducing the offenders' recidivism (risk) and working towards a prosocial life. Instead, to create a GLM-based forensic case formulation, it is essential to integrate the assessment of criminogenic risk factors with the assessment of primary goods satisfaction in relation to the offending behaviour (Willis et al., 2013).

To schematically combine this information, Yates, Kingston, et al. (2009) propose filling out a summary table (see e.g., Figure 11.4).

Figure 11.4 Example of a Summary Table for a GLM-based Case Conceptualization

Scope		Means/ Secondary Goods		Capacity				Relationship to offending	
Primary Goods	Weighting (most valued)	Appropriate	Inappropriate	Internal Capabilities (strengths)	Internal Obstacles (deficits/risks)	External Capabilities (strengths)	External Obstacles (deficits/risks)	Direct	Indirect
Life									
Knowledge									
Excellence in Work									
Excellence in Play									
Excellence in Agency									
Inner Peace									
Relatedness									
Community									
Spirituality									
Creativity									
Pleasure									

Notes. Adapted with permission from the summary table in Yates, Kingston & Ward (2009). *The self-regulation model of the offence and re-offence process: A guide to assessment and treatment planning using the integrated good lives/self-regulation model of sexual offending* (p. 148).

11.5.4 Good Lives Plan

Next, based on a GLM-based forensic case formulation, intervention goals can be planned in collaboration with the juvenile, in the form of a Good Lives Plan (GLP). A GLP provides a detailed future-oriented roadmap for working towards enhanced well-being and reduced recidivism (risk). Consequently, this intervention plan should include the offender's personally relevant, prosocial and realistic approach goals, linked to their important primary goods (Mann et al., 2004; Ward, Mann, et al., 2007). In this phase, the professional can ask the juvenile questions about what, in their view, should be strengthened, built, acquired or changed in order to achieve their goals. Focusing on the offender's own goals (i.e., primary goods) can increase treatment motivation and elicit 'change talk' (known from Motivational Interviewing; Miller & Rollnick, 2002), where the offender themselves can identify and acknowledge the obstacles that criminogenic risk factors may pose (McMurran, 2009; Miller & Rollnick, 2002; Tafrate & Luther, 2014).

Subsequently, targeting the criminogenic risk factors that are incorporated in the GLP helps to remove or reduce the obstacles in the way of prosocially achieving the personally relevant goals. Assessing both risk factors and primary goods satisfaction will uncover the important life domains that can become the main focus of the intervention plan (Willis et al., 2012, 2013). As we have seen in our findings, the important primary goods commonly coincide with the important criminogenic risk factors (see also Section 11.6). Still, the difference and additional value that a GLM-based approach could provide lies in adopting a positive and holistic view of the young offender. When conducting both a risk assessment interview and a GLM primary goods interview, we experienced that the latter allows for more openness and positivity (see Chapter 8).

11.5.5 *Specific Recommendations for Juvenile Offenders*

Over the course of this research, it has become clear that a 'good life' according to the GLM is considered objective (innate and applicable to all people) through its proposal of the 11 universal primary goods. Simultaneously, the GLM can be viewed as pluralistic and subjective in its emphasis on social, cultural and individual differences in which primary goods are deemed more or less important, and the different ways individuals seek to achieve them (Ward & Marshall, 2007; Ward & Maruna, 2007). As our findings imply (see Section 11.1), the developmental period of adolescence also impacts what constitutes a 'good' life for this age group. It is thus important for professionals working with young offenders to be careful not to impose their own interpretations, perceptions and values. Instead, during the assessment and GLP implementation, open-ended questions and using the juveniles' own terminology and language are recommended (Fortune et al., 2014; Print, 2013).

The latter can also be helpful as the GLM's original ideas and terminology are sometimes difficult to understand for young(er) offenders. For example, at G-Map, a GLM-based intervention for adolescent sex offenders has been developed, which proposes adapted terminology for assessing youth. As discussed in Chapter 9 (Section 9.4.7), G-Map adapted the terminology of the GLM's primary goods and reduced them from 11 to 8: 'having fun', 'performing', 'having an identity and autonomy', 'having people in my life', 'having a purpose and making a difference', 'being emotionally healthy', 'being sexually healthy' and 'being physically healthy'. Additionally, they translated the terms 'primary goods' as 'my needs'; 'secondary goods' as 'how I meet my needs'; 'internal capabilities' as 'strengths and skills I have to help me meet my needs'; 'external capabilities' as 'how others can help me meet my needs'; and criminogenic risk factors as 'obstacles' (Fortune et al., 2014; Print, 2013).

Alternatively, creative assessment methods have also been suggested, such as using (self-made/chosen) pictures, cartoons and music related to the offender's important primary goods (Print, 2013; Wanzeele & Oltenfreiter, 2020). These alternative assessment methods might elicit more responsiveness and motivation from juveniles in general, and juveniles with a preference for visual learning and/or those with intellectual disabilities in particular (Fortune et al., 2014; Print, 2013). An example of an age-appropriate adapted case conceptualization can be found in the proposed summary table by Prescott (2018), and Prescott and Dent (2018) for young adolescent offenders (see Figure 11.5).

Figure 11.5 Summary Table of a GLM-based Case Conceptualization for Working with Adolescents

Good Life Goal	Ways to Attain this Goal	How I Will Know I Am Attaining this Goal	How Others Will Know I Am Attaining This Goal	Obstacles I Will Need to Overcome	Ways to Overcome Obstacles
Having Fun					
Being an Achiever					
Being My Own Person					
Being Connected to Other People					
Having a Purpose in Life					
Meeting My Emotional Needs					
Meeting My Sexual Needs					
Being Physically Healthy					

Notes. From Prescott, D. (2018). *Becoming who I want to be: A good lives workbook for young men* (pp. 126-127). Copyright 2018 by Safer Society Press. Reprinted with permission. Also available online: https://safersocietypress.org/store/good-life-plan-at-a-glance-young-men/.

When constructing the Good Lives Plan (GLP) with juveniles, it is recommended to subdivide larger, long-term goals into a number of small, specific, measurable, achievable, realistic steps, with time periods (also known as the SMART technique). As adolescents are known to be less inclined to make long-term plans and have a more limited capacity to delay gratification (Wehmeyer & Shogren, 2017; Wehmeyer et al., 2017), smaller steps will help them to stay motivated and achieve their (intermediate) goals more readily (Fortune et al., 2014; Print, 2013; Wehmeyer & Shogren, 2017).

Furthermore, as minors are usually restricted because of rules and regulations set by their parent(s), caregiver(s) and/or (legal) authorities, it is important to construct age-appropriate goals (Fortune et al., 2014; Print, 2013). The latter also points us to the importance of considering the (social) environments that the juveniles reside in and/or will return to after detention. The GLP should take into account what social, psychological and material resources will be (or need to be) available to the juvenile (Clinkinbeard & Murray, 2012; Ward & Gannon, 2006; Ward & Maruna, 2007). Ultimately, intervention goals included in a GLP should consist of strengthening and building internal capacity and skills (i.e., psychological capital), and maximizing external resources and social support (i.e., social capital) to help the juvenile satisfy their primary goods in socially acceptable ways (Fortune et al., 2014; Print, 2013; Ward, Mann, et al., 2007). Strengthening juveniles' psychological and social capital is especially important as they are the building blocks of a (prosocial) identity (Clinkinbeard & Murray, 2012; Emmons, 1989; Erikson, 1968; Mulvey et al., 2004; Na & Jang, 2019; Putnam, 2001; Ward & Marshall, 2004, 2007; Ward & Maruna, 2007; Wright et al., 2001; see also Chapter 9).

11.6 Important Intervention Goals for Adolescent Offenders

The question then arises as to what types of specific intervention goals could enhance adolescent offenders' psychological and social capital. Based on our results, essential life domains that were consistently found to be important for young offenders consisted of their family and peer relationships, academic or occupational career, leisure activities and having fun and mental health. As outlined below, working on these life domains and a prosocial identity encompasses the most important GLM primary goods as well as the RNR model's 'central eight' criminogenic risk factors.

11.6.1 Family and Peer Relationships

Antisocial peer relationships and problematic family relationships are both known criminogenic risk factors included in the RNR model (Andrews & Bonta, 2010; Bonta & Andrews, 2017). From our findings it became clear that a trade-off can occur between family and peer relationships. That is, delinquency was predicted by dissatisfaction with family relationships and conversely by more satisfaction with (antisocial) peer relationships. For some, problematic family relationships and parenting issues drove them out of their home and into the streets. This subsequently increases their likelihood of engaging in criminal activity, especially if they live in disadvantaged and high-crime neighbourhoods (Jacobs et al., 2020; Putnam, 2001; Sampson et al., 2002; Wikström & Loeber, 2000).

For these juveniles in particular, strengthening and working on their relationships with prosocial peers, in sports clubs, associations (see also Section 11.6.3) and/or at school is an essential intervention goal to achieve the primary goods of 'relatedness' and 'community' (Dishion & Tipsord, 2011). An extreme example to foster such change in social contacts is moving to a different neighbourhood, which has been found to be an effective turning point in reducing recidivism (Hoeve & van der Laan, 2016). Other (less extreme) examples consist of joining new/other associations and sports clubs, and/or changing schools. For some adolescents, a romantic relationship with a (prosocial) partner may guide them towards prosocial choices (Giordano et al., 2003; Sampson & Laub, 1995).

Focusing on prosocial contacts can automatically diminish engagement with antisocial peers (Dishion & Tipsord, 2011; Warr, 1993). Furthermore, for some it may also be beneficial to work on their social skills and assertiveness, especially when confronted with (antisocial) peer pressure they wish to avoid (Lipsey et al., 2000; Tracey & Hanham, 2015).

Additionally, it is of great importance to aim to repair broken relationships with family and/or (other) caregivers when possible (Wright et al., 2001). A number of detained adolescents in our studies mentioned the active role of their parent(s) in the relationship, and/or parenting conflicts. In these cases, the intervention will also depend on the participation of the parent(s) and/or caregiver(s). Both parenting interventions and family therapy have been proven to be effective in reducing recidivism in juvenile offenders (Latimer, 2001; Lipsey et al., 2010; Woolfenden et al., 2002). This is in line with our findings, where dissatisfaction with family relationships was strongly related to both more delinquency and diminished well-being in (detained) adolescents. Moreover, family relationships were perceived to be among the most important aspects of the detained adolescents' lives. Nevertheless, the offenders' own (delinquent) behaviour often (also) had negative influences on the relationship with their parent(s) and other family members, creating conflicts and problems in achieving the primary good of 'relatedness'. Therefore, pointing out this conflict in achieving one of their most important primary goods can provide a trigger to increase treatment motivation and engagement (McMurran & Ward, 2004; Ward & Laws, 2010). In turn, adequate social support has also proven to help sustain the motivation to desist over time (Panuccio et al., 2012; Wright et al., 2001).

11.6.2 School and Work

Problems at school and work are also important criminogenic risk factors in the RNR model (Andrews & Bonta, 2010; Bonta & Andrews, 2017). Again, these factors could play an especially salient role for youth coming from disadvantaged backgrounds. Those juveniles that (have) experience(d) poverty and financial problems tend to prioritize making money (fast and illegally) at the expense of their academic achievement. Yet, in our Western culture, attending school and obtaining a degree or certificate are important prerequisites for acquiring a well-paying job. Additionally, other factors, such as cognitive limitations, problems with attention deficit and/or impulsivity (i.e., criminogenic risk factors) can make it difficult to perform well in school or in lawful jobs (Katsiyannis et al., 2008). In these situations, expelling students from school is not the appropriate solution and often exacerbates their disadvantage (known as the school-to-prison pipeline; Christle et al., 2005; Moore & McArthur, 2014; Wald & Losen, 2003). Problems at school and in attaining a gratifying job can hamper the primary goods of 'life' by the inability to secure an adequate livelihood; and 'excellence in work', 'excellence in agency' and 'spirituality' by not being able to achieve their (future) aspirations and lacking a purpose in life.

Therefore, it is important to provide (detained) youth with adequate educational and career support, including setting goals to continue their education (and/or work), so that they do not fall further behind (Cuevas et al., 2017). Moreover, successful engagement in education, (satisfying) lawful employment and financial independence are known to effectively reduce recidivism (Hill et al., 2017; Katsiyannis et al., 2008; Niebuhr & Orrick, 2020; van den Berg et al., 2014; Wright & Cullen, 2004; Zagar et al., 2013). To set effective treatment goals regarding the juveniles' academic and/or occupational career (for the primary good of 'excellence in work'), it is important to discover what enables them to feel competent and experience success. For some, this also means exploring more practical, rather than academic, careers and professions.

Additionally, the (criminogenic) obstacles that could hamper the juveniles' career goals should be addressed, such as problems with attention, impulsivity and aggression management. Subsequently, knowing their (future) aspirations and working towards those goals (for the primary good of 'excellence in agency') can give them a sense of purpose in their lives (i.e., satisfy the primary good of 'spirituality'). Furthermore, on their path to adulthood, some (older) adolescents would benefit from working towards independence, not only financially but also in terms of living on their own (i.e., finding accommodation) and taking care of themselves (i.e., for the primary goods of 'life' and 'excellence in agency'). In these cases, it is recommended to carefully set out a collaborative (discharge) plan with the juvenile and their network, to maintain (social) support during their reintegration (Abrams et al., 2008; Van Hecke, Meulewaeter, Vanderplasschen, et al., 2021; Wilson & Tully, 2009).

11.6.3 Leisure Activities and Having Fun

For some juveniles, their (future) aspirations (also) lie in gaining success with their hobbies, such as playing sports or composing (rap) music. As a lack of structured leisure activities is a known criminogenic risk factor (Andrews & Bonta, 2010; Bonta & Andrews, 2017), these aspirations should be encouraged. At the same time, in (detained) young offenders, leaving school has been linked to more passive leisure time activities (Farnworth, 2000), interfering with the primary good of 'excellence in play'. Having no structure or daily activities can lead to a lack of scope in achieving one's primary goods, which in turn can lead to boredom and potential engagement in illegal activities (Drozda, 2006; Newberry & Duncan, 2001; Taylor, 2017; Wainwright & Nee, 2014). Some experience these illegal activities (including substance use) as a source of having fun, related to the primary good of 'pleasure'. This is particularly the case when other legal leisure activities are not available or not sufficiently challenging and fun (Csikszentmihalyi, 2000; Drozda, 2006; Farrington, 1993; Gordon & Caltabiano, 1996; Hansen & Breivik, 2001; Newberry & Duncan, 2001; Putniņš, 2010; Robertson, 1994; Troonbeeckx et al., 2015).

As a result, maintaining, discovering and working on socially acceptable leisure activities that can provide the juveniles with fun (i.e., satisfy the primary good of 'pleasure') as well as challenging experiences (i.e., for the primary good of 'excellence in play') are important treatment goals. Subsequently, barriers in the way of engaging in these activities (such as lack of financial resources, lack of availability and a lack of skills) should be taken into account. In practice, this could mean looking for creative ways to overcome those barriers such as exploring subsidy opportunities, alternative activities in another but nearby city, investing in skills training, etc. (Farnworth, 2000; Robertson, 1994, 2001).

11.6.4 Substance (Ab)use

Another important criminogenic risk factor for criminal and violent recidivism is substance abuse (Andrews & Bonta, 2010; Bonta & Andrews, 2017). A relatively large proportion of (detained) young offenders (occasionally) use substances as a way to experience fun, joy and excitement (i.e., to satisfy the primary good of 'pleasure'). In such cases, monitoring the frequency and severity of the substance use is an important treatment goal as well. Finding alternative ways as a substitute for experiencing this type of enjoyment that is socially acceptable and less harmful, is recommended. Additionally, a proportion of the detained adolescent offenders in our research referred to their substance (ab)use as self-medication to cope with emotional problems and achieve the primary good of 'inner peace'. For some of these adolescents their substance abuse was the main driver of their delinquent behaviour, often in combination with drug dealing to finance their own use. These findings are supported by previous studies that demonstrated substance abuse as a powerful criminogenic risk factor mediating the relationship between mental health issues and delinquency (Craig et al., 2018; Guebert & Olver, 2014; Nguyen & Bouchard, 2013; Wills et al., 2016). Therefore, in cases where substance use has become problematic, substance abuse treatment is recommended with a focus on the underlying mental health issues (Cuellar et al., 2004).

11.6.5 Mental Health and Overall Well-Being

While externalizing behaviour problems (e.g., impulsivity, hostility and aggression) can be considered criminogenic risk factors, internalizing mental health issues are commonly referred to as non-criminogenic (Andrews & Bonta, 2010; Bonta & Andrews, 2017). Indeed, in our sample, internalizing mental health problems, such as depressive and anxiety symptoms were not directly related to the adolescents' delinquent behaviour. They were, however, related to lower levels of overall well-being. A possible explanation for the latter has been suggested by Barnao et al. (2016), stating that psychopathology interferes with the satisfaction of 'inner peace' and other primary goods necessary for well-being, which can thus indirectly increase the risk of offending behaviour. Furthermore, our studies show that, during detention, both externalizing (indirectly through overall well-being) and internalizing mental health problems influence treatment motivation and subsequent recidivism risk. Thus, our and previous studies suggest that working on overall well-being, externalizing *and* internalizing psychopathological problems, should be included as important treatment goals in juvenile offender rehabilitation (Beaudry et al., 2021; Buunk et al., 2016; DiPierro-Sutton et al., 2021; Guebert & Olver, 2014; Leenarts et al., 2013; van Binsbergen et al., 2001; Van Damme, Hoeve, et al., 2015; Van Hecke, Meulewaeter, Rowaert, et al., 2021).

Although some authors suggest that well-being is a stable factor, largely determined by genetic factors (Holte et al., 2014; Steger & Kashdan, 2007; Stubbe et al., 2005), our and other studies demonstrated that overall well-being levels are changeable (Gilman & Handwerk, 2001; Lyubomirsky et al., 2005, 2011; Sheldon & Lyubomirsky, 2009, 2012; Tang & Chan, 2017). In particular, positive emotions are considered to play an important role in the enhancement of well-being. According to Fredrickson's (2004) Broaden-and-Build Theory, positive emotions can broaden people's perspective and encourage them to set more personal growth and approach goals. The experience of positive affect has, furthermore, been demonstrated to enable success in multiple life domains, including work performance, social relationships, physical health and creativity (Lyubomirsky et al., 2005). However, one should keep in mind that it is impossible to experience positive feelings continuously and expecting constant happiness can even be counterproductive. It should, therefore, be equally important to learn to adequately cope with negative emotions that are part of life and to pursue an emotional balance (De Wachter, 2019; Pavot & Diener, 2004).

11.6.6 *Prosocial Identity and Agency*

Finally, an overarching treatment goal includes the formation of a coherent prosocial identity. Antisocial attitudes, beliefs and rationalizations are known criminogenic risk factors (Andrews & Bonta, 2010; Bonta & Andrews, 2017). As such, these attitudes may become obstacles in one's prosocial primary goods satisfaction, that is, they can diminish the belief that the offender is able to lead a prosocial life and achieve their goals in a socially acceptable way (Anderson et al., 2020; Brezina & Topalli, 2012; Johnston et al., 2019). Consequently, a lack of (prosocial) self-efficacy beliefs can hamper the (prosocial achievement of the) primary good of 'excellence in agency' (Bandura et al., 2003; Johnston et al., 2019). Moreover, as long as these antisocial attitudes and (previous) criminal behaviour are considered part of one's identity, desistance from delinquency will be difficult to achieve (Abrams & Aguilar, 2005; Brezina & Topalli, 2012; McMahon & Jump, 2018; Oberlader et al., 2021; Paternoster & Bushway, 2009).

Therefore, identifying the juveniles' self-efficacy beliefs is an important aspect in effective rehabilitative interventions. To sustainably desist, the juveniles will not only need the appropriate skills and resources, but also the belief and confidence that they will succeed (Mahler et al., 2018; McMahon & Jump, 2018). The latter is sometimes referred to as 'desistance self-efficacy' (Brezina, 2020), which has been associated with reduced recidivism (Abrams & Aguilar, 2005; Johnston et al., 2019). Similarly, adopting a prosocial identity and having expectations of a positive future self, have also been related to less offending (Cuevas et al., 2017; Na & Jang, 2019; Oberlader et al., 2021). Establishing (social) support for the offenders' self-determined goals (i.e., related to their primary goods) in the rehabilitation process is considered important for enhancing prosocial self-efficacy and agency, improving the chances to successfully desist (Johnston et al., 2019; Tyler et al., 2020). Furthermore, some authors suggest that with age and maturation, young offenders also leave their criminal identity behind. Over the course of years, they are considered to adopt a more prosocial identity by taking on adult roles, such as living independently, having a relationship and being legally employed (Hill et al., 2016; McCuish et al., 2020; Rocque et al., 2019; Thomas & Vogel, 2019). In our studies we did not include the assessment of the difference in prosocial versus antisocial self-efficacy/agency. Nevertheless, given the existing research we recommend that promoting prosocial self-efficacy/agency and identity should be included in the rehabilitation intervention as an overarching treatment goal.

11.7 Effective Individualized Interventions

After the assessment phase is finished and a GLP has been constructed, the practical implementation of the plan can take many forms. That is, the GLM can be seen as an overarching motivational framework that guides interventions towards the appropriate treatment goals but does not specify exactly how these goals should be achieved during the intervention (Willis et al., 2012). Although it is beyond the scope of this research to address all the possible interventions that could be implemented within a GLM framework, some examples and effective components known from the scientific literature are discussed below.

11.7.1 Residential Interventions as a Last Resort

During the course of rehabilitation, especially during and after secure confinement, a number of barriers might come up that should be taken into account. Examples are barriers related to adapting to and from a restrictive and repressive environment, stigma, debts, accommodation problems, employment, school problems and mental health issues (Abrams, 2006; De Valk et al., 2019; Harder et al., 2011; Janssen-de Ruijter et al., 2019; Van Hecke et al., 2019). Because of the confinement, juveniles may experience a large discrepancy between living and working on their treatment goals 'inside', compared to the realities of life 'outside' (Abrams, 2006). Additionally, while residential treatments can be effective in reducing externalizing and internalizing problems in some cases (De Swart et al., 2012; Knorth et al., 2008), it can also promote antisocial behaviour by 'peer contagion' (Dishion & Tipsord, 2011).

Furthermore, highly structured residential placements can diminish the juveniles' sense of autonomy and negatively influence their treatment motivation and well-being (De Valk et al., 2019; Harder et al., 2012; van der Helm et al., 2014; van der Laan & Eichelsheim, 2013). Instead, open positive living climates have been found to be related to more treatment motivation and better treatment outcomes, as juveniles are given opportunities to develop towards independence and autonomy (Heynen et al., 2017; van der Helm et al., 2014, 2018). Roest et al. (2016) suggest that positive and open group climates should consist of

> a supportive environment in which staff attend to the psychological needs of adolescents and refrain from repressive professional behavior, such as unfair treatment, punitive behavior, and enforcement of incremental rules. (p. 457)

Still, for a number of juveniles (especially low-risk youth), residential interventions in general are not the most suitable. In these cases, outpatient and community-based interventions where the juvenile remains in their social network and environment are recommended (Howell & Lipsey, 2012; Lipsey, 2009; Ryan et al., 2014). Accordingly, in the Netherlands, a number of large-scale secure residential Juvenile Justice Institutions have been closed in recent years to be replaced with small-scale (half-open) facilities for justice-involved youth. These facilities aim to ensure that the juveniles can spend their detention closer to home, focusing on reintegrating in society. While in the facility, they are allowed to visit home during the day and attend their own school and/or go to work (Dienst Justitiële Inrichtingen, 2021). Likewise, the new Juvenile Delinquency Decree in Flanders, Belgium considers a residential placement as a last-resort measure (Put & Leenknecht, 2019). Along these lines, the new decree also introduced 'offence-oriented contextual counselling' as a(n) (alternative) juvenile justice response,[5] which is an overarching term for a range of community-based interventions.

Examples of types of community-based counselling methods that are used include Multi-Systemic Therapy and New Perspectives (see the next section; Gerits, 2019).

11.7.2 Community-based GLM-Compatible Interventions

Multi-Systemic Therapy (MST; Borduin, 1999; Curtis et al., 2004; Henggeler & Schaeffer, 2016) is an example of a community-based intervention that can easily be applied within the GLM framework. Within MST, antisocial or criminal behaviour is considered to arise from an interaction between the individual, the social environment and internal and external risk factors. As a result, the intervention aims to increase the juveniles' capacities (internal resources) and the social systems' capacity (external conditions). This includes targeting individual, family, peer, school and community factors that contribute to and maintain the problematic behaviour. In doing so, the therapist identifies several potential strengths in each domain that can help the juvenile and their network. As in the GLM, different (sub-) interventions or treatments can be combined to address the identified and targeted treatment goals (Borduin, 1999; Henggeler & Schaeffer, 2016). Several meta-analytic studies demonstrated that MST effectively decreases externalizing and internalizing symptoms, out-of-home placements and re-arrest (Curtis et al., 2004; van der Stouwe et al., 2014).

In a similar vein, the Dutch programme 'New Perspectives' (Elling & Melissen, 2007) is a community-based intervention that aims to improve juveniles' quality of life by addressing multiple systems (home, school, peers and neighbourhood). It consists of an intensive three-month coaching phase followed by a three-month after care phase. During the programme, youth care workers are available for 24 hours a day, seven days a week. Components of the programme include setting goals in consultation with the client, motivational interviewing, empowerment and reinforcement of the social network (including peers, parents and teachers), cognitive restructuring, problem-solving skills and modelling (Elling & Melissen, 2007). Compared to treatment as usual in youth care for at-risk juveniles, it has proven to be equally effective in terms of treatment outcomes, such as reducing internalizing problems, externalizing problems and delinquent behaviour (de Vries et al., 2017, 2018).

5 This type of counselling is not always used only as an alternative to a residential placement but can also be combined with or start at the end of a residential stay, to allow for a faster release and/or provide support in transition during re-entry to the community (Gerits, 2019).

11.7.3 General Effective Components

In general, as suggested by the RNR model and demonstrated in many previous studies, cognitive-behavioural therapy techniques are found to be the most effective for (juvenile) offender rehabilitation. While the behavioural component of the intervention focuses on developing appropriate behaviours and skills, the cognitive component targets distorted attitudes and patterns of thinking (Fortune, 2018; Howell & Lipsey, 2012; Lipsey, 2009; Tafrate & Mitchell, 2014).

Additionally, an effective component of all types of interventions is their consistent implementation by all professionals working with the juvenile (Goense et al., 2016; Lipsey, 2009). Continuing supervision and training can help with treatment fidelity and ongoing growth and development of the professionals (Bearman et al., 2017).

Finally, a positive, supportive and open demeanour by staff members working with the juveniles is considered an important factor in effective rehabilitation interventions, especially by improving the treatment alliance. Treatment alliance in turn has been found to increase treatment motivation and treatment effectiveness (Roest et al., 2016).

Such an open and positive demeanour by staff members is also considered an important component within the GLM framework:

> Modern interventions texts repeatedly use language such as 'deficit,' 'deviance,' 'distortion,' and 'risk' (e.g., see Salter, 1988). All such words are associated with negative valuations or expectancies. The GLM is a positive model, based on the assumption that people are more likely to embrace positive change and personal development, and so the kinds of language associated with GLM interventions should be future-oriented, optimistic, and approach-goal focused. (Laws & Ward, 2011, p. 200)

Accordingly, an increasing number of authors (also independent from the GLM) argue for a more positive approach in (juvenile) justice interventions (Nikolic-Ristanovic, 2014; Ronel & Elisha, 2011; Ronel & Segev, 2014; Tweed et al., 2011; Walgrave, 2016; Walgrave et al., 2019). The latter is sometimes referred to as 'positive criminology', inspired by the preceding 'positive psychology' movement:

> Positive psychology and positive criminology have shifted away from the notion of conceiving of an individual as containing a set of problems that 'need to be fixed.' Rather, they promote a more holistic view, which acknowledges that thriving and disengagement from distress, addiction, mental illness, crime, or deviance might be fostered more effectively by enhancing positive

> emotions and experiences, rather than focusing on reducing negative attributes. (Ronel & Segev, 2014, p. 1390)

11.8 CONCLUSION

In sum, effective juvenile justice interventions need to adopt a holistic and positive view of young offenders. Based on our own and previous research, we can cautiously conclude that the GLM can offer a helpful framework for the implementation of such a holistic and positive approach in the juvenile justice system. In essence, turning points, life goals, primary goods, strengths, protective factors, criminogenic risk factors and obstacles are interrelated and often overlapping concepts. Combining all these concepts in explaining juvenile delinquency can provide the tools to effectively reduce recidivism and enhance juvenile justice interventions, by incorporating multiple approaches and perspectives.

REFERENCES

* = Included references in the meta-analysis of Chapter 4.

Abate, A., & Venta, A. (2018). Perceptions of the legal system and recidivism: Investigating the mediating role of perceptions of chances for success in juvenile offenders. *Criminal Justice and Behavior, 45*(4), 541-560. https://doi.org/10.1177/0093854817753264.

*Abdel-Khalek, A. M. (2007). Religiosity, happiness, health, and psychopathology in a probability sample of Muslim adolescents. *Mental Health, Religion & Culture, 10*(6), 571-583. https://doi.org/10.1080/13674670601034547.

*Abdel-Khalek, A. M. (2009). Religiosity, subjective well-being, and depression in Saudi children and adolescents. *Mental Health, Religion & Culture, 12*(8), 803-815. https://doi.org/10.1080/13674670903006755.

*Abdel-Khalek, A. M. (2011). Religiosity, subjective well-being, self-esteem, and anxiety among Kuwaiti Muslim adolescents. *Mental Health, Religion & Culture, 14*(2), 129-140. https://doi.org/10.1080/13674670903456463.

*Abdel-Khalek, A. M. (2012). Subjective well-being and religiosity: A cross-sectional study with adolescents, young and middle-age adults. *Mental Health, Religion & Culture, 15*(1), 39-52. https://doi.org/10.1080/13674676.2010.551324.

*Abdel-Khalek, A. M. (2014a). Religiosity, health and happiness: Significant relations in adolescents from Qatar. *International Journal of Social Psychiatry, 60*(7), 656-661. https://doi.org/10.1177/0020764013511792.

*Abdel-Khalek, A. M. (2014b). Happiness, health, and religiosity: Significant associations among Lebanese adolescents. *Mental Health, Religion & Culture, 17*(1), 30-38. https://doi.org/10.1080/13674676.2012.742047.

*Abdel-Khalek, A. M., & Eid, G. K. (2011). Religiosity and its association with subjective well-being and depression among Kuwaiti and Palestinian Muslim children and adolescents. *Mental Health, Religion & Culture, 14*(2), 117-127. https://doi.org/10.1080/13674670903540951.

Abrams, L. S. (2006). Listening to juvenile offenders: Can residential treatment prevent recidivism? *Child and Adolescent Social Work Journal, 23*(1), 61-85. https://doi.org/10.1007/s10560-005-0029-2.

Abrams, L. S., & Aguilar, J. P. (2005). Negative trends, possible selves, and behavior change: A qualitative study of juvenile offenders in residential treatment. *Qualitative Social Work, 4*(2), 175-196. https://doi.org/10.1177/1473325005052392.

Abrams, L. S., Shannon, S. K. S., & Sangalang, C. (2008). Transition services for incarcerated youth: A mixed methods evaluation study. *Children and Youth Services Review, 30*(5), 522-535. https://doi.org/10.1016/j.childyouth.2007.11.003.

*Addae, E. A. (2020). The mediating role of social capital in the relationship between socioeconomic status and adolescent wellbeing: Evidence from Ghana. *BMC Public Health, 20*(1). https://doi.org/10.1186/s12889-019-8142-x.

Adelman, H. S., Taylor, L., & Nelson, P. (1989). Minors' dissatisfaction with their life circumstances. *Child Psychiatry & Human Development, 20*(2), 135-147. https://doi.org/10.1007/bf00711660.

Aebi, M., Linhart, S., Thun-Hohenstein, L., Bessler, C., Steinhausen, H. C., & Plattner, B. (2015). Detained male adolescent offender's emotional, physical and sexual maltreatment profiles and their associations to psychiatric disorders and criminal behaviors. *Journal of Abnormal Child Psychology, 43*(5), 999-1009. https://doi.org/10.1007/s10802-014-9961-y.

Agnew, R. (1985). A revised strain theory of delinquency. *Social Forces, 64*(1), 151-167. https://doi.org/10.2307/2578977.

Agnew, R. (1990). The origins of delinquent events: An examination of offender accounts. *Journal of Research in Crime and Delinquency, 27*(3), 267-294. https://doi.org/10.1177/0022427890027003004.

Agnew, R. (1992). Foundation for a general strain theory of crime and delinquency. *Criminology, 30*(1), 47-88. https://doi.org/10.1111/j.1745-9125.1992.tb01093.x.

Agnew, R. (2006). *Pressured into crime: An overview of general strain theory*. Roxbury Publishing Company.

Agnew, R. (2010). A general strain theory of terrorism. *Theoretical Criminology, 14*(2), 131-153. https://doi.org/10.1002/9781118923986.ch7.

Agnew, R. (2013). When criminal coping is likely: An extension of general strain theory. *Deviant Behavior, 34*(8), 653-670. https://doi.org/10.1080/01639625.2013.766529.

Agnew, R., & Petersen, D. M. (1989). Leisure and delinquency. *Social Problems, 36*(4), 332-350. https://doi.org/10.1525/sp.1989.36.4.03a00020.

Agnew, R., & White, H. R. (1992). An empirical test of general strain theory. *Criminology, 30*(4), 475-500. https://doi.org/10.1111/j.1745-9125.1992.tb01113.x.

Ainsworth, M. S. (1989). Attachments beyond infancy. *American Psychologist, 44*(4), 709-716. https://doi.org/10.1037/0003-066X.44.4.709.

Alexander, M., Lowenkamp, C. T., & Robinson, C. R. (2013). A tale of two innovations: Motivational interviewing and core correctional practices in United States probation. In P. Ugwudike & P. Raynor (Eds.), *What works in offender compliance* (pp. 242-255). Springer.

*Alshammari, A. S., Piko, B. F., & Fitzpatrick, K. M. (2021). Social support and adolescent mental health and well-being among Jordanian students. *International Journal of Adolescence and Youth, 26*(1), 211-223. https://doi.org/10.1080/02673843.2021.1908375.

Amemiya, J., Kieta, J., & Monahan, K. C. (2017). Adolescent offenders' qualitative reflections on desistance from crime. *Journal of Research on Adolescence, 27*(4), 765-781. https://doi.org/10.1111/jora.12313.

Anderson, A. Y., Weiss, D. B., & Oselin, S. S. (2020). When I grow up: Exploring the link between future expectations and criminal trajectories. *Journal of Developmental and Life-Course Criminology*, 1-24. https://doi.org/10.1007/s40865-020-00136-6.

Andrews, D. A., & Bonta, J. (1994). *The psychology of criminal conduct*. Anderson.

Andrews, D. A., & Bonta, J. (1995). *Level of Service—Revised (LSI-R): An offender assessment system: User's guide*. Multi-Health Systems.

Andrews, D. A., & Bonta, J. (2010). *The psychology of criminal conduct* (5th ed.). Anderson.

Andrews, D. A., Bonta, J., & Hoge, R. D. (1990). Classification for effective rehabilitation: Rediscovering psychology. *Criminal Justice and Behavior, 17*(1), 19-52. https://doi.org/10.1177/0093854890017001004.

Andrews, D. A., Bonta, J., & Wormith, J. S. (2011). The Risk-Need-Responsivity (RNR) model: Does adding the good lives model contribute to effective crime prevention? *Criminal Justice and Behavior, 38*(7), 735-755. https://doi.org/10.1177/0093854811406356.

Andrews, D. A., & Dowden, C. (2006). Risk principle of case classification in correctional treatment: A meta-analytic investigation. *International Journal of Offender Therapy and Comparative Criminology, 50*(1), 88-100. https://doi.org/10.1177/0306624X05282556.

Andrews, D. A., & Dowden, C. (2007). The risk-need-responsivity model of assessment and human service in prevention and corrections: Crime-prevention jurisprudence. *Canadian Journal of Criminology and Criminal Justice, 49*(4), 439-464. https://doi.org/10.3138/cjccj.49.4.439.

Andrews, D. A., Zinger, I., Hoge, R. D., Bonta, J., Gendreau, P., & Cullen, F. T. (1990). Does correctional treatment work? A clinically relevant and psychologically informed meta-analysis. *Criminology, 28*(3), 369-404. https://doi.org/10.1111/j.1745-9125.1990.tb01330.x.

Anvari, F., & Lakens, D. (2021). Using anchor-based methods to determine the smallest effect size of interest. *Journal of Experimental Social Psychology, 96*, 104159, https://doi.org/10.1016/j.jesp.2021.104159.

Aristotle. (1985). *Nicomachean ethics. Translated by Terence Irwin*. Hackett Publishing Company.

Arnett, J. J. (1992). Reckless behavior in adolescence: A developmental perspective. *Developmental Review, 12*(4), 339-373. https://doi.org/10.1016/0273-2297(92)90013-R.

Arnett, J. J. (1996). Sensation seeking, aggressiveness, and adolescent reckless behavior. *Personality and Individual Differences, 20*(6), 693-702. https://doi.org/10.1016/0191-8869(96)00027-X.

Arnett, J. J. (1999). Adolescent storm and stress, reconsidered. *American Psychologist, 54*(5), 317-326. https://doi.org/10.1037//0003-066x.54.5.317.

Arnhart, L. (1998). *Darwinian natural right: The biological ethics of human nature*. SUNY Press.

*Arslan, G. (2017). Psychological maltreatment, social acceptance, social connectedness, and subjective well-being in adolescents. *Journal of Happiness Studies, 19*, 983-100. https://doi.org/10.1007/s10902-017-9856-z.

*Arslan, G. (2019). Mediating role of the self–esteem and resilience in the association between social exclusion and life satisfaction among adolescents. *Personality and Individual Differences, 151*, 1-6. https://doi.org/10.1016/j.paid.2019.109514.

*Arslan, G. (2021). School belongingness, well-being, and mental health among adolescents: Exploring the role of loneliness. *Australian Journal of Psychology, 73*(1), 70-80. https://doi.org/10.1111/ajpy.12274.

*Arslan, G., Allen, K. A., & Ryan, T. (2020). Exploring the impacts of school belonging on youth wellbeing and mental health among Turkish adolescents. *Child Indicators Research, 13*(5), 1619-1635. https://doi.org/10.1007/s12187-020-09721-z.

Aspinwall, L. G., & Staudinger, U. M. (2003). *A psychology of human strengths: Fundamental questions and future directions for a positive psychology*. American Psychological Association.

Assink, M., van der Put, C. E., Hoeve, M., de Vries, S. L. A., Stams, G. J. J. M., & Oort, F. J. (2015). Risk factors for persistent delinquent behavior among juveniles: A meta-analytic review. *Clinical Psychology Review, 42*, 47-61. https://doi.org/10.1016/j.cpr.2015.08.002.

Assink, M., & Wibbelink, C. J. M. (2016). Fitting three-level meta-analytic models in R: A step-by-step tutorial. *The Quantitative Methods for Psychology, 12*(3), 154-174. https://doi.org/10.20982/tqmp.12.3.p154.

*Atienza-Gonzalez, F. L., Martinez, N., & Silva, C. (2020). Life satisfaction and self-rated health in adolescents: The relationships between them and the role of gender and age. *Spanish Journal of Psychology, 23*, Article e4. https://doi.org/10.1017/sjp.2020.10.

Aumeboonsuke, V. (2017). Parents or peers, wealth or warmth? The impact of social support, wealth, and a positive outlook on self-efficacy and happiness. *International Journal of Social Economics, 44*(6), 732-750. https://doi.org/10.1108/IJSE-01-2015-0002.

Austin, J. T., & Vancouver, J. B. (1996). Goal constructs in psychology: Structure, process, and content. *Psychological Bulletin, 120*(3), 338-375. https://doi.org/10.1037/0033-2909.120.3.338.

*Ayten, A., & Acat, B. (2019). Internet addiction, values, and religiosity as predictors of life satisfaction among adolescents: A quantitative study on high school students. *Addicta-*

the Turkish Journal on Addictions, 6(3), 847-870. https://www.addicta.com.tr/Content/files/sayilar/10/21.pdf.

Baier, C. J., & Wright, B. R. (2001). "If you love me, keep my commandments": A meta-analysis of the effect of religion on crime. *Journal of Research in Crime and Delinquency, 38*(1), 3-21. https://doi.org/10.1177/0022427801038001001.

*Balaguer, I., Duda, J. L., & Castillo, I. (2017). Motivational antecedents of well-being and health related behaviors in adolescents. *Journal of Human Kinetics, 59*(1), 121-130. https://doi.org/10.1515/hukin-2017-0152.

Baltodano, H. M., Platt, D., & Roberts, C. W. (2005). Transition from secure care to the community: Significant issues for youth in detention. *Journal of Correctional Education, 56*(4), 372-388. www.jstor.org/stable/23282627.

Bandura, A. (1971). *Social learning theory* (Vol. 1). General Learning Press.

Bandura, A. (1977). Self-efficacy: Toward a unifying theory of behavioral change. *Psychology Review, 84*(2), 191-215. https://doi.org/10.1037//0033-295x.84.2.191.

Bandura, A. (1978). Social learning theory of aggression. *Journal of Communication, 28*(3), 12-29. https://doi.org/10.1111/j.1460-2466.1978.tb01621.x.

Bandura, A. (1982). Self-efficacy mechanism in human agency. *American Psychologist, 37*(2), 122-147. https://doi.org/10.1037/0003-066X.37.2.122.

Bandura, A. (2006). Toward a psychology of human agency. *Perspectives on Psychological Science, 1*(2), 164-180. https://doi.org/10.1111/j.1745-6916.2006.00011.x.

Bandura, A., Caprara, G. V., Barbaranelli, C., Gerbino, M., & Pastorelli, C. (2003). Role of affective self-regulatory efficacy in diverse spheres of psychosocial functioning. *Child Development, 74*(3), 769-782. https://doi.org/10.1111/1467-8624.00567.

Barendregt, C. S., Van der Laan, A. M., Bongers, I. L., & van Nieuwenhuizen, C. (2018). Quality of life, delinquency and psychosocial functioning of adolescents in secure residential care: Testing two assumptions of the good lives model. *Child and Adolescent Psychiatry and Mental Health, 12*(1), 1-10. https://doi.org/10.1186/s13034-017-0209-9.

Barnao, M., Ward, T., & Robertson, P. (2016). The good lives model: A new paradigm for forensic mental health. *Psychiatry, Psychology and Law, 23*(2), 288-301. https://doi.org/10.1080/13218719.2015.1054923.

Barnert, E. S., Perry, R., Azzi, V. F., Shetgiri, R., Ryan, G., Dudovitz, R., Zima, B., & Chung, P. J. (2015). Incarcerated youths' perspectives on protective factors and risk factors for juvenile offending: A qualitative analysis. *American Journal of Public Health, 105*(7), 1365-1371. https://doi.org/10.2105/ajph.2014.302228.

Barnes, J. C., & Beaver, K. M. (2010). An empirical examination of adolescence-limited offending: A direct test of Moffitt's maturity gap thesis. *Journal of Criminal Justice, 38*(6), 1176-1185. https://doi.org/10.1016/j.jcrimjus.2010.09.006.

Barnett, G., & Wood, J. L. (2008). Agency, relatedness, inner peace, and problem solving in sexual offending: How sexual offenders prioritize and operationalize their good livesconceptions. *SexAbuse, 20*(4),444-465.https://doi.org/10.1177/1079063208325202.

Barnett, G. D., Manderville-Norden, R., & Rakestrow, J. (2014). The good lives model or relapse prevention: What works better in facilitating change? *Sex Abuse, 26*(1), 3-33. https://doi.org/10.1177/1079063212474473.

Baron, S. W. (2004). General strain, street youth and crime: A test of Agnew's revised theory. *Criminology, 42*(2), 457-484. https://doi.org/10.1111/j.1745-9125.2004.tb00526.x.

Baron, S. W. (2007). Street youth, gender, financial strain, and crime: Exploring Broidy and Agnew's extension to general strain theory. *Deviant Behavior, 28*(3), 273-302. https://doi.org/10.1080/01639620701233217.

Baron, S. W. (2015). Differential social support, differential coercion, and organized criminal activities. *Justice Quarterly, 32*(6), 1089-1117. https://doi.org/10.1080/07418825.2014.887760.

Baron, S. W., & Hartnagel, T. F. (1998). Street youth and criminal violence. *Journal of Research in Crime and Delinquency, 35*(2), 166-192. https://doi.org/10.1177/0022427898035002003.

*Baroun, K. A. (2006). Relations among religiosity, health, happiness, and anxiety for Kuwaiti adolescents. *Psychological Reports, 99*(3), 717-722. https://doi.org/10.2466/pr0.99.3.717-722.

*Bartels, M., Cacioppo, J. T., van Beijsterveldt, T. C. E. M., & Boomsma, D. I. (2013). Exploring the association between well-being and psychopathology in adolescents. *Behavior Genetics, 43*(3), 177-190. https://doi.org/10.1007/s10519-013-9589-7.

Bartholomew, K. J., Ntoumanis, N., Ryan, R. M., Bosch, J. A., & Thøgersen-Ntoumani, C. (2011). Self-determination theory and diminished functioning: The role of interpersonal control and psychological need thwarting. *Personality and Social Psychology Bulletin, 37*(11), 1459-1473. https://doi.org/10.1177/0146167211413125.

Basanta, J. L., Fariña, F., & Arce, R. (2018). Risk–need–responsivity model: Contrasting criminogenic and noncriminogenic needs in high and low risk juvenile offenders. *Children and Youth Services Review, 85*, 137-142. https://doi.org/10.1016/j.childyouth.2017.12.024.

Bastiaansen, D., Koot, H. M., & Ferdinand, R. F. (2005). Determinants of quality of life in children with psychiatric disorders. *Quality of Life Research, 14*(6), 1599-1612. https://doi.org/10.1007/s11136-004-7711-2.

Baumeister, R. F., & Heatherton, T. F. (1996). Self-regulation failure: An overview. *Psychological Inquiry, 7*(1), 1-15. https://doi.org/10.1207/s15327965pli0701_1.

Baumeister, R. F., & Vohs, K. D. (2004). *Handbook of self-regulation: Research, theory, and applications*. Guilford.

Bearman, S. K., Schneiderman, R. L., & Zoloth, E. (2017). Building an evidence base for effective supervision practices: An analogue experiment of supervision to increase EBT fidelity. *Administration and Policy in Mental Health and Mental Health Services Research, 44*(2), 293-307. https://doi.org/10.1007/s10488-016-0723-8.

Beaudry, G., Yu, R., Långström, N., & Fazel, S. (2021). An updated systematic review and meta-regression analysis: Mental disorders among adolescents in juvenile detention and correctional facilities. *Journal of the American Academy of Child & Adolescent Psychiatry, 60*(1), 46-60. https://doi.org/10.1016/j.jaac.2020.01.015.

Becker, L. C. (1992). Good lives: Prolegomena. *Social Philosophy and Policy, 9*(2), 15-37. https://doi.org/10.1017/S0265052500001382.

Beggs, S. M. (2010). Within-treatment outcome among sexual offenders: A review. *Aggression and Violent Behavior, 15*(5), 369-379. https://doi.org/10.1016/j.avb.2010.06.005.

Ben-Arieh, A., Casas, F., Frønes, I., & Korbin, J. E. (2014a). *Handbook of child well-being: Theories, methods and policies in global perspective*. Springer.

Ben-Arieh, A., Casas, F., Frønes, I., & Korbin, J. E. (2014b). Multifaceted concept of child well-being. In A. Ben-Arieh, F. Casas, I. Frønes, & J. E. Korbin (Eds.), *Handbook of child well-being: Theories, methods and policies in global perspective* (pp. 1-27). Springer. https://doi.org/10.1007/978-90-481-9063-8_134.

*Ben-Zur, H. (2003). Happy adolescents: The link between subjective well-being, internal resources, and parental factors. *Journal of Youth and Adolescence, 32*(2), 67-79. https://doi.org/10.1023/a:1021864432505.

Berkowitz, L. (1989). Frustration-aggression hypothesis: Examination and reformulation. *Psychological Bulletin, 106*(1), 59-73. https://doi.org/10.1037/0033-2909.106.1.59.

Bernasco, W. (2013). *Offenders on offending: Learning about crime from criminals*. Routledge.

Berscheid, E. (2003). The human's greatest strength: Other humans. In L. G. Aspinwall & U. M. Staudinger (Eds.), *A psychology of human strengths: Fundamental questions and future directions for a positive psychology* (pp. 37-47). American Psychological Association. https://doi.org/10.1037/10566-003.

Bielas, H., Barra, S., Skrivanek, C., Aebi, M., Steinhausen, H. C., Bessler, C., & Plattner, B. (2016). The associations of cumulative adverse childhood experiences and irritability with mental disorders in detained male adolescent offenders. *Child and Adolescent Psychiatry and Mental Health, 10*(34), 1-10. https://doi.org/10.1186/s13034-016-0122-7.

Birgden, A. (2004). Therapeutic jurisprudence and responsivity: Finding the will and the way in offender rehabilitation. *Psychology, Crime & Law, 10*(3), 283-295. https://doi.org/10.1080/10683160410001662771.

*Blanca, M. J., Ferragut, M., Ortiz-Tallo, M., & Bendayan, R. (2017). Life satisfaction and character strengths in spanish early adolescents. *Journal of Happiness Studies*. https://doi.org/10.1007/s10902-017-9865-y.

*Blau, I., Goldberg, S., & Benolol, N. (2019). Purpose and life satisfaction during adolescence: The role of meaning in life, social support, and problematic digital use. *Journal of Youth Studies, 22*(7), 907-925. https://doi.org/10.1080/13676261.2018.1551614.

Blazak, R. (2001). White boys to terrorist men: Target recruitment of Nazi skinheads. *American Behavioral Scientist, 44*(6), 982-1000. https://doi.org/10.1177/00027640121956629.

*Bluth, K., & Blanton, P. W. (2014). Mindfulness and self-compassion: Exploring pathways to adolescent emotional well-being. *Journal of Child & Family Studies, 23*(7), 1298-1309. https://doi.org/10.1007/s10826-013-9830-2.

*Bluth, K., Campo, R. A., Futch, W. S., & Gaylord, S. A. (2017). Age and gender differences in the associations of self-compassion and emotional well-being in a large adolescent sample. *Journal of Youth and Adolescence, 46*(4), 840-853. https://doi.org/10.1007/s10964-016-0567-2.

Bonta, J., & Andrews, D. A. (2003). A commentary on Ward and Stewart's model of human needs. *Psychology, Crime, & Law, 9*(3), 215-218. https://doi.org/10.1080/10683/16031000112115.

Bonta, J., & Andrews, D. A. (2017). *The psychology of criminal conduct* (6th ed.). Taylor & Francis.

Boonmann, C., van Vugt, E. S., Jansen, L. M. C., Colins, O. F., Doreleijers, T. A. H., Stams, G. J. J. M., & Vermeiren, R. (2015). Mental disorders in juveniles who sexually offended: A meta-analysis. *Aggression and Violent Behavior, 24*, 241-249. https://doi.org/10.1016/j.avb.2015.06.003.

Borduin, C. M. (1999). Multisystemic treatment of criminality and violence in adolescents. *Journal of the American Academy of Child & Adolescent Psychiatry, 38*(3), 242-249. https://doi.org/10.1097/00004583-199903000-00009.

Bosma, A. Q., Kunst, M. J. J., Dirkzwager, A. J. E., & Nieuwbeerta, P. (2017). Treatment readiness as a determinant of treatment participation in a prison-based rehabilitation program: An exploratory study. *International Journal of Offender Therapy and Comparative Criminology, 61*(8), 857-873. https://doi.org/10.1177/0306624X15605609.

Boudreaux, M., & Ozer, D. (2013). Goal conflict, goal striving, and psychological well-being. *Motivation and Emotion, 37*(3), 433-443. https://doi.org/10.1007/s11031-012-9333-2.

Bouman, Y. H. A., Schene, A. H., & de Ruiter, C. (2009). Subjective well-being and recidivism in forensic psychiatric outpatients. *International Journal of Forensic Mental Health, 8*(4), 225-234. https://doi.org/10.1080/14999011003635647.

Bourgon, G., & Bonta, J. (2014). Reconsidering the responsivity principle: A way to move forward. *Federal Probation, 78*(2), 3-10.

*Bourke, L., & Geldens, P. M. (2007a). Subjective wellbeing and its meaning for young people in a rural Australian center. *Social Indicators Research, 82*(1), 165-187. https://doi.org/10.1007/s11205-006-9031-0.

Bourke, L., & Geldens, P. M. (2007b). What does wellbeing mean?: Perspectives of wellbeing among young people & youth workers in rural Victoria. *Youth Studies Australia, 26*(1), 41.

Bowlby, J. (1969). *Attachment and loss: Vol 1, Attachment.* Hogarth.

Bradburn, N. M. (1969). *The structure of psychological well-being.* Aldine.

Bradt, L., Pleysier, S., Put, J., Siongers, J., & Spruyt, B. (2019). *Jongeren in cijfers en letters 4: Bevindingen uit de JOP-monitor 4, de JOP-kindmonitor en de JOP-schoolmonitor 2.* Acco.

Braun, V., & Clarke, V. (2006). Using thematic analysis in psychology. *Qualitative Research in Psychology, 3*(2), 77-101. https://doi.org/10.1191/1478088706qp063oa.

Brenning, K. M., Antrop, I., Van Petegem, S., Soenens, B., De Meulenaere, J., Rodríguez-Meirinhos, A., & Vansteenkiste, M. (2019). I won't obey!: Psychologically controlling parenting and (non)-clinical adolescents' responses to rule-setting. *Journal of Clinical Psychology, 75*(6), 1034-1046. https://doi.org/10.1002/jclp.22750.

Brezina, T. (2020). Freedom of action, freedom of choice, and desistance from crime: Pitfalls and opportunities in the study of human agency. *Journal of Developmental and Life-Course Criminology, 6*(2), 224-244. https://doi.org/10.1007/s40865-019-00111-w.

Brezina, T., & Azimi, A. M. (2018). Social support, loyalty to delinquent peers, and offending: An elaboration and test of the differential social support hypothesis. *Deviant Behavior, 39*(5), 648-663. https://doi.org/10.1080/01639625.2017.1286190.

Brezina, T., & Topalli, V. (2012). Criminal self-efficacy: Exploring the correlates and consequences of a "successful criminal" identity. *Criminal Justice and Behavior, 39*(8), 1042-1062. https://doi.org/10.1177/0093854812438345.

*Bronk, K., Hill, P. L., Lapsley, D. K., Talib, T. L., & Finch, H. (2009). Purpose, hope, and life satisfaction in three age groups. *The Journal of Positive Psychology, 4*(6), 500-510. https://doi.org/10.1080/17439760903271439.

Bronk, K. C. (2011). The role of purpose in life in healthy identity formation: A grounded model. *New Directions for Youth Development, 2011*(132), 31-44. https://doi.org/10.1002/yd.426.

Bronk, K. C., & Finch, W. H. (2010). Adolescent characteristics by type of long-term aim in life. *Applied Developmental Science, 14*(1), 35-44. https://doi.org/10.1080/10888690903510331.

Brooks, M., & Khan, R. (2015). Psychosocial influences that motivate young offenders to engage in a non-custodial community intervention. *The Journal of Forensic Psychiatry & Psychology, 26*(3), 351-367. https://doi.org/10.1080/14789949.2015.1013973.

Brown, B. B., & Braun, M. T. (2013). Peer relations. In C. Proctor & P. A. Linley (Eds.), *Research, applications, and interventions for children and adolescents* (pp. 149-164). Springer.

Brown, K. W., & Ryan, R. M. (2004). Fostering healthy self-regulation from within and without: A self-determination theory perspective. In P. A. Linley & S. Joseph (Eds.), *Positive psychology in practice* (pp. 105-124). Wiley. https://doi.org/10.1002/9780470939338.ch7.

Brunstein, J. C. (1993). Personal goals and subjective well-being: A longitudinal study. *Journal of Personality and Social Psychology, 65*(5), 1061-1070. https://doi.org/10.1037/0022-3514.65.5.1061.

Brunstein, J. C., Schultheiss, O. C., & Grässman, R. (1998). Personal goals and emotional well-being: The moderating role of motive dispositions. *Journal of Personality and Social Psychology, 75*(2), 494-508. https://doi.org/10.1037//0022-3514.75.2.494.

Brunstein, J. C., Schultheiss, O. C., & Maier, G. W. (1999). The pursuit of personal goals. In J. Brandtstadter & R. M. Lerner (Eds.), *Action & self-development: Theory and research through the lifespan* (pp. 169-196). Sage Publications.

*Buelga, S., Musitu, G., Murgui, S., Pons, J., & Howard, V. N. (2008). Reputation, loneliness, satisfaction with life and aggressive behavior in adolescence. *The Spanish Journal of Psychology, 11*(1), 192-200. https://doi.org/10.1017/S1138741600004236.

Burgess, R. L., & Akers, R. L. (1966). A differential association-reinforcement theory of criminal behavior. *Social Problems, 14*(2), 128-147. https://doi.org/10.2307/798612.

*Burrow, A. L., O'Dell, A. C., & Hill, P. L. (2010). Profiles of a developmental asset: Youth purpose as a context for hope and well-being. *Journal of Youth and Adolescence, 39*(11), 1265-1273. https://doi.org/10.1007/s10964-009-9481-1.

Burrowes, N., & Needs, A. (2009). Time to contemplate change? A framework for assessing readiness to change with offenders. *Aggression and Violent Behavior, 14*(1), 39-49. https://doi.org/10.1016/j.avb.2008.08.003.

Bursik Jr, R. J., & Grasmick, H. G. (1993). Economic deprivation and neighborhood crime rates, 1960-1980. *Law & Society Review, 27*, 263-284. https://doi.org/10.2307/3053937.

Burt, C. H., & Simons, R. L. (2013). Self-control, thrill seeking, and crime: Motivation matters. *Criminal Justice and Behavior, 40*(11), 1326-1348. https://doi.org/10.1177/0093854813485575.

Busseri, M. A., & Sadava, S. W. (2011). A review of the tripartite structure of subjective well-being: Implications for conceptualization, operationalization, analysis, and synthesis. *Personality and Social Psychology Review: An Official Journal of the Society for Personality and Social Psychology, Inc, 15*(3), 290. https://doi.org/10.1177/1088868310391271.

Buunk, A. P., Peiro, J. M., Rocabert, E., & Dijkstra, P. (2016). Life satisfaction and status among adolescent law offenders. *Criminal Behavior and Mental Health, 26*(2), 94-100. https://doi.org/10.1002/cbm.1971.

Byrne, G. (2020). How the good lives model can complement mentalization-based treatments for individuals who have offended with anti-social personality disorder and general forensic mental health needs: Practice update. *International Journal of Offender Therapy and Comparative Criminology, 64*(15), 1587-1606. https://doi.org/10.1177/0306624x20928017.

Caffray, C. M., & Schneider, S. L. (2000). Why do they do it? Affective motivators in adolescents' decisions to participate in risk behaviours. *Cognition and Emotion, 14*(4), 543-576. https://doi.org/10.1080/026999300402790.

*Calmeiro, L., Camacho, I., & de Matos, M. G. (2018). Life satisfaction in adolescents: The role of individual and social health assets. *Spanish Journal of Psychology, 21*, Article e23. https://doi.org/10.1017/sjp.2018.24.

Cantor, N., & Sanderson, C. A. (1999). Life task participation and well-being: The importance of taking part in daily life. In D. Kahneman, E. Diener, & N. Schwarz (Eds.), *Well-being: Foundations of hedonic psychology* (pp. 230-243). Sage Publications.

Cantril, H. (1965). *Pattern of human concerns.* Rutgers University Press.

Carl, L. C., Schmucker, M., & Lösel, F. (2020). Predicting attrition and engagement in the treatment of young offenders. *International Journal of Offender Therapy and Comparative Criminology, 64*(4), 355-374. https://doi.org/10.1177/0306624X19877593.

Carlquist, E., Ulleberg, P., Delle Fave, A., Nafstad, H. E., & Blakar, R. M. (2017). Everyday understandings of happiness, good life, and satisfaction: Three different facets of well-being. *Applied Research in Quality of Life, 12*, 481-505. https://doi.org/10.1007/s11482-016-9472-9.

Carroll, A., Gordon, K., Haynes, M., & Houghton, S. (2013). Goal setting and self-efficacy among delinquent, at-risk and not at-risk adolescents. *A Multidisciplinary Research Publication, 42*(3), 431-443. https://doi.org/10.1007/s10964-012-9799-y.

*Casas, F., Bălţătescu, S., Bertran, I., González, M., & Hatos, A. (2013). School satisfaction among adolescents: Testing different indicators for its measurement and its relationship with overall life satisfaction and subjective well-being in Romania and Spain. *Social Indicators Research, 111*(3), 665-681. https://doi.org/10.1007/s11205-012-0025-9.

*Casas, F., Bello, A., Gonzalez, M., & Aligue, M. (2013). Children's subjective well-being measured using a composite index: What impacts Spanish first-year secondary education students' subjective well-being? *Child Indicators Research, 6*(3), 433-460. https://doi.org/10.1007/s12187-013-9182-x.

*Casas, F., Estrada, R. B., Ramírez, C. F., Carrasco, M. G., Teijón, A. T., Pigem, E. N., & Rodríguez Rodríguez, J. M. (2005). Values and their influence on the life satisfaction of adolescents aged 12 to 16: A study of some correlates. *Psychology in Spain, 9*, 21-33.

*Casas, F., Figuer, C., González, M., & Malo, S. (2007). The values adolescents aspire to, their well-being and the values parents aspire to for their children. *Social Indicators Research, 84*(3), 271-290. https://doi.org/10.1007/s11205-007-9141-3.

*Casas, F., Figuer, C., González, M., Malo, S., Alsinet, C., & Subarroca, S. (2007). The well-being of 12- to 16-year-old adolescents and their parents: Results from 1999 to 2003 Spanish samples. *Social Indicators Research, 83*(1), 87-115. https://doi.org/10.1007/s11205-006-9059-1.

*Casas, F., González, M., Figuer, C., & Malo, S. (2009). Satisfaction with spirituality, satisfaction with religion and personal well-being among Spanish adolescents and young university students. *Applied Research in Quality of Life, 4*(1), 23-45. https://doi.org/10.1007/s11482-009-9066-x.

*Casas, F., Sarriera, J. C., Alfaro, J., González, M., Bedin, L., Abs, D., Figuer, C., & Valdenegro, B. (2015). Reconsidering life domains that contribute to subjective well-being among adolescents with data from three countries. *Journal of Happiness Studies, 16*(2), 491-513. https://doi.org/10.1007/s10902-014-9520-9.

Case, S., & Haines, K. (2007). Offending by young people: A further risk factor analysis. *Security Journal, 20*(2), 96-11. https://doi.org/10.1057/palgrave.sj.8350031.

Case, S., & Haines, K. (2015). Children first, offenders second: The centrality of engagement in positive youth justice. *The Howard Journal of Criminal Justice, 54*(2), 157-175. https://doi.org/10.1111/hojo.12099.

Casey, S., Day, A., & Howells, K. (2005). The application of the transtheoretical model to offender populations: Some critical issues. *Legal and Criminological Psychology, 10*(2), 157-171. https://doi.org/10.1348/135532505X36714.

Casey, S., Day, A., Howells, K., & Ward, T. (2007). Assessing suitability for offender rehabilitation: Development and validation of the Treatment Readiness Questionnaire. *Criminal Justice and Behavior, 34*(11), 1427-1440. https://doi.org/10.1177/0093854807305827.

Cassandro, V. J., & Simonton, D. K. (2003). Creativity and genius. In C. L. M. Keyes & J. Haidt (Eds.), *Flourishing: Positive psychology and the life well-lived* (pp. 163-183). American Psychological Association.

*Cava, M. J., Buelga, S., & Musitu, G. (2014). Parental communication and life satisfaction in adolescence. *Spanish Journal of Psychology, 17*, E98. https://doi.org/10.1017/sjp.2014.107.

*Çelik, E. (2015). Mediating and moderating role of sensation seeking in the relation between self-concealmentand life satisfaction in adolescents. *Egitim Ve Bilim-Education and Science, 40*(181), 349-361. https://doi.org/10.15390/eb.2015.4436.

*Çelik, E., Özcan, N., & Turan, M. E. (2014). The perception of school inefficacy, social prescribed perfectionism and self-appraisal as predictors of adolescents' life satisfaction. *Journal of Theory & Practice in Education (JTPE), 10*(4), 1143-1155.

Chaplin, L. N. (2009). Please may I have a bike? Better yet, may I have a hug? An examination of children's and adolescents' happiness. *Journal of Happiness Studies, 10*(5), 541-562. https://doi.org/10.1007/s10902-008-9108-3.

Chen, B., Vansteenkiste, M., Beyers, W., Boone, L., Deci, E. L., Van der Kaap-Deeder, J., Duriez, B., Lens, W., Matos, L., & Mouratidis, A. (2015). Basic psychological need satisfaction, need frustration, and need strength across four cultures. *Motivation and Emotion, 39*(2), 216-236. https://doi.org/10.1007/s11031-014-9450-1.

Chen, F., Jing, Y., Hayes, A., & Lee, J. (2013). Two concepts or two approaches? A bifactor analysis of psychological and subjective well-being. *An Interdisciplinary Forum on Subjective Well-Being, 14*(3), 1033-1068. https://doi.org/10.1007/s10902-012-9367-x.

*Chen, W., Niu, G. F., Zhang, D. J., Fan, C. Y., Tian, Y., & Zhou, Z. K. (2016). Socioeconomic status and life satisfaction in Chinese adolescents: Analysis of self-esteem as a mediator and optimism as a moderator. *Personality and Individual Differences, 95*, 105-109. https://doi.org/10.1016/j.paid.2016.01.036.

*Chen, W., Zhang, D. J., Pan, Y. G., Hu, T. Q., Liu, G., & Luo, S. L. (2017). Perceived social support and self-esteem as mediators of the relationship between parental attachment and life satisfaction among Chinese adolescents. *Personality and Individual Differences, 108*, 98-102. https://doi.org/10.1016/j.paid.2016.12.009.

*Chirkov, V. I., & Ryan, R. M. (2001). Parent and teacher autonomy-support in Russian and US adolescents – common effects on well-being and academic motivation. *Journal of Cross-Cultural Psychology, 32*(5), 618-635. https://doi.org/10.1177/00220221010320 05006.

Chitsabesan, P., Kroll, L., Bailey, S., Kenning, C., Sneider, S., MacDonald, W., & Theodosiou, L. (2006). Mental health needs of young offenders in custody and in the community. *The British Journal of Psychiatry: The Journal of Mental Science, 188*, 534-540. https://doi.org/10.1192/bjp.bp.105.010116.

Christle, C. A., Jolivette, K., & Nelson, C. M. (2005). Breaking the school to prison pipeline: Identifying school risk and protective factors for youth delinquency. *Exceptionality, 13*(2), 69-88. https://doi.org/10.1207/s15327035ex1302_2.

Chu, C. M., Koh, L. L., Zeng, G., & Teoh, J. (2015). Youth who sexual offended: Primary human goods and offense pathways. *Sex Abuse, 27*(2), 151-172. https://doi.org/10.1177/1079063213499188.

*Chui, W. H., & Wong, M. Y. H. (2016). Gender differences in happiness and life satisfaction among adolescents in Hong Kong: Relationships and self-concept. *Social Indicators Research, 125*(3), 1035-1051. https://doi.org/10.1007/s11205-015-0867-z.

Chung, H. H., & Elias, M. (1996). Patterns of adolescent involvement in problem behaviors: Relationship to self-efficacy, social competence, and life events. *American Journal of Community Psychology, 24*(6), 771-784. https://doi.org/10.1007/bf02511034.

Church, A. T., Katigbak, M. S., Locke, K. D., Zhang, H., Shen, J., De Jesús Vargas-Flores, J., Ibáñez-Reyes, J., Tanaka-Matsumi, J., Curtis, G. J., Cabrera, H. F., Mastor, K. A., Alvarez, J. M., Ortiz, F. A., Simon, J.-Y. R., & Ching, C. M. (2013). Need satisfaction and well-being. *Journal of Cross-Cultural Psychology, 44*(4), 507-534. https://doi.org/10.1177/0022022112466590.

*Cikrikci, O., & Gencdogan, B. (2017). The effects of attachment styles and belongingness on life satisfaction among adolescents. *International Journal of Happiness and Development, 3*(3), 241-255. https://doi.org/10.1504/ijhd.2017.084073.

*Civitci, N., & Civitci, A. (2009). Self-esteem as mediator and moderator of the relationship between loneliness and life satisfaction in adolescents. *Personality and Individual Differences, 47*(8), 954-958. https://doi.org/10.1016/j.paid.2009.07.022.

*Clark, M., Amar-Singh, H. S., & Hashim, L. (2014). The subjective well-being of Malaysian school children: Grade level, gender and ethnicity. *Psychology, 5*(12), 1453-1462. https://doi.org/10.4236/psych.2014.512156.

Clark, M. D. (1998). Strength-based practice: The ABC's of working with adolescents who don't want to work with you. *Federal Probation, 62*, 46.

Clark, M. D. (1999). The ABCs of increasing motivation with juvenile offenders. *Juvenile and Family Court Journal, 50*(1), 33-42. https://doi.org/10.1111/j.1755-6988.1999.tb01276.x.

Clinkinbeard, S. S., & Murray, C. I. (2012). Perceived support, belonging, and possible selves strategies among incarcerated juvenile offenders. *Journal of Applied Social Psychology, 42*(5), 1218-1240. https://doi.org/10.1111/j.1559-1816.2011.00884.x.

Cloward, R. A., & Ohlin, L. E. (1960). *Delinquency and opportunity: A study of delinquent gangs*. Routledge.

*Coccia, C., Darling, C. A., Rehm, M., Cui, M., & Sathe, S. K. (2012). Adolescent health, stress and life satisfaction: The paradox of indulgent parenting. *Stress Health, 28*(3), 211-221. https://doi.org/10.1002/smi.1426.

Cohen, A. K. (1955). *Delinquent boys; The culture of the gang*. The Free Press.

*Cohen, D., Greene, J. A., Toyinbo, P. A., & Siskowski, C. T. (2012). Impact of family caregiving by youth on their psychological well-being: A latent trait analysis. *The Journal of Behavioral Health Services & Research, 39*(3), 245-256. https://doi.org/10.1007/s11414-011-9264-9.

Cohen, J. (1988). *Statistical power analysis for the behavioral sciences*. Academic Press.

Cohen, L. E., & Felson, M. (1979). Social change and crime rate trends: A routine activity approach. *American Sociological Review, 44*(4), 588-608. https://doi.org/10.2307/2094589.

Cohen, P. J., Glaser, B. A., Calhoun, G. B., Bradshaw, C. P., & Petrocelli, J. V. (2005). Examining readiness for change: A preliminary evaluation of the University of Rhode Island Change Assessment with incarcerated adolescents. *Measurement and Evaluation in Counseling and Development, 38*(1), 45-62. https://doi.org/10.1080/07481756.2005.11909768.

Colins, O., Vermeiren, R., Vreugdenhil, C., van den Brink, W., Doreleijers, T., & Broekaert, E. (2010). Psychiatric disorders in detained male adolescents: A systematic literature review. *Canadian Journal of Psychiatry, 55*(4), 255-263. https://doi.org/10.1177/070674371005500409.

Colins, O. F., Vermeiren, R., Schuyten, G., & Broekaert, E. (2009). Psychiatric disorders in property, violent, and versatile offending detained male adolescents. *American Journal of Orthopsychiatry, 79*(1), 31-38. https://doi.org/10.1037/a0015337.

Colvin, M., Cullen, F. T., & Vander Ven, T. (2002). Coercion, social support, and crime: An emerging theoretical consensus. *Criminology, 40*(1), 19-42. https://doi.org/10.1111/j.1745-9125.2002.tb00948.x.

Cooper, H. (2017). *Research synthesis and meta-analysis: A step-by-step approach* (5th ed.). Sage Publications.

Cops, D., & Pleysier, S. (2014). Usual suspects, ideal victims and vice versa: The relationship between youth offending and victimization and the mediating influence of risky lifestyles. *European Journal of Criminology, 11*(3), 361-378. https://doi.org/10.1177/1477370813500886.

Cording, J. R., Beggs, S. M., & Grace, R. C. (2016). Challenges for the theory and application of dynamic risk factors. *Psychology, Crime & Law, 22*(1-2), 84-103. https://doi.org/10.1080/1068316X.2015.1111367.

Cottle, C. C., Lee, R. J., & Heilbrun, K. (2001). The prediction of criminal recidivism in juveniles: A meta-analysis. *Criminal Justice and Behavior, 28*(3), 367-394. https://doi.org/10.1177/0093854801028003005.

Cox, W. M., & Klinger, E. (2004). *Handbook of motivational counseling: Concepts, approaches and assessment.* Wiley.

Craig, J. M., Wilson, A. D., Baglivio, M. T., Wolff, K. T., Piquero, A. R., & Epps, N. (2018). Why they did it? Sex differences in the impact of mental health and substance use on motivations for offending. *Crime & Delinquency, 64*(6), 723-757. https://doi.org/10.1177/0011128717718489.

*Crede, J., Wirthwein, L., McElvany, N., & Steinmayr, R. (2015). Adolescents' academic achievement and life satisfaction: The role of parents' education. *Frontiers in Psychology, 6*, 52, 1-8. https://doi.org/10.3389/fpsyg.2015.00052.

Creswell, J. W., & Poth, C. N. (2016). *Qualitative inquiry and research design: Choosing among five approaches.* Sage Publications.

Csikszentmihalyi, M. (2014). *Applications of flow in human development and education.* Dordrecht: Springer.

Csikszentmihalyi, M. (2000). *Beyond boredom and anxiety.* Jossey-Bass.

Cuellar, A. E., Markowitz, S., & Libby, A. M. (2004). Mental health and substance abuse treatment and juvenile crime. *Journal of Mental Health Policy and Economics,* 59-68. https://doi.org/10.3386/w9952.

Cuevas, C., Wolff, K. T., & Baglivio, M. T. (2017). Self-efficacy, aspirations, and residential placement outcomes: Why belief in a prosocial self matters. *Journal of Criminal Justice, 52,* 1-11. https://doi.org/10.1016/j.jcrimjus.2017.06.006.

Cullen, F. T., Williams, N., & Wright, J. P. (1997). Work conditions and juvenile delinquency: Is youth employment criminogenic? *Criminal Justice Policy Review, 8*(2-3), 119-143. https://doi.org/10.1177/088740349700800201.

Cummins, R. A. (1996). The domains of life satisfaction: An attempt to order chaos. *Social Indicators Research, 38*(3), 303-328. https://doi.org/10.1007/BF00292050.

Cummins, R. A. (2000). Personal income and subjective well-being: A review. *Journal of Happiness Studies, 1*(2), 133-158. https://doi.org/10.1023/A:1010079728426.

Curtis, N. M., Ronan, K. R., & Borduin, C. M. (2004). Multisystemic treatment: A meta-analysis of outcome studies. *Journal of Family Psychology, 18*(3), 411-419. https://doi.org/10.1037/0893-3200.18.3.411.

Damon, W., Menon, J., & Bronk, K. C. (2003). The development of purpose during adolescence. *Applied Developmental Science, 7*(3), 119-128. https://doi.org/10.1207/S1532480XADS0703_2.

d'Andrade, R. G. (1995). *The development of cognitive anthropology.* Cambridge University Press.

*Danielsen, A. G., Samdal, O., Hetland, J., & Wold, B. (2009). School-related social support and students' perceived life satisfaction. *The Journal of Educational Research, 102*(4), 303-320. https://doi.org/10.3200/JOER.102.4.303-320.

Dankulincova Veselska, Z., Jirasek, I., Veselsky, P., Jiraskova, M., Plevova, I., Tavel, P., & Madarasova Geckova, A. (2018). Spirituality but not religiosity is associated with better health and higher life satisfaction among adolescents. *International Journal of Environmental Research and Public Health, 15*(12), 1-9. https://doi.org/10.3390/ijerph15122781.

*Datu, J. A. D., & Mateo, N. J. (2015). Gratitude and life satisfaction among Filipino adolescents: The mediating role of meaning in life. *International Journal for the Advancement of Counselling, 37*(2), 198-206. https://doi.org/10.1007/s10447-015-9238-3.

Davids, E. L., Roman, N. V., & Kerchhoff, L. J. (2017). Adolescent goals and aspirations in search of psychological well-being: From the perspective of self-determination theory.

South African Journal of Psychology, 47(1), 121-132. https://doi.org/10.1177/0081246316653744.

Day, A., Bryan, J., Davey, L., & Casey, S. (2006). The process of change in offender rehabilitation programmes. *Psychology, Crime & Law, 12*(5), 473-487. https://doi.org/10.1080/10683160500151209.

Day, A., Casey, S., Ward, T., Howells, K., & Vess, J. (2010). *Transitions to better lives: Offender readiness and rehabilitation*. Taylor & Francis.

De Bus, S., & Put, J. (2020). Verhouding jeugddelinquentie en jeugdhulp: De derde interventiegrond. *Panopticon, 41*(5), 478.

de Ruigh, E. L., Popma, A., Twisk, J. W. R., Wiers, R. W., van der Baan, H. S., Vermeiren, R., & Jansen, L. M. C. (2019). Predicting quality of life during and post detention in incarcerated juveniles. *Quality of Life Research, 28*(7), 1813-1823. https://doi.org/10.1007/s11136-019-02160-6.

de Ruiter, C., & Hildebrand, M. (2009). *Youth level of service/case management inventory. Handleiding*. Pearson Assessment.

de Swart, J. J. W., van den Broek, H., Stams, G. J. J. M., Asscher, J. J., van der Laan, P. H., Holsbrink-Engels, G. A., & van der Helm, G. H. P. (2012). The effectiveness of institutional youth care over the past three decades: A meta-analysis. *Children and Youth Services Review, 34*(9), 1818-1824. https://doi.org/10.1016/j.childyouth.2012.05.015.

de Valk, S., Kuiper, C., van der Helm, G. H. P., Maas, A. J. J. A., & Stams, G. J. J. M. (2019). Repression in residential youth care: A qualitative study examining the experiences of adolescents in open, secure and forensic institutions. *Journal of Adolescent Research, 34*(6), 757-782. https://doi.org/10.1177/0743558417719188.

de Vries, S. L. A., Hoeve, M., Asscher, J. J., & Stams, G. J. J. M. (2018). The long-term effects of the youth crime prevention program "New Perspectives" on delinquency and recidivism. *International Journal of Offender Therapy and Comparative Criminology, 62*(12), 3639-3661. https://doi.org/10.1177/0306624X17751161.

de Vries, S. L. A., Hoeve, M., Wibbelink, C. J. M., Asscher, J. J., & Stams, G. J. J. M. (2017). A randomized controlled trial of the effectiveness of the youth crime prevention program 'New Perspectives'(NP): Post-treatment changes and moderator effects. *Children and Youth Services Review, 82*, 413-426. https://doi.org/10.1016/j.childyouth.2017.10.011.

De Wachter, D. (2019). *De kunst van het ongelukkig zijn*. Lannoo Meulenhoff-Belgium.

Deci, E. L., & Ryan, R. M. (2000). The "what" and "why" of goal pursuits: Human needs and the self-determination of behavior. *Psychological Inquiry, 11*(4), 227-268. https://doi.org/10.1207/S15327965PLI1104_01.

Deci, E. L., & Ryan, R. M. (2008). Facilitating optimal motivation and psychological well-being across life's domains. *Canadian Psychology/Psychologie Canadienne, 49*(1), 14-23. https://doi.org/10.1037/0708-5591.49.1.14.

Del Bove, G., Caprara, G. V., Pastorelli, C., & Paciello, M. (2008). Juvenile firesetting in Italy: Relationship to aggression, psychopathology, personality, self-efficacy, and school functioning. *European Child & Adolescent Psychiatry, 17*(4), 235-244. https://doi.org/10.1007/s00787-007-0664-6.

DeLisi, M., & Vaughn, M. G. (2008). The Gottfredson–Hirschi critiques revisited: Reconciling self-control theory, criminal careers, and career criminals. *International Journal of Offender Therapy and Comparative Criminology, 52*(5), 520-537. https://doi.org/10.1177/0306624X07308553.

Delle Fave, A., Brdar, I., Freire, T., Vella-Brodrick, D., & Wissing, M. (2011). The eudaimonic and hedonic components of happiness: Qualitative and quantitative findings. *An International and Interdisciplinary Journal for Quality-of-Life Measurement, 100*(2), 185-207. https://doi.org/10.1007/s11205-010-9632-5.

Demuth, S., & Brown, S. L. (2004). Family structure, family processes, and adolescent delinquency: The significance of parental absence versus parental gender. *Journal of Research in Crime and Delinquency, 41*(1), 58-81. https://doi.org/10.1177/0022427803256236.

Den Uyl, D. J. (1991). *The virtue of prudence*. P. Lang.

Derzon, J. H. (2010). The correspondence of family features with problem, aggressive, criminal, and violent behavior: A meta-analysis. *Journal of Experimental Criminology, 6*(3), 263-292. https://doi.org/10.1007/s11292-010-9098-0.

Desmarais, S. L., Simons-Rudolph, J., Brugh, C. S., Schilling, E., & Hoggan, C. (2017). The state of scientific knowledge regarding factors associated with terrorism. *Journal of Threat Assessment and Management, 4*(4), 180-209. https://doi.org/10.1037/tam0000090.

Desmond, S. A., Morgan, K. H., & Kikuchi, G. (2010). Religious development: How (and why) does religiosity change from adolescence to young adulthood? *Sociological Perspectives, 53*(2), 247-270. https://doi.org/10.1525/sop.2010.53.2.247.

DiClemente, C. C., Corno, C. M., Graydon, M. M., Wiprovnick, A. E., & Knoblach, D. J. (2017). Motivational interviewing, enhancement, and brief interventions over the last decade: A review of reviews of efficacy and effectiveness. *Psychology of Addictive Behaviors, 31*(8), 862-887. https://doi.org/10.1037/adb0000318.

DiClemente, C. C., & Velasquez, M. M. (2002). Motivational interviewing and the stages of change. In W. R. Miller & S. Rolnick (Eds.), *Motivational interviewing: Preparing people for change* (2nd ed., pp. 201-216). Guilford.

Diener, E. (2006). Guidelines for national indicators of subjective well-being and ill-being. *The Official Journal of the International Society for Quality-of-Life Studies, 1*(2), 151-157. https://doi.org/10.1007/s11482-006-9007-x.

Diener, E., Emmons, R. A., Larsen, R. J., & Griffin, S. (1985). The satisfaction with life scale. *Journal of Personality Assessment, 49*(1), 71-75. https://doi.org/10.1207/s15327752jpa4901_13.

Diener, E., & Fujita, F. (1995). Resources, personal strivings, and subjective well-being: A nomothetic and idiographic approach. *Journal of Personality and Social Psychology, 68*(5), 926-935. https://doi.org/10.1037/0022-3514.68.5.926.

Diener, E., Fujita, F., Tay, L., & Biswas-Diener, R. (2012). Purpose, mood, and pleasure in predicting satisfaction judgments. *An International and Interdisciplinary Journal for Quality-of-Life Measurement, 105*(3), 333-341. https://doi.org/10.1007/s11205-011-9787-8.

Diener, E., Inglehart, R., & Tay, L. (2013). Theory and validity of life satisfaction scales. *An International and Interdisciplinary Journal for Quality-of-Life Measurement, 112*(3), 497-527. https://doi.org/10.1007/s11205-012-0076-y.

Diener, E., Sandvik, E., Pavot, W., & Gallagher, D. (1991). Response artifacts in the measurement of subjective well-being. *An International and Interdisciplinary Journal for Quality-of-Life Measurement, 24*(1), 35-56. https://doi.org/10.1007/BF00292649.

Diener, E., Scollon, C. K. N., Oishi, S., Dzokoto, V., & Suh, E. (2000). Positivity and the construction of life satisfaction judgments: Global happiness is not the sum of its parts. *Journal of Happiness Studies, 1*(2), 159-176. https://doi.org/10.1023/A:1010031813405.

Diener, E., Suh, E. M., Lucas, R. E., & Smith, H. L. (1999). Subjective well-being: Three decades of progress. *Psychological Bulletin, 125*(2), 276-302. https://doi.org/10.1037/0033-2909.125.2.276.

Diener, E., Tay, L., & Myers, D. G. (2011). The religion paradox: If religion makes people happy, why are so many dropping out? *Journal of Personality and Social Psychology, 101*(6), 1278-1290. https://doi.org/10.1037/a0024402.

Diener, E., Wirtz, D., Tov, W., Kim-Prieto, C., Choi, D. W., Oishi, S., & Biswas-Diener, R. (2010). New well-being measures: Short scales to assess flourishing and positive and negative feelings. *Social Indicators Research, 97*(2), 143-156. https://doi.org/10.1007/s11205-009-9493-y.

Dienst Justitiële Inrichtingen. (2021). *Informatieblad Kleinschalige Voorziening Justitiële Jeugd*. Den Haag.

DiGiuseppe, R., Linscott, J., & Jilton, R. (1996). Developing the therapeutic alliance in child—adolescent psychotherapy. *Applied and Preventive Psychology, 5*(2), 85-100. https://doi.org/10.1016/S0962-1849(96)80002-3.

Dijkstra, J. K., Kretschmer, T., Pattiselanno, K., Franken, A., Harakeh, Z., Vollebergh, W., & Veenstra, R. (2015). Explaining adolescents' delinquency and substance use: A test of the maturity gap: The SNARE study. *Journal of Research in Crime and Delinquency, 52*(5), 747-767. https://doi.org/10.1177/0022427815582249.

Dijkstra, J. K., Lindenberg, S., Veenstra, R., Steglich, C., Isaacs, J., Card, N. A., & Hodges, E. V. (2010). Influence and selection processes in weapon carrying during adolescence: The roles of status, aggression, and vulnerability. *Criminology, 48*(1), 187-220. https://doi.org/10.1111/j.1745-9125.2010.00183.x.

DiPierro-Sutton, M., Fite, P. J., & Gudiño, O. (2021). Assessing the links between internalizing symptoms and treatment motivation in incarcerated juveniles. *Children and Youth Services Review, 121*, 105879. https://doi.org/10.1016/j.childyouth.2020.105879.

*Diseth, Å., Danielsen, A. G., & Samdal, O. (2012). A path analysis of basic need support, self-efficacy, achievement goals, life satisfaction and academic achievement level among secondary school students. *Educational Psychology, 32*(3), 335-354. https://doi.org/10.1080/01443410.2012.657159.

Dishion, T. J., Spracklen, K. M., Andrews, D. W., & Patterson, G. R. (1996). Deviancy training in male adolescent friendships. *Behavior Therapy, 27*(3), 373-390. https://doi.org/10.1016/S0005-7894(96)80023-2.

Dishion, T. J., & Tipsord, J. M. (2011). Peer contagion in child and adolescent social and emotional development. *Annual Review of Psychology, 62*, 189-214. https://doi.org/10.1146/annurev.psych.093008.100412.

Dittmar, H., Bond, R., Hurst, M., & Kasser, T. (2014). The relationship between materialism and personal well-being: A meta-analysis. *Journal of Personality and Social Psychology, 107*(5), 879-924. https://doi.org/10.1037/a0037409.

Dobransky, P. (1999). *Mind OS: How the "Operating System of the Human Mind" is the ultimate solution to every personal or business problem* [Unpublished manuscript]. Denver, Colorado.

Dollard, J., Doob, L., Miller, N., Mower, O., & Sears, R. (1939). *Frustration and aggression.* Yale University Press. https://doi.org/10.1037/10022-000.

Dowden, C., & Andrews, D. A. (1999a). What works for female offenders: A meta-analytic review. *Crime & Delinquency, 45*(4), 438-452. https://doi.org/10.1177/0011128799045004002.

Dowden, C., & Andrews, D. A. (1999b). What works in young offender treatment: A meta-analysis. *Forum on Corrections Research, 11*, 21-24.

Dowden, C., & Andrews, D. A. (2000). Effective correctional treatment and violent reoffending: A meta-analysis. *Canadian Journal of Criminology, 42*, 449-467. https://doi.org/10.3138/cjcrim.42.4.449.

Doyal, L., & Gough, I. (1991). *A theory of human need.* Palgrave Macmillan.

Drieschner, K. H., & Verschuur, J. (2010). Treatment engagement as a predictor of premature treatment termination and treatment outcome in a correctional outpatient sample. *Criminal Behaviour and Mental Health, 20*(2), 86-99. https://doi.org/10.1002/cbm.757.

Drozda, C. (2006). Juveniles performing auto theft: An exploratory study into a deviant leisure lifestyle. *Leisure/Loisir, 30*(1), 111-132. https://doi.org/10.1080/14927713.2006.9651344.

Dubow, E. F., Arnett, M., Smith, K., & Ippolito, M. F. (2001). Predictors of future expectations of inner-city children: A 9-month prospective study. *The Journal of Early Adolescence, 21*(1), 5-28. https://doi.org/10.1177/0272431601021001001.

Duckworth, A. L., Steen, T. A., & Seligman, M. E. P. (2005). Positive psychology in clinical practice. *Annual Review of Clinical Psychology, 1*, 629-651. https://doi.org/10.1146/annurev.clinpsy.1.102803.144154.

Easterbrook, M. J., Wright, M. L., Dittmar, H., & Banerjee, R. (2014). Consumer culture ideals, extrinsic motivations, and well-being in children. *European Journal of Social Psychology, 44*(4), 349-359. https://doi.org/10.1002/ejsp.2020.

Easterlin, R. A. (1995). Will raising the incomes of all increase the happiness of all? *Journal of Economic Behavior and Organization, 27*(1), 35-47. https://doi.org/10.1016/0167-2681(95)00003-B.

Edwards, R., Beech, A. R., Bishopp, D., Erikson, M., Friendship, C., & Charlesworth, L. (2005). Predicting dropout from a residential programme for adolescent sexual abusers using pre-treatment variables and implications for recidivism. *Journal of Sexual Aggression, 11*(2), 139-155. https://doi.org/10.1080/13552600500063641.

Eid, M., & Diener, E. (2004). Global judgments of subjective well-being: Situational variability and long-term stability. *An International and Interdisciplinary Journal for Quality-of-Life Measurement, 65*(3), 245-277. https://doi.org/10.1023/B:SOCI.0000003801.89195.bc.

Eid, M., & Larsen, R. J. (2008). *The science of subjective well-being*. Guilford.

Elling, M., & Melissen, M. (2007). *Handboek Nieuwe Perspectieven*. Adviesbureau Van Montfoort.

Elliot, A. J. (1999). Approach and avoidance motivation and achievement goals. *Educational Psychologist, 34*(3), 169-189. https://doi.org/10.1207/s15326985ep3403_3.

Elliot, A. J., & Church, M. A. (1997). A hierarchical model of approach and avoidance achievement motivation. *Journal of Personality and Social Psychology, 72*(1), 218-232. https://doi.org/10.1037/0022-3514.72.1.218.

Elliot, A. J., & Harackiewicz, J. M. (1996). Approach and avoidance achievement goals and intrinsic motivation: A mediational analysis. *Journal of Personality and Social Psychology, 70*(3), 461-475. https://doi.org/10.1037/0022-3514.70.3.461.

Elliot, A. J., Sheldon, K. M., & Church, M. A. (1997). Avoidance personal goals and subjective well-being. *Personality and Social Psychology Bulletin, 23*(9), 915-927. https://doi.org/10.1177/0146167297239001.

Emmons, R. A. (1986). Personal strivings: An approach to personality and subjective well-being. *Journal of Personality and Social Psychology, 51*(5), 1058. https://doi.org/10.1037/0022-3514.51.5.1058.

Emmons, R. A. (1989). The personal striving approach to personality. In L. A. Pervin (Ed.), *Goal concepts in personality and social psychology* (pp. 87-126). Lawrence Erlbaum Associates, Inc.

Emmons, R. A. (1996). Striving and feeling: Personal goals and subjective well-being. In P. M. Gollwitzer & J. A. Bargh (Eds.), *The psychology of action: Linking cognition and motivation to behavior* (pp. 314-337). Guilford.

Emmons, R. A. (1999). *The psychology of ultimate concerns: Motivation and spirituality in personality*. Guilford.

Emmons, R. A. (2003). Personal goals, life meaning, and virtue: Wellsprings of a positive life. In C. L. M. Keyes & J. Haidt (Eds.), *Flourishing: Positive psychology and the life well-lived* (pp. 105-128). American Psychological Association. https://doi.org/10.1037/10594-005.

Emmons, R. A. (2005). Striving for the sacred: Personal goals, life meaning, and religion. *Journal of Social Issues, 61*(4), 731-745. https://doi.org/10.1111/j.1540-4560.2005.00429.x.

Emmons, R. A., Cheung, C., & Tehrani, K. (1998). Assessing spirituality through personal goals: Implications for research on religion and subjective well-being. *An International and Interdisciplinary Journal for Quality-of-Life Measurement, 45*(1), 391-422. https://doi.org/10.1023/A:1006926720976.

Emmons, R. A., & Diener, E. (1986). A goal-affect analysis of everyday situational choices. *Journal of Research in Personality, 20*(3), 309-326. https://doi.org/10.1016/0092-6566(86)90137-6.

Erikson, E. H. (1968). *Identity: Youth and crisis*. WW Norton & company.

Eryılmaz, A. (2018). Comparison of offender and non-offender young men to setting goals for life and attributing meaning to life. *Journal of Religion and Health, 57*(4), 1350-1362. https://doi.org/10.1007/s10943-017-0478-x.

Farnworth, L. (2000). Time use and leisure occupations of young offenders. *American Journal of Occupational Therapy, 54*(3), 315-325. https://doi.org/10.5014/ajot.54.3.315.

Farrington, D. P. (1986). Stepping stones to adult criminal careers. In D. Olweus, J. Block, & M. Radke-Yarrow (Eds.), *Development of antisocial and prosocial behavior: Research, theories, and issues*. Academic Press.

Farrington, D. P. (1993). Motivations for conduct disorder and delinquency. *Development and Psychopathology, 5*(1-2), 225-241. https://doi.org/10.1017/S0954579400004363.

Farrington, D. P. (2008). *Integrated developmental and life-course theories of offending*. Transaction Publishers.

Farrington, D. P., Coid, J. W., Harnett, L., Jolliffe, D., Soteriou, N., Turner, R., & West, D. J. (2006). *Criminal careers up to age 50 and life success up to age 48: New findings from the Cambridge Study in Delinquent Development* (Vol. 94). Home Office Research, Development and Statistics Directorate.

Farrington, D. P., Gaffney, H., & Ttofi, M. M. (2017). Systematic reviews of explanatory risk factors for violence, offending, and delinquency. *Aggression and Violent Behavior, 33*, 24-36. https://doi.org/10.1016/j.avb.2016.11.004.

Farrington, D. P., Ttofi, M. M., & Piquero, A. R. (2016). Risk, promotive, and protective factors in youth offending: Results from the Cambridge study in delinquent development. *Journal of Criminal Justice, 45*, 63-70. https://doi.org/10.1016/j.jcrimjus.2016.02.014.

Fattore, T., Mason, J., & Watson, E. (2007). Children's conceptualisation(s) of their well-being. *Social Indicators Research, 80*(1), 5-29. https://doi.org/10.1007/s11205-006-9019-9.

Faul, F., Erdfelder, E., Buchner, A., & Lang, A.-G. (2009). Statistical power analyses using G*Power 3.1: Tests for correlation and regression analyses. *Behavior Research Methods, 41*(4), 1149-1160. https://doi.org/10.3758/brm.41.4.1149.

Feij, J. A. (2006). De psychologie van de kick. *Justitiële Verkenningen, 4*(5), 63-81. www.bjutijdschriften.nl/tijdschrift/justitieleverkenningen/2006/05/JV_2006_004_005_005.

*Ferrer-Cascales, R., Albaladejo-Blazquez, N., Ruiz-Robledillo, N., Clement-Carbonell, V., Sanchez-SanSegundo, M., & Zaragoza-Marti, A. (2019). Higher adherence to the mediterranean diet is related to more subjective happiness in adolescents: The role of health-related quality of life. *Nutrients, 11*(3), 1-12. https://doi.org/10.3390/nu11030698.

Field, A. (2009). *Discovering statistics using SPSS* (3rd ed.). Sage Publications.

Fisher, D., Beech, A., & Browne, K. (1998). Locus of control and its relationship to treatment change and abuse history in child sexual abusers. *Legal and Criminological Psychology, 3*(1), 1-12. https://doi.org/10.1111/j.2044-8333.1998.tb00348.x.

Fisher, D., Morgan, J., & Leeson, S. (2010). Working with juveniles with sexually abusive behaviour in the UK: The G-map approach. In R. E. Longo, D. S. Prescott, J. Bergman, & K. Creeden (Eds.), *Current perspectives and applications in neurobiology: Working with young persons who are victims and perpetrators of sexual abuse* (pp. 185-198). Neari Press.

Florsheim, P., Shotorbani, S., Guest-Warnick, G., Barratt, T., & Hwang, W.-C. (2000). Role of the working alliance in the treatment of delinquent boys in community-based programs. *Journal of Clinical Child Psychology, 29*(1), 94-107. https://doi.org/10.1207/s15374424jccp2901_10.

Fortune, C.-A. (2018). The good lives model: A strength-based approach for youth offenders. *Aggression and Violent Behavior, 38*, 21-30. https://doi.org/10.1016/j.avb.2017.11.003.

Fortune, C.-A., & Heffernan, R. (2019). The psychology of criminal conduct: A consideration of strengths, weaknesses and future directions. *Psychology, Crime & Law, 25*(6), 659-674. https://doi.org/10.1080/1068316X.2018.1560445.

Fortune, C. A., & Heffernan, R. (2021). Strengths and weaknesses of the psychology of criminal conduct: Implications for the conceptualisation, assessment and treatment of antisocial personality pattern. *Behavioral Sciences & the Law, 39*(5), 678-693. https://doi.org/10.1002/bsl.2545.

Fortune, C.-A., Ward, T., & Print, B. (2014). Integrating the good lives model with relapse prevention: Working with juvenile sex offenders. In D. S. Bromberg & W. T. O'Donohu (Eds.), *Toolkit for working with juvenile sex offenders* (pp. 405-426). Elsevier.

*Frasquilho, D., de Matos, M. G., Neville, F., Gaspar, T., & de Almeida, J. M. C. (2016). Parental unemployment and youth life satisfaction: The moderating roles of satisfaction with family life. *Journal of Child and Family Studies, 25*(11), 3214-3219. https://doi.org/10.1007/s10826-016-0480-z.

Fredrickson, B. L. (2004). The broaden and build theory of positive emotions. *Philosophical Transactions of the Royal Society B: Biological Sciences, 359*(1449), 1367-1377. https://doi.org/10.1098/rstb.2004.1512.

*Freire, T., & Ferreira, G. (2020). Do I need to be positive to be happy? Considering the role of self-esteem, life satisfaction, and psychological distress in Portuguese adolescents' subjective happiness. *Psychological Reports, 123*(4), 1064-1082. https://doi.org/10.1177/0033294119846064.

*Frison, E., Subrahmanyam, K., & Eggermont, S. (2016). The short-term longitudinal and reciprocal relations between peer victimization on Facebook and adolescents' well-being. *Journal of Youth and Adolescence, 45*(9), 1755-1771. https://doi.org/10.1007/s10964-016-0436-z.

Gadermann, A. M., Schonert-Reichl, K. A., & Zumbo, B. D. (2010). Investigating validity evidence of the satisfaction with life scale adapted for children. *Social Indicators Research, 96*(2), 229-247. https://doi.org/10.1007/s11205-009-9474-1.

Gallagher, M. W., & Lopez, S. J. (2007). Curiosity and well-being. *The Journal of Positive Psychology, 2*(4), 236-248. https://doi.org/10.1080/17439760701552345.

*Gallego, G., Perez, M., Fernandez, F., Alcantara-Lopez, M., & Saez, C. (2021). Life satisfaction in adolescents: Relationship with parental style, peer attachment and emotional intelligence. *Electronic Journal of Research in Educational Psychology, 19*(1), 51-74. https://doi.org/10.25115/ejrep.v19i53.3425.

Gamble, A., & Gärling, T. (2012). The relationships between life satisfaction, happiness, and current mood. *An Interdisciplinary Forum on Subjective Well-Being, 13*(1), 31-45. https://doi.org/10.1007/s10902-011-9248-8.

Gannon, T. A., King, T., Miles, H., Lockerbie, L., & Willis, G. M. (2011). Good lives sexual offender treatment for mentally disordered offenders. *The British Journal of Forensic Practice, 13*(3), 153-168. https://doi.org/10.1108/14636641111157805.

Garcia, D., Al Nima, A., Kjell, O. N. E., Granjard, A., & Sikström, S. (2020). The (mis) measurement of happiness: Words we associate to happiness (semantic memory) and narratives of what makes us happy (episodic memory). In S. Sikström & D. Garcia (Eds.), *Statistical semantics: Methods and applications* (pp. 165-189). Springer. https://doi.org/10.1007/978-3-030-37250-7_10.

*Garcia, D., & Moradi, S. (2013). The affective temperaments and well-being: Swedish and Iranian adolescents' life satisfaction and psychological well-being. *Journal of Happiness Studies, 14*(2), 689-707. https://doi.org/10.1007/s10902-012-9349-z.

Gatner, D. T., Douglas, K. S., Hart, S. D., & Kropp, P. R. (2021). Structured Professional Judgment (SPJ) violence risk case formulation and psychopathic personality disorder. *International Journal of Forensic Mental Health, 21*(1), 20-36. https://doi.org/10.1080/14999013.2021.1895378.

Gendreau, P., Little, T., & Goggin, C. (1996). A meta-analysis of the predictors of adult offender recidivism: What works! *Criminology, 34*(4), 575-608. https://doi.org/10.1111/j.1745-9125.1996.tb01220.x.

Gerits, R. (2019). *Delictgericht contextbegeleiden en samen-werken tussen private organisaties en gemeenschapsinstellingen*. Intersentia.

*Gillham, J., Adams-Deutsch, Z., Werner, J., Reivich, K., Coulter-Heindl, V., Linkins, M., Winder, B., Peterson, C., Park, N., Abenavoli, R., Contero, A., & Seligman, M. E. P. (2011). Character strengths predict subjective well-being during adolescence. *Journal of Positive Psychology, 6*(1), 31-44. https://doi.org/10.1080/17439760.2010.536773.

*Gilman, R., Ashby, J. S., Sverko, D., Florell, D., & Varjas, K. (2005). The relationship between perfectionism and multidimensional life satisfaction among Croatian and American youth. *Personality and Individual Differences, 39*(1), 155-166. https://doi.org/10.1016/j.paid.2004.12.014.

Gilman, R., & Barry, J. (2003). Life satisfaction and social desirability among adolescents in a residential treatment setting: Changes across time. *Residential Treatment for Children & Youth, 21*(2), 19-42. https://doi.org/10.1300/J007v21n02_02.

Gilman, R., & Handwerk, M. L. (2001). Changes in life satisfaction as a function of stay in a residential setting. *Residential Treatment for Children & Youth, 18*(4), 47-65. https://doi.org/10.1300/J007v18n04_05.

Gilman, R., & Huebner, E. S. (2000). Review of life satisfaction measures for adolescents. *Behaviour Change, 17*(03), 178-195. https://doi.org/10.1375/bech.17.3.178.

Gilman, R., & Huebner, E. S. (2003). A review of life satisfaction research with children and adolescents. *School Psychology Quarterly, 18*(2), 192-205. https://doi.org/10.1521/scpq.18.2.192.21858.

*Gilman, R., & Huebner, E. S. (2006). Characteristics of adolescents who report very high life satisfaction. *Journal of Youth and Adolescence, 35*(3), 311-319. https://doi.org/10.1007/s10964-006-9036-7.

Gilman, R., Huebner, E. S., & Laughlin, J. E. (2000). A first study of the multidimensional students' life satisfaction scale with adolescents. *An International and Interdisciplinary Journal for Quality-of-Life Measurement, 52*(2), 135-160. https://doi.org/10.1023/A:1007059227507.

Ginsburg, J. I. D., Mann, R. E., Rotgers, F., & Weekes, J. R. (2002). Motivational interviewing with criminal justice populations. In W. Miller & S. Rollnick (Eds.), *Motivational interviewing: Preparing people for change* (Vol. 2, pp. 333-347). Guildford Press.

Giordano, P. C. (2020). Continuing education: Toward a life-course perspective on social learning. *Criminology, 58*(2), 199-225. https://doi.org/10.1111/1745-9125.12244.

Giordano, P. C., Cernkovich, S. A., & Holland, D. D. (2003). Changes in friendship relations over the life course: Implications for desistance from crime. *Criminology, 41*(2), 293-328. https://doi.org/10.1111/j.1745-9125.2003.tb00989.x.

Giordano, P. C., Cernkovich, S. A., & Rudolph, J. L. (2002). Gender, crime, and desistance: Toward a theory of cognitive transformation. *American Journal of Sociology, 107*(4), 990-1064. https://doi.org/10.1086/343191.

Glaser, B. G., & Strauss, A. L. (1967). *Discovery of grounded theory: Strategies for qualitative research*. Routledge.

Glueck, S., & Glueck, E. (1950). *Unraveling juvenile delinquency*. Commonwealth Fund.

Goense, P. B., Assink, M., Stams, G. J. J. M., Boendermaker, L., & Hoeve, M. (2016). Making 'what works' work: A meta-analytic study of the effect of treatment integrity on outcomes of evidence-based interventions for juveniles with antisocial behavior. *Aggression and Violent Behavior, 31*, 106-115. https://doi.org/10.1016/j.avb.2016.08.003.

Goldbeck, L., Schmitz, T., Besier, T., Herschbach, P., & Henrich, G. (2007). Life satisfaction decreases during adolescence. *An International Journal of Quality of Life Aspects of Treatment, Care and Rehabilitation – Official Journal of the International Society of Quality of Life Research, 16*(6), 969-979. https://doi.org/10.1007/s11136-007-9205-5.

*Góngora, V. C. (2014). Satisfaction with life, well-being, and meaning in life as protective factors of eating disorder symptoms and body dissatisfaction in adolescents. *Eating Disorders, 22*(5), 435-449. https://doi.org/10.1080/10640266.2014.931765.

*Góngora, V. C., & Castro Solano, A. (2014). Well-being and life satisfaction in Argentinean adolescents. *Journal of Youth Studies, 17*(9), 1277-1291. https://doi.org/10.1080/13676261.2014.918251.

*Gonzalez, C., Varela, J., Sanchez, P. A., Venegas, F., & De Tezanos-Pinto, P. (2021). Students' participation in school and its relationship with antisocial behavior, academic performance and adolescent well-being. *Child Indicators Research, 14*(1), 269-282. https://doi.org/10.1007/s12187-020-09761-5.

González, M., Coenders, G., Saez, M., & Casas, F. (2010). Non-linearity, complexity and limited measurement in the relationship between satisfaction with specific life domains and satisfaction with life as a whole. *Journal of Happiness Studies, 11*(3), 335-352. https://doi.org/10.1007/s10902-009-9143-8.

Goodman, A., Lamping, D. L., & Ploubidis, G. B. (2010). When to use broader internalising and externalising subscales instead of the hypothesised five subscales on the Strengths and Difficulties Questionnaire (SDQ): Data from British parents, teachers and children. *Journal of Abnormal Child Psychology, 38*(8), 1179-1191. https://doi.org/10.1007/s10802-010-9434-x.

Goodman, R. (1997). The strengths and difficulties questionnaire: A research note. *Journal of Child Psychology and Psychiatry, 38*(5), 581-586. https://doi.org/10.1111/j.1469-7610.1997.tb01545.x.

Goodman, R. (2001). Psychometric properties of the strengths and difficulties questionnaire. *Journal of the American Academy of Child & Adolescent Psychiatry, 40*(11), 1337-1345. https://doi.org/10.1097/00004583-200111000-00015.

Gordon, W. R., & Caltabiano, M. L. (1996). Urban-rural differences in adolescent self-esteem, leisure boredom, and sensation-seeking as predictors of leisure-time usage and satisfaction. *Adolescence, 31*(124), 883.

*Goswami, H. (2012). Social relationships and children's subjective well-being. *Social Indicators Research, 107*(3), 575-588. https://doi.org/10.1007/s11205-011-9864-z.

*Goswami, H. (2014). Children's subjective well-being: Socio-demographic characteristics and personality. *Child Indicators Research, 7*(1), 119-140. https://doi.org/10.1007/s12187-013-9205-7.

Gottfredson, M. R., & Hirschi, T. (1990). *A general theory of crime*. Stanford University Press.

Gray, J. S., Ozer, D. J., & Rosenthal, R. (2017). Goal conflict and psychological well-being: A meta-analysis. *Journal of Research in Personality, 66*, 27-37. https://doi.org/10.1016/j.jrp.2016.12.003.

Grieger, L., & Hosser, D. (May 2014). Which risk factors are really predictive? An analysis of Andrews and Bonta's "central eight" risk factors for recidivism in German youth correctional facility inmates. *Criminal Justice and Behavior, 41*(5), 613-634. https://doi.org/10.1177/0093854813511432.

Griffin, J. (1996). *Value judgement: Improving our ethical beliefs*. Oxford University Press.

Grisso, T. (2008). Adolescent offenders with mental disorders. *Future of Children, 18*(2), 143-164. https://doi.org/10.1353/foc.0.0016.

*Gross, E. F., Juvonen, J., & Gable, S. L. (2002). Internet use and well-being in adolescence. *Journal of Social Issues, 58*(1), 75-90. https://doi.org/10.1111/1540-4560.00249.

Gubbels, J., van der Stouwe, T., Spruit, A., & Stams, G. J. J. M. (2016). Martial arts participation and externalizing behavior in juveniles: A meta-analytic review. *Aggression and Violent Behavior, 28*, 73-81. https://doi.org/10.1016/j.avb.2016.03.011.

Gudjonsson, G. H., & Sigurdsson, J. F. (2007). Motivation for offending and personality. A study among young offenders on probation. *Personality and Individual Differences, 42*(7), 1243-1253. https://doi.org/10.1016/j.paid.2006.10.003.

Guebert, A. F., & Olver, M. E. (2014). An examination of criminogenic needs, mental health concerns, and recidivism in a sample of violent young offenders: Implications for risk, need, and responsivity. *International Journal of Forensic Mental Health, 13*(4), 295-310. https://doi.org/10.1080/14999013.2014.955220.

Gunnell, K. E., Crocker, P. R. E., Mack, D. E., Wilson, P. M., & Zumbo, B. D. (2014). Goal contents, motivation, psychological need satisfaction, well-being and physical activity: A test of self-determination theory over 6 months. *Psychology of Sport & Exercise, 15*(1), 19-29. https://doi.org/10.1016/j.psychsport.2013.08.005.

Hachtel, H., Vogel, T., & Huber, C. G. (2019). Mandated treatment and its impact on therapeutic process and outcome factors. *Frontiers in Psychiatry, 10*, 1-8. https://doi.org/10.3389/fpsyt.2019.00219.

Hamilton, H. A., Noh, S., & Adlaf, E. M. (2009). Perceived financial status, health, and maladjustment in adolescence. *Social Science & Medicine, 68*(8), 1527-1534. https://doi.org/10.1016/j.socscimed.2009.01.037.

Hanniball, K. B., Viljoen, J. L., Shaffer, C. S., Bhatt, G., Tweed, R., Aknin, L. B., Gagnon, N., Douglas, K. S., & Dooley, S. (2018). The role of life satisfaction in predicting youth violence and offending: A prospective examination. *Journal of Interpersonal Violence, 36*(11-12), 5501-5529. https://doi.org/10.1177/0886260518805103.

Hansen, E. B., & Breivik, G. (2001). Sensation seeking as a predictor of positive and negative risk behaviour among adolescents. *Personality and Individual Differences, 30*(4), 627-640. https://doi.org/10.1016/S0191-8869(00)00061-1.

Hanson, R. K., Bourgon, G., Helmus, L., & Hodgson, S. (1 September 2009). The principles of effective correctional treatment also apply to sexual offenders: A meta-analysis. *Criminal Justice and Behavior, 36*(9), 865-891. https://doi.org/10.1177/0093854809338545.

Hanson, R. K., & Morton-Bourgon, K. (2004). *Predictors of sexual recidivism: An updated meta-analysis*. Public Safety and Emergency Preparedness Canada.

Hanson, R. K., & Morton-Bourgon, K. (2005). The characteristics of persistent sexual offenders: A meta-analysis of recidivism studies. *Journal of Consulting and Clinical Psychology, 73*(6), 1154-1163. https://doi.org/10.1037/0022-006x.73.6.1154.

Haranin, E. C., Huebner, E. S., & Suldo, S. M. (2007). Predictive and incremental validity of global and domain-based adolescent life satisfaction reports. *Journal of Psychoeducational Assessment, 25*(2), 127-138. https://doi.org/10.1177/0734282906295620.

Harder, A. T., Knorth, E. J., & Kalverboer, M. E. (2011). Transition secured? A follow-up study of adolescents who have left secure residential care. *Children and Youth Services Review, 33*(12), 2482-2488. https://doi.org/10.1016/j.childyouth.2011.08.022.

Harder, A. T., Knorth, E. J., & Kalverboer, M. E. (2012). Securing the downside up: Client and care factors associated with outcomes of secure residential youth care. *Child & Youth Care Forum, 41*(3), 259-276. https://doi.org/10.1007/s10566-011-9159-1.

Harder, A. T., Knorth, E. J., & Kalverboer, M. E. (2015). Risky or needy? Dynamic risk factors and delinquent behavior of adolescents in secure residential youth care. *International Journal of Offender Therapy and Comparative Criminology, 59*(10), 1047-1065. https://doi.org/10.1177/0306624x14531036.

Harder, A. T., Knorth, E. J., & Kalverboer, M. E. (2017). The inside out? Views of young people, parents, and professionals regarding successful secure residential care. *Child and Adolescent Social Work Journal, 34*(5), 431-441. https://doi.org/10.1007/s10560-016-0473-1.

Harkins, L., Flak, V. E., Beech, A. R., & Woodhams, J. (December 2012). Evaluation of a community-based sex offender treatment program using a good lives model approach. *Sex Abuse, 24*(6), 519-543. https://doi.org/10.1177/1079063211429469.

Harper, C. A., Lievesley, R., Blagden, N., Akerman, G., Winder, B., & Baumgartner, E. (2020). Development and validation of the Good Lives Questionnaire. *Psychology, Crime & Law, 27*(7), 678-703. https://doi.org/10.1080/1068316X.2020.1849695.

Harper, R., & Hardy, S. (2000). Research note. An evaluation of motivational interviewing as a method of intervention with clients in a probation setting. *British Journal of Social Work, 30*(3), 393-400. https://doi.org/10.1093/bjsw/30.3.393.

Harris, D. A., Pedneault, A., & Willis, G. (2019). The pursuit of primary human goods in men desisting from sexual offending. *Sexual Abuse, 31*(2), 197-219. https://doi.org/10.1177/1079063217729155.

Hart, J., & Collins, K. (2014). A 'back to basics' approach to offender supervision: Does working alliance contribute towards success of probation? *European Journal of Probation, 6*(2), 112-125. https://doi.org/10.1177/2066220314543747.

Hart, S. D., & Logan, C. (2011). Formulation of violence risk using evidence-based assessments: The structured professional judgment approach. In P. Sturmey & M. McMurran (Eds.), *Forensic case formulation* (pp. 83-106). Wiley-Blackwell.

Hart, S. D., Sturmey, P., Logan, C., & McMurran, M. (2011). Forensic case formulation. *International Journal of Forensic Mental Health, 10*(2), 118-126. https://doi.org/10.1080/14999013.2011.577137.

Hartup, W. W., & Stevens, N. (1997). Friendships and adaptation in the life course. *Psychological Bulletin, 121*(3), 355. https://doi.org/10.1037/0033-2909.121.3.355.

Harwood, A., Lavidor, M., & Rassovsky, Y. (2017). Reducing aggression with martial arts: A meta-analysis of child and youth studies. *Aggression and Violent Behavior, 34*, 96-101. https://doi.org/10.1016/j.avb.2017.03.001.

*Haworth, C. M. A., Carter, K., Eley, T. C., & Plomin, R. (2017). Understanding the genetic and environmental specificity and overlap between well-being and internalizing symptoms in adolescence. *Developmental Science, 20*(2), 1-9. https://doi.org/10.1111/desc.12376.

Hayes, A. F. (2017). *Introduction to mediation, moderation, and conditional process analysis: A regression-based approach*. Guilford.

Hayes, A. F., Montoya, A. K., & Rockwood, N. J. (2017). The analysis of mechanisms and their contingencies: PROCESS versus structural equation modeling. *Australasian Marketing Journal (AMJ), 25*(1), 76-81. https://doi.org/10.1016/j.ausmj.2017.02.001.

*He, D., Shi, M., & Yi, F. (2014). Mediating effects of affect and loneliness on the relationship between core self-evaluation and life satisfaction among two groups of Chinese adolescents. *Social Indicators Research, 119*(2), 747-756. https://doi.org/10.1007/s11205-013-0508-3.

Healy, D. (2013). Changing fate? Agency and the desistance process. *Theoretical Criminology, 17*(4), 557-574. https://doi.org/10.1177/1362480613494991.

Heffernan, R., & Ward, T. (2015). The conceptualization of dynamic risk factors in child sex offenders: An agency model. *Aggression and Violent Behavior, 24*, 250-260. https://doi.org/10.1016/j.avb.2015.07.001.

Heffernan, R., & Ward, T. (2017). A comprehensive theory of dynamic risk and protective factors. *Aggression and Violent Behavior, 37*, 129-141. https://doi.org/10.1016/j.avb.2017.10.003.

Heffernan, R., & Ward, T. (2019). Dynamic risk factors, protective factors and value-laden practices. *Psychiatry, Psychology and Law, 26*(2), 312-328. https://doi.org/10.1080/13218719.2018.1506721.

Heffernan, R., & Ward, T. (2020). Reformulating dynamic risk factors and practice implications. In H. Heffernan & T. Ward (Eds.), *Dynamic risk factors for sexual offending* (pp. 43-64). Springer. https://doi.org/10.1007/978-3-030-58275-3_4.

Heffernan, R., Ward, T., Vandevelde, S., & Van Damme, L. (2019). Dynamic risk factors and constructing explanations of offending: The Risk-Causality Method. *Aggression and Violent Behavior, 44*, 47-56. https://doi.org/10.1016/j.avb.2018.11.009.

Heffernan, R., Wegerhoff, D., & Ward, T. (2019). Dynamic risk factors: Conceptualization, measurement, and evidence. *Aggression and Violent Behavior, 48*, 6-16. https://doi.org/10.1016/j.avb.2019.06.004.

*Heizomi, H., Allahverdipour, H., Asghari Jafarabadi, M., & Safaian, A. (2015). Happiness and its relation to psychological well-being of adolescents. *Asian Journal of Psychiatry, 16*, 55-60. https://doi.org/10.1016/j.ajp.2015.05.037.

Hemphill, J. F. (2003). Interpreting the magnitudes of correlation coefficients. *American Psychologist, 58*(1), 78-79. https://doi.org/10.1037/0003-066X.58.1.78.

Hemphill, J. F., & Howell, A. J. (2000). Adolescent offenders and stages of change. *Psychological Assessment, 12*(4), 371-381.

Henggeler, S. W., & Schaeffer, C. M. (2016). Multisystemic Therapy®: Clinical overview, outcomes, and implementation research. *Family Process, 55*(3), 514-528. https://doi.org/10.1111/famp.12232.

Henry, S., Henaghan, M., Sanders, J., & Munford, R. (2015). Engaging youth in youth justice interventions: Well-being and accountability. *Youth Justice-An International Journal, 15*(3), 240-255. https://doi.org/10.1177/1473225414562636.

Heynen, E., van der Helm, G. H. P., Cima, M., Stams, G. J. J. M., & Korebrits, A. (2017). The relation between living group climate, aggression, and callous-unemotional traits in delinquent boys in detention. *International Journal of Offender Therapy and Comparative Criminology, 61*(15), 1701-1718. https://doi.org/10.1177/0306624X16630543.

Higley, C. A., Lloyd, C. D., & Serin, R. C. (2019). Age and motivation can be specific responsivity features that moderate the relationship between risk and rehabilitation outcome. *Law and Human Behavior, 43*(6), 558-567. https://doi.org/10.1037/lhb0000348.

Hill, J. M., Blokland, A. A., & van der Geest, V. R. (2016). Desisting from crime in emerging adulthood: Adult roles and the maturity gap. *Journal of Research in Crime and Delinquency, 53*(4), 506-535. https://doi.org/10.1177/0022427816628586.

Hill, J. M., van der Geest, V. R., & Blokland, A. A. (2017). Leaving the bank of mum and dad: Financial independence and delinquency desistance in emerging adulthood. *Journal of Developmental and Life-Course Criminology, 3*(4), 419-439. https://doi.org/10.1007/s40865-017-0058-5.

Hilterman, E. L., Nicholls, T. L., & van Nieuwenhuizen, C. (2014). Predictive validity of risk assessments in juvenile offenders: Comparing the SAVRY, PCL: YV, and YLS/CMI with unstructured clinical assessments. *Assessment, 21*(3), 324-339. https://doi.org/10.1177/1073191113498113.

*Hirschi, A. (2009). Career adaptability development in adolescence: Multiple predictors and effect on sense of power and life satisfaction. *Journal of Vocational Behavior, 74*(2), 145-155. https://doi.org/10.1016/j.jvb.2009.01.002.

Hirschi, T. (2017). *Causes of delinquency*. Routledge.

Hirschi, T., & Stark, R. (1969). Hellfire and delinquency. *Social Problems, 17*(2), 202-213.

Hoeben, E. M., & Weerman, F. M. (2016). Why is involvement in unstructured socializing related to adolescent delinquency? *Criminology, 54*(2), 242-281. https://doi.org/10.1111/1745-9125.12105.

Hoeve, M., Colins, O. F., Mulder, E. A., Loeber, R., Stams, G. J. J. M., & Vermeiren, R. (2014). Trauma and mental health problems in adolescent males: Differences between childhood-onset and adolescent-onset offenders. *Criminal Justice and Behavior, 42*(7), 685-702. https://doi.org/10.1177/0093854814558505.

Hoeve, M., Colins, O. F., Mulder, E. A., Loeber, R., Stams, G. J. J. M., & Vermeiren, R. (2015). The association between childhood maltreatment, mental health problems, and aggression in justice-involved boys. *Aggressive Behavior, 41*(5), 488-501. https://doi.org/10.1002/ab.21586.

Hoeve, M., Dubas, J. S., Eichelsheim, V. I., Van der Laan, P. H., Smeenk, W., & Gerris, J. R. M. (2009). The relationship between parenting and delinquency: A meta-analysis. *Journal of Abnormal Child Psychology, 37*(6), 749-775. https://doi.org/10.1007/s10802-009-9310-8.

Hoeve, M., Dubas, J., S., Gerris, J. R. M., van der Laan, P. H., & Smeenk, W. (2011). Maternal and paternal parenting styles: Unique and combined links to adolescent and early adult delinquency. *Journal of Adolescence, 34*(5), 813-827. https://doi.org/10.1016/j.adolescence.2011.02.004.

Hoeve, M., Jak, S., Stams, G. J. J. M., & Meeus, W. H. J. (2016). Financial problems and delinquency in adolescents and young adults: A 6-year three-wave study. *Crime & Delinquency, 62*(11), 1488-1509. https://doi.org/10.1177/0011128714541190.

Hoeve, M., McReynolds, L. S., & Wasserman, G. A. (2013). The influence of adolescent psychiatric disorder on young adult recidivism. *Criminal Justice and Behavior, 40*(12), 1368-1382. https://doi.org/10.1177/0093854813488106.

Hoeve, M., Stams, G. J., van der Zouwen, M., Vergeer, M., Jurrius, K., & Asscher, J. J. (2014). A systematic review of financial debt in adolescents and young adults: Prevalence, correlates and associations with crime. *PLoS One, 9*(8), e104909. https://doi.org/10.1371/journal.pone.0104909.

Hoeve, M., & van der Laan, P. H. (2016). *Persisters and desisters in crime from adolescence into adulthood: Explanation, prevention and punishment*. Routledge.

Hoffmann, J. P. (2020). Academic underachievement and delinquent behavior. *Youth & Society, 52*(5), 728-755. https://doi.org/10.1177/0044118X18767035.

Hoge, R. D., & Andrews, D. A. (2006). *Youth level of service/case management inventory (YLS/CMI)*. Multi-Heath Systems.

Hoge, R. D., & Andrews, D. A. (2011). *Youth level of service/case management inventory 2.0 (YLS/CMI 2.0): User's manual*. Multi-Health Systems.

*Holder, M. D., Coleman, B., Krupa, T., & Krupa, E. (2016). Well-being's relation to religiosity and spirituality in children and adolescents in Zambia. *Journal of Happiness Studies, 17*(3), 1235-1253. https://doi.org/10.1007/s10902-015-9640-x.

Holmqvist, R., Hill, T., & Lang, A. (2007). Treatment alliance in residential treatment of criminal adolescents. *Child Youth Care Forum, 36*, 163-178. https://doi.org/10.1007/s10566-007-9037-z.

Holte, A., Barry, M. M., Bekkhus, M., Borge, A. I. H., Bowes, L., Casas, F., Friborg, O., Grinde, B., Headey, B., Jozefiak, T., Lekhal, R., Marks, N., Muffels, R., Nes, R. B., Røysamb, E., Thimm, J. C., Torgersen, S., Trommsdorff, G., Veenhoven, R., ... Zachrisson, H. D. (2014). Psychology of child well-being. In A. Ben-Arieh, F. Casas, I. Frønes, & J. E. Korbin (Eds.), *Handbook of child well-being: Theories, methods and policies in global perspective* (pp. 555-631). Springer. https://doi.org/10.1007/978-90-481-9063-8_13.

Hope, N. H., Holding, A. C., Verner-Filion, J., Sheldon, K. M., & Koestner, R. F. (2019). The path from intrinsic aspirations to subjective well-being is mediated by changes in basic psychological need satisfaction and autonomous motivation: A large prospective test. *Motivation and Emotion, 43*(2), 232-241. https://doi.org/10.1007/s11031-018-9733-z.

Horstkötter, D., Berghmans, R., De Ruiter, C., Krumeich, A., & de Wert, G. (2012). "We are also normal humans, you know?" Views and attitudes of juvenile delinquents on antisocial behavior, neurobiology and prevention. *International Journal of Law and Psychiatry, 35*(4), 289-297. https://doi.org/10.1016/j.ijlp.2012.04.006.

Hortop, E., Wrosch, C., & Gagné, M. (2013). The why and how of goal pursuits: Effects of global autonomous motivation and perceived control on emotional well-being. *Motivation and Emotion, 37*(4), 675-687. https://doi.org/10.1007/s11031-013-9349-2.

Houben, M., Van Den Noortgate, W., & Kuppens, P. (2015). The relation between short-term emotion dynamics and psychological well-being: A meta-analysis. *Psychological Bulletin, 141*(4), 901-930. https://doi.org/10.1037/a0038822.

Howell, A. J., Passmore, H.-A., & Buro, K. (2013). Meaning in nature: Meaning in life as a mediator of the relationship between nature connectedness and well-being. *Journal of Happiness Studies, 14*(6), 1681-1696. https://doi.org/10.1007/s10902-012-9403-x.

Howell, J. C., & Lipsey, M. W. (2012). Research-based guidelines for juvenile justice programs. *Justice Research and Policy, 14*(1), 17-34.

Howell, R. T., & Howell, C. J. (2008). The relation of economic status to subjective well-being in developing countries: A meta-analysis. *Psychological Bulletin, 134*(4), 536-560. https://doi.org/10.1037/0033-2909.134.4.536.

Howells, K., & Day, A. (2003). Readiness for anger management: Clinical and theoretical issues. *Clinical Psychology Review, 23*(2), 319-337. https://doi.org/10.1016/s0272-7358(02)00228-3.

Howells, K., & Day, A. (2007). Readiness for treatment in high risk offenders with personality disorders. *Psychology, Crime & Law, 13*(1), 47-56. https://doi.org/10.1080/10683160600869767.

Hsieh, C.-m. (2016). Domain importance in subjective well-being measures. *An International and Interdisciplinary Journal for Quality-of-Life Measurement, 127*(2), 777-792. https://doi.org/10.1007/s11205-015-0977-7.

Hubbard, D. J. (2007). Getting the most out of correctional treatment: Testing the responsivity principle on male and female offenders. *Federal Probation, 71*(1), 2-8.

Huebner, E., Seligson, J., Valois, R., & Suldo, S. (2006). A review of the Brief Multidimensional Students' Life Satisfaction Scale. *An International and Interdisciplinary Journal for Quality-of-Life Measurement, 79*(3), 477-484. https://doi.org/10.1007/s11205-005-5395-9.

Huebner, E. S. (1995). The Students' Life Satisfaction Scale: An assessment of psychometric properties with black and white elementary school students. *Social Indicators Research, 34*(3), 315-323. https://doi.org/10.1007/BF01078690.

*Huebner, E. S., Funk, B. A., & Gilman, R. (2000). Cross-sectional and longitudinal psychosocial correlates of adolescent life satisfaction reports. *Canadian Journal of School Psychology, 16*(1), 53-64. https://doi.org/10.1177/082957350001600104.

Hughes, W. (2012). Promoting offender engagement and compliance in sentence planning: Practitioner and service user perspectives in Hertfordshire. *Probation Journal, 59*(1), 49-65. https://doi.org/10.1177/0264550511429844.

Huta, V., & Ryan, R. M. (2010). Pursuing pleasure or virtue: The differential and overlapping well-being benefits of hedonic and eudaimonic motives. *Journal of Happiness Studies, 11*(6), 735-762. https://doi.org/10.1007/s10902-009-9171-4.

Iselin, A. M., Mulvey, E. P., Loughran, T., Chung, H. H., & Schubert, C. A. (2012). A longitudinal examination of serious adolescent offenders' perceptions of chances for success and engagement in behaviors accomplishing goals. *International Society for Research in Child and Adolescent Psychopathology, 40*(2), 237-249. https://doi.org/10.1007/s10802-011-9561-z.

Jackson, D., & Turner, R. (2017). Power analysis for random-effects meta-analysis. *Research Synthesis Methods, 8*(3), 290-302. https://doi.org/10.1002/jrsm.1240.

Jacobs, B. A., & Wright, R. (1999). Stick-up, street culture, and offender motivation. *Criminology, 37*(1), 149-174. https://doi.org/10.1111/j.1745-9125.1999.tb00482.x.

Jacobs, L. A., Ashcraft, L. E., Sewall, C. J. R., Folb, B. L., & Mair, C. (2020). Ecologies of juvenile reoffending: A systematic review of risk factors. *Journal of Criminal Justice, 66*, 101638. https://doi.org/10.1016/j.jcrimjus.2019.101638.

Janssen-de Ruijter, E., Mulder, E., Bongers, I., Omlo, L., & van Nieuwenhuizen, C. (2019). Looking into the crystal ball: Quality of life, delinquency, and problems experienced by young male adults after discharge from a secure residential care setting in the

Netherlands. *Child and Adolescent Psychiatry and Mental Health, 13*(1), 45. https://doi.org/10.1186/s13034-019-0305-0.

JeugdOnderzoeksPlatform. (2018). *Technisch verslag JOP-schoolmonitor 2.* www.jeugdonderzoeksplatform.be/files/Technischverslag_JOP-schoolmonitor_2018.pdf.

Jochems, E. C., Duivenvoorden, H. J., Van Dam, A., Van Der Feltz-Cornelis, C. M., & Mulder, C. L. (2017). Motivation, treatment engagement and psychosocial outcomes in outpatients with severe mental illness: A test of self-determination theory. *International Journal of Methods in Psychiatric Research, 26*, e1537. https://doi.org/10.1002/mpr.1537.

Johnson, B. R., De Li, S., Larson, D. B., & McCullough, M. (2000). A systematic review of the religiosity and delinquency literature: A research note. *Journal of Contemporary Criminal Justice, 16*(1), 32-52. https://doi.org/10.1177/1043986200016001003.

Johnston, T. M., Brezina, T., & Crank, B. R. (2019). Agency, self-efficacy, and desistance from crime: An application of social cognitive theory. *Journal of Developmental and Life-Course Criminology, 5*(1), 60-85. https://doi.org/10.1007/s40865-018-0101-1.

Jongeren Welzijn. (2011). *Differentiatie nota van het aanbod in gemeenschapsinstellingen.* Vlaamse Overheid.

Jørgensen, I. S., & Nafstad, H. E. (2004). Positive psychology: Historical, philosophical, and epistemological perspectives. In P. A. Linley & S. Joseph (Eds.), *Positive psychology in practice* (pp. 15-34). Wiley. https://doi.org/10.1002/9780470939338.ch2.

Joussemet, M., Vitaro, F., Barker, E. D., Côté, S., Nagin, D. S., Zoccolillo, M. S., & Tremblay, R. E. (2008). Controlling parenting and physical aggression during elementary school. *Child Development, 79*(2), 411-425. https://doi.org/10.1111/j.1467-8624.2007.01133.x.

Jovanović, V. (2015). Beyond the PANAS: Incremental validity of the Scale of Positive and Negative Experience (SPANE) in relation to well-being. *Personality and Individual Differences, 86*, 487-491. https://doi.org/10.1016/j.paid.2015.07.015.

*Jovanović, V., & Brdaric, D. (2012). Did curiosity kill the cat? Evidence from subjective well-being in adolescents. *Personality and Individual Differences, 52*(3), 380-384. https://doi.org/10.1016/j.paid.2011.10.043.

*Jovanović, V., & Gavrilov-Jerkovic, V. (2014). The good, the bad (and the ugly): The role of curiosity in subjective well-being and risky behaviors among adolescents. *Scandinavian Journal of Psychology, 55*(1), 38-44. https://doi.org/10.1111/sjop.12084.

Jovanović, V., Joshanloo, M., Đunda, D., & Bakhshi, A. (2016). Gender differences in the relationship between domain-specific and general life satisfaction: A study in Iran and Serbia. *Applied Research in Quality of Life, 12*, 185-204. https://doi.org/10.1007/s11482-016-9461-z.

Jozefiak, T., & Sonnichsen Kayed, N. (2015). Self- and proxy reports of quality of life among adolescents living in residential youth care compared to adolescents in the general population and mental health services. *Health Qual Life Outcomes, 13*, 104. https://doi.org/10.1186/s12955-015-0280-y.

Jung, S., & Choi, E. (2017). Life satisfaction and delinquent behaviors among Korean adolescents. *Personality and Individual Differences, 104*, 104-110. https://doi.org/10.1016/j.paid.2016.07.039.

Junger-Tas, J., & Marshall, I. H. (1999). The self-report methodology in crime research. *Crime and Justice, 25*, 291-367. https://doi.org/10.1086/449291.

Kahneman, D. (1999). Objective happiness. In D.Kahneman, E. Diener, & N. Schwarz (Eds.), *Well-being: The foundations of hedonic psychology* (pp. 3-25). Sage Publications.

Kashdan, T. B., Biswas-Diener, R., & King, L. A. (2008). Reconsidering happiness: The costs of distinguishing between hedonics and eudaimonia. *The Journal of Positive Psychology, 3*(4), 219-233. https://doi.org/10.1080/17439760802303044.

Kashdan, T. B., & Silvia, P. J. (2009). Curiosity and interest: The benefits of thriving on novelty and challenge. In C. R. Snyder & S. J. Lopez (Eds.), *Oxford handbook of positive psychology* (2nd ed., pp. 367-374). https://doi.org/10.1093/oxfordhb/9780195187243.013.0034.

Kasser, T. (2002). *The high price of materialism*. MIT Press.

Kasser, T. (2004). The good life or the goods life? Positive psychology and personal well-being in the culture of consumption. In P. A. Linley & S. Joseph (Eds.), *Positive psychology in practice* (pp. 55-67). Wiley. https://doi.org/10.1002/9780470939338.ch4.

Kasser, T. (2016). Materialistic values and goals. *Annual Review of Psychology, 67*, 489-514. https://doi.org/10.1146/annurev-psych-122414-033344.

Katsiyannis, A., Ryan, J. B., Zhang, D., & Spann, A. (2008). Juvenile delinquency and recidivism: The impact of academic achievement. *Reading & Writing Quarterly, 24*(2), 177-196. https://doi.org/10.1080/10573560701808460.

Kekes, J. (1989). *Moral tradition and individuality*. Princeton University Press.

Kekes, J. (1995). *Moral wisdom and good lives*. Cornell University Press.

Kelly, R. E., Mansell, W., & Wood, A. M. (2015). Goal conflict and well-being: A review and hierarchical model of goal conflict, ambivalence, self-discrepancy and self-concordance. *Personality and Individual Differences, 85*, 212-229. https://doi.org/10.1016/j.paid.2015.05.011.

Kelly, W. (2003). Some correlates of sleep disturbance ascribed to worry. *Individual Differences Research, 1*, 137-146.

Keyes, C. L. M. (2002). The mental health continuum: From languishing to flourishing in life. *Journal of Health and Social Behavior, 43*(2), 207-222. https://doi.org/10.2307/3090197.

Keyes, C. L. M., & Annas, J. (2009). Feeling good and functioning well: Distinctive concepts in ancient philosophy and contemporary science. *The Journal of Positive Psychology, 4*(3), 197-201. https://doi.org/10.1080/17439760902844228.

Keyes, C. L. M., Shmotkin, D., & Ryff, C. D. (2002). Optimizing well-being: The empirical encounter of two traditions. *Journal of Personality and Social Psychology, 82*(6), 1007-1022. https://doi.org/10.1037/0022-3514.82.6.1007.

King, L. A., Eells, J. E., & Burton, C. M. (2004). The good life, broadly and narrowly considered. In P. A. Linley & S. Joseph (Eds.), *Positive psychology in practice* (pp. 35-54). Wiley. https://doi.org/10.1002/9780470939338.ch3.

*Kjell, O. N., Nima, A. A., Sikstrom, S., Archer, T., & Garcia, D. (2013). Iranian and Swedish adolescents: Differences in personality traits and well-being. *PeerJ, 1*, e197. https://doi.org/10.7717/peerj.197.

Klepfisz, G., Daffern, M., & Day, A. (2016). Understanding dynamic risk factors for violence. *Psychology, Crime & Law, 22*(1-2), 124-137. https://doi.org/10.1080/1068316X.2015.1109091.

Klug, H., & Maier, G. (2015). Linking goal progress and subjective well-being: A meta-analysis. *An Interdisciplinary Forum on Subjective Well-Being, 16*(1), 37-65. https://doi.org/10.1007/s10902-013-9493-0.

Knee, C. R., & Neighbors, C. (2002). Self-determination, perception of peer pressure, and drinking among college students. *Journal of Applied Social Psychology, 32*(3), 522-543. https://doi.org/10.1111/j.1559-1816.2002.tb00228.x.

Knight, K., Hiller, M. L., Broome, K. M., & Simpson, D. D. (29 June 2000). Legal pressure, treatment readiness, and engagement in long-term residential programs. *Journal of Offender Rehabilitation, 31*(1-2), 101-115. https://doi.org/10.1300/J076v31n01_07.

Knorth, E. J., Harder, A. T., Zandberg, T., & Kendrick, A. J. (2008). Under one roof: A review and selective meta-analysis on the outcomes of residential child and youth care. *Children and Youth Services Review, 30*(2), 123-140. https://doi.org/10.1016/j.childyouth.2007.09.001.

*Kocayörük, E., Altintas, E., & Içbay, M. A. (2015). The perceived parental support, autonomous-self and well-being of adolescents: A cluster-analysis approach. *Journal of Child and Family Studies, 24*(6), 1819-1828. https://doi.org/10.1007/s10826-014-9985-5.

Koehler, J. A., Lösel, F., Akoensi, T. D., & Humphreys, D. K. (2013). A systematic review and meta-analysis on the effects of young offender treatment programs in Europe. *Journal of Experimental Criminology, 9*(1), 19-43. https://doi.org/10.1007/s11292-012-9159-7.

Koh, L. L., Day, A., Klettke, B., Daffern, M., & Chu, C. M. (2020). The predictive validity of youth violence risk assessment tools: A systematic review. *Psychology, Crime & Law, 26*(8), 776-796. https://doi.org/10.1080/1068316X.2020.1734200.

Koo, T. K., & Li, M. Y. (2016). A guideline of selecting and reporting intraclass correlation coefficients for reliability research. *Journal of Chiropractic Medicine, 15*(2), 155-163. https://doi.org/10.1016/j.jcm.2016.02.012.

*Kor, A., Pirutinsky, S., Mikulincer, M., Shoshani, A., & Miller, L. (2019). A longitudinal study of spirituality, character strengths, subjective well-being, and prosociality in middle school adolescents. *Frontiers in Psychology, 10*, 377. https://doi.org/10.3389/fpsyg.2019.00377.

Kroll, C. (2011). Different things make different people happy: Examining social capital and subjective well-being by gender and parental status. *An International and Interdisciplinary Journal for Quality-of-Life Measurement, 104*(1), 157-177. https://doi.org/10.1007/s11205-010-9733-1.

Kuykendall, L., Boemerman, L., & Zhu, Z. (2018). The importance of leisure for subjective well-being. In E. Diener, S. Oishi, & L. Tay (Eds.), *Handbook of well-being* (pp. 1-14). DEF Publishers.

Kuykendall, L., Tay, L., & Ng, V. (2015). Leisure engagement and subjective well-being: A meta-analysis. *Psychological Bulletin, 141*(2), 364-403. https://doi.org/10.1037/a0038508.

Kyvsgaard, B. (1991). The living conditions of law violators in Denmark. *International Journal of Offender Therapy and Comparative Criminology, 35*(3), 235-247. https://doi.org/10.1177/0306624X9103500306.

Labrecque, R. M., Campbell, C. M., Elliott, J., King, M., Christmann, M., Page, K., McVay, J., & Roller, K. (2018). An examination of the inter-rater reliability and rater accuracy of the level of service/case management inventory. *Corrections, 3*(2), 105-118. https://doi.org/10.1080/23774657.2017.1323253.

*Laghi, F., Pallini, S., Baumgartner, E., & Baiocco, R. (2016). Parent and peer attachment relationships and time perspective in adolescence: Are they related to satisfaction with life? *Time & Society, 25*(1), 24-39. https://doi.org/10.1177/0961463x15577282.

Laird, R. D., Marks, L. D., & Marrero, M. D. (2011). Religiosity, self-control, and antisocial behavior: Religiosity as a promotive and protective factor. *Journal of Applied Developmental Psychology, 32*(2), 78-85. https://doi.org/10.1016/j.appdev.2010.12.003.

Lanctôt, N., Cernkovich, S., & Giordanoi, P. (2007). Delinquent behavior, official delinquency, and gender: Consequences for adulthood functioning and well-being. *Criminology, 45*(1), 131-157. https://doi.org/10.1111/j.1745-9125.2007.00074.x.

Landenberger, N. A., & Lipsey, M. W. (2005). The positive effects of cognitive–behavioral programs for offenders: A meta-analysis of factors associated with effective treatment. *Journal of Experimental Criminology, 1*(4), 451-476. https://doi.org/10.1007/s11292-005-3541-7.

Langlands, R. L., Ward, T., & Gilchrist, E. (2009). Applying the good lives model to male perpetrators of domestic violence. *Behaviour Change, 26*(2), 113-129. https://doi.org/10.1375/bech.26.2.113.

Larsen, R. J., Diener, E., & Emmons, R. A. (1985). An evaluation of subjective well-being measures. *An International and Interdisciplinary Journal for Quality-of-Life Measurement, 17*(1), 1-17. https://doi.org/10.1007/BF00354108.

Latessa, E. J., & Lowenkamp, C. T. (2006). What works in reducing recidivism. *University of St. Thomas Law Journal, 3*, 521-535.

Latimer, J. (2001). A meta-analytic examination of youth delinquency, family treatment, and recidivism. *Canadian Journal of Criminology, 43*(2), 237-253. https://doi.org/10.3138/cjcrim.43.2.237.

*Lau, M., & Bradshaw, J. (2018). Material well-being, social relationships and children's overall life satisfaction in Hong Kong. *Child Indicators Research, 11*(1), 185-205. https://doi.org/10.1007/s12187-016-9426-7.

Laub, J. H., & Sampson, R. J. (1993). Turning points in the life course: Why change matters to the study of crime. *Criminology, 31*(3), 301-325. https://doi.org/10.1111/j.1745-9125.1993.tb01132.x.

Laub, J. H., & Sampson, R. J. (2001). Understanding desistance from crime. *Crime and Justice, 28*, 1-69. https://doi.org/10.1086/652208.

Laub, J. H., & Sampson, R. J. (2003). *Shared beginnings, divergent lives*. Harvard University Press.

Laws, D. R., & Ward, T. (2011). *Desistance from sex offending: Alternatives to throwing away the keys*. Guilford.

LeBel, T. P., Burnett, R., Maruna, S., & Bushway, S. (2008). The 'chicken and egg' of subjective and social factors in desistance from crime. *European Journal of Criminology, 5*(2), 131-159. https://doi.org/10.1177/1477370807087640.

Lee, A. H., & DiGiuseppe, R. (2018). Anger and aggression treatments: A review of meta-analyses. *Current Opinion in Psychology, 19*, 65-74. https://doi.org/10.1016/j.copsyc.2017.04.004.

Leenarts, L. E. W., Hoeve, M., Van de Ven, P. M., Lodewijks, H. P. B., & Doreleijers, T. H. (2013). Childhood maltreatment and motivation for treatment in girls in compulsory residential care. *Children and Youth Services Review, 35*(7), 1041-1047. https://doi.org/10.1016/j.childyouth.2013.04.001.

Leibrich, J. (1994). What do offenders say about supervision and going straight. *Federal Probation, 58*, 41.

Lent, R. W. (2004). Toward a unifying theoretical and practical perspective on well-being and psychosocial adjustment. *Journal of Counseling Psychology, 51*(4), 482-509. https://doi.org/10.1037/0022-0167.51.4.482.

*León, J., & Liew, J. (2017). Profiles of adolescents' peer and teacher relatedness: Differences in well-being and academic achievement across latent groups. *Learning and Individual Differences, 54*, 41-50. https://doi.org/10.1016/j.lindif.2017.01.009.

Leroux, E. (2019). *Understanding the experiences of justice-involved youth at the intersection of the criminal justice and mental health systems* [Unpublished doctoral dissertation]. Carleton University. https://doi.org/10.22215/etd/2019-13504.

*Leung, J. P., & Leung, K. (1992). Life satisfaction, self-concept, and relationship with parents in adolescence. *Journal of Youth and Adolescence, 21*(6), 653-665. https://doi.org/10.1007/BF01538737.

*Leung, J. P., & Zhang, L. W. (2000). Modelling life satisfaction of Chinese adolescents in Hong Kong. *International Journal of Behavioral Development, 24*(1), 99-104. https://doi.org/10.1080/016502500383520.

Levenson, J. S., & Macgowan, M. J. (2004). Engagement, denial, and treatment progress among sex offenders in group therapy. *Sexual Abuse: A Journal of Research and Treatment, 16*(1), 49-63. https://doi.org/10.1177/107906320401600104.

Levenson, J. S., Macgowan, M. J., Morin, J. W., & Cotter, L. P. (2009). Perceptions of sex offenders about treatment: Satisfaction and engagement in group therapy. *Sexual Abuse, 21*(1), 35-56. https://doi.org/10.1177/1079063208326072.

Levenson, J. S., Prescott, D. S., & D'Amora, D. A. (2010). Sex offender treatment: Consumer satisfaction and engagement in therapy. *International Journal of Offender Therapy & Comparative Criminology, 54*(3), 307-326. https://doi.org/10.1177/0306624x08328752.

*Leversen, I., Danielsen, A. G., Birkeland, M. S., & Samdal, O. (2012). Basic psychological need satisfaction in leisure activities and adolescents' life satisfaction. *Journal of Youth and Adolescence, 41*(12), 1588-1599. https://doi.org/10.1007/s10964-012-9776-5.

*Lewis, A., Huebner, E. S., Malone, P. S., & Valois, R. F. (2011). Life satisfaction and student engagement in adolescents. *Journal of Youth & Adolescence, 40*(3), 249-262. https://doi.org/10.1007/s10964-010-9517-6.

Lewis, G., & Doyle, M. (2009). Risk formulation: What are we doing and why? *International Journal of Forensic Mental Health, 8*(4), 286-292. https://doi.org/10.1080/14999011003635696.

Lim, C., & Putnam, R. (2010). Religion, social networks, and life satisfaction. *American Sociological Review, 75*(6), 914-933. https://doi.org/10.1177/0003122410386686.

*Lin, L., & Shek, D. T. L. (2019). The influence of meaning in life on adolescents hedonic well-being and risk behaviour: Implications for social work. *British Journal of Social Work, 49*(1), 5-24. https://doi.org/10.1093/bjsw/bcy029.

*Lin, L., Wang, S., & Li, J. G. (2021). Association between the search for meaning in life and well-being in Chinese adolescents. *Applied Research in Quality of Life, 16*, 2291-2309. https://doi.org/10.1007/s11482-021-09913-x.

Lindsay, W. R., Ward, T., Morgan, T., & Wilson, I. (2007). Self-regulation of sex offending, future pathways and the good lives model: Applications and problems. *Journal of Sexual Aggression, 13*(1), 37-50. https://doi.org/10.1080/13552600701365613.

Lippke, R. L. (2003). Diminished opportunities, diminished capacities: Social deprivation and punishment. *Social Theory and Practice, 29*(3), 459-485. https://doi.org/10.5840/soctheorpract200329322.

Lipsey, M. W. (2009). The primary factors that characterize effective interventions with juvenile offenders: A meta-analytic overview. *Victims & Offenders, 4*(2), 124-147. https://doi.org/10.1080/15564880802612573.

Lipsey, M. W., & Cullen, F. T. (2007). The effectiveness of correctional rehabilitation: A review of systematic reviews. *Annual Review of Law and Social Science, 3*, 297-320. https://doi.org/10.1146/annurev.lawsocsci.3.081806.112833.

Lipsey, M. W., Howell, J. C., Kelly, M. R., Chapman, G., & Carver, D. (2010). *Improving the effectiveness of juvenile justice programs*. Center for Juvenile Justice Reform at Georgetown University.

Lipsey, M. W., & Wilson, D. B. (2001). *Practical meta-analysis*. Sage Publications.

*Liu, K., Chen, W. W., Wang, H. X., Geng, J. Y., & Lei, L. (2021). Parental phubbing linking to adolescent life satisfaction: The mediating role of relationship satisfaction and the moderating role of attachment styles. *Child Care Health and Development, 47*(2), 281-289. https://doi.org/10.1111/cch.12839.

Llosada-Gistau, J., Montserrat, C., & Casas, F. (2015). The subjective well-being of adolescents in residential care compared to that of the general population. *Children and Youth Services Review, 52*, 150-157. https://doi.org/10.1016/j.childyouth.2014.11.007.

Lo, K. Y., & Matsunobu, K. (2014). Role of art and creativity in child culture and socialization. In A. Ben-Arieh, F. Casas, I. Frønes, & J. E. Korbin (Eds.), *Handbook of child well-being: Theories, methods and policies in global perspective* (pp. 1053-1078). Springer. https://doi.org/10.1007/978-90-481-9063-8_185.

Loeber, R., & Stouthamer-Loeber, M. (1986). Family factors as correlates and predictors of juvenile conduct problems and delinquency. *Crime and Justice, 7*, 29-149. https://doi.org/10.1086/449112.

Logan, C., & Johnstone, L. (2010). Personality disorder and violence: Making the link through risk formulation. *Journal of Personality Disorders, 24*(5), 610-633. https://doi.org/10.1521/pedi.2010.24.5.610.

Loney, D. M., & Harkins, L. (2018). Examining the good lives model and antisocial behaviour. *Psychology, Crime & Law, 24*(1), 38-51. https://doi.org/10.1080/1068316X.2017.1371304.

Looman, J., & Abracen, J. (2013). The risk need responsivity model of offender rehabilitation: Is there really a need for a paradigm shift? *International Journal of Behavioral Consultation and Therapy, 8*(3-4), 30-36. https://doi.org/10.1037/h0100980.

Looman, J., Dickie, I., & Abracen, J. (2005). Responsivity issues in the treatment of sexual offenders. *Trauma, Violence, & Abuse, 6*(4), 330-353. https://doi.org/10.1177/1524838005280857.

Lopez, V. (2008). Understanding adolescent property crime using a delinquent events perspective. *Deviant Behavior, 29*(7), 581-610. https://doi.org/10.1080/01639620701839401.

López-Pérez, B., Sánchez, J., & Gummerum, M. (2016). Children's and adolescents' conceptions of happiness. *Journal of Happiness Studies, 17*(6), 2431-2455. https://doi.org/10.1007/s10902-015-9701-1.

*Lopez-Zafra, E., Ramos-Alvarez, M. M., El Ghoudani, K., Luque-Reca, O., Augusto-Landa, J. M., Zarhbouch, B., Alaoui, S., Cortes-Denia, D., & Pulido-Martos, M. (2019). Social support and emotional intelligence as protective resources for well-being in Moroccan adolescents. *Frontiers in Psychology, 10*, 1529. https://doi.org/10.3389/fpsyg.2019.01529.

Lord, A. (2016). Integrating risk, the good lives model and recovery for mentally disordered sexual offenders. *Journal of Sexual Aggression, 22*(1), 107-122. https://doi.org/10.1080/13552600.2014.975164.

Lösel, F., & Schmucker, M. (2005). The effectiveness of treatment for sexual offenders: A comprehensive meta-analysis. *Journal of Experimental Criminology, 1*(1), 117-146. https://doi.org/10.1007/s11292-004-6466-7.

Lowenkamp, C. T., & Latessa, E. J. (2004). Understanding the risk principle: How and why correctional interventions can harm low-risk offenders. *Topics in Community Corrections*, 3-8.

Lowenkamp, C. T., Latessa, E. J., & Holsinger, A. M. (2006). The risk principle in action: What have we learned from 13,676 offenders and 97 correctional programs? *Crime & Delinquency, 52*(1), 77-93. https://doi.org/10.1177/0011128705281747.

Lu, Y., Avellaneda, F., Torres, E. D., & Temple, J. R. (2020). Adolescent bullying and weapon carrying: A longitudinal investigation. *Journal of Research on Adolescence, 30*, 61-65. https://doi.org/10.1111/jora.12469.

Lyons, M. D., Huebner, E. S., Hills, K. J., & Van Horn, M. L. (2013). Mechanisms of change in adolescent life satisfaction: A longitudinal analysis. *Journal of School Psychology, 51*(5), 587-598. https://doi.org/10.1016/j.jsp.2013.07.001.

Lyons, M. D., Otis, K. L., Huebner, E. S., & Hills, K. J. (2014). Life satisfaction and maladaptive behaviors in early adolescents. *School Psychology Quarterly, 29*(4), 553-566. https://doi.org/10.1037/spq0000061.

Lyubomirsky, S., Dickerhoof, R., Boehm, J. K., & Sheldon, K. M. (2011). Becoming happier takes both a will and a proper way: An experimental longitudinal intervention to boost well-being. *Emotion, 11*(2), 391-402. https://doi.org/10.1037/a0022575.

Lyubomirsky, S., King, L., & Diener, E. (2005). The benefits of frequent positive affect: Does happiness lead to success? *Psychology Bulletin, 131*(6), 803-855. https://doi.org/10.1037/0033-2909.131.6.803.

Lyubomirsky, S., & Lepper, H. S. (1999). A measure of subjective happiness: Preliminary reliability and construct validation. *Social Indicators Research, 46*(2), 137-155. https://doi.org/10.1023/A:1006824100041.

*Ma, C. Q., & Huebner, E. S. (2008). Attachment relationships and adolescents' life satisfaction: Some relationships matter more to girls than boys. *Psychology in the Schools, 45*(2), 177-190. https://doi.org/10.1002/pits.20288.

MacDonald, J. M., Piquero, A. R., Valois, R. F., & Zullig, K. J. (2005). The relationship between life satisfaction, risk-taking behaviors, and youth violence. *Journal of Interpersonal Violence, 20*(11), 1495-1518. https://doi.org/10.1177/0886260505278718.

Maguin, E., & Loeber, R. (1996). Academic performance and delinquency. *Crime and Justice, 20*, 145-264.

Mahler, A., Fine, A., Frick, P. J., Steinberg, L., & Cauffman, E. (2018). Expecting the unexpected? Expectations for future success among adolescent first-time offenders. *Child Development, 89*(6), e535-e551. https://doi.org/10.1111/cdev.12977.

Mahler, A., Simmons, C., Frick, P. J., Steinberg, L., & Cauffman, E. (2017). Aspirations, expectations and delinquency: The moderating effect of impulse control. *Journal of Youth and Adolescence, 46*(7), 1503-1514. https://doi.org/10.1007/s10964-017-0661-0.

*Mahon, N. E., & Yarcheski, A. (2002). Alternative theories of happiness in early adolescents. *Clinical Nursing Research, 11*(3), 306-323. https://doi.org/10.1177/10573802011003006.

*Mahon, N. E., Yarcheski, A., & Yarcheski, T. J. (2005). Happiness as related to gender and health in early adolescents. *Clinical Nursing Research, 14*(2), 175-190. https://doi.org/10.1177/1054773804271936.

Mallion, J. S. (2021). Good lives model: Importance of interagency collaboration in preventing violent recidivism. *Societies, 11*(3), 1-13. https://doi.org/10.3390/soc11030096.

Mallion, J. S., & Wood, J. L. (2020). Good lives model and street gang membership: A review and application. *Aggression and Violent Behavior, 52*, 101393. https://doi.org/10.1016/j.avb.2020.101393.

Mallion, J. S., Wood, J. L., & Mallion, A. (2020). Systematic review of 'Good Lives' assumptions and interventions. *Aggression and Violent Behavior, 55*, 101510. https://doi.org/10.1016/j.avb.2020.101510.

Mann, R., Webster, S., Schofield, C., & Marshall, W. (2004). Approach versus avoidance goals in relapse prevention with sexual offenders. *Official Journal of the Association for the Treatment of Sexual Abusers (ATSA), 16*(1), 65-75. https://doi.org/10.1023/B:SEBU.0000006285.73534.57.

Mann, R. E., Ginsburg, J. I., & Weekes, J. R. (2002). Motivational interviewing with offenders. In M. Mcurran (Ed.), *Motivating offenders to change: A guide to enhancing engagement in therapy* (pp. 87-102). Wiley.

Mann, R. E., Hanson, R. K., & Thornton, D. (2010). Assessing risk for sexual recidivism: Some proposals on the nature of psychologically meaningful risk factors. *Sexual Abuse, 22*(2), 191-217. https://doi.org/10.1177/1079063210366039.

Mann, R. E., & Hollin, C. R. (2007). Sexual offenders' explanations for their offending. *Journal of Sexual Aggression, 13*(1), 3-9. https://doi.org/10.1080/13552600701365621.

Markus, H., & Nurius, P. (1986). Possible selves. *American Psychologist, 41*(9), 954. https://doi.org/10.1037/0003-066X.41.9.954.

*Marques, S., Lopez, S. J., & Mitchell, J. (2013). The role of hope, spirituality and religious practice in adolescents' life satisfaction: Longitudinal findings. *Journal of Happiness Studies, 14*(1), 251-261. https://doi.org/10.1007/s10902-012-9329-3.

Marshall, L. E., & Marshall, W. L. (2012). The risk/needs/responsivity model: The crucial features of general responsivity. In E. Bowen & S. Brown (Eds.), *Perspectives on evaluating criminal justice and corrections* (Vol. 13, pp. 29-45). Emerald Group Publishing Limited.

Marshall, L. E., Marshall, W. L., Fernandez, Y. M., Malcolm, P. B., & Moulden, H. M. (2008). The Rockwood Preparatory Program for sexual offenders: Description and preliminary appraisal. *Sexual Abuse, 20*(1), 25-42. https://doi.org/10.1177/1079063208314818.

Marshall, W., & Serran, G. (2004). The role of the therapist in offender treatment. *Psychology, Crime & Law, 10*(3), 309-320. https://doi.org/10.1080/10683160410001662799.

Marshall, W. L., Fernandez, Y. M., Serran, G. A., Mulloy, R., Thornton, D., Mann, R. E., & Anderson, D. (2003). Process variables in the treatment of sexual offenders: A review of the relevant literature. *Aggression and Violent Behavior, 8*(2), 205-234. https://doi.org/10.1016/S1359-1789(01)00065-9.

Marshall, W. L., Serran, G. A., Fernandez, Y. M., Mulloy, R., Mann, R. E., & Thornton, D. (2003). Therapist characteristics in the treatment of sexual offenders: Tentative data on their relationship with indices of behaviour change. *Journal of Sexual Aggression, 9*(1), 25-30. https://doi.org/10.1080/355260031000137940.

Martin, P. (2005). *Making happy people: The nature of happiness and its origins in childhood.* HarperCollins UK.

*Martinez, C. J., Martin, A. J., Liem, G. A. D., & Colmar, S. (2012). A longitudinal analysis of physical and psychological wellbeing amongst late adolescents: Exploring the transition from school to postschool life. *The Australian Educational and Developmental Psychologist, 29*(1), 17-43. https://doi.org/10.1017/edp.2012.1.

Martinson, R. (1974). What works? Questions and answers about prison reform. *The Public Interest, 35*, 22-54.

Marttinen, E., & Salmela-Aro, K. (2012). Personal goal orientations and subjective well-being of adolescents. *Japanese Psychological Research, 54*. https://doi.org/10.1111/j.1468-5884.2012.00521.x.

Maruna, S. (2001). *Making good: How ex-convicts reform and rebuild their lives*. American Psychological Association.

Maslow, A. H. (1962). *Toward a psychology of being*. Simon and Schuster.

Massey, E. K., Gebhardt, W. A., & Garnefski, N. (2008). Adolescent goal content and pursuit: A review of the literature from the past 16 years. *Developmental Review, 28*(4), 421-460. https://doi.org/10.1016/j.dr.2008.03.002.

Massey, E. K., Gebhardt, W. A., & Garnefski, N. (2009). Self-generated goals and goal process appraisals: Relationships with sociodemographic factors and well-being. *Journal of Adolescence, 32*(3), 501-518. https://doi.org/10.1016/j.adolescence.2008.07.003.

Mayone, M., & Arneklev, B. (2015). Curiosity, low self-control and deviance: An exploratory study. *FAU Undergraduate Research Journal, 4*(1), 1-13.

McCormick, S., Peterson-Badali, M., & Skilling, T. A. (2015). Mental health and justice system involvement: A conceptual analysis of the literature. *Psychology, Public Policy, and Law, 21*(2), 213-225. https://doi.org/10.1037/law0000033.

McCormick, S., Peterson-Badali, M., & Skilling, T. A. (2017). The role of mental health and specific responsivity in juvenile justice rehabilitation. *Law and Human Behavior, 41*(1), 55-67. https://doi.org/10.1037/lhb0000228.

McCuish, E., Lussier, P., & Rocque, M. (2020). Maturation beyond age: Interrelationships among psychosocial, adult role, and identity maturation and their implications for desistance from crime. *Journal of Youth and Adolescence, 49*(2), 479-493. https://doi.org/10.1007/s10964-019-01178-w.

McGraw, K. O., & Wong, S. P. (1996). Forming inferences about some intraclass correlation coefficients. *Psychological Methods, 1*(1), 30-46. https://doi.org/10.1037/1082-989X.1.1.30.

McGregor, I., & Little, B. R. (1998). Personal projects, happiness, and meaning: On doing well and being yourself. *Journal of Personality and Social Psychology, 74*(2), 494-512. https://doi.org/10.1037//0022-3514.74.2.494.

McGregor, I., McAdams, D. P., & Little, B. R. (2006). Personal projects, life stories, and happiness: On being true to traits. *Journal of Research in Personality, 40*(5), 551-572. https://doi.org/10.1016/j.jrp.2005.05.002.

McKnight, C. G., Huebner, E. S., & Suldo, S. (2002). Relationships among stressful life events, temperament, problem behavior, and global life satisfaction in adolescents. *Psychology in the Schools, 39*(6), 677-687. https://doi.org/10.1002/pits.10062.

McMahon, G., & Jump, D. (2018). Starting to stop: Young offenders' desistance from crime. *Youth Justice, 18*(1), 3-17. https://doi.org/10.1177/1473225417741223.

McMurran, M. (2002). *Motivating offenders to change: A guide to enhancing engagement in therapy*. Wiley.

McMurran, M. (2009). Motivational interviewing with offenders: A systematic review. *Legal and Criminological Psychology, 14*(1), 83-100. https://doi.org/10.1348/135532508X278326.

McMurran, M., & Theodosi, E. (2007). Is treatment non-completion associated with increased reconviction over no treatment? *Psychology, Crime & Law, 13*(4), 333-343. https://doi.org/10.1080/10683160601060374.

McMurran, M., & Ward, T. (2004). Motivating offenders to change in therapy: An organizing framework. *Legal and Criminological Psychology, 9*(2), 295-311. https://doi.org/10.1348/1355325041719365.

McMurran, M., & Ward, T. (2010). Treatment readiness, treatment engagement and behaviour change. *Criminal Behaviour and Mental Health, 20*(2), 75-85. https://doi.org/10.1002/cbm.762.

McNeill, F. (2012). Four forms of 'offender' rehabilitation: Towards an interdisciplinary perspective. *Legal and Criminological Psychology, 17*(1), 18-36. https://doi.org/10.1111/j.2044-8333.2011.02039.x.

McNeill, F., Farrall, S., Lightowler, C., & Maruna, S. (2012). *How and why people stop offending: Discovering desistance*. Insights evidence summary to support social services in Scotland. www.iriss.org.uk/sites/default/files/iriss-insight-15.pdf.

Meldrum, R. C., Barnes, J. C., & Hay, C. (2015). Sleep deprivation, low self-control, and delinquency: A test of the strength model of self-control. *Journal of Youth and Adolescence, 44*(2), 465-477. https://doi.org/10.1007/s10964-013-0024-4.

Merton, R. K. (1938). Social structure and anomie. *American Sociological Review, 3*(5), 672-682. https://doi.org/10.2307/2084686.

Messersmith, E. E., & Schulenberg, J. E. (2010). Goal attainment, goal striving, and well-being during the transition to adulthood: A ten-year U.S. national longitudinal study. *New Directions for Child and Adolescent Development, 2010*(130), 27-40. https://doi.org/10.1002/cd.279.

Metler, S. J., & Busseri, M. A. (2017). Further evaluation of the tripartite structure of subjective well-being: Evidence from longitudinal and experimental studies. *Journal of Personality, 5*(2), 192-206. https://doi.org/10.1111/jopy.12233.

Miller, L. (2014). Juvenile crime and juvenile justice: Patterns, models, and implications for clinical and legal practice. *Aggression and Violent Behavior, 19*(2), 122-137. https://doi.org/10.1016/j.avb.2014.01.005.

Miller, T., & Vuolo, M. (2018). Examining the antiascetic hypothesis through social control theory: Delinquency, religion, and reciprocation across the early life course. *Crime & Delinquency, 64*(11), 1458-1488. https://doi.org/10.1177/0011128717750393.

Miller, W., & Rollnick, S. (2002). *Motivational interviewing: Preparing people for change.* Guildford.

Milyavskaya, M., Gingras, I., Mageau, G. A., Koestner, R. F., Gagnon, H., Fang, J., & Boiché, J. (2009). Balance across contexts: Importance of balanced need satisfaction across various life domains. *Personality and Social Psychology Bulletin, 35*(8), 1031-1045. https://doi.org/10.1177/0146167209337036.

Milyavskaya, M., & Koestner, R. F. (2011). Psychological needs, motivation, and well-being: A test of self-determination theory across multiple domains. *Personality and Individual Differences, 50*(3), 387-391. https://doi.org/10.1016/j.paid.2010.10.029.

Milyavskaya, M., Philippe, F. L., & Koestner, R. F. (2013). Psychological need satisfaction across levels of experience: Their organization and contribution to general well-being. *Journal of Research in Personality, 47*(1), 41-51. https://doi.org/10.1016/j.jrp.2012.10.013.

Moffitt, T. E. (1993). Adolescence-limited and life-course-persistent antisocial behavior: A developmental taxonomy. *Psychological Review, 100*(4), 674-701. https://doi.org/10.1037/0033-295X.100.4.674.

Moffitt, T. E. (2018). Male antisocial behaviour in adolescence and beyond. *Nature Human Behaviour, 2*(3), 177-186. https://doi.org/10.1038/s41562-018-0309-4.

*Moksnes, U. K., Eilertsen, M. B., Ringdal, R., Bjørnsen, H. N., & Rannestad, T. (2019). Life satisfaction in association with self-efficacy and stressor experience in adolescents – self-efficacy as a potential moderator. *Scandinavian Journal of Caring Sciences, 33*(1), 222-230. https://doi.org/10.1111/scs.12624.

*Moksnes, U. K., Lohre, A., & Espnes, G. A. (2013). The association between sense of coherence and life satisfaction in adolescents. *Quality of Life Research, 22*(6), 1331-1338. https://doi.org/10.1007/s11136-012-0249-9.

*Moljord, I. E., Moksnes, U. K., Eriksen, L., & Espnes, G. A. (2011). Stress and happiness among adolescents with varying frequency of physical activity. *Perceptual and Motor Skills, 113*(2), 631-646. https://doi.org/10.2466/02.06.10.13.pms.113.5.631-646.

Moore, T., & McArthur, M. (2014). If only I, they, we had done things differently: Young people talk about school difficulties and crime. *Children and Youth Services Review, 44*, 249-255. https://doi.org/10.1016/j.childyouth.2014.06.015.

*Moreira, P. A., Cloninger, C. R., Dinis, L., Sa, L., Oliveira, J. T., Dias, A., & Oliveira, J. (2014). Personality and well-being in adolescents. *Frontiers Psychology, 5*, 1494. https://doi.org/10.3389/fpsyg.2014.01494.

*Morgan, M. L., Vera, E. M., Gonzales, R. R., Conner, W., Bena Vacek, K., & Dick Coyle, L. (2011). Subjective well-being in urban adolescents: Interpersonal, individual, and community influences. *Youth & Society, 43*(2), 609-634. https://doi.org/10.1177/0044118X09353517.

Mortelmans, D. (2020). *Handboek kwalitatieve onderzoeksmethoden.* Acco Leuven.

Mortelmans, D., & Dehertogh, B. (2007). *Regressieanalyse.* Acco.

Mulvey, E. P., Schubert, C. A., Pitzer, L., Hawes, S., Piquero, A., & Cardwell, S. (2016). An examination of change in dynamic risk of offending over time among serious juvenile offenders. *Journal of Criminal Justice, 45*, 48-53. https://doi.org/10.1016/j.jcrimjus.2016.02.008.

Mulvey, E. P., Steinberg, L., Fagan, J., Cauffman, E., Piquero, A. R., Chassin, L., Knight, G. P., Brame, R., Schubert, C. A., Hecker, T., & Losoya, S. H. (1 July 2004). Theory and research on desistance from antisocial activity among serious adolescent offenders. *Youth Violence and Juvenile Justice, 2*(3), 213-236. https://doi.org/10.1177/1541204004265864.

Muris, P., Meesters, C., & van den Berg, F. (1 February 2003). The Strengths and Difficulties Questionnaire (SDQ). *European Child & Adolescent Psychiatry, 12*(1), 1-8. https://doi.org/10.1007/s00787-003-0298-2.

Murphy, M. C. (2001). *Natural law and practical rationality.* Cambridge University Press.

Na, C., & Jang, S. J. (2019). Positive expected selves and desistance among serious adolescent offenders. *Journal of Developmental and Life-Course Criminology, 5*(3), 310-334. https://doi.org/10.1007/s40865-019-00109-4.

Navarro, D., Montserrat, C., Malo, S., González, M., Casas, F., & Crous, G. (2017). Subjective well-being: What do adolescents say? *Child & Family Social Work, 22*(1), 175-184. https://doi.org/10.1111/cfs.12215.

Nee, C., Ellis, T., Morris, P., & Wilson, A. (November 2013). Addressing criminality in childhood: Is responsivity the central issue? *International Journal of Offender Therapy and Comparative Criminology, 57*(11), 1347-1373. https://doi.org/10.1177/0306624x12460377.

Netto, N. R., Carter, J. M., & Bonell, C. (2014). A systematic review of interventions that adopt the "good lives" approach to offender rehabilitation. *Journal of Offender Rehabilitation, 53*(6), 403-432. https://doi.org/10.1080/10509674.2014.931746.

Newberry, A. L., & Duncan, R. D. (2001). Roles of boredom and life goals in juvenile delinquency. *Journal of Applied Social Psychology, 31*(3), 527-541. https://doi.org/10.1111/j.1559-1816.2001.tb02054.x.

*Newland, L. A., Giger, J. T., Lawler, M. J., Carr, E. R., Dykstra, E. A., & Roh, S. (2014). Subjective well-being for children in a rural community. *Journal of Social Service Research, 40*(5), 642-661. https://doi.org/10.1080/01488376.2014.917450.

*Newland, L. A., Lawler, M. J., Giger, J. T., Roh, S., & Carr, E. R. (2015). Predictors of children's subjective well-being in rural communities of the United States. *Child Indicators Research, 8*(1), 177-198. https://doi.org/10.1007/s12187-014-9287-x.

Ng, J. Y. Y., Ntoumanis, N., Thøgersen-Ntoumani, C., Deci, E. L., Ryan, R. M., Duda, J. L., & Williams, G. C. (2012). Self-Determination Theory applied to health contexts:A meta-analysis. *Perspectives on Psychological Science, 7*(4), 325-340. https://doi.org/10.1177/1745691612447309.

*Ng, Z. J., Huebner, E. S., & Hills, K. J. (2015). Life satisfaction and academic performance in early adolescents: Evidence for reciprocal association. *Journal of School Psychology, 53*(6), 479-491. https://doi.org/10.1016/j.jsp.2015.09.004.

Nguyen, H., & Bouchard, M. (2013). Need, connections, or competence? Criminal achievement among adolescent offenders. *Justice Quarterly, 30*(1), 44-83. https://doi.org/10.1080/07418825.2011.589398.

Niebuhr, N., & Orrick, E. A. (2020). Impact of employment satisfaction and stress on time to recidivism. *Corrections, 5*(3), 170-187. https://doi.org/10.1080/23774657.2018.1441761.

Nikolic-Ristanovic, V. (2014). Making people happy is the best crime prevention: Towards happy-making criminology. *European Journal of Criminology, 11*(4), 401-409. https://doi.org/10.1177/1477370814536323.

Noom, M. J., Deković, M., & Meeus, W. H. (1999). Autonomy, attachment and psychosocial adjustment during adolescence: A double-edged sword? *Journal of Adolescence, 22*(6), 771-783. https://doi.org/10.1006/jado.1999.0269.

Nurmi, J. E. (1991). How do adolescents see their future? A review of the development of future orientation and planning. *Developmental Review, 11*(1), 1-59. https://doi.org/10.1016/0273-2297(91)90002-6.

Nurmi, J. E., & Salmela-Aro, K. (2002). Goal construction, reconstruction and depressive symptoms in a life-span context: The transition from school to work. *Journal of Personality, 70*(3), 385-420. https://doi.org/10.1111/1467-6494.05009.

Nussbaum, M. C. (2001). *Women and human development: The capabilities approach* (Vol. 3). Cambridge University Press.

Oberlader, V., Banse, R., Beier, S., & Schmidt, A. F. (2021). *Law-abiding versus criminal identity and self-efficacy: A quantitative approach to unravel psychological factors supporting desistance from crime* [Unpublished manuscript]. Rheinische Friedrich Wilhelms-Universität Bonn. https://doi.org/10.31234/osf.io/wp6m8.

Oberwittler, D. (2004). A multilevel analysis of neighbourhood contextual effects on serious juvenile offending: The role of subcultural values and social disorganization. *European Journal of Criminology, 1*(2), 201-235. https://doi.org/10.1177/1477370804041248.

Ogilvie, D. M., Rose, K. M., & Heppen, J. B. (2001). A comparison of personal project motives in three age groups. *Basic and Applied Social Psychology, 23*(3), 207-215. https://doi.org/10.1207/S15324834BASP2303_7.

Ogilvie, J. M., Stewart, A. L., Chan, R. C. K., & Shum, D. H. K. (2011). Neuropsychological measures of executive function and antisocial behavior: A meta-analysis. *Criminology, 49*(4), 1063-1107. https://doi.org/10.1111/j.1745-9125.2011.00252.x.

Ogloff, J. R. P., & Davis, M. R. (2004). Advances in offender assessment and rehabilitation: Contributions of the risk-needs-responsivity approach. *Psychology Crime & Law, 10*(3), 229-242. https://doi.org/10.1080/10683160410001662735.

Oishi, S., & Diener, E. (2009). Goals, culture, and subjective well-being. In E. Diener (Ed.), *Culture and well-being* (pp. 93-108). Springer. https://doi.org/10.1007/978-90-481-2352-0_5.

Oishi, S., Diener, E., Lucas, R. E., & Suh, E. M. (2009). Cross-cultural variations in predictors of life satisfaction: Perspectives from needs and values. In E. Diener (Ed.), *Culture and well-being* (pp. 109-127). Springer. https://doi.org/10.1007/978-90-481-2352-0_6.

Oishi, S., Diener, E., Suh, E., & Lucas, R. E. (1999). Value as a moderator in subjective well-being. *Journal of Personality, 67*(1), 157-184. https://doi.org/10.1111/1467-6494.00051.

Olson, J., Martin, R. L., & Connell, N. M. (2020). Satisfaction with life and crime: Testing the link. *Psychology, Crime & Law, 27*(7), 631-655. https://doi.org/10.1080/1068316X.2020.1849692.

Olver, M. E., Stockdale, K. C., & Wong, S. C. P. (2012). Short and long-term prediction of recidivism using the youth level of service/case management inventory in a sample of serious young offenders. *Law and Human Behavior, 36*(4), 331-344. https://doi.org/10.1037/h0093927.

Olver, M. E., Stockdale, K. C., & Wormith, J. S. (2009). Risk assessment with young offenders: A meta-analysis of three assessment measures. *Criminal Justice and Behavior, 36*(4), 329-353. https://doi.org/10.1177/0093854809331457.

Olver, M. E., Stockdale, K. C., & Wormith, J. S. (2011). A meta-analysis of predictors of offender treatment attrition and its relationship to recidivism. *Journal of Consulting and Clinical Psychology, 79*(1), 6-21. https://doi.org/10.1037/a0022200.

Olver, M. E., Stockdale, K. C., & Wormith, J. S. (2014). Thirty years of research on the level of service scales: A meta-analytic examination of predictive accuracy and sources of variability. *Psychological Assessment, 26*(1), 156-176. https://doi.org/10.1037/a0035080.

Onder, F. C., & Yilmaz, Y. (2012). The role of life satisfaction and parenting styles in predicting delinquent behaviors among high school students. *Educational Sciences: Theory and Practice, 12*(3), 1744-1748.

Op de Beeck, H. (2012). *Strain en jeugddelinquentie: een dynamische relatie. Een toets van twee centrale verklaringsmechanismen uit Agnews General Strain Theory.* Boom Lemma.

Ortuno-Sierra, J., Aritio-Solana, R., de Luis, E. C., Nalda, F. N., & Fonseca-Pedrero, E. (2019). Subjective well-being in adolescence: New psychometric evidences on the satisfaction with life scale. *European Journal of Developmental Psychology, 16*(2), 236-244. https://doi.org/10.1080/17405629.2017.1360179.

Oyserman, D., & Markus, H. (1990). Possible selves in balance: Implications for delinquency. *Journal of Social Issues, 46*(2), 141-157. https://doi.org/10.1111/j.1540-4560.1990.tb01927.x.

Oyserman, D., & Saltz, E. (1993). Competence, delinquency, and attempts to attain possible selves. *Journal of Personality and Social Psychology, 65*(2), 360-374. https://doi.org/10.1037//0022-3514.65.2.360.

Page, G. L., & Scalora, M. J. (2004). The utility of locus of control for assessing juvenile amenability to treatment. *Aggression and Violent Behavior, 9*(5), 523-534. https://doi.org/10.1016/S1359-1789(03)00047-8.

*Palen, L. A., & Coatsworth, J. D. (2007). Activity-based identity experiences and their relations to problem behavior and psychological well-being in adolescence. *Journal of Adolescence, 30*(5), 721-737. https://doi.org/10.1016/j.adolescence.2006.11.003.

*Pallini, S., Milioni, M., Laghi, F., & Vecchio, G. M. (2016). The ant and the grasshopper: Adolescents' time perspective, satisfaction with life and the mediating role of hope. *Journal of Happiness Studies, 19*, 351-364. https://doi.org/10.1007/s10902-016-9821-2.

Panuccio, E. A., Christian, J., Martinez, D. J., & Sullivan, M. L. (2012). Social support, motivation, and the process of juvenile reentry: An exploratory analysis of desistance. *Journal of Offender Rehabilitation, 51*(3), 135-160. https://doi.org/10.1080/10509674.2011.618527.

Parhar, K. K., Wormith, J. S., Derkzen, D. M., & Beauregard, A. M. (2008). Offender coercion in treatment: A meta-analysis of effectiveness. *Criminal Justice and Behavior, 35*(9), 1109-1135. https://doi.org/10.1177/0093854808320169.

Park, N. (2004). The role of subjective well-being in positive youth development. *The Annals of the American Academy of Political and Social Science, 591*(1), 25-39. https://doi.org/10.1177/0002716203260078.

*Park, N., & Huebner, E. S. (2005). A cross-cultural study of the levels and correlates of life satisfaction among adolescents. *Journal of Cross-Cultural Psychology, 36*(4), 444-456. https://doi.org/10.1177/0022022105275961.

Parliamentary Acts Flemish Parliament No. 1670/1. (2017-2018). Explanatory memorandum to the draft decree on juvenile delinquency law. https://docs.vlaamsparlement.be/pfile?id=1427106.

Paternoster, R., & Bushway, S. (2009). Desistance and the "feared self": Toward an identity theory of criminal desistance. *The Journal of Criminal Law and Criminology, 99*(4), 1103-1156.

Patterson, G. R., & Dishion, T. J. (1985). Contributions of families and peers to delinquency. *Criminology, 23*(1), 63-79. https://doi.org/10.1111/j.1745-9125.1985.tb00326.x.

Pavot, W., & Diener, E. (2004). Findings on subjective well-being: Applications to public policy, clinical interventions, and education. In P. A. Linley & S. Joseph (Eds.), *Positive psychology in practice* (pp. 679-693). Wiley.

Peach, H. D., & Gaultney, J. F. (2013). Sleep, impulse control, and sensation-seeking predict delinquent behavior in adolescents, emerging adults, and adults. *Journal of Adolescent Health, 53*(2), 293-299. https://doi.org/10.1016/j.jadohealth.2013.03.012.

Peets, K., & Hodges, E. V. E. (2018). Authenticity in friendships and well-being in adolescence. *Social Development, 27*(1), 140-153. https://doi.org/10.1111/sode.12254.

Penner, M. J. (1982). The role of selected health problems in the causation of juvenile delinquency. *Adolescence, 17*(66), 347.

Peterson, C., Park, N., & Seligman, M. E. P. (2005). Orientations to happiness and life satisfaction: The full life versus the empty life. *An Interdisciplinary Forum on Subjective Well-Being, 6*(1), 25-41. https://doi.org/10.1007/s10902-004-1278-z.

Peterson, R. A., & Brown, S. P. (2005). On the use of beta coefficients in meta-analysis. *Journal of Applied Psychology, 90*(1), 175-181. https://doi.org/10.1037/0021-9010.90.1.175.

Petrich, D. M. (2020). A Self-Determination Theory perspective on human agency, desistance from crime, and correctional rehabilitation. *Journal of Developmental and Life-Course Criminology, 6*, 353-379. https://doi.org/10.1007/s40865-020-00141-9.

Petrich, D. M., Liu, H., & Nedelec, J. L. (2020). The longitudinal associations between motivation, self-regulatory capacities, and future-oriented cognition and behavior among serious young offenders. *Law and Human Behavior, 44*(5), 424-436. https://doi.org/10.1037/lhb0000421.

Petrie, R. (2013). *Late-adolescent well-being: The balance of life domains*. Pace University.

Pflugradt, D., & Allen, B. (2019). The application of the good lives model to women who commit sexual offenses. *Current Psychiatry Reports, 21*(12), 1-7. https://doi.org/10.1007/s11920-019-1115-z.

Pham, T. B., Schapiro, L. E., John, M., & Adesman, A. (2017). Weapon carrying among victims of bullying. *Pediatrics, 140*(6), e20170353. https://doi.org/10.1542/peds.2017-0353.

Pinquart, M. (2017). Associations of parenting dimensions and styles with externalizing problems of children and adolescents: An updated meta-analysis. *Developmental Psychology, 53*(5), 873. https://doi.org/10.1037/dev0000295.

Piquero, A. R., & Brezina, T. (2001). Testing Moffitt's account of adolescence-limited delinquency. *Criminology, 39*(2), 353-370. https://doi.org/10.1111/j.1745-9125.2001.tb00926.x.

Piquero, A. R., Cardwell, S. M., Piquero, N. L., Jennings, W. G., & Reingle Gonzalez, J. M. (2016). How well do the adolescent risk factors predict re-arrest frequency across race/

ethnicity among serious adolescent offenders? *Journal of Crime and Justice*, 1-21. https://doi.org/10.1080/0735648X.2015.1106070.

Pleysier, S. (2019). Een 'evidence based' jeugddelinquentierecht: What's in a name? In J. Put & J. Leenknecht (Eds.), *Het Vlaamse jeugddelinquentierecht in essentie* (pp. 177-189). Larcier.

Polaschek, D. L. L. (2012). An appraisal of the risk–need–responsivity (RNR) model of offender rehabilitation and its application in correctional treatment. *Legal and Criminological Psychology, 17*(1), 1-17. https://doi.org/10.1111/j.2044-8333.2011.02038.x.

Polaschek, D. L. L., & Ross, E. C. (2010). Do early therapeutic alliance, motivation, and stages of change predict therapy change for high-risk, psychopathic violent prisoners? *Criminal Behaviour and Mental Health, 20*(2), 100-111. https://doi.org/10.1002/cbm.759.

Porporino, F. (2010). Bringing sense and sensitivity to corrections: From programmes to 'fix'offenders to services to support desistance. In J. Brayford, F. Cowe, & J. Deering (Eds.), *What else works? Creative work with offenders* (pp. 61-85). Willan Publishing.

*Poulou, M., & Norwich, B. (2020). Psychological needs, mixed self-perceptions, well-being and emotional, and behavioral difficulties: Adolescent students' perceptions. *European Journal of Psychology of Education, 35*(4), 775-793. https://doi.org/10.1007/s10212-019-00457-1.

*Povedano-Diaz, A., Muniz-Rivas, M., & Vera-Perea, M. (2020). Adolescents' life satisfaction: The role of classroom, family, self-concept and gender. *International Journal of Environmental Research and Public Health, 17*(1), 19. https://doi.org/10.3390/ijerph17010019.

Pratt, T. C., & Cullen, F. T. (2000). The empirical status of Gottfredson and Hirschi's general theory of crime: A meta-analysis. *Criminology, 38*(3), 931-964. https://doi.org/10.1111/j.1745-9125.2000.tb00911.x.

Prescott, D. S. (2018). *Becoming who I want to be. A good lives workbook for young men.* Safer Society Press.

Prescott, D. S., & Dent, T. (2018). *Becoming who I want to be. A good lives workbook for young women.* Safer Society Press.

Prescott, D. S., & Willis, G. M. (2021). Using the good lives model (GLM) in clinical practice: Lessons learned from international implementation projects. *Aggression and Violent Behavior*, 101717. https://doi.org/10.1016/j.avb.2021.101717.

Print, B. (2013). *The good lives model for adolescents who sexually harm.* Safer Society Foundation Brandon.

Prochaska, J. O., & DiClemente, C. C. (1986). Toward a comprehensive model of change. In W. R. Miller & N. Heather (Eds.), *Treating addictive behaviors* (pp. 3-27). Springer.

Prochaska, J. O., DiClemente, C. C., & Norcross, J. C. (1992). In search of how people change: Applications to addictive behaviors. *Addictions Nursing Network, 5*(1), 2-16. https://doi.org/10.1037//0003-066x.47.9.1102.

Prochaska, J. O., & Levesque, D. A. (2002). Enhancing motivation of offenders at each stage of change and phase of therapy. In M. McMurran (Ed.), *Motivating offenders to change: A guide to enhancing engagement in therapy* (pp. 57-73). Wiley.

Proctor, C. L., & Linley, P. A. (2014). Life satisfaction in youth. In G. A. Fava & C. Ruini (Eds.), *Increasing psychological well-being in clinical and educational settings* (pp. 199-215). Springer.

Proctor, C. L., Linley, P. A., & Maltby, J. (2009). Youth life satisfaction: A review of the literature. *Journal of Happiness Studies, 10*(5), 583-630. https://doi.org/10.1007/s10902-008-9110-9.

Purvis, M. (2010). *Seeking a good life: Human goods and sexual offending.* Lambert Academic Press.

Purvis, M., Ward, T., & Willis, G. M. (2011). The good lives model in practice: Offence pathways and case management. *European Journal of Probation, 3*(2), 4-28. https://doi.org/10.1177/206622031100300202.

Purvis, M., Ward, T., & Willis, G. M. (2014). Applying the good lives model of offender rehabilitation to sex offenders. In M. S. Carich & S. E. Mussack (Eds.), *The safer society handbook of sexual abuser assessment and treatment.* (pp. 193-220). Safer Society Press.

Put, J. (2020). Hulpverlening en sanctie in het Vlaamse Jeugddelinquentiedecreet: A perfect (mis) match? *Tijdschrift voor Familie-en Jeugdrecht, 2020*(3), 77-80.

Put, J., & Leenknecht, J. (2019). *Het Vlaamse jeugddelinquentierecht in essentie.* Larcier.

Put, J., & Pleysier, S. (2018). De ontwikkeling van een nieuw Vlaams jeugddelinquentierecht: een juridisch-criminologische reflectie. *Agora, 34*(2), 18-24.

Putnam, R. (2001). Social capital: Measurement and consequences. *Canadian Journal of Policy Research, 2*(1), 41-51.

Putniņš, A. L. (2010). An exploratory study of young offenders' self-reported reasons for offending. *The Journal of Forensic Psychiatry & Psychology, 21*(6), 950-965. https://doi.org/10.1080/14789949.2010.491552.

Pyle, N., Flower, A., Fall, A. M., & Williams, J. (2016). Individual-level risk factors of incarcerated youth. *Remedial and Special Education, 37*(3), 172-186. https://doi.org/10.1177/0741932515593383.

*Raboteg-Šaric, Z., Brajsa-Žganec, A., & Šakic, M. (2009). Life satisfaction in adolescents: The effects of perceived family economic status, self-esteem and quality of family and peer relationships. *Journal for General Social Issues, 18*(3), 547-564.

Rapp, C. A., & Goscha, R. J. (2012). *The strengths model: A recovery-oriented approach to mental health services.* Oxford University Press.

Rask, K., Astedt-Kurki, P., Paavilainen, E., & Laippala, P. (2003). Adolescent subjective well-being and family dynamics. *Scandinavian Journal of Caring Sciences, 17*(2), 129-138. https://doi.org/10.1046/j.0283-9318.2002.00118.x.

Rask, K., Åstedt-Kurki, P., Tarkka, M., & Laippala, P. (2002). Relationships among adolescent subjective well-being, health behavior, and school satisfaction. *Journal of School Health, 72*(6), 243-249. https://doi.org/10.1111/j.1746-1561.2002.tb07337.x.

Rasmussen, D. B. (1999). Human flourishing and the appeal to human nature. *Social Philosophy and Policy, 16*(1), 1-43. https://doi.org/10.1017/S0265052500002235.

Rawls, J. (1978). *A theory of justice*. Harvard University Press.

Rebellon, C. J. (2002). Reconsidering the broken homes/delinquency relationship and exploring its mediating mechanism(s). *Criminology, 40*(1), 103-136. https://doi.org/10.1111/j.1745-9125.2002.tb00951.x.

Reese, L. E., Vera, E. M., Thompson, K., & Reyes, R. (2001). Qualitative investigation of perceptions of violence risk factors in low-income African American children. *Journal of Clinical Child Psychology, 30*(2), 161-171. https://doi.org/10.1207/s15374424jccp3002_4.

Regnerus, M. D. (2003). Religion and positive adolescent outcomes: A review of research and theory. *Review of Religious Research, 44*(4), 394-413. https://doi.org/10.2307/3512217.

Reid, J. A., Richards, T. N., Loughran, T. A., & Mulvey, E. P. (2017). The relationships among exposure to violence, psychological distress, and gun carrying among male adolescents found guilty of serious legal offenses: A longitudinal cohort study. *Annals of Internal Medicine, 166*(6), 412-418. https://doi.org/10.7326/m16-1648.

Reis, H. T., Sheldon, K. M., Gable, S. L., Roscoe, J., & Ryan, R. M. (2000). Daily well-being: The role of autonomy, competence, and relatedness. *Personality and Social Psychology Bulletin, 26*(4), 419-435. https://doi.org/10.1177/0146167200266002.

Rescher, N. (1990). *Human interests: Reflections on philosophical anthropology* (Vol. 6). Stanford University Press.

Richards, K. (2011). What makes juvenile offenders different from adult offenders? *Trends and Issues in Crime and Criminal Justice, 409*, 1-8.

Robertson, B. J. (1994). Leisure in the lives of male adolescents who engage in delinquent activity for excitement. *Journal of Park and Recreation Administration, 12*(4), 29-46.

Robertson, B. J. (2001). The leisure education of incarcerated youth. *World Leisure Journal, 43*(1), 20-29. https://doi.org/10.1080/04419057.2001.9674216.

Rocque, M., Beckley, A. L., & Piquero, A. R. (2019). Psychosocial maturation, race, and desistance from crime. *Journal of Youth and Adolescence, 48*(7), 1403-1417. https://doi.org/10.1007/s10964-019-01029-8.

Rocque, M., & Plummer-Beale, J. (2014). In the eye of the beholder? An examination of the inter-rater reliability of the LSI-R and YLS/CMI in a correctional agency. *Journal of Criminal Justice, 42*(6), 568-578. https://doi.org/10.1016/j.jcrimjus.2014.09.011.

Rodríguez-Meirinhos, A., Antolín-Suárez, L., Brenning, K., Vansteenkiste, M., & Oliva, A. (2020). A bright and a dark path to adolescents' functioning: The role of need satisfaction and need frustration across gender, age, and socioeconomic status. *Journal of Happiness Studies, 21*(1), 95-116. https://doi.org/10.1007/s10902-018-00072-9.

Roedelof, A., Bongers, I. L., & van Nieuwenhuizen, C. (2013). Treatment engagement in adolescents with severe psychiatric problems: A latent class analysis. *European Child & Adolescent Psychiatry, 22*(8), 491-500. https://doi.org/10.1007/s00787-013-0385-y.

Roest, J. J., Van der Helm, G. H. P., & Stams, G. J. J. M. (2016). The relation between therapeutic alliance and treatment motivation in residential youth care: A cross-lagged panel analysis. *Child and Adolescent Social Work Journal, 33*(5), 455-468. https://doi.org/10.1007/s10560-016-0438-4.

Rojas, M. (2006). Life satisfaction and satisfaction in domains of life: Is it a simple relationship? *An Interdisciplinary Forum on Subjective Well-Being, 7*(4), 467-497. https://doi.org/10.1007/s10902-006-9009-2.

Ronel, N., & Elisha, E. (2011). A different perspective: Introducing positive criminology. *International Journal of Offender Therapy and Comparative Criminology, 55*(2), 305-325. https://doi.org/10.1177/0306624X09357772.

Ronel, N., & Segev, D. (2014). Positive criminology in practice. *International Journal of Offender Therapy and Comparative Criminology, 58*(11), 1389-1407. https://doi.org/10.1177/0306624x13491933.

*Ronen, T., Hamama, L., Rosenbaum, M., & Mishely-Yarlap, A. (2016). Subjective well-being in adolescence: The role of self-control, social support, age, gender, and familial crisis. *Journal of Happiness Studies, 17*(1), 81-104. https://doi.org/10.1007/s10902-014-9585-5.

Rotter, J. B. (1966). Generalized expectancies for internal versus external control of reinforcement. *Psychological Monographs: General and Applied, 80*(1), 1-28. https://doi.org/10.1037/h0092976.

Ruchkin, V. V., Schwab-Stone, M., Koposov, R., Vermeiren, R., & Steiner, H. (2002). Violence exposure, posttraumatic stress, and personality in juvenile delinquents. *Journal of the American Academy of Child & Adolescent Psychiatry, 41*(3), 322-329. https://doi.org/10.1097/00004583-200203000-00012.

Rudd, M., Aaker, J., & Norton, M. I. (2014). Getting the most out of giving: Concretely framing a prosocial goal maximizes happiness. *Journal of Experimental Social Psychology, 54*, 11-24. https://doi.org/10.1016/j.jesp.2014.04.002.

Russo-Netzer, P., & Shoshani, A. (2020,). Authentic inner compass, well-being, and prioritization of positivity and meaning among adolescents. *Personality and Individual Differences, 167*, 110248. https://doi.org/10.1016/j.paid.2020.110248.

Ryan, J. P., Abrams, L. S., & Huang, H. (March 2014). First-time violent juvenile offenders: Probation, placement, and recidivism. *Social Work Research, 38*(1), 7-18. https://doi.org/10.1093/swr/svu004.

Ryan, M., McCauley, M., & Walsh, D. (2019). The virtuous circle: A grounded theory exploration of the good lives model. *Sexual Abuse: A Journal of Research and Treatment, 31*(8), 908-929. https://doi.org/10.1177/1079063218780730.

Ryan, R. M., & Deci, E. L. (2000a). Intrinsic and extrinsic motivations: Classic definitions and new directions. *Contemporary Educational Psychology, 25*(1), 54-67. https://doi.org/10.1006/ceps.1999.1020.

Ryan, R. M., & Deci, E. L. (2000b). Self-determination theory and the facilitation of intrinsic motivation, social development, and well-being. *American Psychologist, 55*(1), 68-78. https://doi.org/10.1037//0003-066x.55.1.68.

Ryan, R. M., & Deci, E. L. (2001). On happiness and human potentials: A review of research on hedonic and eudaimonic well-being. *Annual Review of Psychology, 52*(1), 141-166. https://doi.org/10.1146/annurev.psych.52.1.141.

Ryan, R. M., & Deci, E. L. (2017a). Identity development, self-esteem, and authenticity. In R. M. Ryan & E. L. Deci (Eds.), *Self-determination theory: Basic psychological needs in motivation, development, and wellness* (pp. 382-400). Guilford.

Ryan, R. M., & Deci, E. L. (2017b). *Self-determination theory: Basic psychological needs in motivation, development, and wellness.* Guilford. https://doi.org/10.1521/978.14625/28806.

Ryan, R. M., Huta, V., & Deci, E. L. (2013). Living well: A self-determination theory perspective on eudaimonia. In A. Delle Fave (Ed.), *The exploration of happiness* (pp. 117-139). Springer. https://doi.org/10.1007/978-94-007-5702-8_7.

Ryff, C. D. (1989). Beyond Ponce de Leon and life satisfaction: New directions in quest of successful ageing. *International Journal of Behavioral Development, 12*(1), 35-55. https://doi.org/10.1177/016502548901200102.

Ryff, C. D., & Singer, B. H. (1998). The contours of positive human health. *Psychological Inquiry, 9*(1), 1-28. https://doi.org/10.1207/s15327965pli0901_1.

Ryff, C. D., & Singer, B. H. (2008). Know thyself and become what you are: A eudaimonic approach to psychological well-being. *An Interdisciplinary Forum on Subjective Well-Being, 9*(1), 13-39. https://doi.org/10.1007/s10902-006-9019-0.

*Saha, R., Huebner, E. S., Hills, K. J., Malone, P. S., & Valois, R. F. (2014). Social coping and life satisfaction in adolescents. *Social Indicators Research, 115*(1), 241-252. https://doi.org/10.1007/s11205-012-0217-3.

*Saha, R., Huebner, E. S., Suldo, S. M., & Valois, R. F. (2010). A longitudinal study of adolescent life satisfaction and parenting. *Child Indicators Research, 3*(2), 149-165. https://doi.org/10.1007/s12187-009-9050-x.

Salavera, C., & Usan, P. (2020). The relationship between eudaimonic wellbeing, emotional intelligence and affect in early adolescents. *Current Psychology*. https://doi.org/10.1007/s12144-020-01208-y.

Salavera, C., Usan, P., Teruel, P., & Antonanzas, J. L. (2020). Eudaimonic well-being in adolescents: The role of trait emotional intelligence and personality. *Sustainability, 12*(7), 2742. https://doi.org/10.3390/su12072742.

Salmela-Aro, K. (2010). Personal goals and well-being: How do young people navigate their lives? *New Directions for Child and Adolescent Development, 2010*(130), 13-26. https://doi.org/10.1002/cd.278.

*Salmela-Aro, K., & Tuominen-Soini, H. (2010). Adolescents' life satisfaction during the transition to post-comprehensive education: Antecedents and consequences. *Journal of Happiness Studies, 11*(6), 683-701. https://doi.org/10.1007/s10902-009-9156-3.

*Salmela-Aro, K., & Tynkkynen, L. (2010). Trajectories of life satisfaction across the transition to post-compulsory education: Do adolescents follow different pathways? *Journal of Youth and Adolescence, 39*(8), 870-881. https://doi.org/10.1007/s10964-009-9464-2.

Sampson, R. J., & Groves, W. B. (1989). Community structure and crime: Testing social-disorganization theory. *American Journal of Sociology, 94*(4), 774-802. https://doi.org/10.1086/229068.

Sampson, R. J., & Laub, J. H. (1995). *Crime in the making: Pathways and turning points through life*. Harvard University Press.

Sampson, R. J., Morenoff, J. D., & Gannon-Rowley, T. (2002). Assessing "neighborhood effects": Social processes and new directions in research. *Annual Review of Sociology, 28*(1), 443-478. https://doi.org/10.1146/annurev.soc.28.110601.141114.

Sampson, R. J., Raudenbush, S. W., & Earls, F. (1997). Neighborhoods and violent crime: A multilevel study of collective efficacy. *Science, 277*(5328), 918-924. https://doi.org/10.1126/science.277.5328.918.

Schimmack, U. (2008). The structure of subjective well-being. In M. Eid & R. J. Larsen (Eds.), *The science of subjective well-being* (pp. 97-123). Guilford.

Schimmack, U., & Oishi, S. (2005). The influence of chronically and temporarily accessible information on life satisfaction judgments. *Journal of Personality and Social Psychology, 89*(3), 395-406. https://doi.org/10.1037/0022-3514.89.3.395.

Schmuck, P. E., Kasser, T., & Ryan, R. M. (2000). Intrinsic and extrinsic goals: Their structure and relationship to well-being in German and U.S. college students. *An International and Interdisciplinary Journal for Quality-of-Life Measurement, 50*(2), 225-241. https://doi.org/10.1023/A:1007084005278.

Schmuck, P. E., & Sheldon, K. M. (2001). *Life goals and well-being: Towards a positive psychology of human striving*. Hogrefe & Huber Publishers.

Schoenthaler, S., & Bier, I. (1985). Diet and delinquency: Empirical testing of seven theories. *International Journal of Biosocial Research, 7*(2), 108-131.

Schubert, C. A., Mulvey, E. P., Loughran, T. A., & Losoya, S. H. (2012). Perceptions of institutional experience and community outcomes for serious adolescent offenders. *Criminal Justice and Behavior, 39*(1), 71-93. https://doi.org/10.1177/0093854811426710.

Schwalbe, C. S. (2007). Risk assessment for juvenile justice: A meta-analysis. *Law and Human Behavior, 31*(5), 449-462. https://doi.org/10.1007/s10979-006-9071-7.

Schwarz, N., & Strack, F. (1991). Evaluating one's life: A judgment model of subjective well-being. In F. Strack, M. Argyle, & N. Schwarz (Eds.), *Subjective well-being. An interdisciplinary perspective*. Pergamon.

Schwarz, N., & Strack, F. (1999). Reports of subjective well-being: Judgmental processes and their methodological implications. In D. Kahneman, E. Diener, & N. Schwarz (Eds.), *Well-being: The foundations of hedonic psychology* (pp. 61-84). Sage Publications.

Sebire, S. J., Standage, M., & Vansteenkiste, M. (2009). Examining intrinsic versus extrinsic exercise goals: Cognitive, affective, and behavioral outcomes. *Journal of Sport and Exercise Psychology, 31*(2), 189-210. https://doi.org/10.1123/jsep.31.2.189.

Seligman, M. E. P. (2004). *Authentic happiness: Using the new positive psychology to realize your potential for lasting fulfillment*. Simon and Schuster.

Seligman, M. E. P. (2011). *Flourish: A visionary new understanding of happiness and well-being*. Simon and Schuster.

Seligman, M. E. P., & Csikszentmihalyi, M. (2000). Positive psychology: An introduction. *American Psychologist, 5*(1), 5-14. https://doi.org/10.1037//0003-066x.55.1.5.

Semenza, D. C. (2018). Health behaviors and juvenile delinquency. *Crime & Delinquency, 64*(11), 1394-1416. https://doi.org/10.1177/0011128717719427.

Sen, A. (2001). *Development as freedom*. Oxford Paperbacks.

Serie, C. M. B., Pleysier, S., & Weber, A. (2017a). *Satisfaction with Life Scale–Child Version (SWLS-CV - Dutch/Flemish translation)*. https://commondatastorage.googleapis.com/eddiener/uploads/version/file/166/SWLS-C_Dutch_Flemish.pdf.

Serie, C. M. B., Pleysier, S., & Weber, A. (2017b). *Scale of positive and negative experience (SPANE - Dutch/Flemish Version)*. https://commondatastorage.googleapis.com/eddiener/uploads/version/file/165/SPANE_Dutch_Flemish.pdf.

Serin, R. C., & Lloyd, C. D. (2009). Examining the process of offender change: The transition to crime desistance. *Psychology, Crime & Law, 15*(4), 347-364. https://doi.org/10.1080/10683160802261078.

Serin, R. C., & Lloyd, C. D. (2017). *Understanding the risk need, responsivity (RNR) model and crime desistance perspective and integrating them into correctional practice* [Unpublished manuscript]. Carleton University.

Serin, R. C., Lloyd, C. D., Helmus, L., Derkzen, D. M., & Luong, D. (2013). Does intra-individual change predict offender recidivism? Searching for the Holy Grail in assessing offender change. *Aggression and Violent Behavior, 18*(1), 32-53. https://doi.org/10.1016/j.avb.2012.09.002.

Shafran, R., & Mansell, W. (2001). Perfectionism and psychopathology: A review of research and treatment. *Clinical Psychology Review, 21*(6), 879-906. https://doi.org/10.1016/S0272-7358(00)00072-6.

Sharkey, J. D., Shekhtmeyster, Z., Chavez-Lopez, L., Norris, E., & Sass, L. (2011). The protective influence of gangs: Can schools compensate? *Aggression and Violent Behavior, 16*(1), 45-54. https://doi.org/10.1016/j.avb.2010.11.001.

Shaw, C. R., & MacKay, H. D. (1969). *Juvenile delinquency and urban areas: A study of rates of delinquency in relation to differential characteristics of local communities in American cities.* University of Chicago Press.

Shek, D., & Lin, L. (2016). What predicts adolescent delinquent behavior in Hong Kong? A longitudinal study of personal and family factors. *An International and Interdisciplinary Journal for Quality-of-Life Measurement, 129*(3), 1291-1318. https://doi.org/10.1007/s11205-015-1170-8.

*Shek, D. T. L. (1997a). The relation of family functioning to adolescent psychological well-being, school adjustment, and problem behavior. *Journal of Genetic Psychology, 158*(4), 467-479. https://doi.org/10.1080/00221329709596683.

*Shek, D. T. L. (1997b). The relation of parent-adolescent conflict to adolescent psychological well-being, school adjustment, and problem behavior. *Social Behavior and Personality, 25*(3), 277-290. https://doi.org/10.2224/sbp.1997.25.3.277.

*Shek, D. T. L. (1997c). Family environment and adolescent psychological well-being, school adjustment, and problem behavior: A pioneer study in a Chinese context. *Journal of Genetic Psychology, 158*(1), 113-128. https://doi.org/10.1080/00221329709596656.

*Shek, D. T. L. (1998a). A longitudinal study of the relations between parent-adolescent conflict and adolescent psychological well-being. *Journal of Genetic Psychology, 159*(1), 53-67. https://doi.org/10.1080/00221329809596134.

*Shek, D. T. L. (1998b). Longitudinal study of the relationship between family functioning and adolescent psychological well-being. *Journal of Youth Studies, 1*(2), 195-209. https://doi.org/10.1080/13676261.1998.10593006.

Shek, D. T. L. (2003). Economic stress, psychological well-being and problem behavior in Chinese adolescents with economic disadvantage. *Journal of Youth and Adolescence, 32*(4), 259-266. https://doi.org/10.1023/a:1023080826557.

*Shek, D. T. L., & Li, X. (2016). Perceived school performance, life satisfaction, and hopelessness: A 4-year longitudinal study of adolescents in Hong Kong. *Social Indicators Research, 126*(2), 921-934. https://doi.org/10.1007/s11205-015-0904-y.

*Shek, D. T. L., & Liang, L. Y. (2018). Psychosocial factors influencing individual well-being in Chinese adolescents in Hong Kong: A six-year longitudinal study. *Applied Research in Quality of Life, 13*(3), 561-584. https://doi.org/10.1007/s11482-017-9545-4.

Sheldon, K. M., & Bettencourt, B. A. (2002). Psychological need-satisfaction and subjective well-being within social groups. *British Journal of Social Psychology, 41*, 25-38. https://doi.org/10.1348/014466602165036.

Sheldon, K. M., Cummins, R. A., & Kamble, S. (2010). Life balance and well-being: Testing a novel conceptual and measurement approach. *Journal of Personality, 78*(4), 1093-1134. https://doi.org/10.1111/j.1467-6494.2010.00644.x.

Sheldon, K. M., & Elliot, A. J. (1998). Not all personal goals are personal: Comparing autonomous and controlled reasons for goals as predictors of effort and attainment. *Personality and Social Psychology Bulletin, 24*(5), 546-557. https://doi.org/10.1177/0146167298245010.

Sheldon, K. M., & Elliot, A. J. (1999). Goal striving, need satisfaction, and longitudinal well-being: The self-concordance model. *Journal of Personality and Social Psychology, 76*(3), 482. https://doi.org/10.1037/0022-3514.76.3.482.

Sheldon, K. M., Elliot, A. J., Kim, Y., & Kasser, T. (2001). What is satisfying about satisfying events? Testing 10 candidate psychological needs. *Journal of Personality and Social Psychology, 80*(2), 325-339. https://doi.org/10.1037/0022-3514.80.2.325.

Sheldon, K. M., Elliot, A. J., Ryan, R. M., Chirkov, V., Kim, Y., Wu, C., Demir, M., & Sun, Z. (2004). Self-concordance and subjective well-being in four cultures. *Journal of Cross-Cultural Psychology, 35*(2), 209-223. https://doi.org/10.1177/0022022103262245.

Sheldon, K. M., & Houser-Marko, L. (2001). Self-concordance, goal attainment, and the pursuit of happiness: Can there be an upward spiral? *Journal of Personality and Social Psychology, 80*(1), 152. https://doi.org/10.1037/0022-3514.80.1.152.

Sheldon, K. M., Howells, K., & Patel, G. (2010). An empirical evaluation of reasons for non-completion of treatment in a dangerous and severe personality disorder unit. *Criminal Behaviour and Mental Health, 20*(2), 129-143. https://doi.org/10.1002/cbm.760.

Sheldon, K. M., & Kasser, T. (1995). Coherence and congruence: Two aspects of personality integration. *Journal of Personality and Social Psychology, 68*(3), 531-543. https://psycnet.apa.org/doi/10.1037/0022-3514.68.3.531.

Sheldon, K. M., & Kasser, T. (1998). Pursuing personal goals: Skills enable progress, but not all progress is beneficial. *Personality and Social Psychology Bulletin, 24*(12), 1319-1331. https://doi.org/10.1177/01461672982412006.

Sheldon, K. M., & Lyubomirsky, S. (2009). Change your actions, not your circumstances: An experimental test of the sustainable happiness model. In A. K. Dutt & B. Radcliff (Eds.), *Happiness, economics, and politics: Towards a multi-disciplinary approach* (pp. 324-342). Edward Elgar Publishing. https://doi.org/10.4337/9781849801973.00024.

Sheldon, K. M., & Lyubomirsky, S. (2012). The challenge of staying happier: Testing the hedonic adaptation prevention model. *Personality and Social Psychology Bulletin, 38*(5), 670-680. https://doi.org/10.1177/0146167212436400.

Sheldon, K. M., & Niemiec, C. (2006). It's not just the amount that counts: Balanced need satisfaction also affects well-being. *Journal of Personality and Social Psychology, 91*(2), 331-341. https://doi.org/10.1037/0022-3514.91.2.331.

Sheldon, K. M., Ryan, R. M., Deci, E. L., & Kasser, T. (2004). The independent effects of goal contents and motives on well-being: It's both what you pursue and why you pursue it. *Personality and Social Psychology Bulletin, 30*(4), 475-486. https://doi.org/10.1177/0146167203261883.

Sheldon, K. M., Ryan, R. M., & Reis, H. T. (1996). What makes for a good day? Competence and autonomy in the day and in the person. *Personality and Social Psychology Bulletin, 22*(12), 1270-1279. https://doi.org/10.1177/01461672962212007.

*Shin, K., & You, S. (2013). Leisure type, leisure satisfaction and adolescents' psychological wellbeing. *Journal of Pacific Rim Psychology, 7*(2), 53-62. https://doi.org/10.1017/prp.2013.6.

Shong, T. S., Abu Bakar, S. H., & Islam, M. R. (2019). Poverty and delinquency: A qualitative study on selected juvenile offenders in Malaysia. *International Social Work, 62*(2), 965-979. https://doi.org/10.1177/0020872818756172.

Shortt, J. W., Capaldi, D. M., Dishion, T. J., Bank, L., & Owen, L. D. (2003). The role of adolescent friends, romantic partners, and siblings in the emergence of the adult antisocial lifestyle. *Journal of Family Psychology, 17*(4), 521-533. https://doi.org/10.1037/0893-3200.17.4.521.

Shrout, P. E., & Fleiss, J. L. (1979). Intraclass correlations: Uses in assessing rater reliability. *Psychological Bulletin, 86*(2), 420-428. https://doi.org/10.1037//0033-2909.86.2.420.

*Siddall, J., Huebner, E. S., & Jiang, X. (2013). A prospective study of differential sources of school-related social support and adolescent global life satisfaction. *American Journal of Orthopsychiatry, 83*(1), 107-114. https://doi.org/10.1111/ajop.12006.

Silver, I. A., Nedelec, J. L., & Pompoco, A. (2020). Specific responsivity: An assessment of the effect of verbal and math cognitive abilities on the completion of prison programs. *Corrections, 5*(2), 130-148. https://doi.org/10.1080/23774657.2018.1433086.

Silverman, D. (2013). *Doing qualitative research: A practical handbook.* Sage Publications.

Silvey, P. E. (2014). Imagination, play, and the role of performing arts in the well-being of children. In A. Ben-Arieh, F. Casas, I. Frønes, & J. E. Korbin (Eds.), *Handbook of child well-being: Theories, methods and policies in global perspective* (pp. 1079-1097). Springer. https://doi.org/10.1007/978-90-481-9063-8_39.

Simons, D. A., McCullar, B., & Tyler, C. (2006). *Evaluation of the good lives model approach to treatment planning.* 25th annual association for the treatment of sexual abusers research and treatment conference, Chicago, IL.

Singh, A. (1979). Reliability and validity of self-reported delinquency studies: A review. *Psychological Reports, 44*(3), 987-993. https://doi.org/10.2466/pr0.1979.44.3.987.

Singh, J. P., Desmarais, S. L., Sellers, B. G., Hylton, T., Tirotti, M., & Van Dorn, R. A. (2014). From risk assessment to risk management: Matching interventions to adolescent offenders' strengths and vulnerabilities. *Children and Youth Services Review, 47*, 1-9. https://doi.org/10.1016/j.childyouth.2013.09.015.

Sirgy, M. J., Kim, M. Y., Joshanloo, M., Lee, D. J., & Bosnjak, M. (2019). The relationship between domain satisfaction and domain importance: The moderating role of depression. *Journal of Happiness Studies, 21*, 2007-2030. https://doi.org/10.1007/s10902-019-00168-w.

Sirgy, M. J., & Lee, D. J. (2018). The psychology of life balance. In E. Diener, S. Oishi, & L. Tay (Eds.), *Handbook of well-being* (pp. 1-18). DEF Publishers.

Sirgy, M. J., & Wu, J. (2009). The pleasant life, the engaged life, and the meaningful life: What about the balanced life? *Journal of Happiness Studies, 10*(2), 183-196. https://doi.org/10.1007/s10902-007-9074-1.

Skowyra, K. R., & Cocozza, J. J. (2007). *Blueprint for change: A comprehensive model or the identification and treatment of youth with mental health needs in contact with the juvenile justice system.* https://ncyoj.policyresearchinc.org/img/resources/Blueprint-for-Change-A_Comprehensive_Model-638003.pdf.

Skrzypiec, G. (2017). Adolescents' intentions to engage in criminal activity: A cross-disciplinary approach linking theories from social psychology and criminology. *Journal of Forensic Psychology Research and Practice, 17*(5), 305-337. https://doi.org/10.1080/24732850.2017.1374720.

Smith, P., Gendreau, P., & Swartz, K. (2009). Validating the principles of effective intervention: A systematic review of the contributions of meta-analysis in the field of corrections. *Victims and Offenders, 4*(2), 148-169. https://doi.org/10.1080/15564880802612581.

Soenens, B., Vansteenkiste, M., Van Petegem, S., Beyers, W., & Ryan, R. M. (2017). How to solve the conundrum of adolescent autonomy? On the importance of distinguishing between independence and volitional functioning. In B. Soenens, M. Vansteenkiste, & S. Van Petegem (Eds.), *Autonomy in Adolescent Development* (pp. 1-32). Psychology Press.

*Spithoven, A. W. M., Lodder, G. M. A., Goossens, L., Bijttebier, P., Bastin, M., Verhagen, M., & Scholte, R. H. J. (2017). Adolescents' loneliness and depression associated with friendship experiences and well-being: A person-centered approach. *Journal of Youth and Adolescence, 46*(2), 429-441. https://doi.org/10.1007/s10964-016-0478-2.

Sroufe, L. A. (2005). Attachment and development: A prospective, longitudinal study from birth to adulthood. *Attachment & Human Development, 7*(4), 349-367. https://doi.org/10.1080/14616730500365928.

Steger, M., & Kashdan, T. (2007). Stability and specificity of meaning in life and life satisfaction over one year. *An Interdisciplinary Forum on Subjective Well-Being, 8*(2), 161-179. https://doi.org/10.1007/s10902-006-9011-8.

Stephenson, Z., Harkins, L., & Woodhams, J. (2013). The sequencing of interventions with offenders: An addition to the responsivity principle. *Journal of Forensic Psychology Practice, 13*(5), 429-455. https://doi.org/10.1080/15228932.2013.850318.

Stogner, J., & Gibson, C. L. (2010). Healthy, wealthy, and wise: Incorporating health issues as a source of strain in Agnew's general strain theory. *Journal of Criminal Justice, 38*(6), 1150-1159. https://doi.org/10.1016/j.jcrimjus.2010.09.003.

Stogner, J., & Gibson, C. L. (2011). The influence of health strain on the initiation and frequency of substance use in a national sample of adolescents. *Journal of Drug Issues, 41*(1), 69-93. https://doi.org/10.1177/002204261104100104.

Stouthamer-Loeber, M., & Loeber, R. (2002). Lost opportunities for intervention: Undetected markers for the development of serious juvenile delinquency. *Criminal Behaviour and Mental Health, 12*(1), 69-82. https://doi.org/10.1002/cbm.487.

Stubbe, J. H., Posthuma, D., Boomsma, D. I., & De Geus, E. J. (2005). Heritability of life satisfaction in adults: A twin-family study. *Psychological Medicine, 35*(11), 1581-1588. https://doi.org/10.1017/s0033291705005374.

Sturgess, D., Woodhams, J., & Tonkinm, M. (2016). Treatment engagement from the perspective of the offender. *International Journal of Offender Therapy and Comparative Criminology, 60*(16), 1873-1896. https://doi.org/10.1177/0306624X15586038.

*Sujoldžić, A., & De Lucia, A. (2007). A cross-cultural study of adolescents – BMI, body image and psychological well-being. *Collegium Antropologicum, 31*(1), 123-130.

*Suldo, S. M., & Huebner, E. S. (2004). The role of life satisfaction in the relationship between authoritative parenting dimensions and adolescent problem behavior. *Social Indicators Research, 66*(1-2), 165-195. https://doi.org/10.1023/B:SOCI.0000007498.62080.1e.

*Suldo, S. M., Shaffer, E. J., & Riley, K. N. (2008). A social-cognitive-behavioral model of academic predictors of adolescents' life satisfaction. *School Psychology Quarterly, 23*(1), 56-69. https://doi.org/10.1037/1045-3830.23.1.56.

Sumter, M., Wood, F., Whitaker, I., & Berger-Hill, D. (2018). Religion and crime studies: Assessing what has been learned. *Religions, 9*(6), 193-208. https://doi.org/10.3390/rel9060193.

Sun, R., & Shek, D. (2013). Longitudinal influences of positive youth development and life satisfaction on problem behaviour among adolescents in Hong Kong. *Social Indicators Research, 114*(3), 1171-1197. https://doi.org/10.1007/s11205-012-0196-4.

*Sun, R. C., & Shek, D. T. L. (2010). Life satisfaction, positive youth development, and problem behaviour among Chinese adolescents in Hong Kong. *Social Indicators Research, 95*(3), 455-474. https://doi.org/10.1007/s11205-009-9531-9.

*Sun, R. C., & Shek, D. T. L. (2012). Positive youth development, life satisfaction and problem behaviour among Chinese adolescents in Hong Kong: A replication. *Social Indicators Research, 105*(3), 541-559. https://doi.org/10.1007/s11205-011-9786-9.

Sutherland, E. H., & Cressey, D. R. (1960). *Principles of criminology*. Altamira Press.

Sutton, A. J., Duval, S. J., Tweedie, R. L., Abrams, K. R., & Jones, D. R. (2000). Empirical assessment of effect of publication bias on meta-analyses. *BMJ*, 320(7249), 1574-1577. https://doi.org/10.1136/bmj.320.7249.1574.

Sutton, C. (2021). What counts as happiness for young people: A qualitative study. *Children & Society, 35*(1), 18-33. https://doi.org/10.1111/chso.12387.

Sweeten, G. (2012). Scaling criminal offending. *Journal of Quantitative Criminology, 28*(3), 533-557. https://doi.org/10.1007/s10940-011-9160-8.

Tadesse, M. E. (2017). Martial arts and adolescents: Using theories to explain the positive effects of Asian martial arts on the well-being of adolescents. *Journal of Martial Arts Anthropology, 17*(2), 9-23. https://doi.org/10.14589/ido.17.2.2.

Tafrate, R. C., & Luther, J. D. (2014). Integrating motivational interviewing with forensic CBT: Promoting treatment engagement and behavior change with justice-involved clients. In R. C. Tafrate & D. Mitchel (Eds.), *Forensic CBT: A handbook for clinical practice* (pp. 411-435). Wiley.

Tafrate, R. C., & Mitchell, D. (2014). *Forensic CBT: A handbook for clinical practice*. Wiley.

Tang, K. N., & Chan, C. S. (2017). Life satisfaction and perceived stress among young offenders in a residential therapeutic community: Latent change score analysis. *Journal of Adolescence, 57*, 42-53. https://doi.org/10.1016/j.adolescence.2017.03.005.

Tang, M., Wang, D., & Guerrien, A. (2020). A systematic review and meta-analysis on basic psychological need satisfaction, motivation, and well-being in later life: Contributions of self-determination theory. *PsyCh Journal, 9*(1), 5-33. https://doi.org/10.1002/pchj.293.

Taormina, R. J., & Gao, J. H. (2013). Maslow and the motivation hierarchy: Measuring satisfaction of the needs. *The American Journal of Psychology, 126*(2), 155-177. https://doi.org/10.5406/amerjpsyc.126.2.0155.

Taxman, F. S., & Caudy, M. S. (2015). Risk tells us who, but not what or how: Empirical assessment of the complexity of criminogenic needs to inform correctional programming. *Criminology & Public Policy, 14*(1), 71-103. https://doi.org/10.1111/1745-9133.12116.

Tay, L., & Diener, E. (2011). Needs and subjective well-being around the world. *Journal of Personality and Social Psychology, 101*(2), 354-365. https://doi.org/10.1037/a0023779.

Tay, L., Li, M., Myers, D., & Diener, E. (2014). Religiosity and subjective well-being: An international perspective. In C. Kim-Prieto (Ed.), *Religion and spirituality across cultures* (pp. 163-175). Springer. https://doi.org/10.1007/978-94-017-8950-9_9.

Taylor, A., & Leys, M. (2013). *Jongeren met een complexe gedragsproblematiek in Nederlandstalige voorzieningen in Brussel en West-Vlaams-Brabant*. Vrije Universiteit Brussel.

Taylor, E. (2017). 'I should have been a security consultant': The good lives model and residential burglars. *European Journal of Criminology, 14*(4), 434-450. https://doi.org/10.1177/1477370816661743.

Taylor, T. E. (2013). Well-being and prudential value. *Philosophy and Public Policy Quarterly, 31*(2), 10-17.

Teevan, J. J., & Dryburgh, H. B. (2000). First person accounts and sociological explanations of delinquency. *Canadian Review of Sociology/Revue canadienne de sociologie, 37*(1), 77-93. https://doi.org/10.1111/j.1755-618X.2000.tb00587.x.

Telef, B. B. (2013). The scale of positive and negative experience: A validity and reliability study for adolescents. *Anatolian Journal of Psychiatry, 14*(1), 62-68. https://doi.org/10.5455/apd.36692.

*Telef, B. B. (2016). Investigating the relationship among internet addiction, positive and negative affects, and life satisfaction in Turkish adolescents. *International Journal of Progressive Education, 12*(1), 128-135.

Thakker, J., & Ward, T. (2010). Relapse prevention: A critique and proposed reconceptualisation. *Behaviour Change, 27*(3), 154-175. https://doi.org/10.1375/bech.27.3.154.

Theodossiou, I. (1998). The effects of low-pay and unemployment on psychological well-being: A logistic regression approach. *Journal of Health Economics, 17*(1), 85-104. https://doi.org/10.1016/s0167-6296(97)00018-0.

Thogersen-Ntoumani, C., Ntoumanis, N., & Nikitaras, N. (2010). Unhealthy weight control behaviours in adolescent girls: A process model based on self-determination theory. *Psychology and Health, 25*(5), 535-550. https://doi.org/10.1080/08870440902783628.

Thomas, K. J., & Vogel, M. (2019). Testing a rational choice model of "desistance:" Decomposing changing expectations and changing utilities. *Criminology, 57*(4), 687-714. https://doi.org/10.1111/1745-9125.12223.

Thornberg, R. (2012). Informed grounded theory. *Scandinavian Journal of Educational Research, 56*(3), 243-259. https://doi.org/10.1080/00313831.2011.581686.

Tierney, D. W., & McCabe, M. P. (2002). Motivation for behavior change among sex offenders: A review of the literature. *Clinical Psychology Review, 22*(1), 113-129. https://doi.org/10.1016/s0272-7358(01)00084-8.

Tomyn, A. J., Tyszkiewicz, M. D. F., & Cummins, R. A. (2013). The personal wellbeing index: Psychometric equivalence for adults and school children. *Social Indicators Research, 110*(3), 913-924. https://doi.org/10.1007/s11205-011-9964-9.

Tracey, D., & Hanham, J. (2015). Applying positive psychology to illuminate the needs of adolescent males transitioning out of juvenile detention. *International Journal of Offender Therapy and Comparative Criminology, 61*(1), 64-79. https://doi.org/10.1177/0306624X15591242.

Treffers, P. D. A., & Van Widenfelt, B. M. (2000). *Dutch translation of the strengths and difficulties questionnaire (SDQ)*. Leiden University Medical Center Academic Center for Child and Adolescent Psychiatry, Curium.

Troonbeeckx, S., Cops, D., Op de Beeck, H., Pleysier, S., & Put, J. (2012). Delinquentie tijdens de jongvolwassenheid: De rol van 'agency' versus 'structure'. *Tijdschrift voor Criminologie, 54*(2), 118-135.

Troonbeeckx, S., Put, J., & Pleysier, S. (2015). Agency en structure in de ervaringen van jongeren: een andere kijk op de verklaring van jeugddelinquentie. *Sociologos, 36*(4), 310-332.

*Trzcinski, E., & Holst, E. (2008). Subjective well-being among young people in transition to adulthood. *Social Indicators Research, 87*(1), 83-109. https://doi.org/10.1007/s11205-007-9160-0.

Tweed, R. G., Bhatt, G., Dooley, S., Spindler, A., Douglas, K. S., & Viljoen, J. L. (2011). Youth violence and positive psychology: Research potential through integration. *Canadian Psychology/Psychologie Canadienne, 52*(2), 111-121. https://doi.org/10.1037/a0020695.

Tyler, N., Heffernan, R., & Fortune, C.-A. (2020). Reorienting locus of control in individuals who have offended through strengths-based interventions: Personal agency and the good lives model. *Frontiers in Psychology, 11*, 2297. https://doi.org/10.3389/fpsyg.2020.553240.

*Uçanok, Z., & Güre, A. (2014). Perceived economic strain and psychological well-being: The mediational role of parental relations in Turkish early adolescents. *Journal of Early Adolescence, 34*(6), 685-711. https://doi.org/10.1177/0272431612450948.

Underwood, L. A., & Washington, A. (2016). Mental illness and juvenile offenders. *International Journal of Environmental Research and Public Health, 13*(2), 228-242. https://doi.org/10.3390/ijerph13020228.

United Nations. (1989). The United Nations convention on the rights of the child. www.ohchr.org/en/professionalinterest/pages/crc.aspx.

*Uusitalo-Malmivaara, L. (2012). Global and school-related happiness in Finnish children. *Journal of Happiness Studies, 13*(4), 601-619. https://doi.org/10.1007/s10902-011-9282-6.

*Uusitalo-Malmivaara, L., & Lehto, J. E. (2013). Social factors explaining children's subjective happiness and depressive symptoms. *Social Indicators Research, 111*(2), 603-615. https://doi.org/10.1007/s11205-012-0022-z.

Vahl, P., Colins, O. F., Lodewijks, H. P., Lindauer, R., Markus, M. T., Doreleijers, T. A., & Vermeiren, R. (2016). Psychopathic traits and maltreatment: Relations with aggression and mental health problems in detained boys. *International Journal of Law and Psychiatry, 46*, 129-136. https://doi.org/10.1016/j.ijlp.2016.02.006.

*Valkenburg, P. M., & Peter, J. (2007). Online communication and adolescent well-being: Testing the stimulation versus the displacement hypothesis. *Journal of Computer-Mediated Communication, 12*(4), 1169-1182. https://doi.org/10.1111/j.1083-6101.2007.00368.x.

*Valkenburg, P. M., Peter, J., & Schouten, A. P. (2006). Friend networking sites and their relationship to adolescents' well-being and social self-esteem. *Cyberpsychology, Behavior, and Social Networking, 9*(5), 584-590. https://doi.org/10.1089/cpb.2006.9.584.

Valois, R. F., Paxton, R. J., Zullig, K. J., & Huebner, E. S. (2006). Life satisfaction and violent behaviors among middle school students. *Journal of Child and Family Studies, 15*(6), 695-707. https://doi.org/10.1007/s10826-006-9043-z.

Valois, R. F., Zullig, K. J., Huebner, E. S., & Drane, J. W. (2001). Relationship between life satisfaction and violent behaviors among adolescents. *American Journal of Health Behavior, 25*(4), 353-366. https://doi.org/10.5993/ajhb.25.4.1.

Valois, R. F., Zullig, K. J., Huebner, E. S., Kammermann, S. K., & Drane, J. W. (2002). Association between life satisfaction and sexual risk-taking behaviors among adolescents. *Journal of Child and Family Studies, 11*(4), 427-440. https://doi.org/10.1023/A:1020931324426.

van Beek, G., de Vogel, V., & van de Mheen, D. (2021). The relationship between debt and crime: A systematic and scoping review. *European Journal of Probation, 13*(1), 41-71. https://doi.org/10.1177/2066220320964896.

van Binsbergen, M. H., Knorth, E. J., Klomp, M., & Meulman, J. J. (2001). Motivatie voor behandeling bij jongeren met ernstige gedragsproblemen in de intramurale justitiële jeugdzorg. *Kind en adolescent, 22*(4), 193. https://doi.org/10.1007/bf03060824.

Van Damme, L., Colins, O., De Maeyer, J., Vermeiren, R., & Vanderplasschen, W. (2015). Girls' quality of life prior to detention in relation to psychiatric disorders, trauma exposure and socioeconomic status. *Quality of Life Research, 24*(6), 1419-1429. https://doi.org/10.1007/s11136-014-0878-2.

Van Damme, L., Colins, O., Pauwels, L. J. R., & Vanderplasschen, W. (2015). Relationships between global and domain-specific self-evaluations and types of offending in community boys and girls. *Journal of Community Psychology, 43*(8), 986-1004. https://doi.org/10.1002/jcop.21727.

Van Damme, L., Colins, O., & Vanderplasschen, W. (2020). Vervulling van basisbehoeften bij meisjes voor en na een verblijf in een gemeenschapsinstelling. *Welwijs, 31*(1), 29-33.

Van Damme, L., Colins, O. F., & Vanderplasschen, W. (2014). Gender differences in psychiatric disorders and clusters of self-esteem among detained adolescents. *Psychiatry Research, 220*(3), 991-997. https://doi.org/10.1016/j.psychres.2014.10.012.

Van Damme, L., Fortune, C. A., Hoeve, M., Vanderplasschen, W., & Colins, O. F. (2022). The role of personal resilience and interpersonal support in building fulfilling and prosocial lives: Examining the good lives model among young women four years after youth detention. *International Journal of Offender Therapy and Comparative Criminology, 66*(1), 123-144. https://doi.org/10.1177/0306624x21994055.

Van Damme, L., Fortune, C.-A., Vandevelde, S., & Vanderplasschen, W. (2017). The good lives model among detained female adolescents. *Aggression and Violent Behavior, 37*(Supplement C), 179-189. https://doi.org/10.1016/j.avb.2017.10.002.

Van Damme, L., Hoeve, M., Vanderplasschen, W., Vermeiren, R., Grisso, T., & Colins, O. F. (2015). Detained girls' treatment engagement over time: The role of psychopathology and quality of life. *Children and Youth Services Review, 59*, 47-56. https://doi.org/10.1016/j.childyouth.2015.10.010.

Van Damme, L., Hoeve, M., Vermeiren, R., Vanderplasschen, W., & Colins, O. F. (2016). Quality of life in relation to future mental health problems and offending: Testing the good lives model among detained girls. *Law and Human Behavior, 40*(3), 285-294. https://doi.org/10.1037/lhb0000177.

Van Damme, L., Vanderplasschen, W., Fortune, C.-A., Vandevelde, S., & Colins, O. F. (2019). Determinants of female adolescents' quality of life before, during and after detention: A four-wave follow-up study examining a theory of individual quality of life. *Applied Research in Quality of Life, 16*, 401-434. https://doi.org/10.1007/s11482-019-09775-4.

*van de Wetering, E. J., van Exel, N. J. A., & Brouwer, W. B. F. (2010). Piecing the jigsaw puzzle of adolescent happiness. *Journal of Economic Psychology, 31*(6), 923-935. https://doi.org/10.1016/j.joep.2010.08.004.

van den Berg, C., Bijleveld, C., Hendriks, J., & Mooi-Reci, I. (2014). The juvenile sex offender: The effect of employment on offending. *Journal of Criminal Justice, 42*(2), 145-152. https://doi.org/10.1016/j.jcrimjus.2013.09.001.

van den Berg, J. W., Smid, W., Schepers, K., Wever, E., van Beek, D., Janssen, E., & Gijs, L. (2018). The predictive properties of dynamic sex offender risk assessment instruments: A meta-analysis. *Psychological Assessment, 30*(2), 179. https://doi.org/10.1037/pas0000454.

Van den Broeck, A., Schreurs, B., Proost, K., Vanderstukken, A., & Vansteenkiste, M. (2019). I want to be a billionaire: How do extrinsic and intrinsic values influence youngsters' well-being? *Annals of the American Academy of Political and Social Science, 682*(1), 204-219. https://doi.org/10.1177/0002716219831658.

van der Helm, G. H. P., Beunk, L., Stams, G. J. J. M., & van der Laan, P. H. (2014). The relationship between detention length, living group climate, coping, and treatment motivation among juvenile delinquents in a youth correctional facility. *The Prison Journal, 94*(2), 260-275. https://doi.org/10.1177/0032885514524884.

van der Helm, G. H. P., Kuiper, C. H. Z., & Stams, G. J. J. M. (2018). Group climate and treatment motivation in secure residential and forensic youth care from the perspective of self-determination theory. *Children and Youth Services Review, 93*, 339-344. https://doi.org/10.1016/j.childyouth.2018.07.028.

van der Helm, G. H. P., Wissink, I. B., De Jongh, T., & Stams, G. J. (2012). Measuring treatment motivation in secure juvenile facilities. *International Journal of Offender Therapy and Comparative Criminology, 57*(8), 996-1008. https://doi.org/10.1177/0306624X12443798.

van der Kaap-Deeder, J., Audenaert, E., Vandevelde, S., Soenens, B., Van Mastrigt, S., Mabbe, E., & Vansteenkiste, M. (2017). Choosing when choices are limited: The role of perceived afforded choice and autonomy in prisoners' well-being. *Law and Human Behavior, 41*(6), 567-578. https://doi.org/10.1037/lhb0000259.

van der Kooi, M. (2020). Developmental outcomes and meanings in martial arts practice among youth: A review. *European Journal for Sport and Society, 17*(2), 96-115. https://doi.org/10.1080/16138171.2020.1737421.

van der Laan, A., & Eichelsheim, V. (2013). Juvenile adaptation to imprisonment: Feelings of safety, autonomy and well-being, and behaviour in prison. *European Journal of Criminology, 10*(4), 424-443. https://doi.org/10.1177/1477370812473530.

van der Laan, A. M., Blom, M., Verwers, C., & Essers, A. (2006). *Jeugddelinquentie*. Boom Juridische Uitgevers.

van der Put, C. E., & De Ruiter, C. (2016). Child maltreatment victimization by type in relation to criminal recidivism in juvenile offenders. *BMC Psychiatry, 16*(1), 16-24. https://doi.org/10.1186/s12888-016-0731-y.

van der Stouwe, T., Asscher, J. J., Hoeve, M., van der Laan, P. H., & Stams, G. J. J. M. (2018). The influence of treatment motivation on outcomes of social skills training for juvenile delinquents. *International Journal of Offender Therapy and Comparative Criminology, 62*(1), 108-128. https://journals.sagepub.com/doi/pdf/10.1177/0306624X16648130.

van der Stouwe, T., Asscher, J. J., Stams, G. J. J. M., Deković, M., & van der Laan, P. H. (2014). The effectiveness of multisystemic therapy (MST): A meta-analysis. *Clinical Psychology Review, 34*(6), 468-481. https://doi.org/10.1016/j.cpr.2014.06.006.

van Dierendonck, D. (2012). Spirituality as an essential determinant for the good life, its importance relative to self-determinant psychological needs. *An Interdisciplinary*

Forum on Subjective Well-Being, 13(4), 685-700. https://doi.org/10.1007/s10902-011-9286-2.

van Dierendonck, D., & Mohan, K. (2006). Some thoughts on spirituality and eudaimonic well-being. *Mental Health, Religion and Culture, 9*(03), 227-238. https://doi.org/10.1080/13694670600615383.

van Geel, M., Vedder, P., & Tanilon, J. (2014). Bullying and weapon carrying: A meta-analysis. *JAMA Pediatrics, 168*(8), 714-720. https://doi.org/10.1001/jamapediatrics.2014.213.

van Gemert, F. H. M. (2019). Kickboksen, een Marokkaanse route naar succes? *Tijdschrift voor veiligheid, 18*(3-4), 56-74. https://doi.org/10.5553/TvV/187279482019018304004.

Van Hecke, N., Meulewaeter, F., Rowaert, S., van Nieuwenhuizen, Ch., Van Damme, L., Vanderplasschen, W., & Vandevelde, S. (2021). Adolescents' quality of life and mental health needs during the initial phase in a closed institution. *International Journal of Forensic Mental Health*. Advance online publication. https://doi.org/10.1080/14999013.2021.1934195.

Van Hecke, N., Meulewaeter, F., Vanderplasschen, W., Van Damme, L., Naert, J., Rowaert, S., & Vandevelde, S. (2021). Formerly detained adolescents' narratives: On the interplay between quality of life and desistance. *International Journal of Offender Therapy and Comparative Criminology*. Advance online publication. https://doi.org/10.1177/0306624X211023922.

Van Hecke, N., Vanderplasschen, W., Van Damme, L., & Vandevelde, S. (2019). The bumpy road to change: A retrospective qualitative study on formerly detained adolescents' trajectories towards better lives. *Child and Adolescent Psychiatry and Mental Health, 13*(1), 10-35. https://doi.org/10.1186/s13034-019-0271-6.

van Nieuwenhuizen, Ch., Schene, A., & Koeter, M. (2002). Quality of life in forensic psychiatry: An unreclaimed territory? *International Review of Psychiatry, 14*(3), 198-202. https://doi.org/10.1080/09540260220144993.

Van Petegem, S., Beyers, W., Vansteenkiste, M., & Soenens, B. (2012). On the association between adolescent autonomy and psychosocial functioning: Examining decisional independence from a self-determination theory perspective. *Developmental Psychology, 48*(1), 76-88. https://doi.org/10.1037/a0025307.

Van Petegem, S., Soenens, B., Vansteenkiste, M., & Beyers, W. (2015). Rebels with a cause? Adolescent defiance from the perspective of reactance theory and self-determination theory. *Child Development, 86*(3), 903-918. https://doi.org/10.1111/cdev.12355.

Van Petegem, S., Zimmer-Gembeck, M., Baudat, S., Soenens, B., Vansteenkiste, M., & Zimmermann, G. (2019). Adolescents' responses to parental regulation: The role of communication style and self-determination. *Journal of Applied Developmental Psychology, 65*, 101073. https://doi.org/10.1016/j.appdev.2019.101073.

Van Ryzin, M. J., Gravely, A. A., & Roseth, C. J. (2009). Autonomy, belongingness, and engagement in school as contributors to adolescent psychological well-being. *Journal of Youth and Adolescence, 38*(1), 1-12. https://doi.org/10.1007/s10964-007-9257-4.

van Vianen, A. E. (2018). Person–environment fit: A review of its basic tenets. *Annual Review of Organizational Psychology and Organizational Behavior, 5*, 75-101. https://doi.org/10.1146/annurev-orgpsych-032117-104702.

Van Widenfelt, B. M., Goedhart, A. W., Treffers, P. D., & Goodman, R. (2003). Dutch version of the strengths and difficulties questionnaire (SDQ). *European Child & Adolescent Psychiatry, 12*(6), 281-289. https://doi.org/10.1007/s00787-003-0341-3.

Vanassche, S., Sodermans, A. K., Matthijs, K., & Swicegood, G. (2014). The effects of family type, family relationships and parental role models on delinquency and alcohol use among Flemish adolescents. *Journal of Child and Family Studies, 23*(1), 128-143. https://doi.org/10.1007/s10826-012-9699-5.

Vansteenkiste, M., Niemiec, C. P., & Soenens, B. (2010). The development of the five mini-theories of self-determination theory: An historical overview, emerging trends, and future directions. *Advances in Motivation and Achievement, 16*, 105-165. https://doi.org/10.1108/S0749-7423(2010)000016A007.

Vansteenkiste, M., & Ryan, R. M. (2013). On psychological growth and vulnerability: Basic psychological need satisfaction and need frustration as a unifying principle. *Journal of Psychotherapy Integration, 23*(3), 263. https://doi.org/10.1037/a0032359.

Vansteenkiste, M., & Sheldon, K. M. (2006). There's nothing more practical than a good theory: Integrating motivational interviewing and self-determination theory. *British Journal of Clinical Psychology, 45*(1), 63-82. https://doi.org/10.1348/014466505X34192.

*Veldorale-Griffin, A., Coccia, C. C., Darling, C. A., Rehm, M., & Sathe, S. (2013). The role of parental indulgence and economic stress in life satisfaction: Differential perceptions of parents and adolescents. *Journal of Family Social Work, 16*(3), 205-224. https://doi.org/10.1080/10522158.2013.786776.

Vella-Brodrick, D. A., Park, N., & Peterson, C. (2009). Three ways to be happy: Pleasure, engagement, and meaning—findings from Australian and US samples. *Social Indicators Research, 90*(2), 165-179. https://doi.org/10.1007/s11205-008-9251-6.

*Vera, E. M., Moallem, B. I., Vacek, K. R., Blackmon, S., Coyle, L. D., Gomez, K. L., Lamp, K., Langrehr, K. J., Luginbuhl, P., Mull, M. K., Telander, K. J., & Steele, J. C. (2012). Gender differences in contextual predictors of urban, early adolescents' subjective well-being. *Journal of Multicultural Counseling and Development, 40*(3), 174-183. https://doi.org/10.1002/j.2161-1912.2012.00016.x.

*Vera, E. M., Vacek, K., Blackmon, S., Coyle, L., Gomez, K., Jorgenson, K., Luginbuhl, P., Moallem, I., & Steele, J. C. (2012). Subjective well-being in urban, ethnically diverse adolescents the role of stress and coping. *Youth & Society, 44*(3), 331-347. https://doi.org/10.1177/0044118X11401432.

Verdonck, E. (2017). *De aantrekkelijkheid van geweld. Een onderzoek naar de rol van intrinsieke aspecten in de betekenisgeving en verklaring van fysiek geweld bij jongeren.* KU Leuven.

Verdonck, E., Pleysier, S., Cops, D., & Put, J. (2011). *Jongeren en geweld. Dader-en slachtofferschap gemeten en beleefd.* Acco.

Vermeiren, R., Jespers, I., & Moffitt, T. (2006). Mental health problems in juvenile justice populations. *Child and Adolescent Psychiatric Clinics of North America, 15*(2), 333-351. https://doi.org/10.1016/j.chc.2005.11.008.

Veronneau, M. H., Koestner, R. F., & Abela, J. R. Z. (2005). Intrinsic need satisfaction and well-being in children and adolescents: An application of the self-determination theory. *Journal of Social and Clinical Psychology, 24*(2), 280-292. https://doi.org/10.1521/jscp.24.2.280.62277.

*Verzeletti, C., Zammuner, V. L., Galli, C., & Agnoli, S. (2016). Emotion regulation strategies and psychosocial well-being in adolescence. *Cogent Psychology, 3*, Article 1199294. https://doi.org/10.1080/23311908.2016.1199294.

Viechtbauer, W. (2010). Conducting meta-analyses in R with the metafor package. *Journal of Statistical Software, 36*(3), 1-48. https://doi.org/10.18637/jss.v036.i03.

Vieira, T. A., Skilling, T. A., & Peterson-Badali, M. (2009). Matching court-ordered services with treatment needs: Predicting treatment success with young offenders. *Criminal Justice and Behavior, 36*(4), 385-401. https://doi.org/10.1177/0093854808331249.

Viljoen, J. L., Bhanwer, A. K., Shaffer, C. S., & Douglas, K. S. (2018). Assessing protective factors for adolescent offending: A conceptually informed examination of the SAVRY and YLS/CMI. *Assessment, 27*(5), 959-975. https://doi.org/10.1177/1073191118768435.

Viljoen, J. L., Shaffer, C. S., Gray, A. L., & Douglas, K. S. (2017). Are adolescent risk assessment tools sensitive to change? A framework and examination of the SAVRY and the YLS/CMI. *Law and Human Behavior, 41*(3), 244. https://doi.org/10.1037/lhb0000238.

Villeneuve, M.-P., F.-Dufour, I., & Turcotte, D. (2019). The transition towards desistance from crime among serious juvenile offenders: A scoping review. *Australian Social Work, 72*(4), 473-489. https://doi.org/10.1080/0312407X.2019.1586967.

Vujcic, M. T., Brajsa-Zganec, A., & Franc, R. (2019). Children and young peoples' views on well-being: A qualitative study. *Child Indicators Research, 12*(3), 791-819. https://doi.org/10.1007/s12187-018-9559-y.

Wainwright, L., & Nee, C. (2014). The good lives model – new directions for preventative practice with children? *Psychology, Crime and Law, 20*(2), 166-182. https://doi.org/10.1080/1068316X.2013.770851.

Wald, J., & Losen, D. J. (2003). Defining and redirecting a school-to-prison pipeline. *New Directions for Youth Development, 2003*(99), 9-15. https://doi.org/10.1002/yd.51.

Walgrave, L. (2016). Positive criminology, criminology of trust and restorative justice. *Restorative Justice, 4*(3), 424-434. https://doi.org/10.1080/20504721.2016.1243858.

Walgrave, L., Ward, T., & Zinsstag, E. (2019). When restorative justice meets the good lives model: Contributing to a criminology of trust. *European Journal of Criminology, 18*(3), 444-460. https://doi.org/10.1177/1477370819854174.

Wallander, J. L., & Koot, H. M. (2016). Quality of life in children: A critical examination of concepts, approaches, issues, and future directions. *Clinical Psychology Review, 45*, 131-143. https://doi.org/10.1016/j.cpr.2015.11.007.

Walters, G. D. (2002). Maintaining motivation for change using resources available in an offender's natural environment. In M. McMurran (Ed.), *Motivating offenders to change: A guide to enhancing engagement in therapy* (pp. 121-135). Wiley. https://doi.org/10.1002/9780470713471.ch8.

Wang, A., Peterson, G. W., & Morphey, L. K. (2007). Who is more important for early adolescents' developmental choices? Peers or parents? *Marriage & Family Review, 42*(2), 95-122. https://doi.org/10.1300/J002v42n02_06.

Wanzeele, W., & Oltenfreiter, S. (2020). De zoektocht naar een behandelkader dat werkt: wat kunnen we leren van de Risk–Need–Responsivity principes en het good lives model? In K. Goethals, M. De Boeck, T. Dilliën, W. Huys, & N. Nuyts (Eds.), *Handboek behandeling van seksueel afwijkend gedrag* (pp. 203-234). Gompel-Scavina.

Ward, M., & Attwell, P. (2014). Evaluation of two community outreach forensic psychological services. *Journal of Forensic Practice, 16*(4), 312-326. https://doi.org/10.1108/JFP-04-2013-0027.

Ward, T. (2002a). Good lives and the rehabilitation of offenders: Promises and problems. *Aggression and Violent Behavior, 7*(5), 513-528. https://doi.org/10.1016/S1359-1789(01)00076-3.

Ward, T. (2002b). The management of risk and the design of good lives. *Australian Psychologist, 37*(3), 172-179. https://doi.org/10.1080/00050060210001706846.

Ward, T. (2010). The good lives model of offender rehabilitation: Basic assumptions, etiological commitments, and practice implications. In F. McNeill, P. Raynor, & C. Trotter (Eds.), *Offender supervision: New directions in theory, research and practice* (pp. 41-64). Willan Publishing.

Ward, T. (2013). Addressing the dual relationship problem in forensic and correctional practice. *Aggression and Violent Behavior, 18*, 92-100. https://doi.org/10.1016/j.avb.2012.10.006.

Ward, T. (2016). Dynamic risk factors: Scientific kinds or predictive constructs. *Psychology, Crime & Law, 22*(1-2), 2-16. https://doi.org/10.1080/1068316X.2015.1109094.

Ward, T. (2019). Why theory matters in correctional psychology. *Aggression and Violent Behavior, 48*, 36-45. https://doi.org/10.1016/j.avb.2019.08.015.

Ward, T., & Beech, A. R. (2015). Dynamic risk factors: A theoretical dead-end? *Psychology, Crime & Law, 21*(2), 100-113. https://doi.org/10.1080/1068316X.2014.917854.

Ward, T., & Brown, M. (2003). The risk-need model of offender rehabilitation: A critical analysis. In T. Ward, D. Laws, & S. M. Hudson (Eds.), *Sexual deviance: Issues and controversies* (pp. 338-353). Sage Publications. https://doi.org/10.4135/9781483328751.n19.

Ward, T., & Brown, M. (1 September 2004). The good lives model and conceptual issues in offender rehabilitation. *Psychology, Crime & Law, 10*(3), 243-257. https://doi.org/10.1080/10683160410001662744.

Ward, T., & Carter, E. (2019). The classification of offending and crime related problems: A functional perspective. *Psychology, Crime & Law, 25*(6), 542-560. https://doi.org/10.1080/1068316X.2018.1557182.

Ward, T., Day, A., Howells, K., & Birgden, A. (2004). The multifactor offender readiness model. *Aggression and Violent Behavior, 9*(6), 645-673. https://doi.org/10.1016/j.avb.2003.08.001.

Ward, T., & Fortune, C.-A. (2013). The good lives model: Aligning risk reduction with promoting offenders' personal goals. *European Journal of Probation, 5*(2), 29-46. https://doi.org/10.1177/206622031300500203.

Ward, T., & Fortune, C.-A. (2016). The role of dynamic risk factors in the explanation of offending. *Aggression and Violent Behavior, 29*, 79-88. https://doi.org/10.1016/j.avb.2016.06.007.

Ward, T., & Gannon, T. A. (2006). Rehabilitation, etiology, and self-regulation: The comprehensive good lives model of treatment for sexual offenders. *Aggression and Violent Behavior, 11*(1), 77-94. https://doi.org/10.1016/j.avb.2005.06.001.

Ward, T., Hudson, S. M., & France, K. G. (1993). Self-reported reasons for offending behavior in child molesters. *Annals of Sex Research, 6*(2), 139-148. https://doi.org/10.1007/BF00849304.

Ward, T., & Laws, D. R. (2010). Desistance from sex offending: Motivating change, enriching practice. *International Journal of Forensic Mental Health, 9*(1), 11-23. https://doi.org/10.1080/14999011003791598.

Ward, T., & Mann, R. E. (2004). Good lives and the rehabilitation of offenders: A positive approach to sex offender treatment. In P. Alex Linley & S. Joseph (Eds.), *Positive psychology in practice* (pp. 598-616). Wiley. https://doi.org/10.1002/9780470939338.ch36.

Ward, T., Mann, R. E., & Gannon, T. A. (2007). The good lives model of offender rehabilitation: Clinical implications. *Aggression and Violent Behavior, 12*(1), 87-107. https://doi.org/10.1016/j.avb.2006.03.004.

Ward, T., & Marshall, B. (2007). Narrative identity and offender rehabilitation. *International Journal of Offender Therapy and Comparative Criminology, 51*(3), 279-297. https://doi.org/10.1177/0306624x06291461.

Ward, T., & Marshall, W. L. (2004). Good lives, aetiology and the rehabilitation of sex offenders: A bridging theory. *Journal of Sexual Aggression, 10*(2), 153-169. https://doi.org/10.1080/13552600412331290102.

Ward, T., & Maruna, S. (2007). *Rehabilitation*. Routledge.

Ward, T., Melser, J., & Yates, P. M. (2007). Reconstructing the risk–need–responsivity model: A theoretical elaboration and evaluation. *Aggression and Violent Behavior, 12*(2), 208-228. https://doi.org/10.1016/j.avb.2006.07.001.

Ward, T., & Stewart, C. A. (2003a). Criminogenic needs and human needs: A theoretical model. *Psychology, Crime & Law, 9*(2), 125-143. https://doi.org/10.1080/1068316031000116247.

Ward, T., & Stewart, C. A. (2003b). The relationship between human needs and criminogenic needs. *Psychology, Crime & Law, 9*(3), 219-224. https://doi.org/10.1080/1068316031000112557.

Ward, T., & Stewart, C. A. (2003c). The treatment of sex offenders: Risk management and good lives. *Professional Psychology: Research and Practice, 34*(4), 353-360. https://doi.org/10.1037/0735-7028.34.4.353.

Ward, T., Vess, J., Collie, R. M., & Gannon, T. A. (2006). Risk management or goods promotion: The relationship between approach and avoidance goals in treatment for sex offenders. *Aggression and Violent Behavior, 11*(4), 378-393. https://doi.org/10.1016/j.avb.2006.01.001.

Ward, T., & Willis, G. M. (2016). Responsivity dynamic risk factors and offender rehabilitation: A comparison of the good lives model and the risk-need model. In D. Laws & W. O'Donohue (Eds.), *Treatment of sex offenders* (pp. 175-190). Springer. https://doi.org/10.1007/978-3-319-25868-3_8.

Ward, T., Yates, P. M., & Willis, G. M. (January 2012). The good lives model and the risk need responsivity model: A critical response to Andrews, Bonta, and Wormith (2011). *Criminal Justice and Behavior, 39*(1), 94-110. https://doi.org/10.1177/0093854811426085.

Warr, M. (1993). Age, peers, and delinquency. *Criminology, 31*(1), 17-40. https://doi.org/10.1111/j.1745-9125.1993.tb01120.x.

Warr, M. (2002). *Companions in crime: The social aspects of criminal conduct*. Cambridge University Press.

Warr, M., & Stafford, M. (1991). The influence of delinquent peers: What they think or what they do? *Criminology, 29*(4), 851-866. https://doi.org/10.1111/j.1745-9125.1991.tb01090.x.

Waterman, A. S. (2008). Reconsidering happiness: A eudaimonist's perspective. *The Journal of Positive Psychology, 3*(4), 234-252. https://doi.org/10.1080/17439760802303002.

Waterman, A. S., Schwartz, S. J., & Conti, R. (2008). The implications of two conceptions of happiness (hedonic enjoyment and eudaimonia) for the understanding of intrinsic motivation. *Journal of Happiness Studies, 9*(1), 41-79. https://doi.org/10.1007/s10902-006-9020-7.

Watson, D., Clark, L. A., & Tellegen, A. (1988). Development and validation of brief measures of positive and negative affect: The PANAS scales. *Journal of Personality and Social Psychology, 54*(6), 1063-1070. https://doi.org/10.1037//0022-3514.54.6.1063.

*Weber, M., & Huebner, E. S. (2015). Early adolescents' personality and life satisfaction: A closer look at global vs. domain-specific satisfaction. *Personality and Individual Differences, 83*, 31-36. https://doi.org/10.1016/j.paid.2015.03.042.

Weber, S., Jud, A., & Landolt, M. A. (2016). Quality of life in maltreated children and adult survivors of child maltreatment: A systematic review. *Quality of Life Research, 25*(2), 237-255. https://doi.org/10.1007/s11136-015-1085-5.

Wehmeyer, M. L., & Shogren, K. A. (2017). Goal setting and attainment and self-regulation. In K. Hogren, M. Wehmeyer, & N. Singh (Eds.), *Handbook of positive psychology in intellectual and developmental disabilities* (pp. 231-245). Springer. https://doi.org/10.1007/978-3-319-59066-0_16.

Wehmeyer, M. L., Shogren, K. A., Little, T. D., & Lopez, S. J. (2017). *Development of self-determination through the life-course*. Springer. https://doi.org/10.1007/978-94-024-1042-6.

Weijers, I. (2020). Jonge veelplegers en hun worsteling om te stoppen met criminaliteit. *Tijdschrift voor Criminologie, 62*(2-3), 228-246. https://doi.org/10.5553/TvC/0165182X2020062203006.

Wells, J., Armstrong, T., Boisvert, D., Lewis, R., Gangitano, D., & Hughes-Stamm, S. (2017). Stress, genes, and generalizability across gender: Effects of MAOA and stress sensitivity on crime and delinquency. *Criminology, 55*(3), 548-574. https://doi.org/10.1111/1745-9125.12147.

White, L. M., Lau, K. S. L., & Aalsma, M. C. (2016). Detained adolescents: Mental health needs, treatment use, and recidivism. *The Journal of the American Academy of Psychiatry and the Law, 44*(2), 200-212.

Whitehead, P. R., Ward, T., & Collie, R. M. (2007). Time for a change: Applying the good lives model of rehabilitation to a high-risk violent offender. *International Journal of Offender Therapy and Comparative Criminology, 51*(5), 578-598. https://doi.org/10.1177/0306624X06296236.

WHOQOL. (1995). The world health organization quality of life assessment (WHOQOL): Position paper from the World Health Organization. *Social Science & Medicine, 41*, 1403-1409. https://doi.org/10.1016/0277-9536(95)00112-k.

Wibbelink, C. J. M., Hoeve, M., Stams, G. J. J. M., & Oort, F. J. (2017). A meta-analysis of the association between mental health disorders and juvenile recidivism. *Aggression and Violent Behavior, 33*, 78-90. https://doi.org/10.1016/j.avb.2017.01.005.

Wikström, P.-O. H. (2014). Why crime happens: A situational action theory. In G. Manzo (Ed.), *Analytical sociology: Actions and networks* (pp. 74-94). Wiley. https://doi.org/10.1002/9781118762707.ch03.

Wikström, P. O. H., & Loeber, R. (2000). Do disadvantaged neighborhoods cause well-adjusted children to become adolescent delinquents? A study of male juvenile serious offending, individual risk and protective factors, and neighborhood context. *Criminology, 38*(4), 1109-1142. https://doi.org/10.1111/j.1745-9125.2000.tb01416.x.

Williams, D. J. (2003). "Quality of life" as perceived by sex offenders on early release in a halfway house: Implications for treatment. *Journal of Offender Rehabilitation, 38*(2), 77-93. https://doi.org/10.1300/J076v38n02_05.

Williams, D. J., & Strean, W. B. (2002). The transtheoretical model and quality of life promotion: Towards successful offender rehabilitation. *Probation Journal, 49*(3), 217-226. https://doi.org/10.1177/026455050204900305.

Williams, D. J., & Strean, W. B. (2003). Quality of life promotion: The foundation of offender rehabilitation? *Forum on Corrections Research, 14*(2), 43-45.

Williams, G. C., Niemiec, C. P., Patrick, H., Ryan, R. M., & Deci, E. L. (2009). The importance of supporting autonomy and perceived competence in facilitating long-term tobacco abstinence. *Annals of Behavioral Medicine, 37*(3), 315-324. https://doi.org/10.1007/s12160-009-9090-y.

Willis, G. M., & Grace, R. C. (June 2008). The quality of community reintegration planning for child molesters: Effects on sexual recidivism. *Sex Abuse, 20*(2), 218-240. https://doi.org/10.1177/1079063208318005.

Willis, G. M., Prescott, D. S., & Yates, P. M. (2013). The good lives model (GLM) in theory and practice. *Sexual Abuse in Australia and New Zealand, 5*(1), 3-9.

Willis, G. M., & Ward, T. (2011). Striving for a good life: The good lives model applied to released child molesters. *Journal of Sexual Aggression, 17*(3), 290-303. https://doi.org/10.1080/13552600.2010.505349.

Willis, G. M., & Ward, T. (2013). The good lives model: Does it work? Preliminary evidence. In L. Craig, L. Dixon, & T. A. Gannon (Eds.), *What works in offender rehabilitation: An evidence-based approach to assessment and treatment* (pp. 305-317). Wiley. https://doi.org/10.1002/9781118320655.ch17.

Willis, G. M., Yates, P. M., Gannon, T. A., & Ward, T. (2012). How to integrate the good lives model into treatment programs for sexual offending: An introduction and overview. *Sex Abuse, 25*(2), 123-142. https://doi.org/10.1177/1079063212452618.

Wills, T. A., Simons, J. S., Sussman, S., & Knight, R. (2016). Emotional self-control and dysregulation: A dual-process analysis of pathways to externalizing/internalizing symptomatology and positive well-being in younger adolescents. *Drug and Alcohol Dependence, 163*, S37-S45. https://doi.org/10.1016/j.drugalcdep.2015.08.039.

Wilson, A., & Tully, P. (2009). Reintegrating young offenders into the community through discharge planning: A review of interventions and needs of youth in secure care. *Australian Journal of Primary Health, 15*(2), 166-172. https://doi.org/10.1071/py08063.

Wilson, H. W., Stover, C. S., & Berkowitz, S. J. (2009). Research review: The relationship between childhood violence exposure and juvenile antisocial behavior: A meta-analytic review. *Journal of Child Psychology and Psychiatry, 50*(7), 769-779. https://doi.org/10.1111/j.1469-7610.2008.01974.x.

Wilson, L. C., & Scarpa, A. (2011). The link between sensation seeking and aggression: A meta-analytic review. *Aggressive Behavior, 37*(1), 81-90. https://doi.org/10.1002/ab.20369.

Wilson, R. J., & Yates, P. M. (2009). Effective interventions and the good lives model: Maximizing treatment gains for sexual offenders. *Aggression and Violent Behavior, 14*(3), 157-161. https://doi.org/10.1016/j.avb.2009.01.007.

Wittouck, C., & Vander Beken, T. (2019). Recovery, desistance, and the role of procedural justice in working alliances with mentally ill offenders: A critical review. *Addiction Research & Theory, 27*(1), 16-28. https://doi.org/10.1080/16066359.2018.1518434.

Wolfowicz, M., Litmanovitz, Y., Weisburd, D., & Hasisi, B. (2020). A field-wide systematic review and meta-analysis of putative risk and protective factors for radicalization outcomes. *Journal of Quantitative Criminology, 36*(3), 407-447. https://doi.org/10.1007/s10940-019-09439-4.

*Wong, S. S., & Lim, T. (2009). Hope versus optimism in Singaporean adolescents: Contributions to depression and life satisfaction. *Personality and Individual Differences, 46*(5-6), 648-652. https://doi.org/10.1016/j.paid.2009.01.009.

Wood, J. L. (2014). Understanding gang membership: The significance of group processes. *Group Processes & Intergroup Relations, 17*(6), 710-729. https://doi.org/10.1177/1368430214550344.

Wood, J. L., & Alleyne, E. (2010). Street gang theory and research: Where are we now and where do we go from here? *Aggression and Violent Behavior, 15*(2), 100-111. https://doi.org/10.1016/j.avb.2009.08.005.

Wooden, W. S., & Blazak, R. (1995). *Renegade kids, suburban outlaws: From youth culture to delinquency*. Wadsworth.

Wooditch, A., Tang, L. L., & Taxman, F. S. (2014). Which criminogenic need changes are most important in promoting desistance from crime and substance use? *Criminal Justice and Behavior, 41*(3), 276-299. https://doi.org/10.1177/0093854813503543.

Woods, S. B., Farineau, H. M., & McWey, L. M. (2013). Physical health, mental health, and behaviour problems among early adolescents in foster care. *Child: Care, Health and Development, 39*(2), 220-227. https://doi.org/10.1111/j.1365-2214.2011.01357.x.

Woolfenden, S. R., Williams, K., & Peat, J. K. (2002). Family and parenting interventions for conduct disorder and delinquency: A meta-analysis of randomised controlled trials. *Archive of Disease in Childhood, 86*(4), 251-256. https://doi.org/10.1136/adc.86.4.251.

Wormith, J. S., Gendreau, P., & Bonta, J. (2012). Deferring to clarity, parsimony, and evidence in reply to Ward, Yates, and Willis. *Criminal Justice and Behavior, 39*(1), 111-120. https://doi.org/10.1177/0093854811426087.

Wormith, J. S., & Olver, M. (2002). Offender treatment attrition and its relationship with risk, responsivity, and recidivism. *Criminal Justice and Behavior, 29*(4), 447-471. https://doi.org/10.1177/0093854802029004006.

Wright, J. P., & Cullen, F. T. (2001). Parental efficacy and delinquent behavior: Do control and support matter? *Criminology, 39*(3), 677-706. https://doi.org/10.1111/j.1745-9125.2001.tb00937.x.

Wright, J. P., & Cullen, F. T. (2004). Employment, peers, and life-course transitions. *Justice Quarterly, 21*(1), 183-205. https://doi.org/10.1080/07418820400095781.

Wright, J. P., Cullen, F. T., & Miller, J. T. (2001). Family social capital and delinquent involvement. *Journal of Criminal Justice, 29*(1), 1-9. https://doi.org/10.1016/S0047-2352(00)00071-4.

Wright, R., & Topalli, V. (2013). Choosing street crime. In F. T. Cullen & P. Wilcox (Eds.), *Oxford handbook of criminological theory* (pp. 475-493). Oxford University Press. https://doi.org/10.1093/oxfordhb/9780199747238.013.0024.

Wrzesniewski, A., Rozin, P., & Bennett, G. (2003). Working, playing, and eating: Making the most of most moments. In C. L. M. Keyes & J. Haidt (Eds.), *Flourishing: Positive psychology and the life well-lived* (pp. 185-204). American Psychological Association. https://doi.org/10.1037/10594-008.

Wylie, L. A., & Griffin, H. L. (2013). G-map's application of the good lives model to adolescent males who sexually harm: A case study. *Journal of Sexual Aggression, 19*(3), 345-356. https://doi.org/10.1080/13552600.2011.650715.

*Xie, X. C., Zhao, F. Q., Xie, J. L., & Lei, L. (2016). Symbolization of mobile phone and life satisfaction among adolescents in rural areas of China: Mediating of school-related relationships. *Computers in Human Behavior, 64*, 694-702. https://doi.org/10.1016/j.chb.2016.07.053.

Yalçın, Ö. (2012). Parental behavioral and psychological control relationships to self-esteem, life satisfaction, depression, and antisocial behaviors. *International Journal of Human Sciences, 9*(2), 1581-1590.

Yang, Y., Knight, K., Joe, G. W., Rowan-Szal, G. A., Lehman, W. E. K., & Flynn, P. M. (1 November 2013). The influence of client risks and treatment engagement on recidivism. *Journal of Offender Rehabilitation, 52*(8), 544-564. https://doi.org/10.1080/10509674.2013.840353.

*Yang, Y., Li, P. P., & Kou, Y. (2017). Orientations to happiness and subjective well-being in Chinese adolescents. *Child Indicators Research, 10*(4), 881-897. https://doi.org/10.1007/s12187-016-9410-2.

*Yap, S. T., & Baharudin, R. (2016). The relationship between adolescents' perceived parental involvement, self-efficacy beliefs, and subjective well-being: A multiple mediator model. *Social Indicators Research, 126*(1), 257-278. https://doi.org/10.1007/s11205-015-0882-0.

Yates, P. M., Kingston, D. A., & Ward, T. (2009). *The self-regulation model of the offence and re-offence process: A guide to assessment and treatment planning using the integrated good lives/self-regulation model of sexual offending.* Pacific Psychological Assessment Corporation.

Yates, P. M., & Prescott, D. S. (2011). *Building a better life: A good lives and self-regulation workbook.* Safer Society Press.

Yates, P. M., Prescott, D. S., & Ward, T. (2010). *Applying the good lives and self-regulation model to sex offender treatment: A practicial guide for clinicians.* Safer Society Press.

Yates, P. M., Simons, D. A., Kingston, D. A., & Tyler, C. (2009). *The good lives model of rehabilitation applied to treatment: Assessment and relationship to treatment progress and compliance.* 28th Annual Convention of the Association for the Treatment of Sexual Abusers (ATSA), Dallas, TX.

Yates, P. M., & Ward, T. (2008). Good lives, self-regulation, and risk management: An integrated model of sexual offender assessment and treatment. *Sexual Abuse in Australia and New Zealand, 1*(1), 2-19.

*Yeung, D. Y., Ho, S. M., & Mak, C. W. (2015). Brief report: Attention to positive information mediates the relationship between hope and psychosocial well-being of adolescents. *Journal of Adolescence, 42,* 98-102. https://doi.org/10.1016/j.adolescence.2015.04.004.

*Yildiz, M. A. (2016). Serial multiple mediation of general belongingness and life satisfaction in the relationship between attachment and loneliness in adolescents. *Educational Sciences-Theory & Practice, 16*(2), 553-578. https://doi.org/10.12738/estp.2016.2.0380.

Yong, A. D., Williams, M. W. M., Provan, H., Clarke, D., & Sinclair, G. (2015). How do offenders move through the stages of change? *Psychology, Crime & Law, 21*(4), 375-397. https://doi.org/10.1080/1068316X.2014.989166.

*You, S., Lim, S. A., & Kim, E. K. (2017). Relationships between social support, internal assets, and life satisfaction in Korean adolescents. *Journal of Happiness Studies, 19*, 897-915. https://doi.org/10.1007/s10902-017-9844-3.

Zagar, R. J., Grove, W. M., & Busch, K. G. (2013). Delinquency best treatments: How to divert youths from violence while saving lives and detention costs. *Behavioral Sciences & the Law, 31*(3), 381-396. https://doi.org/10.1002/bsl.2062.

Zamble, E., & Porporino, F. (1988). *Coping, behavior, and adaptation in prison inmates.* Springer Science & Business Media.

Zeccola, J., Kelty, S. F., & Boer, D. (2021). Does the good lives model work? A systematic review of the recidivism evidence. *The Journal of Forensic Practice, 23*(3), 285-300. https://doi.org/10.1108/JFP-03-2021-0010.

Zhu, X. Q., & Shek, D. T. L. (2020a). The influence of adolescent problem behaviors on life satisfaction: Parent–child subsystem qualities as mediators. *Child Indicators Research, 13*, 1767-1789. https://doi.org/10.1007/s12187-020-09719-7.

Zhu, X. Q., & Shek, D. T. L. (2020b). Predictive effect of positive youth development attributes on delinquency among adolescents in mainland China. *Frontiers in Psychology, 11*, 3570. https://doi.org/10.3389/fpsyg.2020.615900.

Zhu, X. Q., & Shek, D. T. L. (2021). Problem behavior and life satisfaction in early adolescence: Longitudinal findings in a Chinese context. *Journal of Happiness Studies, 22*, 2889-2914. https://doi.org/10.1007/s10902-020-00346-1.

Zirkel, S. (1992). Developing independence in a life transition: Investing the self in the concerns of the day. *Journal of Personality and Social Psychology, 62*(3), 506-521. https://doi.org/10.1037/0022-3514.62.3.506.

Zirkel, S., & Cantor, N. (1990). Personal construal of life tasks: Those who struggle for independence. *Journal of Personality and Social Psychology, 58*(1), 172-185. https://doi.org/10.1037/0022-3514.58.1.172.

Ziv, R. (2016). *Moving beyond the RNR and GLM models: Building a new vision for offender rehabilitation*. University of Cincinnati.

Ziv, R. (2018). *The future of correctional rehabilitation: Moving beyond the RNR model and good lives model debate*. Routledge.

*Zou, R., Niu, G. F., Chen, W., Fan, C. Y., Tian, Y., Sun, X. Y., & Zhou, Z. (2017). Socioeconomic inequality and life satisfaction in late childhood and adolescence: A moderated mediation model. *Social Indicators Research, 136*, 305-318. https://doi.org/10.1007/s11205-016-1542-8.

Zuckerman, M. (1971). Dimensions of sensation seeking. *Journal of Consulting and Clinical Psychology, 36*(1), 45. https://doi.org/10.1037/h0030478.

Zuckerman, M. (1994). *Behavioral expressions and biosocial bases of sensation seeking.* Cambridge University.

Žukauskienė, R. (2014). Adolescence and well-being. In A. Ben-Arieh, F. Casas, I. Frønes, & J. E. Korbin (Eds.), *Handbook of child well-being: Theories, methods and policies in global perspective* (pp. 1713-1738). Springer. https://doi.org/10.1007/978-90-481-9063-8_67.

Zullig, K., & White, R. (2011). Physical activity, life satisfaction, and self-rated health of middle school students. *The Official Journal of the International Society for Quality-of-Life Studies, 6*(3), 277-289. https://doi.org/10.1007/s11482-010-9129-z.

Zullig, K. J., Valois, R. F., Huebner, E. S., Oeltmann, J. E., & Drane, J. W. (2001). Relationship between perceived life satisfaction and adolescents' substance abuse. *Journal of Adolescent Health, 29*(4), 279-288. https://doi.org/10.1016/S1054-139X(01)00269-5.

www.ingramcontent.com/pod-product-compliance
Lightning Source LLC
Chambersburg PA
CBHW080936240926
51849CB00004BA/475
* 9 7 8 9 4 6 2 3 6 4 2 5 7 *